A Special Issue of
Language and Cognitive Processes

Experimental and Theoretical Advances in Prosody

Edited by

Duane G. Watson
University of Illinois, USA

Michael Wagner
McGill University, Canada

and

Edward Gibson
Massachusetts Institute of Technology, USA

Routledge
Taylor & Francis Group
LONDON AND NEW YORK

First published 2010 by Psychology Press

Published 2019 by Routledge
2 Park Square, Milton Park, Abingdon, Oxon, OX14 4RN
52 Vanderbilt Avenue, New York, NY 10017

Routledge is an imprint of the Taylor & Francis Group, an informa business

British Library Cataloguing in Publication Data
A catalogue record for this book is available from the British Library

Cover design by Jim Wilkie
Typeset in India by Datapage (India) Private Limited, Chennai

ISBN 13: 978-1-84872-740-3 (hbk)
ISSN 0169-0965

Contents*

---

*This book is also a special issue of the journal *Language and Cognitive Processes*, and forms issues 7, 8, & 9 of Volume 25 (2010). The page numbers are taken from the journal and so begin with p. 905

LANGUAGE AND COGNITIVE PROCESSES
2010, 25 (7/8/9), 905–945

Psychology Press
Taylor & Francis Group

Experimental and theoretical advances in prosody: A review

Michael Wagner[1,2] and Duane G. Watson[3]

[1]*Cornell University, Ithaca, NY, USA,* [2]*Department of Linguistics, McGill University, Montreal, QC, Canada,* [3]*Department of Psychology, University of Illinois at Urbana-Champaign, Champaign, IL, USA*

Research on prosody has recently become an important focus in various disciplines, including Linguistics, Psychology, and Computer Science. This article reviews recent research advances on two key issues: prosodic phrasing and prosodic prominence. Both aspects of prosody are influenced by linguistic factors such as syntactic constituent structure, semantic relations, phonological rhythm, pragmatic considerations, and also by processing factors such as the length, complexity, or predictability of linguistic material. Our review summarises recent insights into the production and perception of these two components of prosody and their grammatical underpinnings. While this review only covers a subset of a broader set of research topics on prosody in cognitive science, these topics are representative of a tendency in the field towards a more interdisciplinary approach.

Keywords: Prosody; Intonation; Comprehension; Production.

Prosody can be roughly defined as a level of linguistic representation at which the acoustic-phonetic properties of an utterance vary independently of its lexical items. This admittedly vague definition encompasses a variety of phenomena: emphasis, pitch accenting, intonational breaks, rhythm, and intonation. Some aspects of the prosody of an utterance are mere reflexes of

---

Correspondence should be addressed to Duane G. Watson, Department of Psychology, University of Illinois at Urbana-Champaign, 603 E Daniel St., Champaign, IL 61820, USA. E-mail: dgwatson@illinois.edu

We would like to thank Mara Breen, Ted Gibson, and Laura Dilley for comments on earlier drafts of this paper. The first author was supported by FQRSC Grant NP-132516, SSHRC Canada Research Chair 212482, and NSF Grant 0642660, and the second author by NIH Grant R01DC008774 from the National Institute on Deafness and Other Communication Disorders during the writing of this paper.

http://www.psypress.com/lcp DOI: 10.1080/01690961003589492

processing during speech production, others have been conventionalised and encode grammatical information. In this article, we focus on two aspects of prosody that are central in current research: boundary strength and relative prominence among words. These two components of prosody and the precise way in which various factors influence them have become an important area of research in recent years in various fields, including semantics, syntax, computational linguistics, and psycho- and neuro-linguistics.

A little over 10 years before the publication of this paper, Cutler, Dahan, and van Donselaar (1997) and Shattuck-Hufnagel and Turk (1996) each wrote comprehensive reviews of work on prosody in both linguistics and psychology up to that time. Since then, there has been an explosion in the number of studies investigating the role of prosody in cognition and linguistics, as well as improvements in techniques for examining prosody. In this article, we attempt to pick up where those two papers left off and review some of the recent work in prosody. Because it would be impossible to provide a review of the entire field in so small a space, we have tried to cover areas that lie at the interface of theoretical and experimental approaches to prosody, and at the interface of linguistics, psycholinguistics, and computational linguistics.

In so doing, we focus on two aspects of prosody that are central in current research: boundary strength and the relative prominence between words. Within these domains, similar questions have arisen in recent years: What is the relationship between prosody, discourse, and syntactic structure? What are the acoustic correlates of prosody? What information does prosody convey and are the cognitive processes that underlie it primarily production centred or comprehension centred?

WHAT IS PROSODY?

Every utterance in human speech comes with certain properties that are referred to as its "prosody". One way to define "prosody" is by its function. "Prosody" is often used to refer to those phonetic and phonological properties of speech that are crucially *not* due to the choice of lexical items, but rather depend on other factors such as how these items relate to each other semantically and/or syntactically, how they are grouped rhythmically, where the speaker places emphasis, what kind of speech act the utterance encodes, whether turn taking in conversation is being negotiated, and they can reflect the attitude and emotional state of the speaker. While these factors can also determine the choice of lexical material, they can affect the signal directly without any mediation by a lexical morpheme with segmental content, and it is this kind of information that is often referred to as the prosody of an utterance (cf. discussions in Ferreira, 2002; Ladd, 2008).

Another, quite different way to define "prosody" is by its form, which includes its phonetic and phonological substance. A common definition of prosody is that it comprises the "suprasegmental" (Lehiste, 1970) aspects of the speech stream, i.e., properties such as syllable structure, intonation, and reflexes of prosodic structure, which are acoustically reflected in fundamental frequency, duration, and intensity. Both of these definitions, the one that puts more emphasis on the function of prosody and the one emphasising its form, have their virtues and flaws. An issue with the first definition is that it excludes suprasegmental properties in the lexicon, such as lexical tone, syllable structure, and lexical stress, yet many researchers understand the term "prosody" as including these. An issue with the second definition is that it presupposes an analysis that divides the information in the speech stream cleanly into a segmental and prosodic component, but at the signal level, there is no separation of prosodic and segmental information. Both use the same channel and encode information by the same phonetic correlates, e.g., fundamental frequency, duration, and intensity. Whichever definition one may favour, boundary strength and prominence, the two topics on which the remainder of this review will focus, would count as prosody under either.

BOUNDARIES

An utterance of more than two words in it often has a perceptible subgrouping (Lehiste, 1973). Prosodic grouping can be produced and perceived even in the absence of identifiable words (cf. de Pijper & Sanderman, 1994; Larkey, 1983). Thus, perceived grouping is not simply due to the semantic relationship or the co-occurrence frequency between words, although of course these factors might add to, or be confounded with, the effects of prosody on perceived grouping in actual speech. Below we discuss the main acoustic correlates of prosodic grouping—duration, fundamental frequency, and intensity—and how they signal grouping and boundaries, and we discuss the nature of their relationship to syntax and language processing.

Phonetic and phonological correlates

Duration

Lehiste (1973) used ambiguity resolution to study acoustic correlates of prosodic boundaries and to understand the extent to which these correlates reflect syntactic bracketing. Lehiste (1973) identified duration as the most reliable cue in disambiguating syntactic structures based on their bracketing. The main durational cues affecting boundary strength perception are preboundary lengthening, pauses, and domain-initial strengthening.

Klatt (1975) showed that segments are lengthened preceding boundaries, even in the absence of pauses. Pre-boundary lengthening has been shown to correlate closely with the strength of the following boundary (Byrd & Saltzman, 1998; Price, Ostendorf, Shattuck-Hufnagel, & Fong, 1991; Shattuck-Hufnagel & Turk, 1996; Wightman, Shattuck-Hufnagel, Ostendorf, & Price, 1992). Pre-boundary lengthening correlates with other acoustic cues that reflect that articulatory gestures of segments preceding boundaries are spatially more extreme, i.e., hyperarticulated (Byrd & Saltzman, 2003; Edwards, Beckman, & Fletcher, 1991; Fougeron & Keating, 1997), and are spaced further apart (Byrd & Saltzman, 2003). Final lengthening affects the syllable left adjacent to the boundary, and, according to Berkovits (1994), extends to the closest stressed syllable. Turk and White (1999) found lengthening in all material from the boundary to the rime of the syllable carrying main stress. The degree of pre-boundary lengthening of a segment decreases with the distance from the prosodic boundary (Byrd, Krivokapic, & Lee, 2006).

Closely related to pre-boundary lengthening are the presence and length of pauses at boundaries. Pre-boundary lengthening and pause duration are closely related and have been argued to contribute to a single percept of pause or juncture, and listeners report hearing pauses even when there are no unfilled pauses in the signal (Martin, 1970). O'Malley, Kloker, and Dara-Abrams (1973) found evidence that different amounts of pause duration can code different degrees of boundary, a finding that was confirmed in Fant and Kruckenberg (1996).

Apart from final lengthening and pausing, a third duration-related phenomenon is *domain-initial strengthening.* Cho (2002), Fougeron and Keating (1997), Jun (1993), Keating, Cho, Fougeron, and Hsu (2003) and Lavoie (2001) show that the phonetic realisation of segments depends on the strength of a preceding boundary. Evidence from production experiments using electro-palatography suggests that initial strengthening increases cumulatively with the strength of the preceding prosodic boundary. Keating et al. (2003) provides evidence that domain-initial strengthening occurs cross-linguistically in typologically distinct languages with very different prosodic systems. Even languages that are not stress-based such as French, Korean, and Taiwanese, show very similar patterns of domain-initial strengthening to English, although they are quite different when it comes to pitch-related cues to phrasing, suggesting that domain-initial strengthening is a general reflex of prosodic organisation. In addition to lengthening segments at the beginning of prosodic domains, new segments can also be inserted in order to strengthen the beginning of a domain. Dilley, Shattuck-Hufnagel, and Ostendorf (1996) and Redi and Shattuck-Hufnagel (2001) show evidence that glottal stop insertion is more likely at stronger prosodic domain breaks compared with weaker boundaries.

Fundamental frequency

A second important acoustic dimension in cueing prosodic boundaries is fundamental frequency and its perceptual correlate pitch. There are two major sources of information on prosodic phrasing in the pitch curve of an utterance: pitch excursions at prosodic boundaries and the scaling of pitch accents relative to each other.

The first type of pitch cue for boundaries is pitch events that occur at the edges of strong prosodic domains. They are commonly analysed as boundary tones (following Pierrehumbert, 1980). These boundary tones are aligned relative to the end or beginning of a prosodic domain. Some boundary tones, especially sentence-final ones, are often linked to semantic or pragmatic meaning, and are sometimes treated as intonational morphemes in their own right (Gussenhoven, 1984, 2004; Pierrehumbert & Hirschberg, 1990). It is not clear, however, whether every pitch event at a boundary can be analysed in this way.[1]

A second type of pitch cue to prosodic phrasing is the relative scaling of pitch accents within an utterance. Pitch accents on individual words are often scaled relative to preceding ones, and the precise scaling pattern depends on the prosodic phrasing (and other factors, e.g., focus, see below). Féry and Truckenbrodt (2005) and Ladd (1988) looked at the following type of coordination structure in English and German, respectively, where A, B, and C stand in for sentences:

(1a) A but (B and C)
(1b) (A and B) but C

The pitch accent scaling distinguishes the two types of structures. In structures of type (1a), conjunct C has a lower F0 than B, and B in turn has a lower F0 than A. The pitch level goes down from accent to accent. In structures of type (1b), on the other hand, C and B are at about the same level, but both are set to a lower pitch compared to A.

This contrast in pitch scaling was used to argue for a prosodic representation that reflects the syntactic difference between (1a) and (1b). For example, Ladd (1988) proposes to explain the difference in pitch scaling by a hierarchical metrical representation that allows a recursive nesting of intonational phrases. Within each level of coordinate structure, conjuncts are downstepped relative to the preceding conjunct. In structures of type (1b), conjunct C is downstepped relative to the first conjunct (A and B). This has

[1] Boundary tones also play an important role in negotiating turn-taking. We will not discuss these discourse functions of boundary tones in this review, because our main focus is how boundaries are signaled.

the effect that the pitch of an accent in C is lower than the maximal pitch in (A and B), but it is not lower than the pitch in a preceding conjunct, in this case B. Further evidence for this kind of scaling is presented in van den Berg, Gussenhoven, and Rietveld (1992), who propose that the pitch level of entire domains containing accents can be downstepped relative to preceding domains, using reference lines.

Related to the relative scaling of pitch accents are resets. They are perceived as discontinuities and are interpreted as a cue for strong boundaries (de Pijper & Sanderman, 1994). Truckenbrodt (2002) argued that phrase-initial F0 reset, i.e., a resetting of the reference pitch line, acts as an additional correlate of intonational phrases in certain dialects of German, and is used in very much the same way as boundary tones to signal phrasing.

There are other cues related to the voice source that correlate with prosodic boundaries. A common phenomenon is voice quality changes at the end of a prosodic domain. For example, creaky voice is a common cue to end a prosodic domain in English and many other languages, as observed already in Lehiste (1973).

Intensity

A third source of information for prosodic boundaries apart from fundamental frequency and duration is intensity, although this cue has been less studied as a signal for boundaries. Kim, Yoon, Cole, and Hasegawa-Johnson (2006) report that some speakers in the Switchboard corpus show a difference between two boundary types differing in strength (intermediate vs. intonational phrase in ToBI terms), such that the stronger boundary was associated with lower intensity of the material preceding the boundary. This difference, however, was not consistent across speakers.

Gradient or categorical?

A common assumption in the linguistic literature is that prosodic boundaries can be categorised according to a very limited inventory of boundary types that are organised in a "prosodic hierarchy". The prosodic hierarchy proposed in Selkirk (1986) includes six categories: the utterance, intonational phrase, phonological phrase, phonological word, foot, and syllable. Each utterance contains at least one instance of each category; each category higher up on the hierarchy consists of one or more elements of the next lower category. Different boundary strengths are interpreted as categorical phonological differences between boundary types.

This assumption of a prosodic hierarchy is shared by the ToBI annotation system of American English (Silverman et al., 1992). It assumes three categories, intonation phrase, intermediate phrase, and word—lower prosodic categories are not encoded in the ToBI labelling system since the annotation scheme does not label within-word prosody. The ToBI system has proven useful in making prosodic information available in speech corpora. ToBI was originally developed to transcribe the intonation of American English but has since been adapted to transcribe a wide variety of languages (Jun, 2005).

A problem for the categorical view of boundary strength, however, is that often when boundaries of different strengths can be discerned, the differences are quantitative rather than qualitative. Experiments based on pitch accent scaling and on the various durational cues to prosodic boundary strength reviewed above suggest that many correlates of boundary strength show gradient and cumulative effects. Another source of evidence comes from durational evidence for a relative scaling of the strength of boundaries relative to earlier-produced boundaries in production (Wagner, 2005). Some researchers conclude that we need to distinguish between intonational phrases of different strengths above and beyond the categorical distinctions that have been proposed (cf. discussion in Kim et al., 2006; Ladd, 2008).

Since Price et al. (1991), the ToBI system includes a boundary strength annotation, the *break index*, which is based on boundary type differences. Syrdal and McGory (2000), however, found poor inter-labeller agreement in ToBI with respect to the precise boundary type but high agreement with respect to whether or not there is a boundary. And according to de Pijper and Sanderman (1994), both naïve and trained listeners have very similar and very reliable intuitions about *relative* boundary strength, but are not very reliable at categorising boundaries. A recurring theme in the literature on investigating prosodic boundaries is that researchers decide to annotate whether or not a boundary is present rather than trying to distinguish the precise ToBI type (de Pijper & Sanderman, 1994; Watson & Gibson, 2004b).

An alternative annotation system that is compatible with relative notions of boundary strength and prominence is the *Rhythm and Pitch* annotation system developed and tested in Dilley, Breen, Bolivar, Kraemer, and Gibson (2006) and Dilley and Brown (2005). This system dissociates the precise nature of the tonal implementation from perceived grouping and prominence relations, and is thus more apt to account for gradient and relative distinctions that are not accompanied by categorical differences. A study comparing inter-labeller agreement of RaP and ToBI annotations (Dilley et al., 2006) found a higher inter-labeller agreement with respect to boundary type for RaP, a system in which boundary labels are based on perceived degree of disjuncture compared to ToBI where boundary labels are based on perceived disjuncture and the identity of boundary tones.

Relationship to syntactic structure

The relationship between prosodic phrasing and syntactic structure is an area of particularly diverging opinions. Models differ in how closely they assume prosodic phrasing matches up with syntactic constituent structure, and conversely how complicated a mapping function they postulate at the interface between the two representations. Early work in the phonetic and psycholinguistic tradition explored the extent to which the phonetic realisation of an utterance directly reflected syntactic structure. It was felt that the surface acoustic form of a sentence might reveal something about the underlying syntactic representation, and this was supported by researchers who found greater segmental lengthening and pause insertion at points in a sentence that corresponded with phrase structure boundaries (Klatt, 1975; Lehiste, 1973). However, other researchers have found evidence that the relationship is less transparent, and developed models to explain apparent discrepancies between syntax and prosody. We review some of these proposals below.

Prosody reflects syntax

According to recent proposals in categorial grammar (Steedman, 1991), the surface prosodic phrasing *is* the syntax. Categorical grammar is a theory of how syntax and meaning composition go hand in hand. It provides a range of operations that can effectively re-bracket the phrase structure of an expression in unconventional ways. In English, for example, both (S)(VO) and (SV)(O) are permitted as syntactic bracketings, reflecting the fact that both prosodic phrasings are possible. Categorial grammar thus provides an account of syntax that matches prosodic constituency, and assures surface compositionality even in cases where at first blush the prosodic bracketing seems to contradict the syntactic one.

Compatible with this viewpoint is recent work on bracketing paradoxes (Wagner, 2005, 2010), which provides syntactic evidence that at least some apparent cases of mismatches between syntax and prosody actually involve a syntactic structure that in fact matches the prosody. A complex meaning can often be constructed in more than one way, and the choice between structures comes with different prosodies. An apparently mismatching prosodic phrasing may in fact reveal a different syntactic choice about how a complex meaning is constructed. The motivation for the choice between these different structures may ultimately lie in processing factors, e.g., extraposing a relative clause avoids a nested structure, which may be difficult to process.

Algorithmic approaches

There are a number of factors that affect prosody that do not appear to be mediated by syntax. Many researchers concluded that the mapping between phrase structure and the acoustics of an utterance is not one to one, and a tradition started that sought to characterise this link, both in the literature on phonological theory (Nespor & Vogel, 1986; Selkirk, 1984, 1986; Truckenbrodt, 1995) and in the processing literature (Cooper & Paccia-Cooper, 1980; Ferreira, 1988; Gee & Grosjean, 1983; Grosjean & Collins, 1979; Watson & Gibson, 2004b). These approaches were algorithmic, and derived prosodic properties such as pause length based on a syntactic representation and a set of mapping rules.

Developments in prosodic theory in the early 1980s introduced the notion of prosodic and phonological constraints, which were purported to influence pausing and the duration of words independent of syntax, and these principles were incorporated into algorithms (Ferreira, 1988; Gee & Grosjean, 1983; Watson & Gibson, 2004b). For example, pauses are relatively unlikely to occur between phonologically light items like function words and nearby content words that are phonologically heavy (Nespor & Vogel, 1986; Selkirk, 1984). Other work suggested that speakers tend to produce pauses such that the resulting prosodic phrases are roughly the same length (Cooper & Paccia-Cooper, 1980). As a consequence, syntax and prosodic structure can diverge such that pauses might occur at a relatively minor syntactic boundary over a more major boundary. A sentence like (2) with a large pause between "understand" and "the politicians" is well formed with a pause between the verb and the direct object instead of between the subject and the verb.

(2) I don't understand // the politician's policies.

Researchers like Gee and Grosjean (1983; henceforth, GG) incorporated these observations into their algorithm, predicting pauses using both syntactic constraints and prosodic constraints like phonological phrasing and prosodic balancing. This model did quite well in predicting pause lengths, accounting for (in GG's article) 92% of the variance, an improvement over earlier accounts without prosodic constraints, such as the model in Cooper and Paccia-Cooper (1980; henceforth, CPC), whose model accounted for only 56% on the same data. However, this model also includes a large number of steps and parameters for building a prosodic representation. GG's algorithm contained a total of eight steps, and because these steps were highly interrelated, it is difficult to know which aspects of the algorithm were doing the heavy lifting in predicting pause length. As pointed out by GG, the goal of these models was not to provide an explanation of the cognitive mechanisms that underlie speech, but rather to provide a description of where pauses were likely to occur.

Ferreira (1988, 1993) proposed two improvements to models by GG and CPC in her algorithm. First, she introduced the linguistic notion of the prosodic phrase boundary to the algorithmic approach, arguing that psycholinguists should be trying to account for the presence (and absence) of prosodic boundaries rather than pause length. If one assumes that the presence or absence of intonational phrases is binary, aggregating over pause lengths gave the appearance that GG and CPC's models were predicting pause duration. She argued that in reality CPC and GG were predicting the relative likelihood of a boundary occurring at a word boundary. Ferreira (1993) found that the actual extent of pause duration and pre-pausal lengthening was determined by the segmental properties of the pre-boundary word, with segmental duration engaging in a trading relationship with pause length. Words with shorter intrinsic vowel length had a longer pause than words with a longer intrinsic vowel length although the total duration of the word and pause together was roughly the same when controlling for sentence position.

Ferreira's second improvement to the algorithmic approach was the incorporation of semantic constraints into an algorithm. Work by Selkirk (1984) suggests that semantic structure can constrain prosodic structure. She proposed the Sense Unit Condition which roughly states that constituents that do not have a dependency relationship cannot co-occur within the same intonational phrase. For example, (3a) sounds unacceptable because "in the moon" and "is a myth" are not semantically related yet occur within the same intonational phrase. According to Selkirk, if a boundary occurs after "moon" such that the PP and the VP are in separate phrases, the sentence is more acceptable.

(3a) The man // in the moon is a myth.
(3b) The man // in the moon // is a myth.

However, note that Watson and Gibson (2004a) found that in acceptability surveys, (3a) and (3b) were both unacceptable compared to a sentence in which no boundary occurred. They argue that the poor acceptability of (3a) and (3b) was driven by interrupting the local dependency relationship between the modifier PP and the subject noun.

Ferreira (1988) proposed a model of prosodic phrasing based on X-bar theory (Jackendoff, 1977). Because X-bar theory instantiates different types of dependency relationships into the syntactic representation, she proposed that the likelihood of an intonational phrase boundary could be predicted by the X-bar structure of the sentence, which serves as a proxy for the semantic closeness of dependents. Within her algorithm, boundaries are least likely to occur between semantically related words like a head and its argument while boundaries are more likely to occur between weakly related constituents like a head and an adjunct or between two unrelated adjuncts. In a series of production experiments, Ferreira shows that this model performs significantly better than previous algorithms.

Within the phonological literature, a theory that has gained wide currency is the edge-alignment theory of prosodic phrasing. Based on observations on the phrasing of tone sandhi domains in Taiwanese (Chen, 1987) and related phenomena, Selkirk (1986) proposes that the left and right edge of certain syntactic constituents are aligned with the right and left edge of certain prosodic constituents. Today, this is often implemented using optimality theory, and output constraints such as "Align XP" (Selkirk, 1995) and "Wrap XP" (Truckenbrodt, 1995, 1999) are used to force certain prosodic phrasings. Differences in the prosodic phrasing between languages are taken to be due to different rankings of the constraints. The edge-alignment theory crucially assumes a set of syntactic categories (e.g., Maximal Projection: XP), and a set of phonological categories (e.g., phonological phrase, intonational phrase), since it is certain *types* of prosodic boundaries that align with certain *types* of syntactic edges.

More recently, there has been a resurgence in trying to understand whether algorithmic approaches can provide a useful account of intonational boundaries. Watson and Gibson (2004b) proposed that much of the success enjoyed by previous theories was due to their incorporation of two factors: (1) predicting a high likelihood of a boundary before a long constituent and (2) predicting a high likelihood of a boundary after a long constituent. In addition, Watson and Gibson showed that an algorithm incorporating these two factors, along with constraints against boundaries occurring when a constituent is not complete and between heads and arguments, did as well as the previous algorithms. Watson and Gibson propose that ultimately, boundary production is related to planning and recovery processes. Boundaries occur before long constituents to give the speaker planning time, and boundaries occur after long constituents to provide speakers with time for recovery. Follow up work by Watson, Breen, and Gibson (2006a) suggests that the optionality of a dependent, in addition to its argument status, influences boundary placement. Speakers are reluctant to place boundaries between a head and an obligatory argument. Watson et al. (2006a) argue that the obligatoriness constraint stems from heads and obligatory dependents being more likely to be planned together at the boundary before the head, negating a need for the intervening boundary. Turk (2008) proposes that prosodic phrasing, just like prosodic prominence, reflects local predictability, thus also invoking a processing explanation rather than a grammatical mapping.

The link between planning and prosodic structure has been supported by findings from the literature. Ferreira (1991) found that pauses were longer before syntactically complex object phrases. Wheeldon and Lahiri (1997) also found that initiation times for a sentence increased with the number of phonological words in the subject.

Ferreira (2007) points out that production factors are unlikely to account for all aspects of intonational phrasing, noting that boundaries and pausing may also result from the metrical structure of a sentence. It is also clear that boundaries play a role in the signalling of pragmatic and semantic information as in the case of asides, appositives, and nonrestrictive relative clauses (Nespor & Vogel, 1986; Shattuck-Hufnagel & Turk, 1996; Watson & Gibson, 2004b).

Ferreira (2007) has recently challenged the use of the algorithmic approach by itself in understanding boundary placement in production. She points out that in testing these algorithms, different researchers have used different syntactic structures as test sets. Because there is no principled way to select the stimuli to compare these algorithms, it is difficult to evaluate these theories with respect to one another. Both the algorithmic approach and a more traditional approach in which specific properties of matched sentences are manipulated to examine the likelihood of intonational boundaries at specific word boundaries will be important for understanding boundaries in production.

Boundaries and parsing

Resolving ambiguities

There is a great deal of work in the literature demonstrating that listeners can take advantage of the close mapping between syntax and prosodic boundaries to resolve ambiguities in language processing. There is an excellent review by Cutler et al. (1997) that surveys work on listeners' use of prosody in syntactic parsing up to that time.

One of the big questions in the 1990s was understanding whether intonational boundaries can be used to resolve syntactic ambiguities in online processing. This question was asked in the context of a larger debate about the modularity of sentence processing: is syntactic information the only source of information used in the initial stages of processing (e.g., Frazier & Clifton, 1996) or is information from other domains used in these early stages as well (e.g., Tanenhaus, Spivey-Knowlton, Eberhard, & Sedivy, 1995)? Studies suggest that nonsyntactic information is used very rapidly in processing, though researchers disagree over whether the effects occur immediately or upon re-analysis or re-processing. Research over the past 20 years strongly suggests that prosody is one of the many factors that are rapidly integrated into the linguistic representation (Grabe, Warren, & Nolan, 1994; Kjelgaard & Speer, 1999; Marslen-Wilson, Tyler, Warren, Grenier, & Lee, 1992; Snedeker & Trueswell, 2003; Watson & Gibson, 2005 to name just a few).

Given that boundaries clearly play a role in sentence processing, researchers have focused on two questions: (1) what sort of information do intonational boundaries provide and (2) do speakers consistently produce boundaries for the listener? We discuss the second question in the next section, and explore the first question here.

The literature unequivocally demonstrates that boundaries can disambiguate certain types of syntactic structures. Interestingly, certain types of ambiguities are much more easily disambiguated than others. For example, prosody appears to play a stronger role in disambiguating sentences in which the difference between interpretations lies in how the two meanings are grouped. Consider the examples in (4) below.

(4a) When Roger leaves // the house is dark. (Kjelgaard & Speer, 1999)
(4b) When Roger leaves the house // it's dark.

Work by Speer and colleagues (Kjelgaard & Speer, 1999; Speer, Kjelgaard, & Dobroth, 1996) and others (Warren, Grabe, & Nolan, 1995) suggests that boundaries can help to resolve local ambiguities in sentences like (4). Although listeners typically interpret the noun following the verb in the subordinate clause as a direct object (instead of the subject of the main clause), placing a boundary between the noun and the verb such that the noun is grouped with the main clause reduces this bias.

(5a) Pat // or Jay and Lee convinced the bank president to extend the mortgage. (Clifton, Frazier, & Carlson, 2006)
(5b) Pat or Jay //and Lee convinced the bank president to extend the mortgage.

Similarly, conjunctions like those in (5) have been shown to be disambiguated by prosodic phrasing (Clifton et al., 2006; Lehiste, 1973; Streeter, 1978; Wagner, 2005). An early boundary in (5) groups Jay and Lee together while a later boundary groups Pat and Jay together.

(6a) Mary maintained // that the CEO lied when the investigation started. (Carlson, Clifton, Charles, & Frazier, 2001)
(6b) Mary maintained that the CEO lied // when the investigation started.

Finally, boundaries can play a role in signalling the presence of long distance dependencies (Kraljic & Brennan, 2005; Schafer, Speer, & Warren, 2005; Snedeker & Trueswell, 2003). The boundary in (6a) biases listeners towards attaching the adverbial phrase to the local verb "lied", whereas the boundary in (6b) creates a bias towards attachment to the matrix verb "maintained".

(7) The detective showed the blurry picture of the diamond // to the client.

Boundaries can also facilitate processing unambiguous structures likes the one in (7). Listeners rated sentences with a boundary between "diamond" and "to the client" as being easier to understand than sentences without this boundary (Watson & Gibson, 2005). They also found that a boundary between a head and a local dependent in an unambiguous sentence disrupts processing.

When do intonational boundaries not help? Different researchers have made the same general claim: boundaries can resolve ambiguities in which the surface bracketing of a sentence differs across interpretations, but cannot resolve ambiguities in which they do not (Lehiste, 1973; Lieberman, 1967; Shattuck-Hufnagel & Turk, 1996). For example, (8) below is globally ambiguous. "Flying" can be interpreted as either a gerund or an adjective. Lieberman (1967) points out that the prosodic phrasing of this sentence cannot disambiguate it.

(8) Flying airplanes can be dangerous.

Lieberman attributes this observation to the similar surface structure but differing deep structure of the two interpretations, arguing that boundaries may only play a role in disambiguation when surface structure differs. The major syntactic breaks in the sentence are in the same location across interpretations even though the sentence meanings differ. This generalisation also explains why sentences like (9) have yielded inconsistent results in the literature.

(9a) Mary knows the boy on the bench.
(9b) Mary knows the boy is sleeping.

The structures in (9) contain a local ambiguity at the noun phrase "the boy". It can either be interpreted as the subject of a sentential complement (9b) or as the direct object of the verb (9a) and listeners have a preference for the latter interpretation. A large number of researchers have investigated whether resolution of this ambiguity might be influenced by prosody, but the results from the literature are mixed. Some studies have found that speakers are more likely to produce a boundary (or at least acoustic correlates of boundaries) after the verb in the sentential complement continuation (Nagel, Shapiro, Tuller, & Nawy, 1996; Warren, 1985). Recent work by Anderson and Carlson (2004) suggests that speakers produce cues in this structure less consistently than they do in early closure/later closure ambiguities like the one in (4). Beach (1991) and Marslen-Wilson et al. (1992) found that listeners interpret a boundary after the verb as indicating the SC continuation. However, Stirling and Wales (1996) and Watt and Murray (1996) found no such difference. To complicate the picture, Gahl and Garnsey (2004) found that lengthening of the verb depends on verb bias. Certain verbs like "believe" occur more frequently with sentential complements than direct objects. Conversely, verbs like "confirmed" occur more frequently with direct objects than sentential complements. Gahl and Garnsey (2004) found that verbs were lengthened and preceded a longer pause when they occurred with the dispreferred continuation.

If it is the case that prosodic disambiguation of the structure in (9) is less frequent than other structures, one possible reason is a lack of difference in the surface structure of the two interpretations. Both the sentential complement and direct object continuation enjoy the same type of relationship with the verb. Like the ambiguity in (8), the difference between interpretations lies in their syntactic categories and not in their syntactic relationships. Similarly, classic sentences like (10), which are locally ambiguous and contain a verb ("raced") that can be either interpreted as the main verb of the sentence or a verb in a reduced relative clause, cannot be disambiguated prosodically (Fodor, 2002).

(10a) The horse raced past the barn fell.
(10b) The horse raced past the barn and fell.

Again, although the surface structure labels differ between these interpretations, the syntactic relations between constituents do not.

There have been two types of explanations for why boundaries can only disambiguate ambiguous sentences that have interpretations that differ in their surface structure. One is that the link between syntactic structure and prosodic breaks is formalised in the grammar as prosodic structure (e.g., Selkirk, 2000; Truckenbrodt, 1999), and prosodic structure provides cues to syntactic structure through knowledge of the grammar. The other is that prosodic boundaries serve as a means by which the listener organises the incoming linguistic signal for language processing. The latter is discussed below, and of course, the two possibilities are not mutually exclusive.

Psychologists have proposed two types of processing accounts, but both accounts assume that the central role of boundaries in processing is to provide information about how the linguistic signal is organised. One class of theories argues that boundaries group words into processing units (Frazier & Clifton, 1998; Schafer, 1997), while the other argues that boundaries mark points of disjuncture in a sentence (Marcus & Hindle, 1990; Pynte & Prieur, 1996; Watson & Gibson, 2005). At first glance, these theories may appear to make similar predictions; however, if we consider sentences like (6) above, the differences become clearer.

Theories based on grouping argue that words that occur within the same intonational phrase are processed together at the same processing stage (e.g., Schafer, 1997). Effects of boundaries on ambiguity resolution are driven by whether ambiguously attached constituents appear in the same prosodic phrase as an attachment site. Thus in (6), a boundary after the matrix verb "maintained" causes the verb in the embedded clause, "lied", and the adverbial phrase "when the investigation started" to be processed together in the same processing chunk. This temporal proximity in the processing system creates a preference for low attachment. When a boundary occurs after the embedded verb "lied", the adverbial phrase is not processed in the same unit as either verb. According to grouping theories, a second boundary should not influence attachment preferences. However, this runs counter to findings in the literature that a boundary before an ambiguously attached constituent biases listeners towards high attachment (e.g., Carlson et al., 2001; Schafer et al., 2005; Snedeker & Trueswell, 2003).

Theories based on disjuncture, like Watson and Gibson's (2004a, 2005) anti-attachment hypothesis, argue that boundaries primarily serve as a signal of nonlocal attachment. The boundary after "maintained" in (6) signals that the verb is unlikely to receive future attachment, thus facilitating low attachment to the embedded verb. A boundary after the embedded verb "lied" signals that the adverbial phrase does not attach locally. One shortcoming of this theory lies in its explanation of low attachment. A boundary after "maintained" signals that the main verb is unlikely to receive further attachment, but in actuality, it does attach locally to the embedded clause, although it does not receive attachment down stream. This predicts that this boundary should increase sentence difficulty because it provides incorrect information about nonlocal attachment, while still aiding in resolving the ambiguity. Whether this is actually the case is unclear.

Neither theory provides an adequate explanation of the data, and it is likely that a hybrid of the two approaches will provide a fuller account. That is, the presence of a boundary acts as a signal that two elements are not associated while the absence of a boundary can signal that two elements are grouped together. Listeners may very well use both types of information in parsing syntactic structure.

Another question is understanding whether boundaries provide information about the local syntactic context in which they appear or whether they can provide information about other locations in the sentence. Carlson and colleagues (2001) have argued that listeners use global prosodic structure when processing syntactic information. They found that in sentences like (6), an early boundary after the verb "maintained" reduced the high attachment preference driven by the boundary after the embedded verb "lied". Similarly a boundary after "lied" reduced the effect of the early boundary on low attachment. In addition, the magnitude of the boundary (i.e., whether the boundary was an intermediate or full intonational phrase) modulated the effect. Snedeker and Casserly (2010 this issue) also find effects of global prosodic structure on ambiguity resolution although they find effects of both the global prosodic structure and absolute boundary size on attachment.

Frazier, Carlson, and Clifton (2006) argue that this is evidence against approaches that argue that boundaries provide information about the local syntactic context (e.g., Watson & Gibson, 2004a, 2005). However, this line of argument conflates two definitions of locality. On the one hand, locality may describe whether a boundary provides information about its local syntactic context. In another sense, locality may describe whether a listener interprets a boundary only at the position at which it is encountered. These are two independent empirical questions. Watson and Gibson (2004a, 2005) argue that boundaries provide local information in the first sense, whereas Frazier et al. (2006) provide evidence that boundaries are nonlocal in the second. For example, Carlson et al.'s (2001) evidence is consistent with the early and late boundary providing local information about their syntactic contexts, and the listener integrating over these boundaries across the sentence in making an attachment preference.

Audience design

Recent work in understanding intonational boundaries and parsing has come to focus on the role of boundaries at the interface of language comprehension and language production. Traditionally, psycholinguists have used ambiguity resolution as a tool for understanding the underlying mechanisms of the language comprehension system. A natural question that has followed from this research tradition is understanding whether speakers consistently provide listeners with prosody that disambiguates a sentence.

The evidence thus far has been mixed. Allbritton, McKoon, and Ratcliff (1996) found that naïve speakers did not reliably disambiguate sentences prosodically for listeners, while expert speakers did. Findings by Snedeker and Trueswell (2003) are consistent with Allbritton et al.'s findings from naïve speakers. In a referential communication task, speakers instructed their partners to tap objects in a real world display using utterances like (11).

(11) Tap the frog with the flower.

Here, the prepositional phrase "with the flower" can be interpreted as either an instrument of the verb or a modifier of "frog". Verb attachment is associated with a boundary after "frog", while NP attachment is associated with a boundary after the verb "Tap". Snedeker and Trueswell (2003) found that speakers only disambiguated the sentence for listeners if they were aware of the ambiguity. Based on these findings, some have concluded that speakers do not typically disambiguate syntactic structure for listeners during the course of normal conversation.

The above findings conflict with other work in the literature. Schafer and colleagues (2005) found that speakers consistently disambiguate sentences similar to (11) for listeners in a referential communication task. Similarly, Kraljic and Brennan (2005) found that speakers consistently disambiguate structures like (12) below.

(12) Put the dog in the basket on the star.

In (12), the listener is being instructed by another subject to move either a dog that is in a basket onto a star, or to move a dog into a basket that is on a star. Kraljic and Brennan (2005) found that speakers consistently disambiguated the sentence by placing an intonational phrase boundary at the right-hand constituent boundary of the direct object depending on the intended interpretation, independent of whether they were aware of the ambiguity or not, and independent of whether the context was actually ambiguous or not. They conclude that the production of prosodic structure is constrained by speaker-centred processes rather than listener-centred processes.

A speaker-centred explanation may explain the seemingly inconsistent results of Snedeker and Trueswell (2003). The sentences produced in Snedeker and Trueswell's experiment were shorter than those used in Kraljic and Brennan (2005) or Schafer et al. (2005). If speakers' productions of intonational boundaries are largely driven by the length of syntactic constituents (Watson & Gibson, 2004b), then speakers are unlikely to produce intonational boundaries in short sentences, whether they are ambiguous or not. Thus, the effect of speaker awareness found by Snedeker and Trueswell may be due in large part to sentence length. Speakers' awareness of the ambiguity may have encouraged more boundary use than normal in short sentences.

If Kraljic and Brennan's (2005) speaker-centred view is correct, speakers may produce intonational boundaries for reasons related to planning, rather than for the listener. Listeners may be sensitive to the distribution of these boundaries, inferring syntactic and semantic structure from boundary placement. MacDonald (1999) has proposed this type of model to provide a general account of the interface between production and comprehension, arguing that the distribution of syntactic structures constrains listeners' parsing preferences.

Clifton and colleagues (2006) propose a similar model specifically for prosodic structure. Under the Rational Speaker Hypothesis, speakers produce intonational boundaries based on factors such as syntactic structure, constituent length, and pragmatics. Clifton and colleagues argue that listeners are sensitive to the likely underlying causes of boundary placement and weight these boundaries accordingly. Consider (13):

(13a) Pat // or Jay and Lee convinced the bank president to extend the mortgage.
(13b) Pat or Jay // and Lee convinced the bank president to extend the mortgage.
(13c) Patricia Jones // or Jacqueline Frazier and Letitia Connolly convinced the bank president to extend the mortgage.
(13d) Patricia Jones or Jacqueline Frazier // and Letitia Connolly convinced the bank president to extend the mortgage.

A boundary in (13) can tell a listener how to group the three referents in the subject. Clifton and colleagues (2006) found that listeners were less likely to use boundaries to group the nouns when the nouns were phonologically longer (as in 13c and 13d) and more likely to use the boundaries for grouping when the referents were shorter. Clifton et al. (2006) argue that in (13c) and (13d), listeners attribute the boundaries to constituent length rather than to disambiguating the grouping of the subject.

Implicit prosody

Recently, there has been a great deal of interest in how the prosodic structure of a language potentially influences language comprehension in reading. With the exception of punctuation, there is no explicit prosody available to readers. Researchers have proposed that listeners construct a prosodic representation on the fly in reading called implicit prosody (Bader, 1998; Fodor, 2002).

Bader (1998) was the first to propose that implicit prosody may be more than an epiphenomenon of reading and may affect parsing decisions. He argued that the degree of difficulty of recovering from a garden path results partly from having to re-analyse both the prosodic structure of a sentence and the syntactic structure of a sentence. Readers experience more difficulty when both syntax and prosodic structure must be re-processed or re-analysed than when syntax alone must be re-processed or re-analysed. For example, Bader claims that NP/S ambiguities like (9) result in less severe garden paths than early/late closure ambiguities like (4). According to Nespor and Vogel's (1986) formulation of prosodic structure, the two interpretations in (9) share the same prosodic structure, while the two interpretations in (4) have different prosodic structures. Because re-analysis in the latter interpretation requires an additional change to the prosodic representation, the garden path is more severe.

Fodor (1998, 2002) has proposed a more direct role for implicit prosody in parsing decisions and has argued that it can provide a broad explanation for an unsolved problem in the field: understanding cross-linguistic differences in attachment preferences. Although there seems to be a general cross-linguistic locality preference for constituents to be attached to more recent material (Frazier & Clifton, 1998; Gibson, 2000), globally ambiguous sentences like the one below result in different preferences in different languages.

(14) Frank knows the secretary of the linguist who quit her job.

The relative clause "who quit her job" can modify either "secretary" or "linguist". In English, there is a preference towards attaching to the most recent or lowest node in the sentence (low attachment), in this case "linguist". However in Spanish, there is a preference to attach to the highest node, "secretary". Although there have been a variety of proposals, there has been no satisfactory explanation as to why speakers of different languages have different attachment preferences (see Fodor, 1998 for a review). Fodor and colleagues have argued that implicit prosody plays a role. The claim is that readers construct a prosodic structure that fits the prosodic constraints of their language, and that this representation, in turn, can influence attachment preferences. For example, shorter relative clauses are associated with low attachment cross-linguistically. Fodor argues that shorter relative clauses are less likely to be preceded by an intonational boundary because listeners disprefer to place a short relative clause in an intonational phrase by itself (see Selkirk, 2000). The absence of a boundary at this location creates a bias towards low attachment. In contrast, a longer relative clause is more likely to be preceded by a boundary in the implicit prosodic representation, and this boundary creates a bias towards high attachment. Fodor (1998, 2002) argues that languages in which one sees high attachment preferences are those in which prosodic constraints require prosodic breaks at the beginning of constituents (English is not one of these languages). Boundaries are constructed before relative clauses because these breaks are required by the grammar (in Fodor's theory), and these boundaries induce high attachment. Fodor and colleagues (e.g., Hirose, 1999; Lovric, 2003) are testing these hypotheses across a wide class of languages.

Although implicit prosody is providing interesting potential explanations for a variety of phenomena, this type of approach faces a large set of challenges. Because implicit prosody cannot be directly measured, a manipulation of implicit prosody in reading necessarily requires a manipulation of another linguistic factor that is assumed to affect prosody in spoken speech. Thus, it is difficult to know whether implicit prosody or another linguistic factor is the underlying source of any effect that is found.

A cross-linguistic approach like the one offered by Fodor in which one studies links between varying distributions of prosodic structure and syntax across languages, rather than manipulating linguistic variables within a language, may offer the best approach.

PROSODIC PROMINENCE

Phonetic and phonological correlates

Just as in the case of boundary strength and phrasing, the phonetic cues related to prominence include duration, fundamental frequency, and intensity, as shown by Fry (1955, 1958) and Lieberman (1960). Which cues are the most important is still controversial, and also varies vastly between languages. The following discussion is mostly based on research on English.

Duration has been shown in many studies to correlate with prominence in English both to signal word stress, and, at the phrasal level, to signal phrasal prominence. Given that duration also plays a crucial role in signalling phrasing, it seems that the same channel has to do double duty (more than that, really, since duration is also crucial in conveying lexical contrasts between words). However, the precise durational changes related to prominence were argued in Beckman and Edwards (1992) to differ from the durational changes affected by boundary strength. While the durational correlate of prominence (e.g., under focus) is often achieved by increasing phase, that is, decreasing the overlap between gestures, the durational lengthening at the end of prosodic constituents tends to be achieved by a slowing down of the gestures, i.e., a decrease in stiffness.

Fundamental frequency can encode prominence in a number of ways. The location of primary prominence in a word is reflected in the temporal alignment of pitch accents. The degree of prominence on a word can be increased by a higher pitch excursion (Eady, Cooper, Klouda, Mueller, & Lotts, 1986; Rietveld & Gussenhoven, 1985). Furthermore, an increase in pitch range was shown in Ladd and Morton (1997) to be interpreted as encoding a distinction as to whether or not an accented constituent was especially emphasised. Post-focal material is often realised with a reduced pitch range (Xu & Xu, 2005). Relative pitch scaling is thus a main cue in English for encoding relative prominence.

Kochanski, Grabe, Coleman, and Rosner (2005), however, question whether pitch is a reliable cue even if the mean values in experimental studies often show differences. Kochanski et al. (2005) point out the variability of pitch cues across utterances. They demonstrate that pitch is not a good predictor of prominence in an English corpus, and find evidence that loudness is the best acoustic correlate. Beckman and Pierrehumbert (1986) found that duration and intensity together form a reliable correlate of prominence, a finding that was confirmed in a perception study based on synthetic stimuli in Turk and Sawusch (1996).

Finally, spectral slope has also been linked to cueing prominence (Heldner, 2001; Sluijter & van Heuven, 1996). Sluijter and van Heuven found that syllables show a flatter spectral tilt in words carrying contrastive stress.

Relative prominence relations and categorical prominence levels

A controversial issue in the domain of prominence is whether linguistically significant degrees of prominence are gradient and relative or whether they correspond to phonological categories—a debate similar to the one on boundary strength. The categorical view holds that phonology provides a small number of discrete levels of prominence, whose use is determined by grammatical constraints. This controversy can be traced at least to the discussion of the prominence assignment algorithm presented in Chomsky and Halle (1968), in which each syllable was assigned an integer value reflecting the degree of prominence as determined by its place in the syntactic structure. This algorithm was criticised for providing an unrealistic number of degrees of prominence (Vanderslice & Ladefoged, 1972), even though it was explicit in not wanting to provide a phonetic theory of prominence in the first place. The crux of the gradient stress representation in Chomsky and Halle (1968), and also more recent gradient representations such as the "metrical grid" (Liberman, 1975; Liberman & Prince, 1977), was to allow a fine-grained encoding of *relative* prominence relations between syllables and words, because the idea was that relative prominence is what is influenced by syntactic and other factors. The phonetic realisation was assumed to be *compatible* with these relations, but would not necessarily reflect them in all their detail.

A narrower inventory of phonetic prominence distinctions seems plausible at least at the word-stress level, where there is evidence for a small set of distinctions that are phonologically motivated, such as reduced, unreduced, and stressed vowels, although this does not mean that there are no gradient distinctions within these categories. Similar suggestions of a limited set of categorical options have been made for prominence at the sentence level, e.g., whether or not a word is pitch accented is often taken to be a categorical distinction. Related to this is the question of whether there are categorically different types of pitch accents, each associated with distinct semantic/pragmatic import (e.g., Pierrehumbert & Hirschberg, 1990).

Even if it remains controversial how prominence should be represented, it is uncontroversial that relative prominence plays an important role in grammar, e.g., in the information structure of English. The wrong relative prominence relation between words often leads to infelicity:

(15) A: Would you like some coffee?
B: I would love some *coffee*.

If the prominence of "coffee" in (15B) is higher than that of "love", this sentence sounds odd, for reasons to be discussed below. Relative prominence is very salient at the end of phrases and utterances, which is why much of the impressionistic data reported in the literature on sentence-level prominence discusses where the last and main prominence falls in a sentence. Shifting the prominence away from the end of a sentence in cases when it is not motivated or failing to do so when it is motivated, can lead to strong pragmatic deviance. Xu and Xu (2005) argue that such shifts in prominence are achieved by a relative pitch range suppression rather than by a categorical deaccentuation. They show evidence that pitch suppression after (but not before) focused constituents is observed in English, but within the subordinated domain there are still remnants of the pitch movements usually associated with word stress.

Thus the extent to which prominence is mediated by the placement and omission of accents or by gradient adjustments of relative prominence such as pitch range modulation remains controversial, but the fact that prominence encodes important information about the structure of an utterance and its context is not.

Relationship to syntactic structure

Sentence-level prominence can be affected by a number of syntactic factors. In fact, Chomsky and Halle (1968) argued that the relative prominence of words in a sentence is entirely determined by a recursive algorithm that translates phrase structures into a phonological transcription which includes relative prominence. Bolinger (1972) challenged this syntactic approach and argued that accents directly reflect the intentions of the speaker and the information flow of the sentence. Schmerling (1976) also questioned the feasibility of a purely syntactic account of sentence stress assignment, and proposed a number of semantic constraints that affect sentence stress instead. One factor she proposes is that "predicates receive lower stress than their arguments", which accounts for why in German and English a direct object is always more prominent, independent of whether or not the word order is OV or VO. This semantic generalisation is integrated in the theory of sentence stress proposed in Gussenhoven (1984). Gussenhoven presents a system that captures the circumstances under which words are phrased into a single domain carrying a single accent. The decisive factor that makes one constituent integrate into a single accent domain with a second constituent is semantic. If a constituent is the argument of a second argument, they form a single accent domain. The only syntactic condition in this theory is that the two constituents be adjacent to each other. Effects of argument structure on prominence are also discussed in Selkirk (1984).

It is not clear though that a semantic approach to sentence prominence is sufficient. Whether or not a predicate is prosodically subordinated and forms a single accent domain with an adjacent argument depends on its syntactic relation to the argument. Truckenbrodt and Darcy (2010) report that complement clauses in German differ from complement NPs in that the selected predicate remains accented when taking a clausal complement. This observation can be related to the fact that complement clauses in German obligatorily "extrapose", that is, they are treated very differently from other syntactic complements, e.g., they follow the verb instead of preceding it, in contrast to nominal arguments in German. Two influential syntactic approaches that place a higher emphasis on syntax in the negotiation of prominence are Cinque (1993) and Truckenbrodt (1995).

Prominence and information and discourse structure

It is widely accepted that pitch accents play a role in signalling the information and discourse status of the words and constituents in which they appear, although how to characterise this information is under considerable debate. Researchers have proposed that a pitch accent is placed on constituents that are new (e.g., Chafe, 1987; Halliday, 1967; Prince, 1981), important (Bolinger, 1972) or nongiven (Schwarzschild, 1999), focused (Büring, 2007; Jackendoff, 1972; Rooth, 1992; Selkirk, 1995), less accessible (Arnold, 2008), or unpredictable (Aylett & Turk, 2004; Gregory, 2001). Below, these differing perspectives are reviewed.

Givenness

Work in the literature suggests a link between the givenness of a referent and whether it is produced with an accent. New information is argued to be accented while given information is argued to be de-accented, and work from the psycholinguistic literature supports this characterisation. This pattern is also reflected in preferences in comprehension. Both Dahan, Tanenhaus, and Chambers (2002) and Terken and Nooteboom (1987), found that listeners' comprehension of instructions was better when new information was accented and given information was de-accented. Listeners also rate sentences with accented new information and de-accented given information as being more acceptable (Birch & Clifton, 1995).

However, it is also clear that previous mention is not sufficient for a word to be interpreted as given. In a corpus study, Hirschberg (1993) found that previously mentioned information is often accented. De-accented words were very likely to be given, but given words were only de-accented approximately half of the time. Terken and Hirschberg (1994) found that whether speakers produced a word with an accent depended on whether the referent was new and whether it had changed syntactic position, given information produced in a different syntactic role was accented. This may be related to evidence in Wagner (2006) and Williams (1997) that shows that in many cases marking a constituent as given is only possible when there is an antecedent that includes a plausible alternative to its sister constituent. Dahan et al. (2002) found that listeners preferred accents on given information if that information was not salient in the discourse.

To illustrate the issues for a theory in which previously mentioned material is de-accented and new material is accented, consider the following examples (based on examples in Schwarzschild, 1999):

(16a) Patty's cousin likes classical music, but PATTY likes rock 'n' roll.
(16b) Who is Patty's cousin arguing with? She's arguing with PATTY.
(16c) Cathy likes to waltz, but her partner HATES dancing.

In (16a), the second instance of "Patty" is accented to contrast her with her cousin even though "Patty" was previously mentioned. Example (16b) demonstrates that accenting previously mentioned material may be felicitous even without contrast. In (16c), new material like "partner" and "dancing" can forgo accenting even though they are mentioned for the first time.

Researchers have tried two different approaches to solve this problem. One has been to re-define given and new so that it captures the data (see Venditti & Hirschberg, 2003 for a review). Halliday (1967) argues that given information should be defined as information that is recoverable from the discourse while new information is not inferable from the discourse and violates the expectations of the conversational participants. Schwarzschild (1999) argues that the givenness of information depends on whether it is entailed by the discourse. Under these accounts, "Patty" is accented in (16a) and (16b) because it is not predictable from the discourse. "Partner" and "dancing" can be de-accented because they are inferable from the discourse.

Focus structure

Closely related to theories of "givenness" are theories of "focus structure". Jackendoff (1972), e.g., suggested the following: "As Working definitions, we will use the 'focus of a sentence' to denote the information in the sentence that is assumed by the speaker not to be shared by him and the hearer, and 'presupposition of a sentence' to denote the information in the sentence that is assumed by the speaker to be shared by him and the hearer.

Intuitively, it makes sense to speak of a discourse as 'natural' if successive sentences share presuppositions, that is, if the two speakers implicitly agree on what information they have in common".

One particularly influential theory of focus is that of Rooth (1992), who proposed to capture the notion of focus using the alternatives that a focused constituent evokes. In his theory, every constituent in a sentence is assigned a meaning and a set of alternatives. If there is no focused information inside of a constituent, the set of alternatives is the unitary set of that constituent. If there is a constituent marked as focused, then the alternative set includes all constituents that can be built by replacing that constituent with contextually relevant alternatives of the same semantic type. Rooth's theory has the nice property that it accounts for different kinds of focus phenomena, such as question–answer congruence, contrastive stress, and givenness marking with a single formalism. Variations of this type of approach were presented in Büring (2003), Schwarzschild (1999), and Wagner (2006).

It remains controversial, however, whether it is indeed the case that a unique theory can account for the full range of "focus" phenomena. A theory that makes a distinction between focus and anaphoric destressing is proposed in Reinhart (2006), and this distinction is also commonly made in recent Optimality Theory literature on the topic (e.g., Samek-Lodovici, 2002).

Focus projection

Acoustic prominence of a word is often assumed to reflect the information status of the word itself. As has been pointed out in the literature (e.g., in Chomsky, 1971; see also Ladd, 2008 for a discussion), this assumption is problematic because of examples like the one below:

(17a) What does Patty do in her free time?
(17b) Patty likes to ROCK 'n' ROLL.

Here "rock 'n roll" is accented, but the new information, or focused material, is actually the entire VP "likes to rock 'n roll". An entire constituent may require highlighting in the discourse, yet frequently, an accent might only occur on only one of the words in the constituent. There appear to be constraints on which word in a focused constituent can carry an accent. For example, (18b) is a well-formed response to the question in (18a), while (18c) is less acceptable.

(18a) What does Mary like?
(18b) Mary likes the picture of the VASE.
(18c) Mary likes the picture near the VASE.

Gussenhoven (1983) and Selkirk (1984) argue that to prosodically focus a constituent, an accent must occur on an (internal) syntactic argument of the constituent (in this case, "vase"), but there need not be an accent on the head (in this case, "picture"). But adjuncts differ from arguments in that if the head remains unaccented, focus cannot project from a syntactic adjunct of a head. Thus, in (18b), "vase" can project focus to the entire object noun phrase while in (18c) it cannot.

Experimental work by Birch and Clifton (1995, 2002) confirms these claims. Participants rated sentences in which arguments carry an accent to focus a constituent as being more acceptable than sentences in which adjuncts carry the accent. Similar findings are reported by Welby (2003). However, Breen, Fedorenko, Wagner, and Gibson (2010 this issue) found consistent differences between narrow and broad focus in the production of accented words, and point out that the difficulty between perceptually differentiating broad and narrow focus in the case of VP vs. O focus may be that the two conditions have similar prominence relations between verb and object.

Prominence and accessibility

Another strategy to better understand "givenness" and "focus" effects has been to use accounts of discourse focus and accessibility to describe givenness constraints on accenting (Dahan et al., 2002; Venditti & Hirschberg, 2003; Watson, Arnold, & Tanenhaus, 2005). These accounts have traditionally been used to explain speakers' word choice preferences, particularly pronoun usage (see Arnold, 2008 for a review). The assumption is that as a discourse proceeds, information varies in its overall level of activation. Information that is highly activated tends to be highly accessible and is referred to using pronouns or shortened expressions while less accessible material is referred to with a full referring expression (Brennan, 1995; Grosz, Joshi, & Weinstein, 1995; Grosz & Sidner, 1986; Gundel, Hedberg, & Zacharski, 1993). Accessibility is influenced by syntax, topicality, recency of mention, and other factors. It is possible that accessibility plays a role in accenting as well as in the choice between full noun phrases and pronouns; accessible information is de-accented while nonaccessible information is accented. This approach can capture given/new effects since given information is likely to be accessible while new information is not. It also captures the apparent exceptions: nonpreviously mentioned information that can be inferred or derived from the discourse context is likely to be accessible. In addition, previously mentioned information is not always accessible and would thus require an accent.

Prominence and predictability

There is a close relationship between frequency and probability and quantitative measures of prominence (Aylett, 2000; Aylett & Turk, 2004; Bard et al., 2000; Bell, Brenier, Gregory, Girand, & Jurafsky, 2009; Gregory, Healy, & Jurafsky, 2002; Jurafsky, Bell, Gregory, & Raymond, 2001). Watson, Arnold, and Tanenhaus (2008a) found that words that are predictable from task-based constraints are more likely to be shortened, and Gahl and Garnsey (2004) found that verbs occurring with dispreferred arguments tend to be longer in duration. The acoustic length of a syllable correlates with its likelihood in context. The precise modelling of this probabilistic relationship is still an open question.

A model to explain these effects is proposed in Aylett (2000) and Aylett and Turk (2004), whose Smooth Signal Hypothesis holds that the degree of prominence of a syllable depends on its degree of redundancy, and various processes in speech conspire to evenly spread redundancy throughout an utterance. The effects that can be accounted for by the Smooth Signal Hypothesis involve quantitative differences not only in the strength of certain phonetic cues but also categorical choices, such as whether or not a syllable carries a pitch accent.

More recent research by Jaeger (2006) and Levy and Jaeger (2007) shows that choices between different lexical and syntactic options (e.g., the choice between inserting a relative pronoun or not) can be explained by this idea—by inserting a relative pronoun, the redundancy of the signal is increased, and this insertion/omission of the additional morpheme was shown to depend on the redundancy of the surrounding material. They argue that lengthening may be part of a general strategy speakers use to optimally communicate with listeners, the "Uniform Information Density Hypothesis" (Jaeger, 2006; Levy & Jaeger, 2007).

There is also a clear link between predictability and pitch accenting. Highly predictable words are less likely to be accented than nonpredictable words (Bell et al., 2002; Gregory, 2001). Gregory (2001) found that both low frequency and low transitional probabilities predict pitch accenting in corpora of spoken speech. What underlies this relationship? One possibility is that predictability effects simply reflect the statistics of discourse structure. Arnold (1998) found that changes in discourse accessibility are relatively infrequent in conversation. Thus, accenting unpredictable information may simply reflect the effects of accessibility discussed above. Predictability might also have a more direct effect on pitch accenting. Words that are infrequent might be more difficult to produce and require hyperarticulation (see Gahl & Garnsey, 2004 for a discussion). Watson et al. (2008a) found that word lengthening due to unpredictability also correlated with disfluency, suggesting that production difficulty may underlie both. In addition, Fowler and Housum (1987) found that repeated words tend to be reduced, and more recent work by Bard and Aylett (1999) found that this reduction is not always the result of de-accenting, suggesting that it may be the result of something other than marking information for the listener. Bell et al. (2009) argue that lengthening may relate to difficulties with lexical access. Understanding whether pitch accents are primarily speaker or listener centred faces the same challenge this question has faced in other areas of the literature (see Arnold, 2008 for discussion of the debate in the word choice literature). Because production- and listener-centred preferences are intimately linked, untangling the two poses a challenge for the field.

Integrating focus structure, accessibility, and predictability

There is relatively little overlap between the tradition of work on focus and givenness on the one hand, and the work on accessibility and predictability on the other. Often, similar terms used in these traditions can mean very different things, which can be confusing to the novice who is just beginning to explore the literature. For example, the use of the term "focus" in the focus structure tradition differs from its usage in the discourse accessibility tradition discussed above. In the latter tradition, focus refers to given, highly accessible information. In the focus structure tradition, it refers to new, nonaccessible information.

It is very clear that future work in pitch accenting will require cross-talk between these traditions. Researchers in the pragmatic and discourse accessibility tradition will need to integrate findings from focus structure into their work if they wish to successfully predict and understand how pragmatics affects the distribution of accenting. Some of the researchers in this tradition are interested in the computational problem of predicting accent distribution, and integrating focus structure constraints into current models is inevitable. It is also the case that researchers in the focus structure condition who abstract away from the discourse and cognitive constraints that govern importance and pitch accenting do so at their own peril. Evidence for performance constraints on accenting like referent accessibility (e.g., Venditti & Hirschberg, 2003) and repetition effects on pitch accenting (Bard & Aylett, 1999) suggests that a full understanding of information structure and pitch accenting may not be possible if one assumes that the link between accenting and information structure lies only in the grammar. Recent work on coherence relations (Kehler, Kertz, Rohde, & Elman, 2008) can be seen as one attempt at integrating the more formal theory of focus structure with a more elaborate theory of how discourse works.

Pitch accents and online processing

A great deal of controversy surrounds the representations and usages underlying pitch accents, including whether there are different types of accents (e.g., H* vs. LH*), whether these differences are categorical or continuous, and what acoustic properties of pitch accents drive their perception.

One source of this controversy has been the lack of an implicit measure of listeners' perception of an accent. Much of the early work on accent perception relied on the intuitions of researchers or naïve subjects. In either case, judgements are potentially influenced by top-down perception, and in many instances, the differences on which the judgements turn may depend on potentially complex discourse representations, which may be too subtle to intuit with any consistency.

Until recently, researchers have not had the tools to implicitly measure a listener's perception of an accent as it is heard in real time (see Watson, Gunlugson, & Tanenhaus, 2006b for a review). There has been an explosion of recent work using eye tracking in a visual-world paradigm to answer questions about the comprehension of pitch accents. In this paradigm, participants are presented with a visual array, either on a computer screen or a real-life display. The participant is typically given auditory instructions while their fixations are monitored by an eye-tracking system, allowing the researcher to manipulate some aspect of the linguistic signal. Because fixations are driven by a wide array of factors that may have little to do with the language, the participant's task is designed so that verbal instructions play a critical role in completion of the task. The visual-world paradigm has been used by the psycholinguistics community to investigate a wide range of questions about both language production and comprehension, including syntactic ambiguity resolution (e.g., Tanenhaus et al., 1995), verb processing (e.g., Altmann & Kamide, 1999), semantic and discourse processing (e.g., Sedivy, Tanenhaus, Chambers, & Carlson, 1999), conversation (Brown-Schmidt, Campana, & Tanenhaus, 2005), lexical access (Allopenna, Magnuson, & Tanenhaus, 1998), categorical perception (McMurray, Tanenhaus, & Aslin, 2002), and many others.

The visual-world paradigm is ideally suited for investigating questions related to prosody. Fixations are highly sensitive to the acoustic-phonetic signal, making it an ideal tool for investigating prosody. Dahan et al. (2002) used this paradigm to investigate how quickly listeners process pitch-accent information in online comprehension. On a computer display containing eight pictures of objects, participants were instructed to move two objects to different locations in the screen. Critically, two of the objects were a phonetic cohort, sharing their initial segments (e.g., "candy" and "candle").

Typically, when listeners encounter temporarily ambiguous cohort competitors, participants fixate on each cohort picture equally until disambiguating information is encountered. In order to see whether a pitch accent can resolve this ambiguity, and to understand whether pitch accents are rapidly processed in comprehension, Dahan et al. manipulated both the given/new status of one of the cohorts and whether it was produced with a pitch accent.

(19a) Put the candle/candy below the triangle.
(19b) Now put the CANDLE/candle above the square.

When participants heard a pitch accent on the target word in (19b), they fixated on the new referent more often than the given referent. When the critical cohort was de-accented, participants looked to the given referent more than the new referent. These differences appeared approximately 300 ms after the onset of the target cohort, suggesting that not only are pitch accents rapidly detected, but also they can be integrated into the discourse representation in the first moments of processing.

The success of Dahan et al.'s (2002) study has led researchers to adopt this technique to investigate the semantic and acoustic properties of pitch accents. Using the visual-world paradigm, Ito and Speer (2008) and Weber, Braun, and Crocker (2006) found that listeners fixated potential contrast objects when they heard an L+H* on an adjective. Watson, Tanenhaus, and Gunlogson (2008b) have found that the interpretation of L+H* and H* may overlap instead of having complimentary distributions. Chen, den Os, and de Ruiter (2007) have used the paradigm to investigate the semantic properties of different accents. Isaacs and Watson (2010 this issue) manipulated the acoustic properties of pitch accents in a paradigm similar to that used by Dahan et al. (2002) and found that F0 slope contributed more to the perception of accenting and de-accenting than overall F0 and duration.

CONCLUSIONS

In this review we have attempted to summarise some of the advances in our understanding of pitch accents and prosodic boundaries over the past decade. Several themes emerge. There are ongoing debates surrounding how to characterise the acoustic-phonetic properties of both pitch accent and boundaries. Controversy also surrounds how they are linked to discourse, syntactic, and semantic structure. However, there is general agreement that both boundaries and accents are sensitive to a variety of factors. For example, prominence can result from a word being focused in the discourse, important, and unpredictable. A challenge for the next decade will be building theories in which these factors can be understood in a unified framework.

Much of the interdisciplinary work in prosody has focused on pitch accents and intonational phrasing, so it is in these areas that we have focused this review. However, there are wide swaths of research in prosody that we have not mentioned.

There remain questions about the role the utterance level contour or tune plays in signalling pragmatic and semantic information (e.g., Gunlogson, 2003; Pierrehumbert & Hirschberg, 1990) as well as questions about the representations that underlie rhythmic adjustments of prominence (e.g., Dilley, 2005; Gussenhoven, 1991; Selkirk, 1984) and phrasing (e.g., Ghini, 1993; Nespor & Vogel, 1986; Post, 1999; Prieto, 2005). More generally, the basic representations that underlie prosodic structure are still controversial. Although much of the reviewed work above assumes that the acoustic properties of prosody map onto an abstract phonological representation; this view is not shared by all researchers in the field (e.g., see Ladd, 2008 for discussion), some of whom argue that there is a direct mapping between acoustic features and linguistic meaning (e.g., Xu & Xu, 2005). There is debate surrounding the representations that underlie prosody more generally as well as questions about the assumptions that underlie coding systems like ToBI. There are also questions about how prosodic structure fits into models of language production.

Note that the basic questions we review here are about intonational phrasing and pitch accents; questions about acoustic correlates, function, and underlying representations, are also fundamental questions in these other areas of prosody. An interdisciplinary approach, which has been so fruitful in furthering our understanding of pitch accenting and intonational breaks, may also be fruitful in these other areas.

REFERENCES

Allbritton, D. W., McKoon, G., & Ratcliff, R. (1996). Reliability of prosodic cues for resolving syntactic ambiguity. *Journal of Experimental Psychology: Learning, Memory, and Cognition, 22*(3), 714–735. doi:10.1037/0278-7393.22.3.714

Allopenna, P. D., Magnuson, J. S., & Tanenhaus, M. K. (1998). Tracking the time course of spoken word recognition using eye movements: Evidence for continuous mapping models. *Journal of Memory and Language, 38*(4), 419–439. doi:10.1006/jmla.1997.2558

Altmann, G. T., & Kamide, Y. (1999). Incremental interpretation at verbs: Restricting the domain of subsequent reference. *Cognition, 73*(3), 247–264. doi:10.1016/S0010-0277(99)00059-1

Anderson, C., & Carlson, K. (2004, March). *Prosodic phrasing in DO/SC and closure sentences.* Paper presented at the Seventeenth Annual CUNY Conference on Human Sentence Processing, College Park, MD.

Arnold, J. (1998). *Reference form and discourse patterns*. Unpublished doctoral dissertation, Stanford, CA: Stanford University.

Arnold, J. E. (2008). Reference production: Production-internal and addressee-oriented processes. *Language and Cognitive Processes, 23*(4), 495–527. doi:10.1080/01690960801920099

Aylett, M. (2000, October). *Stochastic suprasegmentals: Relationships between redundancy, prosodic structure and care of articulation in spontaneous speech*. Paper presented at the Sixth International Conference on Spoken Language Processing Beijing, China.

Aylett, M., & Turk, A. (2004). The smooth signal redundancy hypothesis: A functional explanation for relationships between redundancy, prosodic prominence, and duration in spontaneous speech. *Language and Speech, 47*(1), 31–56. doi:10.1177/00238309040470010201

Bader, M. (1998). Prosodic influences on reading syntactically ambiguous sentences. In J. Fodor & F. Ferreira (Eds.), *Reanalysis in sentence processing* (pp. 1–46). Dordrecht, the Netherlands: Kluwer.

Bard, E. G., Anderson, A. H., Sotillo, C., Aylett, M., Doherty-Sneddon, G., & Newlands, A. (2000). Controlling the intelligibility of referring expressions in dialogue. *Journal of Memory and Language, 42*, 1–22. doi:10.1006/jmla.1999.2667

Bard, E. G., & Aylett, M. P. (1999). The dissociation of deaccenting, givenness, and syntactic role in spontaneous speech. In J. Ohala, Y. Hasegawa, M. Ohala, D. Granveille, & A. Bailey (Eds.), *Proceedings of the XIVth International Congress of Phonetic Sciences* (pp. 1753–1756). Berkeley, CA: University of California.

Beach, C. M. (1991). The interpretation of prosodic patterns at points of syntactic structure ambiguity: Evidence for cue trading relations. *Journal of Memory and Language, 30*, 644–663. doi:10.1016/0749-596X(91)90030-N

Beckman, M., & Pierrehumbert, J. (1986). Intonational structure in English and Japanese. *Phonology Yearbook, 3*, 255–310.

Beckman, M. E., & Edwards, J. (1992). Intonational categories and the articulatory control of duration. In Y. Tohkura, E. Vatikiotis-Bateson, & Y. Sagisaka (Eds.), *Speech perception, production and linguistic structure* (pp. 359–375). Tokyo: Ohmsha.

Bell, A., Brenier, J. M., Gregory, M., Girand, C., & Jurafsky, D. (2009). Predictability effects on durations of content and function words in conversational English. *Journal of Memory and Language, 60*(1), 92–111. doi:10.1016/j.jml.2008.06.003

Bell, A., Gregory, M., Brenier, J., Jurafsky, D., Ikeno, A., & Girand, C. (2002, September). *Which predictability measure affect content and durations?* Paper presented at the Proceedings of ISCA Tutorial and Research Workshop on Pronunciation Modeling and Lexicon Adaptation for Spoken Language, Estes Park, CO.

Berkovits, R. (1994). Durational effects in final lengthening, gapping, and contrastive stress. *Language and Speech, 37*, 237–250.

Birch, S., & Clifton, C. Jr. (1995). Focus, accent, and argument structure: Effects on language comprehension. *Language and Speech, 38*(4), 365–392.

Birch, S., & Clifton, C. (2002). Effects of varying focus and accenting of adjuncts on the comprehension of utterances. *Journal of Memory and Language, 47*, 571–588. doi:10.1016/S0749-596X(02)00018-9

Bolinger, D. (1972). Accent is predictable (if you're a mind reader). *Language, 48*, 633–644. doi:10.2307/412039

Breen, M., Fedorenko, E., Wagner, M., & Gibson, E. (2010). Acoustic correlates of information structure. *Language and Cognitive Processes, 25*, 1044–1098. doi:10.1080/01690965.2010.504378

Brennan, S. E. (1995). Centering attention in discourse. *Language and Cognitive Processes, 102*, 137–167. doi:10.1080/01690969508407091

Brown-Schmidt, S., Campana, E., & Tanenhaus, M. K. (2005). Real-time reference resolution by naïve participants during a task-based unscripted conversation. In J. C. Trueswell & M. K. Tanenhaus (Eds.), *Approaches to studying world-situated language use: Bridging the language-as-product and language-as-action traditions* (pp. 153–171). Cambridge, MA: MIT Press.

Büring, D. (2003). Focus projection and default prominence. In V. Molnár & S. Winkler (Eds.), *The architecture of focus* (pp. 321–346). Berlin: Mouton De Gruyter.

Büring, D. (2007). Intonation, semantics, and information structure. In G. Ramchand & C. Reiss (Eds.), *The Oxford handbook of linguistic interfaces* (pp. 445–473). Oxford: Oxford University Press.

Byrd, D., Krivokapic, J., & Lee, S. (2006). How far, how long: On the temporal scope of prosodic boundary effects. *The Journal of the Acoustical Society of America, 120*, 1589–1599. doi:10.1121/1.2217135

Byrd, D., & Saltzman, E. (1998). Intragestural dynamics of multiple phrasal boundaries. *Journal of Phonetics, 26*, 173–199. doi:10.1006/jpho.1998.0071

Byrd, D., & Saltzman, E. (2003). The elastic phrase: Modeling the dynamics of boundary-adjacent lengthening. *Journal of Phonetics, 31*(2), 149–180. doi:10.1016/S0095-4470(02)00085-2

Carlson, K., Clifton, C. Jr., & Frazier, L. (2001). Prosodic boundaries in adjunct attachment. *Journal of Memory and Language, 45*(1), 58–81. doi:10.1006/jmla.2000.2762

Chafe, W. (1987). Cognitive constraints on information flow. In R. Tomlin (Ed.), *Coherence and grounding in discourse* (pp. 21–51). Amsterdam: John Benjamins.

Chen, A., den Os, E., & de Ruiter, J. P. (2007). Pitch accent type matters for online processing of information status: Evidence from natural and synthetic speech. *The Linguistic Review, 24*, 317–344. doi:10.1515/TLR.2007.012

Chen, M. Y. (1987). The syntax of Xiamen tone sandhi. *Phonology Yearbook, 4*, 109–149.

Cho, T. (2002). *The effects of prosody on articulation in English*. New York: Routledge.

Chomsky, N. (1971). Deep structure, surface structure, and semantic interpretation. In D. D. Steinberg & L. A. Jakobovits (Eds.), *Semantics: An interdisciplinary reader in philosophy, linguistics, and psychology* (pp. 183–216). Cambridge, UK: Cambridge University Press.

Chomsky, N., & Halle, M. (1968). *The sound pattern of English*. New York: Harper & Row.

Cinque, G. (1993). A null theory of phrase and compound stress. *Linguistic Inquiry, 24*, 239–298.

Clifton, C. J., Frazier, L., & Carlson, K. (2006). Tracking the what and why of speakers' choices: Prosodic boundaries and the length of constituents. *Psychonomic Bulletin & Review, 13*(5), 854–861.

Cooper, W. E., & Paccia-Cooper, J. (1980). *Syntax and speech*. Cambridge, MA: Harvard University Press.

Cutler, A., Dahan, D., & van Donselaar, W. (1997). Prosody in the comprehension of spoken language: A literature review. *Language and Speech, 40*(2), 141–201.

Dahan, D., Tanenhaus, M. K., & Chambers, C. G. (2002). Accent and reference resolution in spoken-language comprehension. *Journal of Memory and Language, 47*(2), 292–314. doi:10.1016/S0749-596X(02)00001-3

de Pijper, J. R., & Sanderman, A. A. (1994). On the perceptual strength of prosodic boundaries and its relation to suprasegmental cues. *The Journal of the Acoustical Society of America, 96*, 2037–2047. doi:10.1121/1.410145

Dilley, L. (2005). *The phonetics and phonology of tonal systems*. Unpublished doctoral dissertation, Cambridge, MA: Massachusetts Institute of Technology.

Dilley, L., Breen, M., Bolivar, M., Kraemer, J., & Gibson, E. (2006, September). *A comparison of inter-coder reliability for two systems of prosodic transcriptions: RaP (rhythm and pitch) and ToBI (tones and break indices)*. Paper presented in the Proceedings of the International Conference on Spoken Language Processing, Pittsburgh, PA.

Dilley, L., & Brown, M. (2005). The RaP (rhythm and pitch) labeling system. v. 1.0, Massachusetts Institute of Technology. Available from http://faculty.psy.ohio-state.edu/pitt/dilley/rap-system.htm.

Dilley, L., Shattuck-Hufnagel, S., & Ostendorf, M. (1996). Glottalization of word-initial vowels as a function of prosodic structure. *Journal of Phonetics*, *24*, 423–444. doi:10.1006/jpho.1996.0023

Eady, S. J., Cooper, W. E., Klouda, G. V., Mueller, P. R., & Lotts, D. W. (1986). Acoustical characteristics of sentential focus: Narrow vs. broad and single vs. dual focus environments. *Language and Speech*, *29*, 233–251.

Edwards, J., Beckman, M. E., & Fletcher, J. (1991). The articulatory kinematics of final lengthening. *The Journal of the Acoustical Society of America*, *89*, 369–382. doi:10.1121/1.400674

Fant, G., & Kruckenberg, A. (1996). On the quantal nature of speech timing. Spoken Language, 1996. *Proceedings of the ICSLP*, pp. 2044–2047

Ferreira, F. (1988). *Planning and timing in sentence production: The syntax-to-phonology conversion*. Unpublished doctoral dissertation, Amherst, MA: University of Massachusetts.

Ferreira, F. (1991). Effects of length and syntactic complexity on initiation times for prepared utterances. *Journal of Memory and Language*, *30*(2), 210–233. doi:10.1016/0749-596X(91)90004-4

Ferreira, F. (1993). Creation of prosody during sentence production. *Psychological Review*, *100*, 233–253. doi:10.1037/0033-295X.100.2.233

Ferreira, F. (2002). Prosody. In L. Nadel (Ed.), *Encyclopedia of cognitive science* (pp. 762–768). London: Macmillan.

Ferreira, F. (2007). Prosody and performance in language production. *Language and Cognitive Processes*, *22*, 1151–1177. doi:10.1080/01690960701461293

Féry, C., & Truckenbrodt, H. (2005). Sisterhood and tonal scaling. *Studia Linguistica*, *59*, 223–243.

Fodor, J. D. (1998). Learning to parse? *Journal of Psycholinguistic Research*, *27*, 285–319. doi:10.1023/A:1023258301588

Fodor, J. D. (2002, April). Psycholinguistics cannot escape prosody. In *Proceedings of speech prosody* (pp. 83–90). Aix-en-Provence, France.

Fougeron, C., & Keating, P. (1997). Articulatory strengthening at edges of prosodic domains. *Journal of the Acoustical Society of America*, *101*, 3728–3740. doi:10.1121/1.418332

Fowler, C., & Housum, J. (1987). Talkers signaling of new and old words produced in various communicative contexts. *Language and Speech*, *28*, 47–56.

Frazier, L., Carlson, K., & Clifton, C. Jr. (2006). Prosodic phrasing is central to language comprehension. *Trends in Cognitive Science*, *10*, 244–249. doi:10.1016/j.tics.2006.04.002

Frazier, L., & Clifton, C. (1996). *Construal*. Cambridge, MA: MIT Press.

Frazier, L., & Clifton, C. (1998). Sentence reanalysis and visibility. In J. D. Fodor & F. Ferreira (Eds.), *Reanalysis in sentence processing* (pp. 143–176). Dordrecht, the Netherlands: Kluwer.

Fry, D. B. (1955). Duration and intensity as physical correlates of linguistic stress. *Journal of the Acoustical Society of America*, *27*, 765–768. doi:10.1121/1.1908022

Fry, D. B. (1958). Experiments in the perception of stress. *Language and Speech*, *1*(2), 126–152.

Gahl, S., & Garnsey, S. M. (2004). Knowledge of grammar, knowledge of usage: Syntactic probabilities affect pronunciation variation. *Language*, *80*(4), 748–775. doi:10.1353/lan.2004.0185

Gee, J., & Grosjean, F. (1983). Performance structures: A psycholinguistic appraisal. *Cognitive Psychology*, *15*, 411–458. doi:10.1016/0010-0285(83)90014-2

Ghini, M. (1993). Phi-formation in Italian: A new proposal. *Toronto Working Papers in Linguistics*, *12*, 41–78.

Gibson, E. (2000). The dependency locality theory: A distance-based theory of linguistic complexity. In Y. Miyashita, A. Marantz, & W. O'Neil (Eds.), *Image, language, brain* (pp. 95–126). Cambridge, MA: MIT Press.

Grabe, E., Warren, P., & Nolan, F. (1994). Resolving category ambiguities-evidence from stress shift. *Speech Communication*, *15*, 101–114. doi:10.1016/0167-6393(94)90045-0

Gregory, M. (2001). *Linguistic informativeness and speech production: An investigation of contextual and discourse-pragmatic effects on phonological variation*. Boulder, CO: University of Colorado.

Gregory, M. L., Healy, A. F., & Jurafsky, D. (2002). *Common ground in production: Effects of mutual knowledge on word duration*. Unpublished manuscript, University of Colorado at Boulder, CO.

Grosjean, F., & Collins, M. (1979). Breathing, pausing, and reading. *Phonetica*, *36*, 98–114. doi:10.1159/000259950

Grosz, B. J., Joshi, A. K., & Weinstein, S. (1995). Centering: A framework for modeling the local discourse. *Computational Linguistics*, *21*(2), 203–225.

Grosz, B. J., & Sidner, C. (1986). Attention, intentions, and the structure of discourse. *Computational Linguistics*, *12*, 175–204.

Gundel, J. K., Hedberg, N., & Zacharski, R. (1993). Cognitive status and the form of referring expressions. *Language*, *69*, 274–307. doi:10.2307/416535

Gunlogson, C. (2003). *True to form: Rising and falling declaratives as questions in English*. New York: Routledge.

Gussenhoven, C. (1983). *A semantic analysis of the nuclear tones of English*. Bloomington, IN: Indiana University Linguistics Club.

Gussenhoven, C. (1984). *On the grammar and semantics of sentence accents*. Cinnaminson, NJ: Foris.

Gussenhoven, C. (1991). The English rhythm rule as an accent assignment rule. *Phonology*, *8*, 1–35. doi:10.1017/S0952675700001263

Gussenhoven, C. (2004). *The phonology of tone and intonation*. Cambridge, UK: Cambridge University Press.

Halliday, M. A. K. (1967). Notes on transitivity and theme in English: Part 2. *Journal of Linguistics*, *3*, 199–244. doi:10.1017/S0022226700016613

Heldner, M. (2001). Spectral emphasis as an additional source of information in accent detection. In M. Bacchiani, J. Hirschberg, D. Litman, & M. Ostendorf (Eds.), *Prosody 2001: ISCA tutorial and research workshop on prosody in speech recognition and understanding* (pp. 57–60), Red Bank, NJ.

Hirose, Y. (1999). *Resolving reanalysis ambiguity in Japanese relative clauses*. Unpublished doctoral dissertation, CUNY, New York, NY.

Hirschberg, J. (1993). Pitch accent in context predicting intonational prominence from text. *Artificial Intelligence*, *63*(1–2), 305–340. doi:10.1016/0004-3702(93)90020-C

Isaacs, A., & Watson, D. G. (2010). Accent detection is a slippery slope: Direction and rate of F0 change drives listeners' comprehension. *Language and Cognitive Processes*, *25*, 1178–1200. doi:10.1080/01690961003783699

Ito, K., & Speer, S. R. (2008). Anticipatory effects of intonation: Eye movements during instructed visual search. *Journal of Memory and Language*, *85*(2), 541–573. doi:10.1016/j.jml.2007.06.013

Jackendoff, R. (1972). *Semantic interpretation in generative grammar*. Cambridge, MA: MIT Press.

Jackendoff, R. S. (1977). *X'-syntax: A study of phrase structure*. Cambridge, MA: MIT Press.

Jaeger, T. F. (2006). *Redundancy and syntactic reduction in spontaneous speech*. Unpublished doctoral dissertation, Stanford, CA: Stanford University.

Jun, S. A. (1993). *The phonetics and phonology of Korean prosody*. Unpublished doctoral dissertation, Columbus, OH: The Ohio State University.

Jun, S. A. (2005). *Prosodic typology: The phonology and intonation and phrasing*. Oxford: OUP.

Jurafsky, D., Bell, A., Gregory, M., & Raymond, W. D. (2001). Probabilistic relations between words: Evidence from reduction in lexical production. In J. Bybee & P. Hopper (Eds.), *Frequency in the emergence of linguistic structure* (pp. 229–254). Amsterdam: John Benjamins.

Keating, P., Cho, T., Fougeron, C., & Hsu, C. (2003). Domain-initial strengthening in four languages. In J. Local, R. Ogden, & R. Temple (Eds.), *Papers in laboratory phonology VI* (pp. 143–161). Cambridge, UK: Cambridge University Press.

Kehler, A., Kertz, L., Rohde, H., & Elman, J.L. (2008). Coherence and coreference revisited. *Journal of Semantics, 25*(1), 1–44. doi:10.1093/jos/ffm018

Kim, H., Yoon, T., Cole, J., & Hasegawa-Johnson, M. (2006). Acoustic differentiation of L- and L-L% in switchboard and radio news speech. In *Proceedings of speech prosody 2006*, Dresden, Germany.

Kjelgaard, M. M., & Speer, S. R. (1999). Prosodic facilitation and interference in the resolution of temporary syntactic closure ambiguity. *Journal of Memory and Language, 40*(2), 153–194. doi:10.1006/jmla.1998.2620

Klatt, D. H. (1975). Vowel lengthening is syntactically determined in a connected discourse. *Journal of Phonetics, 3*, 129–140.

Kochanski, G., Grabe, E., Coleman, J., & Rosner, B. (2005). Loudness predicts prominence: Fundamental frequency lends little. *The Journal of the Acoustical Society of America, 118*, 1038–1054. doi:10.1121/1.1923349

Kraljic, T., & Brennan, S. E. (2005). Prosodic disambiguation of syntactic structure: For the speaker or for the addressee? *Cognitive Psychology, 50*, 194–231. doi:10.1016/j.cogpsych.2004.08.002

Ladd, D., & Morton, R. (1997). The perception of intonational emphasis: Continuous or categorical? *Journal of Phonetics, 25*, 313–342. doi:10.1006/jpho.1997.0046

Ladd, D. R. (1988). Declination and 'reset' and the hierarchical organization of utterances. *Journal of the Acoustical Society of America, 84*, 530–544.

Ladd, D. R. (2008). *Intonational phonology* (2nd edn). Cambridge, UK and New York, NY: Cambridge University Press.

Larkey, L. S. (1983). Reiterant speech: An acoustic and perceptual validation. *The Journal of the Acoustical Society of America, 73*, 1337–1345. doi:10.1121/1.389237

Lavoie, L. (2001). *Consonant strength: Phonological patterns and phonetic manifestations.* New York: Garland.

Lehiste, I. (1970). *Suprasegmentals.* Cambridge, MA: MIT Press.

Lehiste, I. (1973). Phonetic disambiguation of syntactic ambiguity. *Glossa, 7*, 107–122.

Levy, R., & Jaeger, T. F. (2007). Speakers optimize information density through syntactic reduction. In B. Schölkopf, J. Platt, & T. Hoffman (Eds.), *Advances in neural information processing systems 19* (pp. 849–856). Cambridge, MA: MIT Press.

Liberman, M. (1975). *The intonational system of English.* Doctoral dissertation. Cambridge, MA: Massachusetts Institute of Technology.

Liberman, M., & Prince, A. (1977). On stress and linguistic rhythm. *Linguistic Inquiry, 8*(2), 249–336.

Lieberman, P. (1960). Some acoustic correlates of word stress in American English. *Journal of the Acoustical Society of America, 32*(4), 451–454. doi:10.1121/1.1908095

Lieberman, P. (1967). *Intonation, perception, and language.* Cambridge, MA: MIT Press.

Lovric, N. (2003). *Implicit prosody in silent reading: Relative clause attachment in Croatian.* Unpublished dissertation, CUNY, New York, NY.

MacDonald, M. (1999). Distributional information in language comprehension, production, and acquisition: Three puzzles and a moral. In B. MacWhinney (Ed.), *The emergence of language* (pp. 177–196). Mahwah, NJ: Lawrence Erlbaum.

Marcus, M., & Hindle, D. (1990). Description theory and intonation boundaries. In G. Altmann (Ed.), *Cognitive models of speech processing: Psycholinguistic and computational perspectives* (pp. 483–512). Cambridge, MA: MIT Press.

Marslen-Wilson, W., Tyler, L., Warren, P., Grenier, P., & Lee, C. (1992). Prosodic effects in minimal attachment. *The Quarterly Journal of Experimental Psychology Section A, 45*(1), 73–87.

Martin, J. G. (1970). On judging pauses in spontaneous speech. *Journal of Verbal Learning and Verbal Behavior, 9*, 75–78. doi:10.1016/S0022-5371(70)80010-X

McMurray, B., Tanenhaus, M. K., & Aslin, R. N. (2002). Gradient effects of within-category phonetic variation on lexical access. *Cognition, 86*(2), B33–B42. doi:10.1016/S0010-0277(02)00157-9

Nagel, H. N., Shapiro, L. P., Tuller, B., & Nawy, R. (1996). Prosodic influences on the resolution of temporary ambiguity during on-line sentence processing. *Journal of Psycholinguistic Research, 25*(2), 319–344. doi:10.1007/BF01708576

Nespor, M., & Vogel, I. (1986). *Prosodic phonology.* Dordrecht, the Netherlands: Foris.

O'Malley, M., Kloker, D., & Dara-Abrams, B. (1973). Recovering parentheses from spoken algebraic expressions. *IEEE Transactions on Audio and Electroacoustics, 21*(3), 217–220. doi:10.1109/TAU.1973.1162449

Pierrehumbert, J. (1980). *The phonology and phonetics of English intonation.* Unpublished doctoral dissertation, Cambridge, MA: Massachusetts Institute of Technology.

Pierrehumbert, J., & Hirschberg, J. (1990). The meaning of intonational contours in the interpretation of discourse. In P. R. Cohen, J. Morgan, & M. E. Pollack (Eds.), *Intentions in communication* (pp. 271–311). Cambridge, MA: MIT Press.

Post, B. (1999). Restructured phonological phrases in French: Evidence from clash resolution. *Linguistics, 37*(1), 41–63.

Price, P. J., Ostendorf, S., Shattuck-Hufnagel, S., & Fong, C. (1991). The use of prosody in syntactic disambiguation. *Journal of the Acoustical Society of America, 9*, 2956–2970. doi:10.1121/1.401770

Prieto, P. (2005). Syntactic and eurhythmic constraints on phrasing decisions in Catalan. *Studia Linguistica, 59*(2–3), 194–222.

Prince, E. (1981). Toward a taxonomy of given-new information. In P. Cole (Ed.), *Radical pragmatics* (pp. 223–255). New York: Academic Press.

Pynte, J., & Prieur, B. (1996). Prosodic breaks and attachment decisions in sentence parsing. *Language and Cognitive Processes, 11*(1), 165–192. doi:10.1080/016909696387259

Redi, L., & Shattuck-Hufnagel, S. (2001). Variation in the realization of glottalization in normal speakers. *Journal of Phonetics, 29*(4), 407–429. doi:10.1006/jpho.2001.0145

Reinhart, T. (2006). *Interface strategies: Focus: The PF-interface.* Cambridge, MA: MIT Press.

Rietveld, A. C. M., & Gussenhoven, C. (1985). On the relation between pitch excursion size and prominence. On the relation between pitch excursion size and prominence. *Journal of Phonetics, 13*, 299–308.

Rooth, M. (1992). A theory of focus interpretation. *Natural Language Semantics, 1*, 75–116. doi:10.1007/BF02342617

Samek-Lodovici, V. (2002). Prosody-syntax in the expression of focus. *Natural Language & Linguistic Theory, 23*, 687–755. doi:10.1007/s11049-004-2874-7

Schafer, A. (1997). *Prosodic parsing: The role of prosody in sentence comprehension.* Doctoral dissertation, University of Massachusetts, Amherst.

Schafer, A. J., Speer, S. R., & Warren, P. (2005). Prosodic influences on the production and comprehension of syntactic ambiguity in a game-based conversation task. In M. Tanenhaus & J. Trueswell (Eds.), *Approaches to studying world situated language use: Psycholinguistic, linguistic and computational perspectives on bridging the product and action tradition* (pp. 209–225). Cambridge: MIT Press.

Schmerling, S. F. (1976). *Aspects of English sentence stress.* Austin, TX: University of Texas.

Schwarzschild, R. (1999). Givenness, AVOIDF and other constraints on the placement of accent. *Natural Language Semantics, 7*, 141–177. doi:10.1023/A:1008370902407

Sedivy, J. C., Tanenhaus, M. K., Chambers, C. G., & Carlson, G. N. (1999). Achieving incremental semantic interpretation through contextual representation. *Cognition, 71*(2), 109–147. doi:10.1016/S0010-0277(99)00025-6

Selkirk, E. O. (1984). *Phonology and syntax: The relation between sound and structure.* Cambridge, MA: MIT Press.

Selkirk, E. O. (1986). On derived domains in sentence phonology. *Phonology Yearbook*, *3*, 371–405.

Selkirk, E. O. (1995). Sentence prosody: Intonation, stress and phrasing. In J. A. Goldsmith (Ed.), *The handbook of phonological theory* (pp. 550–569). Cambridge, MA: Blackwell.

Selkirk, E. O. (2000). The interaction of constraints on prosodic phrasing. In M. Horne (Ed.), *Prosody: Theory and experiment* (pp. 231–262). Dordrecht, the Netherlands: Kluwer.

Shattuck-Hufnagel, S., & Turk, A. E. (1996). A prosody tutorial for investigators of auditory sentence processing. *Journal of Psycholinguistic Research*, *25*(2), 193–247. doi:10.1007/BF01708572

Silverman, K. E. A., Beckman, M., Pitrelli, J. F., Ostendorf, M., Wightman, C., Price, P., et al. (1992). TOBI: A standard for labeling English prosody. In *Proceedings of the 1992 international conference on spoken language processing* (Vol. 2, pp. 867–870). Banff, Canada.

Sluijter, A. M. C., & van Heuven, V. J. (1996). Spectral balance as an acoustic correlate of linguistic stress. *The Journal of the Acoustical Society of America*, *100*, 2471–2485. doi:10.1121/1.417955

Snedeker, J., & Casserly, E. (2010). Is it all relative? Effects of prosodic boundaries on the comprehension and production of attachment ambiguities. *Language and Cognitive Processes*, *25*, 1234–1264. doi:10.1080/01690960903525499

Snedeker, J., & Trueswell, J. (2003). Using prosody to avoid ambiguity: Effects of speaker awareness and referential context. *Journal of Memory and Language*, *48*, 103–130. doi:10.1016/S0749-596X(02)00519-3

Speer, S. R., Kjelgaard, M. M., & Dobroth, K. M. (1996). The influence of prosodic structure on the resolution of temporary syntactic closure ambiguities. *Journal of Psycholinguistic Research*, *25*(2), 249–271. doi:10.1007/BF01708573

Steedman, M. (1991). Structure and intonation. *Language*, *67*(2), 260–296. doi:10.2307/415107

Stirling, L., & Wales, R. (1996). Does prosody support or direct sentence processing? *Language and Cognitive Processes*, *11*, 193–212. doi:10.1080/016909696387268

Streeter, L. A. (1978). Acoustic determinants of phrase boundary perception. *The Journal of the Acoustical Society of America*, *64*(6), 1582–1592. doi:10.1121/1.382142

Syrdal, A. K., & McGory, J., (2000). Inter-transcriber reliability of ToBI prosodic labeling. In *Proceedings of the ICSLP* (Vol. 3, pp. 235–238), Beijing, China.

Tanenhaus, M. K., Spivey-Knowlton, M. J., Eberhard, K. M., & Sedivy, J. C. (1995). Integration of visual and linguistic information in spoken language comprehension. *Science*, *268*(5217), 1632–1634. doi:10.1126/science.7777863

Terken, J., & Hirschberg, J. (1994). Deaccentuation of words representing "given" information: Effects of persistence of grammatical function and surface position. *Language and Speech*, *37*(2), 125–145.

Terken, J., & Nooteboom, S. (1987). Opposite effects of accentuation and deaccentuation on verification latencies for given and new information. *Language and Cognitive Processes*, *2*(3), 145–163. doi:10.1080/01690968708406928

Truckenbrodt, H. (1995). *Phonological phrases: Their relation to syntax, focus, and prominence.* Cambridge, MA: MIT Press.

Truckenbrodt, H. (1999). On the relation between syntactic phrases and phonological phrases. *Linguistic Inquiry*, *30*(2), 219–255. doi:10.1162/002438999554048

Truckenbrodt, H. (2002). Upstep and embedded register levels. *Phonology*, *19*(1), 77–120. doi:10.1017/S095267570200427X

Truckenbrodt, H., & Darcy, I. (2010). Object clauses, movement, and phrasal stress. In L. Rochman & N. Erteschik-Shir (Eds.), *The sound patterns of syntax* (pp. 189–216). New York, NY: Oxford University Press.

Turk, A. E. (2008, June). *Prosodic constituency signals relative predictability.* Paper presented at Labphon, University of Wellington, New Zealand.

Turk, A. E., & Sawusch, J. R. (1996). The processing of duration and intensity cues to prominence. *Journal of the Acoustical Society of America*, *99*(6), 3782–3790. doi:10.1121/1.414995

Turk, A. E., & White, L. (1999). Structural influences on accentual lengthening in English. *Journal of Phonetics, 27*(2), 171–206. doi:10.1006/jpho.1999.0093

van den Berg, R., Gussenhoven, C., & Rietveld, T. (1992). Downstep in Dutch: Implications for a model. In G. Docherty & R. Ladd (Eds.), *Papers in laboratory phonology, Vol. II: Gesture, segment, prosody* (pp. 335–358). Cambridge, UK: Cambridge University Press.

Vanderslice, R., & Ladefoged, P. (1972). Binary suprasegmental features and transformational word-accentuation rules. *Language, 48*(4), 819–838. doi:10.2307/411990

Venditti, J., & Hirschberg, J. (2003, August). *Intonation and discourse processing*. Proceedings of the International Congress of Phonetic Sciences, Barcelona, Spain.

Wagner, M. (2005). *Prosody and recursion*. Unpublished doctoral dissertation, Cambridge, MA: Massachusetts Institute of Technology.

Wagner, M. (2006). Givenness and locality. In M. Gibson & J. Howell (Eds.), *Proceedings of SALT XVI* (pp. 295–312). Ithaca, NY: CLC.

Wagner, M. (2010). Prosody and recursion in coordinate structures and beyond. *Natural Language & Linguistic Theory, 28*, 183–237.

Warren, P. (1985). *The temporal organization and perception of speech*. Unpublished dissertation, University of Cambridge, Cambridge, UK.

Warren, P., Grabe, E., & Nolan, F. (1995). Prosody, phonology and parsing in closure ambiguities. *Language and Cognitive Processes, 10*(5), 457–486. doi:10.1080/01690969508407112

Watson, D., & Gibson, E. A. (2005). Intonational phrasing and constituency in language production and comprehension. *Studia Linguistica, 59*(2–3), 279–300. doi:10.1111/j.1467-9582.2005.00130.x

Watson, D. G., Arnold, J. E., & Tanenhaus, M. K. (2005, March). *Not just given and new: The effects of discourse and task based constraints on acoustic prominence*. Poster presented at the 2005 CUNY Human Sentence Processing Conference, Tucson, AZ.

Watson, D. G., Arnold, J. E., & Tanenhaus, M. K. (2008a). Tic tac toe: Effects of predictability and importance on acoustic prominence in language production. *Cognition, 106*(3), 1548–1557. doi:10.1016/j.cognition.2007.06.009

Watson, D. G., Breen, M., & Gibson, E. (2006a). The role of syntactic obligatoriness in the production of intonational boundaries. *Journal of Experimental Psychology: Learning, Memory, and Cognition, 32*(5), 1045–1056. doi:10.1037/0278-7393.32.5.1045

Watson, D. G., & Gibson, E. A. (2004a). Making sense of the sense unit condition. *Linguistic Inquiry, 35*, 508–517. doi:10.1162/ling.2004.35.3.508

Watson, D. G., & Gibson, E. A. (2004b). The relationship between intonational phrasing and syntactic structure in language production. *Language and Cognitive Processes, 19*(6), 713–755. doi:10.1080/01690960444000070

Watson, D. G., Gunlugson, C., & Tanenhaus, M. K. (2006b). Online methods for the investigation of prosody. In A. Saube (Ed.), *Methods in empirical prosody research* (pp. 259–282). Leipzig, Germany: Mouton de Gruyter.

Watson, D. G., Tanenhaus, M. K., & Gunlogson, C. (2008b). Interpreting pitch accents in on-line comprehension: H* vs. L+H*. *Cognitive Science, 32*, 1232–1244. doi:10.1080/03640210802138755

Watt, S. M., & Murray, W. S. (1996). Prosodic form and parsing commitments. *Journal of Psycholinguistic Research, 25*(2), 291–318. doi:10.1007/BF01708575

Weber, A., Braun, B., & Crocker, M. W. (2006). Finding referents in time: Eye-tracking evidence for the role of contrastive accents. *Language and Speech, 49*(3), 367–392. doi:10.1177/00238309060490030301

Welby, P. (2003). Effects of pitch accent position, type, and status on focus projection. *Language and Speech, 46*(1), 53–81. doi:10.1177/00238309030460010401

Wheeldon, L., & Lahiri, A. (1997). Prosodic units in speech production. *Journal of Memory and Language, 37*, 356–381. doi:10.1006/jmla.1997.2517

Wightman, C. W., Shattuck-Hufnagel, S., Ostendorf, M., & Price, P. J. (1992). Segmental durations in the vicinity of prosodic phrase boundaries. *Journal of the Acoustical Society of America*, *92*, 1707–1717. doi:10.1121/1.402450

Williams, E. (1997). Blocking and anaphora. *Linguistic Inquiry*, *28*, 577–628.

Xu, Y., & Xu, C. X. (2005). Phonetic realization of focus in English declarative intonation. *Journal of Phonetics*, *33*(2), 159–197. doi:10.1016/j.wocn.2004.11.001

LANGUAGE AND COGNITIVE PROCESSES
2010, 25 (7/8/9), 946–981

Psychology Press
Taylor & Francis Group

The role of prosody in the English dative alternation

Arto Anttila[1], Matthew Adams[1], and Michael Speriosu[2]
[1]*Department of Linguistics, Stanford University, Stanford, CA, USA,*
[2]*Department of Linguistics, The University of Texas at Austin, Austin, TX, USA*

Does prosody influence the ordering of syntactic constituents? One syntactic phenomenon where prosody has occasionally been suggested to play a role is the English dative alternation. Building on proposals in earlier literature, we present a model of the dative alternation based on prosodic constraints interacting in terms of Optimality Theory. The model predicts the possible constituent orderings as well as the relative well-formedness of each ordering for verb phrases of different prosodic types. Data from two corpora that represent informal written and spoken English show that these predictions are

Correspondence should be addressed to Arto Anttila, Department of Linguistics, Stanford University, Stanford, CA 94305-2150, USA. E-mail: anttila@stanford.edu

This work was partially funded by a grant from the Office of the Vice Provost for Undergraduate Education, Stanford University, and by the Department of Linguistics, New York University.

Some of this material is covered in an earlier version that appeared as Anttila (2008). This paper has benefited from presentations at the Berkeley Phonetics and Phonology Forum (May 2005), the Indiana University Phonology Fest (June 2006), the 26th West Coast Conference on Formal Linguistics at the University of California, Berkeley (April 2007), the LSA Linguistic Institute at Stanford University (July 2007), the GLOW Colloquium at Newcastle, U.K. (March 2008), the Stanford Phonology Workshop (April 2008), the Cornell Workshop on Theoretical and Empirical Approaches to Prosody (April 2008), the 39th Meeting of the North East Linguistic Society at Cornell University (November 2008), and at linguistics colloquia at the University of California, Santa Cruz (November 2007), University of Southern California (March 2008), the University of California, San Diego (May 2008), and the University of California, Los Angeles (November 2009). We thank the audiences for their feedback.

We are deeply indebted to Philipp Angermeyer, Rahul Balusu, and Peter Liem for compiling the Blogspot corpus in the summer of 2004, Anna Cueni and Gabe Recchia for compiling the Switchboard dative alternation corpus, Curtis Andrus for programming the T-Order Generator, and Joan Bresnan for sharing her insights and corpora as well as helping us with statistics and R. We also thank Max Bane, Uriel Cohen Priva, Vivienne Fong, Florian Jaeger, Dan Jurafsky, Paul Kiparsky, Anthony Kroch, Beth Levin, Peter Sells, Tom Wasow, Arnold Zwicky, and members of the Stanford Spoken Syntax Lab for useful input. We are solely responsible for any errors.

http://www.psypress.com/lcp DOI: 10.1080/01690960903525481

largely confirmed. We conclude that the dative alternation exhibits prosodic effects that are mostly gradient and variable, yet entirely systematic. The prosodic hypothesis is thus a serious contender that must be taken into account in any attempt to explain the dative alternation in English.

Keywords: Dative alternation; Prosody; Optimality Theory.

English ditransitive verbs like *give* allow several postverbal constituent orderings. Examples are shown in (1)–(3). We call (1) the double object construction; (2) the prepositional construction; and (3) the Heavy NP Shift construction. Syntactic constituents are indicated by square brackets.

(1) The double object construction:
  (a) Dino impact gave [Earth] [the chill]
  (b) She was recommending [me] [designs] and I gladly listened

(2) The prepositional construction:
  (a) How Western New York Gave [Wings] [to the World]
  (b) I am assigning [it] only [to my advanced 5th graders]

(3) The Heavy NP Shift construction:
  (a) A staff sergeant is explaining [to the men] [the rules of the Geneva Convention]
  (b) I'm going to reveal [to you] [the terms of the wager]

Much attention has been devoted to the semantic and pragmatic factors that play a role in the choice of dative construction; see e.g., Erteschik-Shir (1979), Goldberg (1995), Green (1974), Gropen, Pinker, Hollander, Goldberg, and Wilson (1989), Krifka (1999), Levin (1993), Oehrle (1976), and Thompson (1995). One factor that has occasionally been commented on is prosody, but few studies have pursued the matter systematically. The proposal that prosody might influence the ordering of syntactic constituents is controversial; see e.g., Anttila (2008), Inkelas and Zec (1995), Pullum and Zwicky (1988), Schlüter (2005), Speyer (2005), Vogel (2006), Zec and Inkelas (1990), Zubizarreta (1998), and Zwicky and Pullum (1986). This is partly because the data are often variable and the judgements gradient; see e.g., Bresnan, Cueni, Nikitina, and Baayen (2007). In this paper, we present a model of the dative alternation based on prosodic constraints interacting in terms of Optimality Theory. The model predicts the possible constituent orderings as well as the relative well-formedness of each ordering for verb phrases of different prosodic types. We test the predictions on usage data from two corpora: 1,602 sentences of informal written English extracted from www.blogspot.com and 2,349 sentences of informal spoken English extracted from the Switchboard Corpus (Bresnan et al., 2007; Godfrey, Holliman, & McDaniel, 1992). The corpora are briefly described in Appendix 1. Our main conclusion is that the dative alternation exhibits prosodic effects that are mostly gradient and variable, yet entirely systematic. The prosodic hypothesis is thus a serious contender that must be taken into account in any attempt to explain the dative alternation in English.

It is worth emphasising at the outset that we are not claiming prosody to be the only factor that matters to constituent linearisation. This will be evident from our analysis which explicitly refers to syntactic structure. As an anonymous reviewer notes, it is possible that different kinds of constraints (prosodic, syntactic, semantic, and informational) all participate in evaluating the candidates in the optimality-theoretic model. Our goal in this paper is more modest: to put forward an explicit optimality-theoretic synthesis of earlier prosodic proposals and see to what extent this suffices to explain the constituent linearisation facts in two naturalistic corpora, while acknowledging that syntactic, semantic, and discourse variables may also play a role. In this respect, our position is similar to that in e.g., Zubizarreta (1998), and bears a particularly strong resemblance to the analyses in Büring (2001a, 2001b) (constituent order variation in German double object constructions), Büring and Gutiérrez-Bravo (2001) (the expression of focus in English, Spanish, and German), Samek-Lodovici (2005) (the expression of focus in Italian and English), and Vogel (2006) (Scandinavian object shift) which combine prosodic and morphosyntactic constraints to explain constituent linearisation in an optimality-theoretic model. These analyses defend the view that prosody matters to constituent linearisation. We share this view and provide further support for it based on the English dative alternation.

The paper is structured as follows. We first lay out the prosodic hypotheses drawing on proposals in earlier literature. These hypotheses are then formulated in terms of Optimality Theory (Prince & Smolensky, 1993/2004). The analysis specifies a mapping between two representations which we call the input and the output. The inputs are verb phrases that consist of the verb and its two arguments, marked for their lexical phonological properties, in particular lexical stresses, but with no indication as to how the arguments are linearised. The outputs are linearised verb phrases marked for both their lexical and postlexical phonological properties, in particular sentence prosody. For each input, the analysis predicts some number of possible output variants and preferences among them. We then show that the predictions are supported by the corpus evidence. Next, we discuss four specific predictions that relate to the foot structure of the verb (e.g., *téll* vs. *èxpláin*), pronoun sequences (e.g., *I gave her it*), the distribution of filler phrases (e.g., *I'll give you, you know, two to three years*), and the prosodic nature of the Principle of End Weight. The conclusion summarises the results.

EMPIRICAL GENERALISATIONS

Several well-known observations suggest that prosody plays a role in the dative alternation. In this section, we will review three major generalisations that have been frequently suggested to play a role in the dative alternation and that were illustrated in examples (1)–(3): the pronominality of the NPs (e.g., *me* vs. *designs*), the "weight" of the NPs (e.g., *the men* vs. *the rules of the Geneva Convention*), and the length of the verb (*give* vs. *explain*). The view defended here is that these generalisations are essentially prosodic: monosyllabic pronouns behave differently from other NPs because they are lexically unstressed; the "weight" of an NP is a function of the number of lexically stressed words in it; and the number of lexical stresses (= feet) in the verb plays a role in the linearisation of its argument NPs.

We will assume a standard hierarchical representation of prosody that crucially includes the foot, the prosodic word, and the prosodic phrase; see e.g., Selkirk (2003) and references there. In our discussion of word stress, we take "stress" to mean lexical stress. This is a natural choice for two reasons. First, it is methodologically much easier to pin down lexical stress than postlexical stress: the former can be looked up from a dictionary, whereas the latter results from the complex interaction of lexical stress, syntax, pragmatics, speech rate, etc., and is simply not available in the case of written data. Second, it is entirely plausible that the level of prosodic representation relevant for constituent linearisation is lexical prosody, not postlexical prosody, which is itself sensitive to the linear order of constituents. In our discussion of phrase stress, we assume that default stress falls on the rightmost phrase of the VP (Chomsky & Halle, 1968, pp. 15–24). Again, this simplifying assumption is methodologically inevitable in the case of written data and a reasonable first approximation in the case of spoken data.

One perhaps unusual aspect of our study is that we test prosodic hypotheses using two kinds of corpus data: spoken and written. We take the view that the patterns of constituent linearisation in spoken English are reflected in written English. This seems to us a plausible null hypothesis. It is perhaps worth emphasising that there is nothing new in using written sources to study prosody. This method is inevitable in the study of historical prosody where all we have is the written record and indispensable in the study of rhythm and metre in poetry. In the study of currently spoken languages, written data can be a convenient source of evidence. For example, Anttila (1997) used written corpora to study the distribution of secondary stress in Finnish words, building on the auxiliary hypothesis that the distribution of certain suffix variants is conditioned by stress. Naturally, one would expect evidence from different sources to converge, but there seems to be no reason to limit the study of prosody to speech data, to the exclusion of other types of data such as written data, experimental data, or data from well-formedness judgements.

With these introductory remarks behind us, we now proceed to discuss the three prosodic generalisations in more detail.

Lexically unstressed pronouns

The lexically unstressed pronouns *me, you, him, her, it, us,* and *them* behave differently from other NPs in dative constructions. First, it is well known that pronoun themes are avoided in double object constructions:

(4) (a) Pat gave [food] [to Chris] ~ Pat gave [Chris] [food]
(b) Pat gave [it] [to Chris] ~ *Pat gave [Chris] [it]

Following Vogel (2006) and Zwicky (1986), we take this restriction to be prosodic. We assume that every syntactic phrase forms a prosodic phrase, irrespective of whether it contains lexical stresses or not.[1] Adopting a convention that marks prosodic constituents by parentheses, we write (XP). We further assume that a lexical head (verb, preposition) and its adjacent complement can be included in the same prosodic phrase, i.e., (V NP) and (P NP); see e.g., Inkelas and Zec (1995) for discussion. The sentence **Pat gave Chris it* is ill-formed because it contains a prosodic phrase that consists of nothing but a lexically unstressed pronoun. Zwicky (1986, p. 106) calls this the Unaccented Pronoun Constraint and illustrates its role in several constituent ordering phenomena in English, including the dative alternation, the verb-particle alternation, presentational inversion, and quotative inversion. We shall call this constraint *(x) for short. The constraint is stated in (5) and illustrated in (6).[2]

(5) *(x): Lexically unstressed unary prosodic phrases are avoided.

(6)		
(a)	Pat (gave Chris) (some fóod)	lexically stressed, binary
(b)	Pat (gave Chris) (fóod)	lexically stressed, unary
(c)	Pat (gave it) (to him)	lexically unstressed, binary
(d)	*Pat (gave Chris) (it)	*(x)

[1] A different formulation is given in Truckenbrodt (2007) whose constraint StressXP requires that each syntactic phrase contain a beat of stress on the level of the prosodic phrase.

[2] An anonymous reviewer notes that in spoken language pronouns can be accented, citing Wolters and Beaver (2001), and concludes that the unstressed pronoun assumption is only a very rough approximation. Following the standard view in autosegmental-metrical phonology (see e.g., Ladd, 1996), we make a distinction between stress and pitch accent: stress denotes metrical prominence; pitch accents are tones. It is true that pitch accents provide a powerful diagnostic for lexical stress (see e.g., Hayes, 1995, pp. 10–11 for examples from English), but they cannot be identified with lexical stress. We thus cannot conclude from the existence of accented pronouns that pronouns have lexical stress. Indeed, Wolters and Beaver (2001) point out that in most cases accent on pronouns appears to be optional and interpretable as a sign of rhetorical contrast.

The same prosodic generalisation emerges in the verb-particle construction. A lexically stressed particle can form a prosodic phrase on its own, whereas the lexically unstressed pronoun cannot.

(7) The verb-particle construction:

(a)	It (slows down) (the machíne)	lexically stressed, binary
(b)	It (slows the machine) (dówn)	lexically stressed, unary
(c)	It (slows me) (dówn)	lexically stressed, unary
(d)	*It (slows down) (me)	*(x)

An anonymous reviewer points out a possible alternative explanation for the ill-formedness of sentences like **Pat gave Chris it* and **It slows down me.* According to Vogel (2006, p. 1,086), in such examples the right edge of a prosodic phrase is aligned with an unstressed pronoun which does not constitute a prosodic word. However, the reviewer further notes that this incorrectly predicts the phrasing (*I gave it*) (*to my sister*) to be ungrammatical, suggesting that sentence-finality is independently required. The Unstressed Pronoun Constraint *(x) correctly predicts both types of examples: it excludes the former, but admits the latter.

Second, it is well known that verbs like *lower, mutter, donate,* and *return* generally avoid double objects. However, if the goal is a lexically unstressed pronoun, double objects are attested (Grimshaw, 2005). Numerous examples collected from the internet are given in Bresnan and Nikitina (2003) (= B&N 2003).

(8) (a) *I lowered John the box
(b) Buddha lowered him the silver thread of a spider (B&N, 2003)

(9) (a) *Susan muttered Rachel the news
(b) She muttered him a hurried apology (B&N, 2003)

(10) (a) *John donated the charity money
(b) They can get the gullible ones to donate them money (Google)

(11) (a) *John returned the government the money
(b) Judas returned them the money (Google)

This pattern can be explained by appealing to stress clash. Assume that phrasal stress only falls on phrases that already bear lexical stress. If the noun phrase contains a lexical stress, the resulting verb phrase [V NP] contains a sequence of two stressed constituents, i.e., (ˈVˈNP) where a lexical stress from the verb is followed by a phrasal stress from the NP. If the noun phrase does not contain a lexical stress, which is the case with unstressed pronouns, there is no clash, i.e., (ˈV NP).

(12) (a) *John (retúrned the góvernment) (the money) stress clash
(b) Judas (retúrned them) (the money) no stress clash

We define a constraint *CLASH that is violated by a prosodic phrase that combines a lexical stress from the verb with a phrasal stress from the complement phrase.

(13) *CLASH: Stress clashes are avoided within a prosodic phrase.

The effect of *CLASH is vividly illustrated in the attested example (14). Here the writer's choice between the prepositional construction and the double object construction reflects the phonology of the goal phrase (*every good child, them*).

(14) With war still looming in Iraq and Santa having to *deliver presents to every good child in the world* by 24 hrs, I wonder if this year his sleigh will get shot down by a SAM (Surface-to-Air Missile) when he's *delivering them presents* over Iraq. (Google)

Stress clash also provides a rationale for the quantitative asymmetry observed with verbs like *give* which freely allow double objects. The construction type *I gave him the book* is prosodically superior to the construction type *I gave Jim the book* because of stress clash. The resulting quantitative asymmetry is illustrated from the Blogspot and Switchboard data in (15). The percentages in (15a) refer to all double object constructions with an unstressed goal (= lexically unstressed pronoun) and a stressed theme; the percentages in (15b) refer to all double object constructions with a stressed goal and a stressed theme where both are equally heavy in the sense explained in the following section. The large bias in favour of pronominal goals is consistent with the stress clash hypothesis.

(15) The percentage of double objects with stressed vs. unstressed goals

	BLOGSPOT	SWITCHBOARD
(a) I (gáve him) (the book)	94.4%	97.0%
(b) I (gáve Jím) (the book)	25.5%	47.8%

Alternative definitions of *CLASH are possible. For example, we might hypothesise that *CLASH is evaluated at the level of words. A violation would thus consist of two adjacent stressed words: (*gáve Jím*) would violate *CLASH, but (*gáve his són*) would not. We might also hypothesise that *CLASH is evaluated at the level of syllables. A violation would thus consist of two adjacent stressed syllables: (*gáve Jím*) would violate *CLASH, but (*gáve immédiate atténtion*) would not. Finally, it is possible that clash avoidance operates at all three prosodic levels simultaneously, predicting that (*gáve Jím*) should cumulate more violations than (*gáve immédiate atténtion*) which in turn should cumulate more violations than (*gáve his són*). The result would be a more fine-grained categorisation of clash data, with cumulative effects of *CLASH: no violations at all, violations of *CLASH only, violations of *CLASH and *CLASH(word), and violations of *CLASH, *CLASH(word), and *CLASH(syllable). At this point, we do not know to what extent this more fine-grained analysis would improve the predictions of the model. To see this, more corpus annotation would be required.

Alternative hypotheses that do not involve prosody have been proposed to explain the behaviour of lexically unstressed pronouns. One such hypothesis is brought up by an anonymous reviewer: pronouns are used to refer to highly accessible entities, hence one could argue that there is a constraint against highly accessible entities being realised as themes in double object constructions. Under this hypothesis, **I gave Chris it* would be ill-formed, not because *it* is lexically unstressed, but because *it* is a pronoun and thus highly accessible.

While the accessibility of NPs may well play a role in constituent linearisation, it does not seem to cover all the facts. In particular, the accessibility hypothesis sheds no light on the special behaviour of reflexive pronouns. Consider the examples in (16): the theme NP is a lexically stressed noun in (16a), a lexically stressed pronoun in (16b), and a lexically unstressed pronoun in (16c). To our judgement, (16a) and (16b) are appreciably better than (16c).

(16) (a) She gave us Jim as the culprit
(b) He gave us himself as the culprit
(c) ?She gave us him as the culprit

The accessibility hypothesis leads us to expect no difference between (16b) and (16c): both *him* and *himself* are discourse-old. The unstressed pronoun constraint correctly predicts the difference: *himsélf* is lexically stressed; *him* is lexically unstressed. This suggests that the prosodic hypothesis cannot be reduced to the accessibility hypothesis, even though it is possible that both play a role in constituent linearisation. A similar conclusion is reached by Vogel (2006) and Zwicky (1986).

End weight

The second generalisation is that "heavy" constituents come last. This is known as the Principle of End Weight (Wasow, 2002). A familiar example is Heavy NP Shift, illustrated in (17).

(17) (a) A staff sergeant is explaining [to the men] [the rules of the Geneva Convention]
(b) I'm going to reveal [to you] [the terms of the wager]

Various definitions of "grammatical weight" have been offered in the literature; see Wasow (2002, Ch. 2), for a summary and evaluation. One popular operational definition of grammatical weight is the number of orthographical words in the phrase; for a recent example, see e.g., Jäger and Rosenbach (2006, pp. 953–954). There are very few explicit prosodic proposals on record. The only such proposal cited by Wasow (2002, p. 16) is due to Zec and Inkelas (1990, p. 377) who suggest that English Heavy NP Shift is licensed when the NP contains at least two phonological phrases. This would account for the following contrast:

(18) (a) *Mark showed to John (some letters)
(b) Mark showed to John (some letters) (from Paris)

The near-absence of prosodic proposals of course does not mean that prosodic hypotheses would be manifestly wrong or uninteresting. One reason for the apparent neglect of prosody may be that prosodic proposals are difficult to test. Given the currently available annotated corpora, it is much easier to count orthographical words and syntactic nodes than to count moras, syllables, feet, prosodic words, and prosodic phrases. However, it is entirely possible that hypotheses built on such prosodic notions might explain the data better than the alternatives.

In this paper, we propose to derive end weight effects from stress. The intuition behind our analysis is that every lexical stress strives to be within the prosodic phrase that also receives sentence stress. We name this constraint the STRESS-TO-STRESS PRINCIPLE:

(19) STRESS-TO-STRESS PRINCIPLE: Each lexical stress occurs within the prosodic phrase that receives sentence stress.

We assume that in English sentence stress falls by default on the rightmost constituent. This is the Nuclear Stress Rule of Chomsky and Halle (1968, pp. 15–24). The formulation in (20) comes from Selkirk (1995, p. 562).

(20) The Nuclear Stress Rule: The most prominent syllable of the rightmost constituent in a phrase P is the most prominent syllable of P.

An example of phrasal stress assignment in terms of the metrical grid notation is shown in (21). All four words, *volunteer, firemen, save,* and *lives,* are lexically stressed. At the first cycle, phrasal stress falls on *firemen* and *lives*. At the second cycle, phrasal stress falls on *lives*.

(21)

```
                              x
                  x           x
         x        x       x   x
     ((volunteer firemen) (save lives))
```

The Stress-to-Stress Principle is illustrated in (22). Example (22a) has three word stresses that fall outside the constituent with phrasal stress: *gáve, crítical, bácking*. Example (22b) only has two such stresses: *gáve, Búsh*. The second variant is thus better in terms of the Stress-to-Stress Principle. The fact that both variants are possible shows that the Stress-to-Stress Principle is a violable constraint and that other constraints matter as well.

(22) Illustrating the constraint STRESS-TO-STRESS PRINCIPLE

```
                                           x
                 x   x     x               x
(a) Robertson (gave critical backing) (to Bush)  3 violations
                                    x
                 x   x     x        x
(b) Robertson (gave Bush) (critical backing)     2 violations
```

The stress-based theory of end weight makes three novel predictions not made by other theories. First, it predicts that lexically unstressed function words (e.g., *a*/*an*, *the*, *of*, etc.) should not count for weight. The empirical evidence will be presented shortly. This prediction is not made by the various syntactic hypotheses where weight is calculated in terms of orthographical words or syntactic nodes (Wasow, 2002). Neither is this prediction made by the alternative phonological hypothesis that calculates weight in terms of the number of syllables.

Second, the theory predicts that the weight effect should disappear if nuclear stress falls outside the VP. Potential examples are given in (23) where the VP is followed by an adverbial phrase. Since nuclear stress now falls on the adverbial, it follows that the relative ordering of the argument NPs should not show weight effects.

(23) Nuclear stress lured away

(a) never send [someone] [them] in the mail either (B&N, 2003, pp. 19–20)

(b) not to give [children] [it] to avoid possible allergies (B&N, 2003, pp. 19–20)

Third, the Stress-to-Stress Principle predicts that languages where nuclear stress falls on the left should exhibit leftward Heavy NP Shift. A potential example is Japanese; see McCawley (1977, p. 273), cited in Cinque (1993,

p. 271), Hawkins (2006), and Yamashita and Chang (2001) for relevant discussion.

In this section, we have proposed that end weight effects result from the Stress-to-Stress Principle. Under our hypothesis, grammatical weight depends on the number of prosodic words in the phrase. A possible alternative hypothesis would be that grammatical weight depends on the number of feet. This means that both primary and secondary stresses should count for weight, making *Búsh* lighter than *Rúmsfèld*. As we will see shortly, the two hypotheses yield very similar results. For the moment, we will maintain our working version of the Stress-to-Stress Principle and leave the exploration of alternative hypotheses for future work.

Verb length

In addition to the pronominality and weight of the NPs, the dative alternation is also sensitive to the nature of the verb itself. Many different proposals are on record; see e.g., Green (1974), Gropen et al. (1989), Harley (2007), and Krifka (1999), to mention just a few. Here we will explore the prosodic hypothesis formulated in Grimshaw (2005); for a precedent, see Fraser (1998). Grimshaw notes that the core class of alternating verbs have exactly one foot, e.g., (*give*), *a*(*ssign*), whereas the nonalternating verbs have two or more feet, e.g., (*ex*)(*plain*) and (*do*)(*nate*). This captures the well-known contrast in (24).

(24) (a) They (gave) the church money
(b) *They (do)(nated) the church money

Examples of alternating one-foot verbs are given in (25). The first three verbs have an initial unfooted vowel, hence reduction. Examples of nonalternating two-foot verbs are given in (26).

(25) Alternating one-foot verbs (Grimshaw, 2005; Levin, 1993, pp. 45–46)

a(llot)	(give)	(lend)	(owe)	(send)
a(ssign)	(grant)	(loan)	(pass)	(show)
a(ward)	(hand)	(mail)	(pay)	(teach)
(bring)	(leave)	(offer)	(promise)	(tell)

(26) Non-alternating two-foot verbs (Grimshaw, 2005)

(con)(vey)	(do)(nate)	(pre)(sent)	(trans)(fer)
(de)(liver)	(en)(trust)	(re)(mit)	
(dic)(tate)	(ex)(plain)	(re)(turn)	

Just like the other prosodic constraints, the one-foot constraint is violable. It is well known that some two-foot verbs undergo the dative alternation, at least to some extent. Examples are given in (27).

(27) Alternating two-foot verbs (Levin, 1993, pp. 45–46)

(allo)(cate)	(radi)(o)	(tele)(cast)
(cata)(pult)	(sate)(llite)	(tele)(graph)
(guaran)(tee)	(sema)(phore)	(tele)(phone)

What could be the prosodic rationale behind this taxonomy? Grimshaw (2005) explicitly identifies the one-foot constraint, but suggests that it is an arbitrary learnability cue with no connection to the prosodic system of English. However, it seems possible to go further. First, let us assume that the goal NP must always be adjacent to its head, either the verb or the preposition, and that the two form a syntactic constituent. This is the underlying structure assumed by Larson (1988, p. 335). The double object and prepositional constructions would thus have the following syntactic bracketings:

(28) Syntactic bracketing

(a) [V my sister] [the book]	double object construction
(b) [V] [the book] [to my sister]	prepositional construction

Second, we need a principle that regulates the mapping of syntactic phrases to prosodic phrases. Here we adopt Truckenbrodt's (1999) constraint WRAP-XP, defined in (29):

(29) WRAP-XP (Truckenbrodt, 1999, p. 228)
Each syntactic phrase is contained in a prosodic phrase.

Based on these assumptions, the double object construction has the prosodic bracketing shown in (30)

(30) (a) ([give my sister]) ([the book])
(b) *([donate my sister]) ([the book])

We now have a rationale for the relative ill-formedness of (30b). Assuming that the foot structure of the verb is visible to prosodic phrasing, we can explain why the first structure is better than the second: the one-foot verb *give* yields the prosodic structure ((*give*) (NP)); the two-foot verb *donate* yields the prosodic structure ((*do*)(*nate*) (NP)). The first phrase is binary (= foot + phrase), the second ternary (= foot + foot + phrase). Ternarity avoidance is a well-known syndrome in metrical stress systems. In particular, foot inventories usually exclude feet that require counting higher than two. For extensive discussion, examples, and references, see Hayes (1995, Ch. 8). We can now state the prosodic hypothesis: the incompatibility of two-foot verbs and double objects reflects the avoidance of ternary prosodic phrases. The ternarity constraint is stated in (31).

(31) *TERNARY
No ternary prosodic phrases.

The situation is different in the prepositional construction. Given the syntactic difference between the two constructions, the prosodic parse (V) (NP) is now unproblematic and neither verb violates *TERNARY, as shown in (32). This correctly predicts that the prepositional construction should be compatible with both one-foot and two-foot verbs.

(32) (a) ([give]) ([the book]) ([to my sister])
(b) ([donate]) ([the book]) ([to my sister])

As an additional bonus, this analysis correctly rules out double object constructions where the theme precedes the goal, e.g., **give the book my sister* and **donate the book my sister*. These structures are ill-formed because *my sister* is not adjacent to its head, either a verb or a preposition. With these syntactic assumptions in hand, we return to our prosodic analysis.

The ternarity effect also emerges in verb-particle constructions and resultatives. The following examples are from Harley (2007). The prosodic phrasing is ours.

(33) The verb-particle construction (Harley, 2007, p. 23)

(a)	(give it) (up)	*(donate it) (up)
(b)	(offer it) (up)	*(present it) (up)
(c)	(clear it) (up)	*(clarify it) (up)
(d)	(hand it) (out)	*(distribute it) (out)
(e)	(figure it) (out)	*(calculate it) (out)
(f)	(show it) (off)	*(exhibit it) (off)
(g)	(hide it) (away)	*(conceal it) (away)
(h)	(trade it) (in)	*(exchange it) (in)

(34) Resultatives (Harley, 2007, p. 23)

(a)	(cut it) (apart)	*(divide it) (apart)
(b)	(fill it) (full)	*(inflate it) (full)
(c)	(walk yourself) (tired)	*(perambulate yourself) (tired)
(d)	(squeeze it) (empty)	*(compress it) (empty)
(e)	(freeze solid)	*(congeal solid)

Harley (2007, p. 25) points out that verb-particle constructions and resultatives are fine with Anglo-Saxon type verbs, but not many Latinate ones. She notes that the effect is clearly related to prosody: "[i]f the initial weak syllable of a Latinate verb may be clipped, its occurrence with a particle becomes fine: **confess up* is bad, but *'fess up* is perfectly idiomatic". Under our analysis, what is clipped is not a syllable, but a foot. A possible reverse effect is the ban on the prefix *re-* "again" in double objects and particle verbs (Banfield, 2007; Keyser & Roeper, 1992). Many verbs that generally allow the *re*-prefix do not allow it in double object and verb-particle constructions, as illustrated in (35) and (36). Under our analysis, this restriction can be derived from prosody: the word-level prefix /ri:/- adds a foot to the verb which results in a ternary prosodic phrase. The prosodic phrasing is ours.

(35) The complementarity of *re*- and double objects (Keyser & Roeper, 1992, p. 90)

(a)	We (gave him) money	*We (regave him) money
(b)	I (envied him) his shoes	*I (re-envied him) his shoes
(c)	He (left me) a note	*He (releft me) a note
(d)	I (threw him) the ball	*I (rethrew him) the ball

(36) The complementarity of *re*- and the verb particle (Banfield, 2007)

(a)	John (shipped off) his prizes	*John (reshipped off) his prizes
(b)	Let's (build up) our defenses	*Let's (rebuild up) our defenses
(c)	You should (write down) the response	*You should (rewrite down) the response
(d)	It's time to (count out) the money	*It's time to (recount out) the money

We conclude this section with a snapshot of the Blogspot data. The data clearly show that short verbs (= one foot) exhibit a pattern of dative alternation very different from long verbs (= two feet). The corpus consists of 1,602 sentences of informal written English extracted from www.blogspot.com. These sentences contain approximately 100 hits of each of the following verbs: *assign, award, bring, give, offer, promise* (one foot); *administer, bequeath, concede, convey, deliver, donate, explain, guarantee, recommend, reveal* (two feet). The following operational definition was adopted for determining the number of feet (cf. Grimshaw, 2005): a one-foot verb consists of a monosyllabic stem, a disyllabic stem with initial stress and a final unstressed syllable, or a disyllabic stem with final stress and an initial open syllable with a schwa; all the remaining verbs were classified as two-foot verbs. The vowel qualities were determined based on the Merriam-Webster On-Line Dictionary.[3]

The data summary in (37) shows that with one-foot verbs (e.g., *give*), the double object construction and the prepositional construction are about equally common. As one might expect, with two-foot verbs the prepositional construction is strongly favoured, but double objects are also possible (> 100 tokens). As the chi square test shows, the null hypothesis that verb length (one foot vs. two feet) and construction type (double object vs. prepositional)

[3] Under our descriptive taxonomy, one long verb turns out to have three feet: (*ad*)(*mini*)(*ster*). If this description is correct, and if (*ad*)(*mini*)(*ster*) behaves prosodically like a two-foot verb, e.g. (*de*)(*liver*), we would need to say that *TERNARY is violated by prosodic phrases that are ternary or longer.

are independent must be rejected. We wish to emphasise that these quantitative data are preliminary; see the discussion in Appendix 1. Actual examples of two-foot verbs with double objects are listed in Appendix 2.

(37) Choice of construction by verb length in www.blogspot.com (16 verbs, 1,602 sentences)

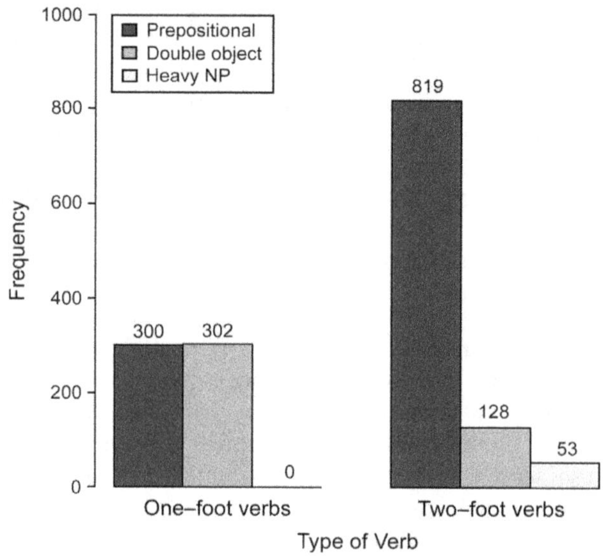

$\chi^2 = 244.7$, df $= 1$, $p < 2.2\text{e}{-16}$ (Heavy NP Shift omitted)

Interestingly, Heavy NP Shift only occurs with two-foot verbs. Is this a coincidence or something we should have expected? To the best of our knowledge, this effect has not been reported in earlier Heavy NP Shift literature, perhaps because it is a quantitative tendency at best. As will become clear in a moment, this generalisation follows from the prosodic analysis outlined above. However, we must first understand how the proposed constraints interact. This topic will be addressed next.

THE PROSODIC MODEL

This section outlines a prosodic model of the English dative alternation. We will take the constraints introduced in earlier sections and study their interaction in terms of Optimality Theory (Prince & Smolensky, 1993/2004). The goal of the analysis is to predict, for any unlinearised verb phrase (= input), its optimal linearisation (= output), given the constraints. Setting up the analysis involves two preliminary tasks. First, in order to make sure that the analysis generalises beyond a few hand-picked examples, we must study its predictions for all possible types of input verb phrases. We will consider the following three binary distinctions:

(38) Defining the space of possible inputs:
  (a) The verb may have either one foot or two feet.
  (b) The goal NP may be either lexically stressed or unstressed.
  (c) The theme NP may be either lexically stressed or unstressed.

Taken together, this yields eight types of possible input verb phrases. Second, for each input verb phrase, we must consider all possible output verb phrases. We will consider the following three binary distinctions:

(39) Defining the space of possible outputs:
  (a) The theme may appear before or after the goal.
  (b) The goal may or may not have the preposition *to*.
  (c) The verb may or may not be parsed together with the adjacent NP.

Taken together, this yields eight types of possible output verb phrases, or in the language of Optimality Theory, output candidates. In (40), we illustrate these output candidates for one particular input: a one-foot verb with a stressed goal and a stressed theme.

(40) Output candidates for one input

(a)	*(give) (the bóok) (to my síster)*	(e)	*(give the bóok) (to my síster)*
(b)	*(give) (to my síster) (the bóok)*	(f)	*(give to my síster) (the bóok)*
(c)	*(give) (the bóok) (my síster)*	(g)	*(give the bóok) (my síster)*
(d)	*(give) (my síster) (the bóok)*	(h)	*(give my síster) (the bóok)*

These initial assumptions define our work space. We wish to emphasise that they represent an idealisation introduced to make the problem analytically manageable. Here we point out two specific assumptions and give our reasons for adopting them as part of our analysis.

First, we are only considering the VP, ignoring the material on its left. As an anonymous reviewer notes, in reality the subject NP may have an effect on the phrasing of the VP. A possible minimal pair is (*I gave*) (*Jim*) (*the book*) and (*Pat*) (*gave Jim*) (*the book*). According to the reviewer, in the former example the verb and the object belong to different prosodic phrases because the lexically unstressed subject is phrased together with the verb, whereas in the latter example the verb and the object are phrased together because the lexically stressed subject forms a prosodic phrase on its own. Studying such putative prosodic effects of the subject would be an interesting undertaking, but beyond the scope of the present work, as it would require annotating the data for the prosodic properties of subjects.

Second, within the VP, we are only considering two phrasings: (V) (XP) (YP) and (V XP) (YP). In particular, we are not considering the phrasing (V XP YP) where the entire VP forms a prosodic phrase. Our choice is based on the theoretical assumption that prosodic phrasing is cyclic. On this assumption, the ternary phrase is possible, but only at the level of the entire VP: ((V) (XP) (YP)). Pursuing the issue of higher-level phrasing would again require a careful consideration of the context of the VP, something that we have not yet studied systematically.

Having now defined the space of possible inputs and possible outputs, we need a grammar to connect the two. In Optimality Theory, the grammar's task is to select the optimal < input, output > mapping from all the logically possible < input, output > mappings. In our example, the picture is slightly more complicated because of variation: some inputs have several optimal outputs. The selection of the optimal mapping is accomplished by the grammatical constraints summarised in (41).

(41) Constraint summary

(a)	Syntax	The goal NP forms an XP with its head.
(b)	Wrap-XP	An XP is contained in a prosodic phrase.
(c)	*(x)	Avoid lexically unstressed unary phrases.
(d)	*Ternary	No ternary prosodic phrases.
(e)	*Clash	No stress clashes within a prosodic phrase.
(f)	Stress-to-Stress	Each lexical stress occurs within the prosodic phrase that receives sentence stress.
(g)	*P-Phrase	Avoid prosodic phrases (gradiently evaluated).
(h)	Focus(Theme)	Focus theme, i.e., put the theme NP under sentence stress.
(i)	Focus(Goal)	Focus goal, i.e., put the goal NP under sentence stress.
(j)	*to	Avoid prepositions.

Many of these constraints were motivated in the preceding section. Some have been directly borrowed from earlier work: *(x) comes from Zwicky (1986); Wrap-XP and *P-Phrase from Truckenbrodt (1999). The last four constraints *P-Phrase, Focus(Theme), Focus(Goal), and *to have not been mentioned until now. The constraint *P-Phrase strives to minimise the number of prosodic phrases. Focus(Theme) requires the theme NP to be rightmost; Focus(Goal) requires the goal NP to be rightmost. Since no linearisation can satisfy both constraints simultaneously, one of them is inevitably violated. Finally, the constraint *to penalises the use of an overt preposition.

Continuing with our example (40) where the input contains a one-foot verb, a stressed goal, and a stressed theme, we now examine the constraint violations incurred by the eight candidate mappings. The violation pattern is summarised in the TABLEAU in (42) where the leftmost column contains the output candidates and the top row contains the constraints. Violations are indicated by asterisks.

(42) The violation pattern for the input "*give*(*my sister, the book*)"

	SYNTAX	WRAP-XP	*(x)	*TERNARY	*CLASH	STRESS-TO-STRESS	*P-PHRASE	FOCUS(Theme)	FOCUS(Goal)	*to
(a) (give)(the book)(to my sister)						*	***	*		*
(b) (give)(to my sister)(the book)						*	***		*	*
(c) (give)(the book)(my sister)	*					*	***	*		
(d) (give)(my sister)(the book)		*				*	***		*	
(e) (give the book)(to my sister)					*	*	**	*		*
(f)(give to my sister)(the book)					*	*	**		*	*
(g) (give the book)(my sister)	*				*	*	**	*		
(h) (give my sister)(the book)					*	*	**		*	

The central observation is that grammatical constraints often CONFLICT. For the moment, let us limit ourselves to candidates (a) and (b). These two candidates have identical violations except for two constraints: candidate (a) violates FOCUS(Theme) because the theme NP (*the book*) is not final in the sentence; candidate (b) violates FOCUS(Goal) because the goal PP (*to my sister*) is not final in the sentence. In other words, there is no way to satisfy both constraints simultaneously. The decision is made by ranking the constraints in order of importance: under the ranking FOCUS(Goal) >> FOCUS(Theme), candidate (a) wins; under the reverse ranking FOCUS(Theme) >> FOCUS(Goal), candidate (b) wins. Leaving the constraints unranked predicts that either ranking can be chosen by the speaker during performance, yielding free variation; see e.g., Anttila (2007) and Kiparsky (1994).

More generally, given a pair of competing candidates and a set of totally ranked constraints, the winning candidate is the one that does better on the highest-ranking constraint that distinguishes the candidates. The OPTIMAL CANDIDATE is the candidate that wins in all pairwise competitions. These elementary definitions reveal an important empirical prediction made by Optimality Theory: grammaticality is COMPARATIVE. An output is grammatical if and only if it is better than all other outputs for the same input. In particular, we cannot determine the grammaticality of a linguistic expression by examining it in isolation. This prediction distinguishes Optimality Theory from many competing theoretical alternatives. Empirical evidence that bears out this prediction will be presented shortly.

Next, we must ask whether we have empirical evidence for ranking any of the constraints. In (43), we propose a partial ranking that divides the constraints into two strata: the top stratum contains the constraints SYNTAX, WRAP-XP, and *(x); the bottom stratum contains all the remaining constraints. The ranking is indicated by a solid line. Within each stratum, the ranking is free.

(43) The partially ranked tableau for the input "*give*(*my sister, the book*)"

	SYNTAX	WRAP-XP	*(x)	*TERNARY	*CLASH	STRESS-TO-STRESS	*P-PHRASE	FOCUS(Theme)	FOCUS(Goal)	*to
(a) → (give)(the book)(to my sister)						*	***	*		*
(b) → (give)(to my sister)(the book)						*	***		*	*
(c) (give)(the book)(my sister)	*					*	***	*		
(d) (give)(my sister)(the book)		*				*	***		*	
(e) → (give the book)(to my sister)					*	*	**	*		*
(f) (give to my sister)(the book)					*	*	**		*	*
(g) (give the book)(my sister)	*				*	*	**	*		
(h) → (give my sister)(the book)					*	*	**		*	

In (43), we use arrows to indicate the candidates that are optimal under some ranking. There are four such candidates: (a), (b), (e), and (h). All other candidates lose out for different reasons. The top-stratum constraint SYNTAX rules out (c) and (g): these are double object constructions where the goal NP is not adjacent to its head. This means that the bottom-stratum constraints are irrelevant for the outcome which is marked by graying out their cells. Another top-stratum constraint WRAP-XP rules out (d): this is a double object construction where the syntactic phrase [V NP] containing the verb and the goal NP is split by a prosodic phrase. This constraint will be crucial for deriving the contrast between one-foot and two-foot verbs. Finally, (f) is ruled out for a particularly interesting reason: it incurs a superset of the violations of (h). This means that (f) can never be optimal because it will always be beaten by (h), no matter how the constraints are ranked. Such candidates are called HARMONICALLY BOUNDED. The remaining four candidates, marked by arrows, are all potentially optimal. Which one is actually optimal depends on the ranking of the bottom-stratum constraints, something decided at the time of performance.

Let us consider one more example. In (44), the input is a one-foot verb with a stressed goal and an unstressed theme. This time, the only possible winner is (e): *give it to my sister*. All other candidates are either ruled out by the three top-stratum constraints or are harmonically bounded. In particular, prosodic phrases that only contain a lexically unstressed pronoun are ruled out by the constraint *(x).

(44) The partially ranked tableau for the input "*give*(*my sister, it*)"

	SYNTAX	WRAP-XP	*(x)	*TERNARY	*CLASH	STRESS-TO-STRESS	*P-PHRASE	FOCUS(Theme)	FOCUS(Goal)	*to
(a) (give)(it)(to my sister)			*				***	*		*
(b) (give)(to my sister)(it)			*			*	***		*	*
(c) (give)(it)(my sister)	*		*				***	*		
(d) (give)(my sister)(it)		*	*			*	***		*	
(e) → (give it)(to my sister)							**	*		*
(f) (give to my sister)(it)			*		*	*	**		*	*
(g) (give it)(my sister)	*						**	*		
(h) (give my sister)(it)			*		*	*	**		*	

What are the possible optimal outputs for all 12 possible inputs, given our grammar? The predictions are summarised in (45):

(45) Summary of predictions. Inputs are presented in the form verb (goal, theme).

	INPUT	NP+NP	NP+PP	HNPS
(a)	give(her, it):	–	yes	–
	return(her, it):	–	yes	–
	give(my sister, it):	–	yes	–
	return(my sister, it):	–	yes	–
(b)	give(her, the book):	yes	yes	–
(c)	give(my sister, the book):	yes	yes	yes
	return(my sister, the book):	yes	yes	yes
	return(her, the book):	yes	yes	yes
(d)	give(my sister, the old book):	yes	yes	yes
	return(my sister, the old book):	yes	yes	yes
	give(my little sister, the book):	yes	yes	yes
	return(my little sister, the book):	yes	yes	yes

Two categorical predictions are made. First, verb phrases with an unstressed theme should only allow the prepositional construction, e.g., *I gave it to her*/**I* *gave her it*/**I gave to her it*. Second, verb phrases with a one-foot verb, an unstressed goal, and a stressed theme should not allow Heavy NP Shift, e.g., *I gave the book to her*/*I gave her the book*/**I gave to her the book*. All the remaining verb phrases are predicted to allow all three variants. The inputs in (45d) take into account the end weight effect by adding one more binary choice: inputs with a stressed goal and a stressed theme may differ in whether the goal is heavier than the theme or vice versa.

These predictions are in the right direction, but they do not get us very far. We now know that all the inputs allow all the outputs, except for (45a) which only allows the prepositional construction and (45b) which disallows Heavy NP Shift. The interesting question is what happens in the variable cases. Are all the predicted constructions equally good for all the inputs? That seems unlikely. For example, *give her the book* sounds more natural than *give my little sister the book* although both are predicted to be possible. In the next section, we will see that such preferences already follow from the analysis.

QUANTITATIVE PREDICTIONS

What does the grammar predict about variation? In order to determine the limits of variation, we examine the factorial typology derived by our grammar. The FACTORIAL TYPOLOGY is the set of all languages predicted to be possible considering all the different inputs (= 12) and all the different constraint rankings (= 7! = 5,040), assuming that SYNTAX, WRAP-XP, and (*x) are always ranked in the top stratum. The factorial typology can be computed using OTSoft (Hayes, Tesar, & Zuraw, 2003). All in all, 30 distinct languages are predicted. To save space, we only display the result for two inputs. We write "D" for the double object construction, "P" for the prepositional construction, and "H" for the Heavy NP Shift construction.

(46) The predictions for two inputs in the 30 possible languages

INPUTS	OUTPUT LANGUAGES							
	1	2	3	4	5	6	7	8
'give(my sister, the old book)':	P	H	D	P	H	D	P	H
'give(her, the book)':	D	D	D	D	D	D	P	D

	9	10	11	12	13	14	15	16
'give(my sister, the old book)':	H	H	H	P	D	D	P	P
'give(her, the book)':	D	D	D	D	D	D	P	D

	17	18	19	20	21	22	23	24
'give(my sister, the old book)':	D	P	D	D	D	D	D	D
'give(her, the book)':	D	P	D	D	D	D	D	D

	25	26	27	28	29	30
'give(my sister, the old book)':	D	D	D	D	D	D
'give(her, the book)':	D	D	D	D	D	D

The double object constructions "D" have been shaded. An interesting asymmetry emerges: shading in the upper row implies shading in the lower row, but not vice versa. The following prediction is thus made: if the double object construction *give my sister the old book* is possible in a language, then the double object construction *give her the book* is also possible in the same language, but not vice versa. Such TYPOLOGICAL ENTAILMENTS are a consequence of Optimality Theory; see e.g., Prince (2006, 2007) for discussion. A typological entailment can be expressed as an implication that relates two <input, output> mappings. In this case:

(47) <"give(my sister, the old book)", *give my sister the old book*> →
<"give(her, the book)", *give her the book*>

Are there other typological entailments hidden in our grammar? It turns out that there are 168 typological entailments in all. We call the set of all typological entailments derived by a grammar a TYPOLOGICAL ORDER, or T-ORDER for short. T-orders are hard to figure out from factorial typologies with paper and pencil, but easy to find using a computer. All the T-orders in this paper have been produced by T-ORDER GENERATOR (Anttila & Andrus, 2006), a free open-source Python programme for computing and visualising T-orders. The programme is available at http://www.stanford.edu/~anttila/research/software.html.

How do T-orders matter to variation? Let us assume the Multiple Grammars Theory of variation (Kiparsky, 1994; Kroch, 1989) which proposes that variation arises from competing invariant grammars within an individual. In Optimality Theory, this means that the speaker has simultaneous access to several different total rankings of the same constraints and chooses among the rankings at the time of performance (speaking, writing); see e.g., Anttila (2007) and McCarthy (2008, pp. 260–264).[4] Consider an individual with four constraint rankings that yield the patterns 1, 3, 7, and 8:

[4] The Multiple Grammars Theory is a generic theory of variation that can be implemented in different ways. For example, Stochastic Optimality Theory (Boersma & Hayes, 2001) posits grammatical constraints with numerical weights called RANKING VALUES. The ranking value of each constraint is fixed, but at evaluation time a small amount of normally distributed noise is added to each constraint. This leads to limited variation in performance: constraints that are close together in weight are highly likely to reverse their mutual ranking from evaluation to evaluation, whereas constraints that are far apart in weight are highly unlikely to do so. The speaker's competence thus consists of a single grammar with numerically weighted constraints, but in actual performance we have multiple grammars evaluated in the standard optimality-theoretic fashion.

(48) An individual with four grammars 1, 3, 7, 8

	1	3	7	8
'give(my sister, the old book)':	P	D	P	H
'give(her, the book)':	D	D	P	D

At the moment of speaking, the individual will draw a grammar from this set. A quantitative prediction now follows: the input "give(my sister, the old book)" should yield at most as many double objects as the input "give(her, the book)". This is a robust prediction: it holds true no matter how the individual selects her grammars from the factorial typology in the course of learning, and no matter whether she favours or disfavours certain grammars during the speaking performance for stylistic reasons.

The T-order for our grammar is displayed in (49) as a directed graph. In order to make the large graph fit on a printed page, we have split it into three parts: (49a) shows the prepositional constructions; (49b) shows the double object constructions; and (49c) shows the Heavy NP Shift constructions. The need to split the connected graph explains the broken arrows.

(49) T-order (168 entailments)

(a) The prepositional construction

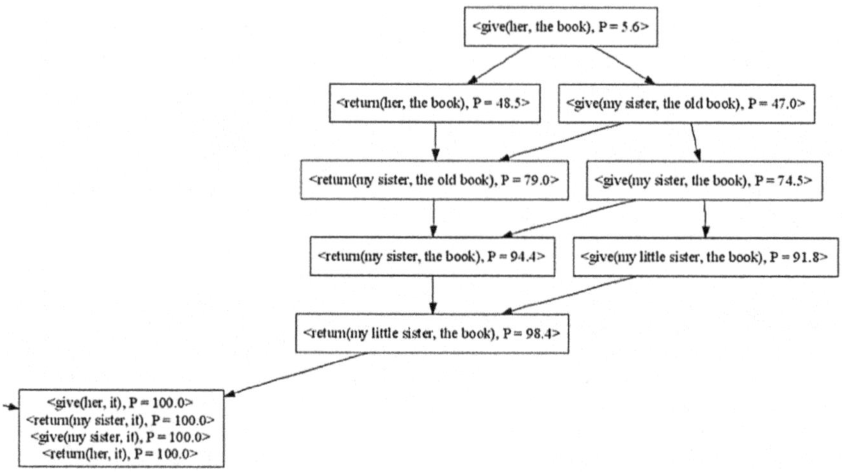

(b) The double object construction:

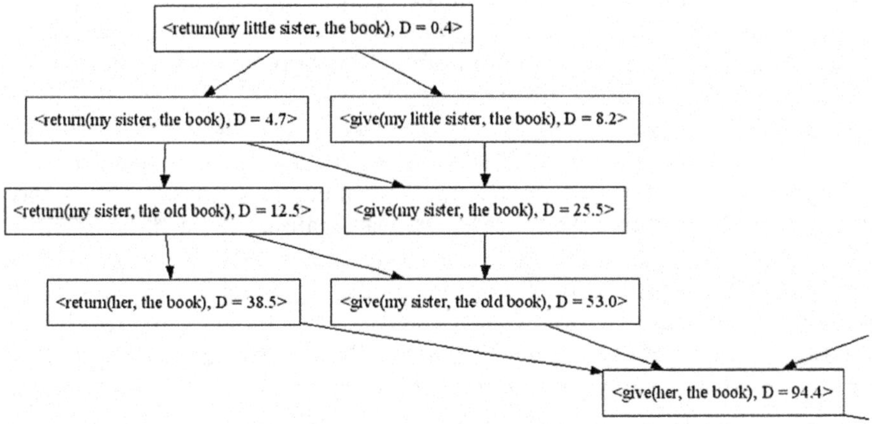

(c) The Heavy NP Shift construction

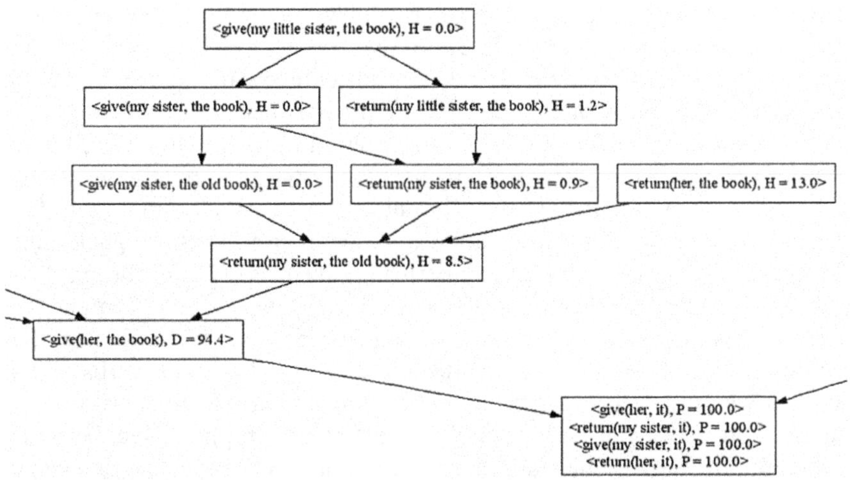

The graph is to be interpreted as follows. The boxes are <input, output> mappings; the arrows are entailments among these mappings. For example, in graph (49a), the arrow connecting < give(her, the book), *P*> (= the top node) and give(my sister, the old book), *P*> reveals the following prediction: if the first input can be expressed as a prepositional construction (i.e., *give the book to her*), so can the second (i.e., *give the old book to my sister*). To put it differently, the first mapping is more marked, the second mapping less marked. The graph has been simplified in two ways to make it visually clearer: transitive arrows have been omitted and mappings that entail one another (= cycles) have been enclosed in a box.

The empirically interesting question is whether the graph correctly captures the quantitative distribution of construction variants in the corpus. To return to our example, the analysis predicts that the first input should yield at most as many prepositional constructions as the second input. In order to see whether this prediction is correct, we have annotated each node in the graph by the Blogspot percentage of the mapping depicted in the node. In this particular case, the first input is realised as a prepositional construction 5.6% of the time, the second input 47.0% of the time. The quantitative asymmetry is thus correctly predicted by the model. Insofar as the analysis is correct, we would expect the empirical numbers to grow in the direction of the arrows, from top to bottom. This prediction is by and large confirmed, with some minor discrepancies in the Heavy NP Shift graph where the data are relatively sparse.

In order to get a slightly more accurate measure of how well the predictions and observations match, we can calculate PRECISION and RECALL for the T-order. Precision is a ratio that indicates how many of the predicted orderings are empirically true. In this case, precision = 0.988, i.e., 99% of the arrows go in the right direction. Recall is a ratio that indicates how many of the empirically true orderings are predicted. In this case, recall = 0.490, i.e., 49% of the orderings in the data are captured by the T-order.

As noted earlier, the Blogspot data are preliminary and the quantitative results must be confirmed on other corpora. We tested the predictions of our model on the Switchboard dative alternation corpus and found that the orderings are identical, with Switchboard showing consistently higher rates of double objects than Blogspot (Speriosu, 2007a, p. 7). However, this positive result comes with a caveat. Compared to Blogspot (1,602 sentences), Switchboard is larger (2,349 sentences), but less diverse. In particular, the Switchboard dative alternation corpus contains no two-foot verbs. This means that we only have data for half of the nodes in graphs (49a) and (49b) and no data at all for the Heavy NP Shift part of the graph in (49c) because the Switchboard dative alternation corpus contains no examples of Heavy NP Shift. Somewhat paradoxically, the written Blogspot data are a better source of prosodic evidence than the spoken Switchboard data.

SPECIFIC PREDICTIONS

At the beginning of the paper, we reviewed three classes of empirical generalisations about the dative alternation. These generalisations related to lexically unstressed pronouns, end weight, and verb length. In each case, we proposed prosodic constraints that seemed intuitively relevant. However, without a theoretical framework, we could not examine the interaction of the proposed constraints or derive any specific predictions, quantitative or otherwise. With the optimality-theoretic framework in hand, we can now examine four specific predictions made by our analysis and present empirical corpus evidence for them. These predictions relate to the foot structure of the verb (e.g., *téll* vs. *èxpláin*), the relative well-formedness of pronoun sequences (e.g., *I gave her it*), the distribution of filler phrases (e.g., *I'll give you, you know, two to three years*), and the prosodic nature of the principle of end weight.

Heavy NP Shift and verb length

The analysis predicts that Heavy NP Shift should be better with two-foot verbs than one-foot verbs, all else being equal. This prediction is visible from the T-order. In the Blogspot data the pattern is categorical: Heavy NP Shift only occurs with two-foot verbs.

(50) Heavy NP Shift with different input types in the Blogspot Corpus

return [to her] [the book]	31	give [to her][the book]	0
return [to my sister] [the old book]	17	give [to my sister] [the old book]	0
return [to my little sister] [the book]	3	give [to my little sister] [the book]	0
return [to my sister] [the book]	2	give [to my sister] [the book]	0

How does this prediction arise? This is illustrated in tableaux (51)–(52), which compare two inputs that are prosodically identical except for the verb: *give* vs. *reveal.*

(51) No Heavy NP Shift with one-foot verbs

'give(her, the book)'	*TERNARY	*P-PHRASE	* to
(a) ([(give)])([to her])([the book])		***	*
(b)→ ([(give)(her)])([the book])		**	

(52) Heavy NP Shift with two-foot verbs

'reveal(her, the truth)'	*TERNARY	*P-PHRASE	*to
(a) → ([(re)(veal)])([to him])([the truth])		***	*
(b) → ([(re)(veal)(him)])([the truth])	*	**	

The grammar predicts that **give to her the book* should be ill-formed, but that *reveal to him the truth* should be well-formed. This may be initially surprising because both constructions incur exactly the same violations as shown in (51a) and (52a). Why should the judgements differ? The answer is characteristically optimality-theoretic: the two expressions compete against different alternatives. The Heavy NP Shift variant **give to her the book* faces a hopeless competition against the prosodically superior double object variant *give her the book* which renders Heavy NP Shift harmonically bounded. In contrast, *reveal to him the truth* competes against the prosodically inferior *reveal him the truth* which suffers from a ternarity violation. The upshot is that Heavy NP Shift is favoured with two-foot verbs because the alternatives are prosodically worse, but disfavoured with one-foot verbs because the alternatives are prosodically better. Phenomena of this sort provide striking support for a fundamental tenet of Optimality Theory: grammaticality is comparative. The well-formedness of an expression depends on the well-formedness of alternative expressions for the same meaning.

Pronoun sequences

Another prediction relates to the well-formedness of pronoun sequences; see Gast (2007) for a recent discussion of such patterns in dialects of British English. It has been observed that there are dialects like (53a) and (53b), but no dialects like (53c).

(53)	(a)	(b)	(c)
	I gave her it	*I gave her it	*I gave her it
	*I gave my sister it	*I gave my sister it	I gave my sister it
	(Hawkins, 1994, p. 312)	(Erteschik-Shir, 1979, p. 452)	no such dialect

As it stands, our analysis only predicts dialect (53b). This is because (*gáve her*) (*it*) and (*gáve my síster*) (*it*) both contain an unary unstressed prosodic phrase which violates the top-stratum constraint *(x). As a result, only the prepositional construction is possible: (*gave it*) (*to her*), (*gave it*) (*to my sister*). This prediction is visible from the bottom node of (49). However, if we relax the ranking and allow *(x) to be dominated we derive the more interesting T-order in (54):

(54) A partial T-order with *(x) as a dominated constraint

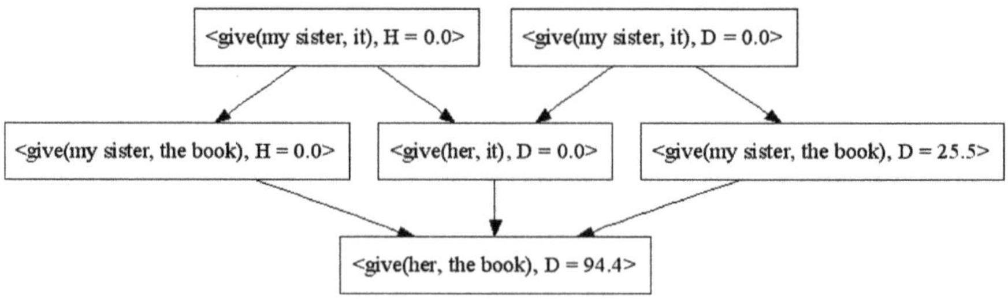

The main observation is that *give my sister it* entails *give her it*. Both have 0% occurrence rate in the Blogspot data, but the prediction is clear: the first should be worse than the second, or else the two should be equal. The reason for this asymmetry is *CLASH: *I (gáve my síster) (it)* violates *CLASH, whereas *I (gáve her) (it)* does not. This explains the typological asymmetry.

(55) (a) ?I (gáve her) (it) –
(b) *I (gáve my síster) (it) *CLASH

We have already seen that the same contrast emerges quantitatively in *I gave him the book* vs. *I gave Jim the book*. The data are repeated in (56). Clash avoidance thus emerges in two ways: typologically across dialects as well as quantitatively within a dialect.

(56) The percentage of double objects affected by *CLASH

	BLOGSPOT	SWITCHBOARD
(a) I (gáve him) (the book)	94.4%	97.0%
(b) I (gáve Jím) (the book)	25.5%	47.8%

Filler phrases

One major difference between spoken language (Switchboard) and written language (Blogspot) is that spoken language contains filler phrases such as *uh* and *you know*. Earlier research has found that filler phrases may signal the presence of new information; see e.g., Arnold, Tanenhaus, Altmann, and Fagnano (2004). Filler phrases are interesting for our purposes because they entail the presence of a prosodic phrase boundary. Our model makes the following prediction: filler phrases should never appear between the verb and an unstressed pronominal NP. This prediction is borne out in the Switchboard dative alternation corpus. The well-formed examples in (57) come from the corpus. The ill-formed examples are constructed.

(57) No filler phrases between a verb and a lexically unstressed pronoun
(a) I'll give you, you know, two to three years
*I'll give, you know, you two to three years
(b) The Constitution gives, uh, the individual the right to own firearms
*The Constitution gives, uh, him the right to own firearms

How does this prediction arise? The prosodically well-formed phrasing (*give you*) (*you know*) (NP) allows the unstressed *you* to be phrased together with the verb. The prosodically ill-formed phrasing *(*give*) (*you know*) (*you*) (NP) forces the unstressed *you* to form a prosodic phrase on its own. The ill-formed phrasing violates several constraints, including *P-PHRASE which strives to minimise the number of prosodic phrases, as well as the top-stratum constraint *(x) which militates against prosodic phrases that consist of nothing but an unstressed pronoun (Zwicky, 1986).

The prosodic nature of end weight

Recall the prediction that unstressed function words such as *a/an, the*, and *of* should not count for weight. This follows from our hypothesis that end weight effects are a consequence of the Stress-to-Stress Principle. We tested this prediction on the prosodically annotated version of the Switchboard dative alternation corpus (Speriosu, 2007b). Joan Bresnan's essential help with the statistical analysis is gratefully acknowledged.

Several measures of "weight" were considered, including log(number of syllables), log(number of orthographic words), log(number of stresses), and crucially, log(number of primary stresses). The frequencies have been logarithmically transformed following a common practice in dealing with frequency data in the language processing literature. In order to find out which of these factors were most closely correlated with the response (the double object construction vs. the prepositional construction), we calculated Spearman's rho squared which shows the rank correlation between two variables. The result in (58) shows that the factor most closely correlated with the response is log(number of primary stresses of the theme).

(58) Spearman's ρ^2

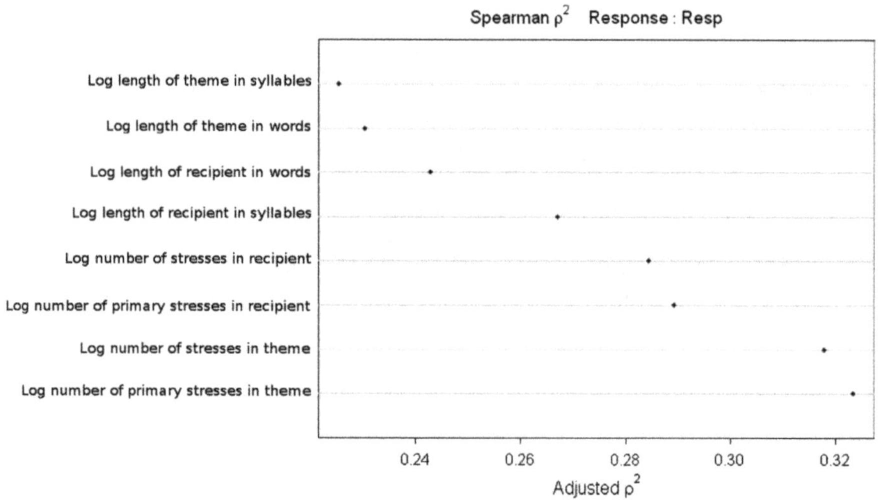

We then used logistic regression to find out whether length in primary stresses is a better predictor of end weight than length in orthographic words. The modelling was done in the *R* computational statistics programming environment (Baayen, 2008). The model summary is shown in (59).[5]

(59) A logistic regression model that compares weight in words to weight in primary stresses

Frequencies of Responses

Prepositional	Double Object
1852	497

	Coefficent	Standard Error	Wald Z	P
Intercept	0.8608	0.1624	5.30	0.0000
Log length of recipient in words	−0.3294	0.3161	−1.04	0.2972
Log length of theme in words	0.3237	0.2152	1.50	0.1325
Log number of primary stresses in theme	−4.2955	0.3083	−13.93	0.0000
Log number of primary stresses in recipient	3.6864	0.3165	11.65	0.0000

Factor	Chi-Square	df	P
Log length of recipient in words	1.09	1	0.2972
Log length of theme in words	2.26	1	0.1325
Log number of primary stresses in theme	194.18	1	<.0001
Log number of primary stresses in recipient	135.65	1	<.0001
TOTAL	497.69	4	<.0001

The binary response variable was the construction type: double object construction (= 0) vs. the prepositional construction (= 1). The positive coefficient of log number of primary stresses in recipient reveals a strong positive correlation between the log of the number of primary stresses in the recipient and the prepositional construction. The negative coefficient of log number of primary stresses in theme reveals a strong negative correlation between the log of the number of primary stresses in the theme and the prepositional construction. In contrast, the number of orthographic words is not significant. We conclude that primary stress is a better predictor of end weight than the number of words. Indeed, the number of words is irrelevant. This result calls for a detailed comparison with the Bresnan et al. (2007) regression model of the dative alternation which uses a large set of syntactic, semantic, and discourse variables to explain the choice of dative construction.

We conclude by commenting on one specific issue that merits further investigation. Our analysis predicts that only the relative number of stresses

[5] Since the different length variables are correlated, including them all in the model results in collinearity. Including only orthographic words and primary stresses results in a better model. To determine this, we used the vif() function from R's Design library which shows collinearity to be within acceptable limits (< 4). We thank Joan Bresnan and an anonymous reviewer for drawing our attention to this problem and for suggesting ways to deal with it.

should matter to end weight. For example, consider the competition between (*gáve crítical bácking*) (*to Búsh*) vs. (*gáve Búsh*) (*crítical bácking*). In terms of the Stress-to-Stress Principle, the prepositional construction loses with the violation ratio of 3:2. Adding one word to the theme causes the prepositional construction to lose with an even larger margin: (*gáve crítical polítical bácking*) (*to Búsh*) vs. (*gáve Búsh*) (*crítical polítical bácking*) has the violation ratio of 4:2. However, because grammaticality is comparative, absolute numbers are irrelevant: in both cases the double object construction is optimal. Based on evidence from English possessives, Jäger and Rosenbach (2006) have argued that this prediction of Optimality Theory is false and that weight effects are actually cumulative. However, their study was based on an orthographic definition of weight. A prosodic reanalysis of Jäger and Rosenbach's data would thus be of interest. If the cumulative effect turned out to persist, we would have prima facie evidence against the optimality-theoretic analysis of end weight proposed here.

CONCLUSION

In this paper, we have studied the English dative alternation in an attempt to answer the question of whether prosody influences constituent ordering. Most of the prosodic hypotheses we examined are familiar from earlier literature. Our main contribution is in providing a theoretical framework that connects these hypotheses and derives a large number of explicit and empirically testable predictions, including quantitative predictions. Based on a preliminary study of two data sets that represent both spoken and written English, we showed that these predictions are largely confirmed. The prosodic effects are mostly gradient and variable, yet entirely systematic. We conclude that the prosodic hypothesis is a serious contender that must be taken into account in any attempt to explain the dative alternation in English.

REFERENCES

Anttila, A. (1997). Deriving variation from grammar. In F. Hinskens, R. van Hout, & L. Wetzels (Eds.), *Variation, change and phonological theory* (pp. 35–68). Amsterdam/Philadelphia: John Benjamins.

Anttila, A. (2007). Variation and optionality. In P. de Lacy (Ed.), *The Cambridge handbook of phonology* (pp. 519–536). Cambridge: Cambridge University Press.

Anttila, A. (2008). Phonological constraints on constituent ordering. In C. B. Chang & H. Haynie (Eds.), *Proceedings of the 26th West Coast Conference on Formal Linguistics* (pp. 51–59). Somerville, MA: Cascadilla Press.

Anttila, A., & Andrus, C. (2006). T-Order Generator, software package. Stanford University, CA. Retrieved February 19, 2009, from http://www.stanford.edu/ ~anttila/research/software.html

Arnold, J. E., Tanenhaus, M. K., Altmann, R., & Fagnano, M. (2004). The old and thee, uh, new. *Psychological Science, 15*, 578–582. doi:10.1111/j.0956-7976.2004.00723.x.

Baayen, R. H. (2008). *Analyzing linguistic data: A practical introduction to statistics using R.* Cambridge: Cambridge University Press.

Banfield, A. (2007). *Beckett's Tattered Syntaxes.* [Handout of a colloquium talk] Department of Linguistics, Stanford University, CA, April 6, 2007.

Boersma, P., & Hayes, B. (2001). Empirical tests of the Gradual Learning Algorithm. *Linguistic Inquiry, 32*, 45–86. doi:10.1162/002438901554586.

Bresnan, J., Cueni, A., Nikitina, T., & Baayen, R. H. (2007). Predicting the dative alternation. In G. Bouma, I. Kraemer, & J. Zwarts (Eds.), *Cognitive foundations of interpretation* (pp. 69–94). Amsterdam: Royal Netherlands Academy of Science.

Bresnan, J., & Nikitina, T. (2003). *On the gradience of the dative alternation.* Unpublished manuscript, Stanford University, Stanford, CA. Retrieved February 19, 2009, from http://www-lfg.stanford.edu/bresnan/download.html

Büring, D. (2001a). Let's phrase it! – Focus, word order, and prosodic phrasing in German double object constructions. In G. Müller & W. Sternefeld (Eds.), *Competition in syntax. Studies in generative grammar 49* (pp. 69–105). Berlin & New York: Mouton de Gruyter.

Büring, D. (2001b). What do definites do that indefinites definitely don't? In C. Féry & W. Sternefeld (Eds.), *Audiatur Vox Sapientiae: A Festschrift for Arnim von Stechow* [Let the voice of wisdom be heard] (Vol. 52, pp. 70–100). Berlin: Akademie Verlag.

Büring, D., & Gutiérrez-Bravo, R. (2001). *Focus-related constituent order variation without the NSR: A prosody-based crosslinguistic analysis. Syntax at Santa Cruz 3.* Santa Cruz, CA: University of California.

Chomsky, N., & Halle, M. (1968). *The sound pattern of English.* New York: Harper and Row.

Cinque, G. (1993). A null theory of phrase and compound stress. *Linguistic Inquiry, 24*, 239–298.

Erteschik-Shir, N. (1979). Discourse constraints on dative movement. In T. Givón (Ed.), *Discourse and syntax: Syntax and semantics* (Vol. 12, pp. 441–467). New York: Academic Press.

Fraser, B. (1998). *A phonological constraint on the alternate to-dative Form.* Unpublished manuscript, Boston University, Boston, MA.

Gast, V. (2007). *I gave it him* – on the motivation of the "alternative double object construction" in varieties of British English. *Functions of Language, 14*, 31–56. doi:10.1075/fol.14.1.04gas.

Godfrey, J., Holliman, E., & McDaniel, J. (1992). SWITCHBOARD: Telephone speech corpus for research and development. In *Proceedings of ICASSP-92* (pp. 517–520). San Francisco, CA: International Conference on Acoustics, Speech, and Signal Processing.

Goldberg, A. (1995). *Constructions: A construction grammar approach to argument structure.* Chicago, IL: University of Chicago Press.

Green, G. (1974). *Semantics and syntactic regularity.* Bloomington, IN: Indiana University Press.

Grimshaw, J. (2005). *Words and structure.* Stanford, CA/Chicago, IL: CSLI/University of Chicago Press.

Gropen, J., Pinker, S., Hollander, M., Goldberg, R., & Wilson, R. (1989). The learnability and acquisition of the dative alternation in English. *Language, 65*, 203–257.

Harley, H. (2007, March 1). *The bipartite structure of verbs cross-linguistically (or: Why Mary can't exhibit John her paintings)*. Paper presented at ABRALIN, Belo Horizonte, Brazil.

Hawkins, J. (1994). *A performance theory of order and constituency.* Cambridge: Cambridge University Press.

Hawkins, J. (2006). Gradedness as relative efficiency in the processing of syntax and semantics. In G. Fanselow, C. Féry, R. Vogel, & M. Schlesewsky (Eds.), *Gradience in grammar: Generative perspectives* (pp. 207–226). Oxford: Oxford University Press.

Hayes, B. (1995). *Metrical stress theory: Principles and case studies.* Chicago: The University of Chicago Press.

Hayes, B., Tesar, B., & Zuraw, K. (2003). OTSoft 2.1, software package. Retrieved January 15, 2010, from http://www.linguistics.ucla.edu/people/hayes/otsoft/

Inkelas, S., & Zec, D. (1995). Syntax-phonology interface. In J. A. Goldsmith (Ed.), *The handbook of phonological theory* (pp. 535–549). Oxford: Blackwell.

Jäger, G., & Rosenbach, A. (2006). The winner takes it all – almost: Cumulativity in grammatical variation. *Linguistics, 44*, 937–971. doi:10.1515/LING.2006.031.

Keyser, S. J., & Roeper, T. (1992). Re: The abstract clitic hypothesis. *Linguistic Inquiry, 23*, 89–125.

Kiparsky, P. (1994). *An OT perspective on phonological variation*. Retrieved February 12, 2010, from http://www.stanford.edu/ ~kiparsky/Papers/nwave94.pdf

Krifka, M. (1999). *Manner in dative alternation*. Paper presented at the West Coast Conference on Formal Linguistics 18, April 9–11, 1999, Tucson, Arizona.

Kroch, A. (1989). Reflexes of grammar in patterns of language change. *Language Variation and Change, 1*, 199–244.

Ladd, D. R. (1996). *Intonational phonology*. Cambridge: Cambridge University Press.

Larson, R. K. (1988). On the double object construction. *Linguistic Inquiry, 19*, 335–391.

Levin, B. (1993). *English verb classes and alternations*. Chicago: The University of Chicago Press.

McCarthy, J. J. (2008). *Doing optimality theory*. Malden, MA: Blackwell.

McCawley, J. (1977). Accent in Japanese. In L. Hyman (Ed.), *Studies in stress and accent* (pp. 261–302). Los Angeles, CA: Department of Linguistics, University of Southern California.

Oehrle, R. T . (1976). *The grammar of the English dative alternation*. PhD thesis, Massachusetts Institute of Technology, Cambridge, MA.

Prince, A. (2006). *Implication & impossibility in grammatical systems: What it is & how to find it*. Rutgers Optimality Archive, ROA-880. Retrieved February 15, 2010, from http://roa.rutgers.edu.files/880-1006/880-PRINCE-0-0.PDF.

Prince, A. (2007). The pursuit of theory. In P. de Lacy (Ed.), *The Cambridge handbook of phonology* (pp. 33–60). Cambridge: Cambridge University Press.

Prince, A., & Smolensky, P. (1993/2004). *Optimality theory: Constraint interaction in generative grammar*. Malden, MA: Blackwell.

Pullum, G. K., & Zwicky, A. M. (1988). The syntax-phonology interface. In F. J. Newmeyer (Ed.), *Linguistics: The Cambridge survey, Vol. I, linguistic theory: Foundations* (pp. 255–280). Cambridge: Cambridge University Press.

Samek-Lodovici, V. (2005). Prosody-syntax interaction in the expression of focus. *Natural Language and Linguistic Theory, 23*, 687–755.

Schlüter, J. (2005). *Rhythmic grammar: The influence of rhythm on grammatical variation and change in English*. Berlin: Mouton de Gruyter.

Selkirk, E. (1995). Sentence prosody: Intonation, stress, and phrasing. In J. A. Goldsmith (Ed.), *The handbook of phonological theory* (pp. 550–569). Oxford: Blackwell.

Selkirk, E. (2003). The prosodic structure of function words. In J. J. McCarthy (Ed.), *Optimality theory in phonology: A reader* (pp. 464–482). Malden, MA: Blackwell.

Speriosu, M. (2007a). *A phonological analysis of the dative alternation in spoken English*. Unpublished manuscript, Stanford University, Stanford, CA.

Speriosu, M. (2007b). *Prosodically analyzing the English dative alternation*. Lab report, August 31, 2007, Unpublished manuscript, Stanford University, Stanford, CA.

Speyer, A. (2005). Topicalization and the trochaic requirement. *Penn Working Papers in Linguistics, 10*, 243–256.

Thompson, S. A. (1995). The iconicity of "dative shift" in English: Considerations from information flow in discourse. In M. E. Landsberg (Ed.), *Syntactic iconicity and linguistic freezes* (pp. 155–175). Berlin: Mouton de Gruyter.

Truckenbrodt, H. (1999). On the relation between syntactic phrases and phonological phrases. *Linguistic Inquiry, 30*, 219–255. doi:10.1162/002438999554048.

Truckenbrodt, H. (2007). The syntax-phonology interface. In P. de Lacy (Ed.), *The Cambridge handbook of phonology* (pp. 435–456). Cambridge: Cambridge University Press.
Vogel, R. (2006). Weak function word shift. *Linguistics, 44*, 1059–1093. doi:10.1515/LING.2006.034.
Wasow, T. (2002). *Postverbal behavior.* Stanford, CA: CSLI.
Wolters, M., & Beaver, D. (2001). What does *he* mean? In J. D. Moore & K. Stenning (Eds.), *Proceedings of the twenty-third annual meeting of the cognitive science society* (pp. 1176–1180). Mahwah, NJ: Lawrence Erlbaum.
Yamashita, H., & Chang, F. (2001). "Long before short" preference in the production of a head-final language. *Cognition, 81*, B45–B55. doi:10.1016/S0010-0277(01)00121-4.
Zec, D., & Inkelas, S. (1990). Prosodically constrained syntax. In S. Inkelas & D. Zec (Eds.), *The phonology-syntax connection* (pp. 365–378). Chicago: The University of Chicago Press.
Zubizarreta, M. L. (1998). *Prosody, focus, and word order.* Cambridge, MA: The MIT Press.
Zwicky, A. (1986). The unaccented pronoun constraint in English. *OSU Working Papers in Linguistics, 32*, 100–113.
Zwicky, A., & Pullum, G. K. (1986). Two spurious counterexamples to the principle of phonology-free syntax. *OSU Working Papers in Linguistics, 32*, 92–99.

APPENDIX 1: THE CORPORA

The Blogspot corpus was compiled by Philipp Angermeyer, Rahul Balusu, and Peter Liem at New York University in the summer of 2004. The corpus consists of 1,602 sentences of informal written English extracted from www.blogspot.com. Data were collected on six one-foot verbs (*assign, award, bring, give, offer, promise*) and 10 two-foot verbs (*administer, bequeath, concede, convey, deliver, donate, explain, guarantee, recommend*, and *reveal*). The following operational definition was adopted for determining the number of feet: a one-foot verb consists of a monosyllabic stem, a disyllabic stem with initial stress and a final unstressed syllable, or a disyllabic stem with final stress and an initial open syllable with a schwa; all the remaining verbs were classified as two-foot verbs. The vowel qualities were determined based on the Merriam-Webster On-Line Dictionary. The goal was to include the first 100 hits of finite dative constructions for each verb. The search was terminated as soon as 100 examples were found. All hits were checked manually. This included checking the surrounding text to make sure that it appeared to be authored by a native speaker of (some variety of) English.

The internet is an excellent source of data on rare constructions such as Heavy NP Shift and the double object construction with two-foot verbs. However, there are many problems in guaranteeing the validity of the data, especially quantitative data. For this reason, the Blogspot data must be considered preliminary. The searches were initially conducted using the base and past tense forms of the verb as search keys. However, it soon became clear that this resulted in a prohibitively large number of spurious hits. One procedure that was successfully used for several verbs was to narrow down the search space by searching for the verb in auxiliary frames in the following order:

Step 1. Find all verbs in the frame {am, are, is, was, were} V-ing.
Step 2. Find all verbs in the frame {has, have, had} V-ed.
Step 3: Find all verbs in the frame {will, shall, can, must, may} V

Despite our efforts to keep the sample random, not all verbs were searched using the same set of search keys in the same order. While we have no particular reason to believe that this would have skewed the relative distributions of the different constructions in any significant way, the quantitative results should be taken as suggestive until they can be independently verified in subsequent studies.

The Switchboard dative alternation corpus was kindly provided to us by Joan Bresnan. The corpus contains 2,349 instances of dative constructions drawn from the Switchboard Corpus of American English (Godfrey et al., 1992), a collection of recorded and transcribed telephone conversations. The dative alternation corpus contains 1,852 instances of the double object construction and 497 instances of the prepositional construction. Heavy NP Shift constructions were not included because of their extreme rarity. The original corpus was annotated for dozens of syntactic, semantic, and discourse variables, including the number, person, animacy, definiteness, and accessibility of the NPs, as detailed in Bresnan et al. (2007). For the purposes of our project, we further annotated the corpus for a number of prosodic variables, including the number of syllables and stresses (both primary and secondary) in the NPs, as well as higher-level variables such as violations of *(x), *CLASH, and STRESS-TO-STRESS PRINCIPLE. The annotation project took place in June–August 2007 and is documented in Speriosu (2007b).

APPENDIX 2: TWO-FOOT VERBS WITH DOUBLE OBJECTS IN THE BLOGSPOT CORPUS

Examples of two-foot verbs with double objects in the Blogspot data are listed below. Seven of the 10 verbs occur in the double object construction at least once. There are large differences among individual verbs. The list is headed by *guarantee* (85 hits) and *bequeath* (30 hits). Not a single instance of the double object construction is found for *convey*, *deliver*, and *donate*.

guarantee (85 hits):

> Our Just and Glorious Leader has guaranteed [them] [trials] to be held in private no later than 2014, so if they have done nothing wrong, they have nothing to fear
> The very language of the Second Amendment refutes any argument that it was intended to guarantee [every citizen] [an unfettered right to any kind of weapon]

bequeath (30 hits):

> The pharmacy fairy bequeathed [me] [three bottles of hydrocodone cough syrup]
> Instead, they had bequeathed [the country] [what Hawke's industry minister, John Button, described as an "industrial museum"]

recommend (6 hits):

> Grrr!!! Every single person who has recommended [me] [a site] has given me one that's not accepting new sign ups!!
> This gal was into everything from Led Zeppelin to Mars Volta and she was recommending [me] [so many bands that I never even heard of]

concede (5 hits):

> "If readers will concede [me] [a bit of patience], I will try to put into the same context the willful destruction of the World Trade Center towers and Britney Spears, one of the most popular entertainment figures in American life, who performed semiclothed last week at the MTV music awards, with a snake".

Plymouth had won 51 games that season, third-most in OHL history, and many had conceded [the Whalers] [a free pass to the Memorial Cup]

administer (1 hit):

We finally get up there and I'm like "oh yeah I need to take a written test" and she's like "okay I need your permit" and I give her the plastic part and she just looks at me like I'm a dumbass and she's like "uhm … no the other part" and I was like "uhm … I don't have it, Top Driver said I wouldn't need it" and she's all "oooh well I can't administer [you] [a test] unless you have it" and I'm like "dude! it went through the freakin' washing machine, my plastic part is right there just gimme a freakin' test!"

explain (1 hit):

I am explaining [you] [the concepts] in Chinese because you bloody can't understand them in English, so stop using your horrendous English with me

reveal (1 hit):

On the other hand, it had revealed [me] [a spiritual view that I didn't see previously]

LANGUAGE AND COGNITIVE PROCESSES
2010, 25 (7/8/9), 982–1023

Psychology Press
Taylor & Francis Group

Turning points, tonal targets, and the English L- phrase accent

Jonathan Barnes[1], Nanette Veilleux[2], Alejna Brugos[3], and Stefanie Shattuck-Hufnagel[4]

[1]*CAS Program in Linguistics, Boston University, Boston, MA, USA,*
[2]*Department of Computer Science, Simmons College, Boston, MA, USA,*
[3]*GRS Program in Applied Linguistics, Boston University, Boston, MA, USA,*
[4]*Speech Communication Group, Research Laboratory of Electronics, Massachusetts Institute of Technology, Cambridge, MA, USA*

This study of the alignment of L- in the H* L-H% contour of American English finds the strongest predictor of the location of the retracted phrase-accent "elbow" to be the location of the accent-related F0 peak, rather than one of a set of metrical "attractors" investigated. A strong correlation between peak height and elbow sharpness suggests that the elbow may arise from interaction between peak height and perception-based constraints on the implementation of postnuclear deaccenting: F0 must become low immediately after the Nuclear-Pitch-Accented syllable, to prevent the percept of a pitch accent on a following accentable syllable. Relativised Area Under the Curve (R-AUC), a global measure for characterising F0 contours, distinguishes this H* L- from contrasting contours (e.g., H* L*) more reliably than a turning point-based approach focused on the location/scaling of an F0 elbow. The R-AUC measure is sensitive to perceptually significant, but difficult-to-quantify, changes in contour shape, while avoiding the pitfalls of purely shape-based theories.

Keywords: Intonation; Phonology.

Correspondence should be addressed to Jonathan Barnes, Boston University, 621 Commonwealth Ave., Boston, MA 02215, USA. E-mail: jabarnes@bu.edu

We wish to thank Michael Wagner, as well as two anonymous reviewers, for valuable feedback on an earlier draft of this paper. We also wish to thank Mariapaola D'Imperio, Sónia Frota, Bob Ladd, Lisa Selkirk, Susan Hertz, Draga Zec, and other audience members at the Cornell Prosody conference in April 2008 for insightful comments and suggestions regarding this work. We gratefully acknowledge the support of the National Science Foundation, Grants #BCS-0643134, #BCS 0643054 and #BCS 0643019.

http://www.psypress.com/lcp DOI: 10.1080/01690961003599954

INTRODUCTION

F0 turning points, like great art or pornography, are things most researchers feel they recognise when they encounter, even while generally applicable criteria for their identification remain surprisingly elusive.[1] Our ability to locate turning points in the F0 curve with some degree of precision has undeniably proven a useful tool in addressing questions about the nature of phonological representations in intonation systems. The discovery of systematic patterns of alignment between turning points and salient elements in the segmental string has moreover been of decisive importance in swinging the weight of opinion in the field away from models of intonation based primarily on pitch movements (i.e., contours, rises, falls), and towards a model taking level-tone targets (primarily Highs and Lows) as its primitives (Bruce, 1977; Ladd, 1996, 2008; Pierrehumbert, 1980). The resulting family of approaches to intonational phonology, typically referred to as Autosegmental-Metrical (hereafter AM, Ladd, 1996, 2008), holds that phonological representations consist of a string of level-tone targets associated with certain positions in the segmental string, and it is also commonly assumed that these targets are realised phonetically as a sequence of turning points in the F0 curve, between which points pitch is simply interpolated more-or-less linearly.[2] For some researchers, the correspondence between phonological tones and concrete phonetic turning points is quite direct, indeed essentially one-to-one (e.g., Bruce, 1977): a corner in the F0 track implies a tone in the phonology, and a tone, conversely, implies a corner. Others view the relationship as in one sense or another less direct. Arvaniti and Ladd (2009), for example, liken the relationship between F0 turning points and the phonological tones that give rise to them to the relationship between an F2 maximum in the acoustic record and a glide /j/ between two low vowels: the turning points are the "most obvious manifestation" of the phonological entity, but cannot be equated with it in any deep or metaphysical sense.

Such differences notwithstanding, current argumentation about the phonological representation of intonation contours generally presupposes a certain level of operational equivalence between turning points and tones; disputes are routinely adjudicated on the basis of the precise locations of identifiable turning points relative to particular segmental landmarks,

[1] To borrow the famous words of US Supreme Court Justice Potter Stewart (Jacobellis v. Ohio, 378 US 184, 197 [1964]).

[2] Throughout, we will use the term *turning point* to refer to a concrete event in the F0 curve, and the terms *tone* and *tonal target* to refer to phonological specifications of pitch level. Likewise, we will use the terms *align* and *alignment* to refer to the phonetic synchronisation of a turning point and its segmental anchor, and the terms *associate* and *association* to refer to the relationship between a phonological tonal autosegment and the Tone-Bearing Unit (TBU) on which it docks.

despite the fact that these observations can frequently be ambiguous (Frota, 2002; del Giudice, Shosted, Davidson, Salihe, & Arvaniti, 2007; Welby, 2003; others). Indeed, we believe it is fair to say that most researchers working in AM models of intonational phonology, however else they may differ, nonetheless operate (with differing degrees of consistency) under the influence of two standard practical assumptions that, for purposes of clarity, it is worth stating explicitly at the outset:

(1) Systematically occurring turning points in the F0 curve imply the presence of tonal targets in the phonology.
(2) Systematic differences in the alignment of these turning points with respect to the segmental string imply different patterns of tonal association in the phonology.

The first of these inferences is near-universal in its application within the AM tradition. The second, however, is generally not applied in certain kinds of cases—for example, when differences in alignment appear gradiently variable, as in cases of tonal crowding (Arvaniti & Ladd, 2009; Silverman & Pierrehumbert, 1990), or when they lead to representations encoding phonetic distinctions involving a level of detail that might end up obscuring fundamental similarities between analogous structures across languages or dialects (e.g., Arvaniti, Ladd, & Mennen, 2006; Ladd, 2006, on Prieto, D'Imperio, & Gili-Fivela, 2005). The goal of this study is to investigate comprehensively the application of these assumptions to a particular problem in the intonational phonology of American English, a problem in which the role played by these two kinds of inferences has been particularly great over the years: the behaviour of "phrase accents" in American English. Much of the disagreement in the literature about the nature of phrase accents and their realisation, we suspect, derives from problematic inferences based on the two assumptions given above concerning the relationship between F0 turning points and phonological tonal targets. It is therefore our goal here to provide a reassessment of those inferences.

Turning points, phrase accents, and English (rise)–fall–rise

The phrase accent, i.e., the tonal target(s) governing the region of the F0 contour between the final pitch accent of a phrase and the boundary tone, has been a feature of the AM approach to intonational phonology since the earliest days of the model (Ladd, 1996, 2008; Pierrehumbert, 1980; Pierrehumbert & Beckman, 1988; and prefigured by Bruce, 1977). The definition has evolved somewhat from its earliest days—currently, phrase accents are held to be boundary tones corresponding to the ends of Intermediate Phrases in the prosodic phrasal parse, symbolised as H- or

L- in the ToBI-family of transcription systems (**To**nes and **B**reak **I**ndices) (Beckman & Pierrehumbert, 1986; Jun, 2005; Silverman et al., 1992). They are thus distinct from boundary tones proper, H% or L%, which signal the end of higher-level Intonational Phrases.

What makes phrase accents interesting for us here, however, is an oft-remarked propensity to "retract" from the licensing phrase boundary, so that they seem to be realised at some distance from, or over some domain broader than, the boundary-adjacent syllable. This is illustrated for the English (rise)–fall–rise contour H* L-H% (expressing incredulity à la Ward & Hirschberg, 1985) in the figures below. Figure 1 shows H* L-H% realised on a relatively short phrase, with just two weak syllables intervening between the nuclear pitch accent (hereafter NPA) and the end of the phrase. Here, the low F0 arising from the L- phrase accent seems readily identifiable with a single F0 turning point, occurring within the final syllable. And if all contours containing Low phrase accents looked just like this one in terms of their realisation, it seems unlikely we would hurry to investigate possible analyses of the phrase accent involving tone spreading, secondary association, or the like. In autosegmental terms, we could simply claim that the Low tonal target associates with a single TBU, giving rise to an F0 turning point at some predictable location in the vicinity. The reason we might ever move beyond such a simple analysis, though, is that not all contours look this unambiguous on the surface.

In Figure 2, for example, the region between the NPA on the first syllable and the right phrase edge is quite long (seven syllables). Within this postnuclear region, the F0 curve describes first a sharp fall from the NPA's peak, then a long, low trough region, terminating at last in a rise at the end of the phrase. Here then, rather than a single L- tonal target reflected in a

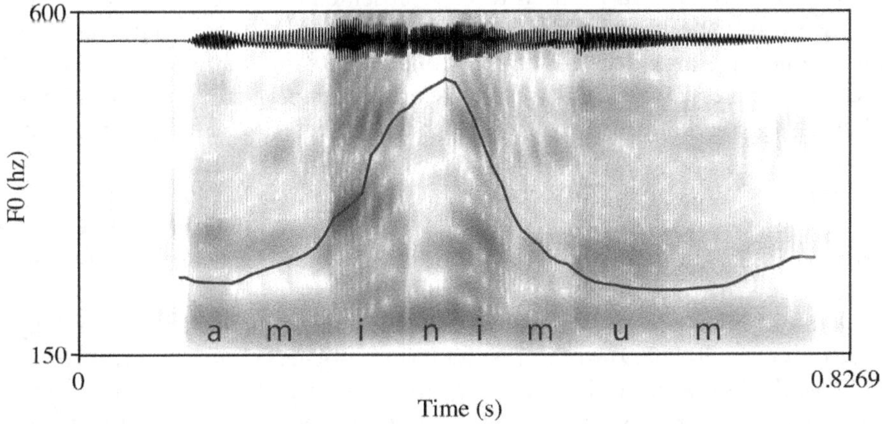

Figure 1. The H* L-H% Incredulity contour realised on the short phrase, *A minimum???!!!*

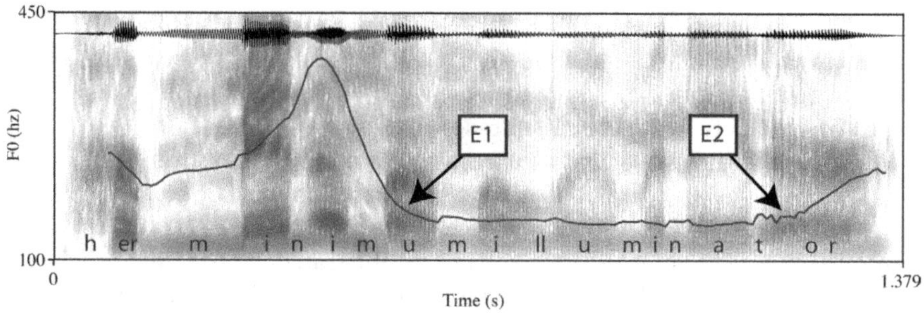

Figure 2. The H* L-H% Incredulity contour realised over a longer phrase, *Her minimum illuminator???!!!*, with an obvious low trough created in the region between the NPA and the phrase end.

clear F0 minimum near the phrase edge, we have what appear to be two low turning points, neither of which is obviously a unique minimum for the region. Inflection points bounding more-or-less level regions such as this are commonly known as "elbows" in the literature.

For clarity's sake, throughout this paper we will refer to the F0 elbows bounding low postnuclear troughs such as that seen in Figure 2 as E1 and E2, respectively. Options for the formal representation of the "extended" phrase accent domain bounded by E1 and E2 include autosegmental spreading of the phrase accent, yielding a single phonological L tone associated with all the syllables in the trough, or long-distance copying (Grice, Ladd, & Arvaniti, 2000; Gussenhoven, 2000), yielding a copy of the L- at the beginning of the trough, another copy at the end, and linear interpolation between the two. For any theory, though, such utterances generate two questions: First, is the extended domain in fact phonological? That is, do both E1 and E2 need to be represented phonologically? Or could a single tonal specification suffice, with the shape of the trough (in cases where one appears) derived from phonetic implementation conventions? Second, if both E1 and E2 are represented phonologically as Low tones, what are the docking sites with which they associate? Which is to say, what attracts the L- leftward in this way?

Consider now how Assumptions 1 and 2 have borne on proposed resolutions of these questions. First, if the only tonal target intervening between the H* of the pitch accent and the H% boundary tone was a single L- associated with a syllable at (or near) the right edge of the phrase, the "target-and-interpolation" model of intonational phonetics and phonology (Arvaniti & Ladd, 2009) would predict a (more-or-less) linear fall from H to L. Since the fall we see in Figure 2 appears to consist of not one, but two line segments, however, Assumption 1 tells us that there must be an additional tonal target in this region, to account for the observed turning point E1.

(See, for example, Pierrehumbert 1980, pp. 84–85, who reasons explicitly in this way regarding an analogous situation with a High target: "There is a H% boundary tone, which is responsible for the F0 maximum at the end of the phrase; however, the contour does not rise smoothly from the L* to this H%, but rather rises, forms a plateau, and then rises again. Thus, an additional H tone is needed to define the corner. This is the H- phrase accent".) This is now the standard assumption in the literature.

Having decided to represent E1 phonologically, we must now also, in line with Assumption 2, examine the pattern of this turning point's phonetic alignment for clues to the docking site of the corresponding L tone in the phonology. Of this enterprise, Pierrehumbert (1980, p. 85) says:

> It is much less clear what principles control the alignment of the phrase accent with the text. In order to investigate this question, a corpus of 350 F0 contours with focus early in the utterance was collected. [. . .] This set of F0 contours was instructive, but still left many questions unanswered.

While tentatively postulating an association between the phrase accent and the end of the word bearing the NPA, Pierrehumbert further notes:

> . . . due to the curvature of the interpolation between [accentual, trailing] H- and L-, and to the interference of segmental effects, it was very difficult to decide where the L- was located. There were many cases where a person with a different theory could have located the L- a syllable to the left or to the right of the word boundary. The interpretation that would first jump to mind varied for repetitions of the same sentence. (Pierrehumbert, 1980, p. 86)

Difficulties notwithstanding, patterns of phrase accent association and the factors triggering them have been analysed in an array of languages in a landmark paper on the nature of phrase accents by Grice et al. (2000). They observe in the literature a variety of candidate "attractors" that might be responsible for luring phrase accents to an earlier location. Among these were: (1) the right edge of the NPA-bearing word (Pierrehumbert & Beckman, 1988); (2) a metrical prominence in the postnuclear trough (demonstrated by Grice et al. to be the case in a number of languages); and (3) a general, leftward imperative, formalised as an ALIGN constraint (Gussenhoven, 2000), possibly interacting with one or both other factors (e.g., mandating association with the leftmost stress in the trough).

For the English H* L-H% contour depicted above, though, Grice et al. analyse the copy of the L- phrase accent reflected in the E1 turning point as the manifestation of a phonological secondary association of the phrase accent with the NPA-bearing syllable itself, alongside the later copy of L-, reflected in E2, which manifests the phrase accent's primary association with a postnuclear lexical stress. Barnes, Shattuck-Hufnagel, Brugos, and Veilleux

(2006) investigated the influence of these and other factors on the realisation of the L- phrase accent in H* L-H% experimentally. Their results supported the conclusions of Grice et al. regarding the end of the L- domain (i.e., the beginning of the final rise): E2 did indeed appear to occur earlier when the penultimate syllable of a phrase was lexically stressed than when it was not, which could point to preferential association of L- with a postnuclear metrical prominence. However, the F0 turning point constituting the beginning of the extended domain, i.e., E1, was difficult to assess for the very reasons detailed by Pierrehumbert above. Nonetheless, a suggestive appearance of some influence of metrical structure on the location of E1 in those results made us eager to investigate further.

It is important to note, before moving on, another key dispute in the literature, concerning not so much the realisation as the phonological identity of our putative phrase accents. The assumption that the turning points at issue here reflect a tonal target distinct from the pitch accent and intervening between it and the final boundary tone, has been challenged by data from a variety of languages suggesting that the relevant tones are not in fact distinct phonological entities, but rather integral parts of the pitch accent itself. Under such an analysis the (rise)–fall–rise contour exemplified above would be viewed not as an H* pitch accent followed by an L- phrase accent and H% boundary tone, but rather as a bitonal HL pitch accent (H*+L, perhaps) preceding a single boundary-related tonal target, H%. This view has been espoused in the AM tradition for English and other West Germanic languages, perhaps most famously and consistently by Gussenhoven (1984, *et seq.*), who attributes the insight to earlier British school analyses (e.g., Halliday, 1970; O'Connor & Arnold, 1973). Similar arguments have been made for certain Romance languages as well, e.g., Frota (2002) on the nuclear H*+L falling contour in European Portuguese, and D'Imperio and House (1997) on Neapolitan Italian.

Goals of this paper

In what follows, we present a comprehensive experimental investigation of the extended postnuclear low F0 region in English, with an eye to evaluating the competing claims detailed above. Specifically, what are the factors that influence the location of the low turning point E1 that begins the low postnuclear trough in our contour (is E1 attracted to metrical prominences? to the boundary of the NPA-bearing word? to the NPA-bearing syllable itself?), and how consistently is this turning point realised? More generally, is E1 in fact the reflection of a phonological Low tone? If so, is E1 better analysed as a copied/spread L- phrase accent, or as a trailing L tone in a complex pitch accent? If E1 is not the reflection of a phonological Low tone, then what is it, and why does the F0 curve fall so sharply from the peak, instead of following an interpolated path to a (single) L- target near the phrase boundary?

To address these questions, we elicited the well-known (rise)–fall–rise contour illustrated above (H* L-H% in ToBI terms), under a range of distinct metrical and prosodic conditions that were strategically designed to adjudicate among competing hypotheses regarding the realisation of the extended postnuclear low domain in American English. In the 'Results' section below (page 999), we demonstrate that, for our data, the strongest predictor of the location of E1 turns out to be the location of the F0 maximum or peak associated with the H* pitch accent. This dependence might be taken to suggest that E1 is in fact a reflection of the trailing tone of a complex pitch accent, rather than of a phrase accent, as is standardly assumed.

On the other hand, we also identify an apparent attraction of E1 to metrical prominences in the trough, an effect that seems to argue in turn for the correctness of the phrase-accent account (to the extent that trailing tones are not known to show such behaviours.) This attraction, however, turns out to lend itself surprisingly poorly to characterisation in terms of the alignment of F0 turning points with a segmental anchor, and correspondingly to characterisation as a consequence of phonological tone association. The effect, while robust, is of a relatively small magnitude, and appears gradiently implemented, meaning that E1 appears to move marginally closer to a potential attractor, but nonetheless to a location that is no closer than several syllables away.

In the section called 'Gradient implementation of E1 and the phonology of elbows' (page 1010), we present another worrying result for a turning point-based account of the postnuclear trough: A strong correlation between peak height and the salience of the E1 turning point suggests that the very presence or absence of an F0 turning point identifiable as E1 in the relevant region of the F0 curve may be far less categorical than is usually assumed. Evidence that the implementation of this turning point is in fact gradiently related to peak height, taken together with the above, lead us to the conclusion that E1 is not, in fact, a reflection of a Low tone of any kind. We propose rather that the appearance of a turning point in this region is epiphenomenal, the result of a constraint on the phonetic implementation of deaccenting in the postnuclear region: The fall from the level of the H* maximum to the level of the eventual L- at the phrase boundary (i.e., E2) must be accomplished sufficiently swiftly to avoid creating the percept of a pitch accent (L* or downstepped H*, for example) on a lexically stressed syllable within the postnuclear region. Pilot perceptual results suggest that a linear fall from the peak to a following lexically stressed syllable, of the kind that might be expected in the absence of such an implementation constraint, has precisely this undesirable effect on contour interpretation.

In the section called 'Relativised Area Under the Curve (R-AUC)' (page 1013), we present a quantitative account of the shape of the postnuclear trough region that does not rely on the location of F0 turning points for its implementation. In it, we introduce a gestalt measure of F0 curve shape that we call Relativised Area Under the Curve (R-AUC), one of the family of global measures we have developed that yield precise, non-turning-point-based characterisations of perceptually relevant aspects of global contour shape. The purpose of R-AUC is to characterise the time-course of the postnuclear fall without relying on the phonologist's (or the listener's) ability to recover the precise location of the fall's "end". It does so by quantifying the overall "Highness" or "Lowness" of the F0 curve within the relevant region. It is thus compatible with the notion that intonational phonology involves sequenced level-tone targets, and views the alignment of F0 turning points as just one of several possible tools for implementing the alignment of a tonal target.

Our conclusion, then, is that the time-course of the sharp fall from the accentual peak to the beginning of the postnuclear trough is not, in the end, driven by the need to align a low turning point with a specific segmental or metrical anchor, but rather, to achieve a specific R-AUC value for the region between the peak and the nearest accentable syllable in the trough, where the R-AUC value that has traditionally been interpreted as the result of one or more L targets instead serves as a cue to the deaccenting of the region as a whole.

METHODS

To assess the influence of the factors listed above on the alignment behaviour of E1, carefully controlled utterances differing in crucial respects in the prosodic structure of the postnuclear trough region were elicited from 15 speakers of American English.

Target utterances

Target elements were two-word noun–noun compounds or adjective–noun phrases with eight syllables, pronounced in isolation as complete Intonational Phrases, e.g., *Minimum illumination!!!???* (In certain target phrases, for the sake of contextual naturalness these two-word phrases were preceded by a monosyllabic function word, such as the indefinite article. This minor difference had no discernible effect on our results, however.) As described below in the section called 'Participants and elicitation' (page 993), training and elicitation were conducted in such a way as to ensure that the NPA was always on the initial syllable of the first word of the target phrase, guaranteeing a lengthy postnuclear region for E1 to locate its preferred alignment patterns. Within this region, we systematically varied the location of candidate attractors for E1: (1) the word boundary; (2) the first postnuclear stressed syllable (here *-lu-*); and (3) the most prominent postnuclear stressed syllable (here *-na-*). Target phrases consisted primarily of sonorant consonants and vowels, to facilitate reliable F0 tracking.

The first four phrase types involve the crossing of two factors (Table 1). The first factor, Word One Type, affects the length and prosodic structure of the first word. The second factor, Word Two Type, involves an important difference in the morphological and prosodic structure of the second word of the phrase.

Word One Type involves an opposition between two critically distinct phrase types. The first is the *lúminàry* phrase type (after one of its exponents, *luminary nominator*), a nominal compound in which Word One contains three posttonic syllables, with the penultimate syllable bearing a secondary stress (as in *lúminàry*). Word Two contains four syllables and begins with a lexically stressed syllable (as in *nóminàtor*). This class of phrases contrasts with the *lánolin* phrase type (after one of its exponents, *lanolin eliminator*), which differs from the *lúminàry* type in that its Word One contains just two posttonic syllables, both of them metrically weak (as in *lánolin*), while Word Two consists of five syllables, with the first always weak (as in *elíminàtor*).

These two phrase types differ in two crucial respects at once. First, *lúminàry* phrases position a lexically stressed syllable close to the main-stress syllable carrying the NPA, with a single weak syllable intervening (*luminar-*). *Lánolin* phrases, by contrast, follow the NPA with a string of three metrically weak syllables (*lanolin e-*). If, as we had suspected, E1 is driven to seek alignment with a lexically stressed syllable in the postnuclear trough, and if, as has been hypothesised (Gussenhoven, 2000), earlier realisation is better, then E1 should be aligned with the leftmost metrically prominent syllable in the trough in both cases, i.e., earlier in *lúminàry* phrases than in *lánolin*.

TABLE 1
Phrase types elicited, with acute accents marking lexical primary stresses and grave accents marking secondary stresses. The first word receives the nuclear pitch accent in each

		Word 2 Type: ATOR vs. ATION	
		Primary stress early	*Primary stress late*
Word 1 type:	1. Three posttonic syllables, strong penult	A. Lúminàry nóminàtor	B. Lúminàry nòminátion
	2. Two posttonic syllables, both weak	A. Lánolin elíminàtor	B. Lánolin elìminátion

(Which is to say, hypothetical spread/copied L could dock on the third syllable of *lúminàry nóminàtor*, but only on the fifth syllable of *lánolin elíminàtor.*) On the other hand, if E1 is attracted to the right edge of the pitch-accented word, then we should observe the reverse: In *luminary* phrases, the boundary between the two words occurs three syllables after the NPA, while in *lanolin* phrases, only two syllables intervene.

The second factor we manipulated, Word Two Type, involves the metrical structure of the second word. Table 1 shows each phrase under Word One Type in two variants. In the first, called –ATOR types for reasons to become apparent, both *luminary* and *lanolin* phrases contain deverbal agentive nouns ending in *–ator* (e.g., *luminary nominator, lanolin eliminator*). Thus, lexical primary stress comes early in that second word, on the initial syllable of *nóminator* types, and on the peninitial of *elíminator*. Such –ATOR phrases contrast in Word Two Type with –ATION phrases. –ATION phrases contain deverbal nouns sharing a stem with their –ATOR counterparts, but end in *–átion*, rather than *–ator*, causing local prominence relations to be reversed: where –ATOR nouns have early primary stress, with secondary stress on the penult, –ATION nouns have early secondary stress, with primary stress on the penult (e.g., *nóminàtor* vs. *nòminátion, elíminàtor* vs. *elìminátion*). Since the primary stress of the second word is also the strongest metrical prominence in the postnuclear region, the difference between –ATOR and –ATION types ensures that, if what attracts E1 is in fact the strongest prominence in the trough, then the E1 should fall earlier in –ATOR phrases than in –ATION. These differences, and their predictions for the hypothesised factors driving the realisation of phrase accents in English, are summarised in Table 2.[3]

One last phrase type included in the study, henceforth the *terminally* type (after one of its exponents, *términally malárial*), is like the now-familiar *luminary* type, in that it places the word boundary three syllables from the pitch-accented phrase-initial syllable. Unlike *luminary* or *lanolin* types, however, this type contains a metrical lapse of four weak syllables between the strong initial and the next lexical stress in the phrases. If E1 is attracted to the earliest lexically stressed syllable in the trough, then *términally* types should stand out from all other phrase types by beginning the L- domain very late (because of the particularly long gap between the NPA and the next lexical stress). By contrast, if E1 seeks out the most prominent stress in the

[3] As discussed below in footnote 12, prominence relations in English are known to be subject to alterations under certain circumstances generally relating to concerns of eurhythmy. While this will become important later in this text, for purposes of the assumptions made here, we know of no reason why the prominence relations we describe would be altered in the contexts we have constructed, nor do we have any evidence that subjects implemented such reversals at any point.

TABLE 2
Potential effects of prosodic class on E1 realisation: crucial comparisons. First syllable in phrase always bears nuclear pitch accent

Prosodic attractor	*Earlier E1 predicted*	*Later E1 predicted*
1. Most prominent postnuclear σ	Lánolin elíminàtor	Lánolin elìminátion
	Word 2 primary stress early	*Word 2 primary stress late*
2. Word boundary	Lánolin # elíminàtor	Lúminàry # nóminàtor
	Two syllables to boundary	*Three syllables to boundary*
3. Leftmost postnuclear stress	lúminàry nóminàtor	Lánolin elíminàtor
	Two syllables to next stress	*Four syllables to next stress*

trough, then *términally* phrases will not stand out as late, but will look comparable to –ATION phrases (both with strongest postnuclear stresses relatively late). These five target phrase classes contained five phrases each, which are listed below in Appendix 1.

Participants and elicitation

Fifteen university-aged native speakers of American English produced four repetitions of each of the 25 target phrases (100 tokens per speaker, 1,500 in all). To ensure that the correct intonation contour was elicited consistently from subjects throughout, some amount of training was necessary. Our previous work (Barnes, Shattuck-Hufnagel, Brugos, & Veilleux, 2006; Brugos, Barnes, Shattuck-Hufnagel, & Veilleux, 2006, Brugos, Barnes, Shattuck-Hufnagel, & Veilleux, 2008) showed that without explicit training, speakers vary their contours to a surprising degree. In elicitations of incredulous (rise)–fall–rise, for example, speakers often default to the low-rise question contour (L* H-H%). In this instance, subjects were first told that the study involved intonation in American English (where the notion of intonation was briefly explained), and that the goal of the experiment was for them to produce a particular intonational pattern in a number short dialogues with an experimenter. The meaning of the contour was explained to subjects as involving energetic disbelief on the part of the speaker, and prerecorded examples of the contour were presented to subjects. To avoid biasing subjects in their subsequent productions of E1, training employed short phrases with little opportunity for extended postnuclear troughs, e.g., "*Hats??!!*", and "*BLUE hats??!!*". For two-word phrases such as the latter, it was explained to subjects that in these instances it should be only the first word about which they were expressing incredulity, i.e., the blueness of the hats in the foregoing. Subjects were asked to confirm that they recognised the contour, and then practiced repeating it, until they could consistently produce the correct pattern on the training phrases.

Subsequently, target utterances were embedded in short, incredulity-enhancing dialogues read with an experimenter. Note that several facts about these dialogues served to ensure that subjects reliably placed the NPA on the first syllable of the target phrase. (For the noun–noun compounds used here, initial primary stress would be the default, but this is not true of the adjective phrases such as *terminally malarial.*) Firstly, the intended word was underlined in the materials from which subjects read their parts in these dialogues, suggesting greater emphasis. Secondly, contexts were all such that the first word of the phrase would most naturally receive contrastive focus, and hence the NPA. (E.g., below, *terminally malarial,* as opposed to *just a little malarial.*) Lastly, the target phrase is in all cases actually produced by the experimenter in the first part of the dialogue with primary stress on the first word (although not with the H* L-H% contour).

Sample Dialogues

(1) Experimenter: George is a thoughtful sort of divorce lawyer—I go to him whenever I need a palimony ruminator.
Subject: A palimony ruminator???!!! (H* L-H%) I thought he was figuring out your plumbing problems!

(2) Experimenter: I'm afraid this patient is terminally malarial.
Subject: Terminally malarial???!!! (H* L-H%) But the doctor just told me he's only a little bit malarial!

Elicitations were recorded in a sound-attenuated room using professional digital recording equipment. Analysis of the recorded speech signals was conducted using Praat (Boersma & Weenink, 2005).

Screening

Tokens were screened by the experimenters to include only fluent (rise)–fall–rise productions with NPA on the first content word of the phrase. A total of 156 tokens were excluded owing to production errors (disfluencies, speech errors) or incorrect contours (e.g., low-rise, i.e., ToBI L* H-H%, or final fall, ToBI H* L-L%).[4] An additional 142 tokens were excluded for irremediable pitch-tracking errors at key points, e.g., gaps in the F0 track or clear distortions (halving, doubling, or unexplained jumps). In all, 21% of the

[4] One speaker with a particularly narrow pitch range typically produced very little final rise in his productions. Many tokens concluded with a rise of 1 semitone or less, which was perceived as largely flat by the authors. Other tokens had no distinguishable final rise in the F0 contour, nor did they have a final fall. As tokens from this speaker formed a continuum from virtually flat to slightly rising to more audibly rising, all such tokens were included as rise-fall-rise contours, and deemed variations in that speaker's unique, rather flaccid production of the desired contour.

TABLE 3
Number of tokens used in anaylsis and gender of each subject

Subject ID	*Gender*	*Tokens used*
1	Male	65
2	Male	79
3	Female	97
4	Female	63
5	Female	70
6	Male	91
7	Female	85
8	Female	79
9	Male	53
10	Female	92
11	Female	97
12	Female	95
13	Female	76
14	Female	47
15	Female	83
Totals	Male: $N = 4$ Female: $N = 11$	1,172

original tokens (including several more noted below) were excluded, reflecting the fact that, although the use of a large number of speakers and tokens provides increased analytic power, there is a practical drawback, in that F0 extraction parameters cannot be tuned for each token. Table 3 shows the number of tokens used for each speaker in the analysis.

Analysis

Recordings were analysed by three labellers trained to locate and annotate the following crucial F0 turning points and segmental locations: Segmental labels included the beginning of the pitch-accented vowel, the midpoint of the following ambisyllabic consonant, the word boundary, and the midpoint of the vocalic nucleus of all syllables following the pitch-accented syllable. Syllable midpoints were used to estimate the relative timing and F0 of postnuclear syllables, because even sonorant consonants can sometimes produce proportionally large F0 perturbations during a long low trough. (See Figure 3.) This was important, to the extent that F0 measures from the trough were necessary to calculate F0 slopes between points such as the accentual peak or the elbow and various attractors. In cases without clear segmental boundaries between syllables, e.g., in V–V sequences (as in *annihilation*), explicit guidelines ensured that labellers converged on a standard location. An example of a labelled Praat TextGrid is shown in Figure 4, with descriptions of labels used in Table 4.

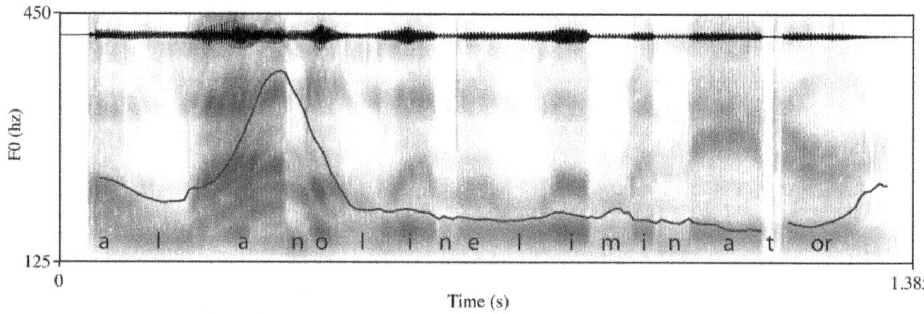

Figure 3. An example of a bumpy low postnuclear trough, with F0 perturbations caused by segmental interference. Segmentally induced F0 variation could make comparison of the F0 of E1 with the F0 of candidate attractors misleading.

Labelled F0 turning points included the pitch-accent peak, and the point judged to represent the end of the fall from peak (i.e., E1). F0 peaks were located semiautomatically by labellers, using a Praat menu command to locate the highest F0 point in a selected region. Identifying the end of the fall, however, was substantially less straightforward. As noted above, E1 rarely represents an actual F0 minimum, either owing to segment-related disturbances within the trough, or to the fact that, after an elbow, the "flat" trough region often continues to fall gradually throughout its duration. Indeed, researchers labelling "the end of the fall" by eye alone typically seem to be referring not to the actual end of the fall (a measurable, physical pattern, i.e., a region of declining F0), but rather to the end of any fall judged "relevant". Some researchers report that "eyeballing" elbows in the F0 curve such as these is quite straightforward, yielding high interlabeller agreement (or agreement with the common algorithmic procedures discussed below; Arvaniti & Ladd, 2009; Knight & Nolan, 2006). Our experience supports the

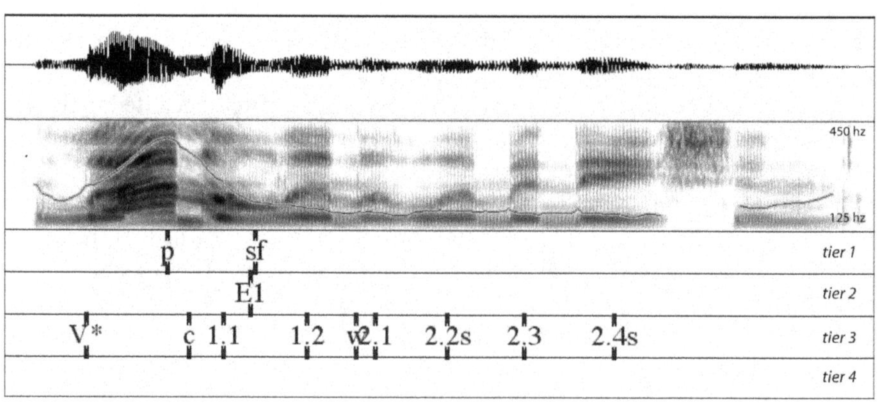

Figure 4. An example of a labelled token of *lanolin eliminator*, produced by a female speaker.

TABLE 4
Description of labelled Praat TextGrid, with label examples from Figure 4

Tier	*Description*		*Label examples from Figure 4*
Tier 1	F0 turning points (hand-labelled)	p	Maximum f0 from accent peak region
		sf	End of "sharp fall," elbow located by labeller's eye
Tier 2	F0 turning point (via algorithm)	E1	Elbow found via semi-automatic line-fitting algorithm
Tier 3	Segmental points	V*	Left edge of pitch-accented vowel
		c	Midpoint of ambisyllabic consonant
		1.1	Midpoint of first post-accent syllable nucleus, word 1
		1.2	Midpoint of second post-accent syllable nucleus, word 1
		w	Word boundary
		2.1	Midpoint of first syllable nucleus, word 2
		2.2s	Midpoint of stressed second syllable nucleus, word 2
		2.3	Midpoint of third syllable nucleus, word 2
		2.4s	Midpoint of stressed fourth syllable nucleus, word 2
Tier 4	Comments		(Used to make comment on disfluencies, f0 tracking errors, wrong contour, etc.)

view that there is often some point (or area) in the F0 track that stands out as an elbow, and here labellers generally agree on location to a reasonable degree. We therefore did task labellers with eyeballing an elbow. (In cases where labellers saw more than one elbow, such as in Figure 6 below, they were instructed to indicate both locations.) In some instances, however, the choice of elbow location was ambiguous enough that the adoption of more rigorous methods was clearly warranted. Figures 5–8 illustrate elbows of increasing obscurity.

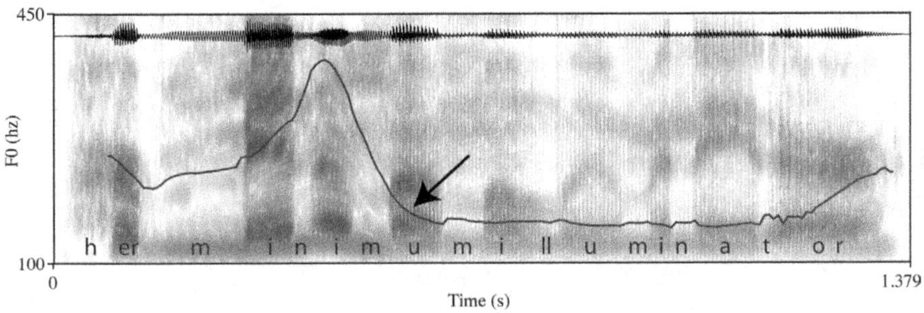

Figure 5. A contour with a readily identifiable "elbow" (arrow indicates placement by line-fitting algorithm described below).

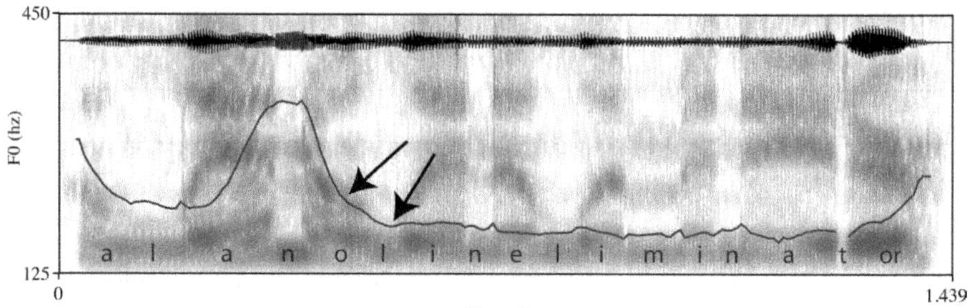

Figure 6. A less straightforward example, with two candidates elbows.

Data extraction and automatic elbow-finding

Fortunately, difficulty in locating F0 turning points (particularly elbows) is a familiar problem, and researchers have devised a number of algorithmic solutions to it. Perhaps the most widely used (and most successful—del Giudice et al., 2007), is a semi-automatic line-fitting algorithm developed by Mary Beckman and her students. (See, e.g., Frota, 2002; D'Imperio, 2000; Welby, 2003; Welby & Loevenbruck, 2006, for applications.) This algorithm fits two lines to the F0 in a region of interest by minimising the residuals from the least-squares fit between the F0 values and the lines, and works well in cases where a piece-wise linear approximation is appropriate. Using hand-labels demarcating the segmental interval from the peak to the second syllable of the second word (by which time the long flat section had consistently been reached), the algorithm finds lines approximating the slope of the fall and the slope of the long low region, respectively. The intersection of these two lines is labelled as the elbow.

A comparison of our hand-labelled and automatically placed elbows yielded a high-degree of agreement, with a mean difference between the two of 26 ms ($SD = 25$). This level of variation seemed sufficiently low to

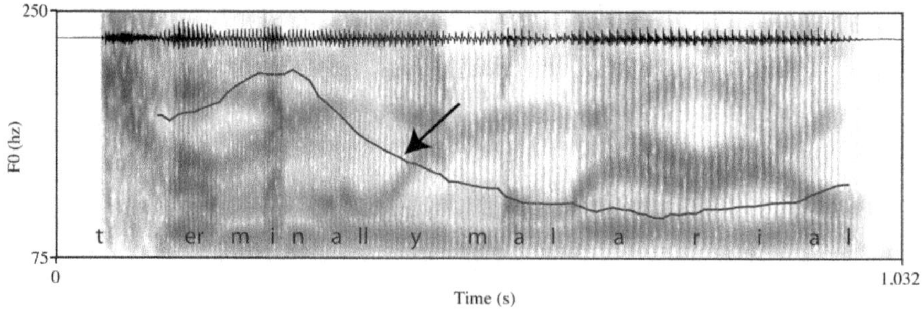

Figure 7. A contour with no obvious elbow (arrow indicates automatic placement).

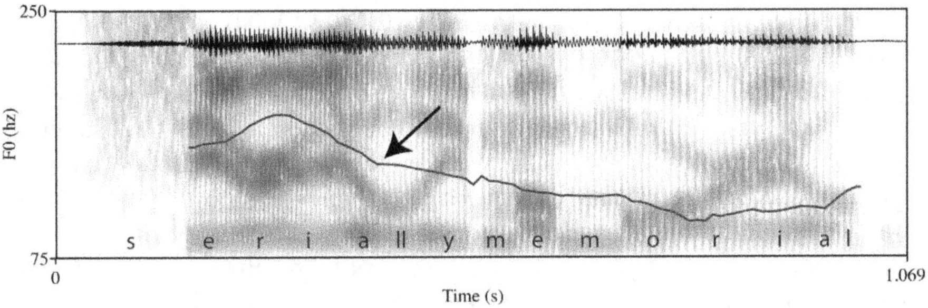

Figure 8. A contour in which the selected elbow seems likely to be a "microprosodic" segmental effect.

convince us that the line-fitting algorithm is finding a point that corresponds closely to what hand-labellers identify as the elbow, such that, in what follows, all reported results involve the automatically placed elbows. Hand-labels for E1 were used as a check on the reliability of the algorithm. Tokens in which the automatic E1 was placed more than three standard deviations from the mean distance between these two points were discarded, resulting in a total of 1,172 files labelled for segmental and prosodic landmarks for analysis.

RESULTS

Correlation analyses

Perhaps the first salient aspect of our results is their opacity to simple interpretation. The elbow as placed by the line-fitting algorithm fell in a relatively consistent region, between the first syllable following the NPA and the first syllable of the second word in the phrase. However, enough variability was observed (even within a single phrase type from a given speaker) that it quickly became apparent that no simple picture of phonological association differences (e.g., elbow within syllable X in one pattern, but syllable Y in another) was likely to emerge. Any systematicity in elbow placement would clearly be subtle, and less visibly categorical. To identify such patterns, we used a variety of analytic procedures.

While the timing of F0 turning points has been used as evidence for distinctions between phonological representations at least since the early days of the AM model, the methods we will use to assess potential patterns of early Low tone association in our data will rely on a set of assumptions made most explicit in the literature on what has come to be known as Segmental Anchoring. The foundational observations for this line of research appear in Arvaniti, Ladd, and Mennen (1998), and are developed especially in later work, such as Atterer and Ladd (2004), Ladd, Faulkner, Faulkner, and Schepman (1999), and Ladd, Mennen, and Schepman (2000). The key notions (Ladd, 2006) are that F0 turning points arise through the phonetic implementation of phonological tonal targets, and that furthermore, phonological association between a tone and a TBU should also involve a predictable timing relationship between the corresponding F0 turning point and some segmental anchoring point affiliated with that TBU. This timing relationship could, but need not, result in temporal co-occurence: the now-famous Greek prenuclear LH aligns its two turning points outside the edges of the syllable ostensibly bearing the pitch accent (Arvaniti et al., 1998). In principle, then, we might expect to find our E1 elbow aligning at some distance from the phonological host of the Low tone giving rise to it. Perhaps most crucially, segmental anchoring predicts that changes to segment durations between stably aligned turning points (whether inherent, rate-related, or otherwise) should result in changes to the duration of the corresponding pitch movements. That is, if the beginning of an F0 fall is tied to one syllable, and the end of the fall is tied to another, then as segmental durations between them decrease, the pitch movement should shorten and steepen. Correspondingly, as the distance between endpoints grows, we predict a longer, shallower pitch movement.[5] This predicted correlation between the durations of certain segmental intervals and the duration/shape of F0 movements presents us with a powerful tool for investigating segmental alignment patterns.

To determine whether E1 aligns with any of the candidate attractors listed above, we can investigate the relationship between (1) duration/shape of the F0 fall from peak to elbow; and (2) segmental durations in key regions of our target phrases. We present evidence from two kinds of correlation analyses: (1) correlations between the distance from the elbow to a candidate attractor and the distance from the peak to the same attractor; and (2) correlations between the distance from peak to attractor and the distance from peak to elbow. The crucial relationships are schematised below (Figure 9): If the elbow lies in a stable timing relationship with a given attractor, we expect (1) no correlation between elbow-to-attractor distance and peak-to-attractor distance, i.e., the elbow should stay fixed with respect to the attractor, regardless of where the peak ends up; and (2) a strong correlation between peak-to-attractor distance and peak-to-elbow distance, i.e., as the peak moves closer to the attractor, it approaches the elbow as well. These analyses are presented in the following for each candidate attractor.

[5] This dependence of the duration of pitch movements on independently varying segmental durations lies at the heart of the Autosegmental-metrical argument against traditional "configuration-based" approaches to the characterization of F0 contours.

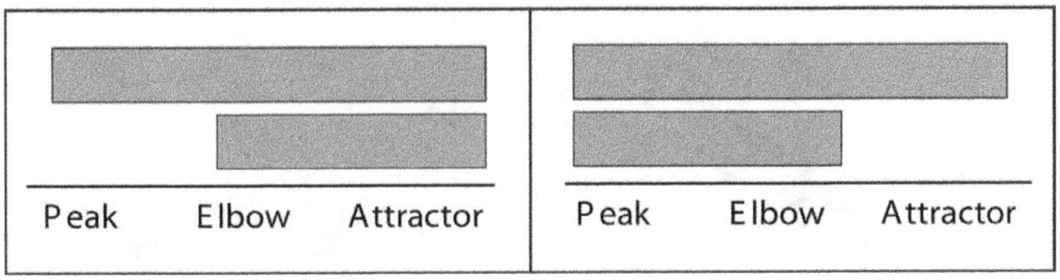

Figure 9. Interval durations correlated to test for segmental alignment patterns. Left: Peak-to-attractor and Elbow-to-attractor intervals. Positive correlation between these durations would imply that the Elbow is aligned with respect to the Peak, and not the Attractor. Lack of correlation might imply the opposite. Right: Peak-to-attractor and Peak-to-Elbow intervals. Positive correlation would imply alignment of Elbow with Attractor. Lack of correlation might imply alignment of Elbow with the Peak.

Leftmost postnuclear stress

Leftmost postnuclear stresses for our various phrase types are: the penult of the first word for *lúminàry nóminàtor/ation* types, and the peninitial of the second word for *lánolin elíminàtor/ation* and *términally malárial* types. If the leftmost postnuclear stress is the attractor with which a putative early L tone associates, then we predict no correlation between the distance from peak to leftmost stress and the distance from E1 to leftmost stress, but instead a strong correlation between the distance from peak to leftmost stress and peak to E1. In fact, our results are precisely the opposite: an extremely strong positive correlation between peak-to-attractor and E1-to-attractor distances, $r(1,172) = .976$, $p < .001$. The elbow, it seems, moves in virtual lockstep with the peak, regardless of where both fall with respect to the attractor. The correlation between peak-to-attractor distance and peak-to-E1 distance, by contrast, is all but nonexistent, $r(1,172) = .129$, $p < .001$ (i.e., sufficient to account for not quite 1.7% of the variation in E1 placement). Scatterplots in Figure 10 underscore this result. We conclude that there is ample evidence here suggesting timing of E1 with respect to the peak, but very little for a stable timing relationship between E1 and leftmost postnuclear stress.

Most prominent postnuclear stress

If E1 is attracted to the strongest stress in the postnuclear trough, the above predictions for its location hold relative to the initial syllable of the second word for *lúminàry nóminàtor* types, the peninitial of the second word for *lánolin elíminàtor* types and *términally malárial* types, and the penult of the second word for both *lúminàry nòminátion* and *lánolin elìminátion* types. Once again we find the opposite: A strong correlation between peak-to-attractor distance and E1-to-attractor distance, $r(1,172) = .968$, $p < .001$, and no meaningful correlation between peak-to-attractor and peak-to-E1

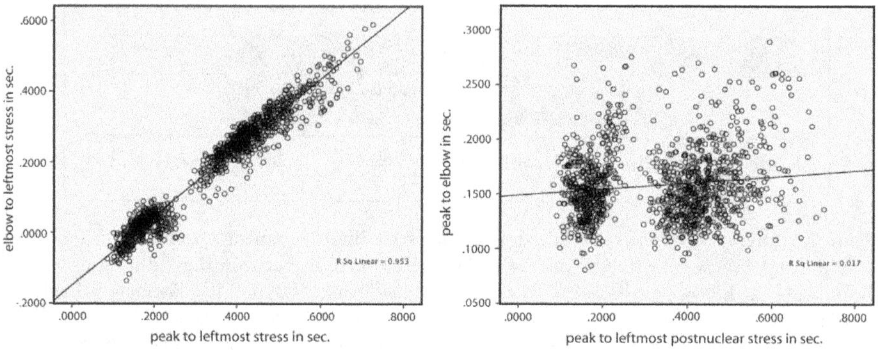

Figure 10. Scatterplots illustrating the relationship between the elbow and one candidate attractor, the leftmost postnuclear stressed syllable. The lefthand plot shows a strong correlation between the distance from peak to attractor and the distance from elbow to attractor. The righthand plot shows a correspondingly weak relationship between the distance from peak to attractor and the distance from peak to elbow. Together, this suggests that the elbow is timed with respect to the peak, not the attractor. (The two clouds arise from the difference between *luminary* phrases and other types in terms of distance from peak to leftmost stress, discussed above in the section called 'Target utterances')

distance, $r(1,172) = .125$, $p < .001$. Once again, E1 seems to move along with the peak, with no evidence for a fixed relationship between it and the attractor.

Word boundary

If the right edge of the pitch-accented word is the target for phonological association of an L tone, then we expect E1 to be timed predictably with respect to that word boundary, predictions holding as above. Again what we find is a strong correlation between peak-to-boundary distance and E1-to-boundary distance, $r(1,172) = .876$, $p < .001$ and little between peak-to-boundary distance and peak-to-E1 distance $r(1,172) = .222$, $p < .001$.

To summarise, correlation analysis finds no evidence for alignment of E1 with any of the candidate attractors investigated. In fact, the extraordinarily strong correlations between peak-to-attractor distance and E1-to-attractor distance suggest that E1 is timed with respect to the peak of the NPA. These findings echo the work of Frota (2002), who concludes (using similar methods) that the end of the nuclear fall associated with the narrow focus H*+L pitch accent in European Portuguese is timed not segmentally, but rather with respect to the accentual peak. In fact, another strong positive correlation, between the distance of the peak from the onset of the accented vowel on the one hand, and the distance of E1 from same, suggests that this is precisely what occurs in American English as well, $r(1,172) = .673, p < .001$: As the peak moves relative to the accented syllable, E1 moves proportionally, meaning that

E1 appears to occur at something like a fixed distance from the F0 peak. (Peaks in our data have a mean location 13 ms after the midpoint of the consonant following the pitch-accented vowel, *SD* = 31 ms, with E1 at a mean distance of 158 ms after peaks, *SD* = 31 ms)

There is, however, an alternative analysis: we would also expect such a positive correlation if *both the peak and the elbow* were segmentally aligned with respect to the pitch-accented syllable. (This might be the phonetic prediction, for example, of Grice et al.'s (2000) suggestion that English phrase accents manifest a phonological secondary association with the syllable bearing the NPA.) In other words, the causal factor behind the movement of the elbow vis-à-vis the accented syllable might not be the movement of the peak *per se*, but rather something else, to which both peak and elbow respond equally, i.e., durational change in the accented syllable. If both peak and elbow were aligned with, say, the end of the pitch-accented vowel, then as that vowel lengthens or shortens, both peak and elbow would move in absolute terms farther from or closer to the onset of the vowel, respectively.

That peaks are aligned with pitch-accented syllables in this fashion appears clear from the strong positive correlation between the distance from vowel onset to peak and the duration of the vowel itself (measured, of necessity, somewhat indirectly as the distance from the vowel onset to the midpoint of the following consonant), $r(1,172) = .592$, $p < .001$. A similar correlation obtains for the distance from vowel onset to elbow, $r(1,172) = .533$, $p < .001$. Note, however, that the correlation between elbow placement and peak placement is substantially stronger than that between elbow placement and vowel duration: .673 vs. .533.

We take the above to be evidence of the alignment of the elbow not with the NPA-bearing syllable *per se*, but rather, with the peak of the accent itself. If the elbow were in fact aligned with some point within the accented syllable, then we would expect the strongest correlation to be between vowel-onset-to-E1 distance on the one hand, and vowel duration on the other. (As vowel duration increases, any possible alignment point within the accented syllable increases in distance from the onset of the syllable, predicting a proportional increase in the distance of E1 from same.) This was seen not to be the case. Instead, the location of E1 appears to vary most stably with location of peak, rather than with any segmental point within the accented syllable. A stepwise multiple regression analysis (see Table 5) underscores this difference: A model taking distance from accented-vowel onset to E1 as a dependent variable, and onset-to-peak distance, vowel duration, and peak height as dependent variables, returns onset-to-peak distance as the strongest predictor of E1 location, $r^2(1,172) = .453$, with vowel duration a distant third, yielding *r*-squared increase of just .022. (Peak F0 is a stronger predictor of

TABLE 5
Linear regression model for factors predicting elbow placement relative to the pitch-accented vowel

Model		*B*	*SE B*	*Beta*
Step 1	(Constant)	0.177	0.004	
	Vowel onset to peak	0.873	0.028	0.673
Step 2	(Constant)	0.048	0.016	
	Vowel onset to peak	0.836	0.028	0.644
	Peak F0	0.001	0.000	0.175
Step 3	(Constant)	0.052	0.016	
	Vowel onset to peak	0.698	0.033	0.538
	Peak F0	0.001	0.000	0.157
	Vowel duration	0.227	0.032	0.185

Note: $r^2 = .453$ for Step 1; $\Delta r^2 = .03$ for Step 2, $\Delta r^2 = .022$ for Step 3, $p < .001$ for all.

E1 location in this model, accounting for an additional 3% of the variability—apparently the fall takes slightly longer with higher peaks.)[6]

[6] An anonymous reviewer questions our dismissal of the .533 correlation coefficient for the relationship between vowel duration and elbow location as indicative of an alignment relationship between the elbow and the pitch-accented syllable. The reviewer notes that we do accept a correlation coefficient of .592 for vowel duration and peak location as indicative of an alignment relationship between the peak and the pitch-accented syllable, and that since elbows are difficult to measure, we might expect the elbow data to be noisier than the peak data, resulting in the slightly lower correlation coefficient, even while the elbow was in fact aligning phonetically with the pitch-accented syllable. The important point here, however, is not the absolute value of any given correlation coefficient, but rather the relative strengths of correlations that offer competing explanations for the phenomenon at hand. The fact that the correlation between peak location and elbow location is stronger than that between vowel duration and elbow location (together with the data from the multiple regression including both vowel duration and peak location as variables) indicates that there is a significant amount of variation in elbow location that we can account for with reference to peak location, but not with reference to vowel duration. (Note too that noise in the elbow data in this case seems not to impede the stronger correlation result.) As to why there should be a relationship as strong as $r = .533$ between vowel duration and elbow location in the first place, this is likely just because vowel duration and peak location, the two competing predictors in this instance, are highly collinear: If peaks are aligned with some point in the pitch-accented syllable, such that peak location is correlated with vowel duration, and if elbows are aligned with respect to peaks, such that elbow location and peak location are correlated, then elbow location and vowel duration will also necessarily be correlated. However, because vowel duration and peak location are not perfectly collinear, the relationship between vowel duration and elbow location will necessarily be weaker than that between peak location and elbow location. Put another way, much of the variation we observe in peak location can be explained with reference to vowel duration. But since some of this variation is either random, or attributable to other sources, if elbow location is in fact determined by peak location, then we expect there to be variation in the placement of the elbow that cannot be accounted for with reference to vowel duration. As we have shown, this is indeed the case.

To summarise, the kinds of correlation analyses typically used in the literature to demonstrate phonetic alignment between a turning point and some segmental host have in this case failed to produce compelling evidence that candidate attractors influence the timing of E1, and hence, by the assumptions outlined above, the association of the corresponding Low tone. Furthermore, there is strong evidence that the crucial factor for determining where the elbow will land is the location of the peak of the H* NPA. In other words, E1 is not aligned segmentally, but rather seems timed relative to another tonal target in the contour.

Another approach to segmental alignment: Analysis of variance

If we have failed to demonstrate categorical stability of the timing of E1 vis-à-vis any attractor, it is still possible that E1 is "aligned" in more subtle, gradient fashion. It could be, for example, that even though location of the peak is the strongest influence on elbow placement, nonetheless there is some tendency for elbow placement to drift leftward or rightward to increase proximity to one or another attractor. To test this, we conducted a two-way analysis of variance with distance in ms from peak to E1 as a dependent variable, and Word One Type and Word Two Type as factors with two levels each. (The following analyses do not include the data from *terminally* type phrases, on which more below.) Recall from above that if E1 is attracted to the leftmost postnuclear stress in the phrase, we would expect to find an effect of Word One Type, with an earlier E1 in *lúminàry nominator/ation* types than in *lánolin eliminator/ation types.* (The mean distance from the peak to the midpoint of the stressed penult of *luminary* is 170 ms, while the mean distance from peak to the midpoint of the stressed peninitial vowel of *eliminator/ation* is much longer, 408 ms.) The reverse trend might be evidence for attraction to the word boundary. (Mean distance to the word boundary is 335 ms in *luminary nominator/ation* types, but just 239 ms in *lanolin eliminator/ation types.*) Likewise, if E1 were attracted to the most prominent postnuclear stress, we would expect a main effect of Word Two Type, with an earlier elbow in –ATOR phrases than in –ATION. (Mean distances from the peak to the midpoint of the most prominent postnuclear vowel are 448 ms and 411 ms for –ATOR phrases from the *luminary* and *lanolin* groups, respectively, but 688 ms and 661 ms for –ATION phrases from the same groups.)

Mean distances and standard deviations are given for each phrase type in Table 6. Results of repeated measures ANOVA carried out by-subject, with Word One Type and Word Two Type as within-subjects factors, shows a marginally significant main effect of Word One Type, $F(1, 14) = 4.905$, $p = .044$, no main effect of Word Two Type, $F(1, 14) = 1.715$, $p > .05$, and no significant interaction, $F(1, 14) = 3.138$, $p > .05$. Results of a two-way

TABLE 6
Mean distances from peak to elbow in ms by phrase type

Phrase type	*Mean*	*SD*	*N*
Lúminàry nòminátion	157	29	236
Lúminàry nóminàtor	159	33	257
Lánolin elìminátion	155	31	232
Lánolin elíminàtor	151	28	232

ANOVA carried out by-item with Word One Type and Word Two Type as between-subjects factors showed a main effect of Word One Type approaching, but not reaching, significance, $F(1, 16) = 3.729$, $p > .05$, no main effect of Word Two Type, $F(1, 16) < 1$, $p > .05$, and no significant interaction, $F(1, 16) = 1.289$, $p > .05$.

If there is any evidence in the foregoing for differences in elbow placement, it is for a small difference, of marginal statistical significance, between *luminary*-type phrases and *lanolin*-type phrases, with the elbow slightly closer on average to the peak in *lanolin* types than in *luminary*. If genuine, as noted above, this difference could be taken as evidence for attraction of E1 to the word boundary. Note, however, that the magnitude of difference in E1 placement between the two types is less than 5 ms, while the difference between the two types in distance from peak to word boundary is quite large—97 ms. This lack of proportionality between hypothetical cause and effect, combined with the questionable perceptual relevance of 5 ms mean difference, and the marginal significance of the effect, makes us hesitant to draw conclusions based on this difference alone. (As we will see below, this small difference ultimately admits of a very different sort of explanation.)

Since the –ATOR/–ATION contrast has been shown not to result in elbow-alignment differences, the next step in our analysis is to pool these types within the *luminary* and *lanolin* groups, and to contrast these two Word One Types individually with the so-far neglected *términally* type phrases. Means and standard deviations for the three phrase types under comparison are given in Table 7. Here, both ANOVA by-item and by-subject yield a striking result: by-subject repeated-measures ANOVA with phrase type as a three level (*luminary, lanolin, and terminally*) within-subjects factor, demonstrates a clear main effect of phrase type on the distance from peak to elbow, $F(2, 28) = 17.535$, $p < .001$. ANOVA conducted by-item, with phrase type as a three level, between-subjects factor, returned a similarly significant effect of phrase type, $F(2, 22) = 13.459$, $p < .001$. Planned comparisons yielded no significant difference between *luminary* and *lanolin*-types, but a highly significant difference between *terminally* types and everything else.

TABLE 7
Mean distances from peak to elbow in ms. by phrase type, pooling –ATOR phrases with –ATION, and including *términally*

Phrase type	*Mean*	*SD*	*N*
Lúminàry	158	31	493
Lánolin	153	30	464
Términally	169	38	215

This result reinforces our skepticism regarding the 5 ms difference between *luminary* types and *lanolin* types, but uncovers a difference between phrase types that the foregoing analysis might not lead us to expect. The later E1 in *términally* type phrases is what we would expect if E1 were attracted to the leftmost prominence in the trough: the strong second syllable of the second word of *términally* phrases (e.g., *–lar* in *terminally malarial*) is farther from the pitch-accented syllable both in terms of number of syllables intervening (4), and in absolute duration in ms (mean = 522, *SD* = 71), than is the leftmost postnuclear prominence in either of the other two classes.

But if this is evidence for gradient attraction of E1 to the leftmost postnuclear stress, something still isn't quite right: Mean peak-to-elbow distances in the *lanolin, luminary,* and *terminally* classes were 153 ms, 158 ms, and 169 ms, respectively. Distances from peak to this attractor, by contrast, were 407 ms, 170 ms, and 522 ms. If the leftmost postnuclear stress truly attracted E1 here, we would expect to find our earliest elbow in *luminary* phrases, a much later elbow in *lanolin,* and a still-later elbow in *terminally.* The similarity of E1 placement in *luminary* and *lanolin* phrases, in other words, remains unexplained.

DISCUSSION

To summarise our results so far, the location of E1 is most robustly predicted by the location of the peak. Correlation analyses gave us no reason to suspect that E1 is aligned with any of the attractors investigated, but ANOVA did turn up a significant difference in E1 location between *terminally* phrases and both other types. This difference cannot be understood as attraction of E1 to the most prominent postnuclear stress, owing to the lack of a significant difference between –ATOR and –ATION types demonstrated above. Attraction of E1 to the leftmost postnuclear stress in *terminally* phrases, however, also fails to account for all the data, as this would leave us unable to explain the apparent lack of significant difference in E1 placement between *lanolin* and *luminary* types.

Phrase accent or trailing tone?

Alignment of E1 with the NPA peak is in principle consistent with either a phrase accent or a trailing +L analysis of this turning point's phonological representation. As noted, Frota (2002) takes the alignment of the elbow with the peak in Portuguese to be evidence for the view that the elbow is not the instantiation of a phrase accent, but rather the trailing tone of a bitonal pitch accent, H*+L. We are not convinced that the alignment data by itself actually speaks to this question. It could be a trailing tone, certainly, but we see no reason in principle to preclude the existence of a phrase accent that is timed with respect to the location of the pitch accent, even if allowing this to be the case does make it difficult to distinguish between a trailing tone and a phrase accent on purely phonetic grounds.[7]

If the facts so far seem to argue for an analysis of E1 as the reflection of a trailing tone of the NPA, however, the later E1 placement observed in the *terminally* class seems to argue otherwise. (Phrase accents, of course, have been argued to seek association with postnuclear metrical prominences, but trailing tones, to our knowledge, have not.) To be fair, this difference is certainly a subtle phonetic effect,[8] but several labellers did independently report noticing unusually gradual falls in the *terminally* class ("bowls" in local parlance). While the statistical effect could in principle arise from a bimodal distribution of peak-to-E1 values for the *terminally class,* some reflecting late alignment, and others earlier, no such distribution was observed for our data. The boxplots presented in Figure 11 below make it clear that while the interquartile range for *terminally* types is not notably wider than that of the other classes, it is notably higher (i.e., reflecting later alignment), as are the median and the 95% confidence interval. A general tendency towards longer peak-to-E1 distances for *terminally* types is thus clearly present here.

Assuming that the effect is genuine, and leaving aside for now the unresolved problem of the early elbows in the *lanolin* class, what might this 10–15 ms average alignment difference mean? It is clearly not the case that E1 is "aligned" in any standard sense with the lexically stressed syllable in the second word of phrases like *terminally malarial*—the correlation analyses presented above demonstrated this. We are left with the possibility that E1 is timed rather strictly relative to the peak—that is, the fall has a relatively

[7] Indeed, as Lisa Selkirk reminds us (personal communication), this was the essence of Bruce's original proposal for the phrase accent in Swedish.

[8] It is also not an effect evidenced by all of our subjects: 2 of 15 subjects showed no trace of it, and for six others, the difference in question was on the order of 5 ms or less.

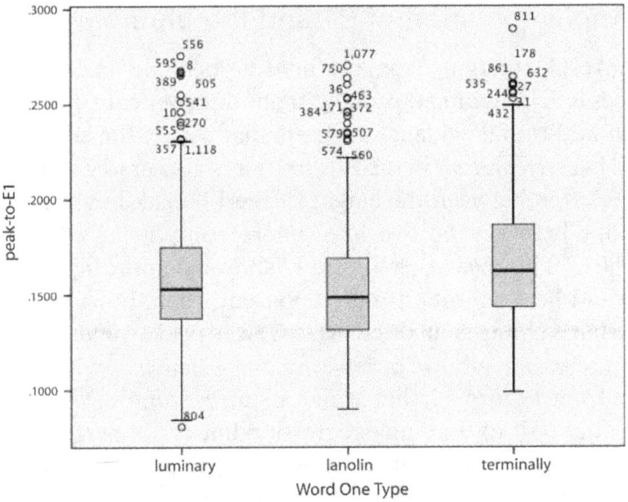

Figure 11. Boxplots representing the distributions of peak-to-E1 distance for the *luminary*, *lanolin*, and *terminally* phrase types.

constant duration—but that within some window of acceptable variability, the elbow might nonetheless be attracted away from the peak in the direction of an attractor, in this case the second, lexically stressed syllable of the second word in phrases like *terminally malarial*.

But what good is served by an elbow location 15 ms closer to a given attractor, if that elbow still ends up a mean 353 ms. from the midpoint of the active attractor? If the lexically stressed syllable is indeed an attractor here, then it is an extremely weak one, drawing the elbow just 4% of the way towards it. That this should count as "better" in any meaningful sense is not at all clear.

Better or not though, it seems highly dubious that this pattern should reflect the difference between two phonologically distinct association patterns for our hypothetical L tone. As noted above for Greek, phonetic turning points need not physically overlap with their phonological host syllables. Still, for that Greek L tone, the turning point occurs on average 5 ms before the accented syllable. Here, our elbow precedes its putative host by over 300 ms, falling two or even three syllables earlier. It seems to us that distances of this magnitude render the notion of phonological association essentially meaningless here. But if the attraction of E1 to the lexical stress in *terminally* phrases cannot credibly be attributed to differences in phonological association of the L- phrase accent, what, then, can it be attributed to?

Gradient implementation of E1 and the phonology of elbows

Here another result emerging from our analysis becomes relevant: not only do any differences in E1 alignment present in our data appear subtle and gradient in nature, but additional evidence suggests that in fact the extent to which an identifiable E1 is *even present* in the F0 contour is also gradient. Our data show a strong correlation between the height of the F0 peak in semitones, and the change in slope between the two lines intersecting at the elbow, $r(1{,}172) = -.619, p < .001$.[9] This means, as Figure 12 shows, that the higher the peak F0, the sharper, and hence more visually apparent, the elbow: high peaks yield elbows with sharp changes in slope, while lower peaks yield changes in slope that are slight, creating elbows of less obvious salience.

It is clear from Figure 12 that while a single, sample-wide correlation is present in the data, fit to the single regression line is not perfect. The problem is that we are pooling data from 15 different speakers, each with a different F0 range. Figure 13 represents the same data with speakers plotted separately, each with a distinct regression line.

A number of things become apparent here. Firstly, as Table 8 below makes clear, there is a significant correlation between peak height and elbow sharpness for all but one of our speakers. (For that speaker, $p = .088$.) The relationship between these two variables is thus real and strong. Differences in pitch ranges between speakers are evident in Figure 13 in the form of

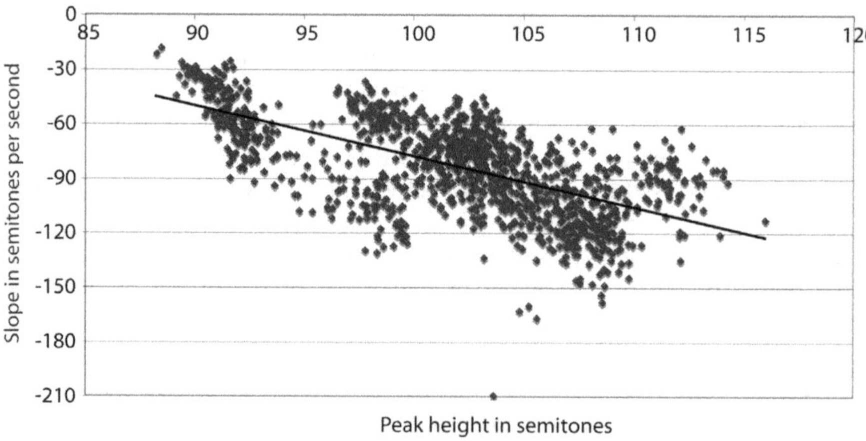

Figure 12. Elbow "sharpness" as a function of peak height.

[9] In fact, the number used in this correlation is just the slope of the first line, which, given the relative lack of variation in the slope of the line representing the low, flat trough, is a strong enough proxy for elbow "sharpness" in general. (The correlation between slope of the first line and change in slope between the two lines calculated directly was over 0.9 for all speakers.)

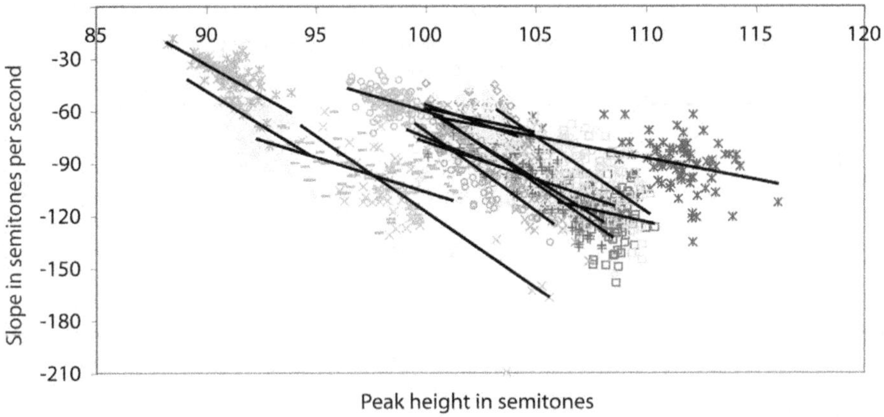

Figure 13. Elbow sharpness as a function of peak height, 15 speakers plotted individually. [To view this figure in colour, please visit the online version of this journal.]

differences in horizontal position and length of the individual trendlines.[10] Differences in vertical placement of trendlines sharing horizontal position and slope demonstrate apparent interspeaker variation in overall levels of elbow sharpness. The significance of the correlation, however, together with the remarkable similarity of the slopes of the trendlines makes clear the basic generalisation: higher peaks lead to sharper, more obvious elbows in a pervasive fashion throughout our data.

Such a tendency, of course, is not unexpected given what we know so far: If peak location is roughly stable for each speaker, and if elbow location and height are also roughly stable (that is, not affected by differences between phrase types, or by peak height), then any variation in peak height will result in changes to the slope of the peak-to-E1 fall. The consequences of this finding, however, are troubling: Elbow sharpness, which is to say, the visual (and possibly auditory) salience of the elbow, appears to vary smoothly along a continuum from extremely salient in the case of high peaks, to unrecognisable in the case of lower peaks. At one end of the continuum, we have utterances in which impressionistic labellers would almost certainly

[10] The four regression lines that seem to follow roughly the same path, beginning at the upper left corner of the chart in Figure 13 represent the four male speakers that took part in the study. The remaining 11 lines represent females. Note that the male speaker with the highest peak F0 values has far steeper slope values than do females with comparable peak F0, resulting in horizontal overlap, but vertical separation, in their plotted results. This is because the male speaker is throughout the elicitation at the top of his pitch range, while the female speaker with comparable F0 is nearer the bottom of hers. An enthusiastic male, in other words, has similar peak F0 to a bored female, with the difference in slope of the fall back to baseline distinguishing the two.

TABLE 8
Pearson correlations between peak height and elbow sharpness by speaker

Speaker	*r*	*N*
1	−.531[a]	65
2	−.656[a]	79
3	−.427[a]	97
4	−.514[a]	63
5	−.737[a]	70
6	−.548[a]	91
7	−.269[b]	85
8	−.806[a]	79
9	−.729[a]	53
10	−.179	92
11	−.341[a]	97
12	−.653[a]	95
13	−.828[a]	76
14	−.317[b]	47
15	−.426[a]	83

[a]Correlation significant at the .001 level (two-tailed); [b]Correlation significant at the .05 level (two-tailed).

note an F0 turning point (e.g., Figure 5, again), and would most likely agree as to its location. At the other end of the continuum (Figure 8, again), we have utterances in which labellers would be unlikely to notice a turning point at all unless explicitly told to do so (as, e.g., the line-fitting algorithm was). It was suggested to us (Mariapaola D'Imperio, personal communication) that perhaps it is wrong to include contours like that in Figure 8 in the same category with those like Figure 5 to begin with. Perhaps in Figure 5 there really is an elbow, reflecting the association of an L tone, while in Figure 8 there simply isn't one: No turning point, after all, implies no tonal target, and hence potentially two distinct patterns of phonological association for the phrase accent, one with retraction, and one without.

This is a sensible conclusion, given only the two ends of the sharpness continuum. The problem is what to do with the range of values in between. If elbow sharpness is in fact gradiently instantiated, then imposing discrete category boundaries on the resulting continuum would be at best arbitrary, at worst misleading. A better analysis would see a single category here, with implementation varying gradiently with peak height. But what would such a representation look like? Is there an elbow, or isn't there? Is there an early L target in the trough, or isn't there?

The question is ultimately this: If we can't be sure whether we have an F0 turning point, can we be sure we have a phonological tonal target? If we are convinced that the salient elbows in high-peak contours represent F0 turning points, and if we are committed to the belief that F0 turning points necessarily reflect the presence of phonological tonal targets, then we might claim that the missing/obscured elbows in low-peak contexts really just reflect something like hypoarticulation: there is always a Low tone associated early in the trough, but it can be hard to measure. (And, potentially, to hear.) Still, this seems unsatisfying as an explanation for our result. The point here is not that elbows are always difficult to measure; indeed, at times they are impossible to miss. The point is that they are *systematically* difficult to measure, i.e., when they occur in particular contexts, and that furthermore, we can predict exactly when and how they will be realised from another, less ambiguous property of the F0 curve: peak height. Since every argument we are aware of for the presence of multiple phonological L tones in the postnuclear trough turns on the need to account for the systematic presence of E1 in the F0 curve, it is of crucial importance to know just how systematic the presence of E1 is. To the extent that it might be possible to account not only for E1's presence, but also for the details of its implementation when it appears, without positing additional elements in the phonological representation of this contour, such an account would be both more accurate, and more economical.

Relativised Area Under the Curve (R-AUC)

Our goal in the following is to present just such an account, one that not only makes quantitatively correct predictions regarding the shape of the F0 curve in the postnuclear trough, but also allows us to resolve the issue of the apparently contradictory behaviour of E1 with respect to the attractors under consideration. On this account, the elbow created by the fall from a high peak is not a part of the phonological representation of the contour, but arises from the interaction of other factors in phonetic implementation: specifically, an unusually high peak, and a constraint requiring F0 to reach a low level that is no longer saliently falling, within a relatively short window following the syllable bearing the NPA. To understand why this should be the case, consider what phrase accents are meant to do in the first place.

Though in formal terms phrase accents are tonal markers of the right boundary of a prosodic constituent, and therefore logically independent of pitch accent, there is a strong intuitive sense among researchers that phrase accents can in certain cases also enhance the prominence of the NPA (e.g., Beckman, 1986, p. 95). This idea, as relates to the magnitude or rapidity of an exiting pitch movement, works most effectively where the NPA and the phrase accent are of opposite polarity (i.e., H* L- or L* H-). A slightly different (and potentially more broadly applicable) view, however, might be that in the case of H* L-, by falling rapidly from the peak of the high NPA, what speakers achieve is a state of affairs whereby any "accentable" syllables within the postnuclear region sound deaccented. Correctly identifying the NPA is of course crucial to the correct interpretation of focus structure in an utterance, and therefore must be reliably achieved. One goal of the long, flat postnuclear region preceding both high and low phrase accents might then just be to ensure that everything within that domain should sound prosodically "uneventful".

That the functional basis for the rapid fall as outlined above is correct is underscored by pilot results suggesting that, when E1 is "removed" from one of our high peak contours, through resynthesis that creates a linear interpolation from the peak to a following accentable syllable, listeners are prone to hear a striking reversal of prominence relations between the two syllables. Whereas in the original contour the H* bears the NPA, in the synthetic, elbow-free contour, the H* now sounds like a prenuclear high accent, and the syllable at which the fall terminates suddenly bears an L* NPA. Apparently, a fall terminating at an accentable syllable is sufficient, at least under some circumstances, to cue the percept of an L*, even in the absence of other typical accent cues (e.g., duration, amplitude, spectral balance). Likewise, if a linear fall from a peak simply passes through an accentable syllable in the trough, terminating in an F0 minimum later, this can cue the very strong percept of a downstepped H* NPA on the accentable syllable, again demoting the actual nuclear syllable in phrase's hierarchy of prominences.

The reason for the appearance of an elbow in our high-peak tokens then becomes clear: in order to achieve a low pitch level relatively soon after an H* NPA, thus avoiding the creation of cues to accentedness on any following accentable syllable, if the peak of the accent is produced relatively high in the speaker's pitch range, then the speaker must produce a steep fall, followed by a relatively flat, low region—the recipe, in other words, for an elbow. By contrast, if the NPA peak is relatively low, the speaker need fall less far to reach the necessary lower level in his/her pitch range. The low-peak fall will thus be shallower, and the elbow less distinct.[11] But what is the time window within which the fall must be accomplished?

Clearly, the bulk of the fall must be completed some time before the next accentable syllable, and our data may suggest how soon. Recall the slightly later E1 in the *términally* type phrases, and recall also the matter of the *lanolin* and *luminary* classes, in which the location of E1 seemed not to follow from the distance to the next lexical stress: *lanolin* and *luminary* behaved similarly, despite major differences in the location of the leftmost stressed

[11] Note that this predicts that for lower-peak utterances, and also for shorter utterances, the contrast between H* L- and H* L* may become perceptually ambiguous. We believe that this is so, and are currently designing studies to test this prediction.

syllable. But what if we were wrong about which lexical stresses are in fact at issue? The crucial distinction lies in the term "accentable".

Throughout, we have taken the set of potential attractors to include all lexically stressed syllables, primary or secondary, regardless of prosodic word affiliation. But it seems intuitive that the secondary stress on the penultimate syllable of *lúminàry* is not an attractor in the same way that the lexical stresses in the second word of the phrase are. In all but the most contrived of metalinguistic contexts this post-main-stress syllable could not meaningfully bear a low accent. Thus, in the target phrase *lúminàry nóminàtor*, if the initial syllable of the phrase bears an H* pitch accent, the next candidate syllable for pitch-accenting under normal circumstances would be the initial syllable of *nóminàtor*. If we, therefore, revise our analysis to focus not on the leftmost lexical stress, but rather on the leftmost accentable syllable, the later elbow placement in *términally* phrases begins to make sense. The mean distances from the H* peak to the midpoint of the vowel of the next accentable syllable in the *lanolin, luminary,* and *terminally* classes are 408 ms, 443 ms, and 522 ms, respectively, as against peak-to-E1 distances of 153 ms, 158 ms, and 169 ms. In other words, the shortest peak-to-E1 distance occurs in the phrase class with the closest following accentable syllable, and likewise, *mutatis mutandis,* for the longest.[12] Under this scenario, E1 doesn't fall later in the *terminally* class because it *must*, in the sense of association with an attractor, but rather just because it *can*. For classes where the distance to the next accentable syllable is shorter, a more rapid fall is required, to avoid cuing a following pitch accent; where the distance to the next accentable syllable is longer, the fall from a given peak height can be more gradual, because there is little risk of creating a spurious percept of a misplaced pitch accent.

Under this scenario, the differences in peak-to-E1 distances between phrase types begin to make sense. But note that the differences are still not entirely proportional to the differences in distance to the next accentable syllable: For the *lanolin* class, the elbow is located a mean distance of 38% of

---

[12] It is important to point out here that we are considering the first syllables of both *nóminàtor* and *nòminátion* type words to be equally accentable. It is true that under most circumstances, if an –ATION word is to be pitch-accented, the pitch accent will fall on the primary-stressed penult, and not the secondary-stressed initial. That said, it is a well-known fact about English that prominence relations in this sense are malleable, with such factors as rhythm and position in the phrase contributing to frequent prominence reversals in words of this type (Shattuck-Hufnagel, Ostendorf, & Ross, 1994). It is thus common enough for syllables of this type to be pitch-accented. (Should Newt Gingrich ever receive the GOP nomination for president, for example, we might quite grammatically refer to him as *Nóminàtion Néwt*.) It may also be of relevance that at the moment when a listener encounters the first syllable of the word *nomination*, both *nomination* and *nominator* are still equally part of the relevant cohort for lexical access, all the more so since prosodic cues to their disambiguation appear to be otherwise severely attenuated in postnuclear position.

the way from peak to accentable syllable. For *luminary* this number is 36%, while for *terminally,* it is just 32%, with ANOVA confirming the significance of this difference. In other words, the elbow in *terminally* tends in the right direction, but seems in fact not to be quite late enough, if our explanation of these facts is correct.

The problem in the foregoing, we think, is with the emphasis on E1 as a pitch event, to the exclusion of the rest of the F0 contour in this region. We have already presented evidence suggesting that E1 in our data is not a "thing-in-itself", not a reflection of an independent phonological tonal target, but rather a phenomenon arising from the interaction of peak height with the proposed constraint on the phonetics of postnuclear deaccenting. This constraint, we argue, requires speakers to reach a low-enough part of their pitch range soon enough after the NPA that any additional further downward progress will not be deemed "salient" by listeners, in a manner that might cue an additional accent, with a resulting prominence reversal. Under these circumstances, we find it unlikely that what listeners are in fact attending to, to determine whether the trough region contains or does not contain pitch accents, is specifically the location and scaling of this nebulous F0 elbow. Rather, we suspect that what is relevant here in determining whether F0 is "sufficiently low" early enough is not what is happening at any given point in the F0 contour, but rather a more general, *gestalt* percept of what the F0 contour is doing during the region in question. In other words, what matters is not whether F0 is low at the moment that E1 occurs (to the extent that this can be determined in the first place), but rather whether F0 is *low in general* in the relevant region.

Of course, quantifying global properties of the F0 contour such as this one, to compute, if you will, a *lowness quotient*, is no simple matter. However, we have been developing just such measures with some degree of success. The measures we are working with share a commitment not to characterising individual points in the F0 contour, but rather to characterising the contour in general within a particular region of the segmental string, in terms of the area under the F0 curve. Measures of area under the F0 curve are of interest because they integrate information from both the time and frequency domains, allowing characterisation of the relative "highness" or "lowness" of a given region without direct reference to any instantaneous value within the region. Such measures also allow changes in contour shape, difficult if not impossible to characterise in terms of turning points, to play a role in the perceptual categorisation of F0 contours. There is by now abundant evidence in the literature on the perception of intonation that both these qualities are desirable—see in particular, D'Imperio (2000) and Niebuhr (2007), as well as Barnes, Brugos, Shattuck-Hufnagel, and Veilleux (2008) for a review. At the same time, this approach allows us to retain a view of intonation based on level-tone targets in the phonology. (We are, after all, still talking about the phonetic realisation of Highs and Lows, rather than of curves that have particular shapes.)

Of course, while the area under the curve (hereafter AUC) appears promising as a measure, it is clear that raw AUC values cannot be used for what we need them to do, owing to a variety of pathological predictions their adoption would make (e.g., that 120 ms of F0 at 80 semitones should sound the same as 80 ms of F0 at 120 semitones, or that a fall with a given area should sound the same as a rise with equivalent area, etc.) In other work we approach this problem by deriving from raw AUC the position of the F0 center of gravity within the region in question, and using that to characterise linguistic distinctions (Barnes, Veilleux, Brugos, & Shattuck-Hufnagel, 2010). What we propose here, for the characterisation of F0 falls of differing shape or rapidity, is a measure we call R-AUC.

Figure 14 demonstrates how this can be accomplished in a coarse fashion for the region between the H* peak and a following attractor, the leftmost accentable syllable. Assuming that our pilot perceptual data are on the right track, i.e., that a linear interpolation between the H*-bearing syllable and the attractor would cue the percept of a pitch accent on the attractor, then this is the configuration speakers are trying to avoid by falling more rapidly. At the other end of a continuum of (theoretically) possible configurations is one that represents completely unambiguous deaccenting: a physiologically impossible instantaneous drop from the level of the peak to the level of the attractor, with a perfectly flat, low region following. Figure 14 represents the hypothetical F0 contour for an L* pitch-accented attractor as a right triangle, the hypotenuse of which is a linear fall from peak to attractor. The area of this triangle thus represents a sufficient AUC value to make a fall of this duration sound like it terminates in an L* pitch accent. The shaded region in Figure 14, by contrast, is topped by a rough two-line stylisation of the deaccented trough contours we elicited, with points representing the times and F0 values of the peak, E1, and attractor midpoint. The area of this region would thus represent an AUC value sufficient to make a fall of this duration sound like a deaccented postnuclear trough. By expressing this raw AUC value not directly, but rather as a percentage of the area of the larger figure (that is, the H* L* triangle), we arrive at a single, contrast-based

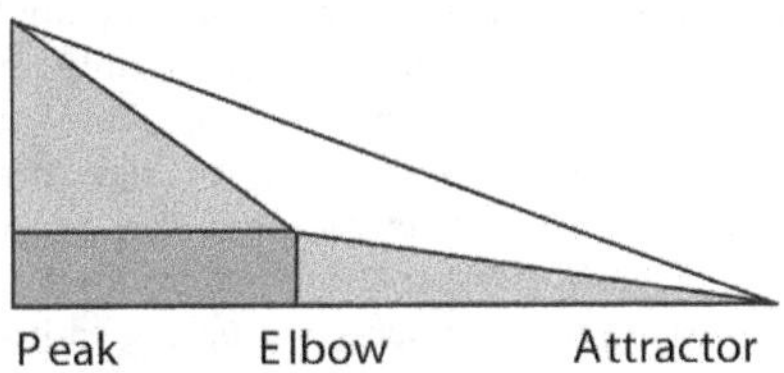

Figure 14. Computing area under the curve in the region between peak and attractor as a percentage of potential area under the curve of a linear interpolation from peak to attractor.

measure expressing how globally low the region in question is. Our hypothetical "instantaneous drop" contour, for example, would have an F0 running along two sides of the larger triangle, thus accruing an AUC of 0, and a R-AUC of 0%, or perfect (indeed, too perfect) deaccenting. Such contours do not occur in nature, of course, but the more rapidly a speaker falls from the F0 level of the peak to the F0 level of the attractor, the closer to that theoretical configuration the resulting contour would come, and the more unambiguously deaccented the attractor would sound.

We are now in a position to ask, ideally in a series of perceptual experiments, how small a R-AUC value needs to be for the region to sound reliably deaccented, or what the identification function would look like in an experiment that presented listeners with a set of contours representing a continuum of R-AUCs. As a first step in this direction, we can ask what R-AUC values looked like for the contours we elicited here, and so determine the extent to which R-AUC values differ between our three phrase types.[13]

The answers are as follows: raw and R-AUC values for the region of the F0 contour between peak and leftmost accentable syllable are given in Table 9 below. Raw AUC is largest for *terminally* phrases and smallest for *lanolin,* with *luminary* somewhere in between. This is to be expected, given what we already know about the duration of this interval in the three phrase types. What we see here then is the whole intonational iceberg (rather than just its tip (not to say elbow), which would be represented by the small differences in peak-to-E1 distance identified by using the turning point-based approach recounted above). Exclusive focus on E1 alignment in fact obscured the larger picture, allowing us to see just a weak local reflection of this larger-scale pattern in contour shape. Looking now at the R-AUC values in Table 9, note that the familiar pattern of differences among our phrase types suddenly disappears. Now, *lanolin* has the smallest R-AUC, *luminary* has the largest, with *terminally* in between. ANOVA conducted by-item and by-subject show these differences not to be significant, however: $F(2, 22) = 2.665$, $p > .05$, $F(2, 28) = 2.166$, $p > .05$. In other words, in terms of R-AUC, all three phrase types look exactly the same: they achieve identical relative lowness over the crucial interval, making it unsurprising that they are judged

[13] Note that the calculation of AUC for our contours is somewhat idealised, assuming as it does linear interpolations between peak, E1, and the attractor midpoint. This assumption allows us to calculate AUC for the region as the sum of the areas of the three geometric figures represented in the shaded region of Figure 14. (Namely, two right triangles and a rectangle.) It would of course be better to calculate AUC directly using integration, or to approximate it using Riemann sums based on successive, short-interval F0 samples over the window in question in our data. We are in fact doing this in several projects in progress, with strong results. For the time being, though, the straight-line stylisation approach seems a reasonable approximation of what we actually recorded. (It also sounds quite natural when resynthesised, as 't Hart 1991, for example, argues that it should.)

TABLE 9
Raw and Relativised Area Under the Curve values for the region of the fall from peak to leftmost accentable syllable given for each of three phrase types

	Raw AUC		*Relativised AUC*	
Phrase Type	*Mean*	*SD*	*Mean*	*SD*
Lanolin	1.64	0.71	0.510	0.090
Lúminàry	1.76	0.67	0.533	0.096
Términally	2.2	0.83	0.527	0.099

(at least informally) as equally deaccented. Differences in "E1 alignment" that seemed to emerge when we focused our attention exclusively on the turning point (such as it was), are seen to vanish in light of this new approach to the characterisation of the falling F0 region. This is a welcome turn of events for a variety of reasons, not the least of which is the deep conviction of the experimenters that (rise)–fall–rise contours with E1-alignment differences on the order of those identified in this study are perceptually indistinguishable from one another, and therefore poor candidates for distinct phonological representations.

CONCLUSION

We have shown that the strongest predictor of the location of the E1 "elbow" in our data, most commonly held to reflect association of an L- phrase accent early in the postnuclear region, is in fact the location of the NPA peak. This result might be taken to suggest that the E1 turning point may not in fact correspond to a phrase accent in the phonology, but rather to the trailing tone of a complex pitch accent. On the other hand, the position of E1 in the trough was demonstrated to vary significantly as a function of the metrical structure of the postnuclear region. This pattern might be taken to support the phrase-accent analysis. While it seemed clear, however, that in *terminally* type phrases, the relatively late postnuclear lexical stress in the second word was somehow responsible for the observed lateness of E1, it appeared impossible to characterise this syllable as an "attractor" for E1 in such a way as to make correct predictions for the placement of E1 in the rest of our data. (Results showed that neither the most prominent, nor the leftmost lexical stress in the trough functioned consistently as an attractor for all phrase types.) Furthermore, the apparent gradience of the attraction of E1 to a metrical prominence was paralleled in our data by a strong correlation between peak height and elbow sharpness, suggesting that the very existence of E1 as a turning point may be a matter of gradient implementation. We argued that not only is E1 probably not the reflection of a phonological phrase accent, but that it is not in fact the reflection of a phonological tonal target of any kind. Rather, it arises from the interaction of peak height with perception-based constraints on the implementation of postnuclear deaccenting, specifically, a need to achieve a low F0 quickly enough after the end of the nuclear syllable to avoid creating the percept of a pitch accent on any following accentable syllable. To demonstrate the fundamental phonetic unity of the falling portions of our (rise)–fall–rise contours across different metrical and prosodic contexts, we introduced the notion of R-AUC. R-AUC is a global measure for the characterisation of F0 contours that is sensitive to subtle changes in contour shape that are difficult to quantify in approaches to tone scaling and alignment that are based solely on F0 turning points. It also succeeds in characterising both the ways in which our different (rise)–fall–rise contours are alike, and how they differ from a contrasting H* L* contour, for example, which a strictly turning point-based approach focused on the location and scaling of a putative F0 elbow cannot do.

This does not mean that F0 turning points are never intentionally aligned with the words, syllables or segments of an utterance, and it certainly does not mean that intonational phonology should abandon the level-based AM approach for a return to configurationist views. We accept a phonology of English intonation that includes phrase accents formalised as High or Low tonal targets, and readily entertain the possibility that those phrase accents are under some circumstances attracted to metrical prominences. We have shown, however, that the extended low domain in the postnuclear region of certain contours is not a reflection of such an attraction, or even necessarily of the phrase accent *per se*, except insofar as there must be a Low target somewhere at the right edge of this domain, to account for the contour fall. The phonological representations of all the (rise)–fall–rise contours under consideration here can thus be identical, consisting of three tonal targets, H*, L-, and H%, each of which are associated phonologically with just one TBU (the nuclear syllable for H*, and then either the phrase-final syllable for both L- and H%, or the penult and final for these two, respectively.) Under this analysis, the sharp fall and low trough, when they occur, arise not from speakers implementing an additional L- tonal target in the form of a segmentally anchored low turning point, but rather from a constraint on the phonetic implementation of deaccenting requiring a specific R-AUC target value over the window between the NPA, and any following potential pitch-accent host. We have also presented what we hope are the first steps towards an understanding of the phonetics and phonology of intonation that includes a prominent role for global characterisations of F0 contours such as the R-AUC we proposed in this context.

REFERENCES

Arvaniti, A., & Ladd, D. R. (2009). Greek wh-questions and the phonology of intonation. *Phonology, 26,* 43–74. doi:10.1017/S0952675709001717

Arvaniti, A., Ladd, D. R., & Mennen, I. (1998). Stability of tonal alignment: The case of Greek prenuclear accents. *Journal of Phonetics, 26,* 3–25. doi:10.1006/jpho.1997.0063

Arvaniti, A., Ladd, D. R., & Mennen, I. (2006). Tonal association and tonal alignment: Evidence from Greek polar questions and contrastive statements. *Language and Speech, 49,* 421–450. doi:10.1177/00238309060490040101

Atterer, M., & Ladd, D. R. (2004). On the phonetics and phonology of "segmental anchoring" of F0: Evidence from German. *Journal of Phonetics, 32,* 177–197. doi:10.1016/S0095-4470(03)00039-1

Barnes, J., Brugos, A., Shattuck-Hufnagel, S., & Veilleux, N. (2008, November). Alternatives to F0 turning points in American English intonation. *Journal of the Acoustical Society of America, 124,* 2497. Poster presented at the 156th meeting of the Acoustical Society of America, Miami, FL, November 10–14, 2008.

Barnes, J., Shattuck-Hufnagel, S., Brugos, A., & Veilleux, N. (2006). The domain of realization of the L- phrase tone in American English. *Speech Prosody 2006: Proceedings of the 3rd International Conference,* Dresden, Germany, May 2–5, 2006, paper 163.

Barnes, J., Veilleux, N., Brugos, A., & Shattuck-Hufnagel, S. (2010). *Tonal center of gravity as a measure of text-tune alignment.* Manuscript in preparation.

Beckman, M. (1986). *Stress and non-stress accent.* Dordrecht: Foris.

Beckman, M., & Pierrehumbert, J. (1986). Intonational structure in Japanese and English. *Phonology, 3,* 255–309. doi:10.1017/S095267570000066X

Boersma, P., & Weenink, D. (2005). *Praat: Doing phonetics by computer (Version 4.3.36).* [Computer program]. Retrieved December 11, 2005, from http://www.praat.org/

Bruce, G. (1977). *Swedish word accents in a sentence perspective.* Lund: Gleerup.

Brugos, A., Barnes, J., Shattuck-Hufnagel, S., & Veilleux, N. (2006, June). A range of intonation patterns produced in an elicitation task. *Journal of the Acoustical Society of America, 119,* 3301. Poster presented at the meeting of the Acoustical Society of America, Providence, RI, June 5–9, 2006.

Brugos, A., Barnes, J., Shattuck-Hufnagel, S., & Veilleux, N. (2008). *(At least) two members of the rise-fall-rise family.* Poster presented at Experimental and Theoretical Advances in Prosody, Cornell University, Ithaca, NY, April 11–13, 2008.

Frota, S. (2002). Tonal association and target alignment in European Portuguese nuclear falls. In C. Gussenhoven & N. Warner (Eds.), *Laboratory phonology* (Vol. 7, pp. 387–418). Berlin/New York: Mouton de Gruyter.

del Giudice, A., Shosted, R., Davidson, K., Salihe, M., & Arvaniti, A. (2007). Comparing methods for locating pitch "elbows". *Proceedings of International Congress of Phonetic Sciences, XVI* (pp. 1117–1120), Saarbrücken, Germany, August 6–10, 2007.

Grice, M., Ladd, D. R., & Arvaniti, A. (2000). On the place of phrase accents in intonational phonology. *Phonology, 17,* 143–185. doi 10.1017/S0952675700003924

Gussenhoven, C. (1984). *On the grammar and semantics of sentence accents.* Dordrecht: Foris.

Gussenhoven, C. (2000). The boundary tones are coming: On the nonperipheral realization of boundary tones. In M. B. Broe & J. B. Pierrehumbert (Eds.), *Papers in laboratory phonology V: Acquisition and the lexicon* (pp. 132–151). Cambridge: Cambridge University Press.

Halliday, M. A. K. (1970). *A course in spoken English: Intonation.* Oxford: Oxford University Press.

't Hart, J. (1991). F0 stylization of speech: Straight lines versus parabolas. *Journal of the Acoustical Society of America, 90,* 3368–3370. doi:10.1121/1.401396

D'Imperio, M. (2000). *The role of perception in defining tonal targets and their alignment.* Doctoral dissertation, Ohio State University, Columbus, OH.

D'Imperio, M., & House, D. (1997). Perception of questions and statements in Neapolitan Italian. *Proceedings of Eurospeech 1997: Fifth European Conference on Speech Communication and Technology*, Rhodes, Greece, September 22–25, 1997.

Jun, S. (Ed.). (2005). *Prosodic typology: The phonology of intonation and phrasing*. Oxford: Oxford University Press.

Knight, R., & Nolan, F. (2006). The effect of pitch span on intonational plateaux. *Journal of the International Phonetic Association, 36*, 21–38. doi:10.1017/S0025100306002349

Ladd, D. R. (1996). *Intonational phonology*. New York: Cambridge University Press.

Ladd, D. R. (2008). *Intonational phonology* (2nd ed.). New York: Cambridge University Press.

Ladd, D. R. (2006). Segmental anchoring of pitch movements: Autosegmental phonology or gestural coordination? *Rivista di Linguistica* [Italian Journal of Linguistics], *18*, 19–38.

Ladd, D. R., Faulkner, D., Faulkner, H., & Schepman, A. (1999). Constant "segmental anchoring" of F0 movements under changes in speech rate. *Journal of the Acoustical Society of America, 106*, 1543–1554. doi:10.1121/1.427151

Ladd, D. R., Mennen, I., & Schepman, A. (2000). Phonological conditioning of peak alignment of rising pitch accents in Dutch. *Journal of the Acoustical Society of America, 107*, 2685–2696. doi:10.1121/1.428654

Niebuhr, O. (2007). The signalling of German rising-falling intonation categories: The interplay of synchronization, shape, and height. *Phonetica, 64*, 174–193. doi:10.1159/000107915

O'Connor, J. D., & Arnold, G. F. (1973). *Intonation of colloquial English*. Bristol: Longman Group.

Pierrehumbert, J. B. (1980). *The phonetics and phonology of English intonation*. Doctoral dissertation, MIT, Cambridge, MA.

Pierrehumbert, J. B., & Beckman, M. (1988). *Japanese tone structure. Linguistic inquiry monograph* (Vol. 15). Cambridge, MA: MIT Press.

Prieto, P., D'Imperio, M., & Gili-Fivela, B. (2005). Pitch accent alignment in Romance: Primary and secondary associations with metrical structure. *Language and Speech, 48*, 359–396. doi:10.1177/00238309050480040301

Silverman, K., Beckman, M., Pitrelli, J., Ostendorf, M., Pierrehumbert, J., Hirschberg, J., et al. (1992). *TOBI: A standard scheme for labeling prosody*. Proceedings of the International Conference on Spoken Language, Banff, Canada, October 12–16, 1992.

Silverman, K., & Pierrehumbert, J. (1990). The timing of prenuclear high accents in English. In J. Kingston & M. Beckman (Eds.), *Between the grammar and physics of speech: Papers in laboratory phonology I* (pp. 72–106). Cambridge: Cambridge University Press.

Ward, G., & Hirschberg, J. (1985). Implicating uncertainty: The pragmatics of fall-rise intonation. *Language, 61*, 747–776.

Welby, P. (2003). *The slaying of Lady Mondegreen, being a study of French tonal association and alignment and their role in speech segmentation*. Doctoral dissertation, Ohio State University, Columbus, OH.

Welby, P., & Loevenbruck, H. (2006). Anchored down in Anchorage: Syllable structure, rate and segmental anchoring in French. *Rivista di Linguistica, 18*, 39–124.

APPENDIX 1: TARGET PHRASES

1. céremòny nùmerátion
   cúlinàry màrinátion
   lúminàry nòminátion
   pálimòny rùminátion
   púlmonàry làminátion

2. céremòny númeràtor
   cúlinàry márinàtor
   lúminàry nóminàtor
   pálimòny rúminàtor
   púlmonàry láminàtor

3. álien annìhilátion
   lánolin elìminátion
   Líllian allèviátion
   Márilyn enùmerátion
   mínimum illùminátion

4. álien anníhilàtor
   lánolin elíminàtor
   Líllian alléviàtor
   Márilyn enúmeràtor
   mínimum illúminàtor

Additionally:
   críminally millénial
   mínimally manéuverable
   nóminally molécular
   sérially memórial
   Términally malárial

LANGUAGE AND COGNITIVE PROCESSES
2010, 25 (7/8/9), 1024–1043

Psychology Press
Taylor & Francis Group

The role of contrastive intonation contours in the retrieval of contextual alternatives

Bettina Braun and Lara Tagliapietra
Max Planck Institute for Psycholinguistics, Nijmegen, the Netherlands

Sentences with a contrastive intonation contour are usually produced when the speaker entertains alternatives to the accented words. However, such contrastive sentences are frequently produced without making the alternatives explicit for the listener. In two cross-modal associative priming experiments we tested in Dutch whether such contextual alternatives become available to listeners upon hearing a sentence with a contrastive intonation contour compared with a sentence with a non-contrastive one. The first experiment tested the recognition of contrastive associates (contextual alternatives to the sentence-final primes), the second one the recognition of non-contrastive associates (generic associates which are not alternatives). Results showed that contrastive associates were facilitated when the primes occurred in sentences with a contrastive intonation contour but not in sentences with a non-contrastive intonation. Non-contrastive associates were weakly facilitated independent of intonation. Possibly, contrastive contours trigger an accommodation mechanism by which listeners retrieve the contrast available for the speaker.

Keywords: Alternative-set semantics; Contrast; Cross-modal priming; Dutch; Intonation.

"Ben stood up and said: 'I still have some work to do'. He said this in such a way as to imply that I was the one who had nothing to do."[1] In reading this

[1] First author's translation of the quotation: 'Ben stand auf. Ich muß noch was tun. Er sagte das so, als sei ich derjenige, der nichts tun muß.' (Timm, 2003, p. 156).

Correspondence should be addressed to Bettina Braun, Max Planck Institute for Psycholinguistics, P.O Box 310, 6500AH Nijmegen, the Netherlands. E-mail: Bettina.Braun@mpi.nl

We thank Kristin Lemhoefer and two anonymous reviewers for valuable comments on an earlier draft of this paper. Further, we are grateful to Marieke Pompe for providing the Dutch stimuli and contrastive associates and for recording them.

http://www.psypress.com/lcp DOI: 10.1080/01690960903036836

passage from a novel aloud, the utterance 'I still have some work to do' is probably produced first with a neutral intonation contour (see Figure 1a). However, in light of the last sentence ('He said this in such a way as to imply that I was the one who had nothing to do'), one would probably reread this sentence in a different, contrastive way, accenting the two words *I* and *work* (Figure 1b). Such contrastive utterances are part of our daily life. They have two peculiarities. First, they are spoken with a characteristic intonation contour. Second, differently from a neutral realisation, sentences with such a contrastive intonation not only assert a fact (e.g., Ben has to go back to work), but also presuppose contrastive alternatives to the accented words (e.g., someone else doesn't have to work). Although speakers do not explicitly disclose these alternatives, they can become part of the interpretation of the sentence. Apparently, listeners automatically retrieve the alternatives that led the speaker to produce a contrastive utterance. In this paper, we investigated whether a contrastive intonation contour per se triggers a process by which listeners have immediate access to these contextually salient alternatives.

One mechanism available for listeners to deal with lacking background information is called 'bridging' (e.g., Clark, 1977) or 'accommodation' (e.g., Lewis, 1979, Stalnaker, 2002). Accommodation is mainly discussed in the semantics and pragmatics literature and describes 'the phenomenon of accommodating (inserting) something into the context that has not been explicitly mentioned' (Kadmon, 2001, p. 174). It has been argued, for instance, that definite articles presuppose the existence of an entity (e.g., 'I have to pick up my sister from the airport') and factive predicates presuppose the truth of the subordinate clause (e.g., 'He was surprised that he passed the test'). All of the above-mentioned theories deal with the accommodation of a common ground, i.e., a set of propositions that speakers take for granted and encode as such (e.g., the proposition 'I have a sister' in 'I have to pick up my sister from the airport'). We believe that a process similar to accommodation can explain the intuition that listeners generate contextually salient alternatives to contrastively accented words in sentences like ' I still have some WORK to do', in which the prosodic

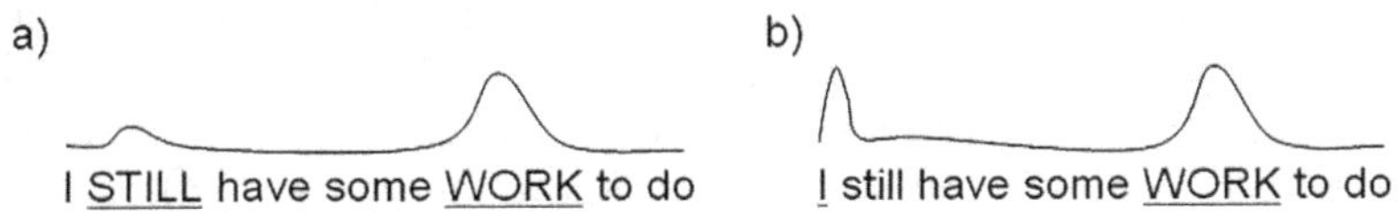

Figure 1. Neutral realisation (a) and contrastive realisation (b). Accents are marked by underscored capitals.

contour signals that the speaker entertains salient alternatives (e.g., *YOU* have *NOTHING* to do).

Alternatives play an important role in the formalisation of accentuation and narrow focus (Jackendoff, 1972; Rooth, 1992; Steedman, 2000, among others). Adapting an example from Steedman, the sentence 'Marcel discovered a SECRET' is formalised via functional abstraction of the accented word, leaving a variable x ('Marcel discovered x', or, more formally, $\lambda x[discovered'(x, Marcel')]$). In this semantic formula, x can be replaced by any contextually or situationally available alternative, resulting in so-called alternative sets (such as {Pluto, a cookie, three dimes} in this example). These alternative sets are more restricted for sentences with a narrow, contrastive focus in which only the focused constituent (i.e., 'a secret' in the above example) contributes new information. Narrow focus sentences serve as answers to specific questions such as 'What did he discover?' Therefore, the alternatives usually have the same syntactic class as the focused constituent (a noun phrase in this example) and belong to the same semantic class ('something that can be discovered' in this example). In contrast, alternative sets become much more varied for sentences with a larger focus domain, such as a verb phrase focus or sentence focus (responses to questions like 'What did he do?' or 'What happened?').

In the experiments that follow we investigated whether this way of formalising sentences with a narrow focus has any psychological reality, i.e., we tested whether relevant contextual alternatives become immediately salient for listeners upon hearing sentences with a contrastive intonation contour. Note that there are already a number of studies that investigated the interpretation of sentences with contrastive intonation contours. Listeners, for instance, successfully exploit intonational information to determine whether the speaker intends to continue with the previously mentioned referent or whether s/he will introduce a new, contrasting one. In an eye-tracking experiment, Dahan, Tanenhaus, and Chambers (2002) used a sequence of two instructions (e.g., 'Move the candle above the triangle. Now move the candy below the square') and asked their participants to click on the respective target object (e.g., 'candy'). An accented referent in the second instruction (e.g., 'Move the candle above the triangle. Now move the CANDY below the SQUARE') led to more fixations to the new, as-yet unmentioned object (e.g., 'candy') compared with an unaccented referent. Since these effects were observed before the speech signal unambiguously identified the target, they can only be attributed to the different prosodic realisations of the instructions. Similarly, upon hearing two instructions (e.g., 'Click on the purple violin. Now click on the red violin') an accented adjective in the 2nd instruction (e.g., 'RED violin') results in more fixations to an object of the same type as in the first instruction (e.g., 'violin') than to another red object (e.g., 'vase') displayed on the screen (Ito & Speer, 2008;

Weber, Braun, & Crocker, 2006). Interestingly, listeners not only make use of pitch accent distribution (i.e., accentuation of referent or adjective) but also appear to be sensitive to pitch accent type: A contrastive pitch accent such as L+H* (high pitch on the stressed syllable preceded by a low tone which results in a steep rise to the peak) creates a strong bias towards contrastive referents, while H* signals both new and contrastive referents (Watson, Tanenhaus, & Gunlogson, 2008). Taken together, these results show that listeners use intonational contrast marking and the situational context (e.g., the objects in the computer display) to identify the intended referents (i.e., new referent, same type of object, or contrastive referent).

However, the results of these eye-tracking studies cannot answer the question whether listeners have access to contrastive alternatives that are *not* explicitly available, i.e., when contrastive sentences are produced without sufficient context (e.g., ' I still have some WORK to do'). Therefore, it is largely unknown how listeners process such sentences, which occur frequently in everyday conversation. The issue, however, can be addressed with the cross-modal associative priming paradigm (Swinney, Onifer, Prather, & Hirschkowitz, 1979; Tabossi, 1996). Differently from eye-tracking experiments, this technique does not offer a preceding context in which contrastive alternatives are explicitly provided. Through these means, implicit rather than explicit alternative processing can be studied. In cross-modal priming experiments, participants first hear a prime (e.g., a word) and then usually perform a lexical decision task on a visually presented target word. Priming effects result in faster lexical decisions (e.g., to CAT) after related auditory primes (e.g., *dog*) than after unrelated ones (e.g., *bus*).[2]

Recently, Norris, McQueen, Cutler, and Butterfield (2006) provided compelling evidence that associative priming is not due to an automatic mechanism following lexical access. Rather, this technique taps into the processing occurring at the level of conceptual representation of the current interpretation of the utterance. Therefore, cross-modal associative priming is sensitive to semantic effects of the context. For example, providing a discourse context incoherent with the association between the prime and the target hampers the recognition of related visual targets (Blutner & Sommer, 1988; Tabossi, 1988; Williams, 1988). Williams (1988), for instance, found priming for visual targets (e.g., TABLE), when primes (e.g., *chair*) were presented in isolation; in random word lists (e.g., 'when brass heard could in that only land as more film to interested to is chair because which came could all ice in'); and in sentences related to the targets (e.g., 'The man entered the dining room and sat down on a chair in eager anticipation of a hearty meal'). On the other hand, priming was not observed when the prime

[2] Throughout this article, auditory primes will be marked by italics and visual targets by capitals.

occurred in sentences that were unrelated to the target (e.g., 'The man found that he could only reach the best apples by standing on a chair because they were all so high up'). Similarly, Tabossi (1988) reported facilitation for visual targets (e.g., FAT) only when sentences underlined aspects of the primes' meaning related to the target (e.g., 'To follow her diet, the woman eliminated the use of butter'); however, there were no reliable effects when the sentences focused on features unrelated to the target (e.g., 'To soften it, the woman heated a piece of butter'). Associative effects are hence subject to the presence of a relevant or 'effective context' (Foss & Ross, 1983; Williams, 1988), which is part of the current interpretation of the utterance (Norris et al., 2006).

More importantly, cross-modal associative priming appears to be sensitive to prosodic effects. A contrastive intonation contour is one of the factors that may encourage deeper semantic processing and hence lead to priming effects (Norris et al., 2006). In Experiment 4C, Norris et al. presented sentences (e.g., 'He suggested that it was really the *date* of the election that mattered') with a contrastive accent on either the prime (e.g., '*date*') or on another word later in the sentence (e.g., 'election'). The visual targets were presented at the offset of the prime (e.g., '*date*'). Priming effects for related targets (e.g., TIME) were detected for both conditions, but were stronger and more reliable after accented primes than after unaccented ones. However, these results cannot be solely attributed to contrastive accentuation as most of the experimental sentences contained syntactic and lexical presupposition triggers (e.g., 'We hoped that . . .', 'The odd thing was . . .') or focus particles (e.g., 'It was only when') that might have drawn listeners' attention to the part of the sentence containing the prime. Therefore, it is conceivable that priming was encouraged also by the syntactic constructions used and not solely by contrastive pitch accents.

Hence, it is still an open question if a contrastive pitch accent per se can serve as an 'effective context' for the recognition of words, and in particular, whether a contrastive pitch accent facilitates the recognition of contrastive alternatives. In two cross-modal priming experiments we investigated the effect of a contrastive intonation on the recognition of words associated to sentence-final primes (e.g., *flamingo*, 'flamingo'). The associated words were either contrastive alternatives (e.g., PELIKAAN, 'pelican'; henceforth: contrastive associates), or generic associates that are not contrastive alternatives (e.g., ROZE, 'pink'; henceforth: non-contrastive associates). More specifically, in Experiment 1a we tested whether contrastive alternatives are easier to recognise upon hearing a sentence with a contrastive intonation contour than after hearing a sentence with a non-contrastive one. In Experiment 1b we tested the effect of the same prosodic contours on the recognition of non-contrastive associates to ascertain whether this effect is specific for contrastive alternatives or whether a contrastive intonation in general makes all kinds of related words more easily accessible.

As contrastive intonation contour we chose a double contrast ('A did B but X did Y'), resulting in a contrast on the first constituent and on the sentence-final prime. Sentences with such a double contrast are unambiguously contrastive (Braun, 2005, 2006), while sentences with only one accent on the sentence-final noun (e.g., 'Marcel discovered a SECRET') may be perceived as ambiguous between a narrow-focus interpretation and a broad-focus interpretation (Bartels & Kingston, 1994; Birch & Clifton, 1995; Ladd, 1983; Welby, 2003). Furthermore, the number and the positions of accented words can be matched in sentences with a double contrast and sentences with a hat pattern, which is the most frequent neutral intonation contour in Dutch (Cohen & 't Hart, 1967; 't Hart, Collier, & Cohen, 1990; see Figure 2a for an illustration). The neutral hat pattern consists of a pitch rise on the first accented word, a slightly declining high plateau, and a fall on the second accented word (see Figure 2b). In our materials, the rise and the fall in the

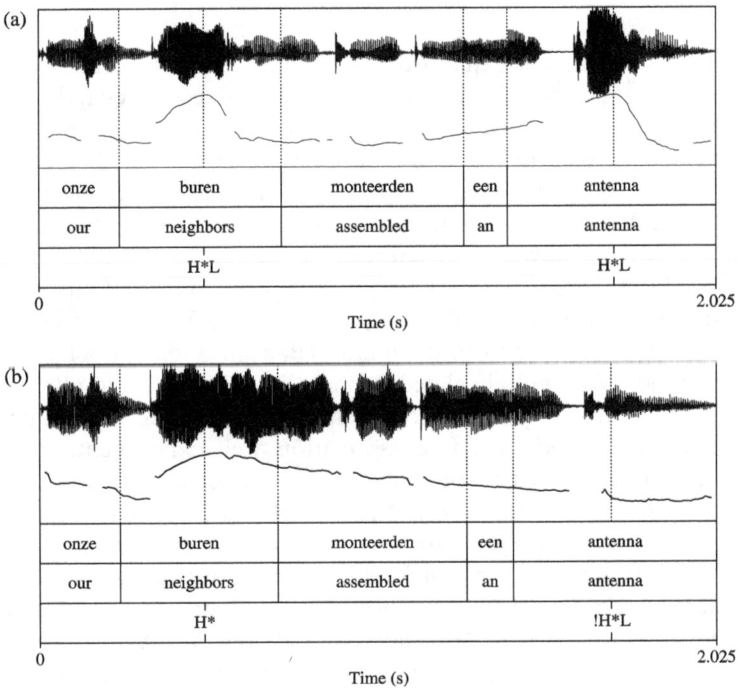

Figure 2. Examples of the hat pattern intonation contour in the non-contrastive condition (a) and of the double peak contour in the contrastive condition (b). The intonational annotation for the sentences following ToDI (Transcription of Dutch Intonation, see Gussenhoven, 2005) is provided on the third tier.

non-contrastive hat pattern are realised on the same words as the two pitch falls in the contrastive intonation contour (on the first content word in the sentence and on the sentence-final word respectively). Hence, the only difference between the two intonation contours is the type of pitch accent on the accented words – i.e., the exact tonal realisation – and not the number or the position of the accented words.

If the semantic formalisation of contrastive focus using alternative sets has any cognitive relevance, we would expect contrastive associates to be more easily accessible and hence facilitated upon hearing a sentence with a contrastive intonation contour but not upon hearing a sentence with a non-contrastive intonation. This explanation only holds, however, if the recognition of non-contrastive associates is not affected by a contrastive intonation contour. If the recognition of non-contrastive associates is modulated by sentence intonation in the same way as the recognition of contrastive associates, then contrastive intonation contours make all kinds of associates more accessible (Norris et al., 2006).

Methods

Materials. Thirty-six quadruplets of Dutch words were selected to use as experimental items. Each quadruplet comprised a related prime (e.g., flamingo, 'flamingo'), a contrastive associate to the related prime (e.g., pelikaan, 'pelican'), a non-contrastive associate to the related prime (e.g., roze, 'pink') and a control prime that was unrelated to each member of the quadruplet (e.g., beroemdheid, 'celebrity'). These quadruplets were created with the following procedure.

Eighty high frequency (> 0.07 occurrences per million) Dutch tri-syllabic mono-morphemic nouns with stress on the second syllable were extracted from the CELEX word form dictionary (Baayen, Piepenbrock, & Gulikers, 1995) for use as potential related primes. Words with large alternative sets (e.g., proper names, places, etc.) were avoided. These 80 related prime candidates were used in a free association web experiment, in which 31 Dutch participants had to produce one free associate in response to each given stimulus. Words that did not elicit a clear associate (i.e., one given by less than 25% of the participants), words that resulted in two equally frequent associates, and words for which participants provided a contrastive alternative (a word of the same word type and semantic class that could be used in sentences such as 'He didn't buy X but Y') were discarded. This selection resulted in 44 related primes that had a frequent non-contrastive associate (produced by 39% of participants, on average). A Dutch native speaker constructed 44 syntactically and semantically neutral sentences (i.e., word orders that do not induce a contrast) that ended in these potential primes. Most of them were subject-verb-object sentences (e.g., 'Our neighbours assembled an antenna'), but there were also three with a preverbal preposition phrase (e.g., 'On Saturday I went to the theatre'), two with an expletive (e.g., 'There was air-conditioning in the cabin'), and two passive constructions (e.g., 'The inflammation was caused by a bacteria'). Further, a semantic alternative for each word in this context to use as contrastive associates was selected (e.g., 'dish' for 'antenna' – which are both means to receive broadcast, 'virus' for 'bacteria' – which are both sources for infection). The association strength between the 44 related primes and their contrastive and non-contrastive associates was then tested in a web-based rating experiment with 20 Dutch participants. Every participant rated a total of 88 words, 44 related ones, and 44 unrelated ones. Each participant rated the relationship between the prime and either the contrastive or the non-contrastive associate (on a scale from 1, 'unrelated' to 7, 'strongly related'). Then, 36 triplets were selected from the set of 44 so that the association strengths of the related primes with the contrastive associate ($M = 5.5$, $SD = 0.77$) and with the non-contrastive associate ($M = 6.2$, $SD = 0.55$) were as balanced as possible. Nevertheless, the relatedness scores for non-contrastive associates were significantly higher than for contrastive ones, $t(35) = 4.9$, $p < .0001$.

The contrastive associates appeared as visual targets in Experiment 1a, and the non-contrastive associates appeared as targets in Experiment 1b. The mean frequency of the eventually selected 36 related primes was 8.6 occurrences per million (o.p.m.), $SD = 11.3$, according to the CELEX database. Contrastive targets were 7.8 letters long on average and had a mean frequency of 19.0 o.p.m. ($SD = 54.2$). Non-contrastive targets were 5.5 letters long with an average frequency of 115.2 o.p.m. ($SD = 203.0$). Given the elicitation procedure for non-contrastive associates and the constraints on the selection of contrastive associates, the lexical frequency and number of characters could not be matched. Contrastive associates were significantly longer than non-contrastive ones, $t(35) = 4.22$, $p < .0001$, and less frequent, $t(35) = 2.77$, $p < .01$.

Finally, for each related prime and its (contrastive and non-contrastive) associates, a control prime unrelated to all three was chosen. Similar to the related primes, control primes were all tri-syllabic words stressed on the second syllable (mean frequency of 10.5 out of a million, $SD = 23.4$); further, control primes could be inserted in the same sentence as their paired related primes. Durations of the experimental and control primes (divided by the respective utterance durations to account for speech rate) did not differ across the two intonational realisations, $t(35) = 1.66$, $p > .1$ for experimental primes, $t(35) = 0.21$, $p > .8$ for control primes. Experimental primes lasted on average 37.8% of the overall utterance duration, control primes 38.5%. All the experimental materials are listed in Appendix 1.

Further, 164 filler sentences and six practice sentences were constructed, structurally and semantically similar to the experimental ones. Eighteen of the filler items had a non-word visual target that was phonologically related to the sentence-final word, 92 had a non-word visual target unrelated to the sentence-final word, and 54 had an existing word as visual target that was unrelated to the sentence final word. The six practice sentences were paired with three word and three non-word visual targets. Filler and practice targets were matched to the experimental targets in terms of the distribution of the number of characters.

All the sentences were recorded by a trained female speaker of Dutch in a soundproof room and directly digitised onto a PC (44 kHz, 16 bit). She read the 36 experimental sentences and the 36 control sentences both neutrally, resulting in a declining hat pattern as shown in Figure 2a, and with a double contrast realised on the first content word of the sentence and the sentence-final prime (Figure 2b). The contrastive intonation was cued by a contrastive precursor and a contrastive connector (e.g., 'WE assembled a SATELLITE dish, but …'). Half of the filler sentences and half of the familiarisation sentences were recorded with a non-contrastive and half with a contrastive intonation contour. As can be seen in Figure 2, the f0-excursion of the pitch fall on the sentence-final prime word was significantly larger in sentences with a contrastive intonation contour than in sentences with an non-contrastive one, $t(71) = 48.6$, $p < .0001$. The excursion was on average 180.0 Hz for contrastive contours compared with 36.3 Hz for non-contrastive ones.[3]

Participants. Eighty Dutch students from the Radboud University Nijmegen, unaware of the purpose of the experiment, participated for a small fee, 40 in each experiment. They had not taken part in the earlier web experiments, had good or corrected vision and no history of hearing problems.

Procedure. Participants were tested individually in a soundproof cabin sitting in front of a computer screen. Each sentence was played in stereo at a comfortable volume via headphones. The visual target appeared in white Arial 72pt characters on black background immediately after the end of the sentence. Participants received written instructions, in which they were asked to press the right button when the string of letters they saw on the screen was a Dutch word or proper name and the left button when it was not. Left-handed participants had to press the left button for 'yes'-responses.

[3] The f0-values were extracted from the middle of the stressed and post-stressed vowel for contrastive contours and in the middle of the pre-stressed and stressed vowel for non-contrastive contours.

Responses slower than 2 seconds after the appearance of the visual target were not recorded.

Four experimental lists were constructed by rotating through the four conditions, crossing the two within-subjects, between-items factors intonation of the target sentence (contrastive or non-contrastive) and prime type (control or related). There were hence nine items per condition. Each list further contained all the practice and filler items, totaling in 206 trials. Two orders were made for each list, avoiding the possibility that two or three subsequent sentences could be interpreted as part of a coherent discourse. Participants were randomly assigned to one of these lists.

Results

Due to an oversight, one control prime was identical to one of the related primes. The two pairs containing these primes were therefore excluded from the analyses.

Experiment 1a – contrastive associates. Six trials were excluded because there was no button press (timeout) and an additional 55 trials were discarded because of an incorrect response. Errors were distributed evenly across conditions and participants. Reaction times for the remaining trials were log-transformed. One participant with exceptionally long reaction times (mean log-RT larger than 2 standard deviations from the overall mean) was not included in the analysis.

Log-RTs within 2 standard deviations of the mean were analysed (range 5.88 to 6.91) using mixed-effects models with participants and items as crossed random factors, and contrast coding for factors ($N = 1280$). This analysis has been chosen over the more traditional separate subject and items analyses as it is less dependent on normality and sphericity assumptions, can cope well with missing data, and allows for the combined analysis of categorical and continuous predictors (e.g., Baayen, 2008; Barr, 2008; Jaeger, 2008; Quené & van den Bergh, 2004). The crucial predictors were intonation (contrastive or non-contrastive) and prime type (control or related prime). Further, the model included a number of predictors that have been shown to affect reaction times in lexical decision experiments, such as log-lexical frequency as extracted from the CELEX word form dictionary, number of characters, the reaction time to the preceding trial, whether the preceding filler trial had a word or non-word target, and the correctness of the preceding response.

The initial model included all predictors and the interaction between intonation and prime type. Predictors with a p-value larger than .1 were removed if this did not deteriorate the fit of the model (as estimated by a likelihood-ratio test). The log-likelihood of the full model was 405.5, that of the final model 405.9 ($\chi^2 = 0.85$, df = 2, $p > .5$). Then, the more parsimonious model was refitted. Data points with residuals larger than 2.5 *SD* were removed. Resulting *p*-values were estimated as the posterior probability of a Markov Chain Monte Carlo (MCMC) simulation with 10000 runs. The results of the final model are summarised in Table 1.

As expected, responses were slower to visual targets with more letters and for which the reaction time to the preceding filler trial was longer. Crucially, results for the contrastive visual targets showed a significant interaction between the intonation of the sentence and the relation between prime and target. Responses were on average 19.3 ms faster after related primes if the sentence containing the prime was spoken with a contrastive intonation contour. There was no facilitation for contrastively related visual targets when sentences had a neutral intonation contour. The mean RT for each condition, calculated on the basis of the statistical model for a mean reaction time to the preceding filler trial (6.47) and a median number of characters for the target (8), are illustrated in Figure 3.

Experiment 1b – non-contrastive associates. Twenty trials with incorrect responses were discarded. Log-RTs within 2 *SD* of the mean were analysed (range 5.85 to 6.79, $N = 1290$). The fitting procedure and predictors were the same as described for Experiment 1a. The log-likelihood of the full model was 588.6 compared with 590.1 for the final model ($\chi^2 = 2.9$, df = 4, $p > .5$). Results of the final model are summarised in Table 2.

Similar to Experiment 1a, responses were slower to visual targets with more letters and for which the reaction time to the preceding filler trial was longer. Furthermore, responses were faster to targets with a higher lexical frequency. Moreover, results for the non-contrastive associates showed a main effect for prime type only. Responses were on average 8.4 ms faster

TABLE 1
Estimates, confidence intervals, and p-values for Experiment 1a. Positive estimates indicate the amount of increase in log-RT relative to the Intercept. For factors, the change from the Intercept applies for the level given in italics.

	Estimate	*Lower Bound*	*Upper Bound*	*p (MCMC)*
Intercept (*non-contrastive intonation, unrelated prime*)	5.732	5.457	6.015	.0001
Intonation (*contrastive*)	0.006	−0.017	0.029	*ns*
Prime Type (*related*)	0.008	−0.015	0.032	*ns*
Previous Log-RT	0.070	0.030	0.111	<.001
Number of characters	0.028	0.016	0.038	<.0005
Intonation: Prime Type (*contrastive intonation, related prime*)	−0.039	−0.073	−0.007	<.05

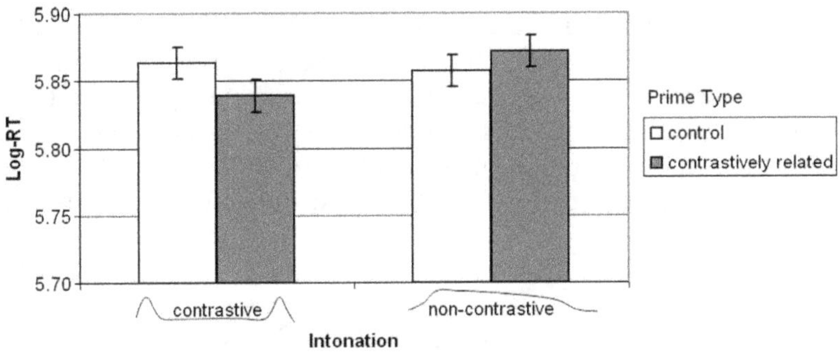

Figure 3. Mean Log-RTs for Experiment 1a (contrastive visual targets) as a function of the experimental conditons: intonation (contrastive vs. non-contrastive) and Prime Type (control vs. related). Error bars represent standard error.

when the auditory prime was related to the visual target than when it was not (on average 538.1 ms for control primes compared with 529.7ms for related ones). There was no effect of intonation, $p(\text{MCMC}) > .5$, and no interaction between intonation and prime type, $p(\text{MCMC}) > .25$. The recognition of generically related visual targets is hence independent of the intonation contour. There is a weak facilitation for related primes, which is consistent with earlier findings in cross-modal priming.[4]

Note that upon hearing a sentence with a contrastive intonation contour the priming effect for non-contrastive targets is smaller than for contrastive ones (8.4 ms vs. 19.3 ms), despite the fact that the non-contrastive targets had a stronger relation to the prime than the contrastive ones. The results of the two experiments cannot be directly compared, however, because of the

TABLE 2
Estimates, confidence intervals, and *p*-values for Experiment 1b.

	Estimate	*Lower Bound*	*Upper Bound*	*p (MCMC)*
Intercept (*non-contrastive intonation, unrelated prime*)	5.645	5.366	5.910	.0001
Prime Type (*related*)	−0.016	−0.031	−0.002	<.05
Previous Log-RT	0.114	0.074	0.152	.0001
Number of characters	0.009	0.003	0.016	<.01
Log-Freq	−0.019	−0.027	−0.011	.0001

[4] Note that while contrastive visual targets were uniformly nouns, four of the non-contrastive visual targets had a different part-of-speech (3 adjectives and 1 verb). This non-uniformity in part-of-speech might influence the priming effects. However, excluding those items does not change the results in any way, so we report the statistical analysis of all items.

lexical differences of the targets across experiments. As reported in the Materials section, non-contrastive targets were shorter and more frequent than the contrastive associates. These differences are probably the reason that participants responded on average 55.9 ms faster to non-contrastive targets than to contrastive ones, $t(2488.7) = 11.4$, $p < .001$, since mean responses per participant for filler trials did not differ across experiments, $t(78) = 0.1$, $p > .9$.

GENERAL DISCUSSION

In two cross-modal priming experiments we manipulated sentence intonation (contrastive vs. non-contrastive) and the relation between prime and visual target (unrelated vs. contrastively and non-contrastively associated). Results showed that contrastive associates – which are contextual alternatives to the primes – are facilitated only when the primes are realised in sentences with a contrastive intonation. On the other hand, non-contrastive associates – which are generic associates that are not contextual alternatives – are weakly facilitated independent of the intonation contour. These results show that a contrastive intonation contour modulates the interpretation of a sentence. In particular, the present results indicate that only a contrastive interpretation of the sentence makes contextually relevant alternatives more accessible and hence easier to recognise.

The observed facilitation of contrastive associates upon hearing a sentence with a contrastive intonation contour appears to be genuinely driven by the interpretation of sentences with a contrastive intonation contour. This effect cannot be simply explained by a more salient production of the primes in sentences with a contrastive intonation. If this explanation were correct, the presence of the larger pitch movement would have also affected the recognition of the non-contrastive associates in Experiment 1b. However, no interaction of prosodic contour and prime-target relation was detected in the second experiment. Also, this effect cannot be explained by the fact that contrastive, category associates generally elicit stronger priming than non-contrastive ones, even when they are barely related to the prime (Fischler, 1977 and Lupker, 1984 for visual-visual priming; Moss, Ostrin, Tyler, & Marslen-Wilson, 1995, for auditory-auditory priming). If this were the case, contrastive associates should have also been facilitated in sentences with a non-contrastive intonation contour.

Finally, one might argue that a contrastive intonation contour only serves the function of attracting attention to the accented words and therefore makes less strongly related associates (i.e., the contrastive associates in this study) also accessible. This explanation would predict the same interaction observed for contrastive associates also for those non-contrastive associates that are only weakly related to the auditory prime. To test this hypothesis, we split the non-contrastive associates into two halves, highly related ones (rating > 6.3) and weakly related ones (rating ≤ 6.3). The weakly related items had a mean rating of 5.8 ($SD = 0.60$) – compared with a mean rating of 5.5 ($SD = 0.77$) for the contrastive associates. These weakly related non-contrastive associates were analysed using the same model as for the contrastive associates. There were neither main effects of intonation or prime type, nor an interaction between the two factors, $p(\text{MCMC}) > .5$. The lack of interaction between intonation and prime type for the weakly related non-contrastive associates suggests that a contrastive intonation contour does not simply have a highlighting function by which less strongly related associates become more accessible. Therefore, it appears more plausible that a contrastive intonation contour especially makes contextually sensible alternatives to the accented words salient.

The present findings support and extend the conclusion drawn by Norris et al. (2006) that prosody alters the interpretation of the sentence. Using syntactically and semantically neutral sentences we could show that prosody per se acts as an 'effective context' (Williams, 1988) and affects sentence interpretation. Furthermore, the effect of prosody proved to be extremely specific. Only contrastive alternatives were facilitated by a contrastive realisation, whereas non-contrastive associates were available for both contrastive and non-contrastive intonation contours. The present results also extend previous findings from the eye-tracking literature. The observed facilitation of contrastive alternatives upon hearing isolated sentences with a contrastive intonation contour shows that contrastive alternatives become accessible even in the absence of linguistic or pragmatic context.

From an intonational perspective, the present data suggest that during the processing of utterances with a non-contrastive intonation contour, only highly related associates (i.e., non-contrastive associates which had a higher rating than the contrastive ones) become accessible and hence are recognised faster. During the processing of utterances with a contrastive intonation, contrastive associates (i.e., contextual alternatives to the accented items) become also salient.

From a linguistic or pragmatic perspective, the present findings support the use of alternative sets to formalise contrastive focus. In sentences with a contrastive intonation contour, in which the alternative sets to the accented words are rather small and of a restricted type, listeners rapidly generate salient contextual alternatives. On the contrary, for sentences with a non-contrastive intonation contour these alternatives are not immediately accessible.

Differently from sentences with only one accent on the sentence-final noun (e.g., 'Marcel discovered a SECRET'), which can be interpreted as neutral or contrastive, the double-peak contour employed in this study (e.g., ' MARCEL discovered a SECRET) unambiguously signals contrast. This prosodic contour, however, encodes contrastive alternatives for both accented words, so that listeners potentially retrieved alternatives for both the sentence-final prime and for the sentence-initial constituent. The additional alternative set for the sentence-initial words may have decreased the facilitation of the contrast associates. Therefore, in sentences with a single contrast on the prime only, this effect might have been larger.

Taken together, the present experiments support the intuition that contrastive accentuation on a word makes contextual alternatives to that word salient to the listener. The fact that salient alternatives are generated upon hearing isolated sentences is especially noteworthy, as listeners frequently encounter utterances that are not sufficiently grounded, i.e., for which the speakers did not provide all the relevant background information beforehand. We suggest that this is due to an accommodation mechanism, through which listeners adopt assumptions implicit in the speaker's use of contrastive marking and generate plausible alternatives. Our data suggest that this accommodation mechanism is automatic and occurs early in the recognition process. Once more, language proves to be an efficient means of communication, as listeners effortlessly exploit prosodic information to accommodate the information that the linguistic structure does not explicitly encode (e.g., contextual alternatives).

REFERENCES

Baayen, R. H. (2008). *Analyzing linguistic data: A practical introduction to statistics using R*. Cambridge: Cambridge University Press.

Baayen, R. H., Piepenbrock, R., & Gulikers, L. (1995). *The CELEX lexical database* [CD-ROM]. Philadelphia, PA: Linguistic Data Consortium, University of Pennsylvania.

Barr, D. J. (2008). Analyzing 'visual world' eyetracking data using multilevel logistic regression. *Journal of Memory and Language, 59*, 457–474.

Bartels, C., & Kingston, J. (1994). Salient pitch cues in the perception of contrastive focus. In P. Bosch & R. van der Sandt (Eds.), *Focus and natural language processing* (pp. 1–10). Heidelberg, Germany: Working Papers of the Institute for Logics and Linguistics.

Birch, S., & Clifton, C. (1995). Focus, accent, and argument structure: Effects on language comprehension. *Language and Speech, 38*, 365–391.

Blutner, R., & Sommer, R. (1988). Sentence processing and lexical access: The influence of the focus-identifying task. *Journal of Memory and Language, 27*, 359–367.

Braun, B. (2005). *Production and perception of thematic contrast in German*. Oxford, UK: Peter Lang Publishing.

Braun, B. (2006). Phonetics and phonology of thematic contrast in German. *Language and Speech*, *49*, 451–493.

Cohen, A., & 't Hart, J. (1967). On the anatomy of intonation. *Lingua*, *19*, 177–192.

Clark, H. (1977). Bridging. In P. Johnson-Laird & P. Wason (Eds.), *Thinking* (pp. 10–63). Cambridge, UK: Cambridge University Press.

Dahan, D., Tanenhaus, M. K., & Chambers, C. G. (2002). Accent and reference resolution in spoken-language comprehension. *Journal of Memory and Language*, *47*, 292–314.

Fischler, I. (1977). Semantic facilitation without association in a lexical decision task. *Memory and Cognition*, *5*, 335–339.

Foss, D. J. & Ross, J. R. (1983). Great expectations: Context effects during sentence processing. In G. Flores D'Arcais & R. J. Jarvella (Eds.), *The process of language understanding* (pp. 169–191). Chichester, UK: Wiley.

Gussenhoven, C. (2005). Transcription of Dutch intonation. In S. Jun (Ed.), *Prosodic typology and transcription: A unified approach* (pp. 118–145). Oxford, UK: Oxford University Press.

't Hart, J., Collier, R., & Cohen, A. (1990). *A perceptual study of intonation: An experimental-phonetic approach to speech melody*. Cambridge Studies in Speech Science and Communication. Cambridge, UK: Cambridge University Press.

Ito, K., & Speer, S. (2008). Anticipatory effects of intonation: Eye movements during instructed visual search. *Journal of Memory and Language*, *58*, 541–573.

Ladd, D. R. (1983). Phonological features of intonational meaning. *Language*, *59*, 721–759.

Jaeger, T. F. (2008). Categorical data analysis: Away from ANOVAs (transformation or not) and towards logit mixed models. *Journal of Memory and Language*, *59*, 434–446.

Jackendoff, R. (1972). *Semantic interpretation in generative grammar*. Cambridge, MA: MIT Press.

Kadmon, N. (2001). *Formal pragmatics: Semantics, pragmatics, presupposition, and focus*. Oxford, UK: Blackwell.

Lewis, D. (1979). Scorekeeping in a language game. *Journal of Philosophical Logic*, *8*, 339–359.

Lupker, S. J. (1984). Semantic priming without association: A second look. *Journal of Verbal Learning and Verbal Behaviour*, *23*, 709–733.

Moss, H. E., Ostrin, R. K., Tyler, L. K., & Marslen-Wilson, W. D. (1995). Accessing different types of lexical semantic information: Evidence from priming. *Journal of Experimental Psychology: Learning, Memory, and Cognition*, *21*, 863–883.

Norris, D., Cutler, A., McQueen, J., & Butterfield, S. (2006). Phonological and conceptual activation in speech comprehension. *Cognitive Psychology*, *53*, 146–193.

Quené, H., & van den Bergh, H. (2004). On multi-level modeling of data from repeated measures designs: A tutorial. *Speech Communication*, *43*, 103–121.

Rooth, M. (1992). A theory of focus interpretation. *Natural Language Semantics*, *1*, 75–116.

Stalnaker, R. (2002). Common ground. *Linguistics and Philosophy*, *25*, 701–721.

Steedman, M. (2000). Information structure and the syntax-phonology interface. *Linguistic Inquiry*, *31*, 649–689.

Swinney, D., Onifer, W., Prather, P., & Hirschkowitz, M. (1979). Semantic facilitation across sensory modalities in the processing of individual words and sentences. *Memory and Cognition*, *7*, 159–165.

Tabossi, P. (1988). Accessing lexical ambiguity in different types of sentential contexts. *Journal of Memory and Language*, *27*, 324–340.

Tabossi, P. (1996). Cross-modal semantic priming. *Language and Cognitive Processes*, *11*, 569–576.

Timm, U. (2003). *Rot*. München, Germany: Deutscher Taschenbuch Verlag.

Watson, D., Gunlogson, C., & Tanenhaus, M. (2008). Interpreting pitch accents in on-line comprehension: H* vs. L+H*. *Cognitive Science, 32*, 1232–1244.

Weber, A., Braun, B., & Crocker, M. (2006). Finding referents in time: Eye-tracking evidence for the role of contrastive accents. *Language and Speech, 49*, 367–392.

Welby, P. (2003). Effects of pitch accent type and status on focus projection. *Language and Speech, 46*, 53–81.

Williams, J. N. (1988). Constraints upon semantic activation during sentence comprehension. *Language and Cognitive Processes, 3*, 165–206.

APPENDIX 1

Materials with English translations. The last two items were not analysed due to a repetition of the word 'vakantie'

Auditory sentence with sentence-final prime	*Control prime*	*Non-contrastive target*	*Contrastive target*
Onze buren monteerden een antenne	trapeze	televisie	schotel
'Our neighbours assembled an antenna'	'trapeze'	'television'	'dish'
De ontsteking werd veroorzaakt door een bacterie	verwonding	ziek	virus
'The inflammation was caused by a bacteria'	'injury'	'ill'	'virus'
Er was airconditioning in de cabine	centrale	vliegtuig	kamer
'There was air-conditioning in the cabin'	'head office'	'plane'	'room'
De kinderen gooiden met confetti	spaghetti	carnaval	serpentine
'The children threw with confetti'	'spaghetti'	'carnival'	'paper streamer'
Mark spiekte tijdens het examen	gefluister	stress	proefwerk
'Mark copied off someone during the exam'	'whispering'	'stress'	'test'
In Florida fotografeerde hij een flamingo	beroemdheid	roze	pelikaan
'In Florida he photographed a flamingo'	'celebrity'	'pink'	'pelican'
Anne is verkleed als gorilla	kabouter	aap	chimpansee
'Anne is dressed up as a gorilla'	'gnome'	'ape'	'chimpanzee'
Roeland repareerde de horloge	insigne	tijd	klok
'Roeland repaired the wrist watch'	'badge'	'time'	'clock'
Henk bestelde een jenever	risotto	drank	brandewijn
'Henk ordered a jenever'	'risotto'	'drink'	'brandy'
Anke noteerde iets op de kalender	papiertje	jaar	rooster
'Anke wrote something down in her calendar'	'piece of paper'	'year'	'schedule'
De keuken ruikt naar kamille	andijvie	thee	lavendel
'The kitchen smells like camomile'	'endive'	'tea'	'lavender'
Marlies voerde de kanarie	koala	vogel	parkiet
'Marlies fed the canary'	'koala'	'bird'	'parakeet'
De slachtoffers sliepen in de kazerne	taveerne	brandweer	sporthal
'The victims slept in the barracks'	'tavern'	'fire brigade'	'gymnasium'

APPENDIX 1 (*Continued*)

Auditory sentence with sentence-final prime	*Control prime*	*Non-contrastive target*	*Contrastive target*
Er waren kokkels in de lagune	terrine	water	rivier
'There were cockles in the lagoon'	'tureen'	'water'	'river'
Marloes ging naar het Lyceum	gebergte	school	mavo
'Marloes attended the lyceum'	'mountain range'	'school'	'lower general sec. education'
De dierenarts moest naar de manege	savanne	paard	boerderij
'The vet had to go to the stables'	'savanna'	'horse'	'farm house'
Mijn broer zit bij de marine	fanfare	boot	luchtmacht
'My brother is at the marines'	'brass band'	'boat'	'air force'
De sculpturen stonden in het museum	noordoosten	kunst	archief
'The sculptures stood in the museum'	'north east'	'art'	'archive'
De kamelendrijver zag een oase	toeriste	woestijn	luchtspiegeling
'The camel-driver saw an oasis'	'tourist'	'desert'	'illusion'
De hond kauwde op een pantoffel'	kastanje	sloffen	slippers
'The dog chewed on a slipper'	'chestnut'	'slippers'	'flip-flop'
De huisarts gaf hem een placebo	verklaring	nep	medicijn
'The GP gave him a placebo'	'explanationt'	'fake'	'medicin'
Mijn buurman werkte voor de provincie	politie	land	gemeente
'My neighbour works for the Province'	'police'	'country'	'community'
De poster hing aan de punaise	piano	prikbord	spijker
'The poster hang from the drawing pin'	'piano'	'notice board'	'nail'
Mijn vader draagt een pyjama	kalkoentje	slapen	nachthemd
'My father wears a pyjama'	'little turkey'	'to sleep'	'nightgown'
Het stel sprak af in de ruine	pagode	kasteel	bunker
'The couple agreed to meet at the ruin'	'pagoda'	'castle'	'bunker'
In de lente gingen zij op safari	karate	jungle	trektocht
'In spring they went on safari'	'karate'	'jungle'	'hiking tour'

APPENDIX 1 (*Continued*)

Auditory sentence with sentence-final prime	*Control prime*	*Non-contrastive target*	*Contrastive target*
Mijn tante ontving een klein salaris	cadeautje	geld	subsidie
'My aunt received a small salary'	'small present'	'money'	'subsidy'
Christel eet het liefst sardine	komkommer	vis	zalm
'Christel preferably eats sardine'	'cucumber'	'fish'	'salmon'
Onze zoon houdt van spinazie	sukade	groente	kool
'Our son loves spinach'	'candied peel'	'vegetable'	'cabbage'
Hans kocht een stuk suede	verlengsnoer	leer	zijde
'Hans bought a piece of suede'	'extension lead'	'leather'	'silk'
Zaterdag ging ik naar het theater	orakel	voorstelling	bioscoop
'On Saturday I went to the theatre'	'oracle'	'performance'	'film theatre'
Zijn lievelingssmaak was vanille	tomaten	ijs	kaneel
'His favourite taste was vanilla'	'tomatoes'	'ice cream'	'cinnamon'
De socialist imponeerde de elite	projectgroep	rijk	burgers
'The socialist impressed the elite'	'project group'	'rich'	'citizens'
De majoor stopte bij de douane	veranda	grens	marechaussee
'The major stopped at the customs'	'veranda'	'border'	'military police'
De technicus werkte in de garage	vakantie	auto	hangar
'The technician worked in the garage'	'holiday'	'car'	'hangar'
De collega gaat op vakantie	auditie	zon	zakenreis
'The colleague went on holidays'	'audition'	'sun'	'business trip'

LANGUAGE AND COGNITIVE PROCESSES
2010, 25 (7/8/9), 1044–1098

Psychology Press
Taylor & Francis Group

Acoustic correlates of information structure

Mara Breen[1], Evelina Fedorenko[2], Michael Wagner[3], and Edward Gibson[2]

[1]*Department of Psychology, University of Massachusetts, Amherst, MA, USA,* [2]*Department of Brain & Cognitive Sciences, Massachusetts Institute of Technology, Cambridge, MA, USA,* [3]*Department of Linguistics, McGill University, Montreal, Canada*

This paper reports three studies aimed at addressing three questions about the acoustic correlates of information structure in English: (1) do speakers mark information structure prosodically, and, to the extent they do; (2) what are the acoustic features associated with different aspects of information structure; and (3) how well can listeners retrieve this information from the signal? The information structure of subject–verb–object sentences was manipulated via the questions preceding those sentences: elements in the target sentences were either focused (i.e., the answer to a wh-question) or given (i.e., mentioned in prior discourse); furthermore, focused elements had either an implicit or an explicit contrast set in the discourse; finally, either only the object was focused (narrow object focus) or the entire event was focused (wide focus). The results across all three experiments demonstrated that people reliably mark (1) focus location (subject, verb, or object) using greater intensity, longer duration, and higher mean and maximum F0, and (2) focus breadth, such that narrow object focus is marked with greater intensity, longer duration, and higher mean and maximum F0 on the object than wide focus. Furthermore, when participants are made aware of prosodic ambiguity present across different information structures, they reliably mark focus type, so that contrastively focused elements are produced with greater intensity, longer duration, and lower mean and maximum F0 than noncontrastively focused elements. In addition to having important theoretical consequences for accounts of semantics and prosody, these experiments demonstrate that linear residualisation successfully removes individual differences in people's productions thereby revealing cross-speaker generalisations. Furthermore,

Correspondence should be addressed to either Mara Breen, Department of Psychology, University of Massachusetts, 522 Tobin Hall, Amherst, MA 01003, USA. E-mail: mbreen@psych.umass.edu or Edward Gibson, Department of Brain and Cognitive Sciences, Massachusetts Institute of Technology, 43 Vassar St., Rm. 3035, Cambridge, MA 02139, USA. E-mail: egibson@mit.edu

http://www.psypress.com/lcp DOI: 10.1080/01690965.2010.504378

discriminant modelling allows us to objectively determine the acoustic features that underlie meaning differences.

Keywords: Prosody; Information structure.

INTRODUCTION

An important component of the meaning of a sentence is its relationship to the context in which it is produced. Some parts of speakers' sentences refer to information already under discussion, while other parts convey information that the speaker is presenting as new for the listener. Depending on the context, the same sentence can convey different kinds of information to the listener. For example, consider the three contexts in (1a)–(1c) for the sentence in (2):

(1) a. Who fried an omelet?
b. What did Damon do to an omelet?
c. What did Damon fry?
(2) Damon fried an omelet.

The event of frying an omelet is already made salient in the context in (1a), and this part of the answer is therefore *given*. Consequently, the sentence *Damon fried an omelet* conveys *Damon* as the *new* or *focused* information.[1] The verb *fried* is the focused information relative to the context in (1b), and the object noun phrase (NP) *an omelet* is the focused information relative to the context in (1c). This component of the meaning of sentences—the differential contributions of different sentence elements to the overall sentence meaning in its relation to the preceding discourse—is called *information structure.*

Three components of information structure have been proposed in the literature: *givenness*, *focus*, and *topic* (see e.g., Féry & Krifka, 2008, for a recent summary). The current paper will be concerned with givenness and focus.[2] Given material is material that has been made salient in the discourse, either explicitly, like the event corresponding to the verb *fried* and the object corresponding to the noun *omelet* in (1a), or implicitly, via inferences based

[1] Numerous terms are used in the literature to refer to the distinction between the information that is old for the listener and the information that the speaker is adding to the discourse: *background* and *foreground*; *given* and *new*; *topic* and *comment*; *theme* and *rheme*, etc. In this paper, we will use the term *given* to refer to the parts of the utterance which are old to the discourse, and *focused* to refer to the part of the utterance which is new to the discourse.

[2] Topic, the third component of information structure, describes which discourse referent focused information should be associated with, as in the mention of Damon in "As for Damon, he fried an omelet". The current studies do not address the prosodic realisation of topic.

on world knowledge (e.g., mentioning *omelet* makes the notion of "eggs" given, Schwarzchild, 1999).

Focused material is what is new to the discourse, or in the foreground. The focus of a sentence can often be understood as the part that corresponds to the answer to the wh-part of wh-questions, like *Damon* in (2) as an answer to (1a) (Jackendoff, 1972; Paul, 1880).

There are two dimensions along which focused elements can differ. The first is contrastiveness. A contrastively focused element, like *Damon* in (3b), indicates that the element in question is one of a set of explicit alternatives or serves to correct a specific item already present in the discourse, as in the following:

(3) a. Did Harry fry an omelet yesterday?
b. Damon fried an omelet yesterday.

Unlike (1a), where there is no explicit set of individuals from which *Damon* is being selected as the "omelet fryer", in (3a) an explicit alternative "omelet fryer" is being introduced: *Harry*. The sentence (3b) in this context thus presents information (i.e., *Damon*) which explicitly contrasts with, or contradicts, some information which has been introduced into the discourse.

There is no consensus in the literature regarding the relationship between noncontrastive focus and contrastive focus. Some researchers have treated noncontrastive focus and contrastive focus as separate categories of information structure (Chafe, 1976; Halliday, 1967; Molnar, 2002; Rochemont, 1986), whereas others have argued that there is no principled difference between the two (e.g., Bolinger, 1961; Rooth, 1985, 1992). According to Rooth (1992), for example, each expression evokes two semantic representations: the expression's actual meaning and a set of alternatives. If a constituent in the expression is focused, then the alternative set contains the expression itself and all expressions with an alternative substituted for the focus-marked constituent; if there is no focus within the expression, the alternative set consists only of the expression itself. Rooth would therefore argue that *Damon* in (1a) is focused and introduces alternative propositions that differ only in the agent of the event ({Damon fried an omelet, Harry fried an omelet, Ada fried an omelet, ...}), even if no alternatives are explicitly mentioned. In (3a), *Damon* also evokes alternative omelet fryers, and therefore has the same focus structure as (1a), but the context makes a specific alternative (*Harry*) more salient than other potential alternatives. Importantly, from Rooth's standpoint, it does not matter whether the alternatives are explicit in the discourse or not: the meaning of the expression is the same.

The second dimension along which focused elements can vary is focus breadth (Gussenhoven, 1983, 1999; Selkirk, 1984, 1995), which refers to the size of the set of focused elements. *Narrow* focus refers to cases where only a single aspect of an event (e.g., the agent, the action, the patient, etc.) is focused, whereas *wide* focus focuses an entire event. Take, for example, the difference between (5) as an answer to (4a) vs. as an answer to (4b):

(4) a. What did Damon fry last night?
    b. What happened last night?
(5) Damon fried an omelet last night.

(4a) narrowly focuses the patient of frying, *omelet* in (5), whereas (4b) widely focuses the entire event of Damon frying an omelet.

The information structure of a sentence element can be conveyed in at least three ways: (1) using word order (i.e., given information generally precedes focused information; e.g., Birner, 1994; Clark & Clark, 1978); (2) using particular lexical items and syntactic constructions (e.g., using cleft constructions such as *It was Damon who fried an omelet*; Lambrecht, 2001); and (3) using prosody. Prosody—which we focus on in the current paper—refers to the way in which words are grouped in speech, the relative acoustic prominence of words, and the overall tune of an utterance. Prosody is comprised of acoustic features such as fundamental frequency (F0), duration, and loudness, the combinations of which give rise to psychological percepts such as phrasing (grouping), stress (prominence), and tonal movement (intonation).

The goal of the current paper is to investigate the prosodic realisation of information structure in simple English subject–verb–object (SVO) sentences like (2), with the goal of addressing the following questions:

(1) First, do speakers mark information structure prosodically?
    a. Do speaker distinguish focused and unfocused elements?
    b. Do speakers distinguish focused elements that have an explicit contrast set in the discourse from those that do not?
    c. Do speakers distinguish sentences in which only the object is focused from those in which the entire event is focused?
(2) What are the acoustic features associated with these different aspects of information structure?
(3) How well can listeners retrieve this information from the signal?

Although the current experiments are all performed on English, the answers to these questions will likely be similar for other West Germanic languages. However, the relationship between prosodic features and information structure across different languages and language groups remains an open question.

In the remainder of the introduction, we briefly lay out two approaches to the study of the relationship between prosody and information structure, and summarise empirical studies which have explored how information structure is realised acoustically and prosodically. We then discuss methodological issues present in previous studies which call into question the generaliseability of the reported findings, and outline how the current methods were designed to better address these questions.

Empirical investigations of prosody and information structure

Two perspectives on the relationship between the acoustics of the speech signal and the meaning associated with various aspects of information structure have been articulated in the literature. According to the *direct-relationship* approach, sets of acoustic features are directly associated with particular meanings (Cooper, Eady, & Mueller, 1985; Eady & Cooper, 1986; Fry, 1955; Lieberman, 1960; Pell, 2001; Xu & Xu, 2005). In contrast, according to the *indirect-relationship* approach (known as the intonational phonology framework), the relationship between acoustics and meaning is mediated by phonological categories (Dilley, 2005; Gussenhoven, 1983; Hawkins & Warren, 1991; Ladd, 1996; Pierrehumbert, 1980). In particular, phonetic prosodic cues are hypothesised to be grouped into prosodic categories which are, in turn, associated with particular meanings. The experiments in the current paper were not designed to decide between these two approaches. However, we will initially discuss our experiments in terms of the direct-relationship approach, because it is more parsimonious. In the general discussion, we will show how the results are also compatible with the indirect-relationship approach.

Turning now to previous empirical work on the relationship between prosody and information structure, we start with studies of focused vs. given elements. Several studies have demonstrated that focused elements are more acoustically prominent than given elements. However, there has been some debate about which acoustic features underlie a listener's perception of acoustic prominence. Some features that have been proposed to be associated with prominence include pitch (i.e., F0; Cooper, Eady, & Mueller, 1985; Eady & Cooper, 1986; Lieberman, 1960), duration (Beckman, 1986; Fry, 1955), loudness (i.e., intensity; Beckman, 1986; Kochanski, Grabe, Coleman, & Rosner, 2005; Turk & Sawusch, 1996), and voice quality (Sluijter & van Heuven, 1996).

In early work on lexical stress, Fry (1955) and Lieberman (1960) argued that intensity and duration of the vowel of the stressed syllable contributed most strongly to the percept of acoustic prominence, such that stressed vowels were produced with a greater intensity and a longer duration than nonstressed vowels. In experiments on phrase-level prominence, Cooper Eady, and Mueller (1985) and Eady and Cooper (1986) also noted that more prominent syllables are longer than their nonprominent counterparts. Cooper et al. (1985) (see also Lieberman, 1960), Rietveld and Gussenhoven (1985), Gussenhoven, Repp, Rietveld, Rump, and Terken (1997), and Terken (1991) argued that F0 was a highly important acoustic feature underlying prominence. Others have argued that the strongest cue to prominence is intensity (e.g., Beckman, 1986). More recently, Turk and Sawusch (1996) also found that intensity (and duration) were better predictors of perceived prominence than pitch, in a perception task. Finally, in a study of spoken corpora, Kochanski et al. (2005) demonstrated that loudness (i.e., intensity) was a strong predictor of labellers' annotations of prominence, while pitch had very little predictive power.

The question of whether contrastively and noncontrastively focused elements are prosodically differentiated by speakers, and perceptually differentiated by listeners, has also been extensively debated. Some have argued that there is no difference in the acoustic features associated with contrastively vs. noncontrastively focused elements (Bolinger, 1961; Cutler, 1977; 't Hart, Collier, & Cohen, 1990), while others have argued that some acoustic features differ between contrastively vs. noncontrastively focused elements (Bartels & Kingston, 1994; Couper-Kuhlen, 1984; Ito, Speer, & Beckman, 2004; Krahmer & Swerts, 2001). For example, Couper-Kuhlen (1984) reported, on the basis of corpus work, that speakers produce contrastive focus with a steep drop after a high F0 target, while high F0 is sustained after noncontrastive focus (see also Krahmer & Swerts, 2001). However, this finding is in contrast to Bartels and Kingston (1994), who have argued, based on a pair of concurrent perception production studies, that the most salient acoustic cue to contrastiveness is the height of the peak on a contrastive word, such that a higher peak is associated with a greater probability of an element being interpreted as contrastive (see also Ladd & Morton, 1997). Finally, Ito et al. (2004) demonstrated that speakers are more likely to use a L+H* accent (i.e., a steep rise from a low target to a high target), compared to a H* accent (i.e., a gradual rise to a high target), to indicate an element that has an explicit contrast set in the discourse.

Krahmer and Swerts (2001) observed that listeners were more likely to perceive a contrastive adjective (e.g., *red* in *red square* preceded by *blue square*) as more prominent than a new adjective when the adjective was presented with a noun compared to when it was presented in isolation. They therefore hypothesised that the lack of a consensus in the literature may be due to the failure of the earlier studies to investigate focused elements in relation to the prosody of the surrounding elements. Consistent with this idea, Calhoun (2005) demonstrated that a model's ability to predict a word's information structure is significantly improved when information about the acoustics of adjacent words is included in the model. These results suggest that a more consistent picture of the acoustic features associated with contrastively and noncontrastively focused elements may emerge if acoustic context is taken into account.

Finally, prior work has investigated whether speakers prosodically differentiate narrow and wide focus. Selkirk (1995), for example, argued that, through a process called *focus projection*, an acoustic prominence on the head of a phrase or its internal argument can project to the entire phrase, thus making the entire phrase focused (see also Selkirk, 1984; see Gussenhoven, 1983, 1999, for a similar claim). According to Selkirk (1984) and Gussenhoven (1983) then a clause containing a transitive verb whose direct object is acoustically prominent is ambiguous between a reading where the object alone is focused and a reading where the entire verb phrase is focused. This hypothesis has been supported in several perception experiments (Birch & Clifton, 1995; Gussenhoven, 1983; Welby, 2003). Welby (2003), for example, demonstrated that listeners rated a sentence like *I read the DISPATCH* with a single acoustic prominence on *dispatch* as a similarly felicitous response to either a question narrowly focusing the object (i.e., *What newspaper do you read?*), or a question widely focusing the entire event (i.e., *How do you keep up with the news?*). However, Gussenhoven (1983) found that, at least in some productions, there is actually a perceptible difference between narrow and wide focus, although listeners cannot use this information to reliably tell in which context the sentence was uttered (see Baumann, Grice, & Steindamm, 2006, for evidence from German showing that speakers do differentiate between narrow and wide focus, with prosodic cues varying across speakers). In contrast to Gussenhoven's perception results, Rump and Collier (1986) found that listeners can accurately discriminate narrow and wide focus using pitch cues.

Limitations of previous work

Although the studies summarised above provide evidence for some systematic differences in the acoustic realisation of different aspects of information structure, no clear picture has yet emerged with regard to any of the three meaning distinctions discussed above (i.e., focused vs. given elements, noncontrastively focused vs. contrastively focused elements, and narrow vs. wide focus). Furthermore, previous studies suffer from several methodological limitations that make the findings inconclusive. Here, we discuss five limitations of previous studies which the current studies seek to address in an effort to reveal a clearer picture of the relationship between acoustic features and information structure.

First, instead of acoustic features, sometimes only Tones and Break Indices (ToBI)[3] annotations are provided (e.g., Birch & Clifton, 1995; Ito et al., 2004), as in the work of researchers who adopt the intonational phonology framework and who therefore believe that using prosodic annotation offers a useful way to extrapolate away from potentially complex interactions among acoustic features which give rise to the perception of specific intonational patterns. One particular problem concerns H* and L+H* accents. As defined in the ToBI system, these accents are meant to be explicit markers of noncontrastive focus and contrastive focus, respectively (Beckman & Ayers-Elam, 1997). However, H* and L+H* are often confused in ToBI annotations (Syrdal & McGory, 2000), and are, in fact, often collapsed in calculating intercoder agreement (Breen, Dilley, Gibson, Bolivar, & Kraemer, 2006; Pitrelli, Beckman, & Hirschberg, 1994; Yoon, Chavarria, Cole, & Hasegawa-Johnson, 2004). Therefore, it is difficult to interpret the results of studies which are based on the difference between H* and L+H* without a discussion of the acoustic differences between these purported categories. In the current studies, we report acoustic features in order to avoid confusion about what the ToBI labels might mean and in order to not presuppose the existence of prosodic categories associated with particular meaning categories of information structure.

A second limitation concerns the method used to generate and select productions for analysis. A common practice involves eliciting productions from a small number of speakers (e.g., Baumann et al., 2006; Krahmer & Swerts, 2001), which results in a potential decrease in experimental power, and could therefore lead to a Type II error. In addition, several previous experiments have excluded speakers' data from analysis for not producing accents consistently (e.g., Cooper et al., 1985; Eady & Cooper, 1986), which could lead to a Type I error. For the current experiments, we recruited between 13 and 18 speakers. In addition, no speakers' productions were excluded from the analyses based on a priori predictions about potential behaviour (e.g., placing accents in particular locations).

A third limitation concerns the tasks used in perception studies. In particular, some studies asked listeners to make judgements about which of two stimuli were more prominent (Krahmer & Swerts, 2001), what accent is acceptable in a particular context (Birch & Clifton, 1995; Welby, 2003), or with which of two questions a particular answer sounded more natural (Gussenhoven, 1983). The problem with these metalinguistic judgements is that they lack a measure of the participants' interpretation of the sentences. In the current studies, we employ a more natural production–comprehension task, in which speakers are trying to communicate a particular meaning of a

[3] The ToBI system was developed in the early 1990s as the standard system for annotation of prosodic features (Silverman et al., 1992).

semantically ambiguous sentence and listeners are trying to understand the intended meaning.

A fourth limitation of previous studies is in how they have dealt with speaker variability. Presenting data from individual subjects separately, as is commonly done, is problematic because it fails to capture the shared aspects of individual productions (e.g., consistent use by most speakers of some set of acoustic features to mark focused elements). In the current studies, we combine data across subjects while simultaneously removing variance due to individual differences using linear regression modelling (e.g., Jaeger, 2008).

A fifth limitation alluded to in the previous section is that many have reported differences between conditions based only on individual acoustic features on single words (Baumann et al., 2006; Cooper et al., 1985; Eady & Cooper, 1986; cf. Krahmer & Swerts, 2001; Calhoun, 2005). If acoustic prominence is perceived in a context-dependent manner, these single-feature/single-word analyses might find spurious differences, or fail to find real differences. In the current studies, we used discriminant modelling on the productions in order to simultaneously investigate the contribution of multiple acoustic features from multiple words in an utterance to the interpretation of information structure of different sentence elements.

EXPERIMENTS: OVERVIEW AND GENERAL METHODS

The current paper presents results from three experiments. Experiment 1 investigated whether speakers prosodically disambiguate focus location (subject vs. verb vs. object), focus type (contrastive vs. noncontrastive), and focus breadth (narrow vs. wide) by eliciting semi-naturalistic productions like that in (3b) (e.g., *Damon fried an omelet this morning*), whose information structure was disambiguated by a preceding question. Experiment 2 investigated whether speakers disambiguate focus location and focus type when the task explicitly required them to communicate a particular meaning to their listeners. Finally, Experiment 3 served as a replication and extension of Experiment 2, in which speakers included an attribution expression (*I heard that*) before the critical sentence.

The acoustic analysis of the productions elicited in all three experiments proceeded in three steps. First, we automatically extracted a series of 24 acoustic features (see Table 2) from the subject, verb, and object of the sentences elicited in Experiments 1–3. Second, we subjected all of these features to a stepwise discriminant function analysis in order to determine which features best discriminated the information structure conditions listed in Table 1 for each of the three experiments. This analysis resulted in a subset of eight acoustic features. Finally, we used discriminant analyses to evaluate whether this subset of eight features could effectively discriminate sets of 2

TABLE 1
Example item from Experiment 1. The target sentence is "Damon fried an omelet this morning"

Condition	*Focus type*	*Focused argument*	*Setup question*
1	Noncontrastive	Wide	What happened this morning?
2	Noncontrastive	S	Who fried an omelet this morning?
3	Noncontrastive	V	What did Damon do to an omelet this morning?
4	Noncontrastive	O	What did Damon fry this morning?
5	Contrastive	S	Did Harry fry an omelet this morning?
6	Contrastive	V	Did Damon bake an omelet this morning?
7	Contrastive	O	Did Damon fry a chicken this morning?

and 3 conditions for each of the three experiments. Specifically, we tested focus location by comparing the features from productions in which each of the elements (subject, verb, object) was focused vs. given. We tested focus type by comparing the features from sentences in which the focused element was contrastively or noncontrastively focused at each of the three syntactic positions. Last, we tested focus breadth by comparing the features for sentences with wide focus to those with narrow object focus. In addition to the analysis of acoustic features, in Experiments 2 and 3 we investigated whether listeners could correctly determine the intended information structure.

EXPERIMENT 1

Method

Participants

Nine pairs of participants were recorded. All participants were self-reported native speakers of American English. All participants were MIT students or members of the surrounding community. Participants were paid for their participation.

Materials

Each trial consisted of a set-up question and a target sentence, which always had an SVO structure (e.g., *Damon fried an omelet this morning*). The target sentence could plausibly answer any one of the seven set-up questions (see Table 1), which served to focus different elements of the sentence or the entire event described in the sentence. The first condition focused the entire event (i.e., *What happened this morning?*). In the remaining conditions, two factors were manipulated: (1) the element in the target sentence that was focused by the question (subject, verb, or object) and (2) the presence of an explicit contrast set for the focused element (absent, i.e., noncontrastively focused element, or present, i.e., contrastively focused element).

All subject and object NPs in the target sentences were bisyllabic with first syllable stress, and all verbs were monosyllabic. All subject NPs were proper names, and object NPs were mostly common inanimate objects, such that the events were nonreversible. Furthermore, all words were comprised mostly of sonorant phonemes. These constraints ensured that words could be more easily compared across items, and facilitated the extraction of acoustic features (which is easier for vowels and sonorant consonants). An adjunct prepositional phrase (PP) was included at the end of each sentence so that differences in the production of the object NP due to the experimental manipulations would be dissociable from prosodic effects on phrase-final, or in this case, sentence-final, words, which are typically lengthened and produced with lower F0 compared to phrase-medial words (e.g., Wightman, Shattuck-Hufnagel, Ostendorf, & Price, 1992).

We constructed 28 sets of materials. Participants saw one condition of each item, following a Latin Square design. A sample item is presented in Table 1. The complete set of materials can be found in Appendix 1.

Procedure

Productions were elicited and prescreened in a two-part procedure. The first part was a training session, where participants learned the intended names for pictures of people, actions, and objects. In the second part, the pairs of participants produced questions and answers for each other. The method was designed to maximise control over what speakers were saying, but also to encourage natural-sounding productions. Pilot testing revealed that having subjects simply read the target sentences resulted in productions with low prosodic variability. After going through the experiment one time, the participants switched roles.

Training session. In the training session, participants learned mappings between 96 pictures and names, so that they could produce the names from memory during the second part of the experiment. In a PowerPoint presentation, each picture, corresponding to a person, an action, an object, or a modifier, was presented with its intended name (see Figure 1, left). The pictures consisted of eight names of people, which were repeated 3–4 items each in the experimental materials, eight colours (which were used in a concurrently run filler experiment), 34 verbs, 44 objects, and two temporal modifiers (*this morning* and *last night*). The pictures were presented in

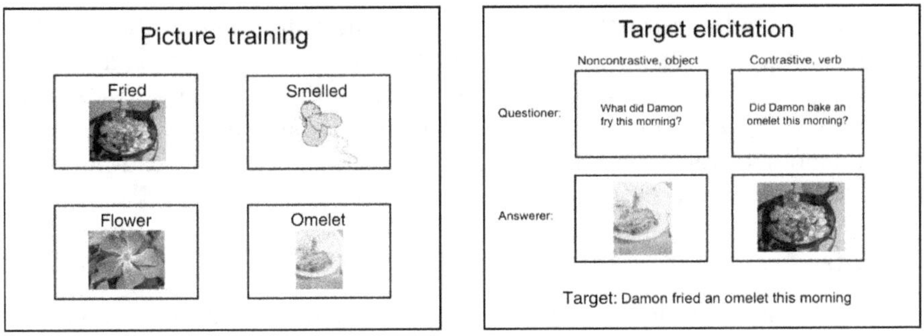

Figure 1. Left: Examples from the picture-training task for Experiment 1. Each square represents a screen shot. Right: Examples of the procedure for the questioner (upper squares) and answerer (lower squares) for Experiment 1. Two conditions are presented: Noncontrastive, object (left), and contrastive, verb (right). The top squares represent screen shots of what the questioner saw on a trial; the bottom squares represent what the answerer saw on a trial.

alphabetical order, to facilitate memorisation and recall. Participants were instructed to learn the mappings by progressing through the PowerPoint at their own pace.

When participants felt they had learned the mappings, they were given a picture-naming test, which consisted of 27 items from the full list of 96. The test was identical for all participants. Participants were told of their mistakes, and, if they made four or more errors, they were instructed to go back through the PowerPoint to improve their memory of the picture–name mappings. Once participants could successfully name 23 or more items on the test, which took between 1 and 3 rounds of testing, they continued with the second part of the experiment. Early in pilot testing, we discovered that subjects had poor recall for the names of the people in the pictures. Therefore, in the actual experiment, subjects could refer to a sheet which had labelled pictures of the people.

Question–answer experiment. The experiment was conducted using Linger 2.92 (available at http://telab.mit.edu/~dr/Linger/), a software platform designed by Doug Rohde for language processing experiments. Participants were randomly paired and randomly assigned to the role of *questioner* or *answerer.* Participants sat at computers in the same room such that neither could see the other's screen. On each trial, as illustrated in Figure 1 (right), the questioner saw a question (e.g., *What did Damon fry this morning?*) which he/she was instructed to produce aloud for the answerer. The answerer was instructed to produce an answer aloud using the information contained in the picture on his/her screen (e.g., *Damon fried an omelet this morning*). The answerer was instructed to produce complete sentences, including the subject, verb, object, and temporal modifier,[4] and to emphasise the part of the sentence that the questioner had asked about, or that he/she was correcting. On a random 20% of trials, the answerer was asked a comprehension question about the answer s/he produced.

Productions were recorded in a quiet room with a head-mounted microphone at a rate of 44 kHz (Table 2).

Results

Of the 504 speaker productions, 87 (17%) were discarded because (1) the answerer failed to use the correct lexical items; (2) the answerer was disfluent; or (3) the production was poorly recorded. The 417 remaining productions were subjected to the acoustic analyses described below.

Acoustic features

Based on previous investigations of prosody and information structure (Bartels & Kingston, 1994; Baumann et al., 2006; Eady & Cooper, 1986; Cooper et al., 1985; Fry, 1955; Krahmer & Swerts, 2001; Lieberman, 1960), we chose a set of acoustic features to analyse (see Table 2). These features were extracted from the productions automatically using the Praat program (Boersma & Weenink, 2006). The measures of F0 computed over portions of the words (e.g., First quarter F0) were chosen in order to investigate how F0 changes across the syllable might contribute to the differentiation of conditions.

Our first goal was to determine which of the 24 candidate acoustic features mediated differences among conditions. We conducted a series of stepwise linear discriminant analyses (LDA)[5] on all of the data collected in Experiments 1–3 reported in the current paper. In order to determine the features to be used in the analyses of all three experiments, we performed a separate stepwise

---

[4] In the absence of explicit instruction to produce complete sentences, with a lexicalised subject, verb, and object, speakers would likely resort to pronouns or would omit given elements altogether (e.g., *What did Damon fry this morning? An omelet*). A complete production account of information structure meaning distinctions should include not just the prosodic cues used by the speakers, but also syntactic and lexical production choices, as well as the interaction among these different production strategies. However, because we focus on prosody in the current investigation, we wanted to be able to compare acoustic features across identical words. Thus, we required that participants always produce a subject, verb, object, and temporal modifier on every trial.

[5] LDA calculates a function, computed as a linear combination of all predictors entered, which results in the best separation of two or more groups. For two groups, only one function is computed. For three groups, the first function provides the best separation of Group 1 from Groups 2 and 3; a second, orthogonal, function provides the best separation of Groups 2 and 3, after partialling out variance accounted for by the first function. *Stepwise* LDA is an iterative procedure which adds predictors based on which of the candidate predictors provide the best discrimination.

TABLE 2
Acoustic features extracted from each word in the target sentence for Experiments 1–3. Stepwise discriminant analyses demonstrated that the measures in bold provided the best discrimination among conditions and were used in all reported analyses

Acoustic feature	*Units*	*Description*
Duration	ms	Word duration excluding any silence before or after the word
Silence	ms	Duration of silence following the word, not due to stop closure
Duration + silence	**ms**	**The sum of the duration of the word and any following silence**
Mean F0	**Hz**	**Mean F0 of the entire word**
Maximum F0	**Hz**	**Maximum F0 value across the entire word**
F0 peak location	0–1	The proportion of the way through the word where the maximum F0 occurs
Minimum F0	Hz	Minimum F0 across the entire word
F0 valley location	0–1	The proportion of the way through the word where the minimum F0 occurs
Initial F0	Hz	Mean F0 of the initial 5% of the word
Early F0	Hz	Mean F0 value of 5% of the word centered at the point 25% of the way through the word
Center F0	Hz	Mean F0 value of 5% of the word centered on the midpoint of the word
Late F0	Hz	Mean F0 value of 5% of the word centered on a point 75% of the way through the word
Final F0	Hz	Mean F0 of the last 5% of the word
First quarter F0	Hz	The difference between initial F0 and early F0
Second quarter F0	Hz	The difference between early F0 and center F0
Third quarter F0	Hz	The difference between center F0 and late F0
Fourth quarter F0	Hz	The difference between late F0 and final F0
Mean intensity	dB	Mean intensity of the word
Maximum intensity	**dB**	**Maximum dB level in the word**
Minimum intensity	dB	Minimum dB level in the word
Intensity peak location	0–1	The proportion of the way through the word where the maximum intensity occurs
Intensity valley location	0–1	The proportion of the way through the word where the minimum intensity occurs
Maximum amplitude	Pascal	Maximum amplitude across the word
Energy	$(\text{Pascal})^2 \times$ Duration	

analysis on the data from each experiment separately. For each analysis we entered all 24 acoustic features across each of the three sentence positions (subject, verb, and object) as possible predictors of the seven experimental conditions, resulting in 72 predictors. Across the three analyses, the acoustic features which consistently resulted in the best discrimination of conditions were (1) duration + silence; (2) mean F0; (3) maximum F0; and (4) maximum intensity on subject, verb, and object. The fact that these 12 features (four acoustic features across three sentence positions) consistently discriminated among conditions across three independent sets of productions (from different speakers and across somewhat different sets of materials) serves as evidence that these features underlie the differentiation of information structure across speakers and materials. Therefore, we use only these 12 features in the LDA reported for the individual experiments in the paper.

Computing residual values

Because of differences among individuals, including age, gender, speech rate, and level of engagement with the task, speakers produce very different versions of the same sentence even within the same experimental condition, thus adding variance to the acoustic features of interest. Similarly, there is likely to be variability associated with different items due to lexical and world knowledge factors. Researchers have previously dealt with the issue of acoustic variability between speakers by normalising pitch and/or duration by speaker (e.g., Shriberg, Stolcke, Hakkani-Tur, & Tur, 2000; Shriberg et al., 1998; Wightman et al., 1992). In order to remove speaker- and item-related variance in the current studies, we computed linear regression models in which speaker (e.g., n=18 in Experiment 1) and item (e.g., n=28 in Experiment 1) predicted each of the 12 acoustic features identified in the stepwise discriminant analyses described in the previous section. From each of these models, we calculated the predicted value of each acoustic feature for a specific item from a specific speaker. We then subtracted this predicted value from every production. The differences among the resulting residual values should reflect differences in the acoustic features due only to the experimental manipulations. All subsequently reported analyses were performed on these residual values.

Focus location

The extent to which a discriminant function analysis can separate data points into two or more groups is calculated with a statistical test, Wilks's Lambda.[6]

To determine how well the acoustic features could differentiate focus location in speakers' productions, we computed a model where the 12 acoustic predictors were used to discriminate among three focus locations:

[6] Wilks's lambda is a measure of the distance between groups on means of the independent variables, and is computed for each function. It ranges in size from 0 to 1; lower values indicate a larger separation between groups. The extent to which the model can effectively discriminate a new set of data is simulated by a leave-one-out classification, in which the acoustic data from each production are iteratively removed from the dataset, the model is computed, and the left-out case is classified by the resultant functions.

subject, verb, or object. In this analysis, we are averaging across the contrastive and noncontrastive condition for each sentence position.

The overall Wilks's Lambda of the model was significant, $\Lambda = .46$, $\chi^2(24) = 271$, $p < .001$, indicating better-than-chance differentiation of subject focus from verb and object focus. In addition, the residual Wilks's Lambda was significant, $\Lambda = .84$, $\chi^2(24) = 62.65$, $p < .001$, indicating that the acoustic predictors could also differentiate verb focus from object focus (see Figure 2). Leave-one-out classification correctly classified 67% of the productions. The model correctly classified subject focus 76% of the time, verb focus 58% of the time, and object focus 66% of the time. Table 3 presents the standardised canonical discriminant function coefficients of the model.[7]

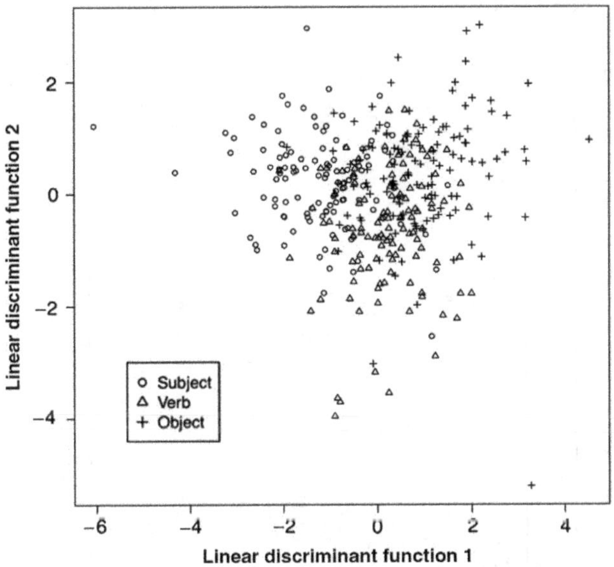

Figure 2. Separation of focus locations on two discriminant functions in Experiment 1. The figure illustrates an effective discrimination among the three groups. Productions of subject focus are clustered in the upper left quadrant; productions of verb focus are clustered in the lower half of the plot; productions of object focus are clustered in the upper right quadrant.

[7] The coefficients in Table 3 indicate which acoustic features best discriminate focus location, such that larger absolute values indicate a greater contribution of that feature to discrimination. For example, inspection of the plot in Figure 2 and the coefficients in the focus location columns of Table 3 shows that the acoustic features of *Damon* score around zero, or lower, on the first function (−0.002, 0.001, −0.01, and −0.06) and around zero on the second function (−0.003, 0.021, −0.016, and −0.101). *Fried* shows a different pattern; specifically, the acoustic features of *fried* have coefficients around zero for the first function, and negative coefficients for the second function. Finally, *omelet* shows a third pattern: its acoustic correlates are centered around zero for the first function, but are high for the second function.

TABLE 3
Standardised canonical coefficients of the discriminant functions computed for Experiment 1

		Focus location		*Focus type*			
		Function 1	*Function 2*	*Subject focus*	*Verb focus*	*Object focus*	*Focus breadth*
Omelet	Duration + silence	−0.001	0.004	0.008	0.003	0.004	0.003
	Mean F0	−0.006	0.011	0.011	−0.014	−0.019	0.000
	Maximum F0	0.002	0.001	−0.002	0.002	0.006	0.003
	Maximum intensity	−0.037	0.181	−0.137	−0.026	0.189	0.199
Fried	Duration + silence	0.007	−0.001	0.007	0.002	−0.001	0.005
	Mean F0	0.024	−0.003	0.000	−0.040	−0.013	−0.025
	Maximum F0	0.002	−0.002	0.004	−0.007	0.013	0.003
	Maximum intensity	0.094	−0.010	−0.076	0.131	−0.043	0.011
Damon	Duration + silence	−0.002	−0.003	0.005	−0.002	0.005	0.003
	Mean F0	0.001	0.021	−0.016	−0.007	−0.014	0.007
	Maximum F0	−0.010	−0.016	−0.012	0.020	−0.011	−0.005
	Maximum intensity	−0.060	−0.101	0.087	0.056	−0.225	−0.123

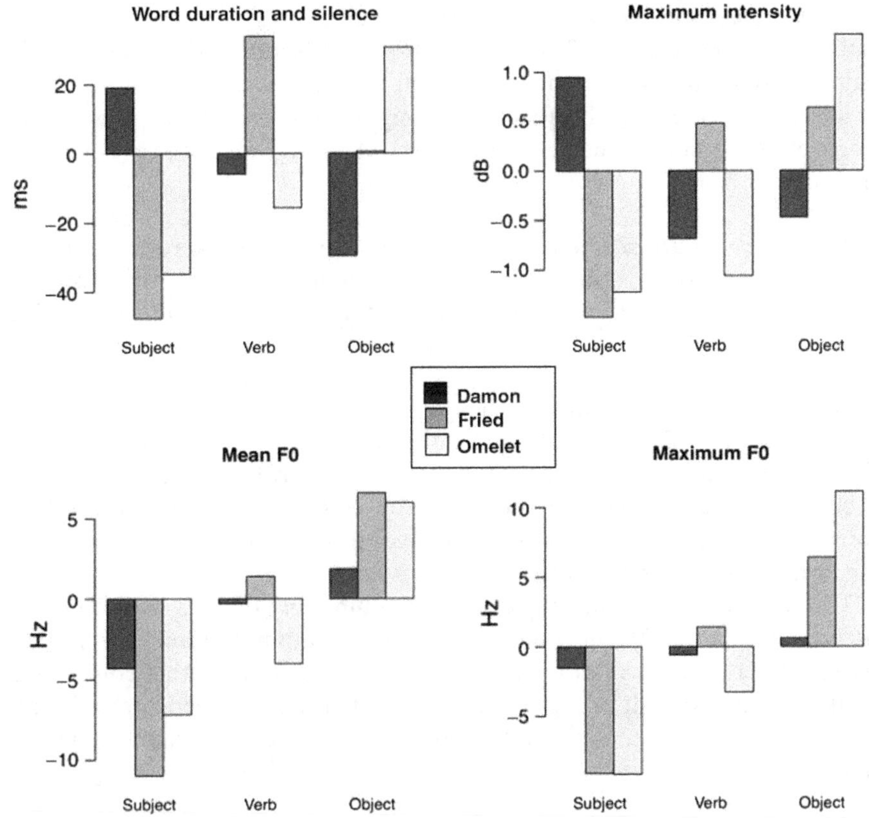

Figure 3. Values of the four discriminating acoustic features of productions of subject, verb, and object focus in Experiment 1.

Figure 3 graphically presents the mean values of the four features, demonstrating that across all three focus locations the intended focus location is produced with the highest maximum intensity, the longest duration and silence, and the highest relative F0.

Focus type

To determine how well the acoustic features could differentiate the type of focus (i.e., noncontrastive vs. contrastive) in speakers' productions, we computed three models in which the 12 acoustic predictors were used to discriminate between two focus groups. The three models investigated differences between noncontrastive and contrastive focus at the three focus locations: subject, verb, and object.

Focus type—subject position. The overall Wilks's Lambda was not significant, $\Lambda = .898$, $\chi^2(12) = 11.95$, $p = .45$, indicating that the acoustic features could not discriminate between noncontrastive and contrastive focus. Because the overall model is not significant, we do not present the scores of the specific acoustic features or the classification statistics here or in the analyses below.

Focus type—verb position. The overall Wilks's Lambda was not significant, $\Lambda = .851$, $\chi^2(12) = 17.92$, $p = .12$, indicating that the acoustic features could not discriminate between noncontrastive and contrastive focus.

Focus type—object position. The overall Wilks's Lambda was significant, $\Lambda = .82$, $\chi^2(12) = 22.63$, $p < .05$, indicating that the acoustic features could discriminate between noncontrastive and contrastive focus above chance level. Leave-one-out classification correctly classified 59% of the productions. The model correctly classified noncontrastive focus 59% of the time and contrastive focus 59% of the time.

The coefficients in the object focus column of Table 3 indicate that intensity and mean F0 contribute most to classification. Figure 4 graphically presents the mean values of the four features, demonstrating that contrastive focus is produced with a higher maximum intensity, a longer duration and silence, and higher maximum F0. Noncontrastive focus is produced with a higher mean F0.

Focus breadth

To determine how well the acoustic features could differentiate focus breadth, we computed a model in which the 12 acoustic predictors were used to discriminate between productions where the entire event was focused and productions where the object was noncontrastively or contrastively focused.

The overall Wilks's Lambda was significant, $\Lambda = .75$, $\chi^2(12) = 47.83$, $p < .001$, indicating that the acoustic features could successfully discriminate between conditions where the entire event is focused and conditions where the object is narrowly focused. Leave-one-out classification correctly classified 72% of the productions. The model correctly classified wide focus 67% of the time and narrow focus 74% of the time.

The standardised canonical discriminant function coefficients in the focus breadth column of Table 3 indicate that maximum intensity contributes most to focus breadth classification. Figure 5 graphically presents the mean values of the four features, demonstrating that wide focus is produced with a more uniform duration + silence and maximum F0 across the sentence than object

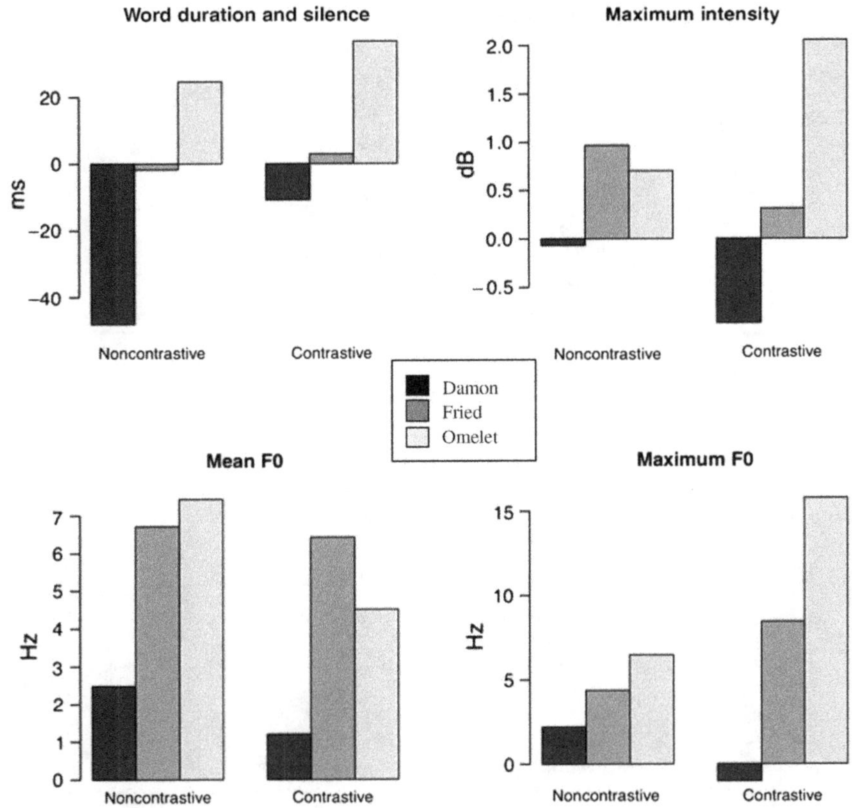

Figure 4. Values of the four discriminating acoustic features of productions of noncontrastive and contrastive object focus when *omelet* is focused in Experiment 1.

focus. Wide focus is also produced with a more uniform, greater intensity than object focus.

Discussion

Focus location

The results demonstrate that speakers consistently provide acoustic cues which disambiguate focus location. Specifically, speakers indicated focus with increased duration, higher intensity, higher mean F0, and higher maximum F0. Furthermore, these results are consistent with the pattern reported in Eady and Cooper (1986), such that the word preceding a focused word is less prominent (produced with shorter duration, lower intensity, and lower F0) than the focused word, and the word following the focused word is less prominent than the word preceding the focused word. Previous studies

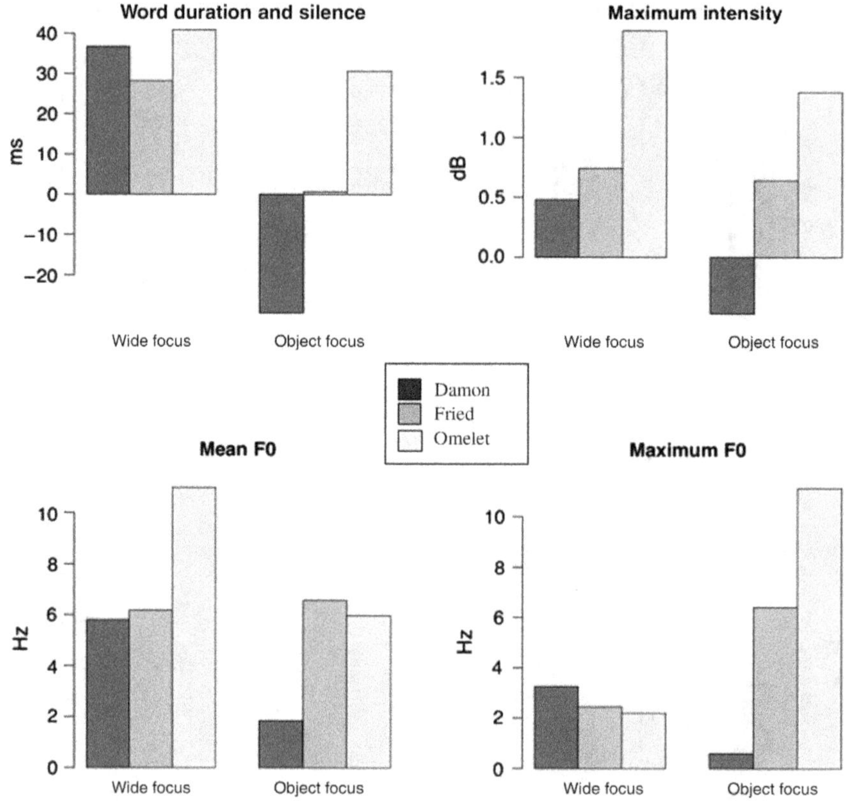

Figure 5. Values of the four discriminating acoustic features of productions of wide and narrow object focus in Experiment 1.

(Eady & Cooper, 1986; Rump & Collier, 1996) have reported this reduction in acoustic prominence following focused elements as being mainly indicated by lower F0 on the postfocal words, though in our data we also find evidence of this reduction in measures of duration and intensity.

Focus type

The results demonstrate that in semi-naturalistic productions speakers do not systematically differentiate between different focus types (focused elements which have explicit contrast sets in the discourse and those which do not). Specifically, at two out of three sentence positions, a discriminant function analysis could not successfully classify speakers' productions of contrastively vs. noncontrastively focused elements. The observation that speakers could not successfully discriminate noncontrastive and contrastive focus in subject or verb positions could be a result of insufficient experimental power, a limitation of the current experiment which will be addressed in Experiments 2 and 3.

Focus breadth

The results demonstrate that speakers do systematically mark focus breadth prosodically. Narrow object focus is produced with the highest maximum F0, longest duration, and maximum intensity of the object noun, relative to the other words in the sentence. For wide focus, the acoustic features are more similar across the sentence; only intensity and mean F0 are higher on the object than on the other words in the sentence. These differences are subtle, but sufficient for the model to successfully discriminate the productions.

The fact that the model failed to systematically classify productions by focus type (with the exception of the object position), while achieving high accuracy in focus location and focus breadth indicates that speakers were not marking focus type with prosody in Experiment 1. However, the method used to elicit productions did not require that subjects be aware of the information structure ambiguity of the materials. Evidence from other production studies suggests that speakers may not prosodically disambiguate ambiguous productions if they are not aware of the ambiguity. Albritton, McKoon, and Ratcliff (1996), for example, demonstrated that speakers did not disambiguate syntactically ambiguous constructions like "Dave and Pat or Bob" unless they were aware of the ambiguity (see also Snedeker & Trueswell, 2003, but cf. Kraljic & Brennan, 2005; Schafer, Speer, Warren, & White, 2000, for evidence that speakers do disambiguate syntactically ambiguous structures even in the absence of ambiguity awareness). Experiment 2 was designed to be a stronger test of speakers' ability to differentiate focus location, focus type, and focus breadth. We used materials similar to those in Experiment 1, with two important methodological modifications. First, instead of producing the answers to questions with no feedback, the speaker's task now involved trying to enable the answerer to choose the question that s/he was answering from a set of possible questions. Moreover, we introduced feedback so that the speaker would always know whether his/her partner had chosen the correct answer. Second, we changed the design from a between- to a within-subjects manipulation. This ensured that speakers were aware of the manipulation, as they were producing the same answer seven times over the course of the experiment with explicit instructions to differentiate their answers for their partner.

In addition to making the speaker's task explicit, the new design also allowed us to analyse the subset of the productions for which the listeners could successfully identify the question-type and which therefore contain sufficient information for differentiating utterances along the three relevant dimensions of information structure.

EXPERIMENT 2

Method

Participants

Seventeen pairs of participants were recorded for this experiment. Subjects were MIT students or members of the surrounding community. All reported being native speakers of American English. None had participated in Experiment 1. Participants were paid for their participation.

Materials

The materials had the same structure as those from Experiment 1, though the critical words differed. Specifically, a larger set of names and a wider variety of temporal modifiers were used, and some verbs and objects differed from Experiment 1. Unlike Experiment 1, each subject pair was presented with all seven versions of each of 14 items, according to a full within-subjects within-items design. All materials can be found in Appendix 2.

Procedure

Two participants sat at computers in the same room such that neither could see the other's screen. One participant was the speaker and the other was the listener. Speakers were told that they would be producing answers to questions out loud for their partners (the listeners), and that the listeners would be required to choose which question the speaker was answering from a set of seven choices.

At the beginning of each trial, the speaker was presented with a question on the computer screen to read silently. After pressing a button, the answer to the question appeared below the question, accompanied by a reminder to the speaker that s/he would only be producing the answer aloud, and not the question. Following this, the speaker had one more chance to read the question and answer, and then he/she was instructed to press a key to begin recording (after being told by the listener that he/she is ready), to produce the answer, and then to press another key to stop recording.

The listener sat at another computer, and pressed a key to see the seven questions that s/he would have to choose his/her answer from. When s/he felt familiar with the questions, s/he told the speaker s/he was ready. After the speaker produced a sentence out loud for the listener, the listener chose the question s/he thought the speaker was answering. If the listener answered incorrectly, his/her computer produced a buzzer sound, like the sound when a contestant makes an incorrect answer on a game show. This cue was included to ensure that speakers knew when their productions did not contain enough information for the listener to choose the correct answer.[8]

Results—production

Two speaker–listener pairs were excluded as the listener did not achieve comprehension accuracy greater than 20%. One further pair was excluded as one member was not a native speaker of American English. Finally, another pair of subjects was excluded because they did not take the task seriously, and produced unnaturally emphatic contrastive accents, often shouting the target word, and laughing while doing so. These exclusions left a total of 13 pairs of participants whose responses were analysed.

Sixty-seven of the 1274 trials (5%) were excluded because (1) the speaker failed to produce the correct words; (2) the speaker was disfluent; or (3) the production was poorly recorded. Analyses were performed on all trials, and on the subset of trials for which the listener correctly identified the question. The results were very similar in the two analyses. For brevity of presentation, we present results from analyses conducted on the correct trials ($n = 660$, 55%). The productions from Experiment 2 were analysed using the acoustic features chosen in the feature-selection procedure described in Experiment 1. All analyses were performed on the residual values of these features, after removing speaker and item variance with the method described in Experiment 1.

Focus location

The overall Wilks's Lambda was significant, $\Lambda = .085$, $\chi^2(24) = 1335$, $p < .001$, indicating that the acoustic features could differentiate subject focus from verb and object focus. In addition, the residual Wilks's Lambda was significant, $\Lambda = .306$, $\chi^2(11) = 641$, $p < .001$, indicating that the acoustic features could also discriminate verb focus from object focus (see Figure 6).

Leave-one-out classification correctly classified 93% of the productions. The model correctly classified subject focus 94% of the time, verb focus 90% of the time, and object focus 95% of the time.

The standardised canonical coefficients in the first two columns of Table 4 indicate that the acoustic features contributing most to the discrimination of focus location are once again mean F0 and maximum intensity, though the

[8] In early pilots in which there was no feedback for incorrect responses, we observed that listeners were at chance in choosing the correct question.

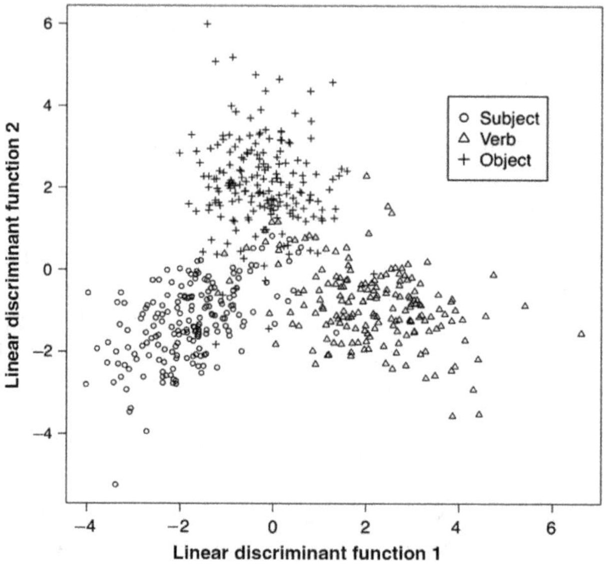

Figure 6. Separation of focus locations on two discriminant functions for Experiment 2. The figure illustrates an effective discrimination among the three groups. Productions of subject focus are clustered in the lower left quadrant of the plot; productions of verb focus are clustered in the lower right quadrant; productions of object focus are clustered in the lower half.

other two features are also contributing. In fact, inspection of the acoustic feature means in Figure 7 demonstrates that the highest value of every acoustic feature is associated with the intended focused item, with the exception of mean F0 when the subject is focused.

Focus type

Focus type—subject position. The overall Wilks's Lambda was significant, $\Lambda = .633$, $\chi^2(12) = 81.41$, $p < .001$, indicating that the acoustic features could discriminate between noncontrastive and contrastive focus better than chance. Leave-one-out classification correctly classified 75% of the productions. The model correctly classified noncontrastive focus 78% of the time and contrastive focus 71% of the time.

The standardised canonical discriminant function coefficients in Table 4 indicate that maximum intensity at all three locations (i.e., large intensity differences between the subject and verb and the subject and object) contributes most to classification. Figure 8 graphically presents the mean values of the four features, demonstrating that, in addition to intensity differences, contrastive focus is produced with longer duration and silence, as well as lower mean and maximum F0.

TABLE 4
Standardised canonica coefficients of all discriminant functions computed for Experiment 2

		Focus location		*Focus type*			
		Function 1	*Function 2*	*Subject focus*	*Verb focus*	*Object focus*	*Focus breadth*
Omelet	Duration + silence	−0.001	0.004	0.004	0.006	0.003	0.003
	Mean F0	−0.006	0.011	−0.003	0.005	−0.023	0.000
	Maximum F0	0.002	0.001	0.004	−0.009	−0.003	0.003
	Maximum intensity	−0.025	0.183	−0.052	−0.171	0.012	0.199
Fried	Duration + silence	0.007	−0.002	0.006	0.002	−0.007	0.005
	Mean F0	0.024	−0.005	0.001	−0.022	0.006	−0.025
	Maximum F0	0.001	−0.002	−0.007	0.001	0.003	0.003
	Maximum intensity	0.093	−0.016	−0.105	0.063	−0.084	0.011
Damon	Duration + silence	−0.002	−0.002	0.002	0.005	0.009	0.003
	Mean F0	0.003	0.021	−0.010	0.004	−0.009	0.007
	Maximum F0	−0.011	−0.015	−0.014	−0.012	−0.006	−0.005
	Maximum intensity	−0.067	−0.097	0.094	−0.014	0.010	−0.123

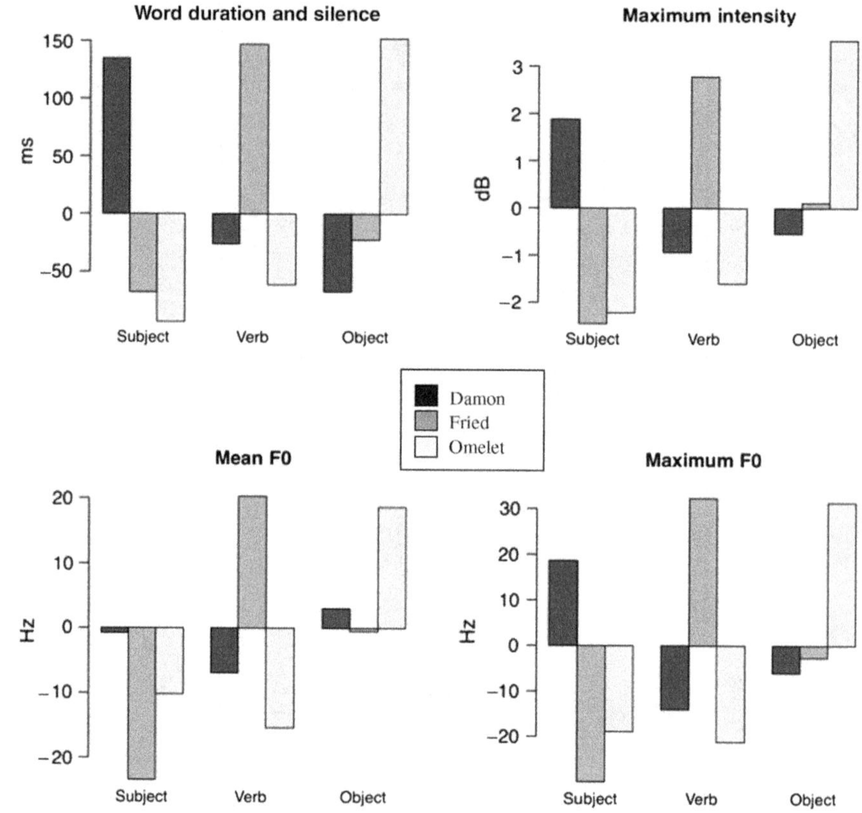

Figure 7. Values of the four discriminating acoustic features of productions of subject, verb, and object focus in Experiment 2.

Focus type—verb position. The overall Wilks's Lambda was significant, $\Lambda = .654$, $\chi^2(12) = 72.27$, $p < .001$, indicating that the acoustic features could discriminate between noncontrastive and contrastive focus better than chance. Leave-one-out classification correctly classified 72% of the productions. The model correctly classified noncontrastive focus 70% of the time and contrastive focus 75% of the time.

The standardised canonical discriminant function coefficients in Table 4 indicate that, once again, maximum intensity contributes most to classification. Figure 9 graphically presents the mean values of the four features, demonstrating that contrastive focus is produced with a higher maximum intensity, and a longer duration and silence, than noncontrastive focus. Once again, noncontrastive focus is produced with higher mean and maximum F0 than contrastive focus.

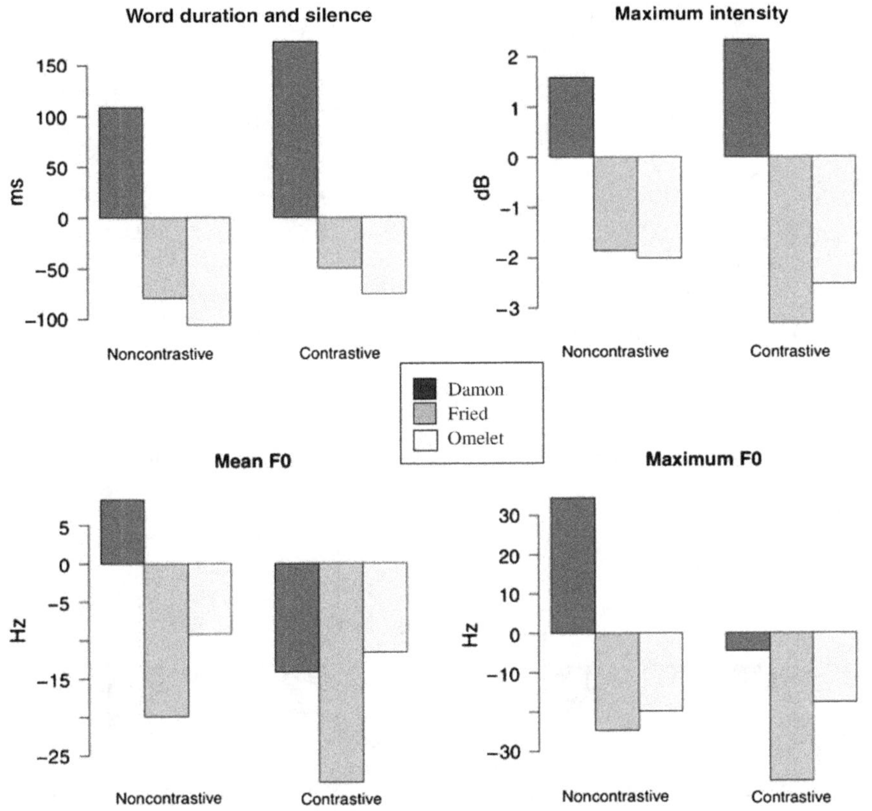

Figure 8. Values of the four discriminating acoustic features of productions of noncontrastive and contrastive object focus when *Damon* is focused in Experiment 2.

Focus type—object position. The overall Wilks's Lambda was significant, $\Lambda = .793$, $\chi^2(12) = 41.3$, $p < .001$, indicating that the acoustic features could discriminate between noncontrastive and contrastive focus better than chance. Leave-one-out classification correctly classified 67% of the productions. The model correctly classified noncontrastive focus 69% of the time and contrastive focus 66% of the time.

The standardised canonical discriminant function coefficients in Table 4 indicate that contrastive focus is most strongly associated with lower mean F0. Figure 10 graphically presents the mean values of the four features, demonstrating that contrastive focus is produced with a lower mean and maximum F0 than noncontrastive focus.

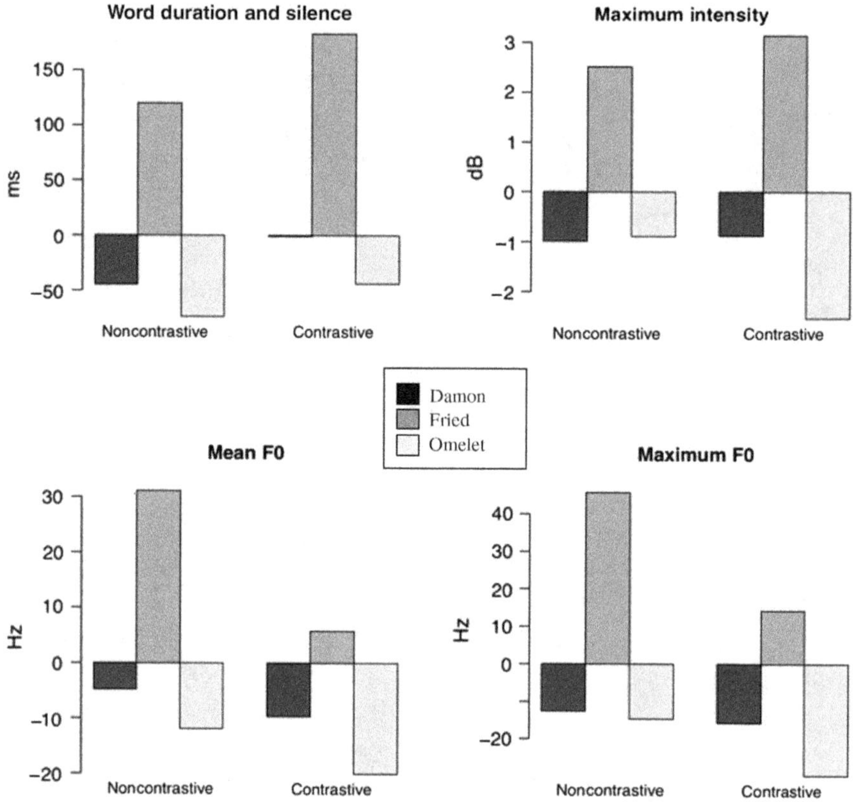

Figure 9. Values of the four discriminating acoustic features of productions of noncontrastive and contrastive object focus when *fried* is focused in Experiment 2.

Focus breadth

The overall Wilks's Lambda was significant, $\Lambda = .59$, $\chi^2(12) = 148$, $p < .001$, indicating that the acoustic features could differentiate between wide focus and narrow object focus. Leave-one-out classification correctly classified 84% of productions; wide focus was correctly classified 77% of the time, and object focus was correctly classified 88% of the time.

The standard canonical coefficients in the "Focus breadth" column of Table 4 indicate that the maximum intensity of each of the target words contributes most strongly to the discrimination of focus breadth. Although intensity is contributing most strongly to classification, inspection of the acoustic means in Figure 11 indicates that wide focus is marked by lesser prominence on the object, reflected in shorter duration, lower F0, and lower

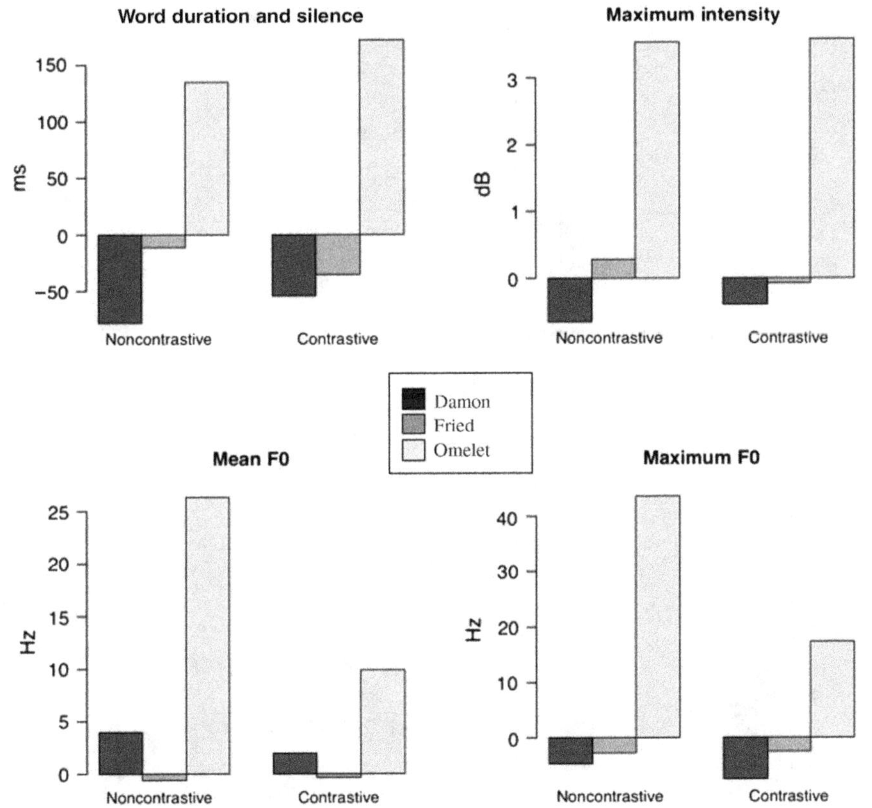

Figure 10. Values of the four discriminating acoustic features of productions of noncontrastive and contrastive object focus when *omelet* is focused in Experiment 2.

intensity; conversely, narrow object focus is marked by greater prominence on the object, reflected in longer duration, higher F0, and higher intensity.

Results—perception

Listeners' choices of question sorted by the intended question are plotted in Figure 12. Listeners' overall accuracy was 55%. To determine whether listeners were able to determine the speaker's intended sentence meaning, we assessed, for focus location and focus type, whether each subject's proportion of correct responses exceeded chance; wide focus productions were excluded from the analysis, so that chance performance for focus location was 0.33, and chance performance for focus type was 0.5. Results demonstrated that listeners were able to successfully identify focus location: all 13 subjects'

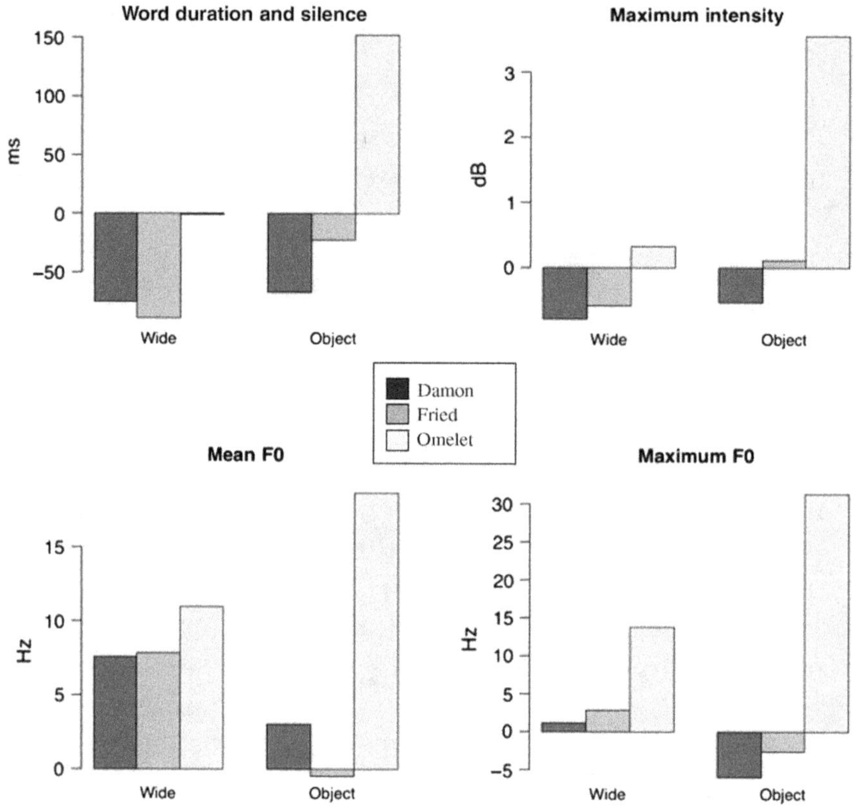

Figure 11. Values of the four discriminating acoustic features of productions of wide and narrow object focus in Experiment 2.

performance significantly exceeded chance performance, $p = .05$, two-tailed. However, listeners were unable to successfully identify focus type: only three of 13 subjects performed at above-chance levels (based on the binomial distribution), $p = .05$, two-tailed. To investigate focus breadth, we assessed, for wide focus and narrow object focus separately, whether each subject's proportion of correct responses exceeded chance. For these analyses, we excluded subject and verb focus productions, so that chance performance was 0.33 for wide focus, and 0.67 for narrow object focus. Results demonstrated that listeners were moderately successful at identifying focus breadth: six out of 13 subjects identified wide focus at rates above chance, and nine out of 13 subjects identified narrow object focus at levels above chance $p = .05$, two-tailed.

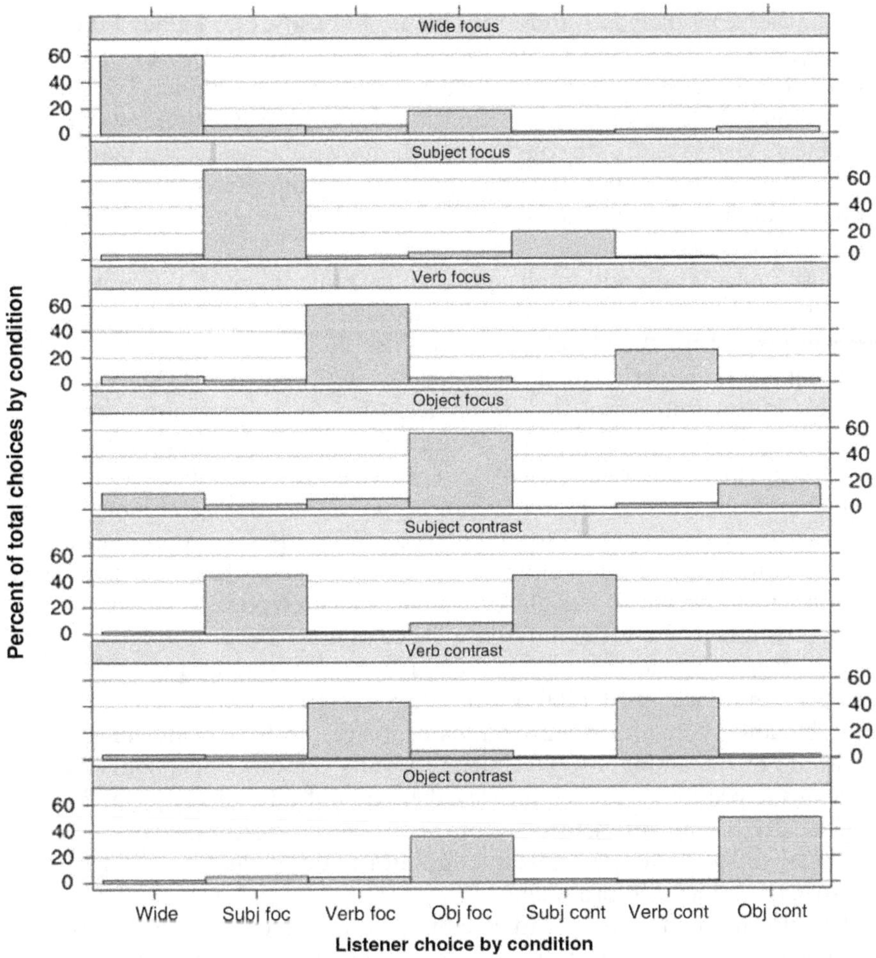

Figure 12. Percentage of Listeners' condition choice by intended sentence type for Experiment 2.

Discussion

The production results replicated the two main findings from Experiment 1, and provided evidence for acoustic discrimination of focus type across sentence positions as well. First, these results demonstrated that focused elements have longer durations than given elements, incur larger F0 excursions, are more likely to be followed by silence, and are produced with greater intensity. Second, speakers consistently differentiate between wide and narrow focus by producing the object in the latter case with higher F0, longer duration, and greater intensity. Specifically, although object focus was indicated by increased duration, higher intensity, and higher F0 on the object than on the subject or the verb, wide focus was indicated by comparatively greater duration, higher intensity, and higher F0 on the subject and the verb, and shorter duration, lower intensity, and lower F0 on the object. These results are consistent with those obtained by Baumann et al. (2006), who demonstrated that narrow focus on an element was indicated with longer duration and a higher F0 peak than wide focus on an event encompassing that element.

Most importantly, although speakers in Experiment 1 did not differentiate conditions with and without an explicit contrast set for the focused element (except for the object position), these conditions were differentiated by speakers in Experiment 2, at every syntactic position. There are two possible interpretations of this difference. First, in Experiment 1, speakers produced only four trials in each of the seven conditions, whereas speakers in Experiment 2 (and Experiment 3, reported below), produced 14 trials in each condition, resulting in greater power in the latter two experiments. The fact that, in Experiment 2, speakers successfully discriminated contrastive and noncontrastive focus in all three positions, suggests that the lack of such an effect in Experiment 1 could be due to a lack of power.

As mentioned above, the difference in the findings between Experiments 1 and 2 is also consistent with results from Albritton et al. (1996) and Snedeker and Trueswell (2003) who demonstrated that speakers do not disambiguate syntactically ambiguous sentences with prosody unless they are aware of the ambiguity. The current results demonstrate a similar effect for acoustic prominence, such that speakers do not differentiate two kinds of acoustically prominent elements (contrastively vs. noncontrastively focused elements) unless they are aware of the information structure ambiguity in the structures they are producing.

The discriminant analyses indicated that contrastively focused words were produced with longer durations and higher intensity than noncontrastively focused words, but that noncontrastively focused words were produced with higher F0 than contrastively focused words.[9] This latter finding is surprising when compared to some previous studies. For example, Ladd and Morton (1997) found that higher F0 and larger F0 range is perceived as more "emphatic" or "contrastive" by listeners. Similarly, Ito and Speer (2008) demonstrated that contrastively focused words were produced with higher F0 than noncontrastive ones. Given the unexpected results, we inspected individual pitch tracks to more closely observe the F0 patterns across the

[9] Importantly, the F0 results are not artefacts of the residualisation procedure employed to remove variance from the acoustic features due to speaker and item. The same numerical pattern of F0 values is observed whether residualisation is employed or not, though only the residualised acoustic features successfully discriminate focus type.

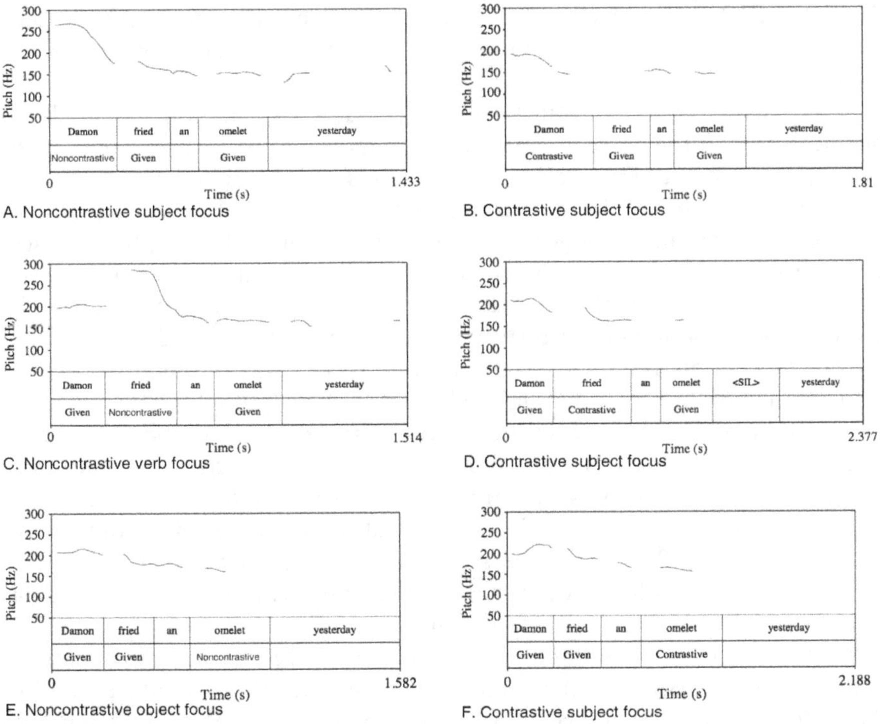

Figure 13. Pitch tracks for noncontrastive and contrastive subject focus, noncontrastive and contrastive verb focus, and noncontrastive and contrastive object focus, respectively, from a typical speaker from Experiment 2.

entire utterances. The pitch tracks presented in Figure 13 were generated from the productions of a typical speaker, and they exemplify the higher F0 observed for noncontrastive focus than contrastive focus in the subject position (A vs. B) and verb position (C vs. D). Contrastive focus on the object is realised with the same F0 as noncontrastive focus on the object (E vs. F).

Note that our finding that noncontrastive focus is realised with higher F0 than contrastive focus is still consistent with the claim that contrastive focus is more prominent than noncontrastive focus. As the graphs in Figures 8–10, and the pitch tracks in Figure 13 indicate, although contrastive elements were consistently produced with lower pitch, they were also consistently produced with longer durations and greater intensity than noncontrastive elements. As reviewed in the introduction, there is evidence that intensity and duration can convey prominence more effectively than higher pitch (Beckman, 1986; Fry, 1955; Kochanski et al., 2005; Lieberman, 1960; Turk &

Sawusch, 1996). Our data are therefore consistent with prior claims that contrastive focus is produced with greater prominence than noncontrastive focus.

As discussed in the introduction, the production elicitation and analysis methods used in the current experiment are more robust than methods used in many previous studies, including those whose results are inconsistent with the current findings. In particular, the current results are based on productions from naïve subjects in a communication task, and the analyses were performed on data with speaker and item variability removed. The current results are therefore more likely to reflect the underlying generalisations about the relationship between acoustics and meaning.

The perception results only partially mirrored the production results. Consistent with the production results, listeners were highly successful in discriminating among the three focus locations. In contrast to the production results, however, listeners were only moderately successful in identifying focus type (noncontrastive vs. contrastive) from the speakers' productions. In fact, listeners most often confused noncontrastive focus with contrastive focus (see Figure 12). These results suggest that, even though speakers may be consistently signalling focus type with their prosody, listeners are not able to exploit those cues for comprehension.

With regard to focus breadth, the perception results are incompatible with a strong version of the focus projection hypothesis (Selkirk, 1995). According to this hypothesis, an acoustic prominence on the object NP can be interpreted as marking the entire clause as focused. Listeners are therefore predicted to treat a production with an acoustically prominent object NP as ambiguous between the narrow object focus reading and the wide focus reading. However, as can be seen in Figure 12, listeners correctly identified narrow object noncontrastive focus 57% of the time, interpreting it as wide focus only 13% of the time, and correctly identified narrow object contrastive focus 49% of the time, interpreting it as wide focus only 6% of the time. These results are not consistent with Gussenhoven's (1983) finding that listeners cannot reliably distinguish between narrow objects focus and wide focus.

Experiments 1 and 2 provide evidence that speakers systematically indicate focus location and focus breadth using a set of four acoustic features. These experiments further suggest that speakers can, but don't always, indicate focus type. In particular, the results suggest that speakers prosodically differentiate contrastive from noncontrastive focus only when they are aware of the meaning ambiguity and/or when the task involves conveying a particular meaning to a listener.

To further investigate the speakers' ability to prosodically differentiate contrastive from noncontrastive focus, we conducted an additional experiment. Acoustic analyses in Experiments 1 and 2 were limited to three words (i.e., subject, verb, and object) in the sentence. However, in natural productions, speakers' utterances are often prefaced by attribution expressions (e.g., *I think* or *I heard*), or expressions of emotional attitudes towards the described events (e.g., *Unfortunately* or *Luckily*). It is therefore possible that contrastive information might be partially conveyed by prosodically manipulating these kinds of expressions. We explored this possibility in Experiment 3, in which we had speakers produce target SVO constructions with a preamble. Experiment 3 was also intended to serve as a replication of the results of Experiment 2; in particular, the somewhat unexpected finding that noncontrastive focus is produced with higher F0 than contrastive focus.

EXPERIMENT 3

Method

Participants

Fourteen pairs of participants (speakers and listeners) were recorded for this experiment. Subjects were MIT students or members of the surrounding community. All reported being native speakers of American English. None had participated in Experiments 1 or 2. Participants were paid for their participation.

Materials

The materials for Experiment 3 were identical to those from Experiment 1 described above with the exception that an attribution expression (I heard that) was appended to the beginning of each target sentence.

Procedure

The procedure for Experiment 3 was identical to that for Experiment 2.

Results—production

Four speaker–listener pairs were excluded as the listener did not achieve comprehension accuracy greater than 20%. These exclusions left a total of 10 pairs of participants whose responses were analysed. Eighty-one of the 980 recorded trials (8%) were excluded because (1) the speaker failed to produce the correct words; (2) the speaker was disfluent; or (3) the production was poorly recorded. Analyses were performed on all trials, and on the subset of trials for which the listener correctly identified the question the speaker produced the sentence in response to. As in Experiment 2, the results were very similar for the two analyses. For brevity of presentation, we present results from analyses conducted on the correct trials ($n = 632$, 70%).

Focus location

In order to investigate the contribution of the prosody of *I heard that* to the differentiation of the focus type in Experiment 2, we performed a stepwise discriminant function analysis which included as predictors measures of the four acoustic features we had selected initially (duration + silence, mean F0; maximum F0, and maximum intensity) (1) for the subject (Damon), verb (fried), and object (omelet) and (2) for each of the first three words of the sentence (*I*, *heard*, *that*). Of the 24 predictors included in the stepwise discriminant function analysis, the features which resulted in the best discrimination of focus type were (1) the duration + silence of *I*; (2) the maximum F0 of *I*; and (3) the maximum intensity of *I*. Based on these results, we conducted an additional analysis in which we included a subset of 16 predictors: the duration + silence, mean F0, maximum F0, and maximum intensity of the subject, verb, object, and *I*.

As in Experiments 1 and 2, we conducted a discriminant analysis to determine whether the measures of (1) duration + silence; (2) maximum F0; (3) mean F0; and (4) maximum intensity of the four critical words in the sentence could predict focus location.

The overall Wilks's Lambda was significant, $\Lambda = .058$, $\chi^2(32) = 1467.09$, $p < .001$, indicating that the acoustic features could differentiate subject focus from verb and object focus. In addition, the residual Wilks's Lambda was significant, $\Lambda = .275$, $\chi^2(15) = 664.75$, $p < .001$, indicating that the acoustic features could also discriminate verb focus from object focus (Figure 14). Leave-one-out classification procedure correctly classified 97% of the productions. At individual focus locations, the model correctly classified subject focus 96% of the time, verb focus 97% of the time, and object focus 97% of the time (Figure 15).

Focus type

Focus type—subject position. The overall Wilks's Lambda was significant, $\Lambda = .39$, $\chi^2(16) = 157.44$, $p < .001$, indicating that the acoustic features could successfully discriminate between noncontrastive and contrastive focus. Leave-one-out classification correctly classified 85% of the productions. The model correctly classified noncontrastive focus 85% of the time and contrastive focus 85% of the time.

The standardised canonical discriminant function coefficients in Table 5 indicate that maximum intensity overall, and specifically, maximum intensity on "I", is contributing most to classification. Figure 16 graphically presents the mean values of the four features, demonstrating that, in addition to intensity differences, contrastive focus is produced with longer duration and silence, and with lower mean and maximum F0.

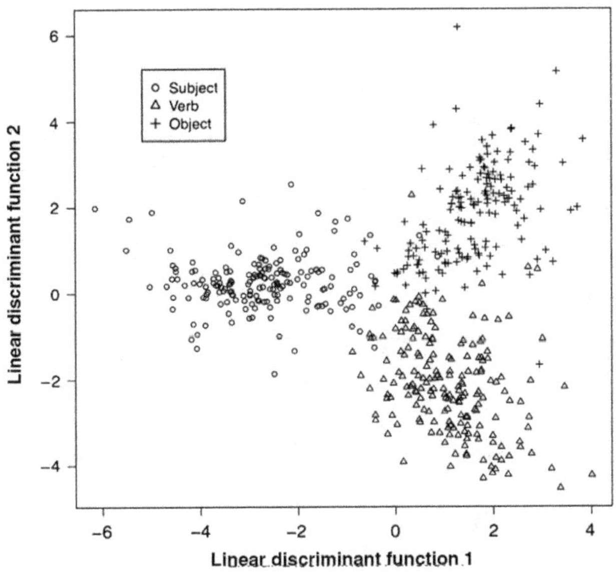

Figure 14. Separation of focus locations on two discriminant functions for Experiment 3. The figure illustrates an effective discrimination among the three groups. Productions of subject focus are clustered in the left half of the plot; productions of verb focus are clustered in the lower right quadrant; productions of object focus are clustered in the upper right quadrant.

Focus type—verb position. The overall Wilks's Lambda was significant, $\Lambda = .46$, $\chi^2(16) = 139.28$, $p < .001$, indicating that the acoustic features could discriminate between noncontrastive and contrastive focus. Leave-one-out classification correctly classified 80% of the productions. The model correctly classified noncontrastive focus 86% of the time and contrastive focus 74% of the time.

The standardised canonical discriminant function coefficients in Table 5 indicate that, intensity on *I* is contributing the most to classification. Figure 17 graphically presents the mean values of the four features, demonstrating that contrastive focus is produced with a higher maximum intensity, and a longer duration and silence, than noncontrastive focus. As in Experiment 2, noncontrastive focus is produced with higher mean and maximum F0 than contrastive focus.

Focus type—object position. The overall Wilks's Lambda was significant, $\Lambda = .40$, $\chi^2(16) = 133.37$, $p < .001$, indicating that the acoustic features could discriminate between noncontrastive and contrastive focus better than chance. Leave-one-out classification correctly classified 83% of the productions. The model correctly classified noncontrastive focus 89% of the time and contrastive focus 76% of the time.

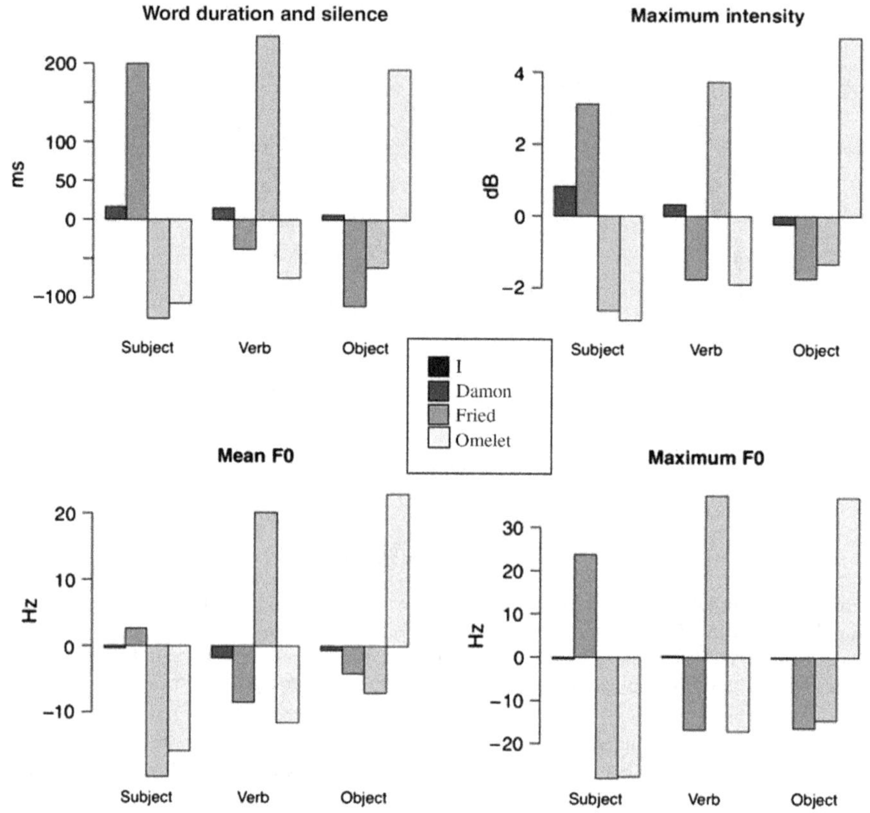

Figure 15. Values of the four discriminating acoustic features of productions of subject, verb, and object focus in Experiment 3.

The standardised canonical discriminant function coefficients in Table 5 indicate that intensity and mean F0 on *I* are contributing the most to accurate classification. Figure 18 graphically presents the mean values of the four features, demonstrating that contrastive focus is produced with a higher mean and maximum F0 than noncontrastive focus.

Focus breadth

The overall Wilks's Lambda was significant, $\Lambda = .48$, $\chi^2(16) = 148$, $p <$ .001, indicating that the acoustic features could differentiate between wide focus and narrow object focus. Leave-one-out classification correctly classified 87% of productions; wide focus was correctly classified 79% of the time, and object focus was correctly classified 92% of the time.

TABLE 5
Standardised canonical coefficients of all discriminant functions computed for Experiment 3

		Focus location		*Focus type*			
		Function 1	*Function 2*	*Subject focus*	*Verb focus*	*Object focus*	*Focus breadth*
Omelet	Duration + silence	0.002	0.003	0.000	0.000	0.003	0.002
	Mean F0	0.005	0.012	−0.013	−0.009	0.005	−0.010
	Maximum F0	0.003	0.000	0.005	0.006	−0.003	0.003
	Maximum intensity	0.069	0.106	−0.037	−0.011	0.007	0.151
Fried	Duration + silence	0.001	−0.003	0.000	0.002	0.001	0.005
	Mean F0	0.025	−0.021	−0.001	−0.002	−0.001	−0.006
	Maximum F0	−0.005	−0.002	−0.001	−0.005	0.000	−0.003
	Maximum intensity	0.091	−0.077	−0.086	−0.015	0.027	−0.048
Damon	Duration + silence	−0.003	0.000	0.002	0.000	0.000	0.002
	Mean F0	0.011	0.011	−0.011	−0.020	0.019	−0.003
	Maximum F0	−0.014	−0.003	−0.001	0.007	−0.014	−0.008
	Maximum intensity	−0.147	0.011	0.159	−0.006	−0.064	−0.123
I	Duration + silence	0.000	0.000	0.004	0.005	0.005	−0.001
	Mean F0	−0.005	0.000	−0.013	−0.008	−0.003	−0.009
	Maximum F0	0.004	−0.002	0.017	0.010	0.014	0.005
	Maximum intensity	−0.021	−0.017	0.142	0.133	0.126	0.014

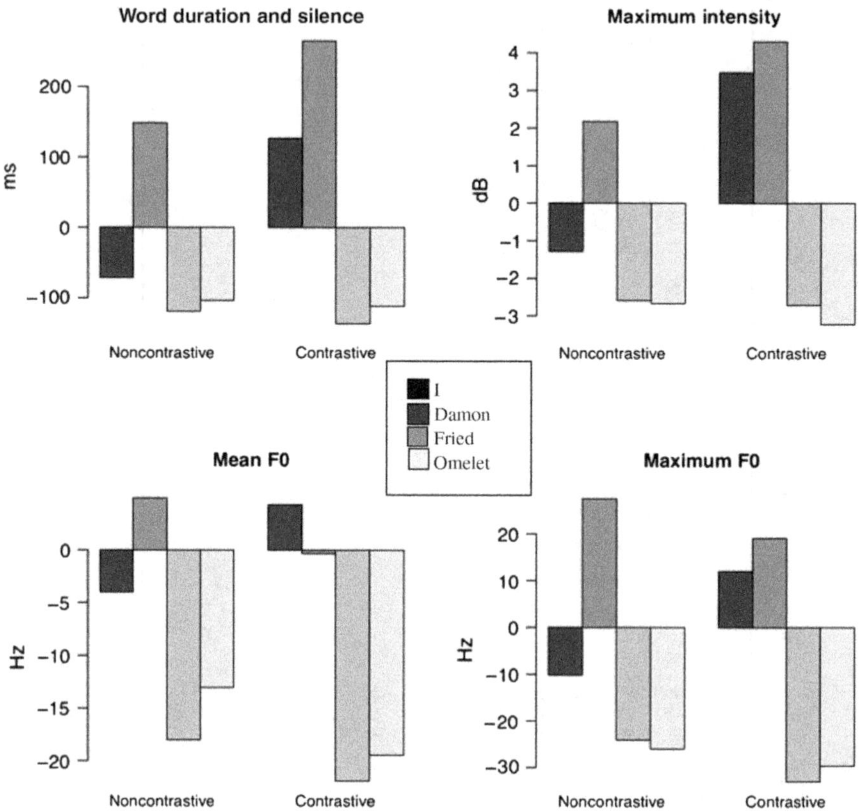

Figure 16. Values of the four discriminating acoustic features of productions of noncontrastive and contrastive object focus when *Damon* is focused in Experiment 3.

The standard canonical coefficients in the "Focus Breadth" column of Table 5 indicate that the maximum intensity of each of the target words contributes most strongly to the discrimination of focus breadth. Specifically, greater intensity on the object is a strong predictor of object focus; less intensity on the subject and the verb is a strong predictor of wide focus. Although intensity is contributing most strongly to classification, inspection of the acoustic means in Figure 19 indicates that wide focus is indicated by lesser prominence on the object, reflected in shorter duration, lower F0, and lower intensity; conversely, narrow object focus is indicated by greater prominence on the object, reflected in longer duration, higher F0, and higher intensity.

Results—perception

Listeners' overall accuracy percentage by condition is plotted in Figure 20. Listeners' overall accuracy was 70%. As described in Experiment 2, we

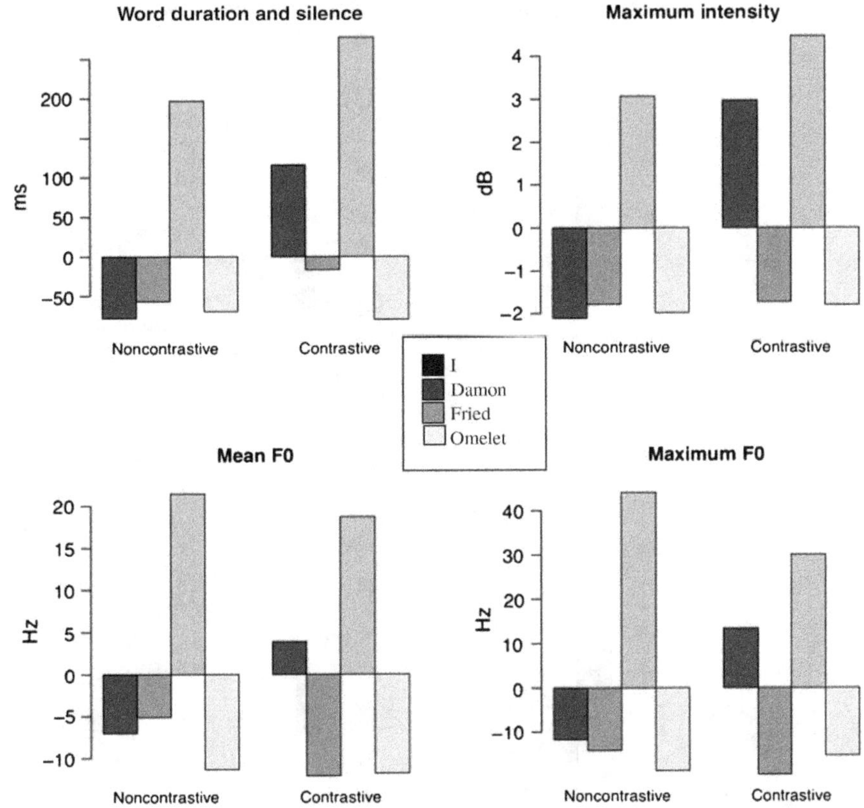

Figure 17. Values of the four discriminating acoustic features of productions of noncontrastive and contrastive object focus when *fried* is focused in Experiment 3.

compared each subject's responses to chance performance. Results demonstrated that listeners were able to successfully identify focus location, as all 10 subjects' performance significantly exceeded chance performance, $p = .05$, two-tailed. Listeners were moderately successful at discriminating focus type, as six of 10 subjects' performance exceeded chance levels, $p = .05$, two-tailed. Listeners successfully identified focus breadth as eight out of 10 subjects identified wide focus at rates above chance, and eight out of 10 subjects identified narrow object focus at levels above chance $p = .05$, two-tailed.

Discussion

Experiment 3 was conducted in order to (1) investigate whether speakers could differentiate focus type with prosody if the sentences contained an attribution expression that could convey contrastive information, in addition

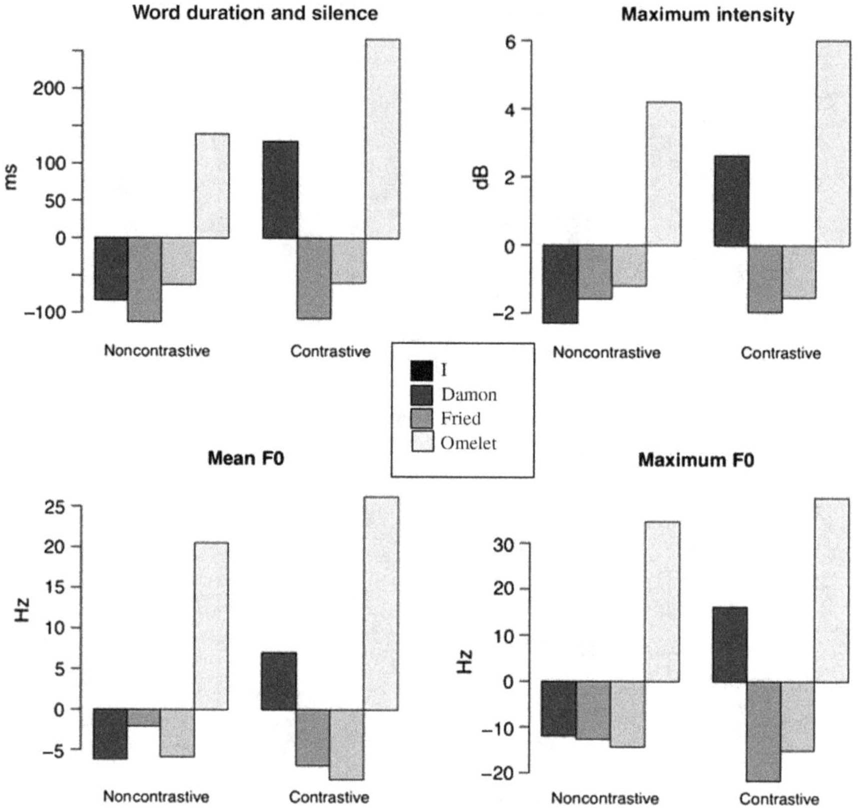

Figure 18. Values of the four discriminating acoustic features of productions of noncontrastive and contrastive object focus when *omelet* is focused in Experiment 3.

to the elements that describe the target event, and (2) replicate the results of Experiment 2.

With regard to the second goal, the production results of Experiment 3 successfully replicated the findings from Experiments 1 and 2. As in Experiments 1 and 2, speakers systematically differentiated focus location and focus breadth with a combination of duration, intensity, and F0 cues. Furthermore, as in Experiment 2, noncontrastive focus was produced with higher F0 than contrastive focus (though only when the subject or verb was focused), and contrastive focus was always produced with greater duration and intensity. As discussed above, these F0 results contrast with prior findings (Bartels & Kingston, 1994; Couper-Kuhlen, 1984; Ladd & Morton, 1997; Ito & Speer, 2008), but can be interpreted in light of more recent evidence that higher intensity is a stronger cue to greater prominence than higher pitch (Kochanski et al., 2005).

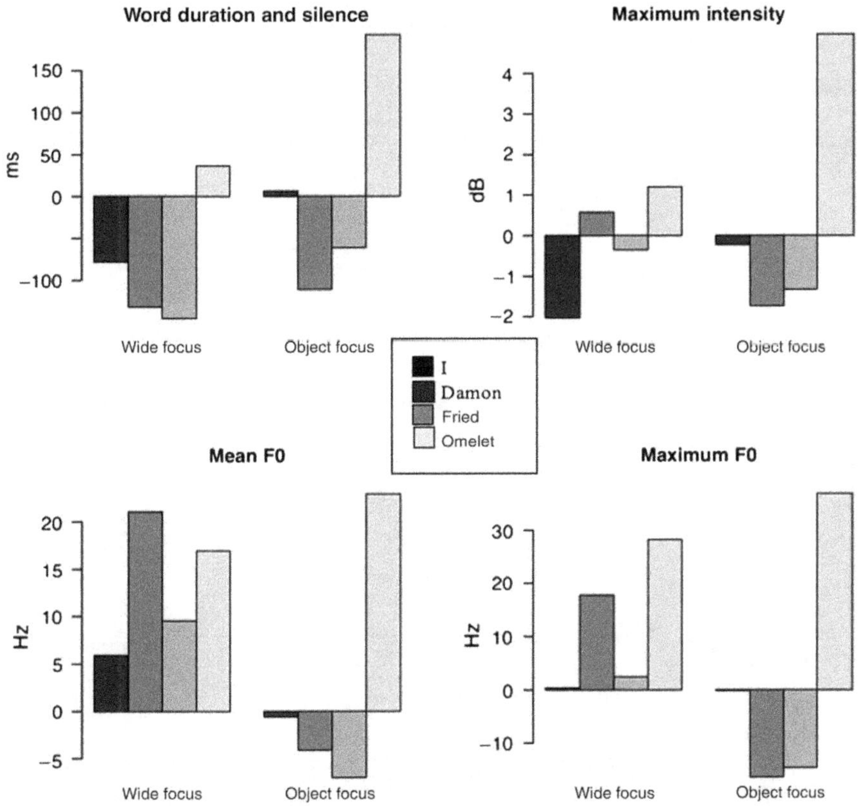

Figure 19. Values of the four discriminating acoustic features of productions of wide and narrow object focus in Experiment 3.

In addition, results from Experiment 3 demonstrated that the strongest cues to discrimination of focus type were the acoustics of *I* (from the attribution expression *I heard that*). Specifically, in contrastive focus conditions, the word *I* was produced with longer duration, higher intensity, and higher mean F0 and maximum F0. Indeed, discrimination of focus type in Experiment 3 was far better than in Experiment 2. It therefore appears that speakers can manipulate prosody on sentence elements outside of the target clause (e.g., in attribution expressions) to convey contrastiveness.

The perception results demonstrated that listeners could accurately determine focus location, similar to the results of Experiment 2. Furthermore, listeners were more accurate in determining focus type than listeners in Experiment 2. This increase in accuracy was likely due to speakers' tendency to prosodically mark *I* in the contrastive conditions.

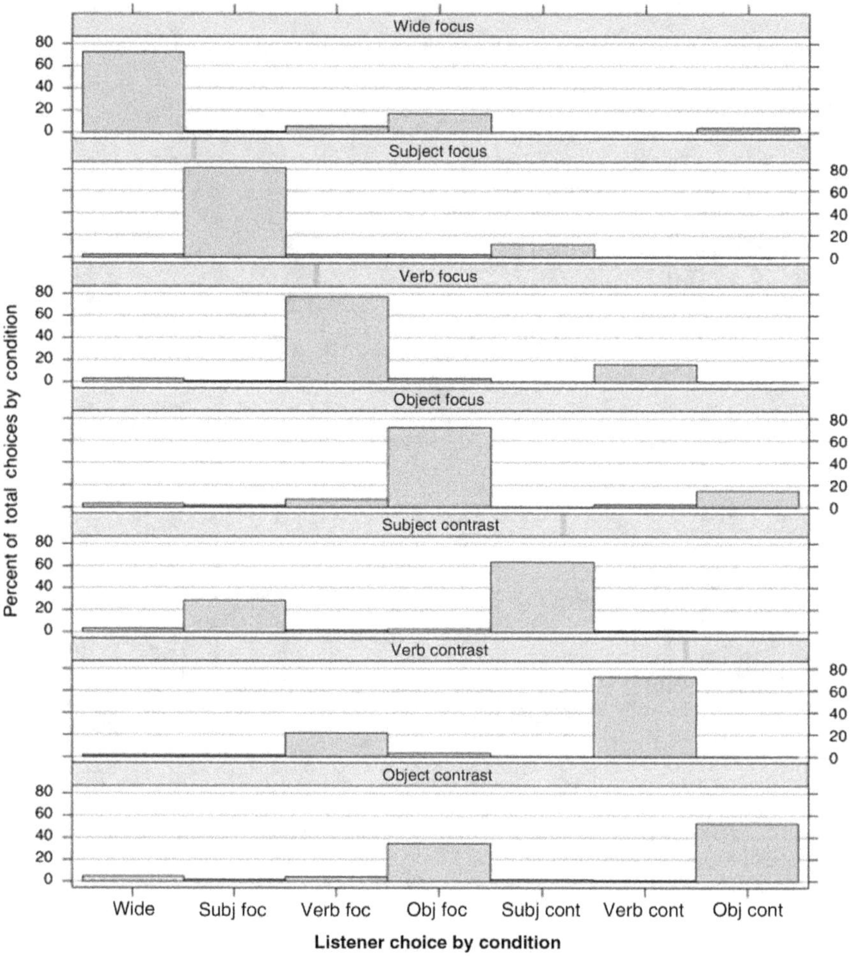

Figure 20. Percentage of listeners' condition choice by intended sentence type for Experiment 3.

GENERAL DISCUSSION

The three experiments reported in the current paper explored the ways in which focus location, focus type, and focus breadth are conveyed with prosody. In each experiment, naïve speakers and listeners engaged in tasks in which the information status of sentence elements in SVO sentences was manipulated via preceding questions. The prosody of the target sentences was analysed using a series of classification models to select a subset from the set of acoustic features that would best be able to discriminate among focus locations and between focus types. In addition, in Experiments 2 and 3, the production results were complemented by the perception results that demonstrated listeners' ability to use the prosodic cues in the speakers' utterances to arrive at the intended meaning.

At the beginning of the paper, we posed three questions about the relationship between acoustics and information structure: (1) do speakers mark information structure prosodically, and, to the extent they do; (2) what are the acoustic features associated with different aspects of information structure; and (3) how well can listeners retrieve this information from the signal? We are now in a position to answer these questions.

First, we have demonstrated that speakers systematically provide prosodic cues to the location of focused material. Across all three experiments, speakers provided cues to focus location whether or not the task explicitly demanded it, across subject, verb and object positions. In addition, across all three experiments, speakers systematically provided cues to focus breadth, such that wide focus was prosodically differentiated from narrow object focus. Finally, we found that speakers can, but don't always, prosodically differentiate contrastive and noncontrastive focus. Specifically, speakers did not prosodically differentiate focus type in Experiment 1, but they did so in Experiment 2 and, even more strongly, in Experiment 3. As discussed above, the fact that speakers did not differentiate focus type in Experiment 1, where they were plausibly not aware of the meaning ambiguity, but did differentiate between contrastive and noncontrastive focus in Experiments 2 and 3, where the task made the meanings more salient, is consistent with results from the literature on intonational boundary production demonstrating that speakers only produce disambiguating boundaries when they are aware of the syntactic ambiguity (Albritton et al., 1996; Snedeker & Trueswell, 2003; cf. Kraljic & Brennan, 2005; Schafer et al., 2000). Furthermore, the results from Experiment 3, where the critical words were preceded by the attribution expression *I heard that*, demonstrated even stronger differentiation of focus type than in Experiment 2, suggesting that speakers are able to convey contrastiveness using words outside of the clause containing the contrastively focused element.

To answer the question of which acoustic features are associated with different meaning categories of information structure, we conducted a series of discriminant function analyses with the goal of objectively identifying which of 24 measures of duration, intensity, and F0 allowed for the best discrimination of conditions. Across all experiments, and across different sentence positions, the best differentiation among conditions was achieved using the following four features: word duration, maximum word intensity, mean F0, and maximum F0. These results are consistent with many previous studies in the literature, implicating these features in conveying aspects of information structure. An important contribution of the current studies is that these results were obtained using a quantitative analysis across many naïve speakers and items, and are therefore more likely to be generalisable.

These data also demonstrate how exactly these four features are used in conveying different aspects of information structure. With regard to focus location, focused material is produced with longer duration, higher F0, and greater intensity than given material. With regard to focus type, noncontrastive focus is realised with higher mean and maximum F0 on the focused word than contrastive focus, whereas contrastive focus is realised with greater intensity on the focused word than noncontrastive focus. Finally, with regard to focus breadth, narrow focus on the object is indicated by higher F0 and longer duration on the object, compared to wide focus, and wide focus is conveyed by higher intensity and F0, and longer duration on prefocal words.

To answer the question of how well listeners can retrieve prosodic information from the signal, we included a perception task in Experiments 2 and 3. When the relevant acoustic cues were present in the input (as demonstrated by successful classification by the models), listeners were also able to classify the utterances, although not quite as successfully as the models. Furthermore, the fact that the model always achieved high classification accuracy suggests that the utterances contained enough acoustic information to make these discriminations, and that we did not leave any particularly informative acoustic features out of the analyses.

Implications for theories of the mapping of acoustics to meaning

While our production and perception results are compatible with a direct relationship between acoustics and meaning, they are also consistent with the existence of mediating phonological categories, as in the intonational phonology framework. For example, a standard assumption within intonational phonology is that there is a phonological category "accent" mediating acoustics and semantic focus, such that a focused element is accented, and an unfocused element is unaccented (e.g., Brown, 1983). Our production and perception results are compatible with this assumption. First, if speakers are signalling focus location by means of placing acoustic features corresponding to a +accent category on focused elements, then we would expect to see strong acoustic differences between focused and given elements, as we have observed. Moreover, if listeners perceive accents categorically, then we would predict successful discrimination of productions on the basis of focus location, as we have observed. Second, when the object is focused, it will be accented, resulting in higher acoustic measures on the object compared to other positions, as we have observed. Furthermore, in the wide focus condition, the subject, verb, and object—all of which are focused—would all receive accents, and would therefore be more acoustically similar to one another than they are in the wide focus condition. This difference in accent placement would lead to successful discrimination between wide and narrow focus by listeners, as we have observed. Finally, there has been much debate in the intonational phonology literature about whether there is a phonological category +/− contrastive. The results of our experiments are perhaps best explained without such a category. In particular, if speakers accent focused elements without differentiating between contrastive and noncontrastive focus, then we would expect similar acoustic results between productions which differ only on focus type, which would lead to poor discrimination by the model. Moreover, listeners would not be successful in discriminating focus type, as we have observed. Our experimental results are thus compatible with an intonational phonological approach which includes an accent category mediating acoustics and meaning, but no category for contrastiveness. Importantly, although our results do not support a categorical difference between noncontrastive and contrastive focus, they do not exclude the possibility that speakers can mark these distinctions with relative differences in prominence (Calhoun, 2006).

Implications for semantic theories of information structure

The current results are relevant to two open questions in the semantics of information structure: (1) whether contrastive and noncontrastive focus constitute two distinct categories and (2) whether focus on the object of a verb can project to the entire verb phrase.

As described in the introduction, Rooth (1992) proposed an account of focus which makes no distinction between noncontrastive focus and contrastive focus. (6) shows the F-marking (focus-marking) that Rooth's account would assign to the conditions in Experiments 1 and 2. Importantly, words and phrases which evoke alternatives, either explicit or implicit, are considered focused (i.e., F-marked).

(6) a. Subject, subject contrast: *Damon*$_F$ fried an omelet last night.
b. Verb, verb contrast: Damon *fried*$_F$ an omelet last night.
c. Object, object contrast: Damon fried *an omelet*$_F$ last night.
d. Wide: [Damon *fried an omelet*]$_F$ last night.

Our results provide tentative support for Rooth's proposal that F-marked constituents do not differ substantively as a function of whether the alternatives they evoke are explicit (our contrastive condition) or implicit (our noncontrastive condition). Although speakers differentiated these two conditions acoustically, they only did so when the contrast between the conditions was made salient (Experiments 2 and 3). Moreover, even when speakers did mark this distinction, listeners were unable to consistently use this information to recover the intended meaning (Experiment 2). These results suggest that there are no consistent semantic differences between foci with explicit alternatives in the discourse and those with implicit alternatives.

The second semantic issue that these results bear upon is whether narrow focus on the object can project to the entire verb phrase. According to the theory of focus projection proposed in Selkirk (1984, 1995), an acoustic prominence on the direct object (*omelet*) can project focus to the entire verb phrase (*fried an omelet*) and then up to the entire clause/sentence. Gussenhoven (1983, 1999) makes a similar claim. Both Selkirk's and Gussenhoven's accounts therefore predict that a verb phrase with a prominence on the object would be ambiguous between a narrow object focus interpretation and a wide focus interpretation. Neither the production nor the perception results were consistent with this prediction. In production, speakers distinguished between narrow object focus and wide focus, and in perception, listeners were able to distinguish these two conditions.

One aspect of the production results (the acoustic realisation of the subject) for the narrow object focus and wide focus conditions is, however, predicted by both Selkirk and Gussenhoven's accounts. In particular, in the wide focus condition, the subject constitutes new information while in the narrow object focus condition the subject is given. Selkirk and Gussenhoven both predict that the subject would be more acoustically prominent in the wide focus condition than in the narrow object focus condition. This is exactly what we observed (especially in Experiments 1 and 3). Nevertheless, as discussed above, speakers also systematically disambiguated wide focus from narrow object focus across all three experiments with their realisation of the object and the verb. Specifically, wide focus was produced with stable or increasing duration, intensity, and F0 across the subject, verb, and object; narrow object focus, on the other hand, was characterised by shorter duration and lower intensity and F0 on the subject and verb, followed by a steep increase in each of these values on the object.

Similar to our production findings, Gussenhoven (1983) found that, at least in some productions, wide focus differed from narrow object focus in that the verb was more prominent under wide focus. Listeners, however, were unable to use this acoustic information to distinguish wide focus from narrow object focus. Gussenhoven took this result as evidence that the two conditions are not reliably distinguished (consistent with his theory). Our results did not replicate this production/perception asymmetry: listeners are able to successfully classify productions with a single prominence on *omelet* as indicating narrow object focus and did not confuse these productions with those from the wide focus condition.

Methodological contributions

A further contribution of the current research to investigations of prosody and information structure is methodological. With regard to the methods used to elicit productions, we used multiple, untrained speakers to ensure that our results are generaliseable to all speakers and are not due to speakers' prior beliefs about what pattern of acoustic prominence signals a particular meaning (see Gibson & Fedorenko, 2010, for similar arguments with respect to linguistic judgements). Furthermore, unlike most previous work in which productions were selected for analysis based on perceptual differentiability or on ratings of the appropriateness of prosodic contours, we elicited and selected for analysis productions using a meaning task. Thus our analyses were based on the communicative function of language. Finally, we did not exclude speakers based on our perceptions of their productions; speakers were excluded for failure to provide information to their listeners.

The analyses used here also constitute an improvement over previous analyses. First, using discriminant modelling, we were able to simultaneously investigate the contribution of multiple sentence elements to acoustic differentiation of conditions. Second, we demonstrated that residualisation is a useful method for controlling for variability among speakers and lexical items. For example, preliminary analyses performed on the productions from Experiment 2 without first computing residual values of the acoustic features revealed a 13% average increase in values of Wilks' Lambda (where lower values indicate better discrimination) and a 7% average decrease in classification accuracy. Third, the discriminant modelling proved successful in objectively determining which acoustic features were the biggest contributors to differences among conditions. The success of the analyses used in the current studies is encouraging for future investigations of prosodic phenomena previously considered too variable for study in a laboratory setting with naïve speakers.

One question that arises from the current set of studies is, to what extent the current results can be generalised to all speakers and all sentences. In production studies, there is always a trade-off between (1) having enough control over what participants are producing to ensure sufficient data for analysis, and (2) ensuring that the speech is as natural as possible. In Experiment 1, we attempted to elicit natural productions, but failed to find systematic differences between focus types. In making the speakers' task—to help their listeners choose the correct question-type—explicit, we may have also encouraged speakers to produce these sentences with somewhat exaggerated prosody. Further experiments and corpus investigations will be necessary to determine whether speakers normally produce contrastive meanings in this way.

In conclusion, the current studies used rigorous scientific methods to explore several important questions about the acoustic correlates of information structure. By providing some initial answers to these questions, along with some implications for semantic theory, and by offering a novel, objective way to approach these and other questions, these studies open the door to future investigations of the relationship between acoustics and meaning.

REFERENCES

Albritton, D., McKoon, G., & Ratcliff, R. (1996). Reliability of prosodic cues for resolving syntactic ambiguity. *Journal of Experimental Psychology: Learning, Memory, and Cognition, 22*, 714–735.

Bartels, C., & Kingston, J. (1994). Salient pitch cues in the perception of contrastive focus. In P. Boach & R. Van der Sandt (Eds.), *Focus & natural language processing* [IBM Working Papers on Logic and Linguistics, v. 6], (pp. 1–10), Heidelberg, Germany.

Baumann, S., Grice, M., & Steindamm, S. (2006). Prosodic marking of focus domains-categorical or gradient? In *Proceedings of speech prosody* (pp. 301–304). Dresden, Germany.

Beckman, M. (1986). *Stress and non-stress accent* [Netherlands Phonetic Archives Series No. 7]. Dordrecht, The Netherlands: Foris.

Beckman, M., & Ayers Elam, G. (1997). *Guidelines for ToBI labeling, version 3*. Ohio State University.

Birch, S., & Clifton, C. (1995). Focus, accent, and argument structure: Effects on language comprehension. *Language and Speech, 38*(4), 365–391.

Birner, B. (1994). Information status and word order: An analysis of english inversion. *Language, 70*(2), 233–259.

Boersma, P., & Weenink, D. (2006). *Praat: Doing phonetics by computer (Version 4.3.10)* [Computer program]. Retrieved from http://www.praat.org/

Bolinger, D. (1961). Contrastive accent and contrastive stress. *Language, 37*, 83–96.

Breen, M., Dilley, L., Gibson, E., Bolivar, M., & Kraemer, J. (2006, March). *Advances in prosodic annotation: A test of inter-coder reliability for the RaP (Rhythm and Pitch) and ToBI (Tones and Break Indices) transcription systems.* Poster presented at the 19th CUNY Conference on Human Sentence Processing, New York, NY.

Brown, G. (1983). Prosodic structures and the given/new distinction. In D. R. Ladd & A. Cutler (Eds.), *Prosody: Models and measurements* (pp. 67–77). Berlin, Germany: Springer.

Calhoun, S. (2005, January). It's the difference that matters: An argument for contextually-grounded acoustic intonational phonology. In *Linguistics Society of America Annual Meeting.* Oakland, CA.

Calhoun, S. (2006). *Information structure and the prosodic structure of English: A probabilistic relationship* (PhD thesis, University of Edinburgh, UK).

Chafe, W. (1976). Givenness, contrastiveness, definiteness, subjects, *topics and points of view*. In C. N. Li (Ed.), *Subject and topic* (pp. 27–55). New York: Academic Press.

Clark, E. V., & Clark, H. H. (1978). Universals, relativity, and language processing. In J. H. Greenberg (Ed.), *Universals of human language* (Vol. I, pp. 225–277). Stanford, CA: Stanford University Press.

Cooper, W., Eady, S., & Mueller, P. (1985). Acoustical aspects of contrastive stress in question-answer contexts. *Journal of Acoustical Society of America*, *77*(6), 2142–2156.

Couper-Kuhlen, E. (1984). A new look at contrastive intonation. In R. Watts & U. Weidman (Eds.), *Modes of interpretation: Essays presented to Ernst Leisi* (pp. 137–158). Tübingen, Germany: Gunter Narr Verlag.

Cutler, A. (1977). The context-independence of "Intonational Meaning". *Chicago Linguistic Society*, (CLS 13), 104–115.

Dilley, L. C. (2005). *The phonetics and phonology of tonal systems*. Unpublished Ph.D. dissertation. Massachusetts Institute of Technology, Cambridge, MA.

Eady, S. J., & Cooper, W. E. (1986). Speech intonation and focus location in matched statements and questions. *Journal of the Acoustical Society of America*, *80*, 402–415.

Féry, C., & Krifka, M. (2008). Information structure: Notional distinctions, ways of expression. In P. van Sterkenburg (Ed.), *Unity and diversity of languages* (pp. 123–136). Amsterdam: John Benjamins.

Fry, D. B. (1955). Duration and intensity as physical correlates of linguistic stress. *Journal of the Acoustical Society of America*, *27*, 765–768.

Gibson, E., & Fedorenko, E. (2010). Weak quantitative standards in linguistics research. *Trends in Cognitive Sciences, 14,* 233–234.

Gussenhoven, C. (1983). Testing the reality of focus domains. *Language and Speech*, *26*, 61–80.

Gussenhoven, C. (1999). On the limits of focus projection in English. In P. Bosch & R. van der Sandt (Eds.), *Focus: Linguistic, cognitive, and computational perspectives* (pp. 43–55). Cambridge, UK: Cambridge University Press.

Gussenhoven, C., Repp, B. H., Rietveld, A., Rump, W. H., & Terken, J. (1997). The perceptual prominence of fundamental frequency peaks. *Journal of the Acoustical Society of America*, *102*, 3009–3022.

Halliday, M. (1967). *Intonation and grammar in British English*. The Hague: Mouton.

Hawkins, S., & Warren, P. (1991). Factors affecting the given-new distinction in speech. In *Proceedings of the 12th International Congress of Phonetic Sciences* (pp. 66–69). Aix en Provence, France.

Ito, K., & Speer, S. (2008). Anticipatory effects of intonation: Eye movements during instructed visual search. *Journal of Memory and Language*, *58*, 541–573.

Ito, K., Speer, S. R., & Beckman, M. E. (2004). Informational status and pitch accent distribution in spontaneous dialogues in English. In *Proceedings of the International Conference on Spoken Language Processing* (pp. 279–282). Nara, Japan.

Jackendoff, R. (1972). *Semantic interpretation in generative grammar*. Cambridge, MA: MIT Press.

Jaeger, T. F. (2008). Categorical data analysis: Away from ANOVAs (transformation or not) and towards logit mixed models. *Journal of Memory and Language*, *59*, 434–446.

Kochanski, G., Grabe, E., Coleman, J., & Rosner, B. (2005). Loudness predicts prominence: Fundamental frequency lends little. *The Journal of the Acoustical Society of America*, *118*(2), 1038–1054.

Krahmer, E., & Swerts, M. (2001). On the alleged existence of contrastive accents. *Speech Communication*, *34*, 391–405.

Kraljic, T., & Brennan, S. E. (2005). Prosodic disambiguation of syntactic structure: For the speaker or for the addressee? *Cognitive Psychology*, *50*, 194–231.

Ladd, D. R. (1996). *Intonational phonology*. [Cambridge Studies in Linguistics 79]. Cambridge, UK: Cambridge University Press.

Ladd, D. R., & Morton, R. (1997). The perception of intonational emphasis: Continuous or categorical? *Journal of Phonetics, 25*, 313–342.

Lambrecht, K. (2001). A framework for the analysis of cleft constructions. *Linguistics, 39*, 463–516.

Lieberman, P. (1960). Some acoustic correlates of word stress in American English. *The Journal of the Acoustical Society of America, 32*(4), 451–454.

Molnar, V. (2002). Information structure in a cross-linguistic perspective. In H. Hasselgård, S. Johansson, B. Behrens, & C. Fabricius-Hansen (Eds.), *Language and computers* (Vol. 39, pp. 147–161). Amsterdam, The Netherlands: Rodopi.

Paul, H. (1880). *Prinzipien der sprachgeschichte* [Principles of the history of language]. Tübingen, Germany: Max Niemeyer.

Pell, M. D. (2001) Influence of emotion and focus location on prosody in matched statements and questions. *Journal of the Acoustical Society of America, 109*(4), 1668–1680.

Pierrehumbert, J. B. (1980). *The phonology and phonetics of English intonation.* Unpublished dissertation, Massachusetts Institute of Technology, Cambridge, MA.

Pierrehumbert, J., & Hirschberg, J. (1990). The meaning of intonational contours in the interpretation of discourse. In P. R. Cohen, J. Morgan, & M. E. Pollack (Eds.), *Intentions in communication* (pp. 271–311). Cambridge, MA: MIT Press.

Pierrehumbert, J., & Steele, S. (1989). Categories of tonal alignment in English. *Phonetica, 46*, 181–196.

Pitrelli, J., Beckman, M., & Hirschberg, J. (1994). Evaluation of prosodic transcription labeling reliability in the ToBI framework. In *Proceedings of the International Conference on Spoken Language Processing* (pp. 123–126). Yokohama, Japan.

Rietveld, A. C. M., & Gussenhoven, C. (1985). On the relation between pitch excursion size and prominence. *Journal of Phonetics, 13*, 299–308.

Rochemont, M. S. (1986). *Focus in generative grammar.* Amsterdam, Philadelphia: John Benjamins.

Rooth, M. (1985). *Association with focus.* Doctoral thesis, University of Massachusetts Amherst, MA.

Rooth, M. (1992). A theory of focus interpretation. *Natural Language Semantics, 1*, 75–116.

Rump, H. H., & Collier, R. (1996). Focus conditions and the prominence of pitch-accented syllables. *Language and Speech, 39*, 1–17.

Schafer, A. J., Speer, S. R., Warren, P., & White, S. D. (2000). Intonational disambiguation in sentence production and comprehension. *Journal of Psycholinguistic Research, 29*, 169–182.

Schwarzchild, R. (1999). GIVENness, AvoidF and other constraints on the placement of accent. *Natural Language Semantics, 7*, 141–177.

Selkirk, E. (1984). *Phonology and syntax: The relation between sound and structure.* Cambridge, MA: MIT Press.

Selkirk, E. (1995). Sentence prosody: Intonation, stress, and phrasing. In J. Goldsmith (Ed.), *The handbook of phonological theory* (pp. 550–569). Oxford: Blackwell.

Shriberg, E., Stolcke, A., Hakkani-Tur, D., & Tur, G. (2000). Prosody-based automatic segmentation of speech into sentences and topics. *Speech Communication, 32*, 127–154.

Shriberg, E., Bates, R., Taylor, P., Stolcke, A., Jurafsky, D., Ries, K., . . . Van Ess-Dykema, C. (1998). Can prosody aid the automatic classification of dialog acts in conversational speech? *Language and Speech, 41*(3–4), 439–487.

Silverman, K. E. A., Beckman, M., Pierrehumbert, J., Ostendorf, M., Wightman, C. W. S., Price, P., et al. (1992). ToBI: A standard scheme for labeling prosody. In *Proceedings of the 2nd International Conference on Spoken Language Processing* (pp. 867–879). Banff, Canada.

Sluijter, A., & van Heuven, V. (1996). Spectral balance as an acoustic correlate of linguistic stress. *Journal of the Acoustical Society of America, 100*, 2471–2485.

Snedeker, J., & Trueswell, J. (2003). Using prosody to avoid ambiguity: Effects of speaker awareness and referential contest. *Journal of Memory and Language, 48*, 103–130.

Stalnaker, R. (2002). Common ground. *Linguistics and Philosophy, 25*, 701–721.

Syrdal, A., & McGory, J. (2000). Inter-transcriber reliability of ToBI prosodic labeling. In *Proceedings of the International Conference on Spoken Language Processing* (pp. 235–238). Beijing, China.

Terken, J. (1991). Fundamental frequency and perceived prominence accented syllables. *Journal of the Acoustical Society of America, 89*, 1768–1776.

't Hart, J., Collier, R., & Cohen, A. (1990). *A perceptual study of intonation.* Cambridge, UK: Cambridge University Press.

Turk, A., & Sawusch, J. (1996). The processing of duration and intensity cues to prominence. *Journal of the Acoustical Society of America, 99*, 3782–3790.

Welby, P. (2003). Effects of pitch accent position, type, and status on focus projection. *Language and Speech, 46*, 53–81.

Wightman, C. W., Shattuck-Hufnagel, S., Ostendorf, M., & Price, P. J. (1992). Segmental durations in the vicinity of prosodic phrase boundaries. *Journal of the Acoustical Society of America, 91*(3), 1707–1717.

Xu, Y., & Xu, C. X. (2005). Phonetic realization of focus in English declarative intonation. *Journal of Phonetics, 33*, 159–197.

Yoon, T., Chavarria, S., Cole, J., & Hasegawa-Johnson, M. (2004). Intertranscriber reliability of prosodic labeling on telephone conversation using ToBI. In *Proceedings of the International Conference on Spoken Language Processing* (pp. 2729–2732). Nara, Japan.

APPENDIX 1

Experiment 1 items

Full items are recoverable as follows: Question A is always "What happened last night?" Questions B–D are wh-questions about the subject, verb, and object, respectively. Questions E–G are questions which introduce the explicit alternative subject, verb, or object, indicated in parentheses.

1. Question A: What happened last night?
   Question B: Who fed a bunny last night?
   Question C: What did Damon do to a bunny last night?
   Question D: What did Damon feed last night?
   Question E: Did Jenny feed a bunny last night?
   Question F: Did Damon pet a bunny last night?
   Question G: Did Damon feed a baby last night?
   Response: Damon fed a bunny last night.
2. Damon (Lauren) caught (pet) a bunny (a squirrel) last night.
3. Damon (Molly) burned (break) a candle (a log) last night.
4. Darren (Lauren) cleaned (eat) a carrot (a chicken) last night.
5. Darren (Molly) peeled (eat) a carrot (a potato) last night.
6. Darren (Nora) found (buy) a diamond (a ring) last night.
7. Darren (Jenny) sold (lose) a diamond (a sapphire) last night.
8. Jenny (Damon) found (lose) a dollar (a quarter) last night.
9. Jenny (Darren) sewed (rip) a dolly (a blanket) last night.
10. Jenny (Logan) read (open) an email (a letter) last night.
11. Jenny (Nolan) smelled (plant) a flower (a skunk) last night.
12. Lauren (Darren) burned (write) a letter (a magazine) last night.

13. Lauren (Logan) mailed (open) a letter (a package) last night.
14. Lauren (Nolan) read (write) a novel (a newspaper) last night.
15. Lauren (Damon) fried (bake) an omelet (a chicken) last night.
16. Logan (Molly) peeled (chop) an onion (an apple) last night.
17. Logan (Nora) fried (chop) an onion (a potato) last night.
18. Logan (Jenny) cleaned (buy) a pillow (a rug) last night.
19. Molly (Logan) dried (wash) a platter (a bowl) last night.
20. Molly (Nolan) sold (find) a platter (a vase) last night.
21. Molly (Damon) poured (drink) a smoothie (a cocktail) last night.
22. Nolan (Nora) pulled (push) a stroller (a sled) last night.
23. Nolan (Jenny) bought (sell) a stroller (a wheelbarrow) last night.
24. Nolan (Lauren) sewed (knit) a sweater (a quilt) last night.
25. Nora (Nolan) killed (trap) a termite (a cockroach) last night.
26. Nora (Damon) changed (wash) a toddler (a baby) last night.
27. Nora (Darren) fed (dress) a toddler (a bunny) last night.
28. Nora (Logan) pulled (push) a wagon (a wheelbarrow) last night.

APPENDIX 2

Items used for Experiments 2–3

Full items are recoverable as follows: Question A always asks "What happened _____?" where the blank corresponds to the temporal adverb. Questions B–D are wh-questions about the subject, verb, and object, respectively. Questions E–G are questions which introduce the explicit alternative subject, verb, or object, indicated in parentheses.

1. a. Context: What happened yesterday?
   b. Context: Who fried an omelet yesterday?
   c. Context: What did Damon do to an omelet yesterday?
   d. Context: What did Damon fry yesterday?
   e. Context: Did Harry fry an omelet yesterday?
   f. Context: Did Damon bake an omelet yesterday?
   g. Context: Did Damon fry a chicken yesterday?
   Target: No, Damon fried an omelet yesterday.
2. (I heard that) (No,) Megan (Jodi) sold (lose) her diamond (her sapphire) yesterday.
3. (I heard that) (No,) Mother (Daddy) dried (wash) a platter (a bowl) last night.
4. (I heard that) (No,) Norman (Kelly) read (write) an email (a letter) last night.
5. (I heard that) (No,) Lauren (Judy) poured (drink) a smoothie (a cocktail) this morning.
6. (I heard that) (No,) Nora (Jenny) sewed (rip) her dolly (her blanket) this morning.
7. (I heard that) (No,) Molly (Sarah) trimmed (wax) her eyebrows (her hair) on Tuesday.
8. (I heard that) (No,) Nolan (Steven) burned (break) a candle (a log) on Tuesday.
9. (I heard that) (No,) Logan (Billy) killed (trap) a termite (a cockroach) last week.
10. (I heard that) (No,) Radar (Fido) caught (lick) a bunny (a squirrel) last week.
11. (I heard that) (No,) Darren (Maggie) pulled (push) a stroller (a sled) on Sunday.
12. (I heard that) (No,) Brandon (Tommy) peeled (eat) a carrot (a potato) on Sunday.
13. (I heard that) (No,) Maren (Debbie) cleaned (buy) a pillow (a rug) on Friday.
14. (I heard that) (No,) Lindon (Kelly) fooled (fight) a bully (a teacher) on Friday.

LANGUAGE AND COGNITIVE PROCESSES
2010, 25 (7/8/9), 1099–1140

Psychology Press
Taylor & Francis Group

How does informativeness affect prosodic prominence?

Sasha Calhoun

School of Philosophy, Psychology & Language Sciences, University of Edinburgh, Edinburgh, UK

A key function of prosodic prominence is to mark the most *informative* words in an utterance. However, informativeness has been conceptualised as, e.g., focus, given/new status or predictability; it is not clear how these are related. Furthermore, prominence is constrained by metrical prosodic structure. We present a new framework for prominence production: informativeness and prosodic factors are constraints on the probabilistic alignment of words with metrical structure. Informativeness operates on two levels, focus and lexical "accentability" (predictability, part-of-speech). Foci align with nuclear accents, however, this is affected by prosodic and "accentability" constraints. Accent prediction models (nuclear, non-nuclear, or unaccented) are presented for the Switchboard corpus. Consistent with our predictions, nuclear accents are more likely later in a phrase, and on focused words. The likelihood of nuclear and non-nuclear accents is affected by prosodic constraints (e.g., rhythm) and "accentability". The implications for the role of prosody in language production are discussed.

Keywords: Prosody; Information structure; Discourse processing.

Correspondence should be addressed to Sasha Calhoun, School of Philosophy, Psychology & Language Sciences, University of Edinburgh, 7 George Square, Edinburgh EH8 9JZ, UK. E-mail: Sasha.Calhoun@ed.ac.uk

The research on which this work is based was completed as part of a Scottish Enterprise Edinburgh–Stanford Link grant. The author is now supported by a British Academy postdoctoral fellowship.

Thanks to Bob Ladd, Fernanda Ferreira and Mark Steedman for useful discussions in developing the ideas presented here and feedback on earlier drafts of this article. I am grateful to Jean Carletta, Jason Brenier, Neil Mayo, Dan Jurafsky, David Beaver, Jonathan Kilgour, and Shipra Dingare for their efforts in constructing the corpus, and Leonardo Badino for his Switchboard *n*-gram data. Also thanks to Martin Corley and an anonymous reviewer for useful suggestions on the statistical analysis and its presentation. Lastly, thanks to the audience at the Experimental and Theoretical Advances in Prosody conference at Cornell in April 2008 for encouraging feedback on the original presentation of this paper.

http://www.psypress.com/lcp DOI: 10.1080/01690965.2010.491682

INTRODUCTION

Words which are prosodically prominent are "highlighted" in relation to the words around them. One of the main reasons speakers do this is to mark the highlighted word as more *informative* than others in the utterance. However, informativeness has been conceptualised in a number of ways in linguistics, psycholinguistics, and computational linguistics, including focus/background, given/new status, or predictability (e.g., Aylett & Turk, 2004; Dahan, Tanenhaus, & Chambers, 2002; Halliday, 1968; Rooth, 1992). It is not clear if these are reducible to a single dimension of "informativeness". Furthermore, prosodic prominence seems to obey regularities which are not related to informativeness, i.e., it is part of *prosodic structure* (e.g., Ladd, 2008). We present a framework within which to understand how informativeness, and prosodic structure, affect the production of prominence in English. We claim informativeness and prosodic factors place constraints on the probabilistic mapping of words onto metrical prosodic structure (Calhoun, 2006, 2010). Informativeness operates broadly on two levels: information structure (focus) and "accentability" (predictability, referent accessibility). This mapping is affected by other constraints, including those inherent in prosodic structure itself.

In support of these proposals, logistic regression models are presented which predict accent status (nuclear, non-nuclear, or unaccented) in a corpus of annotated spontaneous speech, Switchboard (Calhoun et al., 2010; Godfrey, Holliman, & McDaniel, 1992). These models are used to demonstrate that the informativeness and prosodic constraints proposed influence the likelihood of a word being accented or nuclear accented as predicted. Regression analysis of a corpus is a useful method to simultaneously evaluate the effect of many interacting factors on a particular process. It also allows us to use spontaneous speech, which is particularly important for prosody, which can differ greatly from experimental to natural settings (e.g., see Ito & Speer, 2006). However, this does not imply that the regression models are actually realistic models of language production (see Jurafsky, 2003, pp. 89–90). They are rather an important first step to show what factors are involved in this complex system. To our knowledge, no previous study using a corpus of spontaneous speech has considered such a wide range of linguistically motivated predictors of accent status. However, evidently in future work, these results will need to be extended and confirmed using complementary experimental methods working directly with human subjects.

Below, existing treatments of informativeness in the literature are reviewed, along with their claimed effects on prosodic prominence in English. We then review literature on prominence itself. In the following section, we outline our constraint-based framework of how informativeness and prosodic factors affect the realisation of prominence, and relate this to predictions about the likelihood of accents and nuclear accents in our corpus. The accent prediction models are reported in Analysis 1, and the acoustic features of accents by metrical position in Analysis 2. Finally, the implications of these results are discussed, including a speculative discussion of the role of prosody in language production.

Informativeness

Informativeness has been conceptualised in quite different ways in different disciplines. It is not clear how these different notions relate to each other, or indeed, if they are reducible to a single dimension. Here these proposed functions of prominence are reviewed.

Within linguistics, the relationship between prosodic prominence and informativeness has long been described in terms of *information structure.* Each utterance in a discourse has an information structure, i.e., each entity, predication, etc. is marked as to how it refers back to, alters and/or updates the existing discourse model (e.g., Halliday, 1968; Steedman, 2000). The main linguistic marker of information structure is standardly held to be *focus* (e.g., Jackendoff, 1972; Rooth, 1992; Selkirk, 1995). F(ocus)-marked elements contain the asserted or contextually new information, while the presupposition, or contextually given information, is the *background.* This can be seen most clearly in question–answer pairs, such as the following (from the Switchboard corpus, in a conversation recorded in 1991 on the US federal budget deficit, CAPS marks the nuclear accent):

(1) B: my first comments on the budget...

A: ... what would be the first thing you'd cut? defence?

B: Surprisingly, no

B: I would cut [the PRISON systems]$_F$

The part of B's reply contained in the question is the background, while the response to the *wh*-phrase is the focus (F; only the last line is analysed). In standard accounts, the head of the *F*-marked phrase is pitch accented, while the background is unaccented (e.g., Jackendoff, 1972; Selkirk, 1995). However, there are problems with positing a direct relationship between accenting and focus (see Beaver, Clark, Flemming, Jaeger, & Wolters, 2007; Calhoun, 2006, 2010; German, Pierrehumbert, & Kaufmann, 2006), therefore this has alternatively been claimed to be a relationship between focus and nuclear accenting (Büring, 2006; Ladd, 1996, 2008; Truckenbrodt, 1999;

Wagner, 2005; see next section for definition of latter). Early psycholinguistic studies showed that focus plays an important role in sentence processing (see review in Cutler, Dahan, & van Donselaar, 1997, pp. 172–174). For instance, Cutler and Fodor (1979) showed focusing leads to faster responses in phoneme monitoring, even without extra prosodic prominence on the focused word; while Blutner and Sommer (1988) found that multiple meanings of homophones are activated for focused words, but not necessarily other words.

Focusing has been claimed to affect the interpretation of an utterance, e.g., its truth-conditions. It is claimed that *F*-marked elements introduce a presupposition of a contextually appropriate set of alternatives to the focus (Rooth, 1992). For example, for (1) this would be (notation from Rooth, 1992):

(2) $[[\text{I would cut [the prison systems]}_F]]^f =$

$\{\text{cut(I, x)}|x \in E\}$, where *{prison systems, defence, health care, . . . }* are elements of E

That is, the speaker introduces the presupposition that the proposition *cut(I, prison systems)* is one of a set of alternatives including *cut(I, defence)*, etc. The discourse interpretation of this is that the speaker contrasts *prison systems* within the set of *areas of the budget to cut* and thereby negates its alternatives in the discourse model.

Integral to many theories of focus is the claim that words which are *F*-marked (usually by a (nuclear) accent) can "project" focus to other elements in an utterance on the basis of either syntactic or phonological rules (e.g., Büring, 2006; Halliday, 1968; Jackendoff, 1972; Ladd, 2008; Selkirk, 1995; Truckenbrodt, 1999). This accounts for the fact that many utterances appear to have a "default" prosodic realisation which is compatible with multiple focus structures (e.g., see Selkirk, 1995). For instance, if (1) had been said with no preceding context, it could have a *broad focus* interpretation, i.e., the whole utterance would be the assertion (as opposed to *narrow focus,* such as (1), Ladd, 2008), as follows:

(3) $[\text{I would cut the PRISON systems}]_F$

There is debate about whether broad focus implies alternatives to the whole utterance; or whether there is a distinction between "information" focus which can apply to whole phrases and does not imply alternatives (e.g., (3)), and "contrastive" focus which applies to smaller units and does (e.g., (2); see Umbach, 2004). This is related to the debate about whether "contrast" is consistently marked prosodically, e.g., by higher or more emphatic accents on contrastive words (see (Ito & Speer, 2008; Watson, Gunlogson, & Tanenhaus, 2008) vs. (Breen, Fedorenko, Wagner, & Gibson, 2010 this issue; Krahmer & Swerts, 2001; Welby, 2003)), or by lowering the prenuclear pitch range (Xu & Xu, 2005). As these issues are somewhat tangential for us, they will be largely left aside.

Much work in psycholinguistics has looked at how prosodic prominence affects information or *reference status,* i.e., given or new in a discourse. Broadly, deaccentuation biases given reference, though it is less clear that accenting actively biases new reference (for review see Cutler et al., 1997, pp. 174–178; also Chen, den Os, & de Ruiter, 2007; Dahan et al., 2002; Watson, 2008). In production, though, there is far from a direct correspondence between given/new status and accenting (e.g., Bard & Aylett, 1999; Hirschberg, 1993). Further, reference status is not necessarily a dichotomy: the number, recency, and grammatical role of previous mentions are relevant (Terken & Hirschberg, 1994; Watson & Arnold, 2005); while entities that have not been mentioned before may still be mediated or inferable (Prince, 1981, 1992), influencing accent type and prominence (Baumann & Grice, 2006). It has been suggested, therefore, that there is a direct relationship between referent *accessibility* (cf. Ariel, 1990) and prominence (e.g., Watson, 2008). In the semantics literature, on the other hand, it is argued that "relative" givenness, not "discourse" givenness, is relevant to accenting (Schwarzschild, 1999; Wagner, 2006). For example, the realisation in (1) would be appropriate whether or not *prison systems* had been mentioned, as it is new in relation to the proposition *I would cut* ...

Finally, accent prediction studies in the computational literature have shown the effectiveness of much "lower-level" features. Part-of-speech (POS) type is consistently a good predictor of accent status, while uni and bigram predictability lead to small but consistent improvements on it (Chen & Hasegawa-Johnson, 2004; Hirschberg, 1993; Pan, McKeown, & Hirschberg, 2002). The less predictable a word, the more likely it is to be accented; or the more predictable a word, the less information it contains, and therefore the less likely to be prominent (cf. Aylett & Turk, 2004). Content words in particular are usually less predictable/have more information than function words. German et al. (2006) have shown experimentally that POS effects are separable from focus: speakers avoid accenting prepositions even when they are the only "new" or focused information in an utterance. Recently, Nenkova et al. (2007) found that *accent ratio,* i.e., the probability of a lexeme being accented, outperforms these predictability features (see definition in the "Corpus and Features" section of "Corpus Analysis 1"). This suggests storage of accent features on lexemes, e.g., Nenkova et al. (2007) found a reasonable number of fairly high-frequency lexemes in their data which were nonetheless usually accented (note this finding does not preclude accent storage at other levels of representation, e.g., syllables).

It is unclear how these different ways of characterising the relationship between informativeness and prominence fit together. Bolinger (1972) argued that they all reduce to relative informativeness, i.e., the accent is always on the most informative or "newsworthy" word in the utterance. Likewise, Aylett and Turk (2004) propose that there is a direct, inverse relationship between informativeness (or predictability) and prominence. These approaches, however, are hard to reconcile with the apparent regularity of broad focus effects in certain syntactic/prosodic structures regardless of lexical content, e.g., in utterances like *five pounds,* the greater stress is usually on *pounds* not *five,* when *five* is surely the most informative word (assuming the unit of currency is known to speaker and listener, see further in Calhoun, 2006, 2010; Ladd, 2008). Our findings will suggest that informativeness acts on broadly two levels: information structure (focus and relative givenness) and "accentability" (discourse givenness/accessibility, POS, predictability). In the final discussion, this division is motivated in terms of effects at different stages of language production.

Prosodic prominence

In many of the accounts above, prosodic prominence is equated with *(de)accenting.* Accented words are *prominent* or stressed at a phrasal level, i.e., they have higher pitch, greater duration and intensity, less spectral tilt (Sluijter & van Heuven, 1996), and often pitch movement on the lexically stressed syllable (e.g., see Terken & Hermes, 2000). However, rather than accents being independent events that are purely functionally motivated, we contend they are manifestations of strong nodes in metrical structure (cf. Büring, 2006; Ladd, 2008; Truckenbrodt, 1999; Wagner, 2005). In each phrase, syllables map onto a hierarchically organised metrical structure, i.e., a binary branching structure of *s(trong)* and *w(eak)* nodes (Liberman, 1979). Prominence is an inherently *relative* property: there can be multiple *levels* of prominence structure within a phrase beyond [$\pm$accent]. By definition, the node dominated entirely by strong nodes is the most "structurally" prominent, and carries the *nuclear* accent (see Figure 1, Liberman, 1975). It is obligatory in any well-formed (i.e., fluent) phrase and has particular perceptual importance (cf. Ladd, 2008, sec. 4.1.1). Nuclear accenting is much more closely linked to focus than accenting in general (Büring, 2006; Ladd, 1996, 2008; Truckenbrodt, 1999; Wagner, 2005). Strong nodes in prenuclear position may be realised with accents. (For practical reasons, to be explained below, these will be referred to as "prenuclear accents"; however, according to our proposal, these "accents" are the phonetic realisation of metrical stress, rather than directly marking functional properties of the words.) In postnuclear position, strong nodes must be significantly less phonetically prominent, and therefore tend to have

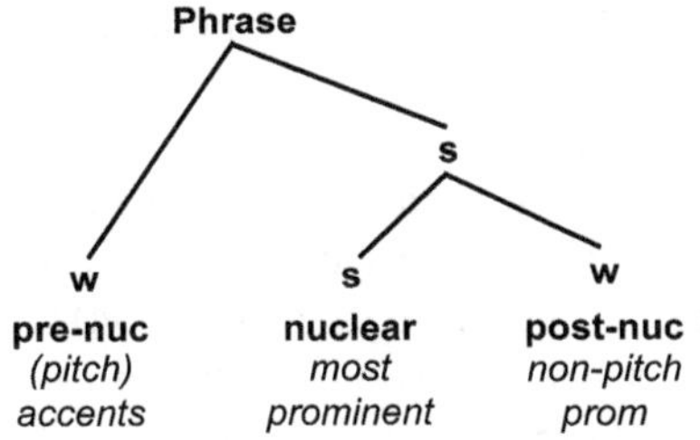

Figure 1. Basic phrase level metrical structure and resulting prominence realisation (cf. Liberman, 1979).

much lower pitch than the nuclear accent (at least if followed by a low phrase boundary, see Ladd, 2008, secs. 4.1.4 and 8.1.2).

Metrical structure has important properties which affect both the production and perception of prominence (see further in Calhoun, 2006 [ch. 3], 2010). In English, the structure is by default *right branching,* i.e., the right branch in each binary node is strong (Ladd, 2008; Liberman, 1979). At the level of the prosodic phrase, this means that the nuclear accent is much more likely to fall at the end of the phrase, given that at the top level of the prominence structure within each phrase, the right branch is likely to be strong (cf. Figure 2; Hayes, 1995; Selkirk, 1984; Truckenbrodt, 2006). In perception, the right-most accent is biased to be heard as the most "structurally" prominent, even if it is not the highest, longest, or loudest (Ayers, 1996; Hermes & Rump, 1994; Rump & Collier, 1996; Terken & Hermes, 2000). The nuclear accent is understood to be "more important" (cf. Ladd, 2008, sec. 7.1.2). Ayers (1996) has shown that response times in a phone-monitoring task were slower for downstepped nuclear accents than other nuclear accents (suggesting they are less phonetically prominent), but the type of nuclear accent (downstepped vs. not) did not affect times in a

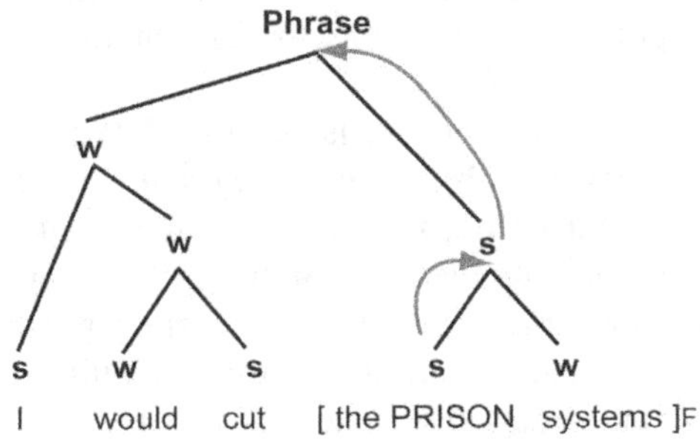

Figure 2. Metrical structure of (1). The accent on prison is nuclear as it is entirely dominated by strong nodes in the phrase (indicated by the arrows). The focus (F) aligns with the nuclear accent.

question-answering task (showing lower phonetic prominence does not affect perception of an accent's importance).

Metrical structure in English is *rhythmically* constrained: stress is manipulated to maintain an alternating pattern of strong and weak nodes at each level of the structure (see Hayes, 1995; Ramus, Nespor, & Mehler, 1999; Shattuck-Hufnagel, Ostendorf, & Ross, 1994). Prenuclear accents are much more susceptible to stress shift, i.e., leftward movement to avoid stress clash, than nuclear accents (Shattuck-Hufnagel et al., 1994); which is what we would expect if the position of nuclear accents were "fixed", and prenuclear accents adjusted in relation to it.

Early psycholinguistic studies showed that the nuclear accent is important for sentence processing (see review in Cutler et al., 1997, pp. 172–174). For instance, words bearing nuclear accents (or "sentence stress") are processed more efficiently (Cutler & Foss, 1977; Shields, McHugh, & Martin, 1974). Some studies found that rhythmic patterns may allow listeners to predict where the nuclear accent falls (Cutler, 1976; Shields et al., 1974), although later studies found only weak evidence for this (Pitt & Samuel, 1990).

The relationship between information structure and prosodic prominence

As we have just shown, there are competing concepts as to what informativeness is, each of which is said to affect prosodic prominence in different ways.

Within the linguistics literature, a number of recent proposals have emphasised the role of nuclear accents in signalling focus within metrical structure. We can think of this as a strong constraint on the mapping between words and metrical structure requiring foci to align with nuclear accents (cf. Büring, 2006; Ladd, 1996, 2008; Truckenbrodt, 1995; Wagner, 2005). For example, in (1), *prison systems* is the focus, and *prison* aligns with the nuclear accent (the nuclear accent falls on *prison* rather than *systems* because it is a compound noun; Prince & Liberman, 1977), as shown in Figure 2.

The position of the nuclear accent is central to the focus interpretation (i.e., (2)). A rendition with both *prison* and *systems* unaccented would not convey the same focus structure, i.e., the nuclear accent has to fall within *prison systems* to get the intended alternative set. In our framework, the scope of focus (narrow vs. broad) is affected by the right-branching bias. In this case, because the nuclear accent falls in the "default" position at the end of the phrase, focus can potentially project to the whole phrase (cf. (3)), i.e., the nuclear accent would fall on *prison* in the broad focus case too. (For more details on the relationship between prosodic structure and focus projection, see Calhoun, 2010.)

Work looking at informativeness in terms of features such as reference status or POS type/unigram predictability, etc. tends to assume a direct relationship between increased informativeness and either increased likelihood of accenting or increased phonetic prominence *per se*. As far as we are aware, there has been little work directly comparing how these different kinds of informativeness affect prominence in the same data set. We propose a framework to test and explain this relationship in language production. Our proposal is that each of the factors outlined above are constraints on the probabilistic mapping of words onto metrical prominence structure. This framework is developed into a full theory of the relationship between informativeness and prosodic prominence, and the implications for both production and perception, in other work (Calhoun, 2006, 2010). This study aims to establish what the key constraints on the realisation of prominence are. Each of the factors discussed above is therefore formulated in terms of features in our corpus. These features are tested to see if they affect the likelihood that a word is accented or nuclear accented in our corpus in the way predicted. From this it is concluded if each factor is a constraint on the mapping of words onto metrical structure.

In our framework, informativeness constraints operate on broadly two levels: focus and lexical "accentability". There is a strong constraint that foci should align with nuclear accents. Therefore, words which are foci are predicted to be likely to be nuclear accented. The effect of lexical "accentability" is separate: words which are more "accentable" because of their POS type, (lack of) predictability, reference status, or accent ratio are constrained to try to align with strong nodes in metrical structure. Therefore, they are predicted to be more likely to be accented in general. It is not clear from previous findings if all these "accentability" properties have distinct effects, so they are treated separately in the corpus model.

We also expect, within our framework, that the properties of prosodic structure itself place constraints on the realisation of prominence, along with the effects of informativeness factors. Therefore, purely prosodic factors should also affect the likelihood of accenting and nuclear accenting. There should be an approximate alternation of strong and weak nodes, because of rhythmic constraints, so prenuclear accents should not be too far apart. For example, in Figure 3, the accents on *I*, *cut,* and *systems* do not seem to imply that these words are focused, e.g., that there is an intended contrast between *cut* and another verb in this context. Such prenuclear accents are problematic for nonmetrically based theories, as there is no principled way to distinguish between them and prenuclear accents which do signal focus, e.g., without reference to the effect of rhythm, what signals that the accent on *cut* is not intended to mark it as focused (see Calhoun, 2006, 2010)? Postnuclear accents should have significantly lower fundamental frequency (F0; cf. Figure 1), as is the case in Figure 3.

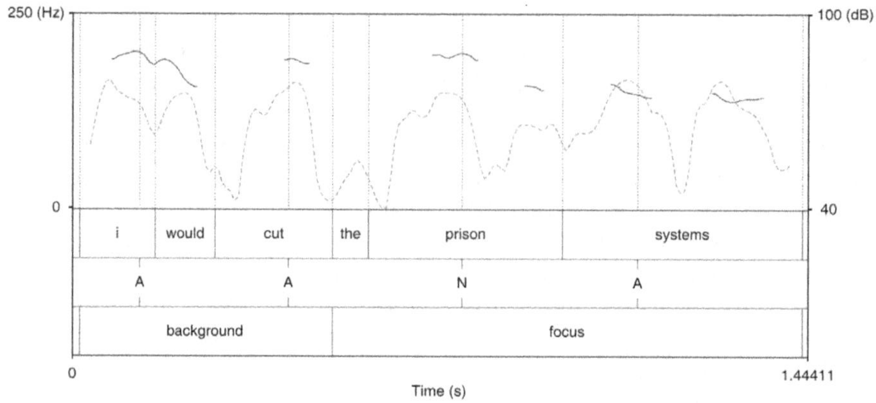

Figure 3. F0 trace (dark solid line) and intensity curve (light dashed line) for (1), along with the word transcript, accent, and focus annotation (A = full non-nuclear accent, N = nuclear accent; see "Corpus and Features" section of "Corpus Analysis 1" for further details).

Nuclear accents are predicted to be more likely to fall towards the end of the phrase they are in, as in (1), consistent with the right-branching bias. Since nuclear accents are defined by their position in metrical structure, phrasing constrains the realisation of prominence; so constraints on phrasing indirectly affect the likelihood of a word being accented or nuclear accented. For instance, there are physiological and processing constraints on phrase length: it becomes progressively harder to both compute and physically produce a prosodic phrase as it gets longer (cf. Watson & Gibson, 2004). Because of rhythmic constraints, the number of accents in a phrase is correlated with phrase length, as the ratio of accents to phrase length should remain stable across different phrase lengths. This implies that, as phrase length increases, each new accent is increasingly less likely, as a phrase of that length is less likely. It is also well-established that syntactic structure strongly constrains prosodic phrasing (e.g., see Ferreira, 2007; Selkirk, 1984; Shattuck-Hufnagel & Turk, 1996; Watson & Gibson, 2004). As this paper concerns prominence and not phrasing, the details of this relationship will not be discussed here. However, syntactic structure features should not affect accent likelihood directly. Rather, it is predicted that syntactic structure constrains prosodic structure, which in turn constrains prominence.

Finally, the overall emphasis in an utterance affects its prosodic realisation (although it does not change the structural prosodic relationships). As the overall pitch for a phrase increases, and/or the speaking rate slows, each strong node in the phrase will be realised with greater phonetic prominence. This increases the proportion of strong nodes that would be called (or annotated as) accented (within the commonly held view that "accenting" reflects some sort of objective level of prominence; Ladd, 2008, ch. 8). Note the discourse factors which influence overall emphasis will not be modelled.

CORPUS ANALYSIS 1: ACCENT PREDICTION

The first corpus analysis reports the results of accent prediction models built using a subset of the Switchboard corpus. The aim of these models is to test whether the constraints just described affect the likelihood of (nuclear) accents in the way claimed; in particular, whether prosodic constraints on the appearance of accents are consistent with the effect of metrical structure on the manifestation of prominence, as claimed above; and whether focus associates more with nuclear accenting, while other types of informativeness more affect accenting in general, as claimed. These claims are tested by evaluating the effectiveness of different features (prosodic and informativeness) in predicting the accent status of words in the corpus.

The features introduced below capture the most important consequences for accent placement of our prosodic and informativeness constraints. There are, however, practical limits to what can be reliably annotated and effectively modelled over a large-scale corpus, leading to a degree of disassociation between our theoretical constraints and the features designed to test them. Likewise, as outlined in the last section, the dependent variable is whether a word has a nuclear accent, non-nuclear accent, or no accent, as these three categories are the most important for our theoretical claims. We return to this issue in the final discussion.

Accent prediction is a well-established task in speech processing. Most previous work has been aimed at improving speech applications, such as speech recognition or synthesis. The goal, therefore, is to maximise accuracy over all words in a corpus suitable for such applications. Accent prediction accuracy using read speech, monologues, or radio news speech is reasonably good (in absolute terms), ranging from 84 to 88% (e.g., Chen & Hasegawa-Johnson, 2004; Conkie, Riccardi, & Rose, 1999; Pan et al., 2002; Sridhar, Bangalore, & Narayanan, 2008). However, read speech tends to use "formuliac" prosody with little variation in focus structure (e.g., see Yuan, Brenier, & Jurafsky, 2005). Accent prediction in such corpora is likely to be both easier and involve different weights on relevant features than in spontaneous speech. Recently, however, there have been a series of accent prediction studies using a similar subset of the Switchboard corpus to ours (Brenier et al., 2006; Nenkova et al., 2007; Sridhar, Nenkova, Narayanan, & Jurafsky, 2008; see also Gregory & Altun, 2004). They report accuracy of between 76 and 79% on detecting accents (without the nuclear/non-nuclear distinction). As discussed above, their best feature was accent ratio, with slight improvement over performance with this feature by adding focus status and word acoustic features. The approach used here is somewhat different. Rather than aiming to maximise accuracy, the aim is to test predictions of our framework by looking at the impact and size of the effect of different features in accent prediction models, i.e., closer to the goals of conventional psycholinguistic experiments. One statistical classifier is used, multinomial logistic regression, enabling fairly straight-forward interpretation of results, and feature importance.

Corpus and features

The data set consists of 18 spontaneous telephone conversations between pairs of American English speakers from the Switchboard corpus (Godfrey et al., 1992). It was used because it is a large collection of spontaneous speech with a broad range of relevant annotations, including the transcription, POS/syntax, reference status, focus, and prosody (Calhoun et al., 2010). In the test set, there are 10,143 words from 33 speakers, approximately 2.5 hours of speech. Below details about the annotations and features extracted using them are given, as motivated by the discussion above (see Appendix 1 for a full list). Data exclusions are also detailed. In order to minimise the effect of extraneous factors (which, in conventional experiments, would be controlled for in the choice of materials and design), a "partially controlled" approach is adopted. Data are excluded which our framework does not claim to explain, such as disfluencies; and data for which all relevant information are not available, such as words not annotated for focus status.

Prosody

The prosodic annotation included accents and phrases. The annotation scheme was based on the Tones and Breaks Indices (ToBI) standards (Beckman & Hirschberg, 1999). However, certain changes were made to concentrate on features most relevant to this study. As well as marking the presence of ***accents,*** one accent in each fluent phrase was marked as *nuclear.* The nuclear accent was defined as the most *structurally* prominent accent in the phrase, normally the right-most one (see discussion above and Ladd, 2008). The annotators were told to mark the "most important" accent, which might not be the most acoustically prominent. Annotators made a further distinction between weak and full non-nuclear accents, the former for cases with ambiguous cues to phrase-level prominence (such as prominence with little F0 movement). These are grouped in our analysis. Tonal accent type was not marked. The accent status of a word *(nuclear, non-nuclear,* or *unaccented)* was the predictee in the models below. Rather than just marking break indices, annotators used the location of ToBI break indices (3, 4, 1p, 2p, and X) to group words into ***prosodic phrases.*** Groups of words starting with one of these indices (or silence) and followed by ToBI break index 3 or 4 were defined as a *phrase.* No distinction was made between 3 and 4 breaks as preliminary analysis suggested the distinction was not useful for accent prediction. Words in disfluent phrases (ending with ToBI 1p and 2p), as well as short phrases containing only discourse fillers (e.g., *um* or *you know)* (ToBI X), were excluded from the data set.

Most of the annotations were done by a paid postgraduate linguistics student at the University of Edinburgh who was trained in using ToBI and who was naive to the goals of this study; and a small number (3) by the author. One conversation side was used to check agreement between the annotator and the author. Kappa agreement on both accent type and presence/absence of accent was .80, on break type .89, and presence/absence of a break 0.91; levels of agreement considered to show good reliability (Carletta, 1996). These scores are also commensurate with those reported for previous ToBI annotations (Pitrelli, Beckman, & Hirschberg, 1994; Yoon, Chavarrla, Cole, & Hasegawa-Johnson, 2004).

Both the accent and phrase annotation were used to extract accent predictor features. Features aimed at capturing rhythmic constraints on accenting included the number of words since the last accent and the number of syllables in the word. For each phrase features were extracted capturing overall emphasis, and therefore likelihood of accenting, such as the mean pitch of the phrase and the speech rate per phrase, in syllables (citation form) per second. All acoustic features were extracted automatically using Praat (Boersma & Weenink, 2008). Pitch features were normalised as a percentage of the speaker's logged pitch range, with outliers excluded (more than 2.5 standard deviations from the mean). Extreme F0 values are commonly the result of F0-doubling or halving errors by F0-extraction programmes (e.g., see Ladd, 2008, online appendix). Speech rate was measured over phrases, rather than larger units. The measure was therefore unreliable for short utterances, although these were uncommon in our data (1% of words were in phrases of one syllable, 3.3% in phrases of two syllables). If larger units had been used (e.g., pause-delimited conversation turns), they would have included variable numbers of phrases, so the effect of phrase-final lengthening on this measure would be uneven.

A "phrase positional" feature, the position of the current phone in the phrase relative to the total number of phones in the phrase, was included to capture the expected constraint of phrase position on accenting. In pretesting, this proved more effective than measuring position by word or syllable. The number of accents in the phrase before the current word, and the total number of phones in the phrase, was also included to capture the length constraint on phrasing. In one of the models below (Pros + Info–Phr), relative phrase positional features are excluded. In this case phrase position was measured in syllables, as this proved more effective than the phone measure for that model. (This measure is never included in the same model as relative phrase position, as they are highly correlated, $r = .59$.)

Focus

Focused words are predicted to be likely to be nuclear accented. A word was defined as a ***focus*** if it was "salient with an implication that this salience is in comparison or contrast to other related words or NPs explicitly or implicitly evoked in the context" (cf. Rooth, 1992). Only "contentful" words (i.e., nouns, verbs, adjectives, adverbs, pronouns, and demonstratives) in full sentences were marked. Focus was marked either at the word or NP level. Words which were not annotated for focus status were excluded from the data set. Words were annotated using focus "types", i.e., discourse contexts which commonly evoke focus: *contrastive,* explicit contrast with a mentioned, semantically related word; *subset,* a member of a more general set mentioned in the context; *adverbial,* a focus-sensitive adverb such as *only* or *even* is associated with the word; *answer,* completes a question (or open proposition) by the other speaker; *correction,* corrects or clarifies a previous word or phrase; or *other,* clearly a focus, but does not fall into one of the other types. All other words were marked ***background*** (see further in Calhoun et al., 2010).

Annotations were done by two paid postgraduate linguistics students at the University Edinburgh who were naive to the goals of this study. Agreement between the two annotators was measured on three conversations. "Blind" agreement (without consultation) on focus type was .67 (kappa), after discussion this rose to 0.85. Although this is lower than might be hoped, it is not unusual. To our knowledge, this is the only large-scale annotation scheme using such a broad definition of focus/contrast. Previous schemes have used much more restrictive definitions, e.g., new information or explicit contrasts (Hedberg & Sosa, 2007; Nakatani, Hirschberg, & Grosz, 1995; Zhang, Hasegawa-Johnson, & Levinson, 2006; though see Buráňová, Hajičová, & Sgall, 2000). It is difficult, therefore, to assess what a "good" level of agreement is (see further in Calhoun et al., 2010).

Below, a ternary distinction is made between *focus:* (marked at) *word level,* and *focus: NP level,* and *background*; all words in a focused marked NP were marked as *focus: NP level.* Focus type was not significant in any of our models, so it is not reported in the analysis. Since our annotation scheme does not capture broad focus, words in syntactic clauses which did not include at least one focused word were excluded (this exclusion was done after the other feature extractions).

Reference status

NPs were marked for reference status as part of an independent project (Nissim, Dingare, Carletta, & Steedman, 2004). As discussed above, it has been claimed that old words are more likely to be unaccented, and new words accented. The annotation was based on Prince's (1992) givenness hierarchy: first mentions of entities were ***new*** and subsequent mentions ***old.*** Entities that were not previously mentioned, but that were generally known or inferable were ***mediated.*** Where a noun was dominated by more than one annotated NP, reference status was taken from the NP most immediately dominating that noun. Since this hierarchy applies to referring expressions, only NPs were annotated, limiting the power of this feature over the whole data set.

Part-of-speech (POS)/syntax

The Penn Treebank annotation (Marcus, Santorini, & Marcinkiewicz, 1993; Taylor, Marcus, & Santorini, 2003) was used to extract a number of syntactic features. These included ***POS,*** grouped into broad classes *(nouns, verbs, adjectives, adverbs, pronouns, and demonstratives,* other parts-of-speech were not included as they were not marked for focus). POS has been shown to be highly predictive of accenting, as noted above. Each word was also marked according to the syntactic ***constituent*** *(subject, predicate, object, and adjunct)* and ***clause*** type *(main, complement, adverbial, relative, and parenthetical)* it was in; along with the position of the word in the constituent/clause relative to the total number of words in the constituent/clause (see further in Calhoun, 2006, ch. 5). Where a word was within an embedded clause or constituent, its position and type were taken from the lowest level of syntactic structure dominating that word. As discussed above, syntactic structure is expected to constrain prosodic phrasing, and therefore indirectly the position of the nuclear accent.

Predictability measures

As noted above, accent ratio has been shown to be a very good predictor of accenting in this corpus (Nenkova et al., 2007). Nenkova et al.'s (2007) accent ratio data are therefore included. The accent ratio of a word is the probability that a particular lexeme is accented, where that likelihood is significantly different from chance, or 0.5 otherwise; that is:

$$AccentRatio(w) = \begin{cases} \frac{k}{n} & \text{if } B(k, n, 0.5) \leq 0.05 \\ 0.5 & \text{otherwise} \end{cases},$$

where n is the total number of times the word w appeared in the corpus, k is the number of times word w appeared accented, and $B(k, n, 0.5)$ is the probability (under a binomial distribution) that there are k successes in n trials if the probability of success and failure is equal (using 60 Switchboard conversations annotated for accenting, Ostendorf, Shafran, Shattuck-Hufnagel, Carmichael,

& Byrne, 2001). For example, *AccentRatio(you)* = *0.3407, AccentRatio(education)* = *0.8666,* and *AccentRatio(probably)* = *0.5.*

Unigram and ***bigram*** predictability have further been shown to correlate negatively with prominence. These features were defined as $\log_{10}(pw)$ and $\log_{10}(pw_i|pw_{i-1})$ respectively, calculated from the Switchboard corpus (3 million words), together with a 17 million word corpus of newspaper text to increase the reliability of the *n*-gram measures (Scottish Herald news from 1998 to 2002, cf. Badino & Clark, 2007). Unigram and bigram measures were calculated using the CMU language modelling toolkit (Clarkson & Rosenfeld, 1997), based on a vocabulary of the 20,000 most frequent words in the combined corpus, with Witten–Bell discounting applied (the lowest frequency for unigrams in the vocabulary in our data set was 37, for bigrams 20, out of 20 million words). For words not in this vocabulary, a floor probability of -10 (logged value) was used. Bigrams were calculated as follows:

$$p(w_i|w_{i-1}) = \begin{cases} \dfrac{p(w_{i-1}, w_i)}{p(w_{i-1})} & \text{if } (w_{i-1}, w_i) \text{ in vocab, else} \\ \dfrac{p^*(w_{i-1})^* p(w_i)}{p(w_{i-1})} & \text{if } (w_{i-1}) \text{ nd } (w_i) \text{ in vocab, else} \\ -10 & \end{cases}$$

when the bigram sequence was not in the corpus, the joint probability was calculated by multiplying a back-off probability of $p^*(w_{i-1})$ by the probability of w_i. When either w or w_{i-1} was not in the vocabulary, the floor probability of -10 was used.

Word prominence

Finally, acoustic prominence features were extracted for the word itself: the relative duration, normalised mean intensity, and normalised median F0 and inter-quartile (I-Q) F0 range of the word. All values were extracted automatically using Praat and F0 normalised as described above. Intensity was normalised relative to the mean for the speaker, and duration relative to the number of syllables in the word. Since by definition accented words should be more phonetically prominent than unaccented words around them (see above), the acoustic correlates of prominence should be higher for accented words.

Correcting for collinearity

As is well-known, correlation between predictors is problematic for regression analysis, as it gives rise to collinearity in models (e.g., Hocking, 2003, ch. 5). While some collinearity is inevitable in a study such as this, steps were taken to reduce it as much as possible. All continuous predictors were *Z*-transformed, which can reduce collinearity. This also makes their regression coefficients easier to interpret, as they are all on the same scale, with an equivalent range to the categorial predictors. The pair-wise correlation between all our predictors was then calculated. Pairs of predictors correlated by $r > .5$ were considered problematic. These were unigram with bigram predictability ($r = .72$); and phrase mean F0 with word median F0 ($r = .72$). In each case, the latter predictor was regressed against the former, and the residuals of the latter used as predictors. Finally, the resulting level of collinearity was tested using to the Variance Inflation Factor (VIF) and Tolerance metrics using a regression model with all potential predictors and accent status as the dependent. Myers (1990) suggests VIF values greater than 10 are unacceptable, while Menard (1995) suggests Tolerance values less than 0.2 merit concern. Table 1 shows that the final level of collinearity between the predictors is therefore acceptable.

Modelling approach

In the models reported below, features are grouped into sets: *prosodic* (rhythmic and phrasal features) and *informativeness* (focus, reference status, POS/syntax, and predictability measures). This was done to gauge the relative efficacy of prosodic structure and informativeness in predicting accent status. For each feature set, all features were included to start and then nonsignificant features excluded one-by-one and the models rerun. The resultant feature sets were combined *(Pros + Info)* and the process repeated. The analysis below concentrates on this model, as it best captures the features which should be available to the language production system in deciding prominence realisation. The combined models, with word prominence features added *(Pros + Info + Word),* and with "phrase positional" features removed *(Pros + Info–Phr),* are also reported. The former is intended as a "check" on the Pros + Info model (more details below); the latter to assess the claim that syntactic phrasing has an indirect effect on prominence. All statistical analyses were conducted using the SPSS statistics package, version 14 for Windows.

Results and discussion

Accent prediction models were built using each group of features. All models had significantly lower log likelihoods than a baseline model, in which all words were unaccented (the most likely category): prosodic, $LL = 17{,}213$, $\chi^2(14, N = 10{,}072) = 2{,}039$, $p < .0005$; informativeness, $LL = 17{,}994$, $\chi^2(32, N = 10{,}026) = 917$, $p < .0005$; Pros + Info, $LL = 16{,}041$, $\chi^2(32, N = 10{,}072) = 3{,}211$, $p < .0005$; Pros + Info–Phr, $LL = 17{,}277$, $\chi^2(42, N = 9{,}955) = 1{,}753$, $p < .0005$; Pros + Info + Word, $LL = 13{,}977$, $\chi^2(38, N = 9{,}401) = 4{,}162$,

TABLE 1
Collinearity diagnostics, Variance Inflation Factor (VIF), and Tolerance (inverse of VIF)

Feature	*Tolerance*	*VIF*
Accents so far	0.386	2.588
Words since last accent	0.533	1.878
Syllables in word	0.545	1.834
Phrase mean F0	0.452	2.211
Speech rate	0.641	1.559
Rel. pos. in phrase	0.243	4.118
Phones in phrase	0.375	2.665
Focus status	0.690	1.448
Info status	0.323	3.096
Part-of-speech	0.288	3.473
Clause type	0.962	1.039
Rel. pos. in clause	0.641	1.560
Words in clause	0.876	1.142
Constituent type	0.508	1.967
Rel. pos. in constituent	0.863	1.159
Accent ratio	0.752	1.330
Unigram	0.444	2.251
Bigram	0.492	2.031
Word median F0	0.444	2.251
Word F0 I-Q range	0.932	1.072
Word mean intensity	0.859	1.165
Word duration	0.474	2.111

These measures were derived from a regression model with accent status as the dependent including all features which were tested in the accent prediction models reported below. Note this model itself is not reported as it includes features which did not turn out to be significant.

$p < .0005$. Table 2 shows the effect on the log likelihood of the Pros + Info model of removing each feature in turn (with replacement). The larger the log likelihood of the reduced model, the greater the importance of that feature to model fit. The effect of feature removal on the log likelihoods for each of the other models is listed in Appendix 1. All models only include significant features ($p \leq .05$).

Table 3 shows the direction and magnitude of the effect of each feature in the *Pros + Info* model on the likelihood of a non-nuclear or nuclear accent. For each feature, the odds ratio *(OR,* equivalent to β coefficients in linear regression) is reported. For ease of interpretation it is converted to *P diff,* i.e., the percentage difference in the likelihood of a (non-)nuclear accent with that variable. For categorial variables, this is the effect of the value of the variable given (e.g., verb for POS) compared to a reference value for that variable (background for focus status, pronoun for POS); only significant values for

TABLE 2
Importance of features in the Pros+Info model: The effect on the log likelihood of the Pros+Info model of removing each feature in turn (with replacement) from the full model

Group	*Feature*	*LL of reduced model*	χ^2 *(df)*
	Full model	16041	–
Prosodic	Rel. pos. in phrase	16865	824.4 (2)*
	Accents so far	16486	444.9 (2)*
	Words since last accent	16140	99.1 (2)*
	Syllables in word	16138	96.9 (2)*
	Speech rate	16083	42.2 (2)*
	Phrase mean F0	16067	26.6 (2)*
	Phones in phrase	16058	17.1 (2)*
Informativeness	Focus status	16460	419.0 (4)*
	Accent ratio	16247	206.2 (2)*
	Part-of-speech	16083	42.1 (10)*
	Unigram	16069	27.9 (2)*

The log likelihoods (LL) of the reduced model in each case and χ^2 tests showing their significance (in comparison to the full model) are given (df = degrees of freedom, *Highly significant, $p < .01$). Features are grouped by type, and then listed according to the magnitude of their importance within each type.

each variable are listed. For continuous variables, this is the effect of a one unit increase on a Z-transformed scale (i.e., one standard deviation for that variable).

Tables 2 and 3 show clear evidence for the prosodic constraints predicted. The most important feature for model fit is relative position in the phrase (*rel. pos. in phrase;* see Table 2). The likelihood of a nuclear accent increases as relative position increases (see Table 3); consistent with the predicted operation of the right-branching bias. Both non-nuclear and nuclear accents become more likely as the number of words since the last accent increases (*words since last accent*), and as the number of syllables in the word increases (*syllables in word*). These effects are consistent with predicted rhythmic constraints: there should not be too long a gap between accented words in a phrase, and the more syllables in a word, the more likely one will align with a strong node (i.e., be accented). The effect of both features is smaller on nuclear accents, consistent with our claim that the nuclear accent is "central", and other prominences adjusted in relation to it (see further final discussion). The feature *accents so far* is also important for model fit (see Table 2). The likelihood of either accent decreases as the number of preceding accents in the phrase increases (see Table 3). This is consistent with the indirect effect of the phrase length constraint, i.e., phrases with many accents are dispreferred. As the number of *phones in the phrase* goes up, the

TABLE 3
Direction and magnitude of the effect of each feature in the Pros+Info model on the likelihood of a non-nuclear or nuclear accent

	Non-nuclear				*Nuclear*			
Feature	*OR*	*OR:CI*	*P diff*	*Wald*	*OR*	*OR:CI*	*P diff*	*Wald*
Increase								
Rel. pos. in phrase	–	–	–	–	3.59	3.24–3.98	30.7%	591.2**
Syllables in word	1.39	1.30–1.48	6.1%	89.9**	1.26	1.18–1.35	5.1%	46.0**
Words since last accent	1.46	1.35–1.57	7.2%	96.3**	1.23	1.15–1.33	4.6%	30.7**
Phrase mean F0	1.14	1.08–1.20	2.3%*	23.2**	1.11	1.05–1.17	2.2%	13.0**
Phones in phrase	1.14	1.05–1.23	2.3%	9.7**	–	–	–	–
Focus: word level	2.01	1.74–2.33	14.2%	87.0**	4.27	3.71–4.93	34.7%	397.9**
Focus: NP level	–	–	–	–	1.61	1.36–1.90	10.9%	31.1**
Noun	1.42	1.16–1.74	6.6%	11.4**	1.42	1.14–1.77	8.0%	9.8**
Demonstrative	1.59	1.26–2.01	9.0%	15.0**	1.31	1.01–1.71	6.1%	4.0*
Verb	1.34	1.14–1.57	5.4%	12.6**	–	–	–	–
Accent ratio	1.53	1.44–1.63	8.2%	176.6**	1.42	1.32–1.52	7.9%	100.1**
Decrease								
Accents so far	0.47	0.43–0.52	−10.2%	263.0**	0.45	0.41–0.49	−14.2%	319.3**
Speech rate	0.82	0.78–0.87	−3.2%	41.1**	0.93	0.87–0.98	−1.6%	6.2*
Unigram	0.86	0.81–0.92	−2.4%	20.5**	0.86	0.81–0.92	−3.1%	22.1**

The odds ratio (OR), confidence interval of the odds ratio (OR:CI) and the percentage (%) change in likelihood (*P* diff) are given, along with the Wald statistic (a measure of the significance of each feature for each outcome; **Highly significant, $p < .01$; *Significant, $.01 \leq p < .05$). For categorical variables the effect of (significant) values of that variable is given, whereas for continuous variables the effect of a one unit increase is shown (on a *Z*-transformed scale). Features are grouped by type: prosodic before informativeness; and then by the magnitude of their effect within each type.

likelihood of a non-nuclear accent increases slightly (with a very small effect on model fit). This is likely due to the fact that longer phrases have more non-nuclear accents (relative to nuclear accents), although in any case the effect of this feature is small. The effect of overall emphasis is also small (in importance and magnitude), but works in the expected direction: as *phrase mean F0* goes up, and *speech rate* goes down, the likelihood of both types of accent rises.

Secondly, as predicted, our two levels of informativeness affect the likelihood of each type of accent differently. *Focus status* is very important to model fit (see Table 2). A single focus makes both types of accent more likely *(focus: word level),* but the magnitude of the effect of this feature is much bigger for nuclear accents and holds for words in focused NPs as well *(focus: NP level)* (see Table 3). This is consistent with our prediction that focus is primarily a constraint on nuclear accents. Among the "accentability" features, *accent ratio,* POS type, and *unigram* predictability all effect the likelihood of both non-nuclear and nuclear accents in the expected direction (see Table 3). The most important of these (to model fit) is accent ratio, consistent with Nenkova et al.'s (2007) findings. However, contrary to their result, accent ratio is less important than focus status (to model fit), and has only a moderate influence on accent likelihood (compared to focus status; see Table 3). This difference is probably because our partially controlled data set allows the effect of focus to be seen fully. POS type and unigram predictability have only a small influence on model fit (see Table 2). The likelihood of both accent types increases if the word is a noun or demonstrative, and the likelihood of a non-nuclear accent increases for verbs (relative to pronouns; see Table 3); these are arguably the most "informative" parts-of-speech. Consistent with previous findings, as unigram predictability goes up, the likelihood of both types of accent goes down, although the magnitude of this effect is small. In line with our predictions, these "accentability" features affect the likelihood of non-nuclear and nuclear accents roughly equally; and are clearly separate from those of focus.

Table 4 presents accent status classification for each feature model, along with overall accuracy, relative to a baseline (all words unaccented), in order to show how accurately nuclear vs. non-nuclear accents are predicted. The predicted outcome for each word was the most likely outcome (unaccented, non-nuclear accent, or nuclear accent) for that word according to each regression model, and the percentages given show the proportion of times the predicted outcome was actually the accent status for that word. Data points correctly predicted by the model are considered to be recognised by the model.

Nuclear accent recognition is much better than non-nuclear accent recognition. This is true across all feature models; even in the final model (Pros + Info + Word) only 45.8% of non-nuclear accents are correctly

TABLE 4
Accent status recognition. Percentages of words correctly classified as having no accent (None), a non-nuclear accent (Non-Nuclear) or a nuclear accent (Nuclear), and overall accuracy (Overall) are shown for models built using each group of features

	Accent status recognition (%)			
	None	*Non-nuclear*	*Nuclear*	*Overall*
Baseline	100	0	0	47.2
Prosodic	81.7	24.2	70.4	59.6
Informativeness	81.9	10.0	65.5	55.8
Pros+Info	83.0	37.3	74.9	64.0
Pros+Info–Phr	84.3	21.6	65.1	58.7
Pros+Info+Word	85.1	45.8	78.3	67.3

recognised, whereas nuclear accent recognition is at 78.3%. This supports our contention that the nuclear accent is much better defined in prosodic structure than accenting in general. That is, the nuclear accent is a well-defined position in prosodic structure (the strongest node in the phrase), whereas "accenting" describes some of the other strong nodes in a phrase, determined according to some externally defined level of phonetic prominence (i.e., external to the prosodic structure; see further Prosodic prominence introduction and final discussion). The prosodic model is more accurate than the informativeness model for both non-nuclear (24.2% vs. 10.0%) and nuclear accents (70.4% vs. 65.5%). This suggests that both accent types are best defined by their place in prosodic structure, as predicted (i.e., accents are manifestations of metrical structure). Combining prosodic and informativeness features has a roughly additive effect on non-nuclear accent recognition (rising to 37.3%), whereas for nuclear accents there is only a moderate increase over the prosodic model (to 74.9%). This suggests that the effect of prosodic and informativeness features on nuclear accent placement are not independent (cf. final discussion). For non-nuclear accents, the effect of prosodic constraints may be weaker (or at least not as well-captured by these features), so the two sets of features are more independent.

Overall accuracy and recognition of both nuclear and non-nuclear accents are substantially worse in the combined model without phrase positional features (Pros+ Info–Phr vs. Pros+ Info). This shows that prosodic phrasing constrains prominence, as is implicit in our model (i.e., nuclear and prenuclear accents are defined by their position in the phrases they are in). For the informativeness and Pros+ Info–Phr models only, features capturing the position of the word in syntactic structure (in the clause and constituent), prove significant (see Appendix 1). Consistent with our predictions, it seems that syntactic structure only indirectly constrains accent placement. Since syntactic structure is known to constrain prosodic phrasing, syntactic structure features should only be significant for accent prediction when prosodic phrasing features are not in the model, as is the case.

The addition of word-level acoustic features substantially improves non-nuclear accent recognition (from 37.3 to 45.8%), but only leads to a small increase in nuclear accent recognition (from 74.9 to 78.3%). The effect of these features is a "check" on the performance of the Pros + Info model. Both types of accent are more acoustically prominent than unaccented words (as is shown by Corpus Analysis 2), so the (lack of) improvement in accuracy with word-level acoustic features is a measure of how well the other features explain accent placement. Therefore, this shows once more that our features are much more effective for nuclear accents than non-nuclear ones, as the improvement in accuracy for nuclear accents is much smaller than that for non-nuclear accents with the addition of word-level features.

Finally, the accuracy of our final model can be compared to previous studies using Switchboard. Overall accuracy is lower (76–79%; Brenier et al., 2006; Nenkova et al., 2007; Sridhar, Nenkova, et al., 2008), however, these studies only make a binary distinction between accented and unaccented words. For comparison, therefore, a logisitic regression model was run with the features from the Pros + Info + Word model to make this binary classification. Overall accuracy was 82.2% (83.4% for accented words and 80.7% for unaccented words), and the model was highly significant (compared to the baseline model) ($-2LL = 7{,}330$, χ^2 $(19,\ N = 9{,}401) = 5{,}631$, $p < .0005$). This is higher than previous results although the task may have been easier because of the more restricted data set. However, it does show that our model is comparable in accuracy to those reported in the automatic speech processing literature.

CORPUS ANALYSIS 2: ACOUSTIC FEATURES OF ACCENTS

The second analysis looks at the acoustic correlates of accents depending on their position in metrical structure: pre, post, or nuclear. The reality of prominence structure is a fundamental postulate of our framework. This analysis therefore tests whether accents in fact carry phonetic cues to their structural position.

Method

The effect of Accent Position *(prenuclear, nuclear, and postnuclear)* on acoustic prominence was tested (measured by its correlates used above: *median F0, F0 I-Q range, mean intensity,* and *duration).* Three covariates *(accents so far, phrase mean F0,* and *rel. pos. in phrase)* were included to control for well-known phrasal pitch and duration effects, such as declination and final lengthening (e.g., Shattuck-Hufnagel & Turk, 1996; Terken & Hermes, 2000). The data set was the same as above, without unaccented words: a total of 5,109 words, of which 1,958 had prenuclear accents, 2,904 nuclear accents, and 247 postnuclear accents.

Results and discussion

Using a one factor multivariate ANCOVA, there was a highly significant main effect of Accent Position, $F(8, 10202) = 26.8$, $p < .0005$, and highly significant main effects for all three covariates: Accents So Far, $F(4, 5100) = 36.3$, $p < .0005$; Phrase Mean F0, $F(4, 5100) = 2{,}267.0$, $p < .0005$; and Rel. Pos. in Phrase, $F(4, 5100) = 159.5$, $p < .0005$. Table 5 shows the direction of the effect of each covariate on each dependent variable. These are generally as expected given the phrasal effects being controlled for. Median F0 tends to decrease as relative position *(rel. pos. in phrase (phones))* and *accents so far* increase; reflecting expected declination. Word median F0 increases as *phrase mean F0* increases, reflecting overall emphasis. Mean intensity follows broadly the same pattern. F0 I-Q range also increases with *phrase mean F0,* although oddly F0 range seems to increase later in the phrase (contrary to the expected effect of declination). Duration tends to increase with relative position, as expected given final lengthening.

Posthoc univariate tests (Bonferroni correction) showed there was a highly significant effect of Accent Position on all four dependents: *median F0,* $F(2, 5103) = 39.4$, $p < .0005$; *F0 I-Q range,* $F(2, 5103) = 24.6$, $p < .0005$;

TABLE 5
Effect of covariates on each dependent acoustic measure

Dependent	*Covariate*	β	*SE*	*t*
Median F0	Rel. pos. in phrase (Phones)	−0.205	0.013	−15.810**
	Accents so far	−0.129	0.011	−11.775**
	Phrase mean F0	0.769	0.008	93.690**
F0 I-Q range	Rel. pos. in phrase (Phones)	0.106	0.025	4.310**
	Accents so far	−0.014	0.021	−0.650
	Phrase mean F0	0.042	0.016	2.716**
Mean intensity	Rel. pos. in phrase (Phones)	−0.285	0.019	−14.646**
	Accents so far	−0.015	0.016	−0.941
	Phrase mean F0	0.189	0.012	15.337**
Duration	Rel. pos. in phrase (Phones)	0.317	0.023	14.046**
	Accents so far	−0.037	0.019	-1.932^{+}
	Phrase mean F0	−0.029	0.014	−2.041*

The β coefficients for each covariate are given by acoustic measure, along with their standard errors (SE) and *t* tests showing their significance (**Highly significant, $p < .01$; *Significant, $.01 \leq p < .05$; $^{+}$Marginally significant, $.05 \leq p < .1$).

mean intensity, $F(2, 5103) = 8.6$, $p < .0005$; and *duration,* $F(2, 5103) = 29.1$, $p < .0005$. Table 6 lists the estimated marginal means for each dependent variable by Accent Position. *Posthoc* comparisons (Bonferroni correction) of the differences between marginal means are also given, showing whether these differences are significant.

Figure 4 shows the estimated marginal means by Accent Position. As these measures are reported in Z-transformed units, zero represents the mean over all words (including unaccented words), and one unit is one standard deviation for that variable. Recall that acoustic measures were normalised before being Z-transformed, so differences should be speaker independent. As can be seen, accent position has a distinct effect on each acoustic measure. Nuclear accents are on average more prominent than pre- and postnuclear accents overall, as might be expected. The most distinctive feature is duration: accented words are longer than the overall average (i.e., the means are greater than zero); and nuclear accents are clearly longer than pre- and postnuclear accents (these differences are highly significant, see Table 6). The latter effect is not often cited in the literature. Postnuclear accents have on average much lower F0 and smaller F0 range than prenuclear or nuclear accents (both differences are highly significant), as

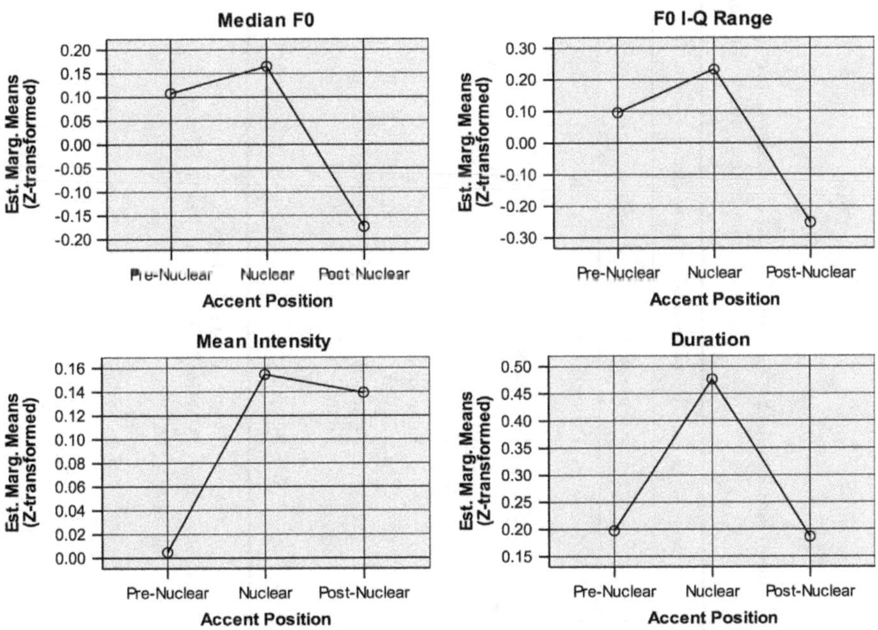

Figure 4. Acoustic profiles of accented words by position (prenuclear, nuclear, postnuclear), controlling for covariates. Estimated marginal means in Z-transformed units for each correlate of acoustic prominence measured.

TABLE 6
Means of dependent acoustic measures by accent position (prenuclear, nuclear, and postnuclear), along with posthoc comparisons between accent positions, controlling for covariates

	Estimated marginal means			*Posthoc comparisons*		
Dependent	*Accent position (i)*	*Mean*	*SE*	*Accent position (j)*	*Mean difference (i – j)*	*SE*
Median F0	Prenuclear	0.108	0.017	Nuclear	–0.057⁺	0.024
	Nuclear	0.164	0.012	Postnuclear	0.338**	0.039
	Postnuclear	–0.174	0.038	Prenuclear	–0.281**	0.043
F0 I-Q range	Prenuclear	0.096	0.032	Nuclear	–0.137**	0.046
	Nuclear	0.232	0.024	Postnuclear	0.485**	0.073
	Postnuclear	–0.252	0.072	Prenuclear	–0.348**	0.082
Mean intensity	Prenuclear	0.005	0.025	Nuclear	–0.150**	0.036
	Nuclear	0.155	0.019	Postnuclear	0.015	0.058
	Postnuclear	0.139	0.057	Prenuclear	0.135	0.065
Duration	Prenuclear	0.197	0.029	Nuclear	–0.279**	0.042
	Nuclear	0.476	0.022	Postnuclear	0.290**	0.067
	Postnuclear	0.186	0.066	Prenuclear	–0.011	0.075

Estimated marginal means (mean) and standard errors (SE) are given in Z-transformed units. The significance of each mean difference is also shown (**Highly significant, $p < .01$; ⁺Marginally significant, $.05 \leq p < .1$)

has been found before (Grice, Ladd, & Arvaniti, 2000). Indeed, median F0 and F0 range for postnuclear accents are lower than the average over all words. Prenuclear accents seem to pattern with nuclear accents in terms of median F0 (the difference between them being marginally significant), while F0 range for prenuclear accents is significantly lower than that for nuclear accents. Postnuclear accents seem to pattern with nuclear accents in terms of intensity (although the difference between pre and postnuclear accents is not significant), while mean intensity for prenuclear accents is little different from the mean over all words. All of this suggests a much more sophisticated manipulation of different correlates of prominence to signal metrical structure than is usually assumed.

Lastly, note that the Analysis 1 results show that these differences are neither necessary nor sufficient for accent recognition (at least by our classifier). While there are, on average, differences in accent realisation depending on metrical structure position, these are not necessarily needed to signal accent position and type, because of the regularities in prosodic structure.

GENERAL DISCUSSION

We have advanced a framework within which to understand how informativeness affects prosodic prominence in English. Our claim is that informativeness and prosodic factors place different constraints on the probabilistic alignment of words with prominence structure. In particular, there are two broad levels of informativeness effects: focused words tend to align with nuclear accents, whereas words which are more "accentable" (because of predictability, POS type, accent ratio, or reference status) are more likely to align with strong nodes in the structure. We further claimed that metrical structure itself has properties, such as a right-branching bias and rhythm, which act as constraints on the realisation of prosodic prominence. Syntactic structure and phrase length act as indirect constraints, as they constrain prosodic phrasing, which in turn constrains prominence realisation. On the basis of this framework, a number of predictions were made about the type and strength of prosodic and informativeness features which probabilistically determine the prominence of a word. These predictions were tested using regression models to predict the accent status (nuclear, non-nuclear accent, and unaccented) of words in an annotated corpus of spontaneous speech, Switchboard. The most important feature was relative position in the phrase, with nuclear accents more likely later in the phrase. This was consistent with the effect of the right-branching bias. Features capturing rhythmic and length constraints also significantly influenced the occurrence of non-nuclear and nuclear accents as expected. Nuclear accents were predicted much more reliably than non-nuclear accents; consistent with our claim that nuclear accents are "central" to prosodic structure. As predicted, focus status proved to be an important feature, and to have a much bigger influence on the likelihood of nuclear accents than non-nuclear accents. Accent ratio was the most important of the "accentability" features, while POS type and unigram predictability had a small effect. All influenced accent likelihood in the predicted direction, having a roughly similar influence on the likelihood of non-nuclear and nuclear accents. Secondly, the acoustic realisation (median F0, F0 range, mean intensity, and duration) of accents by metrical position (pre, post, or nuclear) was analysed. Nuclear accents had higher prominence on all measures, but were best distinguished by increased duration, while prenuclear accents had higher F0 than postnuclear accents, and postnuclear accents had higher intensity than prenuclear accents.

These results provide good empirical support for our prosodic framework. Features capturing the major metrical constraints on prominence: the right-branching bias (relative position in the phrase), rhythm (words since last accent, syllables in word), and the indirect effect of length (accents so far) were significant in all relevant models, and acted in the expected direction. Non-nuclear accents were not very reliably predicted even in our final model, whose features are fairly comprehensive of those suggested to predict accents in the literature. Under the metrical approach, prenuclear accents are manifestations of strong nodes. "Accenting" therefore draws an under-differentiated cut-off between levels of relative prominence in the prenuclear region of a phrase. Analysis 2 found clear acoustic differences between pre-, post-, and nuclear accents consistent with the predictions of metrical theory (see Figure 1). However, Analysis 1 showed that word prominence features were not necessary for accent prediction, at least for nuclear accents.

This supports our claim that accent status is neither signalled nor perceived solely, or even primarily, through phonetic prominence. Nuclear accents were best distinguished by duration. All of this suggests that it is not sufficient to consider accent as a binary property, as the place of an accent in metrical structure has crucial effects on how it is used and perceived; and further that all acoustic correlates of prominence, not just F0, need to be considered (cf. Frazier, Carlson, & Clifton, 2006; Kochanski, Grabe, Coleman, & Rosner, 2005).

Although the prosodic features captured the main consequences of the prosodic constraints in our framework, metrical structure was not implemented directly. This would simply not be feasible in a corpus of this size. There are therefore some limitations to the findings. The relative position in the phrase feature does not distinguish between a right-branching bias and a simple linear order constraint, i.e., the last accent in the phrase should be strongest. Although there are independent reasons to prefer a structural explanation, e.g., it explains where the nuclear accent ends up in after "deaccenting" (see

Calhoun, 2010; Ladd, 2008), teasing apart the effect of these constraints probably requires a different methodology. This is left for future work. Similarly, the words since last accent and syllables in the word features are a somewhat indirect expression of the effect of rhythmic alternation; for a full account of how this constraint operates, see Calhoun, 2010.

There is also a question as to the extent to which the accent annotation definitions used influenced the results. It is difficult to rule this out, however, the annotation guidelines were framed to minimise this as much as possible (see Calhoun, 2006; Calhoun et al., 2010). The nuclear accent was defined as the "most important" rather than the "strongest", and annotators were told it might not be the most acoustically prominent. They were given no information about the relationship between peak height and accent status. There was therefore no necessary relationship between these guidelines and the findings in Analysis 2. Annotators were told that the nuclear accent was normally the right-most strong accent, as this was a necessary part of its definition. This may have contributed to the efficacy of phrase position as a predictive feature. However, annotators could place the nuclear accent earlier, and in 33.4% of cases in our data set the nuclear accent was not on the last word in the phrase. Similarly, the guideline to identify the "most important" accent in each phrase may have influenced annotators to implicitly pay attention to informativeness features, particularly focus, when identifying nuclear accents. No such link was explicitly made to annotators, however, and in our data set 46.8% of focused words were not marked by nuclear accents. Further, the reliability of nuclear accent recognition compared to non-nuclear accents was not a result of annotation reliability, as there was no difference in annotator agreement over all accent types, compared to presence/absence of accent.

Focus and "accentability" features had different weights in predicting nuclear and non-nuclear accents. This is consistent with our claim that these are different levels of informativeness, which cannot be reduced to a single dimension (contra Aylett & Turk, 2004; Bolinger, 1972). This difference is also hard to explain if all accents are functionally motivated (the non-metrical view). On the other hand, "accentability" features (most importantly accent ratio) had similar weights on non-nuclear and nuclear accents. Thus, in relation to the literature on informativeness and prominence, it appears both the focus-based and the predictability-based approaches are valid. However, it remains unclear how and when these two broad factors influence the production process. Below, a model of prosody generation within language production is outlined, consistent with the constraints this study found evidence for.

In the introduction, it was noted that F(ocus)-marking on a word is said to be able to "project" to other words in an utterance. In the corpus study, however, the issue of focus projection was effectively bypassed: focus was marked at the word (or NP) level, and syntactic clauses without a focus were excluded from the data set. Therefore, this study does not directly give evidence for how accent placement works within multiword focus phrases. However, we contend that accent placement within a multiword focus phrase would be the same as accent placement in these models, except without the focus constraint, i.e., the focus constraint would simply specify that the focus must fall somewhere within the focus phrase; all of the other features, e.g., prosodic constraints, would determine which word within the phrase was accented.

Interestingly, reference status was not significant in any of the models, as might have been expected. This may be because it only applied to NPs. It could also be, as suggested by Nenkova et al. (2007), that discourse givenness is more relevant to determining referring expressions than accenting, e.g., a given entity may be referred to using an unaccented pronoun, but this is already captured by the POS feature. It may also be that *relative* givenness is more important for accenting, as discussed above. Entities that are relatively given are usually also discourse given, however, a speaker may treat a discourse given entity as "new" (or focused), if it is not given in relation to the current proposition. Although there is a weak correlation between reference status and accent status in our data [*Spearman's* $r(10{,}141) = .21$, $p < .031$], the relationship does not seem to be direct. Bigram predictability likewise was only significant in the informativeness model, where it had a weak effect on the likelihood of non-nuclear accents (see Appendix 1). This is different to what was found in previous work (Gregory & Altun, 2004; Pan & Hirschberg, 2000), seeming to suggest that contextual predictability effects are captured by our other informativeness features, such as focus or accent ratio.

These results raise intriguing questions about the relationship between prosodic phrasing, syntactic phrasing, and information structure. Nuclear accent placement is strongly constrained by both focus and phrase structure. However, when phrase positional features were not included, syntactic features were significant, suggesting that syntax constrains phrasing. To confirm this, we would need to model phrase boundaries using syntactic features (and vice versa). This is beyond the scope of the present work. In any case, syntactic structure seems to be manipulated to place focal elements in prosodically strong positions. This is interesting since English is usually taken to be a language with a relatively fixed syntax, so that prosody is varied to mark focus (see Ladd, 2008, ch. 6). This would be an interesting area for future research, e.g., to see if focus/prosodic constraints can predict syntactic alternations (cf. Bresnan, Cueni, Nikitina, & Baayen, 2007).

We claimed that the mapping of words onto metrical structure is probabilistic. This is borne out by our accent prediction results which showed there were no absolute relationships between any feature and accent status, which is rather determined probabilistically by multiple weighted factors. However, these statistical models are only meant to show the different constraints on prominence realisation. The development of a full prominence production model remains a (large) area of future research. Below, we sketch what such a model could be like. It would also be interesting to test the consequences of our theory for the role of prominence in perception, e.g., using a formal constraint-based perception model (e.g., Jurafsky, 2003; Tabor, Cornell, & Tanenhaus, 1997; see further in Calhoun, 2006, 2010).

Prosody in language production

In our framework, words are (nuclear) accented in the first place because of their position in prosodic structure. However, from a processing point of view, it is not clear why should there be a separate prosodic structure, rather than simply using prominences and phrases to convey syntactic/information structure. We further claimed that foci align with nuclear accents, which usually occur towards the end of phrases. To achieve this, speakers should try to choose a syntactic structure in which the focused constituent falls towards the end of the phrase. This implies that the planning of prosodic structure should be concurrent with syntactic planning. This is much earlier than in standard models, and is hard to fit with a strictly incremental approach to phonological encoding (e.g., Dell & Burger, 1997; Levelt, 1989). We contend that both of these aspects of our model are necessary, as prosodic structure is a fundamental part of the high-level planning of an utterance (Ferreira, 1993; Frazier et al., 2006; Keating & Shattuck-Hufnagel, 2002).

Frazier et al. (2006) suggest that prosodic structure helps listeners link different representations of the same element (e.g., phones, words, syntax, and semantics) together given that segmentation may be different for each, providing a "skeleton" to which each representation is indexed. As they say, this explains why prosody interacts with every component of grammar. We suggest this "skeleton" is necessary in production as well, i.e., to ensure that the way a message is conveyed is consistent across representations. Prosodic structure is ideal for this because, as was shown above, it has such predictable properties, e.g., rhythm and the right-branching bias. Rhythmical stress has been shown to aid recall in memorisation (Reeves, Schmauder, & Morris, 2000; Sturges & Martin, 1974); while highly regular prosodic patterns are typical of language which must be held in memory, such as nursery rhymes, or with very high-production pressure, such as horse-racing broadcasts.

Keating and Shattuck-Hufnagel (2002) argue that higher-level prosodic structure is planned as a whole in the initial stages of message planning, using a structure derived from, but not identical to, the syntax (see also Ferreira, 1993). As word form encoding progresses, restructuring of this initial structure may occur. As they discuss, Prosodic Words have been the basic units of planning in previous models (e.g., Levelt, 1989; Levelt, Roelofs, & Meyer, 1999). However, it was assumed these are combined into larger prosodic units after word form encoding. Keating and Shattuck-Hufnagel present compelling evidence for the availability of high-level prosodic structure before word form encoding (see their paper for more details). For example, they show that segmental phonetic variation is governed by higher-level prosodic structure (see also Fougeron, 1999). They present arguments based on phonological processes, such as tonal assimilation, speech error data, and "stress clash" resolution studies that speakers must have upcoming prosodic structure available during word form encoding.

These results of this study support a model such as Keating and Shattuck-Hufnagel (2002). Figure 5 sketches our model of prosody generation [following Keating and Shattuck-Hufnagel (2002) this is based on Levelt (1989), assuming without argument the generation of segmental content is the same as in his model]. Information structure (including focus) is part of the *preverbal message* (as per Levelt, 1989, chs. 3 and 4). We propose that *high-level prosodic structure generation* is a component of grammatical encoding (cf. Bock & Levelt, 1994, p. 946).

Rather than being based on the syntax, we suggest that higher-level prosodic structure (including the nuclear accent and major phrase breaks), is based on information structure. Prosodic requirements can therefore influence the syntactic structure used to convey the intended message (in the *positional processing* component): ensuring foci align with nuclear accents, and that the nuclear accent occurs late in the phrase (in line with our findings). This concurs with evidence that the effect of information structure driven syntactic variation is to place focal material in prosodically prominent positions (e.g., see Halliday, 1968; Ward & Birner, 2004). Feedback between the *prosodic structure generation* and *positional processing* components would ensure the resulting structure is syntactically legal, hence the double-headed arrows (it is left to future research whether this could be achieved via a monitoring system, as in Levelt's model). The output, *surface structure,* is again not syntactic, but the prosodic structure itself, with lemma entries at its roots carrying functional and inflectional information (including *F*-marking). Higher-level syntactic structure is discarded, consistent with Frazier et al.'s (2006) proposal for comprehension. This fits with much cross-linguistic evidence that most, if not all, phrase-level phonological processes apply to prosodic structure, not syntax (e.g., Selkirk, 1984; Truckenbrodt, 1999); and with Tyler and Warren's (1987) finding that disruption to higher-level syntax causes less difficulty for comprehension than disruption to higher-level prosodic structure.

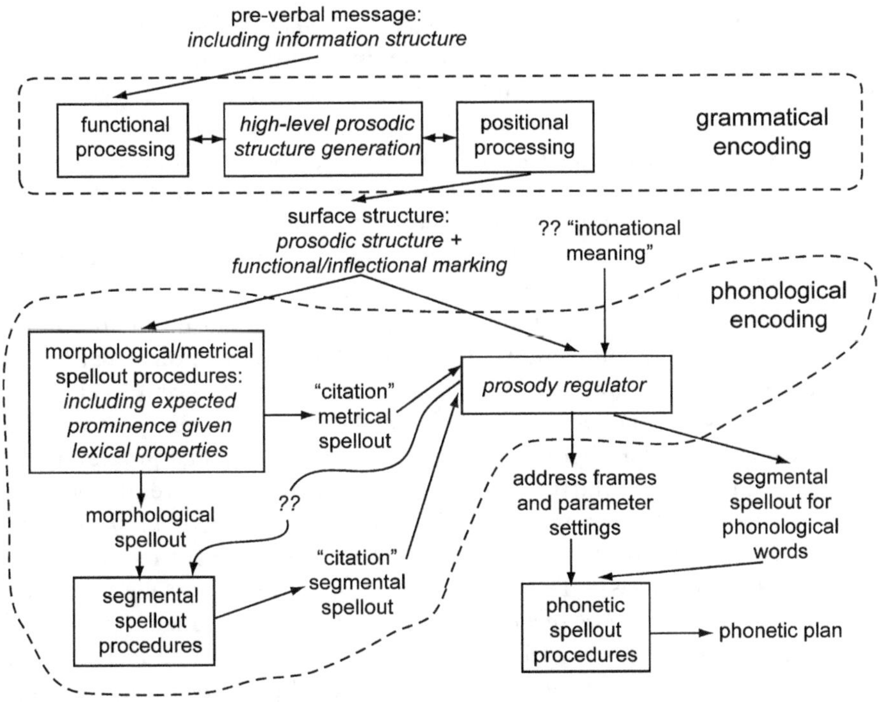

Figure 5. Model sketching proposed role of prosodic structure in the grammatical encoding and phonological encoding processes in language production. The overall model, and details of the phonological encoding processes, is based on Levelt (1989, p. 366), the grammatical encoding processes on Bock and Levelt (1994, p. 946). Text in boxes shows the different processes involved in grammatical and phonological encoding, while open text shows the representations of the message passed between processes. Processes are grouped depending on whether they are part of grammatical or phonological encoding (indicated by the dashed lines), phonetic spell out is considered to be after phonological encoding, and so not part of either group. Differences with Levelt's model are italicised (see text for further details).

In Levelt's model, *surface structure* is input to the *morphological/metrical spellout procedures,* which retrieves the *"citation" metrical spellout* (or prominence structure) for each word. This is posited to be retrieved prior to the segmental content because of "tip-of-the-tongue" evidence, i.e., speakers can often retrieve the metrical form of a word but not its content. We propose that *metrical spellout* also includes the expected prominence of a word given its lexical properties (e.g., accent ratio). This explains why "accentability" influences the likelihood of both nuclear and non-nuclear accents.

The *prosody generator* in Levelt's model is replaced by a *prosody regulator* (see Figure 5). This component integrates the metrical information about each lexeme into the main prosodic structure of the utterance, and generates lower-level prosodic structure (for the *address frames and parameter settings* output). In doing this, it tries to make the final output conform to metrical structure constraints, e.g., rhythm and phrase length limits. The regulator is therefore trying to maintain an alternation between strong and weak syllables (relative to the nuclear accent), while preserving expected prominence (i.e., words that are expected to be prominent should map on to metrically strong positions). It also needs to remain true to the *surface structure* input: in particular, *F*-marked positions must remain metrically strong. Where extra phrases are needed because of length, the *regulator* needs to make sure the nuclear accent for the whole utterance still falls in the same position. These interactions are consistent with our finding that focus, expected prominence, and prosodic constraints all affect accent likelihood. The processing of the *prosodic regulator* therefore involves probabilistic multiple constraint satisfaction, e.g., using a kind of dynamic programming (e.g., see Jurafsky & Martin, 2000). To fit the required overall metrical structure, the *regulator* may make adjustments to the *metrical spellout* of each lexeme which affect its *segmental spellout* (e.g., segment reductions or vowel quality changes). Therefore, the *prosody regulator* may provide feedback to the *segmental spellout procedures* on the final metrical form of the word. As in Levelt's model, phonological encoding can be incremental, given that the *surface structure* encodes the overall prosodic structure. This information is also in the *address frames and parameter settings* output, as it affects phonetic realisation (see Keating & Shattuck-Hufnagel, 2002). Finally, Levelt's model includes another input to the phonological encoding process, *intonational meaning*. It encodes the speaker's emotions and attitudes, and rhetorical force, relevant to the generation of intonation (see Levelt, 1989, ch. 8). Full consideration of this module is beyond the scope of this article.

This approach predicts ambiguity when the outcome of higher-level and lower-level mapping is the same. This is precisely the case with broad/narrow focus ambiguity given a "default" prosodic realisation (e.g., discussion of (1)). A narrow focus realisation could result from a single-word focus mapping onto the nuclear accent during grammatical encoding (e.g., *prison)*. In the broad focus case, the whole prosodic structure would be *F*-marked. Word mapping would then be entirely determined by linear ordering of the constituents, prosodic constraints, and expected prominence (on each *metrical spellout)*. This could result in the same word *(prison)* aligning with the nuclear accent. This model clearly still needs to be fully developed and tested; however, the sketch just given is consistent with our results, and offers new insight into the role of prosody in language production.

REFERENCES

Ariel, M. (1990). *Accessing noun-phrase antecedents.* London: Routledge.

Ayers, G. (1996). *Nuclear accent types and prominence: Some psycholinguistic experiments* (Unpublished doctoral dissertation). Ohio State University, Columbus, OH.

Aylett, M., & Turk, A. (2004). The smooth signal redundancy hypothesis: A functional explanation for relationships between redundancy, prosodic prominence, and duration in spontaneous speech. *Language and Speech, 47*(1), 31–56.

Badino, L., & Clark, R. A. (2007). Issues of optionality in pitch accent placement. In *Proceedings of the ISCA speech synthesis workshop* (pp. 252–257). Bonn, Germany: International Speech Communication Association.

Bard, E., & Aylett, M. (1999). The dissociation of deaccenting, givenness, and syntactic role in spontaneous speech. In J. Ohala, Y. Hasegawa, M. Ohala, D. Granville, & A. Bailey (Eds.), *Proceedings of ICPhS* (pp. 1753–1756). San Francisco, CA: International Phonetics Association.

Baumann, S., & Grice, M. (2006). The intonation of accessibility. *Journal of Pragmatics, 38*, 1636–1657.

Beaver, D., Clark, B., Flemming, E., Jaeger, T. F., & Wolters, M. (2007). When semantics meets phonetics: Acoustical studies of second occurrence focus. *Language, 83*(2), 245–276.

Beckman, M., & Hirschberg, J. (1999). *The ToBI annotation conventions.* Retrieved from http://www.ling.ohio-state.edu/ ~tobi/amejtobi/annotation_conventions.html

Blutner, R., & Sommer, R. (1988). Sentence processing and lexical access: The influence of the focus-identifying task. *Journal of Memory and Language, 27*, 359–367.

Bock, K., & Levelt, W. (1994). Language production: Grammatical encoding. In M. A. Gernsbacher (Ed.), *Handbook of psycholinguistics* (pp. 945–984). San Diego, CA: Academic Press.

Boersma, P., & Weenink, D. (2008). *Praat: Doing phonetics by computer.* Retrieved from http://www.praat.org

Bolinger, D. (1972). Accent is predictable (if you're a mind reader). *Language, 49*, 633–644.

Breen, M., Fedorenko, E., Wagner, M., & Gibson, E. (2010). Acoustic correlates of information structure. *Language and Cognitive Processes, 25*, 1044–1098.

Brenier, J., Nenkova, A., Kothari, A., Whitton, L., Beaver, D., & Jurafsky, D. (2006). The (non)utility of linguistic features for predicting prominence in spontaneous speech. In *Proceedings of IEEE/ACL workshop on spoken language technology* (pp. 54–57). Aruba: IEEE Signal Processing Society.

Bresnan, J., Cueni, A., Nikitina, T., & Baayen, R. (2007). Predicting the dative alternation. In G. Bouma, I. Kraemer, & J. Zwarts (Eds.), *Cognitive foundations of interpretation* (pp. 69–94). Amsterdam: Royal Netherlands Academy of Arts and Sciences.

Buráňová, E., Hajičová, E., & Sgall, P. (2000). Tagging of very large corpora: Topic-focus articulation. In *Proceedings of COLING conference* (pp. 278–284). Saarbriicken, Germany: Morgan Kaufmann.

Büring, D. (2006). Focus projection and default prominence. In V. Molnár & S. Winkler (Eds.), *The architecture of focus* (pp. 321–346). Berlin/New York: Mouton De Gruyter.

Calhoun, S. (2006). *Information structure and the prosodic structure of English: A probabilistic relationship* (Unpublished doctoral dissertation). University of Edinburgh, Edinburgh.

Calhoun, S. (2010). The centrality of metrical structure in signaling information structure: A probabilistic perspective. *Language, 86*, 1–42.

Calhoun, S., Carletta, J., Brenier, J., Mayo, N., Jurafsky, D., Steedman, M., et al. (2010). The NXT-format switchboard corpus: A rich resource for investigating the syntax, semantics, pragmatics and prosody of dialogue. *Language Resources and Evaluation.* Advance online publication. doi:10.1007/s10579-010-9120-1

Carletta, J. (1996). Assessing agreement on classification tasks: The kappa statistic. *Computational Linguistics, 22*(2), 249–254.

Chen, A., den Os, E., & de Ruiter, J. P. (2007). Pitch accent type matters for online processing of information status: Evidence from natural and synthetic speech. *The Linguistic Review, 24*, 317–344.

Chen, K., & Hasegawa-Johnson, M. (2004). An automatic prosody labeling system using ANN-based syntactic-prosodic model and GMM-based acoustic-prosodic model. In *Proceedings of ICASSP* (pp. 509–512). Montreal, Canada: IEEE Signal Processing Society.

Clarkson, P., & Rosenfeld, R. (1997). Statistical language modeling using the CMU-Cambridge toolkit. In *Proceedings of Eurospeech* (pp. 2707–2710). Rhodes, Greece: International Speech Communication Association.

Conkie, A., Riccardi, G., & Rose, R. (1999). Prosody recognition from speech utterances using acoustic and linguistic based models of prosodic events. In *Proceedings of Eurospeech* (pp. 523–526). Budapest, Hungary: International Speech Communication Association.

Cutler, A. (1976). Phoneme-monitoring reaction time as a function of preceding intonation contour. *Perception and Psychophysics, 20*, 55–60.

Cutler, A., Dahan, D., & van Donselaar, W. (1997). Prosody in the comprehension of spoken language: A literature review. *Language and Speech, 40*(2), 141–201.

Cutler, A., & Fodor, J. (1979). Semantic focus and sentence comprehension. *Cognition, 7*, 49–59.

Cutler, A., & Foss, D. (1977). On the role of sentence stress in sentence processing. *Language and Speech, 20*, 1–10.

Dahan, D., Tanenhaus, M., & Chambers, C. (2002). Accent and reference resolution in spoken-language comprehension. *Journal of Memory and Language, 47*, 292–314.

Dell, G., & Burger, L. (1997). Language production and serial order: A functional analysis and a model. *Psychological Review, 104*, 123–147.

Ferreira, F. (1993). Creation of prosody during sentence production. *Psychological Review, 100*(2), 233–253.

Ferreira, F. (2007). Prosody and performance in language production. *Language and Cognitive Processes, 22*(8), 1151–1177.

Fougeron, C. (1999). Prosodically conditioned articulatory variations: A review. *UCLA Working Papers in Phonetics, 97*, 1–74.

Frazier, L., Carlson, K., & Clifton, C. (2006). Prosodic phrasing is central to language comprehension. *Trends in Cognitive Science, 10*(6), 244–249.

German, J., Pierrehumbert, J., & Kaufmann, S. (2006). Evidence for phonological constraints on nuclear accent placement. *Language, 82*(1), 151–168.

Godfrey, J., Holliman, E., & McDaniel, J. (1992). SWITCHBOARD: Telephone speech corpus for research and development. In *Proceedings of ICASSP* (pp. 517–520). San Francisco, CA: IEEE Signal Processing Society.

Gregory, M., & Altun, Y. (2004). Using conditional random fields to predict pitch accent in conversational speech. In *Proceedings of ACL* (pp. 677–683). Barcelona, Spain: Association for Computational Linguistics.

Grice, M., Ladd, D. R., & Arvaniti, A. (2000). On the place of phrase accents in intonational phonology. *Phonology, 17*(2), 143–185.

Halliday, M. (1968). Notes on transitivity and theme in English: Part 3. *Journal of Linguistics, 4*, 179–215.

Hayes, B. (1995). *Metrical stress theory.* Chicago, IL: University of Chicago Press.

Hedberg, N., & Sosa, J. M. (2007). The prosody of topic and focus in spontaneous English dialogue. In C. Lee, M. Gordon, & D. Büring (Eds.), *Topic and focus: Cross-linguistic perspectives on meaning and intonation* (pp. 101–120). Dordrecht: Springer.

Hermes, D., & Rump, H. (1994). Perception of prominence in speech intonation induced by rising and falling pitch movements. *Journal of the Acoustical Society of America, 90*, 97–102.

Hirschberg, J. (1993). Pitch accent in context: Predicting intonational prominence from text. *Artificial Intelligence, 63*, 305–340.

Hocking, R. R. (2003). *Methods and applications of linear models: Regression and the analysis of variance* (2nd ed.). New York: Wiley.

Ito, K., & Speer, S. (2006). Using interactive tasks to elicit natural dialogue production. In S. Sudhoff, D. Lenertová, R. Meyer, S. Pappert, P. Augurzky, I. Mleinek, et al. (Eds.), *Methods in empirical prosody research* (pp. 229–258). New York: Walter de Gruyter.

Ito, K., & Speer, S. (2008). Anticipatory effects of intonation: Eye movements during instructed visual search. *Journal of Memory and Language, 58*(2), 541–573.

Jackendoff, R. S. (1972). *Semantic interpretation in generative grammar*. Cambridge, MA: MIT Press.

Jurafsky, D. (2003). Probabilistic modeling in psycholinguistics: Linguistic comprehension and production. In H. Bod, J. Hay, & S. Jannedy (Eds.), *Probabilistic linguistics* (pp. 39–93). Cambridge, MA: MIT Press.

Jurafsky, D., & Martin, J. (2000). *Speech and language processing: An introduction to natural language processing, computational linguistics, and speech recognition*. Upper Saddle River, NJ: Prentice Hall.

Keating, P., & Shattuck-Hufnagel, S. (2002). A prosodic view of word form encoding for speech production. *UCLA Working Papers in Phonetics, 101*, 112–156.

Kochanski, G., Grabe, E., Coleman, J., & Rosner, B. (2005). Loudness predicts prominence: Fundamental frequency lends little. *Journal of the Acoustical Society of America, 118*(2), 1038–1054.

Krahmer, E., & Swerts, M. (2001). On the alleged existence of contrastive accents. *Speech Communication, 34*(4), 391–405.

Ladd, D. R. (1996). *Intonational phonology*. Cambridge: Cambridge University Press.

Ladd, D. R. (2008). *Intonational phonology* (2nd ed.). Cambridge: Cambridge University Press.

Levelt, W. (1989). *Speaking: From intention to articulation*. Cambridge, MA: MIT Press.

Levelt, W., Roelofs, A., & Meyer, A. (1999). A theory of lexical access in speech production. *Brain and Behavioral Sciences, 22*(1), 1–38.

Liberman, M. (1979). *The intonational system of English* [Outstanding Dissertations in Linguistics 24]. New York: Garland Publishing.

Marcus, M., Santorini, B., & Marcinkiewicz, M. A. (1993). Building a large annotated corpus of English: The Penn Treebank. *Computational Linguistics, 19*, 313–330.

Menard, S. (1995). *Applied logistic regression analysis*. Thousand Oaks, CA: Sage.

Myers, R. (1990). *Classical and modern regression with applications* (2nd ed.). Boston, MA: Duxbury.

Nakatani, C., Hirschberg, J., & Grosz, B. (1995). Discourse structure in spoken language: Studies on speech corpora. In *Working notes of the AAAI spring symposium on empirical methods in discourse interpretation and generation* (pp. 106–112). Stanford, CA: American Association for Artificial Intelligence.

Nenkova, A., Brenier, J., Kothari, A., Calhoun, S., Whitton, L., Beaver, D., et al. (2007). To memorize or to predict: Prominence labeling in conversational speech. In *NAACL human language technology conference* (pp. 9–16). Rochester, NY: Association for Computational Linguistics.

Nissim, M., Dingare, S., Carletta, J., & Steedman, M. (2004, May). An annotation scheme for information status in dialogue. In *Proceedings of LREC* (pp. 638–641). Lisboa, Portugal: European Language Resources Association.

Ostendorf, M., Shafran, I., Shattuck-Hufnagel, S., Carmichael, L., & Byrne, W. (2001). A prosodically labeled database of spontaneous speech. In *Proceedings of the ISCA workshop on prosody in speech recognition and understanding* (pp. 119–121). Red Bank, NJ: International Speech Communication Association.

Pan, S., & Hirschberg, J. (2000). Modeling local context for pitch accent prediction. In *Proceedings of ACL* (pp. 233–240). Hong Kong: Association for Computational Linguistics.

Pan, S., McKeown, K., & Hirschberg, J. (2002). Exploring features from natural language generation for prosody modeling. *Computer Speech and Language, 16*, 457–490.

Pitrelli, J., Beckman, M., & Hirschberg, J. (1994). Evaluation of prosodic transcription labeling reliability in the ToBI framework. In *Proceedings of ICSLP* (Vol. 2, pp. 123–126). Yokohama, Japan: International Speech Communication Association.

Pitt, M., & Samuel, A. (1990). The use of rhythm in attending to speech. *Journal of Experimental Psychology: Human Perception and Performance, 16*, 564–573.

Prince, A., & Liberman, M. (1977). On stress and linguistic rhythm. *Linguistic Inquiry, 8*, 249–336.

Prince, E. (1981). Towards a taxonomy of given-new information. In P. Cole (Ed.), *Radical pragmatics* (pp. 223–255). New York: Academic Press.

Prince, E. (1992). The ZPG letter: Subjects, definiteness, and information-status. In S. Thompson & W. Mann (Eds.), *Discourse description: Diverse analyses of a fund raising text* (pp. 295–325). Philadelphia/Amsterdam: John Benjamins.

Ramus, F., Nespor, M., & Mehler, J. (1999). Correlates of linguistic rhythm in the speech signal. *Cognition, 73*, 265–292.

Reeves, C., Schmauder, A. R., & Morris, R .K. (2000). Stress grouping improves performance on an immediate serial list recall task. *Journal of Experimental Psychology: Learning, Memory and Cognition, 26*(6), 1638–1654.

Rooth, M. (1992). A theory of focus intepretation. *Natural Language Semantics, 1*, 75–116.

Rump, H., & Collier, R. (1996). Focus conditions and the prominence of pitch-accented syllables. *Language and Speech, 39*, 1–17.

Schwarzschild, R. (1999). Givenness, AVOIDF and other constraints on the placement of accent. *Natural Language Semantics, 7*, 141–177.

Selkirk, E. (1984). *Phonology and syntax*. Cambridge, MA: MIT Press.

Selkirk, E. (1995). Sentence prosody: Intonation, stress and phrasing. In J. Goldsmith (Ed.), *The handbook of phonological theory* (pp. 550–569). Cambridge, MA and Oxford: Blackwell.

Shattuck-Hufnagel, S., Ostendorf, M., & Ross, K. (1994). Stress shift and early pitch accent placement in lexical items in American English. *Journal of Phonetics, 22*, 357–388.

Shattuck-Hufnagel, S., & Turk, A. E. (1996). A prosody tutorial for investigators of auditory sentence processing. *Journal of Psycholinguistic Research, 25*(2), 193–247.

Shields, J., McHugh, A., & Martin, J. (1974). Reaction time to phoneme targets as a function of rhythmic cues in continuous speech. *Journal of Experimental Psychology, 102*, 250–255.

Sluijter, A., & van Heuven, V. (1996). Spectral balance as an acoustic correlate of linguistic stress. *Journal of the Acoustical Society of America, 100*(4), 2471–2485.

Sridhar, V. K. R., Bangalore, S., & Narayanan, S. (2008). Exploiting acoustic and syntactic features for automatic prosody labeling in a maximum entropy framework. *IEEE Transactions on Audio, Speech and Language Processing, 16*(4), 797–811.

Sridhar, V. K. R., Nenkova, A., Narayanan, S., & Jurafsky, D. (2008). Detecting prominence in conversational speech: Pitch accent, givenness and focus. In *Proceedings of Speech Prosody* (pp. 453–456). Campinos, Brazil: International Speech Communication Association.

Steedman, M. (2000). Information structure and the syntax-phonology interface. *Linguistic Inquiry, 31*(4), 649–689.

Sturges, P., & Martin, J. (1974). Rhythmic structure in auditory pattern perception and immediate memory. *Journal of Experimental Psychology, 102*, 377–383.

Tabor, W., Cornell, J., & Tanenhaus, M. (1997). Parsing in a dynamical system. *Language and Cognitive Processes, 12*, 211–272.

Taylor, A., Marcus, M., & Santorini, B. (2003). *The Penn Treebank: An overview.* Retrieved from http://citeseer.ist.psu.edu/taylor03penn.html

Terken, J., & Hermes, D. (2000). The perception of prosodic prominence. In M. Horne (Ed.), *Prosody: Theory and experiment. Studies presented to Gösta Bruce* (pp. 89–127). Dordrecht: Kluwer.

Terken, J., & Hirschberg, J. (1994). Deaccentuation of words representing 'given' information: Effects of persistence of grammatical role and surface position. *Language and Speech, 37*, 125–145.

Truckenbrodt, H. (1995). *Phonological phrases: Their relation to syntax, focus and prominence* (Unpublished doctoral dissertation). Cambridge, MA: MIT Press.

Truckenbrodt, H. (1999). On the relation between syntactic phrases and phonological phrases. *Linguistic Inquiry, 30*(2), 219–255.

Truckenbrodt, H. (2006). Phrasal stress. In K. Brown (Ed.), *The encyclopedia of languages and linguistics* (2nd ed., Vol. 9, pp. 572–579). Oxford: Elsevier.

Tyler, L., & Warren, P. (1987). Local and global structure in spoken language comprehension. *Journal of Memory and Language, 26*, 638–657.

Umbach, C. (2004). On the notion of contrast in information structure and discourse structure. *Journal of Semantics, 21*, 155–175.

Wagner, M. (2005). Asymmetries in prosodic domain formation. In N. Richards & M. McGinnis (Eds.), *Perspectives on phrases* (pp. 329–367). Cambridge, MA: MITWPL 49.

Wagner, M. (2006). Givenness and locality. In M. Gibson & J. Howell (Eds.), *Proceedings of SALTXVI* (pp. 295–312). Ithaca, NY: CLC.

Ward, G., & Birner, B. (2004). Information structure and non-canonical syntax. In L. Horn & G. Ward (Eds.), *The handbook of pragmatics* (pp. 153–173). Oxford: Blackwell.

Watson, D. (2008). The role of production factors in acoustic prominence [Abstract]. In *Experimental and Theoretical Advances in Prosody.* New York: Cornell University.

Watson, D., & Arnold, J. (2005). *Not just given and new: The effects of discourse and task-based constraints on acoustic prominence.* Poster presented at the CUNY sentence processing conference. Tucson, AZ.

Watson, D., & Gibson, E. (2004). The relationship between intonational phrasing and syntactic structure in language production. *Language and Cognitive Processes, 19*(6), 713–755.

Watson, D., Gunlogson, C., & Tanenhaus, M. (2008). Interpreting pitch accents in on-line comprehension: H* vs. L+H*. *Cognitive Science, 32*(7), 1232–1244.

Welby, P. (2003). Effects of pitch accent position, type and status on focus projection. *Language and Speech, 46*(1), 53–81.

Xu, Y., & Xu, C. (2005). Phonetic realization of focus in English declarative intonation. *Journal of Phonetics, 33*, 159–197.

Yoon, T-J., Chavarría, S., Cole, J., & Hasegawa-Johnson, M. (2004). Intertranscriber reliability of prosodic labeling on telephone conversation using ToBI. In *Proceedings of ICSLP* (pp. 2729–2732). Jeju, South Korea: International Speech Communication Association

Yuan, J., Brenier, J., & Jurafsky, D. (2005). Pitch accent prediction: Effects of genre and speaker. In *Proceedings of Eurospeech* (pp. 1409–1412). Lisboa, Portugal: International Speech Communication Association.

Zhang, T., Hasegawa-Johnson, M., & Levinson, S. (2006). Extraction of pragmantic and semantic salience from spontaneous spoken English. *Speech Communication, 48*, 437–462.

APPENDIX 1. FEATURES TESTED IN ACCENT PREDICTION MODELS

A list of features tested in the accent prediction models, along with brief descriptions and possible values, grouped by feature type. For continuous variables, the type of value is given, i.e., whole (whole number) or float (other rational number).

Prosodic

Feature	*Description*	*Values*
Rhythmic		
Accents so far	Number of accents in the phrase so far, excluding the current word	*Whole*
Words since last accent	Number of words since the last accent	*Whole*
Syllables in word	Number of syllables in the word	*Whole*
General phrasal		
Phrase mean F0	Mean F0 of the phrase, normalised as a percentage of the speaker's overall range in logged Hz	*Float*
Speech rate	The total number of syllables in the phrase relative to the phrase duration	*Float*
Pos. in phrase	The position of the syllable in the phrase	*Whole*
Phrase positional		
Rel. pos. in phrase	The position of the first phone in the current word relative to the number of phones in the phrase	*Float*
Phones in phrase	The number of phones in the phrase in total	*Whole*

Word prominence

Feature	*Description*	*Values*
Word median F0	Median F0 in the word, normalised as a percentage of the speaker's overall range in logged Hz	*Float*
Word F0 I-Q range	The inter-quartile F0 range in the word, i.e., 0.75–0.25, normalised as a percentage of the speaker's overall range in logged Hz	*Float*
Word mean intensity	The mean intensity in the word, relative to the mean intensity of all words for that speaker	*Float*
Word duration	The duration of the word relative to the number of syllables in the word	*Float*

Informativeness

Feature	*Description*	*Values*
Focus		
Focus status	Whether the word is a focus, at the word level or np level, or background	Focus: word level, focus: NP level, background
Reference status		
Reference status	The reference status of the word (only NPs classified)	Old, med, new, refstat not marked
Part-of-speech/syntax		
Part-of-speech	The part-of-speech of the word, by major group	Noun, verb, pronoun, demonstrative, adjective, and adverb
Clause type	The type of syntactic clause the word is in	Main, complement, relative, adverbial, and parenthetical
Rel. pos. in clause	The position of the current word relative to the number of words in the clause	*Float*
Words in clause	The number of words in the clause in total	*Whole*
Constituent type	The type of constituent the word is in	Subject, predicate, object, and adjunct
Rel. pos. in constituent	The position of the current word relative to the number of words in the constituent	*Float*
Predictability measures		
Accent ratio	Probability that the word is accented, where this is significantly different to chance, or 0.5 otherwise	*Float*
Unigram	Unigram predictability of the word (log(pw))	*Float*
Bigram	Bigram predictability of the word ($\log(pw_i \mid pw_{i-1})$)	*Float*

Impact of features in the different feature group models: The effect on the log likelihood of each feature group model (prosodic, informativeness, Pros+Info–Phr, and Pros+Info+Word) of removing each feature in that model in turn (with replacement)

Feature	Prosodic LL	Prosodic χ^2 (df)	Pros+Info–Phr LL	Pros+Info–Phr χ^2 (df)	Pros+Info+Word LL	Pros+Info+Word χ^2 (df)
Full model	17,213	–	17,277	–	13,977	–
Syllables in word	17,581	368.0 (2)**	17,373	96.0 (2)**	14,265	287.9 (2)**
Words since last accent	17,317	103.8 (2)**	17,373	95.6 (2)**	14,165	187.6 (2)**
Accents so far	17,782	569.6 (2)**	17,681	403.4 (2)**	14,414	436.8 (2)**
Phrase mean F0	17,238	25.1 (2)**	17,312	34.3 (2)**	14,149	171.2 (2)**
Rel. pos. in phrase	18,362	1,149.1 (2)**	n/a	–	15,186	1,208.8 (2)**
Pos. in phrase	n/a	–	17,339	61.4 (2)**	n/a	–
Phones in phrase	17,242	29.0 (2)**	n/a	–		
Speech rate	17,312	98.8 (2)**	17,436	158.4 (2)**	14,021	44.0 (2)**
	Informativeness					
Full model	17,994	–				
Focus status	18,648	654.1 (4)**	17,772	494.3 (4)**	14,180	202.8 (4)**
Part-of-speech	18,111	117.2 (10)**	17,361	83.3 (10)**	14,006	28.3 (10)**
Constituent type	18,048	54.4 (6)**	17,319	41.6 (6)**		
Rel. pos. in constit	18,074	80.0 (2)**	17,355	77.5 (2)**		
Words in clause	18,004	10.1 (2)**	17,286	8.9 (2)*		
Rel. pos. in clause	18,021	27.0 (2)**	17,295	17.7 (2)**		
Accent ratio	18,218	224.2 (2)**	17,460	182.4 (2)**	14,071	93.7 (2)**
Unigram	18,088	94.0 (2)**	17,305	27.6 (2)**	13,991	13.7 (2)**
Bigram	18,006	11.7 (2)**				
				Word median F0	14,291	313.3 (2)**
				Word F0 I-Q range	14,015	37.3 (2)**
				Word mean intensity	14,134	156.6 (2)**
				Word duration	14,529	551.1 (2)**

The log likelihoods (LL) of the reduced model in each case and χ^2 tests showing their significance (in comparison to the full model for that feature group) are given (df = degrees of freedom; **highly significant, $p < .01$; *significant, $.01 \leq p < .05$).

LANGUAGE AND COGNITIVE PROCESSES
2010, 25 (7/8/9), 1141–1177

Psychology Press
Taylor & Francis Group

The role of syntactic structure in guiding prosody perception with ordinary listeners and everyday speech

Jennifer Cole, Yoonsook Mo, and Soondo Baek

Department of Linguistics, University of Illinois at Urbana-Champaign, Urbana, IL, USA

The relationship between syntactic and prosodic phrase structures is investigated in the production and perception of spontaneous speech. Three hypotheses are tested: (1) syntax influences prosody production; (2) listeners' perception of prosodic boundaries is sensitive to acoustic duration; and (3) syntax directly influences boundary perception, (partly) independent of the acoustic evidence for boundaries. Data are from the Buckeye corpus of conversational speech, and the real-time prosodic transcription of those data by 97 untrained listeners. Inter-transcriber agreement codes boundary strength at word junctures, and Boundary scores are shown to be correlated with both the syntactic context and vowel duration of a word. Vowel duration is also correlated with syntactic context, but the effect of syntactic context on boundary perception is not fully explained by vowel duration. Regression analyses show that syntactic clause boundaries and vowel duration are the first and second strongest predictors of boundary perception in spontaneous speech.

Keywords: Prosody perception; Prosody production; Syntax; Spontaneous speech; Prosody transcription.

Correspondence should be addressed to Jennifer Cole, Department of Linguistics, 4080 Foreign Languages Building, University of Illinois at Urbana-Champaign, 707 South Mathews, Urbana, IL 61801, USA. E-mail: jscole@illinois.edu

This work is supported by NSF award IIS-0414117 to the first author and Mark Hasegawa-Johnson. For their varied contributions to the work presented here, we thank three anonymous reviewers, Mark Hasegawa-Johnson, Chilin Shih, Tae-Jin Yoon, Xiaodan Zhuang, and other members of the Prosody-ASR research group, and to José Ignacio Hualde. Special thanks to Zachary Hulstrom and Eun-Kyung Lee for their help with the prosody transcription experiments. Statements in this paper reflect the opinions and conclusions of the authors, and are not endorsed by the NSF or the University of Illinois.

http://www.psypress.com/lcp DOI: 10.1080/01690960903525507

INTRODUCTION

Through prosodic phrasing, languages encode the grouping of words into constituents that cohere semantically (Frazier, Clifton, & Carlson, 2004; Selkirk, 1984), and which can express the preferred rhythmic and intonational patterns of the language (Nespor & Vogel, 1986; Schafer, Speer, Warren, & White, 2000; Watson & Gibson, 2004). The prosodic structure of an utterance, including both phrasing and the marking of prosodic prominence, influences its phonetic expression in many ways, with effects realised at the level of segmental properties (e.g., vowel formant patterns, consonant voicing), and suprasegmental properties (pitch, loudness and duration).[1] Prosody also influences speech comprehension (Cutler, Dahan, & van Donselaar, 1997; Frazier, Carlson, & Clifton, 2006) in that listeners are guided in the interpretation of the syntactic and semantic contents of an utterance by the prosodic structures encoded in its phonetic form.

A simple and direct model of the effect of prosody on sentence comprehension can be characterised as follows. The speaker produces a prosodic structure for an utterance that reflects the grouping of words into syntactic or semantic units. The prosodic structure, part of phonological form, is interpreted in the phonetic implementation, shaping the articulation and resulting in acoustic patterns that encode the prosodic elements marking prominence and phrasing. The listener perceives these acoustic patterns as cues to the prosodic structure produced by the speaker, and interprets the syntactic and semantic properties of the utterance in conformance with the perceived prosodic structure.

The direct syntax–prosody processing model as sketched above is an idealisation, and though it may serve as a useful model of speech processing in laboratory conditions, the facts of speech production and perception in situations of natural speech communication are somewhat more challenging. First, there is the fact that there are many factors that contribute to the assignment of prosodic structure, some of which are related to the linguistic form of the utterance (e.g., syntactic or semantic factors), and others which reflect the speaker's affect, communicative intent, or speaker-selected production factors such as rate or clarity. And, like any other aspect of

[1] Although phonetic implementation of prosody can be seen in evidence from both articulation and acoustics, our project is focused on acoustic correlates and their relation to prosody perception. There are numerous works reporting on a wide range of acoustic parameters as correlates of prosody, of which we cite a few here: Beckman (1986), Beckman and Pierrehumbert (1986), Ladd (1996/2008) for F0; Turk and Sawusch (1997) and Wightman et al. (1992) for duration; Kochanski, Grabe, Coleman, and Rosner (2005) for overall intensity; Heldner (2003) and Sluijter and van Heuven (1996) for spectral emphasis and balance (intensities in sub-bands); van Bergem (1993) for formant structures; Choi, Hasegawa-Johnson, and Cole (2005) for various harmonic and voice source parameters.

speech production, prosody production is also subject to disfluency (DISF) or error. Variability in prosody production that is not due to linguistic form is shown in the Schafer et al.'s (2000) study of English spontaneous speech produced in laboratory conditions, and in the Yoon's (2007) corpus study of radio news announcers' read productions of the same news script. The possibility of variable prosody for a given sentence, even in the absence of structural ambiguity, means that the listener can not have rigid expectations about the prosodic form of an utterance based solely on the word string and prior syntactic context.

A second challenge comes from the fact of inter- and intra-speaker variations in the phonetic encoding of prosody. The acoustic correlates of prosody are variable in all speech styles, but especially so in spontaneous speech. For example, while English speakers producing read speech are fairly consistent in encoding prosodic phrase boundaries through lengthening of the phrase-final syllable rhyme (Wightman, Shattuck-Hufnagel, Ostendorf, & Price, 1992; Yoon, Cole, & Hasegawa-Johnson, 2007), they vary in their use of intensity, F0, glottalisation of phrase-initial vowels (Dilley, Shattuck-Hufnagel, & Ostendorf, 1996), and creaky voicing (laryngealisation) in phrase-final position (Kim, Yoon, Cole, & Hasegawa-Johnson, 2006). Acoustic effects of prosody also vary according to the phonological content of the word or syllable, for example, as shown by Lee and Cole (2007) and Mo (2008), whose studies of radio news speech and spontaneous speech show variability in final lengthening effects on vowels as a function of vowel phoneme.

The third challenge to a model of direct syntax–prosody processing relates to the listener. Listener variability in the perception of prosody has not been discussed as widely in the prosody literature as has speaker variability, but can arise from a number of factors. First, just as there may be DISF or errors in prosody production, the same is true for perception. A listener may fail to detect acoustic cues to prosody that are present in the signal due to performance factors (attention and fatigue), or due to interference from environmental noise or activity. Variability in prosody perception among listeners can also arise due to differences in linguistic experience, e.g., from unfamiliarity with a speaker's voice or his/her phonetic expression of prosody. Evidence for perceptual variability can be seen in studies that report on inter-transcriber agreement rates on tasks of prosody transcription.

Much of the contemporary research on prosody evaluates the prosodic elements of an utterance by means of prosody transcription, using a transcription standard such as the Tones and Break Indices (ToBI) system (Beckman & Ayers, 1997), which is based on the autosegmental–metrical model of prosody (Beckman & Pierrehumbert, 1986; Ladd, 1996/2008). One method for evaluating the reliability of prosody transcription is to employ multiple trained transcribers in the annotation of a common set of materials, and then to assess the agreement rate among them. High agreement is taken to indicate that the transcribers were uniform and consistent in their interpretation of prosody according to the transcription guidelines. Furthermore, if multiple transcribers produce the same prosody annotation for a given utterance, it is assumed that there were sufficiently salient cues to that prosodic structure in the speech signal. Ostendorf, Price, and Shattuck-Hufnagel (1995) conducted a reliability study for the ToBI system using transcriptions of radio broadcast news speech, reporting inter-transcriber agreement rates as high as 91% for the location of prosodic phrase boundaries, and 60% for the location of pitch accent. Dilley, Breen, Bolivar, Kraemer, and Gibson (2006) conducted a similar test of reliability for ToBI transcriptions on a small-scale, combined corpus of radio broadcast news speech and telephone conversational speech, reporting agreement rates of 88% on the location of prosodic phrase boundaries, and 87% on the location of pitch accent. Using a simplified ToBI transcription system (marking only the location and not the tonal type of boundaries and prominent words), Yoon, Chavarría, Cole, and Hasegawa-Johnson (2004) compared transcriber agreement rates for telephone conversational speech, with agreement rates at 89% for boundaries and 86% for pitch accent.

The inter-transcriber agreement rates reported from ToBI reliability studies are well above chance levels, and are taken as validation that the transcription method is generally reliable. But at the same time, they also reveal listener variability, even under idealised listening conditions. The transcription task for each of these studies provides the transcriber with a wealth of information on which to judge prosody, including visual displays of the speech waveform, pitch and intensity tracks and spectrogram, along with an auditory signal, and the transcriber is allowed to listen to the signal as many times as needed, stopping and starting at any location to focus on difficult regions. Transcribers typically undergo rigorous training in preparation for their task, including group discussion and resolution of problem cases. These conditions are far from similar to the conditions under which ordinary listeners perceive and interpret prosody, but even so, these trained transcribers disagree on the prosodic structure of an utterance for 10–30% of its content (counted in words).

There are many differences between the task of prosody transcription by trained transcribers and ordinary prosody perception in the course of everyday speech communication. If we are to take research findings based on expert prosody transcription as representative of what takes place in ordinary speech processing, then we must first establish a parallel between expert transcribers and ordinary listeners in their perception of prosody. A question of particular interest, and the focus of this paper, is whether untrained listeners are guided in their perception of prosody (specifically, prosodic prominence and prosodic phrase boundaries) by information beyond the phonetic form of the utterance, specifically, by information from the syntactic context. Lacking visual information from a graphical speech display or expert linguistic knowledge, is the untrained listener influenced by the syntactic, semantic, and discourse context when making explicit judgements about the prosodic elements in a naturally produced speech utterance? For instance, does the listener have expectations about the prosodic structure of an utterance based on the discourse context, which establishes the information status of each word and phrase, or based on his/her prior experience with utterances containing similar discourse contexts, similar words, or similar syntactic content? And although expert transcribers are trained to focus narrowly on the phonetic evidence for prosody, is there also a possibility of extra-phonetic factors influencing them, too?

The present paper focuses on the relationship between the perception of prosodic phrase boundaries and the syntactic form of an utterance, and is part of a larger study investigating how untrained listeners perceive prosody in spontaneous speech. The goal of this study is to determine the relative strength of (acoustic) phonetic and extra-phonetic factors as correlates of perceived prosody. The approach relies on prosody transcription using multiple, untrained transcribers (15–22 per utterance), and a set of probabilistic prosody features that encode the strength of the prosodic feature (prominence or boundary) based on the proportion of transcribers who perceive that feature. The component of this study presented below addresses the following questions:

- *Variability by listener and speaker.* Do untrained listeners agree with one another in their perception of prosody for a given utterance (listener variability)? Are there differences across speakers in the patterns of prosody as perceived by listeners (speaker variability)?
- *Syntax–prosody association.* What is the relationship between the syntactic properties of an utterance and perceived prosody? How closely do prosodic boundaries perceived by untrained listeners reflect syntactic boundaries, and are there differences among syntactic boundary types in their correlation with perceived prosody? Are there asymmetries in the syntax–prosody correlation for boundaries at the right vs. left edge of syntactic and prosodic domains?
- *Acoustic duration as a cue to syntactic or prosodic phrases.* If syntactic structure is correlated with prosodic phrase structure as perceived by ordinary listeners, is that correlation mediated through the phonetic form?

We turn in the following section to a brief review of prior research on the link between prosody and syntax, both in production and perception. These works paint a complex picture of prosody processing, where a range of linguistic factors, including syntactic factors, interact to determine the prosodic form of an utterance.

LINGUISTIC FACTORS THAT INFLUENCE PROSODY

Prosodic phrases group words together in units that reflect syntactic structure, but syntactic structure does not fully predict prosodic phrasing. This claim follows directly from the observation that speakers vary in the prosody they assign to syntactically similar forms (Schafer et al., 2000; Yoon, 2007), and is reflected in a number of production models that accommodate misalignment of prosodic and syntactic units (Bachenko & Fitzpatrick, 1990; Gee & Grosjean, 1983; Watson & Gibson, 2004, among others). Linguistic theories of prosodic phrase structure recognise patterns of alignment between the edges of prosodic and syntactic constituents, but these constituents are frequently not co-extensive (Selkirk, 1984, 1986, 2000; Shattuck-Hufnagel & Turk, 1996). Yet despite the frequent mismatch between syntactic and prosodic phrases, the syntactic properties of an utterance do play a significant role in determining prosodic structure in speech production. For example, the part-of-speech of a word and the type of phrase it belongs to (e.g., main clause, subordinate clause, adjunct, parenthetical) influence the likelihood that a prosodic phrase boundary will appear before or after the word (Price, Ostendorf, Shattuck-Hufnagel, & Fong, 1991; Schafer et al., 2000; Selkirk, 1984, 1986; Watson & Gibson, 2004).

Syntax is not the only linguistic factor that influences the prosodic structure associated with an utterance. Semantic factors on prosodic phrasing are invoked in Selkirk's (1984) Sense Unit Condition (*elements in an intonational phrase must cohere semantically*) and Frazier et al.'s (2004) Semantic Coherence Constraint (*don't put semantically unrelated elements in the same prosodic phrase*). Other factors influencing prosodic phrasing relate to phonological structure, and include the length of the syntactic phrase, the distance from the previous prosodic boundary, and the location of the nuclear pitch accent (Nespor & Vogel, 1986; Watson & Gibson, 2004). The syntactic, semantic and phonological factors, along with factors related to speaking rate and style, collectively influence the prosodic structure assigned to an utterance, as demonstrated in Calhoun's (2006) work on the automatic prediction of prosody.

Given the complexity of the system that underlies the assignment of prosody, we might expect that the empirical evidence for the role of any single factor will be blunted by the effects of interacting factors. From the perspective of the listener, we may ask if and how acoustic cues to prosody are interpreted in terms of any single conditioning factor. How does the listener determine if the acoustic evidence for a prosodic phrase boundary reflects the syntactic, semantic, or phonological context? Evidence from speech comprehension studies establishes that prosody does contribute to syntactic interpretation (Price et al., 1991; Schafer et al., 2000; Weber, Grice, & Crocker, 2006), but the listener's evaluation of syntactic structure at any location in the utterance seems to depend on the integration of prosodic cues over a larger domain (Frazier et al., 2006). Frazier et al. (2004) state that syntactic structure on its own doesn't force or block any pattern of prosodic phrasing, and they as well as Pynte (2006) claim that a prosodic break may occur in almost any location in a sentence, if motivated by phonological and/or semantic factors.

The production studies cited above find evidence that syntactic structure is (at least partially) encoded in prosodic structure, while the perception and comprehension studies find corresponding evidence that perceived prosody influences the interpretation of syntactic structures. These findings are compatible with the idealised direct syntax–prosody processing model, as described in the Introduction section. The speaker produces a prosodic structure that reflects the syntactic phrasing of the utterance, encoding the prosodic structure in the phonetic implementation of the utterance. The listener perceives the phonetic signal, decodes the prosodic information and uses it to guide an analysis of the syntactic structure for the utterance. The listener's task is complicated by the fact that syntax is not the sole determinant of prosodic structure, so inferences about syntactic structure based on perceived prosody must be tempered by consideration of other factors that shape prosodic structure. For example, the presence of a prosodic phrase boundary preceding sentence-final PP might signal high attachment of the PP, but it may also reflect purely phonological factors, such as the length of the preceding NP, suggesting that the impact of perceived prosody on syntactic judgements must be weighted by taking into account the phonological context (and possibly other factors). Nonetheless, to the extent that syntactic judgements are significantly correlated with perceived prosody, we find support for the model of direct prosody–syntax processing.

TESTING THE PROSODY–SYNTAX RELATIONSHIP IN SPONTANEOUS SPEECH

Our study seeks new empirical evidence for the prosody–syntax relationship, by investigating the perception of prosody in spontaneous, conversational speech. Two hypotheses of the direct prosody–syntax processing model are tested in the experiment presented below: (1) syntactic phrasing influences the prosodic phrase structure a speaker assigns to an utterance, and (2) listeners respond to acoustic cues to prosody in their judgement of the prosodic structure of the utterance. (An additional hypothesis from this model, that the listener's judgement of the prosodic structure influences syntactic interpretation, is not addressed here.) These hypotheses are tested using speech data from a corpus of spontaneous, conversational speech. Perception data are in the form of prosody judgements on these materials, obtained from untrained listeners performing real-time prosodic transcription. Acoustic measures of vowel duration provide production data, and a manual annotation of syntactic phrase structure provides data on the syntactic context of each word in the corpus.

The first hypothesis is tested in two ways: an indirect measure of the influence of syntax on prosody production is from the listeners' perspective, in the relationship between syntactic structure and perceived prosody, and a more direct measure uses acoustic evidence of prosody production, in the correlation between syntactic phrase structure and the acoustic correlates of prosodic phrasing. If syntax influences prosody production, then we expect to observe acoustic effects of prosodic phrase boundaries in locations predicted by the syntax.

We focus our analysis on acoustic effects of prosody in the lengthening of the phrase-final syllable rhyme, which is one of the most studied and robust effects of prosodic phrasing in English (Lehiste, 1972; Wightman et al., 1992; Yoon et al., 2007). Acoustic evidence of final lengthening is measured in the duration of word-final stressed vowels.[2] Unstressed vowels are excluded to avoid durational effects of unstressed vowel reduction, but since over three-quarters of the words in the corpus under study are monosyllabic, the majority of word-final vowels are also stressed.[3]

[2] In addition to durational effects of prosody, we also find overall intensity (Root Mean Square) and acoustic measures of creaky voicing (H1*–H2* and H2*–H4*) to be significantly correlated with the perception of prosodic phrase boundaries for at least some vowel phonemes. We report only the duration findings here, as duration was not only the strongest correlate (based on Pearson's r values), but is also the only acoustic measure that is significantly correlated with boundary perception across most of the vowel phonemes (Mo, 2008). Pause duration is also expected to cue prosodic boundaries, but we have not yet examined pause duration in our materials. For the data reported here, speech excerpts were selected to minimise the occurrence of disfluency within the excerpt, where silent and filled pauses were one of the factors used to identify disfluency. We expect that this selection criterion has skewed the distribution of pause duration at prosodic juncture in these materials. In our ongoing work we are investigating the influence of pause duration on prosody perception with longer excerpts for which pause duration was not a selection criterion.

[3] Prosodic prominence also conditions lengthening of a stressed vowel (e.g., Turk & Sawusch, 1997), so the duration measure examined here may in some cases exhibit combined effects of prominence and boundary lengthening. Prominence is coded in our data with a probabilistic *P*-score assigned to each word, parallel to the assignment of B-scores, which means that we can not simply separate prominent (pitch-accented) words from non-prominent words (unaccented), as has been done in prior studies that are based on ToBI-style prosody transcription. Instead, we

(*continued on next page*)

The second hypothesis is tested by measuring the correlation between the listeners' judgements of prosodic phrase boundaries and stressed vowel duration as the acoustic correlate of prosodic phrase boundary. If listeners are sensitive to the acoustic encoding of prosodic structure, their judgements of prosodic phrase boundary location should coincide with the acoustic evidence of final lengthening. We expect to find longer stressed vowels in words that are perceived as final in the prosodic phrase.

Our study takes the direct prosody–syntax processing model one step further, and tests a third hypothesis about the role of syntax in prosody perception: (3) syntactic phrasing is a direct influence on listeners' perception of prosodic phrase structure. This hypothesis is motivated by considering the effect of the listener's prior linguistic experience on the perception of a new utterance. If the listener's prior experience suggests a strong relationship between syntactic phrase structure of a certain type and the occurrence of a prosodic phrase boundary, then this association could in principle bias the listener to hear a prosodic boundary in the presence of the triggering syntactic form, even if the acoustic evidence for a prosodic boundary was weak or absent. Hypothesis 3 is tested first through the correlation between syntactic phrase structure and listeners' judgements of prosodic phrase boundaries. We expect to find a greater incidence of perceived prosodic phrase boundaries at locations where there is a high-level syntactic phrase boundary (e.g., a clause boundary). A significant correlation could arise due to a direct influence of syntax on prosody perception, but it could also arise if the acoustic evidence supports a judgement of prosodic phrase boundary at locations that coincide with syntactic phrase boundaries. To test for the independence of syntactic phrase structure on prosody perception, we conduct regression analyses with syntactic phrase boundaries and acoustic duration measures as predictors of perceived prosodic phrase boundaries. As shown below, the evidence from regression analysis supports the claim

---

use correlation and regression analysis to look at the relationship between duration, B-scores and *P*-scores. Comparison of correlation coefficients between duration and B-scores (Kendall's tau = .369) vs. duration and *P*-scores (Kendall's tau = .243) shows that duration is more strongly correlated with B-scores (all duration measures are normalised via *z*-transform). The correlation between *P*-scores and B-scores is even weaker (Kendall's tau = .204). Furthermore, regression analysis shows that *P*-scores only very weakly predict B-scores ($r^2 = .027$). Stepwise regression analysis shows that duration is the primary predictor of B-scores ($r^2 = .239$; shown in Table 6, Model B) and *P*-scores as a second factor contribute only marginally as a predictor ($r^2 = .008$). Looking at it from the perspective of duration modelling, we also find that B-scores are stronger predictors of vowel duration ($r^2 = .278$) with *P*-scores again as weak predictors ($r^2 = .039$). These findings demonstrate that boundary effects on duration outweigh prominence effects, and thus that boundary lengthening effects on words marked as prominent cannot be solely attributed to prominence-based lengthening.

that syntactic structure makes an independent contribution to the perception of prosodic phrase structure, beyond that of acoustic vowel duration.[4]

METHODS AND MATERIALS

The speech materials used for the prosody transcription experiment were drawn from the Buckeye corpus of spontaneous, conversation-style speech collected from interviews with adult speakers from Columbus, OH (Pitt et al., 2007). Two excerpts of between 11 and 22 seconds long were extracted from the interviews of 36 speakers, for a total of 72 excerpts, and two similar excerpts taken from one other speaker were used for an initial practice transcription. The excerpts were extracted at junctures between talker turns, often at topic junctures, and always at a natural prosodic break, typically marked by pause. Four stimuli sets were created from these materials. Two sets of test excerpts were constructed each containing one of the two excerpts from 18 speakers, with a third and fourth set containing one of the two excerpts from a second set of 18 speakers. Each test excerpt appeared in only one set, and each speaker is represented by no more than a single excerpt within a set. Each set also contained a practice excerpt from the extra speaker. The test excerpts were randomly sequenced in each set. Orthographic transcripts were created for each excerpt, removing all punctuation and capitalisation, and including

[4] A reviewer asks about the possibility of directly testing the independence of acoustic and lexico-syntactic cues to prosody by testing prosody perception with delexicalised speech—using filters or transformations of the acoustic signal to remove segmental information that reveals the lexical content of the speech. This approach is illustrated in the work of de Pijper and Sanderman (1994) who tested prosodic boundary perception by untrained listeners with delexicalised speech materials which were created by resynthesising speech after replacing the first eight spectral peaks with peaks of fixed frequency and bandwidth, and also manipulating pitch and Linear Predictive Coefficient (LPC) gain. This manipulation has the effect of rendering every vowel as schwa-like in its spectral features, and eliminating consonantal distinctions. The resulting materials were judged by de Pijper and Sanderman to preserve prosodic cues while rendering the utterances otherwise unintelligible; and the procedure was considered more successful than simpler alternative methods involving only low-pass filtering or spectral inversion. We have also considered methods for delexicalisation in our work on prosody perception, but like de Pijper and Sanderman, we have been dissatisfied with the filtering methods we have tested thus far, which were either unsuccessful in removing segmental cues to lexical content or successful in delexicalisation but with distorted or very unnatural sounding prosody. We did not attempt the complex method of spectral peak substitution used by de Pijper and Sanderman, which is unsuitable for our purposes given that we are interested in both segmental and suprasegmental effects of prosody. A related suggestion from this reviewer was to ask transcribers to mark prosody on the text without listening to the associated speech file, in which case lexico-syntactic features alone would guide the annotation. We did not collect such data in the initial phase of this project, whose findings are presented here, but are currently doing so for the second phase of data collection, and expect to report on the findings in our future work.

transcription of DISF and filled pauses. The transcriptions were sequenced to match the auditory presentation of the recorded excerpts, and printed on multiple sheets of paper using 14 pt, Times New Roman font. Listeners provided a coarse prosody annotation for each excerpt by making marks on the printed transcription sheet. The prosody annotation involved marking the location of prosodic phrase boundaries and prominent words in separate tasks (the data on prominence perception are not discussed further here).

Between 15 and 22 listeners transcribed each excerpt for its prosodic content, and the transcriptions were pooled from the entire group to obtain a population-wise, probabilistic measure of the prosodic status of each word. This method is adapted from similar methods used by Buhmann et al. (2002), Streefkerk, Pols, and ten Bosch (1997, 1998), and Swerts (1997).

A total of 97 listeners took part in the transcription experiment, all undergraduate students recruited from introductory level linguistics courses at the authors' home institution. Listeners had no prior training in prosody transcription or prosodic phonology and were monolingual, native speakers of American English. The majority were residents of Illinois from childhood. Data from six listeners were excluded due to failure to follow the transcription guidelines or because they were found not to be monolingual. Listeners were randomly assigned to one of four test groups, corresponding to the four sets of speech materials. Listeners were seated individually at computers in a classroom and told that they would listen through headphones to excerpts from recorded interviews with speakers of American English, and use a pencil to mark the transcript indicating the grouping of words into "chunks" of speech. The experimenter defined chunking by reading the short script in Appendix 1, but no example sound file was played to demonstrate what chunk boundaries might sound like. Subjects were also told that there is no single "right" transcription for an excerpt, and they should not be concerned with how one person's transcription compares to anyone else's.

The participants listened to each excerpt twice in succession, marking the location of "chunk" boundaries with vertical lines between words on the printed transcript. The transcription was performed in real time, and was solely based on auditory impression; listeners were not aided by any visual, graphic display of the speech signal. Listeners also were neither able to start or stop the auditory presentation, nor could they repeat any excerpt after the second presentation. Listeners were allowed to mark changes to their prosody annotation, by striking through a mark to "delete" it, and by circling a stricken mark to recall it. No further changes could be recorded.

Data coding

For each word a probabilistic Boundary score (B-score) is calculated based on the proportion of transcribers from the total group (15–22 per excerpt set), who perceived a prosodic boundary (a juncture between "chunks") following that word. B-score values are between 0 and 1, with extreme high or low scores indicating greater agreement among transcribers, presumably reflecting lesser ambiguity in the prosodic organisation of the utterance, and/or the presence of more salient cues to the presence or absence of a prosodic boundary. Figure 1 shows an example of a partial excerpt, plotting the B-score for each word. This example illustrates a typical finding, namely, that there are many words that transcribers agree are *not* before a boundary, and many fewer words where transcribers reach the same rate of agreement on the positive assignment of a boundary.

In addition to the coding of B-scores, each word is annotated for the highest level syntactic boundary that coincides with its right and left edges, separately, based on a manual syntactic parse based on Penn Treebank annotation guidelines (Marcus, Marcinkiewicz, & Santorini, 1993). The syntactic categories specified in the parse are listed in Table 1.

A sample coding of a partial excerpt is shown in Table 2. The full excerpt from which that sample was taken is shown in (1), with bracketing of the final portion reflecting the location of perceived boundaries labelled by two or more transcribers. This example illustrates the fact that the juncture between any two successive words is coded twice, as a left edge and as a right edge. Consequently, the left and right edge B-scores in the coding are matched: every left edge B-score corresponds to the right edge B-score of the preceding word.

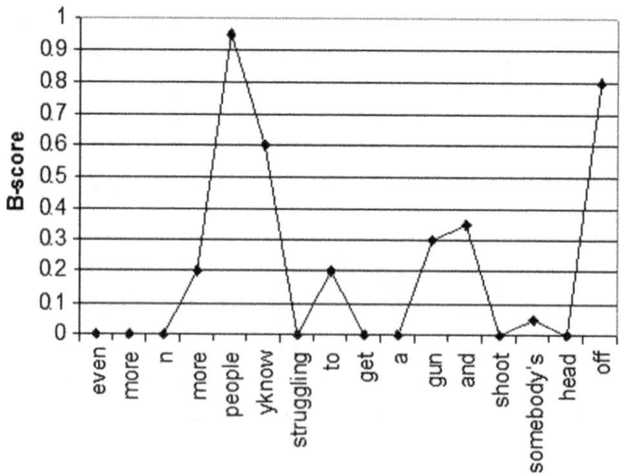

Figure 1. Graph of probabilistic boundary (B) score for each word in a sample utterance from the test corpus. B-scores represent the proportion of transcribers (out of 20 for this excerpt) who perceived a prosodic boundary following the given word.

TABLE 1

Syntactic categories used in the manual annotation in which each word was assigned a "left-edge" label for the highest level syntactic category whose left edge coincides with the left edge of the word

Category	Description and examples
S	matrix S L: uh | *it's just you* ... R: still *live in the city of Columbus* | uh...
S-BAR	subordinate or relative clause L: the fact | *that it was something*... R: *when our kids grew up* | then there was so...
S2	S preceded by (non-coordinating) conjunction or relative pronoun L: the fact that | *it was something*... R: *not defined*
CC-S	coordinating conjunction following or preceding a sentence L: we had standards | *and* there were certain things... R: we had standards *and* | there were certain things...
CC-XP	coordinating conjunction preceding or following an XP L: we did | *or* didn't... R: metal detectors *and* | police
Phrase (XP)	any XP that is not a clause (examples with VP) L: people yknow | *struggling to get*... R: I *like Columbus* | also
Within phrase (W/P)	any word boundary that does not align with a coded syntactic boundary (a non-initial (L) or non-final (R) word) <rarely occurs with boundary label>
Disfluency	filled pause, repetition & repair disfluencies L: in 1981 | *uh* lived... R: and then the protestant | *the uh*...
Discourse marker (DM)	*yknow, like, so, I mean,* ... L: the uh | *sorry* the uh... R: organ playing and *yknow* | praise the Lord...

Note: A "right-edge" label was similarly assigned to the right edge of each word. Other categories with counts less than 10 in this dataset are not shown.

(1)

<start of excerpt> they don't have the money to throw away and like catholic schools they don't have the money to put on those programs so some of those people kind of get pushed aside and so yknow as you can see I'm standing on m soapbox here I do like Columbus public schools but yknow i i i hate when people say yknow look at these test scores [because it really doesn't reflect what's there] [because] [it's like saying] [all kids carry guns to school <end of excerpt>

RESULTS I: LISTENER AND SPEAKER VARIABILITY

To assess the reliability of the prosody transcriptions obtained from untrained listeners, the agreement rate between all transcribers assigned to

TABLE 2
A partial excerpt showing the word sequence (from top to bottom), the left- and right-edge syntactic category for each word, and the B-score associated with that word edge

Left-edge B-score	*Left-edge syntactic category*	*Word*	*Right-edge syntactic category*	*Right-edge B-score*
0.25	**SBAR**	because	SubConj	0
0	S2	it	NP	0
0	VP	really	ADVP	0
0	VP2	doesn't	W/P	0
0	VP2	reflect	W/P	0
0	SBAR	what's	REL	0
0	ADVP	there	**SBAR**	0.45
0.45	**SBAR**	because	**SC**	0.75
0.75	**S2**	it's	W/P	0
0	SBAR	like	SC	0
0	S-ING	saying	**W/P**	0.1
0.1	**SBAR**	all	W/P	0
0	W/P	kids	NP	0
0	VP	carry	W/P	0
0	NP	guns	VP	0
0	PP	to	W/P	0
0	NP	school	SBAR	.

Note: Bold category labels mark locations where two or more listeners marked a right or left prosodic ("chunk") boundary. See Table 1 for definitions of the primary syntactic labels; labels appearing here but not in Table 1 are low-frequency labels in our dataset and are not included in the analysis (e.g., SC "subordinating conjunction").

the same excerpt set was calculated using two measures. Cohen's kappa coefficient (Cohen, 1960) measures the agreement between a pair of transcribers for each word, comparing the boundary labels (boundary and no-boundary). Cohen's kappa is considered a better measure of agreement than the simple percent agreement rate, because it factors in the chance probability of agreement based on the most frequently occurring label. The suggested interpretation of the kappa statistic is that values between 0.41 and 0.6 indicate moderate agreement, and higher values indicate substantial to perfect agreement (Landis & Koch, 1977). We also use Fleiss' kappa statistic (Fleiss, 1981; see also Artstein & Poesio, 2008), which calculates agreement between multiple transcribers over the level expected by chance, and its z-transform for significance testing.

The full results of the reliability analysis, including prominence and B-scores, are presented in Mo, Cole, and Lee (2008). The results for B-scores are summarised here. Cohen's kappa coefficients over the transcriber pairs in each set ($N = 1{,}322$ pairs) show a normal distribution with values ranging from .240 to .850, and a mean kappa of .582, indicating a mean level of moderate agreement above chance. Fleiss' kappa coefficient was calculated separately for the entire group of transcribers assigned to each of the four excerpt sets and Fleiss' kappa coefficients indicate moderate or better agreement above chance levels. The z-normalised kappa scores were tested for significance at a 99% confidence level ($z = 2.32$), and all scores were highly significant ($p < .001$; Set 1: $\kappa = .61$, $z = 19.43$; Set 2: $\kappa = .54$, $z = 21.87$; Set 3: $\kappa = .62$, $z = 25.05$; Set 4: $\kappa = .58$, $z = 26.22$).

From the reliability analysis we conclude that untrained listeners are reliably consistent and systematic in their perception of prosodic boundaries in spontaneous, conversational speech. The distribution of B-scores over all the words in the dataset reveals that agreement is highest for words that listeners judge to be medial in a prosodic phrase, i.e., words with a B-score of zero, and this is the B-score for about 70% of the words in the dataset. The remaining 30% of words are perceived as being final in a prosodic phrase by one or more transcribers (B-score > 0), and the count of words with B-scores at a given level decreases as the B-score increases (i.e., there are few words, which many or all transcribers agree are final in a prosodic phrase).

Looking at the distribution of B-scores across speakers provides an indirect measure of speaker variability in prosody production, because although listeners vary in their perception of prosody, the same group of listeners have transcribed a given set of excerpts, so any differences in the patterns of perceived prosody between speakers can be taken to reflect the individual speaker's implementation of prosody. Figure 2 illustrates speaker variability in a plot of the mean interval between boundary marks and the mean interval between prominent words based on each listener's transcription of each speaker, individually. This plot indicates roughly how frequently listeners hear prominent words and prosodic phrase boundaries for a given speaker, and reveals variation across speakers. For some speakers, listeners perceive on average short intervals between prosodic phrase boundaries, while for other speakers the interval is longer. This variability could be due to differences between speakers in the length of prosodic phrases they assign to their utterances, and/or to the salience of the phonetic cues to prosodic boundary.

An interesting observation from Figure 2 is that speakers vary in the relative intervals between prominent words and boundaries in their speech, as perceived by listeners. Speakers in the group at the left end of the plot have a shorter mean interval between perceived boundaries than between prominent words, indicating that at least some of the prosodic phrases perceived by listeners contain no prominent word, contrary to the prediction from linguistic models of prosody. Speakers in the middle group have roughly equal mean intervals between prominent words and boundaries, which is consistent with a pattern in which listeners identify one prominent word (maybe the nuclear prominence) in each prosodic phrase. The group of speakers at the right of the plot, which is the largest group, have a longer

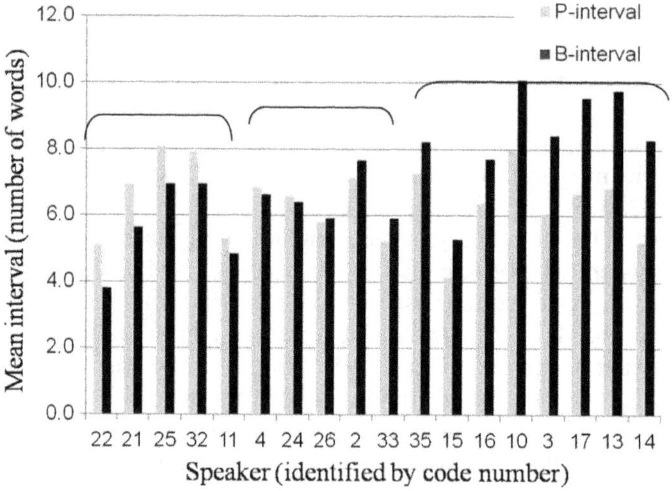

Figure 2. Plot of the mean interval between perceived prominences (P-interval) and boundaries (B-interval) for 18 speakers is shown individually. Intervals are measured in number of words between successive boundaries and prominent labels on an individual transcription, and mean intervals are calculated based on transcriptions from all the transcribers assigned to this excerpt set (16 transcribers for this set), for each speaker. Speakers divide roughly into three groups, as shown, based on the relative length of P-intervals and B-intervals, as described in text.

mean interval between boundaries than between prominent words, indicating that at least some prosodic phrases contain multiple prominent words.

The results presented in this section show that, despite the variability across listeners in the perception of prosodic phrase boundaries, listeners agree on the location of boundaries at levels well above chance. Boundary perception is at least partly systematic, and the next two sections present results showing the contribution of syntactic and acoustic information in predicting listeners' perception of prosodic phrasing. The distribution of B-scores across speakers suggests significant inter-speaker variability as well, which underscores the challenge for the listener in utilising prosodic information to interpret syntactic structures. If speakers vary in the length of prosodic phrases they employ, this might result in a different pattern of association between syntactic and prosodic phrases for different speakers, and listeners must be sensitive to these speaker-based differences to make appropriate use of prosodic cues.

RESULTS II: BOUNDARY PERCEPTION BY SYNTACTIC CATEGORY

Hypothesis 1 of this study states that syntactic phrasing influences the production of prosody. The prediction from this hypothesis is that prosodic phrases will be most likely to occur at the edges of syntactic constituents, with greater probability for higher-level constituents such as clauses than for lower-level constituents such as NPs or VPs. This hypothesis is confirmed indirectly (using perceptual data) in counts of the frequency of boundary marking at the edges of syntactic categories of different types.

Table 3 displays the frequency of boundary marking at the left edge of each syntactic category for about half of the data in this study (excerpts from Sets 1 and 2, the data that were annotated for syntactic structure), under two criteria of boundary marking. The left part of the table (columns 3–5) shows the frequency of boundaries that are labelled by at least half of the transcribers who listened to this subset of the data (18 transcriber for each set), and the right part (columns 6–8) adopts a weaker criterion for boundary marking, counting all boundaries labelled by one or more transcribers. There are two trends to notice in these data. First, the shaded cells mark those syntactic categories with the highest rates of boundary marking (over 25%) at their left edge. Three categories stand out under both criteria for boundary: discourse marker (DM), DISF, and coordinating conjunctions that conjoin clauses (CC-S). Listeners are very likely to perceive the beginning of a prosodic phrase at these locations. Under the weaker criterion of boundary, clauses (S and SBAR) and coordinating conjunctions joining other categories (e.g., CC-NP, CC-VP) also have high rates of boundary marking. Other syntactic categories are less often or even rarely perceived as locations where prosodic phrases begin. Notably, the left edge of a phrase-medial word ("within phrase", W/P) is the least likely location for a prosodic phrase under the stricter criterion of boundary, or is among the three least likely locations under the weaker criterion. Given the large number of W/P syntactic labels (410, or 23% of the total number of syntactic edges), the rarity of perceived prosodic boundaries internal to a syntactic constituent is a significant, though unsurprising pattern in these data.

The bolded percentages in columns 5 and 8 highlight those categories whose left edges contribute more than 10% to prosodic boundary marking. Under both criteria of boundary, the left edge of matrix sentences, conjunctions joining sentences, DISFs, and DMs are the top contributors to perceived boundaries. Under the weaker criterion, the left edges of subordinate or relative clauses (SBAR), noun phrases, and phrase-medial words (W/P) also contribute to perceived boundaries. The finding for phrase-medial words is somewhat surprising. If we think that speakers do not, in fluent speech, actually construct prosodic phrases that begin in the middle of a syntactic constituent, then the occurrence of boundary marks at such locations may be viewed as the error rate for this transcription task with this type of speech. We will see below that the agreement rate (reflected in the B-score) for boundaries in phrase-medial locations is very, very low, lending further support to the view that such boundaries are marked (or perceived)

TABLE 3
The frequency of boundary marking at the *left edge* of each syntactic category

1. Category type	*2. Total number of left edges*	*3. Number of edges with B-score ≥0.5*	*4. Percentage of B-marked edges in syntactic category (%)*	*5. Percentage of B-marked out of total number of B-marked edges (%)*	*6. Number of edges with B-score >0*	*7. Percentage of B-marked edges in syntactic category (%)*	*8. Percentage of B-marked out of total number of B-marked edges (%)*
VP	234	12	5.1	5.19	22	9.4	5.70
ADVP	65	2	3.1	0.87	8	12.3	2.07
ADJP	22	1	4.5	0.43	1	4.5	0.26
W/P	410	9	2.2	3.90	42	10.2	**10.88**
PP	147	6	4.1	2.60	32	21.8	8.29
DM	60	27	45.0	**11.69**	56	93.3	**14.51**
NP	327	22	6.7	9.52	62	19.0	**13.99**
VP	234	12	5.1	5.19	32	13.7	8.29
DISF	78	32	41.0	**13.85**	69	88.5	**17.88**
S	237	52	22.5	**22.51**	117	49.4	**18.13**
CC-NP	19	2	10.5	0.87	14	73.7	2.59
CC-S	76	35	46.1	**15.15**	75	98.7	**13.86**
CC-VP	15	3	20.0	1.30	11	73.3	2.03
SBAR	112	16	14.3	6.93	55	49.1	**10.17**
Total	2036	234		100.00	596		100.00

Note: Column 2 displays the total number of left edges for each syntactic category in a subset of the data representing 18 speakers (excerpt Sets 1 and 2). Column 3 gives a count of those syntactic category left edges that coincide with a prosodic phrase boundary with a B-score of 0.5 or greater, and column 4 represents the same number as a percentage of the total for that category (=(col. 3/col. 2) × 100). Column 5 represents the number in the third column as a percentage of the total number of left-edges boundaries (=234 in this example). Columns 6–8 are the same as columns 3–5, but with the threshold for establishing boundary marking set lower, at one or more transcribers. Bold and shaded cells are discussed in the text.

in error. Finally, the totals at the bottoms of columns 3 and 6 show that boundaries are perceived at the left edges of about 11% of words under the strict criterion, and at about 29% of the words under the weaker criterion.

Table 4 presents the same frequency data for boundary marking at the right edge of syntactic categories.[5] The percentage of boundary marked edges within each syntactic category under the stronger criterion of boundary (column 4) is similar to the pattern observed for left edges in Table 3, with two differences: the right edges of PPs and SBAR are frequently perceived as the end of a prosodic phrase, while the right edges of conjunctions joining clauses (CC-S) are not. Strikingly, under the weaker criterion of boundary (column 7), nearly every syntactic category right edge is frequently perceived as a prosodic phrase boundary, with only phrase-medial words (W/P) and noun phrases displaying a lower rate of boundary perception. The overall high rate of boundary marking (under the weak criterion) at most syntactic right edges (excepting NP edges) suggests that almost any syntactic edge is a potential location for a prosodic phrase boundary, as noted by Frazier et al. (2004) and Pynte (2006). In their contribution to the total number of perceived boundaries (columns 5 and 8), matrix sentences again stand out, this time for their right-edge location, and DMs and DISF also contribute substantially. Unlike with the left-edge boundaries, right edges of noun phrases do not contribute much to boundary perception, and phrase-medial locations are even more likely to be heard as prosodic boundaries.

Overall, the frequency data in Tables 3 and 4 establish that there is a higher rate of boundary marking at the edges of higher-level constituents (matrix sentences) compared to lower-level constituents, and boundaries marked at higher-level syntactic edges contribute more to the total number of perceived prosodic boundaries.

To examine these patterns of boundary marking more closely, we consider next the distribution of B-scores by syntactic category. Figure 3 displays mean B-scores over all the words in the dataset, grouped according to the left- and right-edge syntactic category label of each word. Recall that every word is coded for two B-scores, a left-edge score codes the proportion of transcribers who marked a boundary preceding the word, and a right-edge score similarly coding boundary marking following the word. In the same

[5] Although there are an equal number of left and right syntactic edges coded in this dataset (each word contributes one left and one right edge), the total number of left and right syntactic edges are not equal in Tables 3 and 4 due to categories that are omitted because they have fewer than 10 instances in the dataset, or because they are not coded for both left and right edges. Examples of the latter are the right edges of subordinating conjunctions whose left edge would typically be coded as SBAR, or left edges of gerundive or subject-less infinitival clauses whose right edge would typically be coded as S or SBAR in the guidelines adopted here.

TABLE 4
The frequency of boundary marking at the *right edge* of each syntactic category

1. Category type	*2. Total number of right edges*	*3. number of edges with B-score ≥0.5*	*4. Percentage of B-marked edges in syntactic category (%)*	*5. Percentage of B-marked out of total number of B-marked edges (%)*	*6. Number of edges with B-score >0*	*7. Percentage of B-marked edges in syntactic category (%)*	*8. Percentage of B-marked out of total number of B-marked edges (%)*
VP	134	12	8.96	5.66	49	36.57	8.28
ADVP	49	7	14.29	3.30	14	28.57	2.36
ADJP	5	1	20.00	0.47	4	80.00	0.68
W/P	1016	21	2.07	9.91	125	12.30	**21.11**
PP	7	4	57.14	1.89	5	71.43	0.84
DM	64	26	40.63	**12.26**	57	89.06	9.63
NP	285	11	3.86	5.19	56	19.65	9.46
VP	134	12	8.96	5.66	49	36.57	8.28
DISF	78	37	47.44	**17.45**	76	97.44	**12.84**
S	159	81	50.94	**38.21**	157	98.74	**26.52**
CC-NP	16	2	12.50	0.84	6	37.50	0.92
CC-S	77	11	14.29	4.64	32	41.56	4.90
CC-VP	14	1	7.14	0.42	4	28.57	0.61
SBAR	22	11	50.00	4.64	19	86.36	2.91
Total	2060	237		100.00	653		100.00

Note: The data layout is the same as for Table 3.

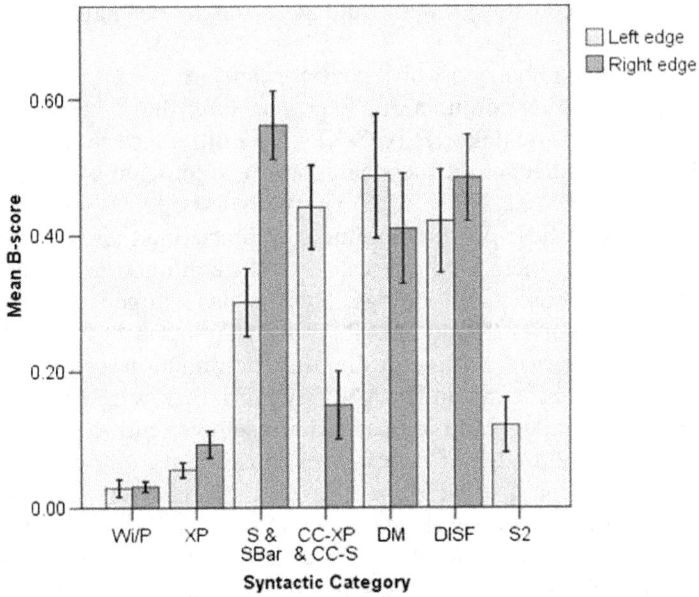

Figure 3. Mean B-scores and error bars (95% CI) by the syntactic category label of the highest syntactic constituent that begins (left edge) or ends (right edge) at the location of the perceived prosodic boundary. Data from all excerpts (Sets 1–4). The XP category (in the XP and CC-XP groups) combines the major phrase categories of NP, VP, ADJP, ADVP, and PP. The S2 category codes subordinate and relative clauses, and is only coded as a right-edge category (see text).

way, each word also contributes two syntactic category labels. Figure 3 plots these left- and right-edge B-scores separately.

These data reveal differences among categories in the overall level of B-scores, as well as asymmetries in the B-scores associated with left vs. right edges. The lowest B-scores are observed at the left and right edges of words that are phrase-medial (W/P) and at the edges of major phrases (XPs) that are not clauses, including NPs, VPs, ADJPs, PPs, and ADVPs. These locations may be marked by one or two transcribers, but rarely more, resulting in low B-scores. Notice that the W/P category was seen to contribute to more than 10% of the total number of marked boundaries in the entire set of transcripts (Tables 3 and 4), but the very low B-scores for phrase-medial words indicate that listeners rarely agree on the perception of a boundary at those locations. The low B-scores of XP and W/P categories contrast with the overall high B-scores of the other category labels, and notably with the higher-level syntactic categories marking clauses (S and SBAR). This difference was tested for significance using the non-parametric Kruskal–Wallis test of mean differences (because sample variances were not homogeneous between the groups), and is found to be highly significant, $\chi^2(2993, 1) = 100.6$, $p < .001$.[6]

A large-edge asymmetry is observed for left or right syntactic edges labelled as coordinating conjunctions (e.g., *but*, *and*) that conjoin sentences (CC-S) or other major categories (CC-XP). The difference in mean B-score between left and right edges for these categories is significant by the Kruskal–Wallis test, $\chi^2(1218) = 52.3$, $p < .001$. The high left-edge B-score indicates that listeners tend to hear prosodic boundaries preceding these conjunctions, rather than following them, and suggests that the conjunction is functioning as a proclitic in the prosodic phonology. There is also a large-edge asymmetry for the clausal categories (S and SBAR), but in the opposite direction from the asymmetry observed with coordinating conjunction categories. This difference is also significant under ANOVA [variances were homogeneous; $F(1, 372) = 52.2$, $p < .001$], and indicates that listeners tend to hear prosodic boundaries at the right edge of clause-level constituents.

A final observation from Figure 3 is that of relatively high B-scores associated with the left and right edges of DMs and DISFs. There are no significant differences between the means of left- and right-edge B-scores by ANOVA. The high B-scores and lack of edge effects indicate that listeners tend to hear DMs and DISFs as separate prosodic domains. We're hesitant to call these prosodic phrases, since it's not clear that they exhibit intonational patterns of a complete phrase, but at a minimum we can say that these elements are not perceived as integrated into the preceding or following prosodic phrases.

The results presented in this section provide indirect measures confirming hypothesis 1. There is a higher rate of boundary marking at the edges of clauses than at the edges of lower-level syntactic constituents or phrase-medial positions. Moreover, listeners agree more on the perception of prosodic boundaries at clause edges, especially right edges, than they do on boundaries in other locations, including the edges of non-clause constituents and medial positions in a syntactic domain. The clause edges have higher B-scores. These findings are predicted by hypothesis 1 if the acoustic evidence of prosodic phrase boundaries is also strongest at clause edges than other locations. We turn next to the analysis of the acoustic evidence.

RESULTS III: ACOUSTIC VOWEL DURATION BY SYNTACTIC CATEGORY

The distributions of B-scores according to syntactic category show differences in the patterns of prosodic boundary perception as a function

[6] All differences reported here as significant by non-parametric analyses of mean differences were also confirmed as significant under ANOVA.

of the syntactic category label of the word preceding and following the boundary. We consider next whether this effect of syntax on boundary perception is mediated through the acoustic signal. Hypothesis 2 of this study is that listeners respond to acoustic cues to prosodic boundaries in their judgement of the boundary status of each word. If the effect of syntactic category on prosodic boundary perception is mediated through the acoustic signal, we expect to find acoustic evidence of prosodic boundaries at those syntactic edges that are associated with higher B-scores. Prior studies show final lengthening is a very robust acoustic effect of prosodic phrase boundaries (Kim et al., 2006; Wightman et al., 1992; Yoon et al., 2007), with increased duration of the syllable-final vowel at increasingly higher levels of prosodic boundary (word < intermediate phrase (ip) < intonational phrase (IP)). Mo (2008) further shows that compared to overall vowel intensity, final vowel duration is a much more consistent correlate of a perceived prosodic phrase boundary across different vowel phonemes, based on the same dataset that is analysed here. Based on these prior findings, we focus on the duration of the final vowel of each word as an acoustic correlate of the perceived boundary following the word. We do not pursue acoustic correlates of the left edge of a perceived prosodic phrase in this paper, leaving that for future research.

Figure 4 displays the (normalised) duration of the word-final vowel and the B-score of each word. Words whose right edges are labelled as DM or DISF are excluded from this step of the analysis, as we have no clear prediction about final lengthening for words of this type. The plot shows a clear trend that words with higher B-scores have longer final vowels, as predicted by hypothesis 2.

Figure 5 shows the distribution of normalised final vowel duration values for five syntactic categories (using the right-edge syntactic label of each word). CC-XP (not shown) has a much skewed distribution and large variance, and is omitted from the analyses that follow. The variable duration patterns for CC-XP, which include conjunctions coordinating NPs, VPs, and other non-clausal phrases, may indicate highly variable patterns in prosodic phrasing, too. These conjunctions may sometimes group prosodically with the conjunct to the left and sometimes with the one to the right, in phrases like "*we did **or** didn't do* ... ". Also excluded from the analysis of vowel duration are the categories DM and DISF, for which the linguistic model makes no strong predictions about vowel duration. Among the five categories shown in Figure 5, there is a trend in longer vowel durations at the end of clauses (S and SBAR), shorter durations following clause-joining conjunctions (CC-S), and the shortest durations at the end of other phrases (XP) and in phrase-medial positions (W/P). The differences in mean vowel duration between the five categories shown in Figure 5 are significant by the Kruskal–Wallis test, $\chi^2(4, 1062) = 118.49$, $p < .001$.

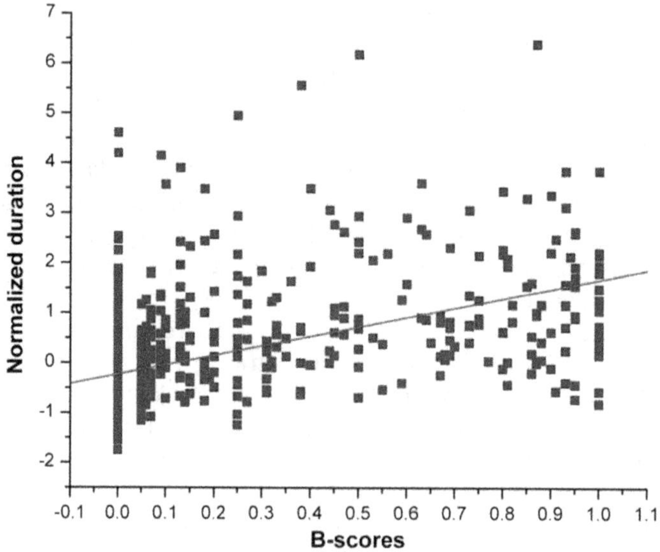

Figure 4. Scatterplot of B-scores and normalised duration of the final vowel of each word in the database, excluding words whose right edges are marked as discourse marker or disfluency ($N = 1422$).

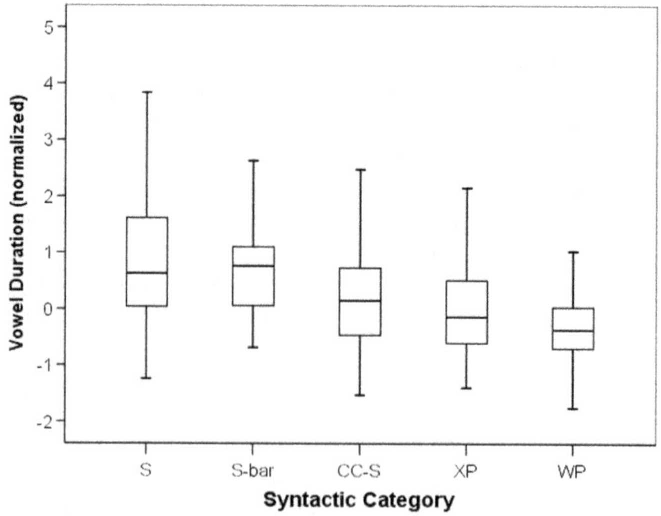

Figure 5. Normalised duration measures (z-transformed) of final vowel for each word grouped by the syntactic category label at its right edge. Excludes discourse markers and disfluency.

The vowel duration measure shows patterned variation that corresponds with B-scores, and with the right-edge syntactic category label of a word. These findings support hypothesis 2, but the question remains whether the syntactic effect on prosodic boundary perception can be fully attributed to the pattern of vowel duration at the right edge of syntactic constituents. To further explore the relationship between vowel duration, syntactic category and prosodic boundary perception, the next section presents correlation analyses of these variables.

RESULTS IV: CORRELATION AND REGRESSION ANALYSES OF BOUNDARY PERCEPTION, SYNTAX, AND ACOUSTIC DURATION

Non-parametric correlation analysis (Kendall's tau) and linear regression analyses are used to test the strength of the relationship between B-scores, right-edge syntactic category labels, and final vowel duration. Left-edge categories are not considered here, due to the expectation of weaker acoustic correlates to the prosodic boundary at the left edge. All regression models except for the final one presented (see Table 7, Model B) exclude words marked at their right edge with the "syntactic" labels marking DISF and DMs. Since there are no inherent numerical values for syntactic categories of different types, this categorical variable is recoded into a series of six binary dummy variables that code, for example, if a word-edge label is XP (yes = 1, no = 0) or if a word-edge label is S or SBAR.

There are significant correlations between each pairing of the three variables under discussion, as shown in Table 5. Separate correlations were tested for each syntactic category, except that the two clause-level categories

TABLE 5
Significant correlations (Kendall's tau) between B-scores, vowel duration, and syntactic category (right edge)

Variables		*Kendall's tau*
B-score	Vowel duration	.369**
B-score	S and SBAR	.541**
	XP	−.049*
	W/P	−.320**
Vowel duration	S and SBAR	.241**
	XP	.047 (p =.059)
	WP	−.208**

Note: Significant correlations marked by *p <.05, **p <.001.

S and SBAR were combined. There were no significant correlations involving the CC-S and CC-XP categories. Looking at the correlations between B-scores and syntactic features, we observe that clause endings (S and SBAR) and phrase-medial locations have a stronger correlation with B-scores than non-clause endings (XP), indicating that listeners are most consistent in hearing prosodic boundaries at the ends of clauses, and are pretty consistent in *not* hearing a boundary in phrase-medial locations, but are much more variable in their perception of boundaries at the ends of non-clausal phrases. The strongest correlation among these variables is between B-scores and the clausal syntactic categories of S and SBAR, and this correlation is even stronger than the correlation between B-scores and vowel duration, or between vowel duration and the S–SBAR syntactic variable. This finding indicates that the effect of syntactic category on B-scores can not be fully attributed to patterns of vowel duration encoding prosodic phrase boundaries at the end of clauses. This finding also supports hypothesis 3 that syntactic context plays a direct role on prosodic boundary perception. The independence of vowel duration and the syntactic categories on B-score prediction is further tested in a hierarchical regression model discussed next.

Table 6 shows results from hierarchical regression models with five syntactic categories combined as the independent variables in one step, and normalised word-final vowel duration as the independent variable in a second step. Model A first evaluates the syntactic category variables, and shows an r^2 value indicating that syntactic category accounts for nearly 30% of the variance in B-score values. Step 2 evaluates the predictive value of normalised duration, which accounts for about an additional 10% of the variance. Model B evaluates the predictor variables in the opposite order, and shows that when duration is evaluated first, it accounts for about 24% of the variance, with syntactic category variables picking up another 16% of the variance. These models show that the set of syntactic category variables and

TABLE 6

Results of two hierarchical linear regression models with syntactic categories (S, SBAR, CC-S, XP, and W/P) and normalised vowel duration as predictor variables and B-scores as dependent variable

		r	r^2	*Significant F* change
Model A	Step 1: syntactic categories	0.545	0.297	<0.001
	Step 2: normalised duration	0.635	0.403	<0.001
Model B	Step 1: normalised duration	0.488	0.239	<0.001
	Step 2: syntactic categories	0.635	0.403	<0.001

Note: Models A and B differ in the order in which the independent variables are evaluated.

vowel duration contribute significantly as predictors of B-score, together accounting for about 40% of the variance in B-scores, confirming our hypothesis that syntactic category contributes to boundary perception beyond what is predicted based on vowel duration patterns. The two models are very similar, with only a small difference in r^2 between them in the first step, where syntactic category variables are stronger predictors of B-score variation than normalised duration. This difference reflects the finding from the non-parametric correlation analysis (Table 5) that syntactic categories have a stronger correlation with B-scores than vowel duration does.

Adding all factors individually to a stepwise regression model indicates which variables contribute the most, and in which order, in predicting B-score variance. Table 7 presents the results from two more stepwise regression models. Model A uses the same dataset and the same predictor variables that went into the hierarchical regression model of Table 6, but does not force all the syntactic category labels to be evaluated in the same step. Here we see that the syntactic variable of clause categories (S and SBAR) emerge as the strongest predictors of B-scores in the first step, with vowel duration as the second step. The syntactic variables of phrase-medial (W/P) and other non-clausal phrase (XP) categories also contribute significantly in Steps 3 and 4. Model B presents the fullest regression model so far, adding back into the dataset the B-scores corresponding to words labelled as DMs and DISF (right edge only), and adding one new dummy variable to code these elements in a single, combined category. The resulting optimal model is like Model A in that clause and vowel duration are the first two strongest predictors, and also shows a strong relationship between the DM and DISF

TABLE 7
Stepwise regression models with full set of syntactic category variables and duration (Model), and with the added "syntactic" variables for discourse markers (DMs) and disfluencies (DISFs)

		r	r^2	*Significant F* change
Model A: excluding DM and DISF	Clause (S and SBAR)	0.596	0.355	<0.001
	Vowel duration	0.678	0.458	<0.001
	W/P	0.680	0.461	0.006
	XP	0.686	0.468	<0.001
Model B: including DM and DISF	Clause	0.537	0.288	<0.001
	Vowel duration	0.640	0.410	<0.001
	DM and DISF	0.686	0.471	<0.001
	W/P	0.688	0.473	0.021

Note: These are the optimal models from stepwise analysis where at each step the variable is selected that is the strongest significant predictor of B-score variance at that step. Predictor variables that are not significant for these models are not shown.

categories and B-scores by adding the variable for these items in the third step, before the variable for phrase-medial words. XP is no longer a significant predictor of B-score variance in Model B.

Summarising the findings from correlation and regression analysis, we find first of all that there are strong three-way correlations between syntactic category information, vowel duration, and perceived prosodic boundaries, confirming expectations based on prior works. Regression analyses show that syntactic category information makes an independent contribution to predicting prosodic boundary perception either before or after the contribution of vowel duration is partialed out. When all the syntactic variables are considered together with vowel duration, it is the clause-level categories and vowel duration that emerge as the two strongest predictors of B-scores, in that order. This result is maintained even when DMs and DISFs are added back into the dataset, with an additional variable.

DISCUSSION

Syntax is reflected in prosody production and perception

The distribution of B-scores at locations marking different kinds of syntactic edges establishes a systematic relationship between syntactic structure and prosody, as expected based on prior works showing a syntax–prosody dependency. The strongest relationship holds for the right edge of a clause-level constituent (S and S bar); listeners are more likely to hear a prosodic boundary in this location than at left edges, which generally supports Selkirk's (1986) analysis of English as a language where syntax and prosody are right-edge aligning. But for coordinating conjunctions linking XPs or clauses, listeners are more likely to hear a prosodic phrase boundary at the left edge of the conjunction than at the right edge, suggesting that conjunctions tend to behave prosodically like proclitics rather than enclitics. The same left-edge bias is observed for elements tagged as DMs.

The acoustic evidence from word-final vowel duration shows that boundary perception correlates with vowel duration, with higher B-scores associated with words that have longer final vowels. Vowel duration is also correlated with syntactic category in the expected direction: words at the end of higher syntactic domains such as clauses have longer duration than words at the end of lower syntactic domains, or words in a medial position of a syntactic domain. Collectively, these findings support hypothesis 1 that speakers' production of prosody reflects the syntactic structure of the utterance, and hypothesis 2 that listeners respond to acoustic cues to prosody in judging the location of prosodic phrase boundaries. The regression analyses also show that the contribution of syntax to boundary perception is a bit larger than the contribution of vowel duration, and that these two factors contribute independently, to some degree. The regression model that best predicts variation in B-scores at the right edges of words is the one that first evaluates the syntactic label at the right edge of the word, and then evaluates the vowel duration. This finding indicates that the relationship between vowel duration and B-scores is different depending on the syntactic category label of the word.

This study considers only one acoustic measure, word-final vowel duration, as the acoustic correlate of prosodic boundaries. As discussed earlier, the choice to use vowel duration as the sole cue is based on findings from prior studies that show duration to be the strongest cue, and the cue that is most consistent across phonological contexts. But we acknowledge here the possibility that other acoustic cues, such as F0, intensity, or glottalisation, may also contribute to listeners' perception of prosodic boundaries, and that regression analysis using a combined set of acoustic variables may show a larger predictive value for acoustic factors overall. In that case, the relative contributions of syntactic and acoustic factors would need to be re-evaluated as well. We are exploring this possibility in our ongoing work. The conclusion we draw from the present analyses is that relative to vowel duration, which is arguably the most robust acoustic cue to prosodic phrase boundaries in English, syntactic factors are even more strongly correlated with boundary perception, suggesting a partial independence between acoustic and syntactic cues to perceived prosody.

The best regression model utilising acoustic vowel duration and the full set of syntactic predictor variables accounts for 46.8% of the variation in B-scores excluding DMs and DISF, and 47.3% of the variation when they are included. Clearly, these factors play a major role in boundary perception, but equally, there must be other factors at play that are not yet included in the best model. We have neither accounted for factors related to focus or information structure, nor phonological factors related to the location of the nearest prominence or boundary to the left or right. We expect significant gains in the model once these factors are included.

B-scores in relation to discrete levels of prosodic boundary

The syntactic context that shows the highest rate of boundary marking, and also the highest rate of inter-listener agreement on boundary perception (i.e., the highest B-scores) is the right edge of a matrix sentence, relative clause, or subordinate clause. Lower-level syntactic categories are not reliably perceived as locations for prosodic phrase boundaries. The autosegmental–metrical model of English intonation (see Ladd, 1996/2008) specifies two levels of prosodic phrasing, the IP and the ip. The IP is higher in the prosodic hierarchy, and comprises one or more ips. These two levels are differentiated acoustically in that the higher-level prosodic boundary (IP) exhibits longer final lengthening, falling F0 contours ending in lower F0 values, lower intensity, and greater incidence of creaky voicing compared to the lower-level ip boundary (Kim et al., 2006). Differences between lower- and higher-level prosodic boundaries in terms of syntactic factors have not to our knowledge been explored, but we expect that the lower-level boundaries are more commonly associated with the edges of lower-level syntactic constituents, or are used in contexts of syntactic embedding.

We hypothesise that untrained listeners performing real-time prosody transcription are marking boundaries in locations that correspond to IPs in a careful ToBI transcription more consistently than in locations that would correspond to the lower-level ips, to the extent that these levels are effectively distinguished by speakers in our database. To test this hypothesis, we conducted a ToBI-style labelling (marking only locations of accent and boundary) with three trained, expert labellers (members of our research group) for a subset of the excerpts from the dataset reported here. The comparison between expert and untrained transcribers is reported in Mo et al. (2008), and the detail that is relevant here is that the words with the highest B-scores based on untrained transcribers correspond to words that are final in a higher-level prosodic phrase (IP) as transcribed by expert labellers. This finding, though based on a small sample from our data, supports our hypothesis that the untrained transcribers are marking higher-level boundaries.

There are several possible explanations for the less frequent perception of lower-level prosodic boundaries by untrained listeners. First, it is possible that the listeners do hear the lower-level boundaries, but simply don't have time to mark everything they hear, and opt to mark the (presumably) more salient higher-level boundaries. A second explanation is that speakers simply do not encode lower-level prosodic boundaries in the spontaneous, conversational speech style represented in our materials, unlike in read speech styles studied in prior works. A third possibility admits that speakers encode both lower- and higher-level boundaries, but are less consistent in the phonetic implementation of the lower-level boundaries, and/or implement these boundaries with subtler cues such that listeners do not reliably perceive them. A relevant observation is that both of the ip boundaries (L- and H-) are potentially ambiguous with the IP boundaries (L–L% and H–L%; among other ambiguities, see Beckman, 1996 for further examples). The lower-level boundaries are distinguished from the higher-level boundaries by the *degree* of F0 lowering, final lengthening or decreased intensity, and by the likelihood of creaky voicing. The inherent ambiguity of IP boundaries is lesser, since in at least some cases there are distinctive F0 contours that derive from the sequence of ip + IP tones, which do not arise with the single tones of the ip boundaries. The third explanation seems the most plausible to us, and is supported by the observation that even expert prosody transcribers struggle to annotate lower-level boundaries. Reliability studies of ToBI-style prosody transcriptions show lower agreement rates for ip compared to IP, and studies using statistical methods to predict boundaries similarly show lower rates of prediction for ip compared to IP (Yoon, 2007). These facts indicate that lower-level prosodic boundaries are not cued as effectively as higher-level boundaries, which may account for the rarity of boundaries perceived at locations marked by lower-level syntactic edges in our study.

The comparison between continuous-valued B-scores and discrete boundary labels such as (ip and IP) in the ToBI system is not intended as a claim that B-scores are an approximation of "true" discrete boundary labels. Our results are also compatible with a prosodic theory based on a continuous-valued boundary feature. Such a theory might posit a unique phonological boundary feature that is (usually) located to align with syntactic edges, but which is phonetically implemented with variation in the strength of the acoustic cues, such that "stronger" boundary cues are present at higher-level syntactic edges, or maybe as conditioned by non-syntactic factors. Prior work that assumes discrete levelled boundary features (e.g., IP and ip), such as our work on the Radio News and Switchboard corpora (Kim et al., 2006), finds significant differences in the acoustic correlates for two or more distinct levels, which suggests that the acoustic features are not drawn from a single uni-modal distribution, but it remains an open question whether there are two or more discrete categories of boundary level, or whether a better analysis is in terms of (one or more) continuous-valued boundary feature, where level distinctions such as IP/ip represent samples drawn from different regions along the continuum.

Sources of variability in prosody production and perception

The variability in the B-scores assigned to words in this study reflects the fact that among the 15–22 listeners transcribing each utterance, there is variability in their rate of inter-transcriber agreement in the perception of prosodic phrase boundaries. This variability in B-scores partly reflects variability among speakers in prosody production. As was shown in Figure 2, there is inter-speaker variation in the mean interval between transcribed boundaries, even with the same set of listeners for a given set of speech excerpts. This variability most likely reflects genuine differences between speakers in the mean length of their prosodic phrases (counted here in number of words), possibly reflecting differences in speech rate or affective factors. Inter-speaker differences in the interval between perceived prosodic phrases may also reflect differences in the salience of the acoustic cues to prosodic phrase boundaries; unless a given phrase boundary bears perceptually salient acoustic cues, it will not be detected and thus not counted in the B-score measure of perceived boundary strength.

Beyond these differences in speakers' production of prosodic phrase boundaries, the listener is another source of variability in observed B-scores, reflecting differences between transcribers in how they perform the task of transcription. Recall that the transcribers were given minimal instructions and no labelled training data or feedback that would have conditioned their transcription practice. It was expected that transcribers would differ in their sensitivity to the speech stimuli, and possibly also in their interpretation of the task and overall attentiveness when transcribing. These differences between transcribers are revealed in differences in the listener's rate of boundary marking. Over a subset of 36 transcribers, the mean interval between transcribed boundaries per listener ranges from 4.91 to 15.5 words (pooling all listeners' transcriptions the mean interval is 8.2 words, SD 2.17). But whereas the speaker-dependent variability in B-scores can be taken as evidence of real differences between speakers in prosody production, the listener-dependent variability in B-scores cannot so readily be taken as evidence of genuine differences between listeners in their perception of prosody. This study counts only those boundaries that listeners explicitly mark in a rapid and attention-demanding transcription task. It is possible that a listener's perceptual sensitivity might be different when gauged from a task of implicit boundary detection, for example, where the listener in some way responds to the perceived prosodic structure without explicitly identifying locations of prosodic boundaries.

We have not yet tested any implicit measures of boundary perception, so we do not offer any direct comparisons between our data and perceived prosodic boundaries based on implicit measures. But given the possibility of task-related factors influencing listeners, and resulting in inter-listener variation, the prosodic boundaries coding in our study cannot be interpreted on its own as direct evidence for the role of prosody in listeners' speech comprehension. We consider that those prosodic boundaries that are marked by listeners in rapid transcription may play a role in speech comprehension, but we do not claim that these are the only elements of prosodic structure that the listener perceives.

Boundary perception in relation to parsing and speech comprehension

Though this study did not test listeners' comprehension of syntax, the findings can be considered in light of models of syntactic parsing and speech comprehension. The coincidence of syntactic boundaries and perceived prosodic boundaries observed here, and their common expression in acoustic effects on vowel duration, supports models of spoken language processing in which prosody perception plays a role in speech comprehension for spontaneous speech, as has previously been shown for more controlled forms such as read speech. To the extent that speakers are consistent in producing longer syllable rhymes at the ends of major syntactic constituents like clauses, listeners may interpret syllable duration as a cue to syntactic structure. Furthermore, the co-occurrence of longer vowels with other acoustic prosodic features (not presented here), such as longer coda consonants, lower overall intensity, and spectral measures of creaky voicing or glottal tenseness (H1*–H2* and H2*–H4) serves to mark these regions in the speech stream as distinct from their surroundings, signalling a phonological and phonetic organisation that is aligned with the syntactic structure of the utterance, and by extension, with aspects of its semantic structure as well. The regular association of acoustic prosodic features with syntactic and semantic structure may condition listeners to perceive the phonological organisation of an utterance—its prosodic structure—where it is predicted by the syntactic context, even in contexts where the acoustic prosodic cues are weak or obscured. The perception of prosodic structure conditioned by comprehension of the syntactic context could explain the pattern of results obtained here, where syntactic factors appear to function at least partly independent of acoustic factors in influencing the perception of prosodic boundaries.

Prosody as a structural interface

Our findings support a model of language in which prosodic structure provides the means by which the phonological, syntactic, and semantic components of an utterance come together. As expressed by Arbisi-Kelm and Beckman (2009), prosodic structure can be considered as the "scaffolding" that marks certain locations in the speech stream as regions of convergence for critical and reliable information about the phonological, syntactic, and semantic content of an utterance. Viewed in this way, we would no sooner say that the perception of prosodic juncture cues syntactic structure than the converse that parsed syntactic structure cues phonological organisation. We further predict that semantic comprehension, e.g., the assignment of arguments identified from the speech stream to positions in lexical semantic structure, may function similarly as a cue to both phonological and syntactic organisation, and that prosody may likewise serve as cue to semantic structure. We leave it for future research to directly test these predictions by comparing the perception of prosody, as done here, with the listeners' comprehension of syntactic and semantic structures.

CONCLUSION

This study demonstrates that speakers encode syntactic structure in their production of prosody in spontaneous, conversational speech, and that the influence of syntax is strongest for clausal constituents at their right edge. In addition, ordinary listeners perceive prosodic boundaries in conversational speech in real-time, and their judgements also show a close relationship between perceived boundaries and syntactic structure. The relationship between syntax and prosodic boundary perception is mediated in part through the acoustic encoding of prosody. Acoustic cues to prosody are strongest at locations predicted by the syntactic structure. But the findings from regression analyses show that syntactic factors, specifically the context of a right-edge clause boundary, are a stronger predictor of boundary perception than the acoustic cue of word-final vowel duration, supporting the conclusion that syntactic factors make an independent contribution to boundary perception, and that relative to durational cues, the syntactic context is a stronger predictor or prosodic phrase boundaries. We conclude that listeners are guided in their perception of prosody by acoustic cues and syntactic context, and that the effect of syntactic context appears to be partly independent of the effect due to final vowel duration, the primary acoustic cue to prosodic phrase boundaries.

REFERENCES

Arbisi-Kelm, T., & Beckman, M. (2009). Prosodic structure and consonant development across languages. In M. Vigário, S. Frota, & M. J. Freitas (Eds.), *Phonetics & phonology: Interactions and interrelations* (pp. 109–136). Amsterdam: John Benjamins.

Artstein, R., & Poesio, M. (2008). Inter-coder agreement for computational linguistics. *Computational Linguistics, 34*(4), 555–596. doi:10.1162/coli.07-034-R2

Bachenko, J., & Fitzpatrick, E. (1990). A computational grammar of discourse-neutral prosodic phrasing in English. *Computational Linguistics, 16*, 155–170.

Beckman, M. (1986). *Stress and non-stress accent*. Dordrecht, the Netherlands: Foris.

Beckman, M., & Ayers, G. (1997). *Guidelines for ToBI labeling* (Version 3.0). Manuscript and accompanying speech materials. The Ohio State University. Retrieved September 10, 2008, from http://www.ling.ohio-state.edu/~tobi/ame_tobi/labelling_guide_v3.pdf

Beckman, M., & Pierrehumbert, J. (1986). Intonational structure in Japanese and English. *Phonology Yearbook, 3*, 255–309. doi:10.1017/S095267570000066X

Buhmann, J., Caspers, J., van Heuven, V. J., Hoekstra, H., Martens, J-P., & Swerts, M. (2002). Annotation of prominent words, prosodic boundaries and segmental lengthening by non-expert transcribers in the spoken Dutch corpus. In M. G. Rodriguez & C. P. S. Araujo (Eds.), *Proceedings of the Third International Conference on Language Resources and Evaluation (LREC)* (pp. 779–785). Paris, France: Evaluations and Language Resources Distribution Agency.

Calhoun, S. (2006). *Information structure and the prosodic structure of English: A probabilistic relationship.* PhD dissertation, University of Edinburgh, UK.

Choi, J-Y., Hasegawa-Johnson, M., & Cole, J. (2005). Finding intonational boundaries using acoustic cues related to the voice source. *Journal of the Acoustical Society of America, 118*(4), 2579–2588. doi:10.1121/1.2010288

Cohen, J. (1960). A coefficient of agreement for nominal scales. *Educational and Psychological Measurement, 20*(1), 37–46. doi:10.1177/001316446002000104

Cutler, A., Dahan, D., & van Donselaar, W. (1997). Prosody in the comprehension of spoken language: A literature review. *Language and Speech, 40*(2), 141–201.

de Pijper, J. R., & Sanderman, A. A. (1994). On the perceptual strength of prosodic boundaries and its relation to suprasegmental cues. *Journal of the Acoustical Society of America, 96*, 2037–2047. doi:10.1121/1.410145

Dilley, L., Breen, M., Bolivar, M., Kraemer, J., & Gibson, E. (2006). A comparison of inter-transcriber reliability for two systems of prosodic annotation: RaR (rhythm and pitch) and ToBI (tones and break indices). In *Proceedings of the International Conference on spoken language processing* (pp. 1619–1622). International Speech Communication Association. Available from http://www.isca-speech.org/archive/interspeech_2006

Dilley, L., Shattuck-Hufnagel, S., & Ostendorf, M. (1996). Glottalization of word-initial vowels as a function of prosodic context. *Journal of Phonetics, 24*, 423–444. doi:10.1006/jpho.1996.0023

Fleiss, J. L. (1981). *Statistical methods for rates and proportions* (pp. 38–46). New York: John Wiley.

Frazier, L., Carlson, K., & Clifton, C., Jr. (2006). Prosodic phrasing is central to language comprehension. *Trends in Cognitive Sciences, 10*, 244–249.

Frazier, L., Clifton, C., Jr., & Carlson, K. (2004). Don't break or do: Prosodic boundary preferences. *Lingua, 114*, 3–27. doi:10.1016/S0024-3841(03)00044-5

Gee, J. P., & Grosjean, F. (1983). Performance structures: A psycholinguistic and linguistic appraisal. *Cognitive Psychology, 15*, 411–458. doi:10.1016/0010-0285(83)90014-2

Heldner, M. (2003). On the reliability of overall intensity and spectral emphasis as acoustic correlates of focal accents in Swedish. *Journal of Phonetics, 31*(1), 39–62. doi:10.1016/S0095-4470(02)00071-2

Kim, H., Yoon, T-J., Cole, J., & Hasegawa-Johnson, M. (2006). Acoustic differentiation of L- and L-L% in switchboard and radio news speech. In R. Hoffmann & H. Mixdorff (Eds.), *Proceedings of the Third International Conference on Speech Prosody 2006*, Dresden, Germany, May 2–5, 2006. Available from ISCA Archive: http://www.isca-speech.org/archive/sp2006.

Kochanski, G., Grabe, E., Coleman, J., & Rosner, B. (2005). Loudness predicts prominence: Fundamental frequency lends little. *Journal of the Acoustical Society of America, 118*, 1038–1054. doi:10.1121/1.1923349

Ladd, D. R. (2008). *Intonational phonology* (2nd ed.). Cambridge: Cambridge University Press. (Original work published 1996)

Landis, J. R., & Koch, G. G. (1977). The measurement of observer agreement for categorical data. *Biometrics, 33*, 159–174. Available from http://www.jstor.org/stable/2529310.

Lee, E-K., & Cole, J. (2007). *Acoustic effects of prosodic boundary on vowels in American English.* Paper presented at the Proceedings of the 42nd meeting of the Chicago Linguistic Society.

Lehiste, I. (1972). The timing of utterances and linguistic boundaries. *Journal of the Acoustical Society of America, 51*, 2018–2024. doi:10.1121/1.1913062

Marcus, M., Marcinkiewicz, M. A., & Santorini, B. (1993). Building a large annotated corpus of English: The Penn Treebank. *Computational Linguistics, 19*(2), 313–330.

Mo, Y. (2008). Duration and intensity as perceptual cues for naïve listeners' prominence and boundary perception. In P. A. Barbosa, S. Madureira, & C. Reis (Eds.), *Proceedings of the Fourth International Conference on Speech Prosody* (pp. 739–742). Campinas, Brazil, May 6–9, 2008. Available from ISCA Archive: http://www.isca-speech.org/archive/sp2008.

Mo, Y., Cole, J., & Lee, E-K. (2008). Naïve listeners' prominence and boundary perception. In P. A. Barbosa, S. Madureira, & C. Reis (Eds.), *Proceedings of the Fourth International Conference on Speech Prosody* (pp. 735–736). Campinas, Brazil, May 6–9, 2008. Available from ISCA Archive: http://www.isca-speech.org/archive/sp2008.

Nespor, M., & Vogel, I. (1986). *Prosodic phonology.* Dordrecht, the Netherlands: Foris.

Ostendorf, M., Price P., & Shattuck-Hufnagel, S. (1995). *The Boston University radio news corpus* (Technical Report ECS-95-001). Boston, MA: Boston University. Retrieved 12/2/2009 from The Linguistic Data Consortium, Philadelphia, PA, http://www.ldc.upenn.edu/Catalog/docs/LDC96S36/bur_crps.ps.

Pitt, M. A., Dilley, L., Johnson, K., Kiesling, S., Raymond, W., Hume, E., et al. (2007). *Buckeye corpus of conversational speech* (2nd release). Columbus, OH: Department of Psychology, Ohio State University. Retrieved March 15, 2006, from www.buckeyecorpus.osu.edu

Price, P. J., Ostendorf, M., Shattuck-Hufnagel, S., & Fong, C. (1991). The use of prosody in syntactic disambiguation. *Journal of the Acoustical Society of America, 90*, 2956–2970. doi:10.1121/1.401770

Pynte, J. (2006). Phrasing effects in comprehending PP constructions. *Journal of Psycholinguist Research, 35*, 245–265. doi:10.1007/s10936-006-9014-y

Schafer, A., Speer, S., Warren, P., & White, S. D. (2000). Intonational disambiguation in sentence production and comprehension. *Journal of Psycholinguistic Research, 29*(2), 169–182. doi:10.1023/A:1005192911512

Selkirk, E. O. (1984). *The relation between sound and structure.* Cambridge: MIT Press.

Selkirk, E. O. (1986). On derived domains in sentence phonology. *Phonology Yearbook, 3*, 371–405. doi:10.1017/S0952675700000695

Selkirk, E. O. (2000). The interaction of constraints on prosodic phrasing. In M. Horne (Ed.), *Prosody: Theory and experiment* (pp. 231–261). Dordrecht, the Netherlands: Kluwer.

Shattuck-Hufnagel, S., & Turk, A. (1996). A prosody tutorial for investigators of auditory sentence processing. *Journal of Psycholinguistic Research, 25*, 193–247. doi:10.1007/BF01708572

Sluijter, A., & van Heuven, V. J. (1996). Spectral balance as an acoustic correlate of linguistic stress. *Journal of the Acoustical Society of America, 100*, 2471–2485. doi:10.1121/1.417955

Streefkerk, B. M., Pols, L. C. W., & ten Bosch, L. F. M. (1997). Prominence in read aloud sentences, as marked by listeners and classified automatically. In R. J. J. H. van Son (Ed.), *Proceedings of the Institute of Phonetic Sciences* (Vol. 21, pp. 101–116). Amsterdam, The Netherlands: University of Amsterdam.

Streefkerk, B. M., Pols, L. C. W., & ten Bosch, L. F. M. (1998). Automatic detection of prominence (as defined by listeners' judgements) in read aloud Dutch sentences. In *Proceedings of the 5th International Conference on Spoken Language Processing* (Vol. 3, pp. 683–686). Sydney, Australia, 30th November–4th December 1998. Available from ISCA Archive, http://www.isca-speech.org/archive/icslp_1998.

Swerts, M. (1997). Prosodic features at discourse boundaries of different strength. *Journal of the Acoustical Society of America, 101*, 514–521. doi:10.1121/1.418114

Turk, A., & Sawusch, J. (1997). The domain of accentual lengthening in American English. *Journal of Phonetics, 25*, 25–41. doi: 10.1006/jpho.1996.0032

van Bergem, D. R. (1993). Acoustic vowel reduction as a function of sentence accent, word stress and vowel class. *Speech Communication, 12*, 1–23.

Watson, D., & Gibson, E. (2004). The relationship between intonational phrasing and syntactic structure in language production. *Language and Cognitive Processes, 19*(6), 713–755. doi:10.1080/01690960444000070

Weber, A., Grice, M., & Crocker, M. (2006). The role of prosody in the interpretation of structural ambiguities: A study of anticipatory eye movements. *Cognition, 99*, B63–B72. doi:10.1016/j.cognition.2005.07.001

Wightman, C. W., Shattuck-Hufnagel, S., Ostendorf, M., & Price, P. J. (1992). Segmental durations in the vicinity of prosodic phrase boundaries. *Journal of the Acoustical Society of America, 91*, 1707–1717. doi:10.1121/1.402450

Yoon, T-J. (2007). *A predictive model of prosody through grammatical interface: A computational approach.* PhD dissertation, University of Illinois at Urbana-Champaign.

Yoon, T-J., Chavarría, S., Cole, J., & Hasegawa-Johnson, M. (2004). Intertranscriber reliability of prosodic labeling on telephone conversation using ToBI. In *Proceedings of the ISCA International Conference on spoken language processing (Interspeech 2004)* (pp. 2729–2732). Jeju Island, Korea, October 4–8, 2004. Available from ISCA Archive, http://www.isca-speech.org/archive/interspeech_2004.

Yoon, T-J., Cole, J., & Hasegawa-Johnson, M. (2007). *On the edge: Acoustic cues to layered prosodic domains.* Paper presented at the Proceedings of the International Congress of Phonetic Sciences, Saarbruecken, Germany.

APPENDIX 1

Scripted instructions read to participants in transcription experiment:

<the first part of the script pertains to prosodic prominence transcription>

...[A] feature of normal speech that we are interested in is the way speakers break up an utterance into **chunks.** These chunks group words in a way that helps the listener interpret the utterance, and are especially important when the speaker produces long stretches of continuous speech. An example of chunking that is familiar to everyone is the chunking that breaks digit sequences down into sub-groups.

For some of the excerpts you will hear, you will be asked to mark the chunks by inserting a vertical line between words that belong to different chunks. It is important for you to know that the boundary between two chunks does not necessarily correspond to the location where you would place a comma, period, or other punctuation mark, so you must really listen and mark the boundary where you here a juncture between two chunks. A chunk may be as small as a single word, or it may contain many words, and speakers can vary quite a bit in the size of the chunks they produce in a given utterance.

LANGUAGE AND COGNITIVE PROCESSES
2010, 25 (7/8/9), 1178–1200

Psychology Press
Taylor & Francis Group

Accent detection is a slippery slope: Direction and rate of F0 change drives listeners' comprehension

Angela M. Isaacs[1] and Duane G. Watson[1,2]

[1]*Department of Psychology, University of Illinois at Urbana-Champaign, Champaign, IL, USA,* [2]*Beckman Institute for Advanced Science and Technology, University of Illinois at Urbana-Champaign, Champaign, IL, USA*

The present study tests whether listeners use F0, duration, or some combination of the two to identify the presence of an accented word in a short discourse. Participants' eye movements to previously mentioned and new objects were monitored as participants listened to instructions to move objects in a display. The name of the target object on critical trials was resynthesised from naturally produced utterances so that it had either high or low F0 and either long or short duration. Fixations to the new object were highest when there was a steep rise in F0. Fixations to the previously mentioned object were highest when there was a steep drop in F0. These results suggest that listeners use F0 slope to make decisions about the presence of an accent, and that F0 and duration by themselves do not solely determine accent interpretation.

Keywords: Prosody; Discourse; Pitch accent; Comprehension.

How you say something can be just as important as what you say. A pitch accent (hereafter simply "accent") is an acoustic prominence associated with a word. It has been argued that prominence is signalled by a number of acoustic changes, which include a rise in fundamental frequency (F0), an increase in duration, and an increase in intensity (Ladd, 1996). Accents can affect the meaning of the utterance by signalling whether information is new, important, in focus, or nonpredictable (Bolinger, 1972; Brown & Yule, 1983;

Correspondence should be addressed to Angela M. Isaacs, Department of Psychology, University of Illinois at Urbana-Champaign, 603 East Daniel St., Champaign, IL 61820, USA. E-mail: aisaacs2@uiuc.edu

This work was supported by NIH Grant R01DC008774-01A1. The first author was supported by NIH Grant T32HD055272. We would like to thank our undergraduate assistants Kathleen Eberhardt and Ahmad Parvinian for help with stimulus preparation and data collection.

http://www.psypress.com/lcp DOI: 10.1080/01690961003783699

Buring, 2007; Halliday, 1967; Levy & Jaeger, 2007; Schwarzschild, 1999; Selkirk, 1995). It is clear that accents play an important role in signalling discourse structure. However, it is less clear which acoustic feature(s) listeners use to determine whether a word is accented. The present study explores listeners' use of F0 and duration in accent detection.

Many theorists have argued that F0 underlies the perception of accenting, though they differ in how they characterise its role. For example, in Pierrehumbert's influential theory (Pierrehumbert, 1980; Pierrehumbert & Hirschberg, 1990), which has been instantiated in the Tone and Break Index labelling system (ToBI; Silverman et al., 1992), accents are composed of tonal targets that are either high (**H**) or low (**L**) and these are defined in relation to the speaker's F0 range. Different targets and different sequences of targets convey different meanings. F0 also plays a critical role in other theories of prominence (Bolinger, 1986; Cruttenden, 1997; Halliday, 1967). For example, Cruttenden (1997) proposed that pragmatic meaning is conveyed by individual F0 contours such as rises, falls, plateaus, and combinations of these features. Two words both containing a rise in F0 may be treated differently depending on the extent of the rise and the path it takes to reach the maximum. Critically, although proponents of these different approaches would argue that duration and intensity correlate with accenting, F0 plays a central role within these theories.

Work in the computational literature also suggests that F0 is used in accent perception. Grabe, Kochanski, and Coleman (2007) tested whether computer-calculated polynomial equations could be used to detect differences between the F0 contours of seven different types of accents in a corpus of hand-labelled speech. The accents included (in their modified ToBI notation) fall (**H*L,%**), fall–rise (**H*L,H%**), high rise (**H*,H%**), rise–plateau (**L*H,%**), rise (**L*H,H%**), late rise (**L*,H%**), and rise–plateau–fall (**L*H,L%**). These equations were first fit with one set of utterances and then tested using a different set of utterances from the same labelled corpora. Comparisons of the coefficients of these seven equations revealed numerous differences between accent types, suggesting that different accent types can be distinguished based on F0 contour. However, in a follow-up experiment, Grabe et al. trained several computer algorithms to classify accents as belonging to one of the seven accent types previously identified by the experimenters. Each classifier was trained to distinguish between two of the seven accent types using the F0 contours of the words. The classifier then categorised novel words as being one of the two accent types on which the classifier had been trained. The classifiers were successful in distinguishing between some, but not all, accent types, suggesting that F0 alone may not be sufficient in distinguishing one accent type from another.

An earlier experiment by Kochanski, Grabe, Coleman, and Rosner (2005) provides some evidence that intensity and duration may fill this gap.

Kochanski et al. developed and tested classifiers designed to identify words in spoken speech that had been labelled as accented by trained labellers. Each classifier was based on a different acoustic measure including F0, intensity, and duration, among others. In contrast to Grabe et al. (2007), the classifier based on F0 contour was one of the worst performers. The most successful classifiers were those based on intensity and duration. Because Kochanski et al. only compared accented to unaccented words (regardless of accent type), this experiment should not be taken as evidence against Grabe et al.'s results showing the importance of F0 contour. However, it does suggest that duration and intensity may be important for listeners to distinguish accented from unaccented words.

Bard and Aylett (1999) found additional evidence for the importance of duration in prominence by examining speech in a referential communication task. Words that were repeated across the discourse were coded using a variant of ToBI and were measured for intelligibility and duration. Bard and Aylett found that, compared to its first realisation, the second realisation of a word was only rarely coded as de-accented but was frequently produced with reduced intelligibility and duration. This is contrary to the well-documented findings that (1) given words are de-accented in speech and (2) reduced intelligibility and duration of given words are due solely to de-accentuation (Bolinger, 1972; Brown & Yule, 1983; Halliday, 1967). This illustrates that for production at least, duration may have an important role to play in conveying givenness.

As a whole, these studies suggest that duration and F0 play an important role in listeners' ability to identify accented words, but it is unclear what role each plays. Research in speech perception and prosody perception provides some possible ways in which F0 and duration might interact. In phoneme perception multiple, redundant phonetic cues exist and sometimes the presence of any one cue is sufficient to indicate the correct phoneme. Repp (1985) termed this type of relationship "cue trading". Beach (1991) found a cue-trading relationship between F0 and duration in the detection of intonational boundaries while resolving locally ambiguous sentences. Listeners may also use a similar relationship between F0 and duration to make inferences about accenting.

Bartels and Kingston (1994) found evidence for a different relationship between F0 and duration. Bartels and Kingston were interested in exploring differences between presentational (**H***) and contrastive (**L+H***) accent types. They synthesised multiple versions of the phrase "Amanda had a banana". For the word "banana", they systematically varied the F0 height on the peak, the F0 height on the dip prior to the peak, the alignment of the F0 peak, and the onset of the F0 peak (i.e., how late the F0 began to rise). Listeners rated whether each utterance had occurred in a discourse context consistent with a contrastive or presentational accent. They found that the cue which best distinguished presentational from contrastive utterances was the F0 slope, which is the direction and rate of F0 change. This suggests that listeners are capable of using F0 slope to distinguish between accent types and raises the possibility that listeners also use F0 slope to distinguish between accented and unaccented words.

The research cited above suggests that listeners may use both duration and F0 to determine when a word is accented. However, these studies relied upon intuitions and data from tasks that are unlike natural comprehension. Although this work has served as an important first step in understanding the acoustics of accents, directly testing the effect of acoustic factors on accent perception in real-time language processing may provide deeper insights into the role F0 and duration play in accent detection.

To investigate this question, we employed a visual-world paradigm (Allopenna, Magnuson, & Tanenhaus, 1998; Eberhard, Spivey-Knowlton, Sedivy, & Tanenhaus, 1995; Tanenhaus, SpiveyKnowlton, Eberhard, & Sedivy, 1995). In this paradigm, the location of participants' gaze within a visual display is recorded over time as participants engage in normal language comprehension or production. Changes in looking preferences over time provide information about the time course of processing. Many studies have used the visual-world paradigm to test questions relating to prosody (e.g., Arnold, 2008; Chen, Os, & De Ruiter, 2007; Dahan, Tanenhaus, & Chambers, 2002; Ito & Speer, 2008; Watson, Tanenhaus, & Gunlogson, 2008; Weber, Braun, & Crocker, 2006; for an overview of the visual-world paradigm and prosody see Watson, Gunlogson, & Tanenhaus, 2006).

Dahan et al. (2002) conducted an important, early study on prominence using the visual-world paradigm that serves as a launching point for the work presented here. Dahan et al. found that participants' gaze location was reliably related to the prosody and given/new status of the critical word. Participants listened to short discourses (see [1] below, capital letters indicate accenting) consisting of two instructions to move objects within a visual display. On critical trials, two of the possible targets were cohort competitors, words which share initial word onsets and are therefore temporarily lexically ambiguous (Allopenna et al., 1998; Marslen-Wilson, 1987). In the first instruction, participants were told to move one of these cohort objects. In the second instruction participants were told to move either the given cohort object (anaphoric condition) or the new cohort object (nonanaphoric condition).

[1] Example discourse from Dahan et al. (2002)

a. Instruction 1 Move the *candy/camel* below the square.
b. Instruction 2 NOW move the *CANDY/candy* above the star.

Dahan et al. (2002) measured participants' fixations to given and new cohort objects during the ambiguous region of the critical word in the second instruction. Consistent with previous research showing that listeners associate accenting with new information (e.g., Birch & Clifton, 2002; Terken & Nooteboom, 1987), they found that when the critical word was produced with an accent, listeners were biased to look at the new cohort object and when the critical word was produced without an accent, they were biased to look at the given cohort object. This suggests that (1) listeners are sensitive to prosodic information, (2) listeners use this information to make rapid predictions about referents in a discourse context, and (3) there is a link between listeners' processing of accents and looking preferences.

The present study will use a modified version of the design used by Dahan et al. (2002). The critical word in the second instruction (i.e., "candy" in [1]) was resynthesised to have either high or low F0 and either long or short duration. Resynthesis was used in this study because of the inherent drawbacks associated with synthesised speech and natural speech. Synthesised speech offers a high degree of control but the resulting audio file does not sound natural. On the other hand, human produced speech sounds very natural but is difficult to control. Resynthesised speech combines the strengths of both approaches. Resynthesis is the process of artificially altering the acoustic properties (like F0, duration, and intensity) of naturally produced audio to produce audio that is both relatively natural sounding and highly controlled. This has made resynthesis a popular tool for exploring questions in prosody and phonology (e.g., Dilley & Brown, 2007; Ladd & Morton, 1997; Ladd & Schepman, 2003; Welby, 2007).

Participants' interpretations of the resynthesised word will be reflected in their looking preferences to the given and new cohort objects. Dahan et al.'s (2002) results suggest that if listeners detect an accent on a word referring to a cohort object, then they should be biased to look at the new cohort object. In Dahan et al.'s study, the speaker produced high F0-peaked accents (**H*** and **L+H***). These accents are associated with a high F0 and a relatively long duration. If listeners detect de-accenting, then they should be biased to look at the given cohort object. Unaccented words are characterised by the absence of a rise in F0 and a short duration. This pattern was confirmed by an analysis of the recordings used for resynthesis, which we present below; accented words are long and are produced with a rise in F0 while unaccented words are short and are produced with a fall in F0.

Several outcomes are possible. If F0 excursion alone is critical for signalling accenting, high F0 should result in more looks to the new cohort object and fewer looks to the given cohort object, independent of duration.

It is also possible that listeners will ignore all F0 information and, instead, use duration alone as a cue to accenting. This would result in a main effect of duration such that long duration, which has been claimed to correlate with accenting (e.g., Kochanski et al., 2005), would result in more looks to the new cohort object than the given cohort object.

Alternately, both F0 and duration may be important. Research suggests two possible interactions: a cue-trading relationship or the use of F0 slope. Beach (1991) found a cue-trading relationship between F0 and duration: either was sufficient for indicating the presence of a boundary tone. Therefore, if a cue-trading relationship exists between F0 and duration in accent perception, then either high F0 or long duration, which are both associated with high F0-peaked accents, will result in more looks to the new cohort object and fewer looks to the given cohort object. The condition in which neither of these cues is present will result in a bias to the given cohort object.

A second possibility is that F0 slope is critical for accent detection. Bartels and Kingston (1994) found that listeners used F0 slope to detect the difference between accent types. In the present study, F0 slope is determined by a combination of both the F0 and duration manipulations. In an initial analysis of stimuli for this experiment that were produced in accented and unaccented contexts, we found that accented words had a positive slope and unaccented words had a negative slope, the latter most likely due to declination that occurs naturally over a sentence. Positive sloped conditions (high F0) are a better match for accented words and should result in more looks to the new cohort object. On the other hand, negative sloped conditions (low F0) are a less good match and should result in more looks away from the new cohort object, and possibly more looks to the given cohort object. In addition, because the F0 contour for the two F0 conditions were set to the same height, conditions with short duration had a steeper slope than conditions with long duration although the absolute F0 excursion is constant within each F0 condition. Bolinger (1986) argues that more abrupt changes in F0 are more salient. Therefore, if slope is important for perceiving the presence of an accent, then there should be more looks to the new cohort object for steep, positive slopes (high F0, short-duration conditions).

METHODS

Participants

Forty-eight native speakers of American English were recruited from the University of Illinois at Urbana-Champaign. Participants received either class credit or $7 compensation for their participation.

Materials

Trials

Participants completed 20 critical trials, 30 filler trials, and four practice trials for a total of 54 trials. Each trial consisted of two separate instructions as in [2] below to move one of the four possible objects. The information status (anaphoric/nonanaphoric) of each trial was determined by the object moved in the first instruction. In the anaphoric condition the same (given) object was moved in both instructions. In the nonanaphoric condition a different (new) object was moved in the second instruction. The F0 and duration manipulations were realised on the critical word in the second instruction (i.e., "camel"). Four different versions of the critical word were resynthesised (described below) resulting in a complete cross of F0 (high/low) and duration (long/short). In both the anaphoric and nonanaphoric conditions the object that served as the destination marker (i.e., "circle" and "triangle" in [2]) was different in the two instructions so that accenting the destination would be felicitous. Because English sentences typically have at least one pitch accent, accenting the destination marker was necessary so that sentences in which the target word might be interpreted as unaccented would still be felicitous.

[2] Instruction 1:

Anaphoric: Move the camel below the circle.
Nonanaphoric: Move the candle below the circle.

Instruction 2:

Now move the *camel* above the triangle.

Information status (anaphoric/nonanaphoric) was a between subjects factor while the acoustic variables, F0 (high/low) and duration (long/short), were within subjects factors. Two cohort items and two distractor items were included on each critical trial for a total of four pictured items (Appendix 1). All cohort pairs were picturable nouns that shared initial phonemes, had equal numbers of syllables, and were matched for lexical frequency (paired $t = 1.373$, df $= 19$, $p > .05$) as reported in the CELEX English database (1993). One member of each pair was randomly chosen to be the critical item in the second instruction. In addition, four stationary geometric figures were present on all trials (Figure 1). Distractor items were not semantically related to the cohort pair and did not share word onsets with the cohort pair.

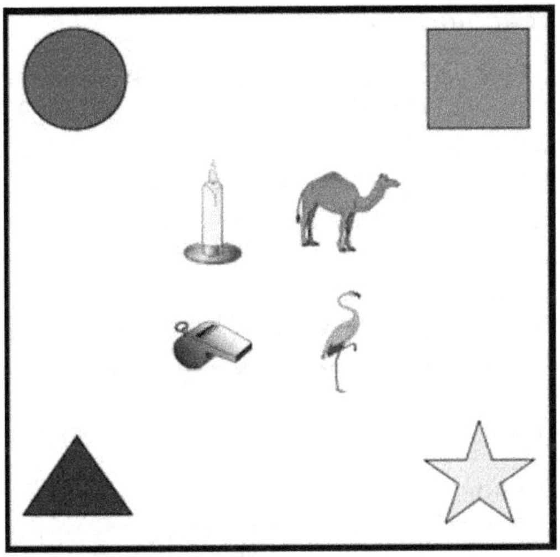

Figure 1. Display at the onset of a critical trial.

Filler trials included anaphoric trials in which the same object was moved in both instructions and nonanaphoric trials in which different objects were moved in each instruction. Filler trials included 10 trials in which no cohort pair was present (five anaphoric and five nonanaphoric), eight trials in which a cohort pair was present but not mentioned (five anaphoric and three nonanaphoric), and two trials in which a cohort pair was present but only one of the cohort objects was mentioned in only one instruction (both nonanaphoric). In addition, there were 10 trials in which a cohort pair was present and was used in both instructions. To help balance the overall information status of all trials, these 10 trials were anaphoric for subjects whose critical trials were nonanaphoric and these 10 trials were nonanaphoric for subjects whose critical trials were anaphoric. One of the filler trials, including the cohort pair "cat"–"cap", was dropped for some participants because earlier participants consistently mistook the target word ("cap") for the cohort competitor ("cat").

Visual stimuli

The 216 pictures used in the visual presentation were selected from the original Snodgrass and Vanderwart (1980) normed picture set, the colourised version of this picture set by Rossion and Pourtois (2001), and from commercial picture databases. All pictures were coloured line drawings or were black and white line drawings, which were colourised using computer software.

Resynthesis of audio files

The critical word for each experimental trial was modified using the Pitch Synchronous Overlap Add (PSOLA) algorithm (Moulines & Verhelst, 1995). This process allowed us to alter the F0 and duration of the critical words in the audio files while leaving all other acoustic features of the soundwave unchanged. Resynthesis took place in three steps, which are discussed below in detail: (1) recording naturally produced audio stimuli (source audio); (2) measurement of median F0 and duration of the critical word across items; and (3) altering F0 and duration values in the critical word of each item, using the measures calculated in step 2 as targets.

Source recordings

It is difficult to know *a priori* what the F0 and duration targets should be for naturally produced accented and unaccented words. Therefore, the source audio had a dual purpose; it served both as the audio which would be resynthesised and the audio from which target acoustic values were calculated. By taking the aggregate duration and F0 of accented and unaccented words in their appropriate discourse contexts, we could estimate appropriate target values for the accented and unaccented words. To this end, we recorded naturally produced accented and unaccented words in nonanaphoric and anaphoric contexts, respectively. Median values of F0 and duration were calculated and these values were used in resynthesis as described below.

For each critical trial, a set of four instructions (see [3] below) was recorded by a male native speaker of American English. Two versions of the second sentence were produced, one in which the critical word was accented and one in which the critical word was unaccented. The information status (anaphoric/nonanaphoric) of the trial was determined by the cohort object moved in the first instruction. Two versions of the first instruction were recorded; in the anaphoric condition the target cohort object (e.g., "camel") was moved and in the nonanaphoric condition the competitor cohort (e.g., "candle") was moved.

[3] Instruction 1:

Anaphoric: Move the camel below the circle.
Nonanaphoric: Move the candle below the circle.

Instruction 2:

Unaccented: Now move the camel above the triangle.
Accented: Now move the CAMEL above the triangle.

The acoustic features of the critical words in the second instructions were analysed to determine the acoustic values to be used in resynthesis. Acoustic comparisons were made between the unaccented items, which tend to have short duration and low F0, and accented items, which tend to have long duration and high F0.

The accented versions (mean = 598 ms, $SD = 90.94$) were significantly longer than the unaccented versions (mean = 497 ms, $SD = 79.75$), paired $t(19) = 7.91$, $p < .001$, one-tailed. A ratio of the duration was measured (unaccented duration to accented duration) for each item. The mean ratio for all 20 items was 0.84.

For each word, F0 was measured by dividing the word into 20 segments of equal duration and measuring the average F0 over each segment. The absolute F0 at any point of a given word is a function of both the accenting on that word and the relative height of the entire utterance in the speaker's range, the F0 baseline. The current experiment used a baselining procedure to isolate the F0 change due to accenting. A constant F0 baseline was measured at the onset of the word "move" for each item and this F0 baseline was subtracted from the F0 means calculated for each segment of the corresponding critical word. This process extracted the F0 contour from the word and corrected for differences in the speaker's range across productions. The algorithms used to extract F0 can occasionally provide spuriously high or low F0 values. Rather than hand-correcting the errors (which may introduce additional error), median values were used to reduce the impact of these outliers on the F0 contour.

The F0 contour for the high F0 condition was generated by calculating the median F0 across all words for each segment. These points are plotted in Figure 2 as grey dots connected by lines. A six-term polynomial equation

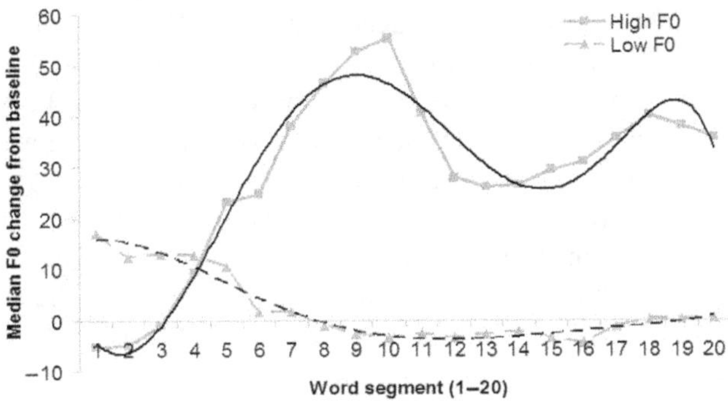

Figure 2. The median F0 values for accented (high F0) and unaccented (low F0) items in 20 equally spaced segments are shown in grey. The graph of the polynomial equations generated to fit these points is shown in black.

(black lines in Figure 2) was generated to fit these 20 F0 points using a line-of-best-fit algorithm in Microsoft Excel. The F0 contour for the low F0 condition was modelled using the same process but with the unaccented items.[1]

Resynthesis

Experimental audio files for each trial were created in Praat (Boersma & Weenink, 2008) using the PSOLA algorithm. The F0 and duration of each critical word were resynthesised to create four distinct versions, all originating from the same source utterance. For this audio set, we found that lengthening a word degraded the word's naturalness. Therefore, resynthesising from an unaccented sound file, which requires lengthening to produce the sound file for the long-duration conditions, resulted in consistently less-natural audio quality for long conditions than short conditions. For this reason, all critical utterances were resynthesised from accented source audio.

The critical word from each accented item was spliced out of the original utterance into a separate audio file. The F0 of each critical word was altered first. The word was divided into 20 segments. For each segment, a new F0 value was created that was equal to the sum of the baseline value for that carrier sentence (calculated as described above) and the target F0 value generated from the polynomials discussed above.

From each raw version of the critical word, two separate audio files were created: one with high F0 and one with low F0. Because these were created from accented sound files (which have naturally long duration), both versions already had long duration. The two audio files for the two short-duration conditions were created by shortening the long versions, resulting in four versions of the critical word. The calculated ratio of 0.84 duration difference between unaccented and accented audio files was deemed by the authors to be too small a difference to produce a sufficient contrast. Other work done in our lab has shown that there are large individual differences in lengthening for accented words (Isaacs & Watson, 2009) but that differences as large as 60% are still naturally produced (Isaacs & Watson, 2007). Therefore, the short-duration audio file was shortened to a value equal to 70% of the original (long) duration.

Figure 3 contains plots of the functions used to generate the F0 contours resynthesised for critical words. To illustrate the difference between short and

[1] F0 values were measured across the entire critical word including both mono- and disyllabic words. Visual comparisons of the F0 contours collapsed across mono- and disyllabic words separately reveal no difference in contour shape. Separate analyses of the fixation data for mono- and disyllabic words show the same pattern of results, so they are collapsed in the results section.

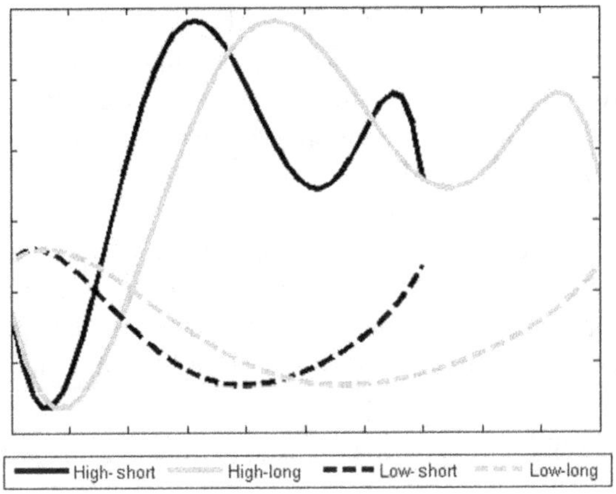

Figure 3. Graphical representations of the functions used to generate F0 contours for the high and low F0 conditions with either long or short duration.

long duration, each equation has been plotted twice: once normally and once with x-axis units that are 70% of the original length.

The four resulting audio files, each containing one version of the critical word (low F0-short duration, low F0-high duration, high F0-short duration, and high F0-long duration), were then spliced into a carrier sentence. The carrier sentence consisted of a preamble (e.g., "Move the") and a destination (e.g., "above the star"). The carrier sentence was taken from the version of each item, which had originally held the unaccented version of the critical item. After splicing, the preamble and destination of the carrier sentence were stylised. Stylisation identifies key points in the F0 contour (local maximums, minimums, and locations of large changes in F0 trajectory) and then interpolates the intermediate F0 values using the PSOLA algorithm. The process maintains the general shape of the F0 contour but introduces a small amount of noise into the recording similar to the type of noise that is present in resynthesised portions of the audio file. The stylisation is generally not noticeable compared to unaltered natural recordings, but the process reduced the contrast between the resynthesised and unresynthesised portions of the utterance, improving the overall coherence of the critical utterances.

Procedure

On each trial, participants listened to two separate instructions as in [2] above. Audio files were played over computer speakers. After each instruction, pictured objects were moved by clicking and dragging the critical object to the specified location.

At the onset of the second instruction, the participants' eye movements were monitored using an Eyelink II eyetracking system. Fixations were compared relative to the onset of the critical word. Because it takes roughly 200 ms to programme an eye movement (Allopenna et al., 1998; Henderson & Ferreira, 2004), we expected prosody-driven fixations to appear 200 ms after the onset of the critical word.

Participants were not able to move objects while audio was being played. If a participant made an error on the first instruction, either by selecting the wrong object or moving it to the wrong location, all objects returned to their original location and the instruction was repeated. Errors made in the second (critical) instruction were not corrected. All errors were noted for later exclusion in data analysis.

RESULTS

After completing the experiment, participants took a survey asking them (1) if they noticed anything unusual and (2) what they thought the experiment was testing. Of the 41 subjects who completed the survey, eight stated that the audio sounded strange or mentioned the audio manipulation in their description of the experiment's purpose.

A total of six trials (0.625% of all trials) were excluded because the participant made an error in the first instruction by selecting the wrong object (two trials) or moving the object to the wrong location (four trials). On an additional 15 trials (1.56% of all trials), participants selected the wrong object in the second instruction. In 14 of these cases, the participants chose the competitor object suggesting that the preferences induced by the manipulation persisted through the end of the trial. Analyses were performed both with and without these 14 trials, both analyses yielded the same result, therefore these trials were retained in the present analyses because it was felt that these errors were related to the manipulation.

Results are reported as Target Advantage Scores (TAS), which are the proportion of fixations to the target minus the proportion of fixations to the competitor over a specified time region (e.g., Arnold, Fagnano, & Tanenhaus, 2003). The resulting value is the difference in the proportion of fixations between the target and competitor. A positive TAS indicates that the participant was looking at the target more than the competitor and a negative TAS indicates more looks to the competitor. Thus, in the anaphoric condition positive values indicate more looks to the given cohort object and negative values indicate more looks to the new cohort object. In the nonanaphoric condition positive values indicate more looks to the new cohort object and negative values indicate more looks to the given cohort

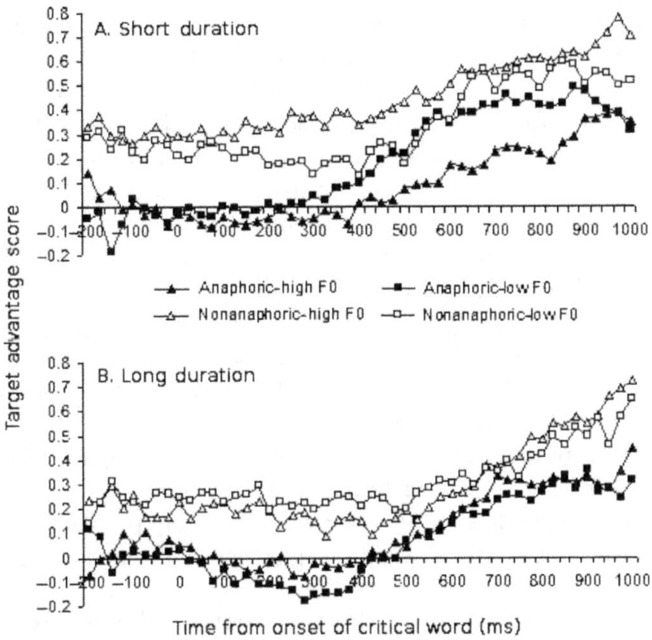

Figure 4. Time course plot of target advantage scores plotted by information status (anaphoric/nonanaphoric) and F0 (high/low) for conditions with short duration (A) and long duration (B) starting at the onset of the critical word (0 ms).

object. Figure 4 shows TAS values plotted over time starting at the onset of the critical word (0 ms).

There was a higher overall TAS for trials in nonanaphoric conditions (Figure 4). In the critical time regions from 200 to 600 ms after critical word onset, nonanaphoric conditions had significantly higher TAS than anaphoric conditions, $t_1(46) = -4.40, p < .001, t_2(38) = -3.97, p < .001$. This bias was even significant in the 400 ms preceding the critical region, $t_1(46) = -5.84, p < .001, t_2(38) = -4.85, p < .001$, which is before participants' eye movements should be affected by the manipulation. This bias replicates the bias found by Dahan et al. (2002).[2]

In the critical time region from 200 to 600 ms after word onset, a reliable Information Status (Anaphoric/Nonanaphoric) × F0 (High/Low) × Duration (Long/Short) interaction was found, $F_1(1, 46) = 8.02, p < .01, F_2(1, 38) = 11.72, p < .005$. Figure 5 illustrates this interaction in the mean TAS values for the critical time region. When duration was long, there was no

[2] Although we find a new bias in this data, replicating Dahan et al. (2002), Arnold (2008) did not find this bias using a slightly different task. This suggests that this bias may be due to task demands rather than a general listener preference to fixate the new item within a contrast set.

difference between high and low F0 conditions as shown by a nonsignificant Information Status (Anaphoric/Nonanaphoric) × F0 (High/Low) interaction for long-duration conditions, $F_1(1, 46) = 1.13$, $p > .05$, $F_2(1, 38) = 1.39$, $p > .05$. This was true in both the anaphoric condition, $t_1(23) = 0.52$, $p > .05$, $t_2(19) = 0.63$, $p > .05$, and the nonanaphoric condition, $t_1(23) = -0.99$, $p > .05$, $t_2(19) = -1.01$, $p > .05$. In contrast, the same analysis performed on short-duration conditions shows that when the duration was short, there was a difference between the high and low F0 conditions, $F_2(1, 46) = 9.51$, $p < .005$, $F_2(1, 38) = 13.18$, $p < .005$. Again, this was true for both the anaphoric condition, $t_1(23) = -2.16$, $p < .05$, $t_2(19) = -2.08$, $p < .10$, and the nonanaphoric condition, $t_1(23) = 2.23$, $p < .05$, $t_2(19) = 3.16$, $p < .01$. In anaphoric conditions, TAS scores were higher if the word was produced with low F0 indicating a looking preference to the given cohort object when the critical word was produced with low F0 as compared to high F0. In contrast, TAS scores were higher in the nonanaphoric condition when the critical word was produced with high F0 indicating a looking preference to the new cohort object when the critical word was produced with high F0 as compared to low F0.

Furthermore, when long- and short-duration conditions are compared, different patterns are found for the anaphoric (Figure 5A) and nonanaphoric (Figure 5B) conditions. In the anaphoric conditions, when F0 was low there was a difference between the long and short duration, $t_1(23) = -2.42$, $p < .05$, $t_2(19) = -2.75$, $p < .05$, but when F0 was high there was no difference between the duration conditions, $ts < 1$. In the nonanaphoric conditions, by comparison, when F0 was low there was no difference between the long- and short-duration conditions, $ts < 1$, but there was a significant difference in the high F0 condition, $t_1(23) = -2.79$, $p < .05$, $t_2(19) = -3.78$, $p < .005$. Thus, both conditions show higher TAS values in the short-duration condition: there was a preference for the given cohort object when F0 was low and a preference for the new cohort object when the F0 was high.

DISCUSSION

Dahan et al. (2002) found that when the critical word was accented, participants looked more at the new cohort object and when the critical word was unaccented, participants looked more at the given cohort object. In this study, we find that accenting is signalled by an interaction between duration and F0 information. The interaction described above rules out the possibility that listeners rely primarily on either F0 or duration alone to make decisions about accenting. As we discuss below, the data here are more consistent with an F0 slope account of accenting than a cue-trading account.

The F0 slope hypothesis predicts that listeners use slope to detect accents. F0 slope is here defined as the direction and rate of F0 change. Accented words in this experiment have high F0 peaks (Figure 3). This positive slope makes listeners more likely to look at the new cohort object. Unaccented words lack this definite peak and, instead, show a general F0 declination over the word. This negative slope makes listeners more likely to look at the given cohort object. Duration affects the rate of this change. Since the absolute amount of F0 change is the same in all conditions within the same F0 condition, a short duration results in steeper slopes than a long duration. Thus, when duration is short, the high F0 condition will have steep positive slope and the low F0 condition will have steep negative slope.

Recall that TAS scores are composed of the difference between the proportion of looks to the target and competitor with positive values indicating more looks to the target and negative values indicating more looks to the competitor. Thus, in the anaphoric condition, positive values indicate more looks to the given cohort object and negative values indicate more looks to the new cohort object. In the nonanaphoric condition, positive values indicate more looks to the new cohort object and negative values indicate more looks to the given cohort object.

In the short-duration conditions, therefore, the F0 slope hypothesis correctly predicts that there should be higher TAS scores for the low F0 condition when the target is anaphoric and higher TAS scores for the high F0 condition when the target is nonanaphoric.

When duration is long, slopes will be less steep both in the high and low F0 condition, which should reduce or eliminate looking preferences both in the anaphoric and nonanaphoric conditions. The F0 slope hypothesis correctly predicts that when duration is long there should be less of a difference in TAS in both the anaphoric and nonanaphoric conditions. Thus, the F0 slope hypothesis correctly predicts the outcome of comparisons between high and low F0.

Since a positive slope leads listeners to look at the new cohort object and negative slopes lead listeners to look more at the given cohort object, when the slope is in the wrong direction for the target condition, listeners should be biased away from the correct target regardless of duration. Thus, the F0 slope hypothesis correctly predicts that there should be no difference in the TAS values for long and short durations in the anaphoric condition when the F0 is high or in the nonanaphoric condition when the F0 is low. However, when the slope is in the correct direction for the information status of the condition, then the looking preference should be largest in the condition in which the slope is steepest, the short-duration condition. Therefore, there should be higher TAS values for the short-duration condition when the F0 is low in the anaphoric condition and when the F0 is high in the nonanaphoric

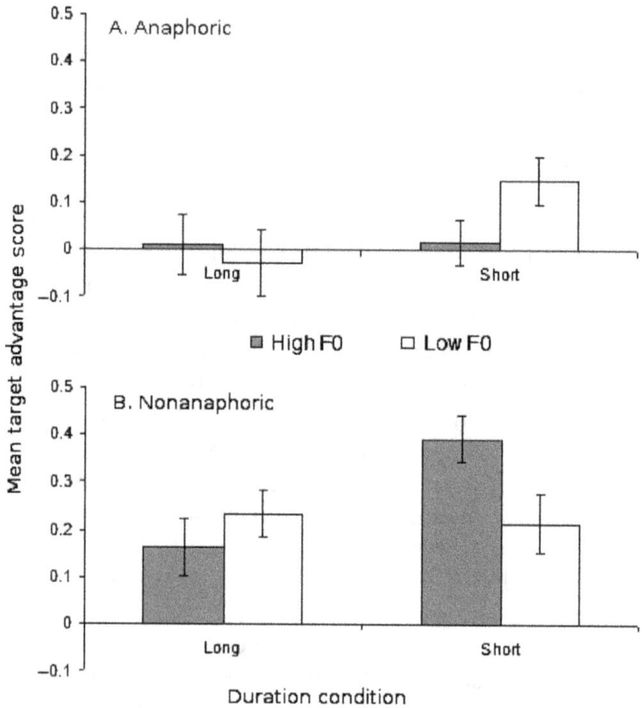

Figure 5. Mean target advantage scores and standard error values plotted by F0 (high/low) and duration (long/short) in the anaphoric (A) and nonanaphoric conditions (B).

condition, which is the pattern observed in Figure 5. The F0 slope hypothesis correctly predicts the results of all eight comparisons between conditions.

In comparison, the cue-trading hypothesis predicts that either of the two cues that indicate accenting, long duration or high F0, should be sufficient to bias listeners towards an accented interpretation. Thus, any condition in which either duration is long or F0 is high should result in a higher proportion of looks to the new cohort object, which would mean higher TAS values for nonanaphoric conditions, and lower TAS values for anaphoric conditions.

Since cue trading predicts that either long duration or high F0 will result in a bias to look at the new cohort object, then any comparison between two items with long duration or high F0 should result in a nonsignificant difference. As predicted, there was no significant difference between F0 conditions with long duration in either the anaphoric condition or the nonanaphoric condition and no significant difference between duration conditions with high F0 in the anaphoric condition. However, contrary to the prediction of cue trading, in nonanaphoric conditions there was a significant difference between duration conditions when F0 was high. Not only is there a significant difference when cue trading predicts there should be none, but also there is actually a preference for the new cohort object when the duration is short. Unlike the F0 slope hypothesis, the cue-trading hypothesis cannot account for this pattern of results.

Cue trading further predicts that any comparison between high and low F0 should result in a larger bias to look at the new cohort object for the high F0 condition. Therefore, in anaphoric conditions, the low F0 condition should have larger TAS values than the high F0 condition and in nonanaphoric conditions the high F0 condition should have larger TAS values than the low F0 condition. In addition, any comparison between long and short duration should result in a larger bias to look at the new cohort object for the long-duration condition. Thus, in anaphoric conditions the short-duration condition should have larger TAS values than the long-duration condition and in nonanaphoric conditions the long-duration condition should have larger TAS values than the short-duration condition.

As predicted, when duration was short, TAS values were higher in the high F0 condition when the target was nonanaphoric and higher in the low F0 condition when the target was anaphoric. However, cue trading predicts that when F0 is low, TAS values should be higher in the long-duration condition than in the short-duration condition when the target is nonanaphoric, but no significant difference was found. Furthermore, there were higher TAS values in the high F0 condition in the nonanaphoric condition when the duration was short than when it was long.

Thus, while cue trading can largely explain the pattern of effects observed in Figure 5, it cannot explain the significant difference between the high F0 conditions in the nonanaphoric condition or the direction of the effect; that there was a greater looking preference to the new cohort object in the high F0 conditions when the duration was short.

Arguably, the version of cue trading that we have outlined above is an extreme version in which any cue to prominence (i.e., high F0 or long duration) is independently sufficient for signalling prominence. In a weaker cue-based theory, cues to prominence might be interpreted additively such that having two cues that signal prominence leads to stronger expectations of prominence than having only a single cue, and the presence of a single cue leads to a stronger perception of prominence than having no cue. Under such a theory, one would predict a difference between conditions in which one cue indicates accenting and conditions in which both cues indicate accenting. However, the difference is in the wrong direction. Even a weaker version cannot explain why looks to the target were greater in the new cohort object condition when F0 was high and duration was short compared to the condition in which F0 was high and duration was long.

Under the strong version of the cue-trading hypothesis, these two conditions should be equal because both contain at least one cue that indicates accenting. Under the weaker, additive version of the cue theory, the long-duration condition should have more looks because it has two cues that indicate accenting (high F0 and long duration) while the short-duration condition only has one (high F0). This suggests that F0 slope and not cue trading, best explains the pattern of looking preferences observed in the present study.

Bartels and Kingston (1994) found that F0 slope was important for listeners to distinguish presentational from contrastive accents and the data presented here suggest that F0 slope may be a general cue used by listeners for accent detection. Although we can only speculate as to why slope might be important, it could simply be that F0 is a salient, easily detectable cue for listeners. Future research will need to explore the degree to which listeners are sensitive to slope differences. The fact that listeners only relied upon slope information when the slope was relatively steep may provide insight into the process used by listeners to detect accents. Several possibilities exist. First, this imbalance may result from limitations in listeners' ability to detect slope. Bolinger (1986) has pointed out that steepness of F0 change makes F0 change more salient. Therefore, listeners' lack of preferences in the less-steep sloped conditions may reflect difficulty in determining slope direction when it is not steep. When they are unsure of the directionality, they fail to posit the presence of an accent and, therefore, do not use prosodic information to disambiguate the cohort object. Alternately, listeners may be sensitive to the fact that less-steep slopes are more likely to be the result of random variation in F0 and, therefore, only use slope as a cue when it is more extreme. Lastly, listeners may make decisions about accenting by attempting to match the F0 contour (the "shape" of the F0 change) to one of a set of prototypes. Steep-sloped conditions might provide a better match for the correct prototype, resulting in an increased likelihood of deciding that an accent is present.

These results also raise questions about accent interpretation. It is unclear what is driving the preference for the given cohort object in the short-low F0 condition. One possibility is that a steep drop in F0 signals de-accenting resulting in an explicit representation of the word as being de-accented which biases listeners towards the given cohort object. Another possibility is that a steep drop in F0 is a reliable indicator of the absence of the high-peaked accent. In this case, the effects seen above reflect fixations away from the new cohort object. This is a subtle difference but one that has important implications for the way that listeners interpret accented and unaccented words. The data here do not differentiate between these two possibilities and either possibility is consistent with the three explanations outlined above for listeners' lack of a looking preference in the less-steep conditions.

Another potential concern is how the nonaccent condition is characterised in this experiment. A drop in F0 is consistent with an **L*** accent, which Pierrehumbert and Hirschberg (1990) argue signals information that is new or salient, but should not be instantiated in the listener's discourse model. This raises a puzzling question: why did listeners not interpret the low F0 conditions as signalling new information since a drop in F0 is consistent with an **L*** accent? We point out that we derived the F0 falling contour from natural productions of nonaccented words. Although **L*** accent may correlate with falling F0, the contour here is consistent with naturally produced nonaccented words, and clearly, the data suggest listeners interpret this contour as cueing given information. Future work will need to determine how the drop in F0 associated with nonaccented words differs from the contour associated with **L***.

Additional questions remain. These results suggest that listeners are using F0 slope to detect the presence of an accent but Ladd, Faulkner, Faulkner, and Schepman (1999) found no consistent relationship between accenting and F0 slope in production. Ladd et al. tested whether F0 contours could be defined in terms of tonal targets that are anchored to points in the speech signal, an idea known as segmental anchoring. Speakers produced a passage under slow, normal, and fast conditions. If segmental anchoring indeed drives accenting, then the presence of tonal targets and their relative alignment should remain the same across speed conditions. This would result in differences in absolute duration and in the F0 slope. On the other hand, if either duration or F0 slope remained constant across the speed conditions then this would be evidence that slope and duration drive accenting. Ladd et al. found no consistent relationship between F0 slope and accenting, supporting the segmental anchoring hypothesis. They conclude that F0 contour in production is determined by F0 alignment and anchoring of tonal targets.

In the present study, the alignment of the F0 peak occurred at the same location within each word in long- and short-duration conditions since the F0 contour was stretched to match the length of the word. Thus, in the present study at least, differences in the duration conditions are not attributable to differences in F0 alignment. Ladd et al. (1999) found that speakers do not produce consistent F0 slope and yet listeners in our experiment used F0 slope to make decisions about accenting. This raises an interesting question. Are listeners using a cue (F0 slope) that speakers do not produce consistently? Further research needs to explore speakers' production of F0 alignment and slope and listeners' use of these features in comprehension.

REFERENCES

Allopenna, P. D., Magnuson, J. S., & Tanenhaus, M. K. (1998). Tracking the time course of spoken word recognition using eye movements: Evidence for continuous mapping models. *Journal of Memory and Language, 38*, 419–439.

Arnold, J. E. (2008). THE BACON not the bacon: How children and adults understand accented and unaccented noun phrases. *Cognition, 108*(1), 69–99.

Arnold, J. E., Fagnano, M., & Tanenhaus, M. K. (2003). Disfluencies signal theee, um, new information. *Journal of Psycholinguistic Research, 32*(1), 25–36.

Bard, E. G., & Aylett, M. P. (1999). *The dissociation of deaccenting, givenness, and syntactic role in spontaneous speech*. Paper presented at ICPhS-99, San Francisco, CA.

Bartels, C., & Kingston, J. (1994). Salient pitch cues in the perception of contrastive focus. *The Journal of the Acoustical Society of America, 95*(5), 2973.

Beach, C. M. (1991). The interpretation of prosodic patterns at points of syntactic structure ambiguity: Evidence for cue trading relations. *Journal of Memory and Language, 30*(6), 644–663.

Birch, S., & Clifton, C. (2002). Effects of varying focus and accenting of adjuncts on the comprehension of utterances. *Journal of Memory and Language, 47*(4), 571–588.

Boersma, P., & Weenink, D. (2008). *Praat: Doing phoenetics by computer*. Amsterdam: Institute of Phoenetic Sciences.

Bolinger, D. (1972). Accent is predictable (if you're a mind-reader). *Language, 48*(3), 633–644.

Bolinger, D. (1986). *Intonation and its parts: Melody in spoken English*. Stanford, CA: Stanford University Press.

Brown, G., & Yule, G. (1983). *Discourse analysis*. Cambridge: Cambridge University Press.

Buring, D. (2007). Semantics, intonation, and information structure. In G. Ramchand & C. Reiss (Eds.), *The Oxford handbook of linguistic interfaces*. Oxford: Oxford University Press.

CELEX English database. (1993). Retrieved September 20, 2006, from http://www.mpi.nl/world/celex

Chen, A., Os, E. D., & De Ruiter, J. P. (2007). Pitch accent type matters for online processing of information status: Evidence from natural and synthetic speech. *Linguistic Review. Special Issue: Prosodic Phrasing and Tunes, 24*(2–3), 317–344.

Cruttenden, A. (1997). *Intonation* (2nd ed.). Cambridge: Cambridge University Press.

Dahan, D., Tanenhaus, M. K., & Chambers, C. C. (2002). Accent and reference resolution in spoken-language comprehension. *Journal of Memory and Language, 47*, 292–314.

Dilley, L. C., & Brown, M. (2007). Effects of pitch range variation on f-sub-0 extrema in an imitation task. *Journal of Phonetics, 35*(4), 523–551.

Eberhard, K. M., Spivey-Knowlton, M. J., Sedivy, J. C., & Tanenhaus, M. K. (1995). Eye movements as a window into real-time spoken language comprehension in natural contexts. *Journal of Psycholinguistic Research, 24*(6), 409–436.

Grabe, E., Kochanski, G., & Coleman, J. (2007). Connecting intonation labels to mathematical descriptions of fundamental frequency. *Language and Speech, 50*(3), 445–474.

Halliday, M. A. K. (1967). *Intonation and grammar in British English*. Paris: Mouton.

Henderson, J. M., & Ferreira, F. (2004). Scene perception for psycholinguists. In J. M. Henderson & F. Ferreira (Eds.), *The interface of language, vision, and action: Eye movements and the visual world* (pp. 1–58). New York: Psychology Press.

Isaacs, A. M., & Watson, D. G. (2007). *Accenting is more than pitch: Word duration and listeners' preferences for discourse referents*. Unpublished manuscript.

Isaacs, A. M., & Watson, D. G. (2009, March). *Speakers and listeners don't agree: Audience design in the production and comprehension of acoustic prominence*. Paper presented at CUNY Sentence Processing Conference, Davis, CA.

Ito, K., & Speer, S. R. (2008). Anticipatory effects of intonation: Eye movements during instructed visual search. *Journal of Memory and Language, 58*(2), 541–573.

Kochanski, G., Grabe, E., Coleman, J., & Rosner, B. (2005). Loudness predicts prominence: Fundamental frequency lends little. *Journal of the Acoustical Society of America, 118*(2), 1038–1054.

Ladd, D. R. (1996). *Intonational phonology.* New York, NY: Cambridge University Press.

Ladd, D. R., Faulkner, D., Faulkner, H., & Schepman, A. (1999). Constant "segmental anchoring" of F0 movements under changes in speech rate. *The Journal of the Acoustical Society of America, 106*(3 Pt. 1), 1543–1554.

Ladd, D. R., & Morton, R. (1997). The perception of intonational emphasis: Continuous or categorical? *Journal of Phonetics, 25*, 313–342.

Ladd, D. R., & Schepman, A. (2003). "Sagging transitions" between high pitch accents in English: Experimental evidence. *Journal of Phonetics, 31*(1), 81–112.

Levy, R., & Jaeger, T. F. (2007). Speakers optimize information density through syntactic reduction. In B. Schlökopf, J. Platt, & T. Hoffman (Eds.), *Advances in neural information processing systems (NIPS) 19* (pp. 849–856). Cambridge, MA: MIT Press.

Marslen-Wilson, W. D. (1987). Functional parallelism in spoken word-recognition. *Cognition. Special Issue: Spoken Word Recognition, 25*(1–2), 71–102.

Moulines, E., & Verhelst, W. (1995). Time-domain and frequency-domain techniques for prosodic modification of speech. In W. B. Kleijn & K. K. Paliwal (Eds.), *Speech coding and synthesis* (pp. 519). New York: Elsevier Science.

Pierrehumbert, J. (1980). *The phonology and phonetics of English intonation* (Unpublished doctoral dissertation). Cambridge, MA: MIT Press.

Pierrehumbert, J., & Hirschberg, J. (1990). The meaning of intonational contours in the interpretation of discourse. In P. R. Cohen, J. Morgan, & M. E. Pollack (Eds.), *Intentions in communication* (pp. 271). Cambridge, MA: MIT Press.

Repp, B. H. (1985). Perceptual coherence of speech: Stability of silence-cued stop consonants. *Journal of Experimental Psychology: Human Perception and Performance, 11*(6), 799–813.

Rossion, B., & Pourtois, G. (2001, May). *Revisiting Snodgrass and Vanderwart's object database: Color and texture improve object recognition.* Paper presented at the 1st Vision Conference, Sarasota, FL.

Schwarzschild, R. (1999). GIVENness, AVOIDF and other constraints on the placement of accent. *Natural Language Semantics, 7*(2), 141–177.

Selkirk, E. (1995). Sentence prosody: Intonation, stress and phrasing. In J.A. Goldsmith (Ed.), *The handbook of phonological theory* (pp. 550–569). London: Blackwell.

Silverman, K., Beckman, M. E., Pitrelli, J., Ostendorf, M., Pierrehumbert, J., Hirschberg, J., & Price, P., (1992, October). *ToBI: A standard for labeling English prosody.* Paper presented at the second international conference on Spoken Language Processing, Banff, Canada.

Snodgrass, J. S., & Vanderwart, M. (1980). A standardized set of 260 pictures: Norms for name agreement, familiarity, and visual complexity. *Journal of Experimental Psychology: Human Learning and Memory, 6*, 174–215..

Tanenhaus, M. K., Spivey-Knowlton, M. J., Eberhard, K. M., & Sedivy, J. C. (1995). Integration of visual and linguistic information in spoken language comprehension. *Science, 268*(5217), 1632–1634.

Terken, J., & Nooteboom, S. G. (1987). Opposite effects of accentuation and deaccentuation on verification latencies for given and new information. *Language and Cognitive Processes, 2*(3–4), 145–163.

Watson, D. G., Gunlogson, C. A., & Tanenhaus, M. K. (2006). Online methods of the investigation of prosody. In A. Steube (Ed.), *Methods in empirical prosody research* (pp. 259–283). New York: Walter de Gruyter.

Watson, D. G., Gunlogson C. A., & Tanenhaus, M. K. (2008). Interpreting pitch accents in on-line comprehension: H* vs L+H*. *Cognitive Science, 32*, 1232–1244.

Weber, A., Braun, B., & Crocker, M. W. (2006). Finding referents in time: Eye-tracking evidence for the role of contrastive accents. *Language and Speech, 49*(3), 367.

Welby, P. (2007). The role of early fundamental frequency rises and elbows in French word segmentation. *Speech Communication, 49*(1), 28–48.

APPENDIX 1
Pictures used for each trial

New cohort object	*Given cohort object*	*Distractor 1*	*Distractor 2*
Bell	Bed	Apple	Pliers
Clown	Cloud	Skeleton	Rolling pin
Skate	Scale	Wagon	Rocket
Rabbit	Raccoon	Calculator	Hanger
Sandwich	Sandal	Barrel	Chocolate bar
Candle	Camel	Whistle	Flamingo
Rooster	Ruler	Vest	Guitar
Pencil	Penguin	Dove	Elk
Rope	Road	Flower vase	Umbrella
Chair	Chain	Backpack	Viola
Plate	Plane	Acorn	Snowman
Pillow	Pickle	Helicopter	Watch
Robe	Rose	Strawberry	Gun
Doll	Dog	Mountain	Net
Chicken	Chimney	Jellyfish	Watch
Carriage	Carrot	Police car	Owl
Sheep	Shield	Giraffe	Violin
Cane	Cake	Shirt	Lemon
Cork	Corn	Ketchup	Nail
Lamb	Lamp	Spinning wheel	Light

LANGUAGE AND COGNITIVE PROCESSES
2010, 25 (7/8/9), 1201–1233

Psychology Press
Taylor & Francis Group

The implicit prosody hypothesis and overt prosody in English

Sun-Ah Jun

Department of Linguistics, University of California, Los Angeles, CA, USA

This study investigates the validity of the Implicit Prosody Hypothesis (IPH) by examining default phrasing in English, a low attachment language, in overt prosody generated by reading aloud sentences where a complex noun phrase serves as the head of a relative clause (NP1 NP2 RC). The prosodic phrasing of 27 sentences collected from 36 speakers was transcribed by three ToBI-trained labellers. Results show that, counter to the predictions of the IPH, the most common prosodic phrasing was (NP1 NP2)//(RC), which would be expected for high attachment preference languages. This default phrasing was found to be influenced by the length of the RC and by syntactically disambiguating properties of the RC verb (i.e., number agreement) only when the RC was short. It was suggested that the prosody generated in silent reading would not necessarily be the same as the prosody generated in reading aloud, especially when reading without skimming the material in advance. Based on the current results and data from previous studies, various ways to access implicit prosody are proposed.

Keywords: Implicit prosody; Overt prosody; Default phrasing; Read aloud.

Correspondence should be addressed to Sun-Ah Jun, Department of Linguistics, University of California, Los Angeles, CA 90095-1543, USA. E-mail: jun@humnet.ucla.edu

This work was supported by a UCLA Faculty Research Grant. Many thanks to Michael Wagner and five anonymous reviewers for providing insightful suggestions and helpful comments. I would also like to thank Janet Fodor, Kiwako Ito, Shari Speer, and the audience at the Conference on Prosody and Language Processing held at Cornell University in 2008 and to Bruce Hayes, Pat Keating, and other members of the UCLA Phonetics Lab for their suggestions and feedback. Special thanks to Janet Fodor and Anouschka Bergmann for sending me helpful references; to J'aime Roemer, Molly Shilman, and Chad Vicenik for their help in prosodic transcriptions; to Timothy Arbisi-Kelm, Peter Graff, and Matthew Weitz for data collection; to Sameer ud Dowla Khan for proofreading the manuscript; and to Kristine Yu, Megha Sundara, Amy Schafer, and UCLA Statistics Consulting Group for their help in statistics.

http://www.psypress.com/lcp DOI: 10.1080/01690965.2010.503658

INTRODUCTION

Since Cuetos and Mitchell's (1988) seminal work, it has been known that languages differ in the attachment preference of a relative clause (RC) when the head noun is a complex noun phrase (i.e., has two nouns) and the relative clause is not biased towards modifying either noun. For example, in (1), the attachment of the RC, *who was on the balcony*, is ambiguous. It can modify the adjacent, embedded head noun *the actress*, i.e., attach low, or the non-adjacent head noun, *the servant*, i.e., attach high.

(1) *Someone shot the servant of the actress who was on the balcony.* (Cuetos & Mitchell, 1988)

In processing sentences like (1), high attachment of an RC is preferred by speakers of Dutch (Brysbaert & Mitchell, 1996), French (Zagar, Pynte, & Rativeau, 1997), German (Hemforth, Konieczny, Scheepers, & Strube, 1998), Japanese (Kamide & Mitchell, 1997), Spanish (Cuetos & Mitchell, 1988), Croatian (Lovric, 2000, 2001), Greek (Papadopoulou & Calhsen, 2003), and Hindi (Vasishth, Agnihotri, Fernandez, & Bhatt, 2004), while low attachment of an RC is preferred by speakers of Arabic (Quinn, Abdelghany, & Fodor, 2000), English (Frazier & Clifton, 1996), Norwegian, Romanian, and Swedish (Ehrlich, Fernández, Fodor, Stenshoel, & Vinereanu, 1999; see Fodor, 1998; Fernández, 2003; Augurzky, 2006 for more details[1]).

This apparent cross-linguistic difference has challenged the universalist view of sentence processing. Psycholinguists have hypothesised that there exists a universal, innate mechanism in human sentence processing which guides a parser (e.g., minimal attachment, late closure, or right association by Kimball, 1973; Frazier & Fodor, 1978; Frazier, 1979; Frazier & Rayner, 1988; Fodor, 1998). The main idea of the universal parsing mechanism is to parse efficiently by not building an unnecessary structure and not changing an existing structure at the level higher than the current clause or phrase, i.e., having fewer syntactic nodes and attaching low. This mechanism explains problems in parsing garden-path sentences (Frazier & Fodor, 1978) and predicts the RC in sentence (1) to attach low cross-linguistically.

In order to explain this cross-linguistic variation of RC attachment, several accounts have been proposed, e.g., the frequency-based *Tuning*

[1] The attachment preference is not fixed even in the same language. The preference varies depending on a variety of factors such as the type of adposition within the complex noun phrase (theta-assigning or not), the type of modifiers (adpositional phrase or relative clause), and the early or late stage of processing (e.g., Carreiras & Clifton, 1993, 1999; De Vencenzi & Job, 1994; Brysbaert & Mitchell, 1996). The attachment preference discussed in this paper is confined to the attachment of the RC in the "NP1 *of* NP2 RC" structure, at a later stage of processing.

Hypothesis (e.g., Cuetos & Mitchell, 1988; Mitchell, 1994; Brysbaert & Mitchell, 1996), memory-based *Predicate Proximity/Recency* (e.g., Gibson, Pearlmutter, Canseco-Gonzales, & Hickock, 1996), argument/adjunct distinction and discourse-based *Construal* (e.g., Gilboy, Sopena, Clifton, & Frazier, 1995; Frazier & Clifton, 1996, 1997), and prominence and discourse-based *Anaphoric Binding* (e.g., Hemforth, Konieczny, Scheepers, & Strube, 1998), but all have encountered counter-examples and have had problems in explaining why the same syntactic structure varying only constituent length triggers different attachment preferences (see below for the effect of length in more detail).

More recently, Fodor (1998, 2002) proposed a new account, the prosody-based *Implicit Prosody Hypothesis (IPH)*. She claims that the cross-linguistic difference in attachment preference is due to a cross-linguistic difference in prosody, specifically the default prosodic phrasing of a sentence, i.e., the prosodic phrasing produced in broad/neutral focus condition or phrasing produced without assuming a specific discourse context. The default phrasing was claimed to favour the syntactic analysis associated with it. Since the attachment preference data were collected from processing a written text, i.e., silent reading, the prosody was not overt but implicit. This hypothesis can explain the effect of constituent length on attachment resolution. Numerous experiments on sentence processing, based on off-line questionnaire data, have shown that an RC tends to attach low when the RC is short but high when the RC is long (e.g., Fernández & Bradley, 1999 on Spanish; Quinn, Abdelghany, & Fodor, 2000 on French, English, and Arabic; Lovric et al., 2000, 2001 on Croatian; Pynte & Colonna, 2000 on French; Fernandez, 2003 on Spanish and English; Hirose, 1999 and Jun & Koike, 2003 on Japanese; Wijnen, 2004 on Dutch; Vasishth, Agnihotri, Fernández, & Bhatt, 2004 on Hindi).

Assuming that implicit prosody is equal to explicit or overt prosody, Fodor and her colleagues (e.g., Maynell, 1999; Quinn et al., 2000; Lovric et al., 2000, 2001) examined prosodic phrasing in overt prosody. They claimed that speakers interpret a prosodic break before an RC (in a sequence of NP1 NP2 RC) as a marker of a stronger syntactic boundary, which prompts high attachment. This suggests that speakers of a language with high attachment preference in silent reading tasks would tend to produce a specific pattern of breaks in their overt prosody: a big prosodic boundary between an RC and its adjacent head noun in the default phrasing of a sentence, but a weak boundary between the two head nouns, NP1 and NP2. Since the processing of boundary strength at one point is relative to the strength of the preceding boundary (e.g., Carlson, Clifton, & Frazier, 2001; Clifton, Carlson, & Frazier, 2002; Frazier, Clifton, & Carlson, 2004), it can be hypothesised that, for speakers of high attachment preference languages, a prosodic break between an RC and the adjacent head noun would be *bigger* than the break between the two head nouns, while the opposite relation would be true for speakers of low attachment preference languages.

This hypothesis was tested using Japanese and Korean data in Jun and Koike (2003) and Jun and Kim (2004), respectively. In both Japanese and Korean, the word order is reversed with respect to that of English. A relative clause comes before a head noun, and the "NP1 *of* NP2" structure (e.g., *servant of the actress*) in English is expressed as "NP2's NP1" structure (e.g., *the actress's servant*). Thus, the default prosodic phrasing is expected to be "(RC) (NP2's NP1)" if these languages prefer high attachment of an RC, but "(RC NP2's) (NP1)" if they prefer low attachment. Assuming that reading out-of-the-blue is representative of the default prosody projected in silent reading, Jun and Koike (2003) examined the prosodic phrasing of 48 ambiguous target sentences in Japanese produced by 30 speakers of Tokyo Japanese (randomised with 36 fillers). Speakers were randomly divided into two groups (Skim group vs. Non-skim group) and read the target sentences out-of-the-blue. The Skim group briefly skimmed the sentences before reading and Non-skim group did not. Three weeks later, the same subjects participated in an off-line questionnaire sentence processing experiment.[2] The target sentences differed in the length of RC, both the length and accentedness (i.e., presence or absence of a lexical pitch accent) of the head noun, as well as the location of the target structure. The RC NP2's NP1 structure was located either sentence-initially (i.e., a complex subject phrase) or sentence-medially (i.e., a complex object phrase); the verb was always sentence-final.

The results showed that Japanese speakers prefer high attachment (66%), confirming previous results (e.g., Kamide & Mitchell, 1997), and produced a bigger prosodic break between an RC and the following head noun than that between the two head nouns (i.e., (RC)//(NP2's NP1), called an *early break*) 67% of the time, supporting the predictions of the IPH. Results also showed an effect of RC length in both production and processing. Longer RCs showed more instances of early breaks than shorter RCs, and longer RCs were attached high more often than short RCs. Even though the length of NP1 and NP2 had no effect on attachment or prosodic phrasing, other non-structural factors such as the accentedness of the head noun affected both production and processing. An unaccented word tended to be phrased together with the following word, thus providing more instances of early breaks when NP2 was unaccented, i.e., (RC)//(unaccented NP2's NP1), and

[2] We did this so that the attachment decisions made by our subjects were not influenced by their familiarity with the sentence materials. However, we later discovered that subjects performed very similarly regardless of how well they remembered the material. Thus, in Jun and Kim's experiment on Korean, the attachment data were collected immediately following the reading task.

showed more instances of high attachment. Furthermore, the location of the RC affected the prosodic phrasing of the structure, although only for the Skim group. More instances of *late breaks*, (RC NP2's)//(NP1), were found sentence-medially than sentence-initially. In sum, the experiment revealed that there is a correlation between prosodic phrasing and the processing of RC attachment[3] and that native speakers' performance is influenced by prosodic factors such as the length of a constituent, the accentedness of a lexical item, and the location of the target structure.

A similar experiment was performed on Korean data (32 target sentences, 32 fillers, and 30 speakers) by Jun and Kim (2004) and Jun (2007). As in the Japanese study, subjects were divided into two Groups (Skim vs. Non-skim), read each sentence out-of-the-blue, and performed an off-line questionnaire processing experiment right after the production experiment. The results showed that Korean speakers also preferred high attachment overall (60%), and the early break pattern was more common in their production when analysed in the revised model of Korean intonation (Jun, 2006, 2007), supporting the IPH. As in Japanese, the effect of RC length was found in both production and processing: longer RCs showed more instances of early breaks (70%) than did shorter RCs (34%), and were attached high more often than were shorter RCs (70% vs. 48%). Unlike Japanese, however, Korean data showed the Skim vs. Non-skim Group effect and RC Location effect only in processing; the Skim group chose high attachment more often than the Non-skim group and a sentence-initial RC triggered more high attachment than a sentence-medial RC. In sum, Korean data also supported the IPH by showing a correlation between RC attachment and overt prosodic phrasing of the target structure.

Since both Japanese and Korean prefer high attachment, it would be important to see if a low attachment preference language such as English also shows prosodic patterns predicted by the IPH. The current study reports a production experiment where English sentences containing the target structure, NP1 NP2 RC, are produced in out-of-the-blue reading. Since English speakers tend to prefer low attachment, we expect to find a smaller prosodic break between the RC and the preceding head noun than the break between the two head nouns, i.e., (NP1)//(NP2 RC), in the majority of cases. In other words, the break after NP1 would be bigger than that after NP2, represented in this paper as "NP1 > NP2".

[3] However, a direct mapping between the attachment and prosodic phrasing of an individual sentence was not good (about 63%). Similar results were found in the studies by Bergmann and her colleagues (see the Discussion section). It was suggested in Jun and Koike (2003) that the correlation is the result of group behavior. It may be a by-product of the common default phrasing being (RC)//(NP1 NP2) and high attachment preference in Japanese.

PRODUCTION EXPERIMENT ON ENGLISH: METHOD

Materials

Twenty-seven target sentences differing in the length of the RC (nine Short RC sentences, nine Medium RC sentences, and nine Long RC sentences) and in the bias of the NP (nine No-bias, nine NP1-bias, and nine NP2-bias sentences) were chosen from the literature on English RC attachment: 14 sentences from Fernandez (2003), seven from Carreiras and Clifton (1993), two from Frazier (1990), and four from Deevy (1999, 2000). All target sentences had the structure "Subject Verb *the* NP1 *of the* NP2 RC". Sentences with a short RC had 10–13 syllables before the RC and a 3–5 syllable RC; sentences with a medium RC had 10–14 syllables before the RC and a 7–10 syllable RC; sentences with a long RC had 13–15 syllables before the RC and a 13–18 syllable RC. The bias of the NP was controlled by manipulating number and gender agreement. (Here, the term "bias" should be interpreted as "disambiguated" either syntactically by number or semantically/pragmatically by gender.)[4] It was expected that varying NP Bias would provide the prosodic phrasing data corresponding to high (NP1-bias) or low (NP2-bias) attachment, providing a reference of phrasing when the phrasing of the target sentences in the No-bias condition was examined. Examples of the three NP Bias types by number and gender agreement are given in (2) and (3), respectively, and the prosodic phrasing predicted by the IPH is shown in (4). In each script, there were 19 Number-bias sentences and 8 Gender-bias sentences in each NP Bias condition.[5] A full list of target sentences used in the experiment is given in Appendix 1.

(2) NP Bias types by number agreement (data modified from Fernandez, 2003)
   a. No-bias
      My friend met the aide of the detective that was fired.
   b. NP1-bias
      My friend met the aide of the detectives that was fired.
   c. NP2-bias
      My friend met the aides of the detective that was fired.

[4] Specifically, the number bias means "syntactically disambiguated towards NP1 or NP2" and the gender bias means "semantically or pragmatically disambiguated towards NP1 or NP2". In this paper, the term "bias" is used for convenience of naming. I thank the reviewer who pointed out the ambiguity and possible inappropriateness of the term "bias".

[5] The experiment was not designed to test any effect of bias types on phrasing, so the number of sentences of the two bias types (Number/Gender) is not balanced. The nineteen Number bias sentences include eight Long RC, four Med RC, and seven Short RC sentences, and the eight Gender bias sentences include one Long RC, five Med RC, and two Short RC sentences.

(3) NP Bias types by gender agreement (data modified from Carreiras & Clifton, 1993)

a. No-bias

The police arrested the sister of the nursemaid who recently gave birth to twins.

b. NP1-bias

The police arrested the sister of the handyman who recently gave birth to twins.

c. NP2-bias

The police arrested the brother of the nursemaid who recently gave birth to twins.

(4) NP Bias types and expected prosodic phrasing by the IPH

No-bias => (NP1)//(NP2 RC)
NP1-bias => (NP1 NP2)//(RC)
NP2-bias => (NP1)//(NP2 RC)

Three scripts were made, each containing different bias types of the 27 target sentences: nine sentences per RC Length type and nine sentences per NP Bias type. Therefore, in each RC Length category, there were three No-bias sentences, three NP1-bias sentences, and three NP2-bias sentences.[6] In each script, 27 target sentences were randomised with 30 filler sentences whose structures varied widely and did not include the target structure. The length of the fillers was similar to that of the target sentences: 10 short sentences (12–18 syllables), 10 medium sentences (20–24 syllables), and 10 long sentences (27–35 syllables). The same fillers were used for all scripts.

Subjects

Thirty-six speakers of American English, mostly undergraduate students at University of California, Los Angeles (UCLA), participated in the experiment. Subjects were randomly assigned to one of three groups (Groups 1, 2, and 3) of equal size. The scripts differed by group, so subjects in each group read only one biased version of each target sentence.

[6] The three NP Bias types were generated from the same sentence by changing the gender or number of relevant head noun or the RC. However, the three RC Length type sentences were not related to each other. That is, Long RC sentences were not created by adding more words to Short RC sentences. Therefore, the data is not designed to compare acoustic durations of the target phrase across NP Bias or RC Length conditions.

Procedures

Subjects read each sentence twice in the sound booth at the UCLA Phonetics Lab. They were told to read it at a comfortable speed without skimming it beforehand. Each sentence was written in one line on a page to avoid any effect of input segmentation on reading (Just, Carpenter, & Woolley, 1982; Ferreira & Henderson, 1990; Gilboy & Sopena, 1996; Swets, Desmet, Hambrick, & Ferreira, 2007; Traxler, 2009). No questions on attachment or the content of the sentences were asked. The recordings were digitised at 22 kHz. The first repetition was segmented for further analysis unless disfluent; when the first repetition was disfluent (which occurred about 15% of the time), the second repetition was used. Three ToBI-trained labellers independently transcribed the tones and break indices of each utterance starting at NP1, following the Mainstream American English Tones and Break Indices (MAE_ToBI) conventions for tones (Beckman & Hirschberg, 1994; Beckman & Ayers-Elam, 1997) and a modified ToBI convention for break indices. In the tone tier, the presence of a pitch accent (but not the type of pitch accent) was transcribed on NP1, NP2, and the first prominent word in the RC. When the end of NP1 or NP2 was marked by a phrasal break, the type of phrase accent (i.e., L- or H-) and/or a boundary tone (i.e., L% or H%) was transcribed after NP1 and NP2. Break indices were labelled only after NP1 and NP2. Labellers determined the tonal categories and break indices by listening to the sound files and referring to the waveforms/spectrograms and pitch tracks displayed in *PitchWorks* (Scicon R&D). The break indices used included 1 (phrase-medial-word boundary), 3 (Intermediate Phrase boundary), 4 (Intonation Phrase boundary), 1- (smaller than a word boundary), 3- (juncture between 1 and 3), and 4- (juncture between 3 and 4), following the MAE_ToBI conventions. For the mismatch cases between tones and break indices, however, a new labelling scheme was used: '1m' was used when the degree of juncture matched that of a phrase-medial word boundary but a phrase accent was nevertheless present, and '3m' was used when the degree of juncture matched that of an Intermediate Phrase boundary but with no accompanying phrase accent. When quantifying the break strength, '1m' was treated as '1' and '3m' was treated as '3'. The uncertainty break indices, 1-, 3-, and 4-, were converted to 0.5, 2, and 3.5, respectively. Thus, the break index (BI) 2 in this paper refers to a juncture between BI 1 and BI 3, not an index for the mismatch between a perceived juncture and a tonally marked prosodic boundary as in MAE_ ToBI.

There were a total of 972 sentences (29 sentences × 36 speakers) transcribed. Three labellers independently transcribed different but overlapping portions of the data as shown in Table 1. Labeller 1 transcribed all three types of NP Bias from 24 speakers (eight speakers in each Group, total 648 sentences), and Labeller 2 transcribed all three types of NP Bias from all

TABLE 1
Number of speakers and sentences transcribed by each labeller

	Number of speakers	*Number of sentences in each bias type*	*Total number of sentences transcribed*
Labeller 1	24 speakers	9 No-bias sentences	216
	24 speakers	9 NP1-bias sentences	216
	24 speakers	9 NP2-bias sentences	216
Labeller 2	36 speakers	9 No-bias sentences	324
	36 speakers	9 NP1-bias sentences	324
	36 speakers	9 NP2-bias sentences	324
Labeller 3	36 speakers	9 No-bias sentences	324

36 speakers (total 972 sentences). Labeller 3 transcribed only No-bias items from all 36 speakers (total 324 sentences). Thus, all No-bias type sentences from 24 speakers were transcribed by all three labellers, and NP1- and NP2-bias type sentences were transcribed by Labellers 1 and 2 only.

RESULTS

There was no Group difference in the phrasing, so results are reported by combining data across groups. Only break index data are presented because tonal transcription data show that NP1, NP2, and at least one word in the RC were always pitch accented and the types of phrase accent or boundary tone did not differ by RC Length and NP Bias type.[7] Due to subjectivity in the perception of the degree of juncture by a transcriber, all three labellers did not always agree on a break index. To show the range of variation in the labelling, the break index data of an individual transcriber are shown separately, except for Figure 2. Though the transcriptions do not always match among the labellers, the inter-transcriber agreement rate was nevertheless fairly good. The agreement rate on raw break index data (based on the nine No-bias items from 24 speakers transcribed by all three labellers)

[7] In general, high (H) tones were more common than low (L) tones after NP1: H occurred 70% of the time in Labeller 1's data, 85% for Labeller 2, and 91% for Labeller 3. After NP2, however, H occurred 35% of the time in Labeller 1's data, 54% for Labeller 2, and 75% for Labeller 3. A higher rate of disagreement among the labellers after NP2 is likely due to the difficulty of categorising tones in a reduced pitch range. However, within each labeller, the distribution of H and L tones after NP1 and NP2 was similar across the RC Length and NP Bias types.

was 53–66% using the stringent method employed in Silverman et al. (1992).[8] When the break index was simplified into two categories[9]—a break index marking the edge of a domain smaller than or equal to the size of a word ($BI \leq 1$) vs. that of a domain larger than a word ($BI > 1$)—the agreement rate increased to 72–88%. Specifically, the agreement rate was 79.5% and 87.8% for the BI after NP1 and NP2, respectively, and 71.6% for the relative break strength between NP1 and NP2. The agreement rate on the relative break strength data of the biased items (18 items from 24 speakers, transcribed by two labellers) was 70%.

Break index after NP1 and NP2

Since English speakers have been shown to prefer low attachment, it was predicted, following the IPH, that the break index after NP1 would be, overall, greater than that after NP2. However, the results show that—counter to the prediction of the IPH—the most common phrasing pattern of the target structure in the No-bias condition was a bigger boundary after NP2 than after NP1, i.e., NP1 < NP2.

Figure 1 shows the proportions of $BI \leq 1$ (a word boundary or smaller) and $BI > 1$ (larger than a word boundary) after each NP in the No-bias condition for each labeller. Labeller 1's data are from 24 speakers and Labellers 2 and 3's data are from 36 speakers. As shown in Figure 1, about half of the breaks after NP1 are larger than word size, and about 90% of the breaks after NP2 are larger than word size. That is, the end of NP2 was more often marked by a bigger break than the end of NP1, for all labellers. The difference between the NP1 break pattern and the NP2 break pattern is significant for all labellers: Labeller 1 ($\chi^2 = 72.07$, df = 1, $p < .001$), Labeller 2 ($\chi^2 = 55.23$, df = 1, $p < .001$), Labeller 3 ($\chi^2 = 83.16$, df = 1, $p < .001$). There was no significant inter-transcriber difference when comparing data from the 24 speakers transcribed by all three.

To make sure that the break after NP2 is larger than the break after NP1 in the same sentence, the relative strength of breaks between NP1 and NP2 in each utterance is measured by the ratio of the break after NP2 to the break

[8] This method was used in calculating labeller agreement in English ToBI data, labelled by Silverman and colleagues (1992). Agreement was calculated across all possible pairs of transcribers for each word. For example, four labellers (a, b, c, and d) would produce six possible transcriber pairs (ab, ac, ad, bc, bd, and cd). If three of four transcribers (a, b, and c) agree, only three of six pairs will match (ab, ac, and bc; but not ad, bd, and cd), and this would result in 50% agreement. If two out of three labellers (a and b) agree, only one of three pairs will match (ab, but not ac and bc), resulting in 33.3% agreement.

[9] This simplification was introduced because the great majority of break indices were either 1 or 3; the small number of breaks transcribed with particular labels made the χ^2 test inappropriate for the data in its original form.

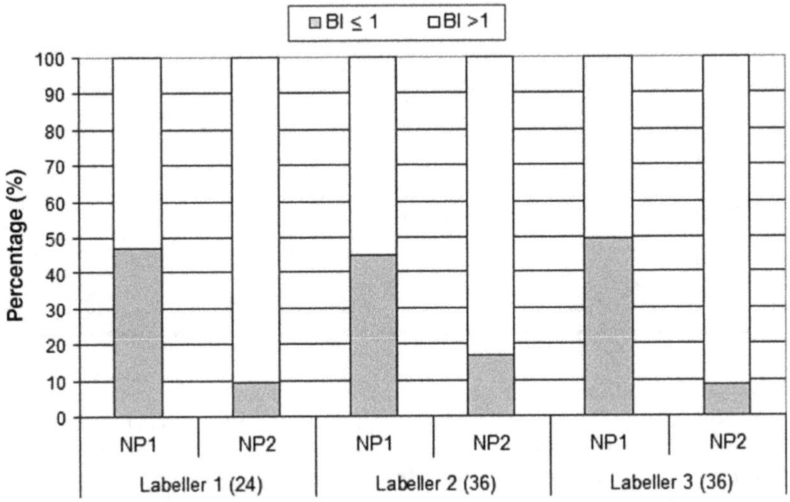

Figure 1. Frequency (in %) of BI ≤ 1 (break index corresponding to a word boundary or smaller) and BI > 1 (break index bigger than a word boundary), after each NP in the no-bias condition, for each labeler. The number in parentheses is the number of speakers each labeler's data is based on.

after NP1 (represented as "NP2/NP1"): if the break after NP2 is bigger than that after NP1, the ratio is > 1; if the break after NP2 is smaller than that after NP1, the ratio is < 1; and if the break after NP2 is the same as that after NP1, the ratio $= 0$. The average ratio of NP2/NP1 was 1.98 for Labeller 1, 1.70 for Labeller 2, and 1.76 for Labeller 3, confirming that speakers generally produced a larger break after NP2 than after NP1 in the same sentence.

The effect of RC length on default phrasing

The length of the relative clause (RC Length) influenced the degree of break after each noun. A stronger effect of RC Length on the degree of juncture was found after NP2 than after NP1. Figure 2 shows the frequency (in %) of raw BI categories found after NP1 and NP2 in each RC Length type in the No-bias condition. Data from the three labellers (24 speakers each) are combined. The observed frequency of each BI category across RC Lengths was marginally significant after NP1 ($\chi^2 = 15.001$, df $= 8$, $p = .057$). Here, the Short RC condition had fewer BI $= 1$ than did the longer RC conditions. On the other hand, the observed distribution of BI categories after NP2 was significantly different across RC Length types ($\chi^2 = 33.981$, df $= 8$, $p < .001$). The Short RC condition had fewer phrase boundaries and more word-size boundaries than did the Long or Medium RC conditions. This pattern is

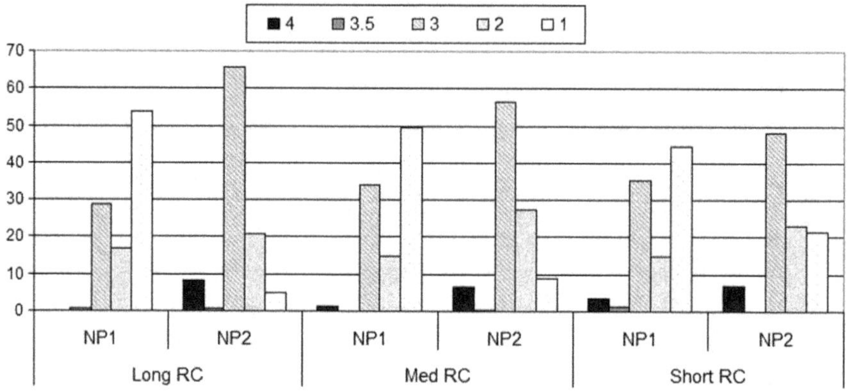

Figure 2. Frequency (in %) of raw BI categories after each NP in the no-bias condition, divided by RC length type. Data from all three labelers are combined (24 speakers per labeler). BI 2 is a juncture between BI 1 (word boundary) and BI 3 (Intermediate Phrase boundary). BI 3.5 is a juncture between BI 3 (Intermediate Phrase boundary) and BI 4 (Intonation Phrase boundary).

TABLE 2
The mean and standard deviation of raw BI values after NP1 and NP2 by RC Length and NP Bias for each labeller

			NP1		*NP2*	
Bias types	*Labellers*	*RC length*	*Mean*	*SD*	*Mean*	*SD*
No-bias	Labeller 1	Long	1.864	0.92	2.921	0.66
		Med	1.944	1.01	2.824	0.80
		Short	2.232	1.10	2.634	0.90
	Labeller 2	Long	1.885	0.91	2.680	0.72
		Med	1.901	0.89	2.554	0.76
		Short	1.922	0.91	2.137	0.92
	Labeller 3	Long	1.835	0.90	2.721	0.69
		Med	1.857	0.93	2.622	0.68
		Short	1.949	0.93	2.556	0.77
NP1-bias	Labeller 1	Long	1.711	0.88	2.936	0.69
		Med	1.992	1.03	2.978	0.68
		Short	1.845	0.94	2.911	0.88
	Labeller 2	Long	1.874	0.87	2.722	0.77
		Med	1.875	0.92	2.690	0.73
		Short	1.833	0.89	2.505	0.89
NP2-bias	Labeller 1	Long	1.697	0.88	2.957	0.76
		Med	1.868	1.08	2.979	0.67
		Short	2.042	1.01	2.528	1.06
	Labeller 2	Long	1.754	0.85	2.725	0.73
		Med	1.792	0.90	2.688	0.73
		Short	2.059	0.89	2.069	0.78

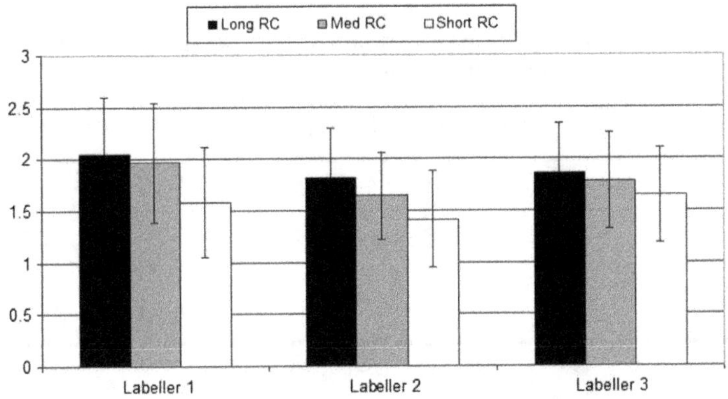

Figure 3. Average ratio of the break after NP2 to the break after NP1 across RC Length types, for each labeler (in the no-bias condition). Error bars reflect standard deviation.

confirmed in the individual labellers' data in Table 2 where the mean and standard deviation of raw BI values after NP1 and NP2 are shown in each RC Length condition.

Again, since what is important in processing is the *relative* strength of boundaries found in the same sentence (e.g., Carlson, Clifton, & Frazier, 2001; Clifton, Carlson, & Frazier, 2002; Frazier, Clifton, & Carlson, 2004), the average ratio of NP2/NP1 for each RC Length, for each labeller, is examined (see Figure 3). All data are from the No-bias condition. Here, the tendency is that the ratio is higher as the RC gets longer. A linear mixed effects model with Speaker as a random effect (model: ratio.np2.np1 ~ group + length + (1|speaker)) shows that, for Labeller 1, the ratio is significantly shorter in the Short RC condition than in the Medium RC condition, and for Labeller 2, the ratio between Medium and Short RC conditions is marginally significant ($p = .052$).[10] Thc ratio across RC Length types was not significant for Labeller 3. The results of the statistics run in R (Baayen, 2008; Bates & Maechler, 2009) are shown in Table 3.

The effect of NP bias on default phrasing

It was expected that NP2-biased sentences would show a smaller break after NP2 than after NP1. That is, the phrasing would be (NP1)(NP2 RC) and the ratio of NP2/NP1 would be < 1 because the RC was forced to attach low (or NP2 and RC form one meaning group). Conversely, NP1-biased sentences were expected to show a bigger break after NP2 than after NP1, i.e., the phrasing would be (NP1 NP2)(RC) and the ratio of NP2/NP1 > 1, as the RC was forced to attach high. However, as shown in Figure 4, the average ratio

[10] The item is not included as a random factor because items are not repeated for RC Length.

TABLE 3
Results of a linear mixed effects model for ratio in No Bias condition, with Group and RC Length as fixed predictors and Speaker as a random effect (model: ratio.np2.np1 ~ group + length + (1|speaker)), for each labeller. Non-significant predictors are shaded in grey and a marginally significant predictor is shaded in light grey.

No bias condition				
Predictor	Coef. β	*SE*(β)	*t*	*p*(MCMC)
Labeller 1 ($R^2 = 0.25$)				
Intercept	1.96	0.22	8.88	1e–4
GROUP(B)	0.04	0.28	0.16	0.85
GROUP(C)	−0.02	0.28	−0.06	0.95
LENGTH(short)	−0.38	0.17	−2.22	0.028
LENGTH(long)	0.15	0.18	0.86	0.40
Labeller 2 ($R^2 = 0.19$)				
Intercept	1.53	0.14	11.03	1e–4
GROUP(B)	0.18	0.17	1.10	0.22
GROUP(C)	0.17	0.17	0.98	0.25
LENGTH(short)	−0.24	0.12	−1.92	0.052
LENGTH(long)	0.17	0.12	1.35	0.18
Labeller 3 ($R^2 = 0.17$)				
Intercept	1.85	0.15	12.24	1e–4
GROUP(B)	−0.18	0.18	−1.01	0.27
GROUP(C)	−0.02	0.19	−0.11	0.90
LENGTH(short)	−0.14	0.13	−1.05	0.30
LENGTH(long)	0.10	0.13	0.78	0.43

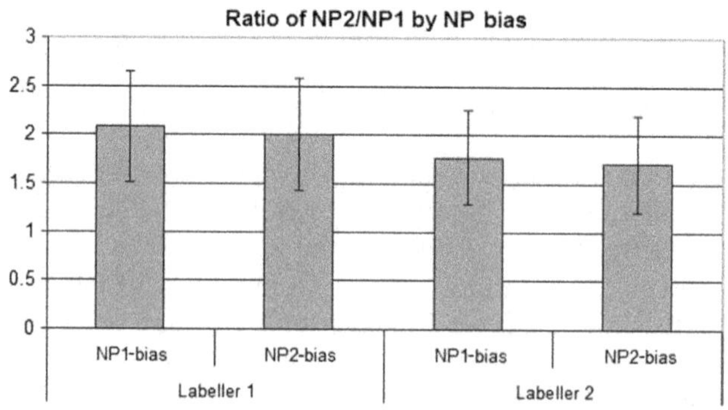

Figure 4. Average ratio of the break after NP2 to the break after NP1 across NP Bias types, for two labelers. Error bars reflect standard deviation.

of NP2/NP1 in each NP Bias condition was > 1 for both labellers (about 2.0 for Labeller 1 and 1.7 for Labeller 2), suggesting that the common default phrasing was (NP1 NP2)(RC) regardless of NP Bias type. A linear mixed effects model with Speaker and Item as random effects (model: ratio.np2.np1 ~ group + np.bias + (1|speaker) + (1|item)) shows that the ratio is not significantly different across NP Bias types for both labellers.

The interaction between RC length and NP bias

However, as shown in Figure 5, the effect of NP Bias varied depending on RC Length for both labellers. The average ratio of break after NP2 to break after NP1 was lower in Short RC than in longer RC conditions for both labellers, but this was true only in No-bias and NP2-bias conditions. (This pattern can be predicted from the raw BI values in Table 2.) In the NP1-bias condition, the ratio was not influenced by RC Length. It seems that the effect of RC Length (i.e., lower NP2/NP1 ratio in Short RC) is over-ridden by the NP1-bias effect (i.e., higher NP2/NP1 ratio).

Table 4 shows the results of a linear mixed effects model for ratio, with Group, RC Length, and NP Bias as fixed predictors and Speaker as a random effect (model: ratio.np2.np1 ~ group + length * np.bias + (1| speaker) for two labellers, combining all three bias conditions. It shows that even though the overall pattern of ratios across NP Bias and RC Length is similar between the two labellers, the NP Bias is not a significant predictor for Labeller 1, while both NP2 Bias and the interaction between NP2 Bias and Short RC were significant predictors for Labeller 2.

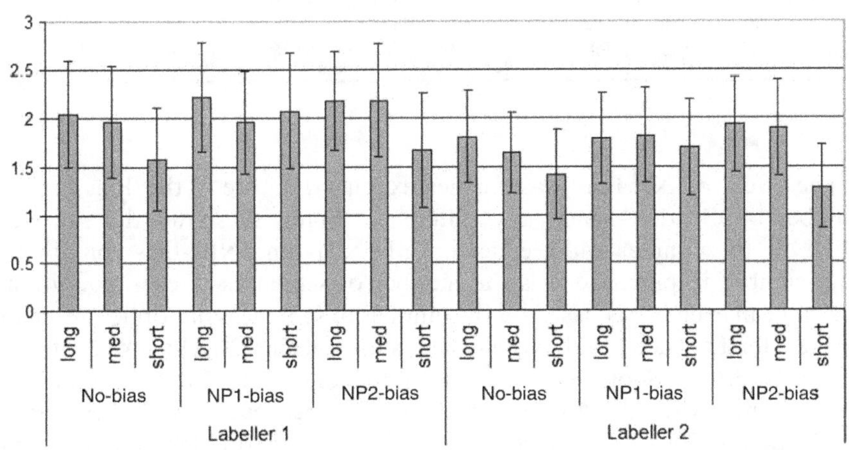

Figure 5. Average ratio of the break after NP2 to the break after NP1 across RC Length in all NP bias conditions for two labelers. Error bars reflect standard deviation.

TABLE 4
Results of a linear mixed effects model for ratio, with Group and RC Length as fixed predictors and Speaker as a random effect (model: ratio.np2.np1 ~ group + length * np.bias + (1|speaker), for two labellers in all three bias conditions. Non-significant predictors and interactions are shaded in grey.

All Bias conditions				
Predictor	Coef. β	*SE*(β)	*t*	*p*(MCMC)
Labeller 1 (R^2 =0.25)				
Intercept	1.91	0.23	8.46	1e-4
GROUP(B)	0.14	0.28	0.51	0.56
GROUP(C)	0.02	0.28	0.06	0.93
LENGTH(short)	−0.39	0.17	−2.26	0.024
LENGTH(long)	0.15	0.18	0.83	0.40
NP BIAS(NP1)	0.03	0.17	0.15	0.89
NP BIAS(NP2)	0.22	0.17	1.27	0.21
LENGTH(short) × NP BIAS(NP1)	0.45	0.24	1.83	0.069
LENGTH(long) × NP BIAS(NP1)	0.16	0.25	0.63	0.52
LENGTH(short) × NP BIAS(NP2)	−0.13	0.24	−0.53	0.60
LENGTH(long) × NP BIAS(NP2)	−0.04	0.25	−0.18	0.87
Labeller 2 (R^2 =0.17)				
Intercept	1.68	0.14	12.42	1e-4
GROUP(B)	−0.08	0.15	−0.54	0.58
GROUP(C)	−0.06	0.15	−0.37	0.72
LENGTH(short)	−0.23	0.13	−1.85	0.07
LENGTH(long)	0.16	0.13	1.31	0.18
NP BIAS(NP1)	0.18	0.13	1.40	0.17
NP BIAS(NP2)	0.27	0.13	2.12	0.032
LENGTH(short) × NP BIAS(NP1)	0.11	0.18	0.62	0.55
LENGTH(long) × NP BIAS(NP1)	−0.19	0.18	−1.06	0.28
LENGTH(short) × NP BIAS(NP2)	−0.39	0.18	−2.17	0.033
LENGTH(long) × NP BIAS(NP2)	−0.15	0.18	−0.81	0.42

The effect of NP Bias was further examined to see if the Bias type—Number or Gender—made any difference. Figure 6 shows the ratio of NP2/NP1 by Number and Gender in only NP1- and NP2-bias conditions. (The number in parenthesis is the number of sentences in each condition. The value in each bar is based on the number of sentences multiplied by eight speakers for Labeller 1 and by 12 speakers for Labeller 2.) The lower ratio of NP2/NP1 in the Short RC and NP2-bias condition shown in Figure 5 is maintained when the NP2 is biased by Number, but to a weaker degree by Gender. A linear mixed effects model for ratio (model: ratio.np2.np1 ~ group + length * np.bias + (1|speaker)) in NP Bias subset analysis shows that the interaction of Short Length and NP2-bias was significant only in

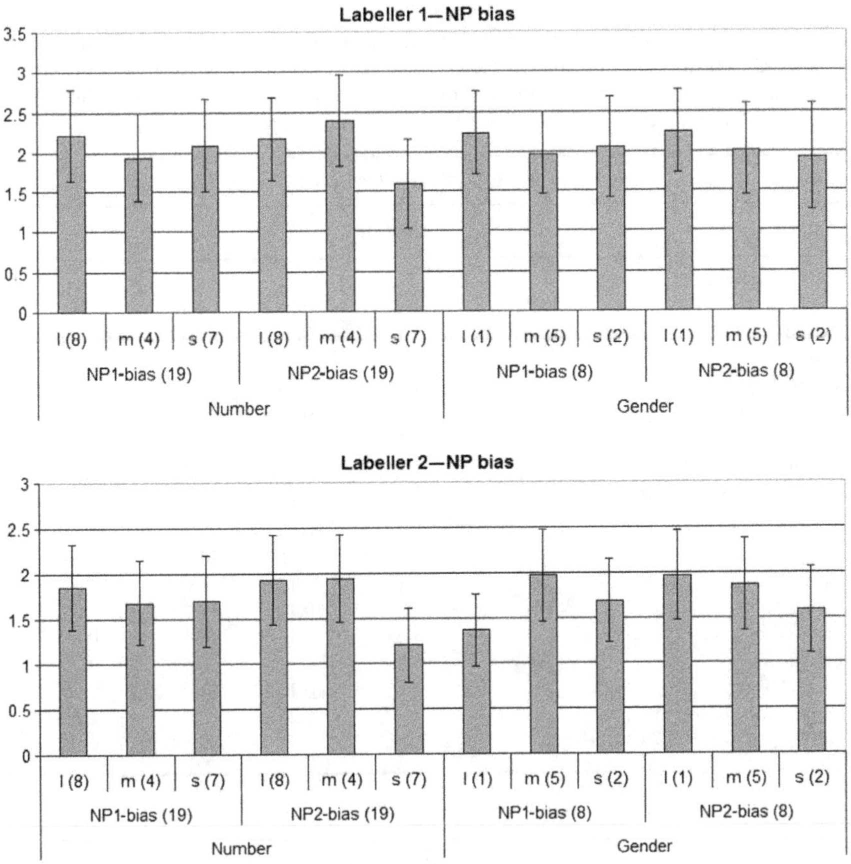

Figure 6. Average ratio of the break after NP2 to the break after NP1 across RC Length in two NP Bias conditions, divided by Number and Gender bias types. Top panel: Labeler 1. Bottom panel: Labeler 2. The number in parenthesis is the number of sentences belonging to each category. Error bars reflect standard deviation.

Number but not in Gender for both labellers.[11] The results of the statistics are shown in Table 5.

In sum, the NP Bias results suggest that both the location and the type of NP Bias are reflected, to some degree, in the prosodic phrasing of a sentence, but the effect of NP Bias on phrasing is much smaller than the overall preference for the default (NP1 NP2)//(RC) phrasing, and is limited to cases where the RC is short.

[11] Results from the linear mixed effects model showed that the effect of Long RC and its interaction with NP1-bias are significant for Labeller 2, but this is not considered meaningful because this is based entirely on one Long RC sentence.

TABLE 5
Results of a linear mixed effects model for ratio in NP bias by Number subset, with Group, RC Length, and NP Bias as fixed predictors and Speaker as a random effect (model: ratio.np2.np1 ~group+length * np.bias + (1|speaker)), for two labellers. Non-significant predictors and interactions are shaded in grey.

NP Bias subset (Number bias)				
Predictor	Coef. β	*SE*(β)	*t*	*p(MCMC)*
Labeller 1 (R^2 =0.29)				
Intercept	1.93	0.28	6.78	1e–4
GROUP(B)	0.13	0.31	0.42	0.63
GROUP(C)	0.08	0.31	0.24	0.78
LENGTH(short)	0.03	0.24	0.12	0.90
LENGTH(long)	0.31	0.23	1.32	0.20
NP BIAS(NP2)	0.39	0.26	1.47	0.15
LENGTH(short) × NP BIAS(NP2)	−0.82	0.33	−2.49	0.014
LENGTH(long) × NP BIAS(NP2)	−0.41	0.33	−1.24	0.22
Labeller 2 (R^2 =0.19)				
Intercept	1.82	0.16	11.10	1e–4
GROUP(B)	−0.22	0.15	−1.43	0.13
GROUP(C)	−0.06	0.16	−0.36	0.74
LENGTH(short)	7e–4	0.17	4e–3	0.99
LENGTH(long)	0.11	0.16	0.67	0.48
NP BIAS(NP2)	0.20	0.19	1.09	0.27
LENGTH(short) × NP BIAS(NP2)	−0.72	0.24	−3.03	2.6e–3
LENGTH(long) × NP BIAS(NP2)	−0.10	0.23	−0.42	0.66

DISCUSSION

Earlier studies on RC attachment in Japanese and Korean (Jun & Koike, 2003; Jun & Kim, 2004; Jun, 2007) showed that speakers prefer high attachment and the most common default phrasing of the "RC NP2*'s* NP1" structure is (RC)//(NP2*'s* NP1), thus supporting the Implicit Prosody Hypothesis (IPH). Studies such as Quinn et al. (2000) and Lovric et al. (2001) also examined attachment preferences as well as the phonetic realisation of overt prosody (f0 and duration) and found support for the IPH.[12]

However, in the current study, it has been found that the default phrasing of the "NP1 NP2 RC" structure in English—a language often described as

[12] Quinn et al. (2000) and Lovric et al. (2001) estimated phrasing based on phonetic data (i.e., f0 values and the duration of the local target nouns) instead of defining it phonologically. They also interpreted the relation of f0 values the same when determining the phrasing in the three languages (i.e., French, English, and Arabic). Please see Jun (2003, pp. 222–223) for concerns regarding the methodology.

preferring low attachment—did not support the IPH, at least when the default prosody is assessed from out-of-the-blue reading. The most common prosodic phrasing of the structure was (NP1 NP2)//(RC), a pattern predicted to correspond to high attachment. The same result was found in recent studies by Bergmann and her colleagues (Bergmann & Ito, 2007; Bergmann, Armstrong, & Maday, 2008). Bergmann and Ito examined the overt prosody and attachment preferences of English RCs by varying the length of NP1 and an RC. They found a preference for low attachment and (NP1 NP2)//(RC) phrasing regardless of length. This finding was confirmed in Bergmann and colleagues' (2008) study where default phrasing of the NP1 NP2 RC structure was examined in English and Spanish. In their study, 10 native speakers of each language read eight ambiguous target sentences without scanning or practicing the sentences first. After reading each sentence, speakers answered questions on attachment. The tones and the degrees of juncture of each utterance were transcribed by three ToBI-trained labellers, similar to the method adopted in the current study. They found a preference for low attachment in English and a preference for high attachment in Spanish, confirming existing findings, but the most common default phrasing pattern of the two languages was the same, i.e., (NP1 NP2)//(RC). Furthermore, they found that, as in Jun and Koike's (2003) Japanese data, the prosodic break patterns that speakers produced did not influence or match their attachment choices. The distribution of high vs. low attachment was about the same regardless of the default phrasing patterns. The main difference between English and Spanish was in the overall number of low and high attachment choices.

Thus, it seems that the most common default phrasing across several languages is to have a bigger break between an RC and the adjacent head noun than between the two head nouns, i.e., (NP1 *of* NP2)//(RC) or (RC)//(NP2*'s* NP1). This leads one to reconsider the validity of the IPH, and if it is valid, the method of assessing implicit prosody by examining overt prosody, the nature of overt prosody through reading aloud out-of-the-blue, and the special status of the NP1 NP2 RC structure.

Implicit prosody in sentence processing

It is now well known that attachment is influenced by prosodic factors such as constituent length—heavy constituents tend to attach high and light constituents tend to attach low—and that languages differ in their prosodic structures and realisations (e.g., languages whose attachment is shown to be influenced by constituent length: Brazilian Portuguese, Croatian, Dutch, English, French, German, Hindi, Japanese, Korean, and Russian; see Augurzky, 2006, Section 3.2.2.2 for more details).

Recent studies examining the effect of working memory on attachment preference also suggest that the attachment is influenced by implicit prosody. Swets et al. (2007) examined the attachment preference of Dutch and English speakers in off-line questionnaire data after assessing subjects' working memory capacity. They found that, when the test sentences were displayed in their entirety, both English and Dutch speakers showed increased preference for high attachment as their working memory capacities decreased. They interpreted this as the effect of prosody. They suggested that low capacity subjects inserted a prosodic break between NP2 and the RC but that high capacity subjects treated the entire NP1 NP2 RC structure as an integrated unit. When they displayed the test sentences in three segments/lines, i.e., NP1 NP2 // RC // matrix VP, they found that the preference for high attachment greatly increased in both English and Dutch speakers regardless of their working memory capacity. Similar results were found in Traxler's (2007, 2009) on-line eye-tracking studies. When the test sentences were displayed in their entirety (Traxler, 2007), the subjects with higher working memory capacity preferred high attachment, the opposite pattern of Swets et al. (2007), probably reflecting differences in tasks, especially on-line vs. off-line. However, when the test sentences were displayed in two lines broken after NP2 (i.e., NP1 NP2 // RC matrix VP), subjects preferred high attachment regardless of their working memory capacity (Traxler, 2009). All these studies suggest that the line break in a sentence, i.e., segmentation, may have triggered an implicit prosodic break, affecting the attachment preference. (See also Gilboy and Sopena (1996) for the effect of segmentation on the self-paced reading task of attachment processing.)

Therefore, it is clear that implicit prosody affects sentence processing. The question remaining is whether implicit prosody is equal to overt prosody, especially the prosody generated by reading aloud, out-of-the-blue.

Is implicit/silent prosody the same as prosody read aloud?

Fodor and her colleagues hypothesised that implicit prosody computed during silent reading is the same as default explicit/overt prosody and examined the prosody of reading aloud to test the IPH (e.g., Fodor, 2002; Lovric et al., 2000, 2001). Overt prosody generated in reading, especially reading aloud out-of-the-blue, is unique. It is different from the prosody generated by other types of overt prosody such as spontaneous speech or disambiguating prosody. Spontaneous speech produces longer pauses but read speech produces more frequent tonal units or prosodic breaks, resulting in smaller prosodic phrases (Howell & Kadi-Hanifi, 1991; Silverman, Blaauw, Spitz, & Pitrelli, 1992; Ayers, 1994). In spontaneous speech or when speakers are trying to disambiguate an ambiguous structure, speakers generate prosody from the information structure they intend to deliver

(Price, Ostendorf, Shattuck-Hufnagel, & Fong, 1991; Allbritten, McKoon, & Ratcliff, 1996; Schafer, Speer, Warren, & White, 2000; Snedeker & Trueswell, 2003; Schafer, Speer, & Warren, 2005; Snedeker & Casserly, 2010 this issue). Therefore, in auditory sentence processing where disambiguating prosody is employed, listeners actively use the prosodic information in the stimuli—over-riding syntactic biases when the prosody cues otherwise—and avoid garden path (e.g., Kjelgaard & Speer, 1999; Snedeker & Trueswell, 2003; Augurzky, 2006). But in the case of reading aloud out-of-the-blue, the text is already given and the speaker is not trying to emphasise or disambiguate any meaning. That is, reading aloud out-of-the-blue would generate "surface" prosody following only the roughest and simplest prosody-syntax mapping constraints, including phonological weight, i.e., rhythm and length (e.g., a break when incoming material is long; Selkirk, 2000; Watson & Gibson, 2004; Krivokapić, 2007) and structural constraints (e.g., a break before a major syntactic constituent; Selkirk, 1986, 2000; Truckenbrodt, 1999).

On the other hand, silent reading during a processing experiment would not generate surface prosody. In general, in a processing experiment where RC attachment is tested off-line, subjects read the questionnaire silently but reading time is not limited (though they are encouraged to answer as quickly as possible). The subjects have the opportunity to read the text multiple times, and as they are trying to answer questions regarding RC attachment, they are presumably reading at a deeper level.

When reading aloud out-of-the-blue, especially when reading without first skimming the sentence in detail and when the speakers are aware that their reading is recorded, the subjects' focus would be on "fluent reading", trying to make the fewest possible mistakes. In this case, a "safe" way to read, or good "performance" of reading aloud, would be to produce each content word prominently, thus putting pitch accent on every content word, and to put a prosodic break more frequently, following phonological and structural constraints (cf. Hudson, Lane, & Pullen, 2005; Rasinski, 2006).

Furthermore, in no-skim reading aloud, the speakers would not be able to prosodify the entire sentence at the beginning. Instead, they would prosodify a few words, as they read along, within their reading span. This can be evidenced by the weak effect of NP Bias, especially the pattern found in the Short RC, in the current experiment. Compared to Med or Long RCs, Short RCs are more likely to form one phrase with the preceding noun, (NP1)// (NP2 RC). However, as shown in Figure 6, the Short RC cases had lower ratios of NP2/NP1 in the NP2-bias conditions, but only when the bias was by Number, not by Gender. This is probably because the lexical item(s) disambiguating the gender information were further away from the head noun than the RC verb that provides the Number information, and also because semantic/pragmatic information (e.g., whether *a boxer* could be male or female) may require a deeper level of processing than syntactic information (cf. Rayner, Carlson, & Frazier, 1983; Mitchell, Corley, & Garnham, 1992).[13]

When the RC is not short, however, it seems that speakers put a break after NP2 before they comprehend the lexically biasing information in the RC. They do so even when the disambiguating information is close to the head noun, i.e., the RC verb for Number bias. This suggests that the surface reading is constrained by length more than by meaning. When speakers put a break before a long RC that is biased to NP2, they may realise in the later part of the RC that their earlier phrasing was not appropriate. So, it is possible that, in order to compensate for their earlier prosodic mis-phrasing, the speakers perform a sort of prosodic repair late in the RC, e.g., putting focus pitch accent on the disambiguating lexical item. This type of prosodic information was not transcribed in the current study, but a re-examination of the sound files revealed that four out of the twelve speakers who put a bigger break before the long RC indeed produced the biased item with hesitation lengthening, and one speaker produced a rising (L+H*) pitch accent on the biased item.[14] This confirms that, in no-skim reading aloud, speakers produce a break before the RC without fully comprehending the meaning of the whole RC. It is very likely that the speakers could only prosodify a smaller piece of a sentence at a time, constrained by the length and syntax of the sentence. These constraints on surface reading could be so strong that it may over-ride any implicit prosody, if it exists, associated with the target structure. This might explain why the string NP1 NP2 RC was predominantly phrased as (NP1 NP2)//(RC) regardless of RC length or bias in the current study. That is, the sequence of two head nouns contains enough syllables to form its own phrase and the relative clause complementiser signals the beginning of a clause. This implies that the most common default phrasing of NP1 NP2 RC structure across languages would be (NP1 NP2)//(RC), if the structure is produced in reading aloud out-of-the-blue without skimming the material in advance. More research on phrasing in low attachment preference languages is needed to confirm this.

Finally, silent reading is also faster than reading aloud (e.g., Taylor, 2006; Rasinski, 2006). As shown in the studies of the effects of speech rate on prosody (e.g., Rietveld & Gussenhoven, 1987; Caspers & van Heuven, 1993; Jun, 1993; Fougeron & Jun, 1998; Zu, Li, & Li, 2006), speakers reorganise

[13] It is therefore also possible that the higher ratio in the NP1-bias by Gender and Short RC condition (Figure 6) is not because speakers processed the gender-bias meaning but because they were influenced by the syntax factor, i.e., a break before RC. In either way, the result on Gender bias should not be given much significance in the current study because the result is based on very small data.

[14] I would like to thank one of the reviewers who directed my attention to the timing of prosodic planning relative to the head noun and bias types and the possibility of prosodic repair.

the prosodic structure of a sentence at faster speech rates. The phrase breaks found at normal speech rates are either reduced or removed at faster speech rates, and this reduction or removal depends on the strength of the break. It is possible that the phrase break before an RC is weak in low attachment languages such as English, and is thus easily deleted or weakened at faster speech rates, while the pre-RC break in French and other high attachment languages is strong and remains even in faster speech rates.[15] More research is needed to explore this possibility.

Accessing implicit prosody in processing

If reading aloud generates "surface" prosody, how could we access the deeper level implicit prosody? One way might be to let the reader be familiar with the written material before reading so that s/he could read it with a deeper level of understanding of the material. Bookheimer and colleagues (Bookheimer, Zeffiro, Blaxton, Gaillard, & Theodore, 1995) claimed that silent reading and oral reading invoke different cognitive processes. Based on the regional cerebral blood flow data using positron emission tomography (PET), they showed that subjects utilise an inferior temporal pathway in silent reading, which is very similar to that involved in object naming (name an object given a visual input), and in which there is direct access to the lexical entry. When reading a word aloud (given an orthographic input), however, subjects engage a superior temporal-inferior parietal route, involving the sequential interpretation of visual elements into phonological sounds, relying on sensorimotor and auditory feedback to monitor oromotor output dynamically. That is, unlike silent reading, reading a word aloud does not activate the brain area responsible for the semantic interpretation but activates the brain area for motor control. This suggests that prosody generated during silent reading may reflect the semantic and pragmatic meaning of the sentence but prosody generated during oral reading might

[15] One of the reviewers asked if the break after the RC in Japanese and Korean (from Jun & Kim, 2004; Jun & Koike, 2003) is bigger than the break before RC in English (the current study). In the prosodic structure of both English and Korean, the most common prosodic break between the RC and the adjacent noun is an Intermediate Phrase (ip) boundary. However, we cannot directly compare the realisations of ip in these two studies because the length and location of the RC is different between the two languages. If we compare the phonetic realisation of the ip in general between the two languages, the English ip has more stable phonetic cues than the Korean ip, as the former normally involves pre-boundary lengthening, phrase accent tone, and pitch reset, while the latter is marked by an optional boundary tone, pitch reset, and minor pre-boundary lengthening. For Japanese, the corresponding break is an Intonation Phrase (IP) boundary in the J_ToBI model, which combines the Intermediate Phrase and Utterance of Beckman and Pierrehumbert's (1986) model. Since the percentage of subcategories (i.e., ip-type or Utterance-type) of Japanese IP is not available in Jun and Koike, we cannot make direct comparisons between English and Japanese, either.

not. Therefore, it is possible that the prosody generated in reading aloud only after thorough comprehension of the sentence is closer to the implicit prosody employed in resolving attachment ambiguities, whether the processing task is on-line or off-line.[16] In fact, this might have been what happened in Fodor and her colleagues' work on overt prosody and the IPH (e.g., Croatian in Lovric et al., 2000, 2001; French, English, and Arabic in Quinn et al., 2000). They asked the subjects to read sentences silently for comprehension first and then read aloud, after which they let subjects answer questions on RC attachment. Allowing the subjects to read for comprehension before reading aloud might be the reason why their phrasing data differed from those found in Bergmann and her colleagues' studies as well as the current study where the subjects were told to read aloud without skimming the sentence first. An experiment is in progress to investigate the effect of reverse ordering (answering attachment questions before reading aloud) on default phrasing.

Another way to access implicit prosody might be to examine on-line processing data using event-related potential (ERP). ERP can reveal an on-line record of processing in a high temporal resolution and provide insights into the brain's activity. Recent ERP studies (e.g., Steinhauer, Alter, & Friederici, 1999; Steinhauer & Friederici, 2001) have shown that the Closure Positive Shift (CPS) component is correlated with a clause boundary cross-linguistically. Thus, observing the CPS component while subjects process an RC attachment may reveal the implicit prosody.

As in other on-line studies on processing using self-paced reading or eye-tracking methodologies (e.g., de Vincenzi & Job, 1993; Kamide & Mitchell, 1997; Kamide, Mitchell, Fodor, & Inoue, 1998; Brysbaert & Mitchell, 2000; Fernandez, 2003; Miyamoto, Nakamura, & Takahashi, 2004), ERP studies on RC attachment in German (Augurzky, 2006) and French (Pynte, Colonna, & Gola, 2003, cited in Augurzky, 2006) found an earlier preference for low attachment and a shift to high attachment when parsing the latter part of a sentence. This shift in attachment preference from low to high through the course of parsing a sentence seems to happen across languages regardless of the attachment preference found in off-line processing studies. This suggests that processing is not guided by a single principle such as late closure or implicit prosody, but by multiple principles in multiple stages of processing. It seems that in silent reading the early part of a sentence is guided by the structural information such as Late Closure and prosodic information, but the processing at the end of a sentence is guided by

[16] Silent/implicit prosody employed in the off-line questionnaire task would be the same as that in the on-line eye-tracking task. But this prosody might be different from that which is employed in the on-line self-paced reading task: in self-paced reading, the reading material is constrained by segmentation chunks, which affect prosody.

pragmatic, thematic, and discourse information. Further research is needed to investigate how many different stages of processing exist and when different parsing mechanisms—including prosody—are integrated.

CONCLUSION

The current study has shown that—counter to the predictions made by the Implicit Prosody Hypothesis—the most common prosodic phrasing of the "NP1 NP2 RC" structure in English, a low attachment preference language, was (NP1 NP2)//(RC), the prosodic phrasing expected to occur with high attachment preference languages. Since this result was based on overt prosody—specifically reading aloud out-of-the-blue—the question of whether this type of overt prosody is equal to the implicit prosody found in silent reading was discussed. It was suggested that the prosody generated in silent reading would not necessarily be the same as the prosody generated in reading aloud, especially when reading without skimming the material in advance. In no-skim reading aloud, speakers seem to prosodify or plan the phrasing of a few words at a time, influenced by the constituent length and syntax of the sentence. The phrasing showed sensitivity to meaning bias only when the relative clause was short and the disambiguating information was near the head noun. Based on these data and data from previous studies, various ways to access implicit prosody such as reading aloud after thorough comprehension of the sentence or reading at a fast rate were suggested.

Since most studies supporting the IPH have investigated the default phrasing of high attachment preference languages, we need to examine more low attachment preference languages to confirm the current findings. Furthermore, we need to examine the default phrasing of various structures in reading aloud to see how the phrasing is influenced by phonological and syntactic constraints. Finally, we need to investigate factors affecting the default phrasing, ways to access implicit prosody, and the attachment difference between on-line and off-line processing experiments.

REFERENCES

Allbritten, D., McKoon, G., & Ratcliff, R. (1996). Reliability of prosodic cues for resolving syntactic ambiguity. *Journal of Experimental Psychology: Learning, Memory, and Cognition, 22*, 714–735.

Augurzky, P. (2006). *Attaching relative clauses in German: The role of implicit and explicit prosody in sentence processing*. MPI Series in Human Cognitive and Brain Sciences 77. Leipzig, Germany.

Ayers, G. (1994). Discourse functions of pitch range in spontaneous and read speech. *OSU Working Papers in Linguistics, 44*, 1–49.

Baayen, R. H. (2008). *Analyzing linguistic data: A practical introduction to statistics using R.* Cambridge, UK: Cambridge University Press.

Bates, D., & Maechler, M. (2009). lme4: Linear mixed effects models using S4 classes. R package version 0.999375-32. Retrieved from http://CRAN.R-project.org/package=lme4

Beckmann, M. E., & Ayers-Elam, G. (1997). *Guidelines for ToBI Labeling.* Unpublished ms. Version 3. Ohio State University.

Beckman, M. E., & Hirschberg, J. (1994). The ToBI annotation conventions. Unpublished ms. Ohio State University, Columbus, OH.

Bergmann, A., Armstrong, M., & Maday, K. (2008). Relative clause attachment in English and Spanish: A production study. *Proceedings of Speech Prosody 2008*, Campinas, Brazil.

Bergmann, A., & Ito, K. (2007). *Attachment of ambiguous RCs: A production study.* Talk given at the 13th annual conference on architectures and mechanisms for language processing (AMLaP), Turku, Finland, Aug, 24–27.

Bookheimer, S. Y., Zeffiro, T. A., Blaxton, T., Gaillard, W., & Theodore, W. (1995). Regional cerebral blood flow during object naming and word reading. *Human Brain Mapping, 3*, 93–106.

Brysbaert, M., & Mitchell, D. C. (1996). Modifier attachment in sentence parsing: Evidence from Dutch. *Quarterly Journal of Experimental Psychology, 49A*(3), 664–695.

Brysbaert, M., & Mitchell, D. C. (2000). The failure to use gender information in parsing: A comment on van Berkum, Brown, and Hagoort (1999). *Journal of Psycholinguistic Research, 29*, 453–466.

Carlson, K., Clifton, C. Jr., & Frazier, L. (2001). Prosodic boundaries in adjunct attachment. *Journal of Memory and Language, 45*, 58–81.

Carreiras, M., & Clifton, C. Jr. (1993). Relative clause interpretation preferences in Spanish and English. *Language and Speech, 36*, 353–372.

Carreiras, M., & Clifton, C. Jr. (1999). Another word on parsing relative clauses: Eyetracking evidence from Spanish and English. *Memory and Cognition, 27*(5), 826–833.

Caspers, J., & van Heuven, V. J. (1993). Effects of time pressure on the phonetic realization of the Dutch accent-lending pitch rise and fall. *Phonetica, 50*, 161–171.

Clifton, C. J., Carlson, K., & Frazier, L. (2002). Informative prosodic boundaries. *Language and Speech, 45*, 87–114.

Cuetos, F., & Mitchell, D. C. (1988). Cross-linguistic differences in parsing: Restrictions on the use of the late closure strategy in Spanish. *Cognition, 30*, 73–105.

De Vincenzi, M., & Job, R. (1995). An investigation of late closure: The role of syntax, thematic structure, and pragmatics in initial and final interpretation. *Journal of Experimental Psychology: Learning, Memory, and Cognition, 21*(5), 1303–1321.

Deevy, P. L. (1999). The Comprehension of English subject-verb agreement. Appendix L: Word by word self-paced reading study materials: Agreement in subject relative clauses. Doctoral dissertation, University of Massachusetts.

Deevy, P. L. (2000). Agreement checking in comprehension: Evidence from relative clauses. *Journal of Psycholinguistic Research, 29*(1), 69–79.

Ehrlich, K., Fernández, E. M., Fodor, J. D., Stenshoel, E., & Vinereanu, M. (1999). *Low attachment of relative clauses: New data from Swedish, Norwegian, and Romanian.* Poster presented at the 12th annual CUNY conference on human sentence processing, New York, March 18–20.

Fernández, E. M. (2003). *Bilingual sentence processing: Relative clause attachment in English and Spanish.* Amsterdam, The Netherlands: John Benjamins.

Fernández, E. M., & Bradley, D. (1999). *Length effects in the attachment of relative clauses in English.* Poster presented at the 12th annual CUNY conference on human sentence processing, New York.

Fernández, E. M., Bradley, D., Igoa, J. M., & Teira, C. (2003). *Prosodic phrasing in the RC-attachment ambiguity: Effects of language, RC-length, and position.* Paper presented at the 9th AMLAP (http://amlap.psy.gla.ac.uk/programme/node29.html), Glasgow, August 25–27.

Ferreira, F., & Henderson, J. (1990). The use of verb information in syntactic parsing: A comparison of evidence from eye-movements and segment-by-segment self-paced reading. *Journal of Experimental Psychology: Learning, Memory, and Cognition, 16*, 555–568.

Fodor, J. D. (1998). Learning to parse. *Journal of Psycholinguistic Research, 27*(2), 285–319.

Fodor, J. D. (2002). Prosodic disambiguation in silent reading. *NELS, 32*, 113–32.

Fougeron, C., & Jun, S.-A. (1998). Rate effects on French intonation: Prosodic organization and phonetic realization. *Journal of Phonetics, 26*, 45–69.

Frazier, L. (1979). *On comprehending sentences: Syntactic parsing strategies.* Doctoral dissertation, University of Connecticut.

Frazier, L. (1990). Parsing modifiers: Special purpose routines in the human sentence processing mechanism? In D. A. Balota, G. G. Flores d'Arcais, & K. Rayner (Eds.), *Comprehension processes in reading* (pp. 303–330). Hillsdale, NJ: Lawrence Erlbaum.

Frazier, L., & Clifton, C. Jr. (1996). *Construal.* Cambridge, MA: MIT Press.

Frazier, L., & Clifton, C. Jr. (1997). Construal: Overview, motivation, and some new evidence. *Journal of Psycholinguistic Research, 26*, 277–295.

Frazier, L., Clifton, C. Jr., & Carlson, K. (2004). Don't break, or do: prosodic boundary preferences. *Lingua, 114*(1), 3–27.

Frazier, L., & Fodor, J. D. (1978). The sausage machine: A new two-stage parsing model. *Cognition, 6*, 291–325.

Frazier, L., & Rayner, K. (1988). Parameterizing the language system: Left- vs. right- branching within and across languages. In J. A. Hawkins (Ed.), *Explaining language universals.* Oxford, UK: Basil Blackwell.

Gibson, E., Pearlmutter, N. J., Canseco-Gonzales, E., & Hickock, G. (1996). Recency preference in the human sentence processing mechanism. *Cognition, 59*, 23–59.

Gilboy, E., & Sopena, J.-M. (1996). Segmentation effects in the processing of complex noun pronouns with relative clauses. In M. Carreiras, J. E. Garcia-Albea, & N. Sebastian (Eds.), *Language processing in Spanish* (pp. 191–206). Hillsdale, NJ: Erlbaum.

Gilboy, E., Sopena, J.-M., Clifton, C. Jr., & Frazier, L. (1995). Argument structure and association preferences in Spanish and English complex NPs. *Cognition, 54*, 131–167.

Hemforth, B., Konieczny, L., Scheepers, C., & Strube, G. (1998). Syntactic ambiguity resolution in German. In D. Hillert (Ed.), *Syntax and semantics: A cross-linguistic perspective* (pp. 293–312). San Diego, CA: Academic Press.

Hirose, Y. (1999). *Resolving reanalysis ambiguity in Japanese relative clauses.* Unpublished doctoral dissertation, CUNY Graduate Center, New York.

Hirschberg, J., & Avesani, C. (2000). Prosodic disambiguation in English and Italian. In A. Botinis (Ed.), *Intonation: Analysis, modelling, and technology* (pp. 87–96). Dordrecht: Kluwer Academic.

Howell, P., & Kadi-Hanifi, K. (1991). Camparison of prosodic properties between read and spontaneous speech material. *Speech Communication, 10*(2), 163–169.

Hudson, R. F., Lane, H. B., & Pullen, P. C. (2005). Reading fluency assessment and instruction: What, why, and how? *The Reading Teacher, 58*(7), 702–714.

Jun, S.-A. (2003a). Prosodic phrasing and attachment preferences. *Journal of Psycholinguistic Research, 32*(2), 219–249.

Jun, S.-A. (2003b). The effect of phrase length and speech rate on prosodic phrasing. *Proceedings of the international congress of phonetic sciences,* Barcelona, Spain: 483–486.

Jun, S.-A. (2006). Intonational Phonology of Seoul Korean Revisited. *Japanese-Korean Linguistics 14* Stanford: CSLI. [Also printed in *UCLA Working Papers in Phonetics* 104: 14–25]

Jun, S.-A. (2007). The intermediate phrase in Korean intonation: Evidence from sentence processing. In C. Gussenhoven & T. Riad (Eds.), *Tones and tunes: Studies in word and sentence prosody.* Berlin: Mouton de Gruyter.

Jun, S.-A., & Kim, S. (2004). Default phrasing and attachment preferences in Korean. *Proceedings of INTERSPEECH-ICSLP*, Jeju, Korea.

Jun, S.-A., & Koike, C. (2003). *Default prosody and RC attachment in Japanese.* Talk given at the 13th Japanese-Korean Linguistics Conference, Tucson, AZ. [Published in *Japanese-Korean Linguistics* 3, 41–53, CSLI, Stanford, in 2008]

Just, M. A., Carpenter, P. A., & Woolley, J. D. (1982). Paradigms and processes in reading comprehension. *Journal of Experimental Psychology: General, 111*, 228–238.

Kamide, Y., & Mitchell, D. C. (1997). Relative clause attachment: Non-determinism in Japanese Parsing. *Journal of Psycholinguistic Research, 26*, 247–254.

Kamide, Y., Mitchell, D. C., Fodor, J. D., & Inoue, A. (1998). *Relative clause attachment ambiguity: Further evidence from Japanese.* Poster presented at the 11th Annual CUNY Conference on Human Sentence Processing, Rutgers.

Kimball, J. (1973). Seven principles of surface structure parsing in natural language. *Cognition, 2*, 15–47.

Kjelgaard, M. M., & Speer, S. R. (1999). Prosodic facilitation and interference in the resolution of temporary syntactic closure ambiguity. *Journal of Memory and Language, 40*, 153–194.

Krivokapiç, J. (2007). Prosodic planning: Effects of phrasal length and complexity on pause duration. *Journal of Phonetics, 35*, 162–179.

Ladd, D. R., Faulkner, D., Faulkner, H., & Schepman, A. (1999). Constant "segmental anchoring" of F0 movements under changes in speech rate. *Journal of the Acoustical Society of America, 106*, 1543–1554.

Lovric, N., Bradley, D., & Fodor, J. D. (2000). *RC attachment in Croatian with and without preposition.* Poster presented at the AMLaP Conference, Leiden.

Lovric, N., Bradley, D., & Fodor, J. D. (2001). *Silent prosody resolves syntactic ambiguities: Evidence from Croatian.* Presented at the SUNY/CUNY/NYU Conference, Stonybrook, NY.

Maynell, L. A. (1999). *Effect of pitch accent placement on resolving relative clause ambiguity in English.* Poster at the 12th CUNY Conference, New York.

Mitchell, D. C. (1994). Sentence parsing. In M. Gernsbacher (Ed.), *Handbook of Psycholinguistics* (pp. 375–409). New York: Academic Press.

Mitchell, D. C., Corley, M. M. B., & Garnham, A. (1992). Effects of context in human sentence parsing: Evidence against a discourse-based proposal mechanism. *Journal of Experimental Psychology: Learning, Memory, and Cognition, 18*(1), 69–88.

Miyamoto, E. T., Nakamura, M., & Takahashi, S. (2004). Processing relative clauses in Japanese with two attachment sites. In K. Moulton & M. Wolf (Eds.), *Proceedings of North Eastern Linguistics Society 34* (pp. 441–452). Amherst: GLSA.

Papadopoulou, D., & Calhsen, H. (2003). Parsing strategies in L1 and L2 sentence processing: A study of relative clause attachment in Greek. *Studies in Second Language Acquisition, 25*, 501–528.

Price, P., Ostendorf, M., Shattuck-Hufnagel, S., & Fong, C. (1991). The use of prosody in syntactic disambiguation. *Journal of the Acoustical Society of America, 90*, 2956–2970.

Pynte, J., & Colonna, S. (2000). Decoupling syntactic parsing from visual inspection: The case of relative clause attachment in French. In A. Kennedy, R. Radach, D. Heller, & J. Pynte (Eds.), *Reading as a perceptual process* (pp. 529–547). Oxford, UK: Elsevier.

Pynte, J., Colonna, S., & Gola, C. (2003). *Can an "unnatural" prosody help parsing?* Poster presented at the 9th AMLaP, Glasgow, August 25–27.

Quinn, D., Abdelghany, H., & Fodor, J. D. (2000). *More evidence of implicit prosody in silent reading: French, English and Arabic relative clauses.* Poster presented at 13th annual CUNY conference on human sentence processing.

R Development Core Team (2009). *R: A language and environment for statistical computing.* R Foundation for Statistical Computing, Vienna. ISBN 3-900051-07-0. Retrieved from http://www.R-project.org

Rayner, K., Carlson, M., & Frazier, L. (1983). The interaction of syntax and semantics during sentence processing: Eye movements in the analysis of semantically biased sentences. *Journal of Verbal Learning and Verbal Behavior, 22*, 358–374.

Rayner, K., & Liversedge, S. P. (2004). Visual and linguistic processing during eye fixations in reading. In F. Ferrreira & J. Henderson (Eds.), *The interface of language, vision and action: Eye movements and the visual world* (pp. 59–104). Hove, UK: Psychology Press.

Rasinski, T. (2006). Issues and trends in literacy: Reading fluency instruction: Moving beyond accuracy, automaticity and prosody. *The Reading Teacher, 59*(7), 704–706.

Rietveld, A. C. M., & Gussenhoven, C. C. (1987). Perceived speech rate and intonation. *Journal of Phonetics, 15*, 273–285.

Schafer, A., Speer, S., Warren, P., & White, S. (2000). Intonational disambiguation in sentence production and comprehension. *Journal of Psycholinguistic Research, 29*, 169–182.

Schafer, A., Speer, S., & Warren, P. (2005). Prosodic influences on the production and comprehension of syntactic ambiguity in a game-based conversation task. In M. K. Tanenhaus & J. C. Trueswell (Eds.), *Approaches to studying world situated language use* (pp. 209–225). Cambridge: MIT Press.

Selkirk, E. (1986). On derived domains in sentence phonology. *Phonology Yearbook, 3*, 371–405.

Selkirk, E. (2000). The interaction of constraints on prosodic phrasing. In M. Horne (Ed.), *Prosody: Theory and experiment (studies presented to Gösta Bruce)* (pp. 231–262). Dordrecht: Kluwer Academic.

Silverman, K., Beckman, M., Pitrelli, J., Ostendorf, M., Wightman, C., Price, P., Pierrehumbert, J., & Hirschberg, J. (1992). ToBI: A standard for labeling English prosody. *Proceedings of international conference on spoken language processing, 2*, 867–870.

Silverman, K., Blaauw, E., Spitz, J., & Pitrelli, J. (1992). A prosodic comparison of spontaneous speech and read speech. *Proceedings of international conference on spoken language processing, 2*, 1299–1302.

Snedeker, J., & Casserly, E. (2010). Is it all relative? Effects of prosodic boundaries on the comprehension and production of attachment ambiguities. *Language and Cognitive Processes, 25*, 1234–1264.

Snedeker, J., & Trueswell, J. C. (2003). Using prosody to avoid ambiguity: Effects of speaker awareness and referential context. *Journal of Memory and Language, 48*, 103–130.

Steinhauer, K., Alter, K., & Friederici, A. D. (1999). Brain potentials indicate the immediate use of prosodic cues in natural speech processing. *Nature Neuroscience, 2*, 191–196.

Steinhauer, K., & Freiderici, A. D. (2001). Prosodic boundaries, comma rules, and brain responses: The closure positive shift in ERPs a universal marker for prosodic phrasing in listeners and readers. *Journal of Psycholinguistic Research, 30*, 267–295.

Swets, B., Desmet, T., Hambrick, D. Z., & Ferreira, F. (2007). The role of working memory in syntactic ambiguity resolution: A psychometric approach. *Journal of Experimental Psychology: General, 136*, 64–81.

Taylor, S. E. (2006). *Fluency in silent reading*. Huntington Station, NY: Taylor Associates/ Communications, Inc. Retrieved from www.readingplus.com

Traxler, M. J. (2007). Working memory contributions to relative clause attachment processing: A hierarchical linear modeling analysis. *Memory and Cognition, 35*, 1107–1121.

Traxler, M. J. (2009). A hierarchical linear modeling analysis of working memory and implicit prosody in the resolution of adjunct attachment ambiguity. *Journal of Psycholinguistic Research, 38*, 491–509.

Truckenbrodt, H. (1999). On the relation between syntactic phrases and phonological phrases. *Linguistic Inquiry, 30*, 219–255.

Vasishth, S., Agnihotri, R. K., Fernández, E. M., & Bhatt, R. (2004). Noun modification preferences in Hindi. In *The Proceedings of Seminar on Construction of Knowledge*, Vidya Bhawan Education Resource Centre, Udaipur, India, pp. 160–171.

Watson, D., & Gibson, E. (2004). The relationship between intonational phrasing and syntactic structure in language production. *Language and Cognitive Processes, 19*, 713–755.

Wijnen, F. (2004). The implicit prosody of jabberwocky and the relative clause attachment riddle. In H. Quené & V. van Heuven (Eds.), *On speech and language. Studies for Sieb G. Nooteboom* (pp. 169–178). Utrecht: Landelijke Onderzoeksschool Taalwetenschap. (LOT Occasional Series 2).

Zagar, D., Pynte, J., & Rativeau, S. (1997). Evidence for early-closure attachment on first-pass reading in French. *Quarterly Journal of Experimental Psychology, 50A*(2), 421–438.

Zu, Y., Li, A., & Li, Y. (2006). Speech rate effects on production features. *Report of Phonetic Research*: 141–144. Beijing, P. R. China: Phonetics Laboratory, Institute of Linguistics, Chinese Academy of Social Sciences.

Appendix 1

Code: F03: Fernandez (2003), CC93: Carreiras and Clifton (1993), Fr90: Frazier (1990), D99: Deevy (1999), D00: Deevy (2000); #a: Neutral, #b: NP1-biased, #c: NP2-biased; 'mod': modified; G: gender biased

Group I

9 Short RC

1a. My friend met the aide of the detective that was fired. (F03)
2b. Rob met the interpreter of the ambassadors that was skinny. (F03mod)
3c. Roxanne read the reviews of the poem that was unfinished. (F03)
4a. Patricia saw the teachers of the students that were in class. (F03)
5b. Lisa couldn't find the refills of the pen that were on sale. (F03)
6c. The doctor called in the son of the pretty nurse who hurt herself (Fr90), G
7a. Jane had inspected the printers of the computers that were stolen (F03)
8b. Peter met the boyfriend of the hostess who was a boxer (CC93 modified), G
9c. John spoke to the secretaries of the lawyer who was out of town. (F03mod)

9 Med RC

1b. The journalist interviewed the daughters of the hostage that were about to exit the airplane. (F03mod)
2c. Someone shot the servants of the actress who was on the balcony. (Fr90)
3a. The hotel director didn't want to see the guides of the tourists that were waiting at the reception desk. (F03)
4b. The police arrested the sister of the handyman who recently gave birth to twins. (CC93), G
5c. The children followed the grandfather of the girl who was wearing a long black skirt. (CC93), G
6a. Jane wrote a story about the uncle of the milkman who was known as a real gentleman. (CC93mod)
7b. Everybody ignored the stepfather of the nun who had a long silky white beard. (CC93 modified), G
8c. An armed robber shot the guard of the actress who had just divorced her husband. (CC93), G
9a. The chef couldn't find the cover of the pan that was in the cupboard on the left. (F03)

9 Long RC

1a. John was excited to meet the niece of the actor who was recently starring in a very successful play. (D00)
2b. Officer Phillips questioned the friend of the housekeepers who was quickly cleaning the motel room where the murder had taken place. (D99)
3c. Dr. Lee conferred with the daughters of the crash victim who was apparently suffering from severe shock. (D99)
4a. The curious reporter talked to the son of the delegate that was watching television in the lobby for the whole afternoon. (F03)
5b. The tall receptionist greeted the clients of the lawyer that were waiting in the conference room in the north hall. (F03)
6c. Kelly argued with the cousins of the farmer who was thoughtlessly fertilizing the fields on windy days. (D99)
7a. Yesterday afternoon I saw the daughter of the madwoman who was trying out some new eye shadow and purple lipstick. (CC93)
8b. Nobody noticed the bodyguards of the ambassador that were talking to the photographer at the party. (F03)
9c. The student read the revisions of the manuscript that was on the list of readings required for the final exam. (F03)

Group II

9 Short RC

1b. My friend met the aide of the detectives that was fired. (F03)
2c. Rob met the interpreters of the ambassador that was skinny. (F03)
3a. Roxanne read the review of the poem that was unfinished. (F03)
5c. Lisa couldn't find the refill of the pens that were on sale. (F03)
4b. Patricia saw the teacher of the students that was in class. (F03)
6a. The doctor called in the sons of the pretty nurses who hurt themselves. (Fr90)
7b. Jane had inspected the printer of the computers that was stolen. (F03)
8c. Peter met the girlfriend of the host who was a boxer. (CC93 modified), G
9a. John called the secretary of the lawyer who was out of town. (F03)

9 Med RC

1c. The journalist interviewed the daughter of the hostages that were about to exit the airplane. (F03 modified)
2a. Someone shot the servant of the actress who was on the balcony. (Fr90)
3b. The hotel director didn't want to see the guide of the tourists that was waiting at the reception desk. (F03)
4c. The police arrested the brother of the nursemaid who recently gave birth to twins. (CC93), G
5a. The children followed the mother of the girl who was wearing a long black skirt. (CC93)
6b. Jane wrote a story about the uncle of the laundress who was known as a real gentleman. (CC93), G
7c. Everybody ignored the stepmother of the monk who had a long white silky beard. (CC93), G
8a. An armed robber shot the maid of the actress who had just divorced her husband. (CC93)
9b. The chef couldn't find the cover of the pans that was in the cupboard on the left. (F03)

9 Long RC

1b. John was excited to meet the niece of the actors who was recently married to a Hollywood star. (D00)
2c. Officer Phillips questioned the cousins of the housekeeper who was quickly cleaning the motel room where the murder had taken place. (D99)
3a. Dr. Lee conferred with the daughter of the crash victim who was apparently suffering from severe shock. (D99)
4b. The curious reporter talked to the sons of the delegate that were watching television in the den for the whole afternoon. (F03)
5c. The tall receptionist greeted the client of the lawyers that were waiting in the conference room in the north hall. (F03)
6a. Kelly MacDonough argued with the wife of the farmer who was thoughtlessly fertilizing the fields on windy days. (D99)
7b. Yesterday afternoon I saw the daughter of the madman who was trying out some new eye shadow and purple lipstick. (CC93), G
8c. Nobody noticed the bodyguards of the ambassador that was talking to the photographer at the party. (F03)
9a. The student read the revisions of the manuscripts that were on the list of readings required for the final exam. (F03)

Group III

9 Short RC

1c. My friend met the aides of the detective that was fired. (F03)
4c. Patricia saw the teachers of the student that was in class. (F03)
7c. Jane had inspected the printers of the computer that was stolen. (F03)
2a. Rob met the interpreter of the ambassador that was skinny. (F03)
5a. Lisa couldn't find the refills of the pens that were on sale. (F03)
8a. Peter met the boyfriend of the host who was a boxer. (CC93 modified)
3b. Roxanne read the review of the poems that was unfinished. (F03)
6b. The doctor called in the son of the pretty nurse who hurt himself. (Fr90), G
9b. John called the secretary of the lawyers who was out of town. (F03)

9 Med RC

1a. The journalist interviewed the daughters of the hostages that were about to exit the airplane. (F03)
2b. Someone shot the servant of the actresses who was on the balcony. (Fr90)
3c. The hotel director didn't want to see the guide of the tourists that were waiting at the reception desk. (F03)
4a. The police arrested the sister of the nursemaid who recently gave birth to twins. (CC93)
5b. The children followed the mother of the boy who was wearing a long black skirt. (CC93), G
6c. Jane wrote a story about the aunt of the milkman who was known as a real gentleman. (CC93), G
7a. Everybody ignored the stepfather of the monk who had a long silky white beard. (CC93)
8b. An armed robber shot the maid of the actor who had just divorced her husband. (CC93), G
9c. The chef couldn't find the covers of the pan that was in the cupboard on the left. (F03)

9 Long RC

1c. John was excited to meet the nieces of the actor who was recently starring in a very successful play. (D00)
2a. Officer Phillips questioned the cousin of the housekeeper who was quickly cleaning the motel room where the murder had taken place. (D99)
3b. Dr. Lee conferred with the daughter of the crash victims who was apparently suffering from severe shock. (D99)
4c. The curious reporter talked to the son of the delegates that were watching television in the den for the whole afternoon. (F03)
5a. The tall receptionist greeted the clients of the lawyers that were waiting in the conference room in the north hall. (F03)
6b. Kelly MacDonough argued with the cousin of the farmers who was thoughtlessly fertilizing the fields on windy days. (D99)
7c. Yesterday afternoon I saw the son of the madwoman who was trying out some new eye shadow and purple lipstick. (CC93), G
8a. Nobody noticed the bodyguards of the ambassador that was talking to the photographer at the party. (F03)
9b. The student read the revisions of the manuscript that were on the list of readings required for the final exam. (F03)

LANGUAGE AND COGNITIVE PROCESSES
2010, 25 (7/8/9), 1234–1264

Psychology Press
Taylor & Francis Group

Is it all relative? Effects of prosodic boundaries on the comprehension and production of attachment ambiguities

Jesse Snedeker[1] and Elizabeth Casserly[1,2]

[1]*Department of Psychology, Harvard University, Cambridge, MA, USA,*
[2]*Department of Linguistics, Indiana University, Bloomington, IN, USA*

While there is ample evidence that prosody and syntax mutually constrain each other, there is considerable uncertainty about the nature of this interface. Here, we explore this issue with prepositional phrase attachment ambiguities (*You can feel$_A$ the cat$_B$ with the feather*). Prior research has been motivated by two hypotheses: (1) the absolute boundary hypothesis (ABH) posits that attachment preferences depend on the size of the prosodic boundary before the ambiguous phrase (boundary B) and (2) the relative boundary hypothesis (RBH) links attachment to the relative size of boundary B and any boundary between the high and low attachment site (boundary A). However, few experiments test the unique predictions of either theory. Study 1 examines how syntax influences prosodic production. The results provide modest support for RBH and stronger support for ABH. In Study 2, we systematically vary the size of both boundaries in an offline comprehension task. We find that absolute boundary strength influences interpretation when relative boundary strength is held constant, and relative boundary strength influences interpretation when absolute boundary strength is held constant. Thus, our theory of the prosody–syntax interface must account for effects of both kinds.

Keywords: Parsing; Prosody; Syntactic ambiguity resolution; Intonational boundaries; Comprehension; Prepositional phrase attachment; Production.

Correspondence should be addressed to Jesse Snedeker, Department of Psychology, Harvard University, 1136 WJH, 33 Kirkland St., Cambridge MA, 02138, USA. E-mail: snedeker@wjh.harvard.edu

We are grateful to Jennifer Venditti, who conducted the ToBI analyses on the utterances from Snedeker and Trueswell (2003), and to Amanda Worek, who kept the lab running smoothly. A special thanks to Stefanie Shattuck-Hufnagel for introducing the authors. This material is based upon work supported by the National Science Foundation (0623845).

http://www.psypress.com/lcp DOI: 10.1080/01690960903525499

Human languages employ several levels of representation: the syllables in an utterance are organised into a prosodic structure, the words into a syntactic structure, and the concepts into a semantic structure. One of the central questions of linguistics is how these partially independent structures are linked together and constrain one another. One of the central questions of psycholinguistics is how information from one level can be used during language comprehension to draw inferences about another. Some of these interfaces are both systematic and well documented, supporting agreement about the content of the interface even when the mechanisms are the subject of dispute. For example, any theory of the syntax–semantics interface must capture the relations between syntactic positions and thematic roles.

In contrast, the study of the prosody–syntax interface is relatively young. Nevertheless, substantial progress has been made. In the past 20 years, we have clearly established that there is a systematic, albeit imperfect, relation between prosodic structure and syntactic form. Manipulations of prosodic structure influence how listeners interpret syntactically ambiguous utterances (Beach, 1991; Carlson, Clifton, & Frazier, 2001; Cooper & Paccia-Cooper, 1980; Lehiste, 1973; Lehiste, Olive, & Streeter, 1976; Price, Ostendorf, Shattuck-Hufnagel, & Fong, 1991; Schafer, 1997; see Cutler, Dahan, & van Donselaar, 1997, for a review). These effects of prosody emerge quickly during online sentence comprehension, suggesting that this is a robust property of the human parser (Kjelgaard & Speer, 1999; Marslen-Wilson, Tyler, Warren, Grenier, & Lee, 1992; Nagel, Shapiro, Tuller, & Nawy, 1996; Pynte & Prieur, 1996; Snedeker & Trueswell, 2003; Steinhauer, Alter, & Friederici, 1999; Warren, Grabe & Nolan, 1995; Weber, Grice, & Crocker, 2006). Naïve speakers systematically vary their prosody depending on the syntactic structure of the utterance and naïve listeners can use this variation to disambiguate the utterance (Kraljic & Brennan, 2005; Schafer, Speer, & Warren, 2005; Snedeker & Trueswell, 2003). Under some circumstances, these prosodic cues disappear when the speaker is unaware of the ambiguity or the context disambiguates the utterance (Allbritton, McKoon, & Ratcliff, 1996; Snedeker & Trueswell, 2003). But in other cases these cues persist, suggesting that they are available to listeners at least some of the time (Kraljic & Brennan, 2005; Schafer et al., 2005). Taken together, these studies indicate that users of a language share implicit knowledge about the relationship between prosody and syntax which they can use during comprehension and production.

However, the precise characterisation of the syntax–prosody mapping is far from clear. Several phenomena suggest that this mapping is unlikely to be simple or deterministic. First, there are major syntactic boundaries which are rarely marked by prosodic boundaries (e.g., the boundary between the subject and the predicate). Second, nonsyntactic factors—such as speech rate, word length, and discourse structure—play a critical role in prosodic structure (for reviews see Beckman, 1996; Cutler et al., 1997; Fernald & McRoberts, 1996; Shattuck-Hufnagel & Turk, 1996; Warren, 1999). Finally, experimental production studies have demonstrated that the same word string, with the same intended structure, in essentially the same discourse context, can be produced with many different prosodic structures (Schafer et al., 2005; Snedeker & Trueswell, 2003).

Theorists have approached the syntax–prosody interface in two ways. Some take on the whole problem, providing an algorithm for converting any syntactic structure into a prosodic structure (Cooper & Paccia-Cooper, 1980; Ferreira, 1988; Gee & Grosjean, 1983; Watson & Gibson, 2004). Other theories focus on a more limited range of phenomena and characterise the mapping within this domain. One commonly explored phenomenon is the prosodic phrasing of syntactic attachment ambiguities (Carlson et al., 2001; Clifton, Carlson, & Frazier, 2002; Schafer, 1997). There are several reasons why this might be a particularly productive place to begin pinning down the syntax–prosody interface.

First, attachment ambiguities are a diverse but clearly defined set of phenomena. The ambiguously attached constituent can vary in its syntactic category, length, and syntactic complexity, allowing experimenters to examine influence of multiple variables. However, all attachment ambiguities have some features in common: in all cases there is an ambiguous phrase which could be linked to the syntactic tree in more than one location. In English, one of the options typically involves incorporating the phrase into the constituent that immediately preceded it, and one of the options involves attaching the constituent at a higher level in the tree. For example, the sentence in (1) has two alternate interpretations. The prepositional phrase ("with flawed data") can be a constituent of the noun phrase as in (2), in which case Amanda is the heroine. Or it can be attached directly to the verb phrase as in (3), making Amanda the villain.

1. Amanda attacked the paper with flawed data.
2. Low attachment: Amanda [attacked [the paper [with flawed data]$_{PP}$]$_{NP}$]$_{VP}$.
3. High attachment: Amanda [attacked [the paper]$_{NP}$ [with flawed data]$_{PP}$]$_{VP}$.

Second, as this example suggests, attachment ambiguities can often remain globally ambiguous. This allows experimenters to examine the influence of prosody on syntax (or syntax on prosody) while holding the string of words constant. One might also expect that the strength of prosody–syntax correspondences would be greatest for globally ambiguous utterances. From a functional perspective, prosodic cues to structure would be most helpful when other information is absent. There is no direct evidence that global ambiguity is marked more clearly than local ambiguity. However, there is evidence that under some circumstances speakers who are aware of a global ambiguity produce clearer prosodic cues than those who are not aware of it (Kraljic & Brennan, 2005; Lehiste, 1973, but see Schafer et al., 2005; Snedeker & Trueswell, 2003). Finally, attachment ambiguities are ubiquitous in everyday conversation, ensuring that we are studying constructions that speakers and listeners have ample experience with, thus maximising our chances of finding systematic, replicable patterns of performance.

To date, there have been two primary ways of thinking about the relation between prosodic structure and the interpretation of attachment ambiguities. Many theorists have focused on the boundary immediately before the ambiguously attached phrase (marked as B in 4), noting that the absence of a boundary in this location favours low attachment, while the presence of a boundary favours high attachment (see e.g., Marcus & Hindle, 1990; Price et al., 1991; Pynte & Prieur, 1996; Watson & Gibson, 2005).

4. Amanda attacked$_{\mathrm{A}}$ the paper$_{\mathrm{B}}$ with flawed data.

On the basis of this data one might conclude that the absolute strength of boundary B was the primary consideration in mapping between prosody and syntax.

More recently, however, other theorists have suggested that the boundary before the ambiguous phrase can only be interpreted in light of the global prosodic structure of the utterance (Carlson et al., 2001; Clifton et al., 2002; Schafer, 1997). This claim is made most explicit in the work of Carlson, Clifton, and Frazier who argue that the boundary at location B is always interpreted with respect to any other boundary that occurs before a constituent that contains the lower attachment site but not the higher attachment site (Clifton et al., 2002). In the utterance above, the only boundary that would be relevant is the one marked A. Specifically, Carlson and colleagues argue that effects of prosody depend on the relative size of these two boundaries: prosodic structures in which A is bigger than B favour low attachment, those in which B is bigger than A favour high attachment, and those in which the two boundaries are equivalent favour neither.

As Carlson and colleagues note, most studies demonstrating that the lower boundary influences attachment are compatible with this relative boundary strength hypothesis. In comprehension studies when a boundary is added in location B, it is typically larger than any relevant boundary A and thus changes the interpretation of the utterance on both hypotheses. In a series of comprehension studies, Carlson and colleagues demonstrate that relative boundary size has an effect on interpretation (Carlson et al., 2001; Clifton et al., 2002). But research to date has not explored whether the absolute size of the final boundary plays a role independent of relative boundary size, and the evidence that the relative boundary size plays a role *independent of absolute boundary size* is limited, coming from a single lab and paradigm (albeit from several constructions). To explore these questions, we introduce two hypotheses which clearly isolate these factors (5 and 6). The absolute boundary hypothesis (ABH) is related to Watson and Gibson's (2005) *anti-attachment hypothesis*, though it is both stronger and more limited in scope. The relative boundary hypothesis (RBH) captures the relevant features of Carlson, Clifton and Frazier's *informative boundary hypothesis* (Clifton et al., 2002).

5. ABH: The absolute size of the prosodic boundary immediately before a constituent (boundary B) predicts syntactic attachment independent of relative boundary size. Larger boundaries are associated with high attachment, smaller boundaries with low attachment.
6. RBH: The relative magnitude of the prosodic boundary immediately before a constituent (boundary B) and any higher relevant boundary (boundary A) predicts syntactic attachment, independent of the absolute size of boundary B. When B is larger than A, high attachment is favoured, when the two are equal there is no preference and when A is larger than B, low attachment is favoured.

These hypotheses are phrased from the perspective of the comprehender, but they could be reframed to make predictions about production as well (in which case prosodic structure would reflect syntactic attachment rather than predicting it).

Notice that both of these hypotheses rely on the notion of boundary strength. Thus to make predictions about the interpretation of particular structures, we need a theory of prosodic boundaries. Like most researchers in this field, we will be describing prosody according to the tones and break indices (ToBI) coding system (Beckman & Hirschberg, 1994), which represents the relative prominence of words in an utterance and their prosodic grouping. According to the prosodic theory underlying ToBI, there are two levels of prosodic structure between the level of the utterance and the prosodic word, the intermediate phrase and the intonational phrase (Beckman & Pierrehumbert, 1986). Each intermediate phrase (or ip) contains at least one pitch accent and ends in a high or low phrase tone. Intermediate phrases are grouped together into intonational phrases (or IP's). An intonational phrase contains at least one intermediate phrase and ends in a high or low boundary tone (which follows the phrase tone of the final intermediate phrase). While prosodic theories vary in the number of hierarchical levels that they recognise, most include levels that roughly correspond to the intermediate and intonational phrase (see e.g., Nespor & Vogel, 1986; Selkirk, 1986). Most researchers exploring the prosody–syntax interface have explicitly argued or implicitly assumed that these two types of boundaries are discrete and categorical. Syntactic structure can influence how an utterance is divided into ip's or IP's, but all boundaries of a given kind are equivalent and thus continuous variation within a category plays no role in syntax–prosody interface. To the best of our knowledge, the experimental evidence for this comes from a single study demonstrating that substantially increasing the salience of an ip boundary does not modify the interpretation of an attachment ambiguity (Experiment 3; Carlson et al., 2001).

By adopting this theory of prosody, we can develop the following predictions about the relation between prosodic structure and syntactic attachment (7 and 8).

7. Predictions about the probability of high attachment under the RBH:

(ip, 0)		(0, 0)		(0, ip)
(IP, 0)	$<$	(ip, ip)	$<$	(0, IP)
(IP, ip)		(IP, IP)		(ip, IP)

8. Predictions about the probability of high attachment under the ABH:

(0, 0)		(0, ip)		(0, IP)
(ip, 0)	$<$	(ip, ip)	$<$	(ip, IP)
(IP, 0)		(IP, ip)		(IP, IP)

Throughout this paper, we will be adopting the convention of describing prosodic structures as ordered pairs in which the first item refers to the boundary at location A and the second to the boundary at location B. Word level breaks are coded as 0, intermediate phrase breaks as ip, and intonational phrase breaks as IP. Notice that the two hypotheses make many of the same predictions. For example on both theories (0, 0) structures result in fewer high attachments than (0, IP) structures. In this paper, we will be focusing our attention on the cases in which one theory predicts that two structures will be equivalent while the other theory predicts a difference. These are the unique predictions of the RBH and ABH, which are listed below (9 and 10).

9. Unique predictions of the relative boundary strength hypothesis:

1a. For utterances with no low boundary: (IP, 0) & (ip, 0) < (0, 0)
1b. For utterances with a low ip boundary: (IP, ip) < (ip, ip) < (0, ip)
1c. For utterances with a low IP boundary: (IP, IP) < (0, IP) & (ip, IP)

10. Unique predictions of the absolute boundary strength hypothesis:

2a. For utterances with equal boundaries: (0, 0) < (ip, ip) < (IP, IP)
2b. For utterances with a larger high boundary: (IP, 0) & (ip, 0) < (IP, ip)
2c. For utterances with a larger low boundary: (0, ip) < (0, IP) & (ip, IP)

Many of these predictions have never been tested or have been tested only indirectly. To examine whether both factors are characteristics of the prosody–syntax interface, we examined these contrasts both in production and comprehension. Study 1 makes use of data from a referential communication task to explore whether speakers use both approaches to disambiguate syntactic attachments. In Study 2, we parametrically varied the strength of the two boundaries in a comprehension task to examine how relative and absolute boundary strength influenced the ultimate interpretation of globally ambiguous utterances.

STUDY 1: RE-ANALYSIS OF PRODUCTION DATA FROM SNEDEKER AND TRUESWELL

Method and prior findings

To begin exploring this question, we re-examined the production data from Snedeker and Trueswell (2003). This study used a referential communication paradigm to examine the prosody–syntax interface in naïve participants. The speaker and the listener were separated by a screen and each given a set of toys, which they believed to be identical. The speaker was then shown a target action using these toys and given a written sentence to produce. The written sentence was removed and the speaker produced the command. The listener followed the command to the best of his/her ability but was not allowed to ask for clarification.

The critical utterances contained ambiguous prepositional phrase attachments ("Tap the frog with the flower"). In Experiment 1, both participants had a toy set which supported both the low and high attachment (e.g., a frog, a frog carrying a flower, a large flower, a block, and a giraffe wearing a coat) and the intended interpretation of the utterance was manipulated within participants. This was done by varying the demonstration that the speaker saw. On high-attachment/instrument trials, the experimenter used the target instrument (the flower) to carry out the action on the unmodified animal (the frog). On low-attachment/modifier trials, she used her hand to carry out the action on the modified animal (the frog carrying a flower). Under these circumstances, listeners were able to use the prosody of the speaker's utterance to arrive at the correct interpretation about 70% of the time. However, the speaker was typically aware of the ambiguity.

In Experiment 2, two changes were made to decrease ambiguity awareness. First, the intended interpretation of the ambiguous utterance was manipulated between speakers. Second, each speaker was given a toy set that only supported the intended interpretation of the ambiguous utterance (e.g., for a low attachment, the flower above would be replaced with a leaf). The listener's toy set remained ambiguous. Under these circumstances, most speakers were unaware of the ambiguity and the listeners were unable to disambiguate the utterance and thus performed at chance.

In analysing the prosodic form of the speakers' utterances, Snedeker and Trueswell implicitly adopted the RBH. Utterances were coded using the ToBI labelling system by a highly-trained coder who was blind to experimental condition, then they were classified according to whether the lower boundary was greater than, lesser than, or equal in size to the higher boundary (see also Schafer, Speer, Warren, & White, 2000). The results were consistent with the RBH. For example, in the experiment with aware speakers, 81% of the utterances in which B was greater than A were intended to have a high attachment, while only 6% of the utterances in which A was greater than B were intended to. However, as we noted earlier, results like this do not uniquely support the RBH. Since most of the utterances had only one prosodic boundary, differences in relative boundary strength were typically accompanied by differences in the absolute strength of boundary B. In fact, when we classify the utterances according to absolute boundary strength, the results are equally strong. In aware speakers, 91% of utterances with an IP break in position B were intended to have a high attachment, while only 9% of the utterances with no break in position B were intended to.

Present analyses and discussion

To explore the unique predictions of the relative and absolute boundary strength hypotheses, we went back to the Snedeker and Trueswell data set to determine how often each prosodic form was used with the intention of communicating low or high attachment. All utterances with ambiguous boundary indices (ToBI codes of 2) were eliminated from this analysis.[1] The frequency of each structure and the proportion which were intended to have a high attachment are listed in Table 1. The first thing to note is that the

[1] These comprised 16% of the tokens in Experiment 1 in which speakers were aware of the ambiguity and 4% of the tokens in Experiment 2 in which they were unaware. All the ambiguous boundaries occurred before the prepositional phrase. In Experiment 1, the proportion of these utterances appearing in high-attachment contexts was intermediate between utterances with a 0 boundary in this location and those with an ip boundary there, suggesting that they were truly ambiguous. In Experiment 2, they were too infrequent to characterise.

TABLE 1
Number of tokens for each prosodic form and the proportion that were produced in the high attachment context

	Production aware speakers		*Production unaware speakers*	
Prosodic form	*Number of tokens*	*Portion with high attachment*	*Number of tokens*	*Portion with high attachment*
0, 0	33	0.21	25	0.48
ip, 0	9	0.00	16	0.44
IP, 0	56	0.04	17	0.12
0, ip	20	0.54	50	0.60
ip, ip	6	0.83	42	0.45
IP, ip	3	0.67	11	0.36
0, IP	62	0.90	29	0.62
ip, IP	24	0.92	12	0.92
IP, IP	13	0.92	9	0.78

nine structures are not equally common. Aware speakers tended to produce utterances with a single IP break or with no internal prosodic boundaries. Unaware speakers were more likely to produce the (ip, ip) or (0, ip) structures. Second, the structures appear to be used in systematically different ways, particularly by aware speakers. Those with no break before the prepositional phrase (top three rows) were typically used for low attachments, while those with an IP break before the ambiguous phrase (bottom three rows) were generally used for high attachments.

To test the unique predictions of each hypothesis, we conducted a series of Fisher's exact tests comparing pairs of forms to determine whether one would be used more often to signal high attachment. The results of these analyses appear in Table 2. The rows of the table evaluate the unique predictions of each hypothesis which were described above (see 9 and 10). Several analyses involved structures that appeared less than 20 times in the data set. These are shaded grey. Obviously no strong conclusions can be drawn from null effects in these cells. Only two predictions of the RBH involve structures that are frequent enough to support a robust analysis. One of these predictions is confirmed: speakers are less likely to use the (IP, 0) structure to signal high attachment than the (0, 0) structure. This is true even for the unaware speakers who make less use of the (IP, 0) structure. The second prediction is that for unaware speakers the (0, ip) structure will be more associated with high attachments than the (ip, ip) structure. This contrast includes a total of 92 data points but fails to reach significance.

The tests of the absolute boundary strength hypothesis were more informative. In aware speakers, six of the seven critical contrasts were reliable, many despite small sample sizes. Structures with no boundary

TABLE 2
Tests of RBH and ABH on production data from aware and unaware speakers

Prediction	*Productions of aware speakers*	*Productions of unaware speakers*
Relative boundary strength		
1a. (IP, 0) <(0, 0)	$p<.05$*	$p<.05$*
1a. (ip, 0) <(0, 0)	$p>.2$	$p>.2$
1b. (IP, ip) <(ip, ip)	$p>.2$	$p>.2$
1b. (ip, ip) <(0, ip)	$p>.2$	$p>.2$
1b. (IP, ip) <(0, ip)	$p>.2$	$p>.2$
1c. (IP, IP) <(0, IP)	$p>.2$	$p>.2$
1c. (IP, IP) <(ip, IP)	$p>.2$	$p>.2$
Absolute boundary strength		
2a. (0, 0) <(ip, ip)	$p<.01$*	$p>.2$
2a. (ip, ip) <(IP, IP)	$p>.2$	$p=.08$
2a. (0, 0) <(IP, IP)	$p<.005$**	$p>.1$
2b. (IP, 0) <(IP, ip)	$p<.05$*	$p>.1$
2b. (ip, 0) <(IP, ip)	$p<.05$*	$p>.2$
2c. (0, ip) <(0, IP)	$p<.005$**	$p>.2$
2c. (0, ip) <(ip, IP)	$p<.05$*	$p<.05$*

Cells in grey include a contrast with fewer than 20 tokens. *$p<.05$, **$p<.005$.

before the prepositional phrase were typically used to convey low attachments, those with IP boundaries in this location were used for high attachments, and those with ip boundaries there were used for both. In unaware speakers, most of these contrasts were unreliable, suggesting that the mapping between syntax and boundary size is less robust when speakers are not deliberately marking the syntactic contrast. However, the contrast between (0, ip) structures and (ip, IP) structures continued to be reliable.

In sum, we find modest support for the relative boundary strength hypothesis and more robust support for the absolute boundary strength hypothesis. The interpretation of these findings is limited by the small numbers of utterances in many cells. Nevertheless, these analyses constrain our model of the interface. By demonstrating that at least one unique prediction of each theory is supported—both in aware and unaware speakers—these data indicate that both relative and absolute boundary strength play a role in the mapping from syntax to prosody.

In Study 2, we continued exploring the predictions of the absolute and relative boundary strength hypotheses. However, we switched our focus from language production to language comprehension. We did this for two reasons. First, as we noted in the introduction, RBH was primarily developed in the context of language comprehension. While aspects of the proposal are motivated by assumptions about the prosodic cues that speakers produce, it is possible that the comprehension system and production system diverge in some respects. Second, our analysis of Study 1 was limited by differences in how often each structure was used. By switching to comprehension, we can ensure that all of the relevant structures are used frequently, thus increasing the power of the study.

STUDY 2: COMPREHENSION OF ATTACHMENT AMBIGUITIES

Methods

Participants

A total of 62 adult native speakers of American English drawn from the Harvard University student body and the greater Cambridge community participated in our experiment. None reported uncorrected hearing or vision problems and all were compensated for their participation with either psychology course credit or five dollars. Two subjects' results were removed from analysis due to equipment malfunction ($n = 1$) or failure to complete the experiment within the allotted time ($n = 1$).

Stimuli

Our critical stimuli consisted of eight base sentences, each containing a prepositional-phrase attachment ambiguity like those in (11) below.[2] These sentences were based on stimuli used in Snedeker and Truswell (2004), which had been designed to provide equal support to the modifier and instrument interpretation, which map on to low and high syntactic attachments, respectively.[3] The eight verbs had been selected on the basis of a sentence completion study and had given rise to roughly equal numbers of instrument and modifier completions. In each case the prepositional object that was paired with the verb had been rated as a moderately plausible instrument for that particular action.

Each utterance was recorded with both a one syllable noun and a three syllable compound noun (11). The three syllable nouns consisted of redundant

[2] We used only eight items for two reasons. First, Snedeker and Trueswell (2004) normed potential instruments for only eight equi-biased verbs and we wished to make use of these norms. Second, the present study served as an offline validation study for a visual-world experiment which employed an act out task to test young children, thus placing additional constraints on the verbs that could be used. Each participant heard the same base sentence in four different prosodies, thus the number of critical items was 32 per participant.

[3] While the only way to semantically interpret the low attachment is as a modifier, the high attachment of a phrase can have several semantic interpretations (accompaniment, location, instrument, etc.). For these particular verbs and prepositional objects, the instrument interpretation was dominant, as evidenced by participants' responses in an act out task (Snedeker & Trueswell, 2004).

forms of the one syllable nouns, which are common in child-directed speech (e.g., *kitty cat*). The goal of this manipulation was to explore the possibility that length of the direct-object noun phrase might play some role in the interpretation of prosodic structure.[4] Because the length manipulation had no reliable effect (and did not interact with the other variables), we will not be discussing it further. A complete list of the sentences can be found in the Appendix.

11. a. You can pinch the dog with the barrette.
    b. You can pinch the puppy dog with the barrette.

Each of these critical sentences was recorded in each of the nine prosodic forms listed in Table 1. The second author, a student of phonetics trained in prosodic analysis, produced all the stimuli. The sentences were then transcribed by a naïve native-English-speaking laboratory assistant to check for naturalness and intelligibility. All utterances were fully intelligible, but sentences spoken with two utterance-internal IP breaks were judged to be highly unnatural and were therefore dropped from the experiment. This left us with 128 critical utterances. The ToBI transcriptions for these utterances appear in Table 3.

The speaker had been instructed to produce each utterance in the most natural manner possible and to produce a consistent prosody across items in the same condition. Consequently, the placement and type of pitch accent was free to vary across conditions. All the target sentences had pitch accents on the direct-object noun and the prepositional object. All had pitch accents on the verb except for a subset of the (0, ip) utterances which had an accent on the sentence subject instead. However, the type of pitch accent on each word varied systematically across conditions, an issue that we return to in the discussion.

To ensure that every utterance was produced with the intended prosody, we measured the duration of each word and the pauses that followed them. We would expect that a break in location A would increase the duration of the verb, while a break in location B would increase the duration of the direct

[4] There are two opposing predictions that might be made about the effects of word length on the interpretation of these utterances. First, on a theory in which listeners evaluate prosodic boundaries according to their informativeness (e.g., Clifton et al., 2002), the use of a longer direct-object noun should make the boundary after it less informative. This would result in more low attachments in the conditions with ip or IP breaks before the prepositional phrase. Second, if we entertain the hypothesis that attachment decisions depend in part on the activation of constituents and that the activation rapidly dissipates (Altmann, 1998), then we might expect that redundant material between the onset of the noun and the ambiguous phrase to decrease the number of low attachments. Thus, the lack of any effect could reflect the opposing effects of these two processes. Or it could suggest that the length manipulation was too weak to exert any effect at all. Across the eight conditions, the long nouns were only 166 ms longer than the short nouns.

TABLE 3
ToBI transcriptions of the stimuli for Study 2

	You	*can*	*verb*		*the*	*DO noun*		*with the*	*pp-object noun*	
IP, 0			L+H*	!H–L%		L*			H*	L–L%
0, IP			H*			!H*	L–H%		H*	L–L%
0, 0			H*			!H*			!H*	L–L%
ip, ip			L*	H–		L*	H–		L+H*	L–L%
ip, 0			H*	L–		H*			!H*	L–L%
0, ip	H* (50%)		L* (50%)			L+H*	L–		L+H*	L–L%
IP, ip			H*	!H–L%		L*	H–		L+H*	L–L%
ip, IP			L*	H–		L*	L–H%		H*	L–L%

object noun. The IP breaks were all accompanied by audible pauses of about 100–300 ms. In contrast most of the ip breaks had no audible pause but many contained short silences (30–100 ms) which were visible when the waveform was visually inspected. Because few of our critical words ended in stop consonants, it was difficult to determine precisely when each word ended and the pause began. For this reason, we calculated the total duration of the critical word and the pause that followed it. These values are given in Table 4. The duration analyses confirm that the IP breaks were produced with more lengthening than the ip breaks which in turn showed more lengthening than the null breaks.

EXPERIMENTAL DESIGN

To avoid fatiguing our participants or eroding their intuitions by requesting many judgments on the same word string, we divided the prosody types into three between-participant conditions (see Table 5) with four prosodic forms appearing in each condition. These conditions were constructed from the perspective of the RBH. We will refer to the between-participant manipulation as Prosody Strength, since the strength of the boundaries was varied across critical cells in these conditions while their relative size was held constant. The within-participant manipulation was termed Prosody Type, because it varied relative boundary strength, and thus, from the perspective of the RBH, the different Prosody Types diverge in the kind of interpretation that they support.

TABLE 4
Durations of critical regions for stimuli for Study 2

Prosodic form	*Verb +pause*	*DO noun +pause*
IP, 0	823 ms CI.95 = ±46	455 ms CI.95 = ±70
0, IP	327 ms CI.95 = ±43	856 ms CI.95 = ±36
0, 0	399 ms CI.95 = ±25	486 ms CI.95 = ±58
ip, ip	608 ms CI.95 = ±49	658 ms CI.95 = ±43
ip, 0	550 ms CI.95 = ±38	440 ms CI.95 = ±43
0, ip	315 ms CI.95 = ±54	644 ms CI.95 = ±38
IP, ip	756 ms CI.95 = ±53	644 CI.95 = ±54
ip, IP	637 ms CI.95 = ±44	916 ms CI.95 = ±51

TABLE 5
Division of the different prosodic forms into three Prosody Strength conditions

	Prosody Strength (between participants)		
Prosody Type (within participant)	*Strong*	*Weak*	*Two breaks*
Neutral no breaks	∅, ∅	∅, ∅	∅, ∅
Neutral ip breaks	ip, ip	ip, ip	ip, ip
High attachment	∅, IP	∅, ip	ip, IP
Low attachment	IP, ∅	ip, ∅	IP, ip

Specifically, each of the Prosody Strength conditions included both the (0, 0) and (ip, ip) utterances, which were predicted to be neutral according to the RBH. In addition, each condition included one prosodic structure with a larger break in position A than in position B (predicted to promote low attachment under the RBH) and one condition with a larger break in position B than in position A (predicted to promote high attachment under the RBH). The nature of these utterances varied across the Prosody Strength conditions. In the strong prosody condition, the asymmetry was created by pitting an IP break against a null break. In the weak prosody condition an ip break was pitted against a null break. In the two-break prosody condition, an IP break was pitted against an ip break (see Table 5). Note that on the relative boundary strength hypothesis, the three Prosody Strength conditions should be equivalent: they each include two prosodies which are neutral with respect to PP-attachment, a prosody more consistent with high attachment, and a prosody more consistent with low attachment.

In addition, the number of syllables in the direct-object noun was manipulated between subjects, resulting in six lists with 32 critical utterances each. On a single list, each base utterance appeared in four different prosodies. Sixteen filler sentences were created: eight contained a relative clause/complement clause ambiguity (12) and eight contained an ambiguous pronoun (13). These filler items were recorded by the same phonetician, who produced four different prosodic forms of each sentence. For example, in sentences such as (13), stress was alternately placed on the words "hippo", "kissed", "horse", or "bored" in order to create four contrasting prosodies and decrease awareness of the critical manipulation.

12. You can tell the zebra who's mean.
13. The hippo kissed the horse because he was bored.

All the fillers were included on each list. Consequently, each participant heard 32 critical stimuli and 64 filler stimuli. The stimuli were presented to participants in four blocks. Each sentence (eight critical and 16 filler) appeared once per block in random order and each prosodic structure appeared twice. The order of presentation was reversed for half of the participants.

Thus, the experiment had four independent variables: Prosody Type (high attachment, low attachment, neutral no breaks, neutral ip breaks) was manipulated within participants and Prosody Strength (strong, weak, and two breaks), Syllable Number (1 or 3), and Order (forward, backward) were manipulated between participants.

PROCEDURE

Participants were told that they were going to hear a series of ambiguous sentences that would repeat over the course of the experiment, said with different "intonation" in each instance. They would be offered two possible interpretations of the sentence and asked to choose "which the speaker intended". Participants were encouraged to respond based on their initial intuitions. Upon agreeing to these instructions, participants were seated at a laptop computer and fitted with noise-cancelling headphones.

The experiment was conducted with PST's E-Prime software. Each session began with two practice trials—identical to session trials—designed to acclimate participants to the presentation mode using unambiguous sentences. In each trial, participants heard an utterance once, with "Listen carefully" displayed on the screen. Then the written form of the sentence appeared on the screen above the question "What does the speaker mean?" and two possible interpretations, A and B. For critical stimuli such as sentence (11a) (*You can pinch the dog with the* barrette), the two options would be: (A) *use the* barrette *to pinch the dog*, and (B) *pinch the dog that has the* barrette. With these items still visible, participants had to press a button to indicate that they were ready to listen to the sentence again, listen and then choose an interpretation by pressing A or B. The instrument and modifier interpretations were randomly assigned to either A or B for each trial across the experiment.

RESULTS

The proportion of high-attachment (instrument) responses in each condition was calculated by subject and by item and submitted to subjects and items ANOVA's with Prosody Strength, Syllable Number, and Order as between-subjects and within-items variables and Prosody Type as a within-subject and within-items variable. Prosody Type distinguished the four prosodic structures within each list and was coded according to the predictions of the relative boundary strength hypothesis (low attachment, high attachment, neutral no breaks, neutral ip breaks). Prosody Strength reflected how the break asymmetry between the low attachment and high attachment conditions was achieved (through a single IP break for strong prosody, a single ip break for weak prosody and an ip and IP break for the two-break condition).

As Figure 1 illustrates there was a robust effect of Prosody Type, $F1(3, 144) = 31.81$, $p < .001$; $F2(3, 21) = 34.95$, $p < .001$. Participants predominately gave high-attachment interpretations to utterances with high-attachment prosody ($M = 0.84$). Utterances with low-attachment prosody only received high-attachment interpretations about half the time ($M = 0.51$), while the two neutral conditions were intermediate ($M = 0.66$ and $M = 0.77$ for neutral no breaks and neutral ip breaks, respectively). However, there was also a reliable effect of Prosody Strength, $F1(2, 48) = 3.59$, $p < .05$; $F2(2, 14) = 6.31$, $p < .05$, and a Prosody Strength by type interaction, $F1(6, 144) = 2.74$, $p < .05$; $F2(6, 42) = 3.91$, $p < .005$. If the direction of relative boundary strength was the only prosodic factor influencing syntactic analysis, then we would expect no effects or interactions involving Prosodic Strength. Thus, this interaction indicates that the mapping between prosody and syntax cannot be reduced to this single factor.[5]

To explore this interaction is greater detail we compared each of the pairs of Prosodic Strength conditions in separate ANOVA's. When the strong and weak prosody conditions were compared, there was no interaction between Prosody Strength and Prosody Type, $F1(3, 96) < 1$, $p > .5$; $F2(3, 21) < 1$, $p > .5$. However, the critical interaction was present in the comparison between the two-break condition and both the strong and the weak prosody conditions, $F1(3, 96) = 3.51$, $p < .05$; $F2(3, 21) = 4.71$, $p < .05$, and $F1(3, 96) = 4.37$, $p < .01$; $F2(3, 21) = 8.08$, $p < .001$, respectively. As Figure 1 suggests, the difference between the low-attachment and high-attachment prosodies was greater when the sentence contained only a single prosodic break. Nevertheless, there was a reliable effect of Prosody Type in all three Prosody Strength conditions strong: $F1(3, 48) = 14.30$; $p < .001$; $F2(3, 21) = 19.43$, $p < .001$; weak: $F1(3, 48) = 17.38$; $p < .001$; $F2(3, 21) = 20.40$, $p < .001$, and two breaks: $F1(3, 48) = 4.37$; $p < .01$; $F2(3, 21) = 6.18$, $p < .005$.

[5] In addition, there was a small but reliable interaction between Prosody Strength and Order, $F1(2, 48) = 3.19$, $p = .05$; $F2(2, 14) = 8.92$, $p = .005$. There were no other reliable effects or interactions. Critically, there was no reliable effect of number of syllables in the direct-object noun, $F1(1, 48) = 1.12$, $p > .2$; $F2(1, 7) = 4.22$, $p = .08$, suggesting that our length manipulation did not have a strong influence on interpretation of the ambiguous phrase.

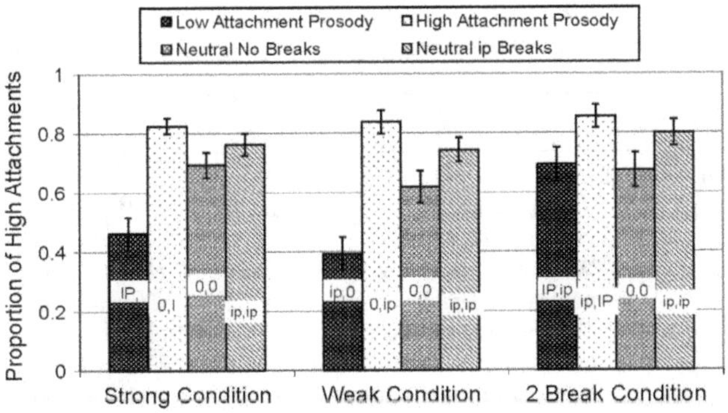

Figure 1. Proportion of high attachment judgements for Study 2.

Next, we examined the unique predictions made by the absolute and relative boundary strength hypotheses in a series of planned comparisons. The results of these tests are given in Table 6.[6] The first thing to notice is that unique predictions of both the RBH and the ABH receive strong support from this data. In particular, the experiment clearly confirms that relative boundary strength influences interpretation when there is no intonational break before the ambiguous phrase (prediction 1a) and that absolute boundary strength influences the interpretation of utterances that would be predicted to have neutral prosody or low-attachment prosody based on relative boundary strength alone (predictions 2a and 2b). Thus, we conclude that both of these factors play some role in syntactic ambiguity resolution.

The second prediction of the relative boundary strength hypothesis receives more modest support from this experiment: when there is an ip break before the ambiguous phrase, the effect of the higher boundary was reliable in the subjects analyses but only marginal in the items analyses (prediction 1b). This suggests that the effect of differences in relative boundary strength is less robust when there is a boundary before the ambiguous phrase, than when there is no boundary in this position (prediction 1a). Such a difference could reflect a fundamental feature of the algorithm mapping prosody to syntax, or it could be driven by the

[6] Where possible, these hypotheses were tested in within-subjects comparisons. However, for some hypotheses between-subjects comparisons were necessary (italics in Table 3). This raises the concern that differences between individual cells could reflect the mix of structures in the two lists rather than differences in the particular cells under consideration. To explore this, we conducted one-way ANOVA's to find out whether the interpretation of the neutral no break (0,0) and the neutral ip break (ip, ip) utterances varied across the three Prosody Strength conditions. We found no evidence that they did (all Fs <1, all ps $>.5$).

TABLE 6
Tests of the RBH and ABH in comprehension judgment data, Study 2

Prediction	*Conditions*[a]	*Result*
Relative boundary strength		
1a. (IP, 0) <(0, 0)	Strong condition: low attachment vs. neutral no breaks	$t1(19) = 4.23$, $p < .001$** $t2(7) = 4.47$, $p < .005$**
1a. (ip, 0) <(0, 0)	Weak condition: low attachment vs. neutral no breaks	$t1(19) = 3.67$, $p < .001$** $t2(7) = 4.15$, $p < .005$**
1b. (IP, ip) <(ip, ip)	Two-break condition: low attachment vs. neutral ip breaks	$t1(19) = 2.43$, $p < .05$* $t2(7) = 1.79$, $p = .058$
1b. (ip, ip) <(0, ip)	Weak condition: neutral ip breaks vs. high attachment	$t1(19) = 1.86$, $p < .05$* $t2(7) = 1.58$, $p = .079$
1b. (IP, ip) <(0, ip)	*Low attachment, two-break condition vs. high attachment, weak condition*	$t1(38) = 2.07$, $p < .05$* $t2(7) = 1.87$, $p = .052$
Absolute boundary strength		
2a. (0, 0) <(ip, ip)	All conditions: neutral no breaks vs. neutral ip breaks	$t1(59) = 3.29$, $p < .001$** $t2(7) = 2.63$, $p < .05$*
2b. (IP, 0) <(IP, ip)	*Low attachment, strong condition vs. low attachment, two-break condition*	$t1(38) = 2.93$, $p < .005$** $t2(7) = 3.43$, $p < .01$*
2b. (ip, 0) <(IP, ip)	*Low attachment, weak condition vs. low attachment, two-break condition*	$t1(38) = 3.78$, $p < .001$** $t2(7) = 6.77$, $p < .001$**
2c. (0, ip) <(0, IP)	*High attachment, weak condition vs. high attachment, strong condition*	$t1(38) < 1$, $p > .3$ $t2(7) < 1$, $p > .3$
2c. (0, ip) <(ip, IP)	*High attachment, weak condition vs. high attachment, two-break condition*	$t1(38) < 1$, $p > .3$ $t2(7) < 1$, $p > .3$

[a]Predictions were tested with within subject comparisons wherever possible. All between subjects tests appear in italics. *$p < .05$, **$p < .005$.

possibility that our measures have greater sensitivity in conditions near the midpoint, relative to conditions near the floor or ceiling.

Finally, one prediction of the absolute boundary strength hypothesis receives no support from this data: for utterances which are predicted to have high attachment under the relative boundary strength hypothesis, absolute boundary has no measurable effect on interpretation (prediction 2c). Again this could reflect a ceiling effect in the data: because participants interpret even (0, ip) utterances as high attachments 84% of the time, there is little room for improvement. Alternately, the lack of any effect here could suggest that ip and IP boundaries are functionally equivalent for the purposes of ambiguity resolution. The strongest version of this hypothesis can be ruled out by the reliable difference between the (IP, ip) and (ip, IP) utterances in the two-break condition, $t1(19) = 2.39$, $p < .05$; $t2(7) = 2.96$, $p < .05$.

However, this leaves open the possibility that IP and ip breaks are equivalent for the purposes of determining *absolute* boundary strength.

GENERAL DISCUSSION

In two studies, we found evidence for both the relative and absolute boundary strength hypotheses. In Study 1, we analysed production data from a referential communication task (Snedeker & Trueswell, 2003) and found that intended syntactic structure influences relative boundary size (even when absolute boundary size is held constant) and influences the absolute size of the final boundary (even when relative boundary size is constant). Even when speakers were unaware of the ambiguity, one unique prediction of each theory was confirmed. In Study 2, we switched our focus to comprehension, which allowed us to gain greater control over the frequency of each structure. The results provided robust support for unique predictions of both the RBH and ABH.

Below we address four issues: (1) we examine the role that variation in pitch accents may have played in Study 2; (2) we compare our findings to those of previous comprehension studies on the RBH; (3) we examine the parallels and divergences between the comprehension and production data; and (4) we explore whether a third hypothesis, the two absolute boundaries hypothesis, might account for these findings.

Disentangling the effects of pitch accents and prosodic phrasing

In the methods section of Study 2, we noted that the pattern of pitch accents in the critical utterances varied systematically across conditions. The speaker was instructed to produce each prosodic structure with the accent pattern that seemed most natural. Because the length (in syllables) of the prosodic phrases varied considerably across conditions, this resulted in systematic differences in the accent pattern. Thus, we must consider the possibility that the effects we observed here reflect differences in the accent pattern instead of, or in addition to, differences in prosodic phrasing. Presumably these effects would be mediated by the connection between accents and discourse functions.

While the precise mapping between accent types and discourse is controversial, most theorists claim that L+H* accents signal new information (Baumann, 2005; Pierrehumbert & Hirschberg, 1990) or discourse themes (Steedman, 2000). The H* accent is often argued to be functionally similar to the L+H* accent but less marked or salient (Baumann, 2005;

Steedman, 2000). In contrast L* accents are typically associated with information that is either given in the discourse or accessible (Baumann, 2005; Pierrehumbert & Hirschberg, 1990). It is unclear how or whether these differences in discourse function might affect syntactic parsing, particularly in the present study where the discourse context is limited. One simple hypothesis is that accents which suggest that constituent is salient and new (e.g., L+H*) might make attachment to that location more probable. Why say more about what is already given?[7]

On this hypothesis, we might predict little or no effect of the accent pattern in cases in which the verb and noun have the same kind of pitch accent. This is true of five of our eight structures: (0, IP), (0, 0), (ip, ip), (ip, 0), and (ip, IP). The three conditions with asymmetric accenting suggest that accenting alone cannot account for our findings. Our (IP, 0) utterances had a stronger accent on the verb (L+H*) than on the noun (L*) but they had one of the lowest proportions of high attachments, as expected on both the RBH and ABH. The (0, ip) utterances had stronger accents on the noun (L+H*) than the verb (L* or no pitch accent at all) but they were consistently interpreted as high attachments. Our (IP, ip) utterances had stronger accents on the verb (H*) than the noun (L*), which might nudge them towards high attachment. These utterances were interpreted as high attachments about 69% of the time, landing in the middle of the structures tested.

None of the critical conclusions in Table 6 can be attributed to differences in accent patterns. For all five tests of the RBH, the predicted effect of accenting is either neutral or goes in the *opposite direction* of the observed and predicted effect of boundary strength. For example, we observed that (0, ip) utterances received more high attachments than (ip, ip) utterances, despite the fact that the (0, ip) utterances had a stronger accent on the noun (L+H*) than the verb (L* or none) which would be predicted to promote low attachment, while the (ip, ip) utterances had L* accents in both positions. Similarly, for the ABH, there are two critical comparisons in which the predicted effect of accenting is either neutral or goes against the observed effect of boundary strength. For example, in support of prediction 2b, we found that (IP, 0) utterances were less likely to be interpreted as high attachments than (IP, ip) utterances even though they had a stronger accent on the verb (L+H*) than (IP, ip) utterances (H*) and the same type of accent on the noun (both L*). Finally, our null findings for prediction 2c of the ABH cannot be attributed to competing effects of boundary strength and accenting. The ABH hypothesis predicts that (0, ip) utterances should receive fewer high attachments than (0, IP) and (ip, IP) utterances. Given the hypothesis sketched above, the accent pattern on these utterances would

[7] This is clearly inspired by Schafer and colleagues' *Focus Attraction Hypothesis* (Schafer et al., 1996), though they cannot be blamed for our particular implementation.

be expected to reinforce this prediction: the (0, ip) utterances have an L + H* accent on the noun and a weak accent (L* or none) on the verb, promoting low attachment, while the other two utterances have the same type of accent in both positions (H* and L*, respectively) creating a more neutral prosody.

In fact, of the 10 comparisons in Table 6, there is only one case in which the variation in accent type offers a competing explanation to hypotheses based on boundary strength. In support of prediction 2b, we found that (ip, 0) utterances received fewer high attachments than (IP, ip) utterances. This is consistent not only with the difference in absolute boundary size, but also with a difference in accenting: the (IP, ip) utterances have a weaker accent on the noun (L*) than on the verb (H*) while the (ip, 0) utterances have H* accents in both positions. But this does not alter our conclusions, as we noted above the other comparison testing prediction 2b cannot be explained by accenting.

In sum, accenting fails to account for the observed data pattern, predicting a reversal of several observed effects, as well as effects that are not present. While accenting may influence syntactic attachment under some circumstances (contrast Lee & Watson, 2008; Schafer, Carter, Clifton, & Frazier, 1996) in the present study, the effects of prosodic phrasing appear to dominate. The question of how accenting, discourse structure, and prosodic phrasing influence syntactic parsing clearly warrants more research.

Comparisons with previous comprehension experiments

To those who have followed the literature on prosody and ambiguity resolution, these results may be somewhat surprising. Over the past 6 years many researchers have adopted some version of the RBH and have found support for it in data from both comprehension (Carlson et al., 2001; Clifton et al., 2002) and production (Kraljic & Brennan, 2005; Schafer et al., 2005, Snedeker & Trueswell, 2003), suggesting that there is ample evidence for this position. But in fact few studies test predictions that are unique to the RBH, and no study to date has focused on exploring the predictions of ABH, while holding relative boundary strength constant. Instead, researchers have conceived of the problem as one of "global" vs. "local" prosody, in which any evidence for global structure having an influence would be evidence against the hypothesis that the interface is purely local.

To determine whether these findings were consistent with prior experiments, we looked at prior experimental studies on the effects of prosody on the resolution of attachment ambiguities. We could find only three papers which tested a unique prediction of either the RBH or ABH. These papers are summarised in Table 7.

TABLE 7
A comparison of the findings of Study 2 and prior experiments testing the relative and absolute boundary hypotheses

Prediction	*Prior study*	*Effect in prior experiments?*	*Effect in study 2?*
Relative boundary strength			
1a. (IP, 0) <(0, 0)		Not tested	√
1a. (ip, 0) <(0, 0)	Schafer (1997), Exp. 1, $p < .05$	√	√
1b. (IP, ip) <(ip, ip)	Carlson et al. (2001), Exp. 3, unreported but likely Clifton et al. (2002), Exp. 2, $p < .05$[a]	√	√
1b. (ip, ip) <(0, ip)	Carlson et al. (2001), Exp. 4, unreported but likely Clifton et al. (2002), Exp. 1, *ns*; Exp. 2, $p < .05$[a]	√	√
1b. (IP, ip) <(0, ip)	Clifton et al. (2002), Exp. 2, $p < .05$	√	√
1c. (IP, IP) <(0, IP)	Clifton et al. (2002), Exp. 1, $p < .05$; Exp. 3, $p < .05$	√	Not tested
1c. (IP, IP) <(ip, IP)		Not tested	Not tested
Absolute boundary strength			
2a. (0, 0) <(ip, ip)		Not tested	√
2a. (ip, ip) <(IP, IP)	Carlson et al. (2001), Exp. 3, unlikely Clifton et al. (2002), Exp. 1, unlikely	X	Not tested
2a. (0, 0) <(IP, IP)		Not tested	Not tested
2b. (IP, 0) <(IP, ip)	Carlson et al. (2001), Exp. 3, unlikely	X	√
2b. (ip, 0) <(IP, ip)		Not tested	√
2c. (0, ip) <(0, IP)	Carlson et al. (2001), Exp. 4, unlikely Clifton et al. (2002), Exp. 1, unlikely	X	X
2c. (0, ip) <(ip, IP)	Carlson et al. (2001), Exp. 4, unlikely	X	X

Note: X, no effect; √, prediction confirmed.
[a]Clifton et al. (2002), Experiment 2, included four different kinds of attachment ambiguities. This contrast was significant in the overall analysis but not for all ambiguity types.

In compiling this table, we entered all cases in which the comparison of interest was analysed with a direct statistical test. However, since the ABH was rarely tested explicitly, we also entered the results of studies in which no planned comparison of the cells was conducted but the outcome was inferable (from the means and the pattern of main effects). In the table, these findings are labelled “likely” and “unlikely”.

For the most part the results of Study 2 converge with the prior findings. Of the 10 predictions that we tested, seven had been previously explored. In four cases, the prediction was confirmed in all studies and in two cases it was not confirmed by any of the studies. In only one case was there an actual difference in the findings. We found more high attachments for (IP, ip) utterances than for (IP, 0) ones, while Carlson et al. (2001) did not. Two details of their experiment may help to explain this discrepancy. First, as the authors point out, the utterances included in the (IP, 0) condition varied in their prosodic structure. About half appeared to contain an intermediate phrase break in position B. Thus the two conditions actually overlapped in structure. Second, both structures were interpreted as low attachments on about 85% of the trials, raising the possibility that ceiling effects limited the sensitivity of the experiment.

Despite these similarities, the present study diverges from the others in finding substantial support for unique predictions of the ABH. Table 7 suggests that this reflects the particular contrasts that were studied. In Study 2, we found reliable evidence for the influence of absolute boundary size when we contrasted ip or IP boundaries with null boundaries. However, we failed to find effects when we contrasted ip boundaries with IP boundaries. The prior work has focused almost exclusively on the latter contrast.

Integrating the findings from production and comprehension

It is difficult to directly compare the results of the comprehension and production studies. The power of the production study varied across the cells but was generally reduced relative to the comprehension study. In the comprehension study, each prosodic structure appeared equally often but participants had a bias towards making high attachments. In the production study, high and low attachments appeared equally often but the participants produced some prosodic structures more than others. Thus, there is a different profile of sensitivity across the cells in each experiment. Nevertheless a few observations can be made.

First, several predictions were confirmed for both producers and comprehenders, suggesting that these are stable features of the prosody–syntax interface. This included the strong contrast between the (IP, 0) and (0, 0) structures, supporting the RBH, which was present in both aware and unaware speakers. In the case of the ABH, all contrasts which pitted an ip or IP boundary in position B against a null boundary were confirmed for the aware speakers and the comprehenders.

Where the two data sets diverged, the interpretation is less clear. This occurred in two places. First, most of the unique predictions of the RBH were confirmed in comprehension but not in production. Here no strong conclusions are possible. The production data are sparse in most of these cells.

It is tempting to conclude that an effect in comprehension implies that the distinction must be reflected in production: Why use a cue which isn't valid? But it is certainly conceivable that two systems could have different operating principles. For example, some relative boundary strength contrasts could be correlated with syntactic attachment during production because each variable is correlated with some third factor (e.g., absolute boundary strength or the length in syllables of the respective constituents). When these confounds are removed (as in the present studies), we would expect to find no effect of syntax on the relevant contrast during production. The comprehension system, however, could have acquired a mapping between relative boundary strength and attachment on the basis of this correlation and might continue to show sensitivity to the contrast under these circumstances.

The second discrepancy is in the final prediction of the ABH. This contrast pits utterances with the (0, ip) structure against those with the (0, IP) or (ip, IP) structure. Producers are more likely to use the latter for high attachments but comprehenders categorically select high attachments for all three utterance types. This difference is intriguing because the comprehension study has considerably more power than the production study. The discrepancy could reflect ceiling effects in the comprehension data. However, our examination of prior studies suggests that this is a fairly robust finding in judgment tasks (see Carlson et al., 2001; Clifton et al., 2002). Alternately, it could reflect a difference in how the effects of absolute boundary strength arise during comprehension and production. Further research on these structures using more parallel materials and tasks would be informative.

Two absolute boundaries?

These data call out for a third hypothesis that can explain the observed effects of both relative and absolute boundary strength. One tempting proposal is that attachment depends on both the absolute strength of the boundary at both position A and the absolute strength of the boundary at position B. We will refer to this hypothesis as the two absolute boundaries hypothesis (2ABH).[8] In contrast with the RBH and ABH (see 7 and 8), 2ABH does not provide a relative ordering of all the possible structures, unless additional assumptions are added about how the sizes of the two boundaries interact. However, it does make the following predictions.

---

[8] Full development of 2ABH would have to specify how the relevant location A is defined. The ABH (as we defined it) grants no role to an earlier boundary. RBH proposals typically argue that multiple boundaries between the high-attachment site and the low-attachment site may be relevant (see e.g., Schafer et al., 2000). In the short simple sentences used in the present study, we can bypass this issue, since there are no likely break locations between position A and B.

14. The size of the boundary at location A should influence attachment

(IP, 0) < (ip, 0) < (0, 0)
(IP, ip) < (ip, ip) < (0, ip)
(IP, IP) < (ip, IP) < (0, IP)

15. The size of the boundary at location B should influence attachment

(IP, 0) < (IP, ip) < (IP, IP)
(ip, 0) < (ip, ip) < (ip, IP)
(0, 0) < (0, ip) < (0, IP)

All the predictions in (15) involve varying the size of the boundary at B and thus are also made by the ABH. Most of the predictions in (14) are also made by the RBH, however, there are two predictions which are unique to the 2ABH:

16. Unique predictions of 2ABH (relative to ABH and RBH)

a. (IP, 0) < (ip, 0)
b. (ip, IP) < (0, IP)

Our data provide scant support for either prediction (see Table 1 and Figure 1). Both of the prosodic structures in 16a are strongly associated with low-attachment contexts in aware speakers and were generally interpreted as low attachments in the comprehension study, while both of the structures in 16b were strongly associated with the high-attachment contexts in aware speakers and interpreted as high attachments in the comprehension study (all $ps > .5$). The data pattern for unaware speakers was murkier. There is a marginal effect suggesting that the (ip, 0) structure appeared more in high-attachment contexts than the (IP, 0) structure ($p = .057$), which would support the prediction in 16a. However, there is also a marginal effect that runs counter to the prediction in 16b: the (ip, IP) structure was more associated with high-attachment contexts than the (0, IP) structure ($p = .073$).

We might also ask whether our data provides any unique support for the RBH or ABH relative to the 2ABH. In the case of the RBH, there are no unique predictions since all predictions which are not shared by the ABH necessarily involve varying the size of the boundary at location A, and thus are also predictions of the 2ABH. However, for the ABH there are several unique predictions relative to both of the other hypotheses.

17. Unique predictions of ABH (relative to 2ABH and RBH)

c. (0, 0) < (ip, ip) < (IP, IP)
d. (ip, 0) < (IP, ip)
e. (0, ip) < (ip, IP)

Our results provide robust support for these predictions. All these predictions were tested and confirmed for aware speakers in Study 1 (see Table 2). Study 2 only tested some of these predictions because (IP, IP) utterances were not included, but two of the three predictions that were tested were confirmed (see Table 6). To account for these findings the 2ABH would have to be supplemented to grant a privileged role to the lower boundary. In sum, our results suggest that the 2ABH does not provide an adequate explanation for the observed attachment patterns.

FINAL WORDS

These studies support unique predictions of both the relative boundary strength hypothesis and the absolute boundary strength hypothesis. Thus our findings imply that neither hypothesis alone is sufficient to account for the relation between prosodic phrasing and the attachment of an ambiguous phrase. In an ideal world, we would now propose an alternate model of the prosody–syntax interface which could account for both sets of findings. Lacking this insight, we can only point to the questions that must be resolved before such a theory can be constructed.

First, greater clarity is needed about the contexts in which ip and IP boundaries have distinct effects and the contexts in which they are treated as equivalent. In our production data, we find robust differences between the two boundary types in comparisons where ABH is in question. However, our comprehension data (and that of Carlson et al., 2001) suggest that the two boundary types are distinct for tests of the RBH but equivalent in tests of the ABH.

Second, it is critical that we know if the effects of relative and absolute boundary strength stem from the same mechanism or different mechanisms. Resolving this question will require on-line experiments that address the unique predictions of each hypothesis and provide information not only about the pattern of interpretation, but also about the processes by which these patterns arise. Our comprehension data hint at the possibility that the two processes may be distinct. Effects of relative boundary size clearly depend on a prosodic representation that distinguishes between ip and IP boundaries. In contrast, effects of absolute boundary size may depend on a coarser representation of prosody in which fails to capture this distinction. This raises the intriguing possibility that the effects of absolute and relative boundary size arise at different points in processing. For example, absolute boundary effects might result from lower-level processes that chunk input for analysis and treat all breaks as identical, while relative boundary effects could result from higher-level processes that attempt to align syntactic structure with a rich representation of prosodic structure.

Finally, in the current paper we have followed the dominant theory of prosodic structure and the dominant practice in psycholinguistics by treating prosodic boundaries as discrete categories and assuming that all variation in interpretation is linked to the categorical status of these boundaries. To the best of our knowledge only one comprehension study has ever tested this assumption (in the context of the prosody–syntax interface). This experiment found the predicted null effect (Experiment 2; Carlson et al., 2001) but additional evidence for this position is critical.

REFERENCES

Allbritton, D., McKoon, G., & Ratcliff, R. (1996). Reliability of prosodic cues for resolving syntactic ambiguity. *Journal of Experimental Psychology: Learning, Memory, and Cognition, 22*, 714–735. doi:10.1.1.122.4

Altmann, G. T. M. (1998). Ambiguity in sentence processing. *Trends in Cognitive Sciences, 2*(4), 146–152. doi:10.1016/S1364-6613(98)01153-X

Baumann, S. (2005, September). *Degrees of givenness and their prosodic marking*. Paper presented at the international symposium on Discourse and prosody as a complex interface, Aix-en-Provence.

Beach, C. M. (1991). The interpretation of prosodic patterns at points of syntactic structure ambiguity: Evidence for cue trading relations. *Journal of Memory and Language, 30*, 644–663. doi:10.1016/0749-596X(91)90030-N

Beckman, M. E. (1996). The parsing of prosody. *Language & Cognitive Processes, 11*, 17–67. doi:10.1080/016909696387213

Beckman, M. E., & Hirschberg, J. (1994). *The ToBI annotation conventions.* Columbus, OH: Ohio State University.

Beckman, M. E., & Pierrehumbert, J. B. (1986). Intonational structure in Japanese and English. *Phonology Yearbook, 3*, 255–309.

Carlson, K., Clifton, C., & Frazier, L. (2001). Prosodic boundaries in adjunct attachment. *Journal of Memory & Language, 45*(1), 58–81. doi:10.1006/jmla.2000.2762

Clifton, C. Jr., Carlson, K., & Frazier, L. (2002). Informative prosodic boundaries. *Language and Speech, 45*, 87–114.

Cooper, W. E., & Paccia-Cooper, J. (1980). *Syntax and speech.* Cambridge, MA: Harvard University Press.

Cutler, A., Dahan, D., & van Donselaar, W. (1997). Prosody in the comprehension of spoken language: A literature review. *Language & Speech, 40*(2), 141–201.

Fernald, A., & McRoberts, G. (1996). Prosodic bootstrapping: A critical analysis of the argument and the evidence. In J. Morgan & K. Demuth (Eds.), *Signal to syntax* (pp. 365–388). Mahwah, NJ: Erlbaum.

Ferreira, F. (1988). *Planning and timing in sentence production: The syntax-to-phonology conversion.* Unpublished dissertation, University of Massachusetts, Amherst, MA.

Gee, J. P., & Grosjean, F. (1983). Performance structures: A psycholinguistic and linguistic appraisal. *Cognitive Psychology, 15*, 411–458.

Kjelgaard, M. M., & Speer, S. R. (1999). Prosodic facilitaion and interference in the resolution of temporary syntactic closure ambiguity. *Journal of Memory and Language, 40*, 153–194. doi: 10.1006/jmla.1998.2620

Kraljic, T., & Brennan, S. E. (2005). Prosodic disambiguation of syntactic structure: For the speaker or for the addressee? *Cognitive Psychology, 50*(2), 194–231.

Lee, E.-K., & Watson, D. (2008, March). *Effects of focal accents on relative clause attachment: Accent effects or memory effects?* Poster presented at the 21st annual CUNY conference on human sentence processing, Chapel Hill, NC.

Lehiste, I. (1973). Phonetic disambiguation of syntactic ambiguity. *Glossa, 7*, 102–122.

Lehiste, I., Olive, J. P., & Streeter, L. A. (1976). Role of duration in disambiguating syntactically ambiguous sentences. *Journal of the Acoustical Society of America, 60*, 1199–1202.

Marcus, M., & Hindle, D. (1990). Description theory and intonation boundaries. In G. Altmann (Ed.), *Cognitive models of speech processing: Computational and psycholinguistic perspectives* (pp. 483–512). Cambridge, MA: MIT Press.

Marslen-Wilson, W. D., Tyler, L. K., Warren, P., Grenier, P., & Lee, C. S. (1992). Prosodic effects in minimal attachment. *Quarterly Journal of Experimental Psychology, 45A*, 73–87. doi:10.1080/14640749208401316

Nagel, H. N., Shapiro, L. P., Tuller, B., & Nawy, R. (1996). Prosodic influences on the resolution of temporary ambiguity during on-line sentence processing. *Journal of Psycholinguistic Research, 25*(2), 319–344.

Nespor, M. A., & Vogel, I. (1986). *Prosodic phonology.* Boston: Kluwer.

Pierrehumbert, J. B., & Hirschberg, J. (1990). The meaning of intonational contours in the interpretation of discourse. In P. R. Cohen, J. Morgan, & M. E. Pollack (Eds.), *Intentions in communication* (pp. 271–311). Cambridge, MA: MIT Press.

Price, P., Ostendorf, M., Shattuck-Hufnagel, S., & Fong, C. (1991). The use of prosody in syntactic disambiguation. *Journal of the Acoustical Society of America, 90*, 2956–2970.

Pynte, J., & Prieur, B., (1996). Prosodic breaks and attachment decisions in sentence parsing. *Language and Cognitive Processes, 11*, 165–192. doi:10.1080/016909696387259

Schafer, A., Carter, J., Clifton, C., & Frazier, L. (1996). Focus in relative clause construal. *Language and Cognitive Processes, 11*(1/2), 135–163. doi:10.1080/016909696387240

Schafer, A., Speer, S., & Warren, P. (2005). Prosodic influences on the production and comprehension of syntactic ambiguity in a game-based conversation task. In J. C. Trueswell & M. K. Tanenhaus (Eds.), *Approaches to studying world situated language use* (pp. 209–226). Cambridge, MA: MIT Press.

Schafer, A., Speer, S., Warren, P., & White, S. (2000). Intonational disambiguation in sentence production and comprehension. *Journal of Psycholinguistic Research, 29*, 169–182.

Schafer, A. J. (1997). *Prosodic parsing: The role of prosody in sentence comprehension.* Unpublished doctoral dissertation, University of Massachusetts, Amherst, MA

Selkirk, E. O. (1986). On derived domains in sentence phonology. *Phonology Yearbook, 3*, 371–405.

Shattuck-Hufnagel, S., & Turk, A. E. (1996). A prosody tutorial for investigators of auditory sentence processing. *Journal of Psycholinguistic Research, 25*(2), 193–247.

Snedeker, J., & Trueswell, J. (2003). Using prosody to avoid ambiguity: Effects of speaker awareness and referential context. *Journal of Memory and Language, 48*, 103–130.

Snedeker, J., & Trueswell, J. C. (2004). The developing constraints on parsing decisions: The role of lexical-biases and referential scenes in child and adult sentence processing. *Cognitive Psychology, 49*(3), 238–299.

Steedman, M. (2000). Information structure and syntax-phonology interface. *Linguistic Inquiry, 31*(4), 649–689.

Steinhauer, K., Alter, K., & Friederici, A. D. (1999). Brain responses indicate immediate use of prosodic cues in natural speech processing. *Nature Neuroscience, 2*, 191–196.

Warren, P. (1999). Prosody and sentence processing. In S. Garrod & M. Pickering (Eds.), *Language processing* (pp. 155–188). Hove, UK: Psychology Press.

Warren, P., Grabe, E., & Nolan, F. (1995). Prosody, phonology and parsing in closure ambiguities. *Language and Cognitive Processes, 10*, 457–486. doi:10.1080/01690969508407112

Watson, D., & Gibson, E. (2004). The relationship between intonational phrasing and syntactic structure in language production. *Language and Cognitive Processes, 19*, 713–755. doi:10.1080/01690960444000070

Watson, D., & Gibson, E. (2005). Intonational phrasing and constituency in language production and comprehension. *Studia Linguistica, 59*, 279–300.

Weber, A., Grice, M., & Crocker, M. W. (2006). The role of prosody in the interpretation of structural ambiguities: A study of anticipatory eye movements. *Cognition, 99*, B63–B72. doi:10.1016/j.cognition.2005.07.001

APPENDIX: SENTENCES FOR STUDY 2

Critical sentences

1. You can turn over the whale/killer whale with the stick.
2. You can point at the dog/puppy dog with the flower.
3. You can drag the cat/kitty cat with the pipe cleaner.
4. You can throw the bear/panda bear with the cup.
5. You can scratch the whale/killer whale with the paper.
6. You can pinch the dog/puppy dog with the barrette.
7. You can feel the cat/kitty cat with the feather.
8. You can blow on the bear/panda bear with the fan.

Pronoun ambiguities (implicit causality)

1. The cow envied the zebra because he is mean.
2. The elephant ignored the monkey because he won the race.
3. The giraffe kicked the lion because he lost his rock.
4. The hippo kissed the horse because he was bored.
5. The horse laughed at the giraffe because she had a new toy.
6. The lion liked the frog because she is happy.
7. The lobster looked at the dolphin because she had eaten too much.
8. The pig whispered to the cow because she made new friends easily.

Relative clause/complement clause ambiguities

1. You can whisper to the little bear who's brown.
2. You can tell the giraffe who's naughty.
3. You can inform the hippo who's hungry.
4. You can show the horse who's new.
5. You can teach the cow who's good.
6. You can ask the lobster who's tired.
7. You can whisper to the lion who yawned.
8. You can tell the zebra who's nice.

LANGUAGE AND COGNITIVE PROCESSES
2010, 25 (7/8/9), 1265–1293

Psychology Press
Taylor & Francis Group

Phoneme restoration methods for investigating prosodic influences on syntactic processing

Iglika Stoyneshka[1], Janet Dean Fodor[1], and Eva M. Fernández[1,2]

[1]*Program in Linguistics, Graduate Center, City University of New York, New York, NY, USA,* [2]*Queens College, City University of New York, New York, NY, USA*

We present a novel method for establishing the preferred interpretation of ambiguities in spoken sentences. It makes use of the phoneme restoration effect (Warren, 1970): when noise replaces phoneme(s) in a word, listeners report that they perceive the word as intact and congruent with the context. If the word disambiguates a potentially ambiguous sentence, the word that is "heard" reveals which interpretation listeners assigned. The advantage of this method is its naturalness: no deliberative judgements, no interrupting task, no attention drawn to the ambiguity, and no reliance on anomalous sentences. Our experiments examined the contribution of prosodic phrasing to syntactic ambiguity resolution, using three different tasks to probe what participants thought they had heard: Visual Word Choice, Sentence Repetition, and Speech Shadowing. All three tasks showed a powerful effect of prosody on the resolution of two syntactic ambiguities in Bulgarian.

Keywords: Phoneme restoration; Syntactic ambiguity; Prosody; Shadowing; Bulgarian; Methodology.

Correspondence should be addressed to Iglika Stoyneshka, Program in Linguistics, Graduate Center, City University of New York, 365 Fifth Avenue, New York, NY 10016-4309, USA. E-mail: idst_r@yahoo.com

We thank the audiences at the conference on Experimental and Theoretical Advances in Prosody (Cornell University, April 2008) and the Charles Clifton Festschrift (The Royal Society of Edinburgh, May 2008), as well as two anonymous reviewers, for comments and suggestions that have improved this paper.

http://www.psypress.com/lcp DOI: 10.1080/01690961003661192

STUDYING AMBIGUITY RESOLUTION

Ambiguity resolution has long been used in sentence processing research as a tool to reveal what the human sentence parsing mechanism finds easy or difficult, allowing researchers to test hypotheses about its architecture and mode of operation. Ambiguity resolution preferences can indicate, for example, whether incoming words tend to be attached high or low, whether anaphors favour local or distant antecedents, and what factors influence such choices. For the relative clause (RC) attachment ambiguity illustrated in (1), potential factors of interest include the length of the RC, whether the RC is restrictive or nonrestrictive, the presence of a preposition between the two nouns in languages where it is optional (e.g., Croatian; Lovrić, 2003), whether the RC is preceded by a comma in writing, and the relative plausibility of the two meanings.

(1) I kissed the brother of the actress who was looking in the mirror.

One factor that has attracted interest in recent psycholinguistic research is the prosodic contour of a spoken sentence. For example, Kjelgaard and Speer (1999) investigated the role of prosody in what they called "late closure" versus "early closure" sentences like those in (2), where the noun phrase (NP) following the first verb could be its object as in (2a) or the subject of the next clause as in (2b). They found that the locus of a prosodic boundary (marked here by the symbol ||) could significantly facilitate or inhibit a particular interpretation.

(2) a. Whenever Roger leaves the house || it's dark.
b. Whenever Roger leaves || the house is dark.

In reading experiments, the subject NP interpretation (2b) was found to be more difficult than the object NP interpretation (2a), indicating a strong bias in this construction to postpone closure of the first clause as long as possible. However, in auditory presentation with a prosodic break after the first verb, as indicated in (2b), the processing disadvantage of "early closure" was eliminated.

The experiments reported here on two ambiguities in Bulgarian provide new evidence of the influence of prosody on ambiguity resolution. However, the primary goal of these experiments was to explore and evaluate a family of novel methods for detecting perceivers' favoured interpretations of auditorily presented ambiguous sentences, methods that exploit the phenomenon of phoneme restoration.

A variety of methods are currently in use for establishing the preferred reading of an ambiguity and the role of prosody. The simplest is a postsentence comprehension question, e.g., *Who was looking in the mirror?* for the ambiguity in (1) (Fernández, 2007) or a postsentence judgement of prosodic acceptability (Frazier, Clifton, & Carlson, 2004). Another technique is cross-modal naming, in which participants read aloud a visually presented word immediately following a spoken sentence fragment, e.g., *Flying planes ARE/IS* (Kjelgaard & Speer, 1999; Marslen-Wilson, Tyler, Warren, Grenier, & Lee, 1992). Schafer, Speer, Warren, and White (2000) designed an interactive board-game providing both production and comprehension data for semi-scripted sentences. Ferreira, Anes, and Horine (1996) developed an auditory moving window paradigm, to parallel standard self-paced reading paradigms. Event-related potential (ERP) methods are now employed to track the perception of prosodic breaks, and to assess sensitivity to prosodic anomalies (Augurzky, 2006; Eckstein & Friederici, 2006; Steinhauer, Alter, & Friederici, 1999). And the visual world paradigm, with spoken input, provides finely timed data about which referents or actions are evoked in the minds of listeners (Snedeker & Trueswell, 2003; Watson, Gunlogson, & Tanenhaus, 2006).

Despite all these options, we have been seeking a new method, one that would satisfy some important criteria of naturalness and unobtrusiveness as well as sensitivity to prosodic influences on parsing. Ideally, this would be a method that is less likely to draw attention to the ambiguity, as postsentence comprehension questions tend to do. It would also avoid drawing attention to the importance of the prosody, as is inevitable when participants are asked to judge prosodic acceptability, or when syntactic constructions are presented with conflicting prosody as is common in ERP studies. Finally, the optimal experimental task would be one in which participants' responses are spontaneous and nondeliberative, because their attention is focused elsewhere than on the phenomenon actually under investigation.

The visual world paradigm, in which participants' eye movements over a carefully constructed visual display are monitored as they listen to auditory inputs, clearly meets these criteria (see Watson et al., 2006). This protocol has been employed for studying prosodic effects, such as the interpretive consequences of contrastive pitch accents (Ito & Speer, 2005; Watson et al., 2006). It can be used also for investigating prosodic effects on syntactic ambiguity resolution, as in the study of PP-attachment (e.g., *Tap the frog with the flower*) by Snedeker and Trueswell (2003). It remains to be seen how adaptable it will prove to be for other syntactic ambiguities, like those in (1) and (2) above, which will depend in part on the practical matter of how readily the different interpretations can be displayed visually.

Our approach, in contrast to existing methods, relies on a lexical disambiguation, similar to the cross-modal task employed by Marslen-Wilson et al. (1992) but without the use of interrupted sentences; the latter may create undue biases if hearers tend to construe the end of the presented sentence fragment as the end of a phrase. Our method takes advantage of the phoneme restoration effect. We ask participants: "What word did you *hear*?"

THE PHONEME RESTORATION EFFECT

The phoneme restoration effect was first described by Warren (1970) on the basis of a very small-scale experiment, with the single item shown in (3). The sentence was recorded and then the *s* in *legislatures* was replaced by a cough before presentation to listeners (for an auditory demonstration, see Warren, 2008, and accompanying sound files).

(3) The state governors met with their respective legi▒latures in the capital city.

(We use the symbol ▒ to indicate the location where one or more phonemes have been replaced.) Warren reported that 19 out of 20 listeners denied that any speech sound was missing; the one person who suspected a missing sound guessed a wrong one. Warren and colleagues and other researchers since (e.g., Bashford & Warren, 1979; Samuel, 1981, 1996; Sherman, 1971) describe this effect as a genuine perceptual illusion, in which listeners are convinced that they are hearing an uninterrupted speech stream even though in fact a portion of it is absent and has been replaced by noise (a cough in (3), but usually white noise). Warren's first experiment was replicated with the whole syllable *gis* in *legislatures* replaced by noise, showing that the restoration effect was not disrupted by stretches of noise up to a few hundred milliseconds (Warren & Warren, 1970).

Many more stringent tests followed (for a review, see Samuel, 1996). Some focused on the nature of the replacing sound, and generally found that the illusion was effective when the noise was loud enough that it could have masked the speech sound had it been present. The strength of the illusion also depended on the acoustic properties of the excised phoneme, as well as on factors such as word/nonword status, word length, and position of the noise in the word. Most relevant for our purposes is the effect of sentential context on phoneme restoration. Early work by Sherman (1971) had found that the noise was typically "heard" as a phoneme that made a word congruent with the rest of the sentence, even when the relevant context occurred *after* the critical word (e.g., the word with noise in *The ▒eel is on the shoe* was heard as *heel* rather than as *meal* or *wheel*). In later work Samuel (1981) noted that participants tended to report *battle* in the context of *soldier* in (4a) and *batter* in the context of *pitcher* in (4b).

(4) a. The soldier's thoughts of the dangerous bat▓ made him very nervous.
b. The pitcher's thoughts of the dangerous bat▓ made him very nervous.

In general, contextually predictable words were reported more often and were more often judged to be intact. Note that the restored phoneme in (4) reveals a semantic (or at least associative) influence on lexical ambiguity resolution.

Our goal was to see whether a restored phoneme can reveal a prosodic influence on syntactic ambiguity resolution. Neither prosody nor syntactic ambiguity has been previously examined using phoneme restoration. Samuel's target sentences were evidently intended to have the same prosodic contour (though recorded separately; Samuel, 1981, p. 487), so they did not allow assessment of prosodic effects. The sentential materials tested by Samuel (1981) and Sherman (1971) were lexically but not structurally ambiguous, and they were disambiguated only by semantic–pragmatic biases.

SELECTION OF MATERIALS FOR TESTING

In all experiments reported here, participants listened to a stimulus sentence that was temporarily structurally ambiguous but could be disambiguated to one analysis or the other by a single later word (cf. the *is* versus *it's* of Kjelgaard and Speer's example (2) above). The disambiguating words were of roughly equal length and prominence in the sentence, and differed by at most two or three phonemes. This minimally different region was excised from the waveform and replaced by white noise in both cases, so that the resulting waveforms now had identical segmental content; they differed only in their prosodic contours. The question of interest was whether participants would restore the missing phoneme(s) in such a way as to create the word that was compatible with the syntactic analysis implied by the prosody.

Detailed description of all the experimental materials is given below. In the present section, we explain what motivated the choice of language and the particular ambiguities within that language, as tools for assessing the efficacy of the phoneme restoration methodology.

Our test language was Bulgarian, a Slavic language with rich morphology including obligatory gender and number agreement, providing ample opportunity to find matched pairs of disambiguating words differing only in morphologically expressed features. Two syntactic constructions were tested: the NP coordination ambiguity in (5) and the RC attachment ambiguity in (6). In (5), number agreement in the second verb (in boldface in the examples) indicates whether or not *Ivan* and *Mimi* form a conjoined NP. If they do, the second verb must be plural; if they do not (i.e., if it is *Ani* and *Ivan* that are conjoined), the verb must be singular. In (6), the gender marking on the relative pronoun (boldface) dictates the antecedent for the relative pronoun, and hence the attachment position of the RC.

(5) a. Nakraia sreshtnahme Ani || i Ivan i Mimi **biaha** vav vaztorg.

[V N1] [N2 N3 V]

In the end meet-past-1p.pl Ani and Ivan and Mimi were in ecstasy

b. Nakraia sreshtnahme Ani i Ivan || i Mimi **beše** vav vaztorg.

[V N1 N2] [N3 V]

In the end meet-past-1p.pl Ani and Ivan and Mimi was in ecstasy

In the end (we) met Annie and Ivan and Mimi were/was ecstatic.

(6) a. Podtseniha advokata || na pevitsata **koiato** kupi imenieto.

[V [N1 [N2 [RC]]]]

Underestimate-past lawyer-m of singer-f who-f buy-past estate-det

b. Podtseniha advokata na pevitsata || **kojto** kupi imenieto

[V [[N1 N2] [RC]]]

Underestimate-past lawyer-m of singer-f who-m buy-past estate-det

(They) underestimated the lawyer of the singer who bought the estate.

In both types of experimental materials, the disambiguating word was a closed class item (a function word): a copula verb for NP coordination sentences as in (5), and a relative pronoun for RC attachment sentences as in (6). Thus, the two disambiguating words for a given sentence did not differ in lexical meaning; their disambiguating role was due solely to their agreement features (number or gender).

We selected these two constructions for testing because their responsiveness to prosodic disambiguation has been studied in other languages and with other methods, providing existing data against which the outcomes of the phoneme restoration tasks can be compared. Coordination ambiguities as in (5) are disambiguated prosodically, perhaps universally, by inserting a prosodic phrase break at one point or another in the sequence of conjuncts. A break after N1 encourages the interpretation in (5a); a break after N2 favours the interpretation in (5b). This ambiguity, and its corresponding prosodic disambiguations, has been the focus of a number of investigations of the relationship between prosody and syntax, dating back to seminal work by Lehiste (1972), Lehiste, Olive, and Streeter (1976), and Streeter (1978). A variant of this construction is featured in instruments designed to detect expressive and perceptive prosody deficits in children (see Peppé & McCann, 2003; Peppé, McCann, Gibbon, O'Hare, & Rutherford, 2007).

Clifton, Carlson, and Frazier (2006) examined English sentences like (7a) containing an ambiguous sequence of three conjoined or disjoined nouns (proper names or common nouns with determiners).

(7) a. Pat or Jay and Lee convinced the bank president to extend the mortgage.

b. Who convinced the bank president?
Pat or (Jay + Lee) (1 or 2 people)   (Pat or Jay) + Lee (2 people)

The sentences were presented auditorily with a prosodic break placed early (after *Pat*) or late (after *Jay*). Participants read a comprehension question following each sentence, and selected one of two visually presented answers, as illustrated in (7b). Prosodic phrasing robustly affected listeners' syntactic/semantic analysis of the ambiguity. With an early break, the second and third nouns were most often grouped together syntactically; with a late break, the first and second nouns were most often grouped together syntactically.

The RC attachment ambiguity illustrated in (6) has also been shown to be sensitive to prosodic disambiguation, in a number of languages including Croatian (Lovrić, 2003), English (Fernández, 2007), German (Augurzky, 2006), Hebrew (Shaked, 2009), and Spanish (Teira & Igoa, 2007). The prosodic contrast involves the insertion of a prosodic break after N1 for the interpretation in (6a), or after N2 for the interpretation in (6b). These RC attachment studies all report asymmetric effects: a prosodic break after N1 has a stronger impact on interpretation than a prosodic break after N2. This may be a point of contrast between the RC attachment and coordination constructions, since there are no reports in the literature, as far as we can tell, of such an asymmetry between the two contours for the coordination ambiguity. It is difficult to know whether this is just a lacuna in data presentation, since data for the two contours are often pooled. Beach, Katz, and Skowronski (1996) and Clifton et al. (2006) do report results separately for the two contours; the numerical data do not suggest any substantial difference in effectiveness between them, but no statistical comparisons are presented.

In short, previous research indicates a strong impact of the location of prosodic boundaries on the preferred interpretation of both of these ambiguous constructions, with the additional finding that a break after N1 has a greater effect than a break after N2 for the RC attachment ambiguity, while this is apparently not so for the coordination ambiguity.

Comparison with these previous findings is an important part of the evaluation of the phoneme restoration method for studying prosody in parsing. The method can be deemed valid to the extent that it reproduces standard observations concerning the association between certain prosodic structures and certain perceived syntactic structures. The method can be deemed sensitive if it registers effects of prosody on syntactic parsing that are at least as powerful, or even more so, than in studies using other methods. Since the quality of the results could be affected by exactly how the phoneme restoration approach is implemented in an experimental protocol, an additional aim of this study was to determine whether one of the three tasks that were used to detect which phoneme was restored (Visual Word Choice, Sentence Repetition, and Speech Shadowing; more details below) is superior to the others. The effects of the tasks could be compared because, aside from their differences with respect to the type and timing of the responses required, all three protocols employed exactly the same auditory target stimuli (more details below). Moreover, the stimuli were described to the participants in the same manner in each case. Participants were told that the experiment concerns how well people can recognise a word that is difficult to hear due to noise, as sometimes happens in everyday life such as when there is poor reception on a telephone, or static interference over the radio.

In presenting the materials in this fashion, our intention was to divert participants' attention away from the syntactic ambiguity, and also away from the prosodic manipulations, by encouraging them to focus on identifying the word "masked" by the noise. In post-task de-briefing, few participants indicated any awareness of the syntactic ambiguity or the role of prosody, but we emphasise that our data do not establish that the participants were in the grip of a true perceptual illusion, and for our purposes it is not essential to do so. Using noise-replaced stimuli is an unobtrusive way of tapping into how listeners' interpretations of ambiguous sentences are influenced by prosody; the procedure can also be used to study how other factors, like word frequency or plausibility, influence ambiguity resolution. This rationale holds whether or not participants sometimes suspect that the relevant phoneme is not actually present. Thus, the status of the phoneme restoration effect as a perceptual illusion is not critical for our investigation; but it is of interest, and we consider it below.

THREE VARIANTS OF THE PHONEME RESTORATION METHOD

We examined three different protocols, all of which exploit the phoneme restoration phenomenon to assess the effect of prosody on the resolution of syntactic ambiguities. They constituted three different ways of detecting which word the listener believed was in the sentence despite its being partially "masked" by noise. In one variant of the method (Visual Word Choice) participants indicated which of two visually presented words they thought had been in the sentence. In another variant they repeated back the sentence (Sentence Repetition). In a third version they repeated the sentence while listening to it (Speech Shadowing). It was unclear in advance whether all three variants would be equally effective; it seemed possible that Visual Word Choice might be the least sensitive, and that shadowing might be too taxing on participants.

Visual Word Choice

In the Visual Word Choice protocol, participants listen to the stimulus, then see two words on the screen, and are asked to indicate which of the two words was in the sentence. Participants are instructed to listen carefully and answer as quickly as possible, and to guess if not sure. This is the least subtle of the three tasks, since it carries at least a hint that two different words *might* have been compatible with the stimulus. Despite this, there are valuable advantages of word choice over a standard comprehension questionnaire. Asking "What word did you hear?" rather than "What does the sentence mean?" can draw attention away from the sentence-level ambiguity. Also, though it is not an on-line task, it helps to minimise the delay between the stimulus and the response because there is no intervening question to parse and comprehend, but just two (short) words to read. For a study of prosodic influence this is especially valuable, since phonological memory is limited, and there is a risk that the mental representation of the prosody of the target item may be overlaid by prosody projected onto an intervening question.

Sentence Repetition

In the Sentence Repetition protocol, the task is to repeat the sentence aloud immediately after hearing it. This task is also known in the literature as *elicited imitation.* It is widely used with children (e.g., Lust, Flynn, & Foley, 1996) and second language learners (e.g., Bley-Vroman & Chaudron, 1994). In our study, the dependent measure was the frequency with which the noise in the critical word in the input was replaced in the participant's output by a phoneme (or phonemes) that created a word compatible with the syntactic structure favoured by the prosodic phrasing.

While still a postsentence task, the Sentence Repetition task goes even further than the Visual Word Choice task in eliminating the processing of intrusive material between the target sentence and the response. Perhaps more important is that by not offering specific word choices, the Sentence Repetition protocol does not draw attention even to the lexical ambiguity of the noise-replaced word. Participants are given no reason to believe that there is any uncertainty at all about what the word really was that they were attempting to hear "through" the noise; their attention is focused on remembering and reproducing the sentence accurately. Note that in asking them to repeat the sentence we did not ask them to reproduce its prosody; the prosody of the stimuli was never mentioned in the instructions. (The extent to which the repetitions do match the prosody of the stimulus can be analysed and may yield results of interest, but it is not the concern of the present report.)

Speech Shadowing

The Speech Shadowing task was first used by Marslen-Wilson (1973). In Speech Shadowing, the listener reproduces the input while still continuing to hear and process the remainder of the sentence or passage. For Marslen-Wilson, the most significant aspect was the discovery of a small proportion of "close shadowers" who could repeat back material at a lag of only 250–300 ms, with evidence of processing at the syntactic and semantic levels within that brief time-span. For our purposes, Speech Shadowing (even if not especially close shadowing) has two advantages. Most obviously, compared with the Sentence Repetition task of Experiment 2, shadowing minimises the time lag between the prosodic disambiguation of the syntax and the participant's response. Also, shadowing is a very demanding task, so participants almost certainly have no attention to spare for thinking about the structure of a sentence and whether or not it is potentially ambiguous. This is the ultimate move in distracting participants' attention from the syntactic ambiguity and its prosodic disambiguation.

Of special interest for present purposes is that Marslen-Wilson (1975) observed spontaneous restoration of contextually appropriate phonemes in place of actual but contextually incorrect phonemes, in the shadowing of normal prose. For example, the nonword *tomorrane* was frequently reproduced as *tomorrow*, and *travedy* as *tragedy*, when the sentential context was syntactically and semantically supportive. Note that these are phonetically highly detectable deviations under normal circumstances; that they were not detected (or not detected rapidly enough to be included in the output) during shadowing may be due to their identifiability being overwhelmed by the high pressure of processing at all levels in the shadowing task. Our shadowing experiment differed from Marslen-Wilson's in that we employed noise-replaced rather than inappropriate phonemes as targets for restoration, and the supporting context was prosodic rather than syntactic/semantic. As in the Sentence Repetition task, the dependent measure was how often the noise in the input was replaced in the participant's output by a phoneme (or phonemes) that created a word compatible with the syntactic analysis cued by the prosody.

GENERAL PROPERTIES OF THE MATERIALS

Identical target materials were used in all three experiments. For each target construction (NP coordination and RC attachment), 24 target sentence pairs were created so as to meet specific syntactic and morphological criteria, described in this section. We also describe here the prosodic properties of the targets.

Morphosyntactic properties of the target stimuli

NP coordination materials were constructed using the following syntactic template (optional elements appear in parentheses; *i* is the coordinating conjunction "and" in Bulgarian):

(8) (Adverbial) (NP) Verb NP1 *i* NP2 *i* NP3 Copula PP

Two of the three postverbal NPs form a coordinate NP, which fills one of two syntactic positions: direct object of the first clause verb or subject of the second clause copula verb. The three NPs in a sentence were either short proper names (12 items) or common nouns (12 items), and were matched within each sentence for animacy and length in syllables. The last noun phrase (NP3) was singular. Since Bulgarian has obligatory subject–verb agreement, the number of the copula verb in the second clause showed whether its subject was just NP3 (singular verb) or the coordination of NP2 and NP3 (plural verb).

RC attachment materials were constructed using the following template:

(9) Verb NP1 Prep NP2 RC

The head nouns of the two NPs were common nouns, matched within a sentence for length in syllables. However, the two nouns in a sentence differed in gender: one masculine and one feminine, order counterbalanced. Since the relative pronoun in Bulgarian obligatorily agrees with the noun that the RC modifies, its gender morphologically disambiguated the attachment of the RC. The RC always consisted of a relative pronoun and a VP, the latter having a transitive verb and a direct object; its length was always two prosodic words (six syllables), which is relatively short for Bulgarian but fully acceptable.

The above templates were used to create pairs of sentences, such that the sentences within a pair were morphologically disambiguated towards opposite readings of the ambiguity; see examples in (5) and (6) above.

All target materials were assessed for plausibility by four judges, native speakers of Bulgarian who were not aware of the purpose of the experiment. They were asked to make judgements regarding the two interpretations of each ambiguity, by reading a context phrase or sentence, followed by two continuations. The examples in (10) and (11), provided here in English, illustrate the procedure.

(10) A chance encounter.
 a. We met Ani and Mimi. Ivan was ecstatic.
 b. We met Ani. Ivan and Mimi were ecstatic.
(11) They televised the granddaughter of the poet.
 a. The granddaughter got an award.
 b. The poet got an award.

Items were used as targets in the experiments reported below only if the two interpretations were judged to be equally plausible by at least three of the four judges. For those items, on a scale from –3 (maximal N1 bias) to +3 (maximal N2 bias), with 0 midpoint (equal bias for both interpretations), the mean rating for NP coordination targets was +0.05, and for RC attachment targets –0.06. Analysis of variance showed that the judges did not significantly differ from each other in their ratings ($F < 1$) and that ratings for the two item types did not differ significantly from each other or from 0, $F(1, 46) = 2.73$, $p > .10$.

Prosodic properties of the target stimuli

For both NP coordination and RC attachment, prosodic disambiguation can be achieved by placing a prosodic boundary immediately following N1 (henceforth, an **N1] break**) or immediately following N2 (henceforth, an **N2] break**). The 24 basic target sentence pairs for each construction were recorded by a trained native speaker (the first author of this paper), each with a contour appropriate to its morphological disambiguation. We used separately recorded sentence versions produced by the trained speaker (rather than creating different versions by splicing or manipulating the prosody digitally) to ensure that the prosodic contours of interest were as natural as possible and to avoid introducing acoustic artifacts into the stimuli—a problem encountered by Samuel (1981); see discussion below. The speech was normally paced (approximately 150 words per minute) and its prosody was clear. The audio stimuli were digitised with a sampling frequency of 44,100 Hz (with a resolution of 16 bits, monaural).

Sentence-internal prosodic breaks in Bulgarian are signalled by pre-boundary lengthening and a rise in pitch optionally followed by a pause (Misheva & Nikov, 1998). Table 1 lists mean durations and pitch movements for N1 and N2 in the target materials; these are the regions where signals of an upcoming prosodic boundary would be acoustically realised. Both the duration and pitch movement data reflect the intended asymmetries in the recordings. As desired, the duration of N1 was greater in N1] stimuli than in N2] stimuli, for both NP coordination materials, $t(23) = 14.40$, $p < .001$ and RC attachment materials, $t(23) = 16.32$, $p < .001$. Also, N1 was systematically produced with a rising intonation in N1] stimuli, and a comparatively flat intonation in N2] stimuli, for both coordination materials, $t(23) = 5.22$, $p < .001$ and RC attachment materials, $t(23) = 9.81$, $p < .001$. In contrast, the duration of N2 was greater in N2] stimuli than in N1] stimuli for both coordination materials, $t(23) = 8.18$, $p < .001$ and RC attachment materials [$t(23) = 10.29$, $p < .001$], and the intonation of N2 was rising in N2] stimuli versus flat in N1] stimuli (coordination: $t(23) = 14.51$, $p < .001$; RC attachment: $t(23) = 18.50$, $p < .001$). Differences between N1] stimuli and N2] stimuli in the duration of a silent pause following N1 or N2 did not reach significance for either construction.

Filler items

The complete set of stimuli in Experiment 1 included 36 filler sentences of several types. Of the fillers, 12 contained an ambiguity different from the two target ambiguities but which also allowed for prosodic disambiguation; the disambiguating words were *se* and *si*, in bold in (12).

TABLE 1
Mean durations for N1 and N2 (and following pauses) and pitch movements for N1 and N2 in acoustic stimuli employed in Experiments 1, 2, and 3.

		Duration (ms)				*Pitch movements (ΔHz)*[a]	
		N1	*Pause*	*N2*	*Pause*	*N1*	*N2*
Coordination ambiguity	N1]	530	444	521	–	+104.4	−8.2
	N2]	445	–	607	464	−4.4	+108.4
RC attachment ambiguity	N1]	720	302	604	–	+76.6	+24.3
	N2]	583	–	701	327	+3.1	+127.8

[a]Pitch movement data are expressed as the difference (Δ) between F_0 measurements (Hz) taken at the stressed syllable and at the offset of the word-final vowel. A positive number indicates a pitch rise, a negative number a pitch fall.

(12) a. Običaše da **se** hvali. || Detsata i te go znaeha.
Like-sg-past to refl boast. Children also they it know-pl-past
He liked to boast. Even the children knew it.

b. Običaše da **si** hvali detsata. || I te go znaeha.
Like-sg-past to one's boast children and they it know-pl-past
He liked to boast of his children. And they knew it.

The prosodic break in materials like (12) aligned with the sentence boundary. *Se/si* ambiguity fillers were recorded in these two versions, each with a falling boundary tone and a following pause between the two sentences.

The other 24 fillers were fully unambiguous; that is, the segment that would be replaced by white noise could be restored in only one way to create a word that would yield a grammatical and meaningful sentence. Of these, six contained one of the verb forms (*beše/biaha*) used in the NP coordination target items, and six contained one of the relative pronouns (*kojto/koiato*) used in the RC attachment target items; but in both cases, unlike the target items, the other word from the pair made the sentence ungrammatical, as illustrated in (13).

(13) Kakto obiknoveno po tova vreme Nina i bliznatsite b▓ na plaža.
As usual at this time Nina and twins-pl w▓ at beach-det.
As usual at this time Nina and the twins *were/*was* at the beach.

The remaining 12 filler sentences contained an adverbial clause beginning with either *kadeto* ("where") or *kakto* ("as, in such manner"), as illustrated in (14). In this example, only *kadeto* is acceptable; *kakto* makes the sentence semantically anomalous. Half of the fillers of this type had *kadeto* as the correct response; the others had *kakto* as the correct response.

(14) Ogleda s pognusa mjastoto, k▓to se nalagaše da prespjat.
Look-past-sg with disgust place-det where refl need-past to sleep-perf-pl.
(S/he) looked with disgust at the place *where/?as* (they) had to spend the night.

All unambiguous fillers were recorded with prosody appropriate to their respective constructions. Thus, a proportion of unambiguous fillers contained a prosodic break, though in a variety of positions. The unambiguous fillers were included to draw attention away from the target stimuli, and to provide accuracy data for screening out inattentive participants.

Phoneme replacement

For the target materials and ambiguous fillers, the disambiguating portion of the critical word was removed from the recordings and replaced with a segment of white noise, synthesised using Praat (with the same sampling rate and bit rate of the recorded stimuli: 44,100 Hz and 16 bits monaural). The duration of the noise used in each sentence of a given pair was the average of the duration of the two versions for that item, to eliminate durational cues. The resulting signal had the same segmental content for the two different versions of each target sentence, but the sentence-level prosody differed between versions. Figure 1 provides waveforms and pitch tracks for the two versions of examples (5) and (6). As the figure illustrates, prosodic cues signalling prosodic boundaries (F_0 rises and pauses) precede the region that has been replaced by noise.

For the unambiguous fillers, white noise replaced the phonemes that differed between the contrasting lexical items used in the relevant filler subtype: for example *kadeto* in sentences like (14).

Three native Bulgarian speakers with a background in linguistics listened to all the noise-replaced stimuli, and confirmed that they sounded natural and that the noise was not disruptive.

EXPERIMENT 1: VISUAL WORD CHOICE

Method

Participants

Twenty-four native speakers of Bulgarian (67% female), undergraduate students at the University of Economics in Varna and Varna Free University, participated successfully in this experiment.

Materials

The 24 NP coordination items and 24 RC attachment items—each in two stimulus versions, differing in their prosody as described earlier—made up the target materials for this experiment. The targets were counterbalanced across two lists (12 items in each of the two experimental conditions for each construction), and were interspersed among the 36 filler items (of which, as discussed in detail above, 12 were presented with one of two different disambiguating prosodies in the different versions/lists, and the others were presented with a single appropriate prosody across versions). Each list was preceded by two practice items, and two additional "warm-up" items at the beginning of the testing session.

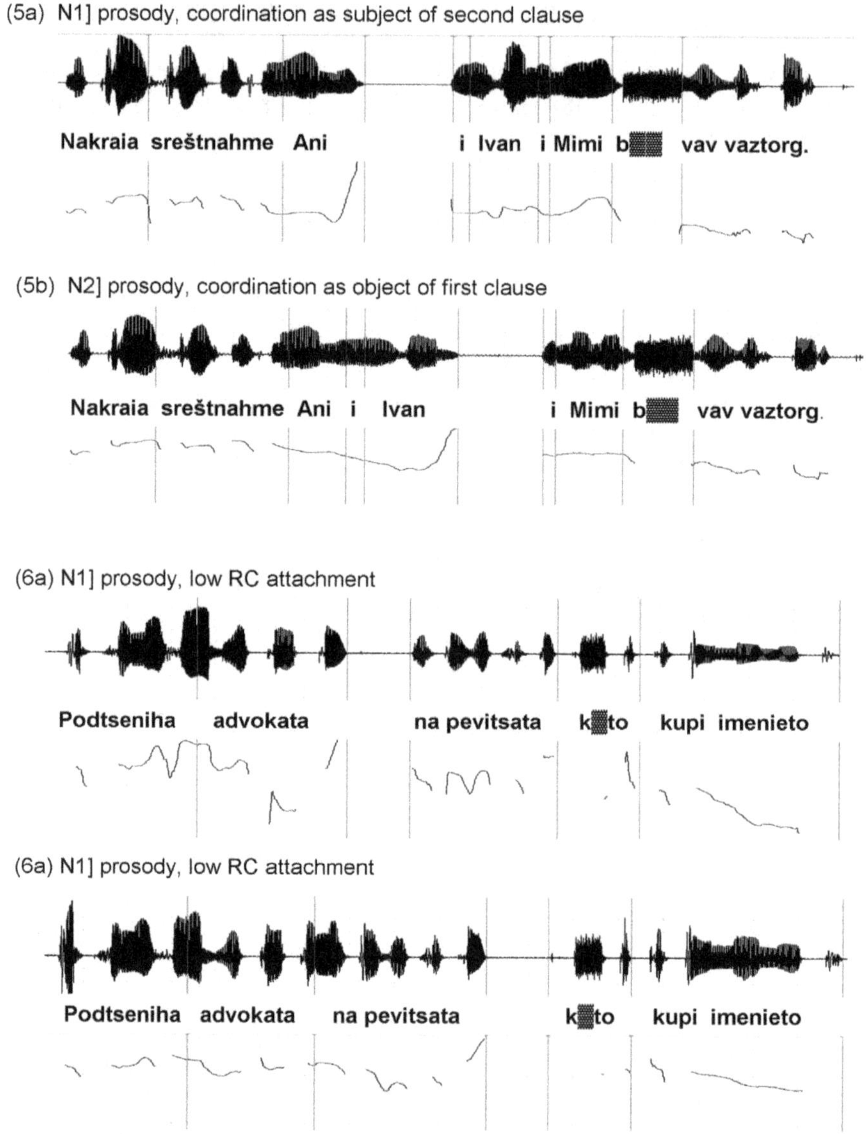

Figure 1. Disambiguating prosodies for target materials illustrated in examples (5) and (6). The waveforms and pitch tracks displayed indicate durational and intonational differences between versions.

Procedure

A computer running DMDX (Forster & Forster, 2003) was used to present the audio stimuli (in a different pseudo-random order for each participant) and collect participant responses. Participants pressed a key on the keyboard to trigger the audio presentation of a given item. Immediately at the offset of the stimulus sentence, two words appeared on the screen. They were the words parts of which had been excised from the acoustic stimuli. For the coordination ambiguity the two words were always *biaha* and *beše*; for the RC attachment ambiguity they were always *koiato* and *kojto*; for ambiguous fillers they were always *se* and *si*. For unambiguous filler sentences the contextually appropriate word was paired with the other word used in the same subtype of fillers, e.g., *kadeto* and *kakto* for fillers like (14).

From the participants' perspective the task was merely to decide which word had been in the sentence. Participants indicated which of the two words they thought had appeared in the preceding sentence by pressing one of two marked keys. They had been instructed to listen to the sentence carefully and to answer as quickly as possible and guess if not sure. There was a fixed timeout of 9,000 ms for responding to the Visual Word Choice.

Data treatment

The data were cast as percent congruent phoneme restorations—that is, as the percentage of word choices indicating a syntactic disambiguation congruent (as established on the basis of prior studies; see above) with the prosodic contour of the stimulus sentence. The response timeout for the word choice resulted in a negligible (0.2%) amount of missing data.

Results

In the data presentation for this and the other two experiments, we begin in each case with a basic assessment of the sensitivity of the task: the degree of congruence between the syntactic structure indicated by the phoneme restoration data and the syntactic structure cued by the prosody. We then examine in each case, minor variations that may be of theoretical interest.

Data for Experiment 1 are reported in Figure 2 (leftmost panel in each of the bar graphs), which clearly shows that for both the NP coordination and the RC attachment ambiguities the overwhelming majority (ranging between 83 and 95%) of phoneme restorations in Experiment 1 were restorations that were congruent with the prosody of the stimuli.

Turning now to the details: with NP coordination materials, N1] and N2] prosody elicited similar amounts of congruent restorations (F_1, $F_2 < 1$), as was tentatively expected in the absence of previous reports to the contrary. With RC attachment materials, N1] prosody elicited significantly more congruent restorations than N2] prosody, $F_1(1, 22) = 7.22$, $p = .013$;

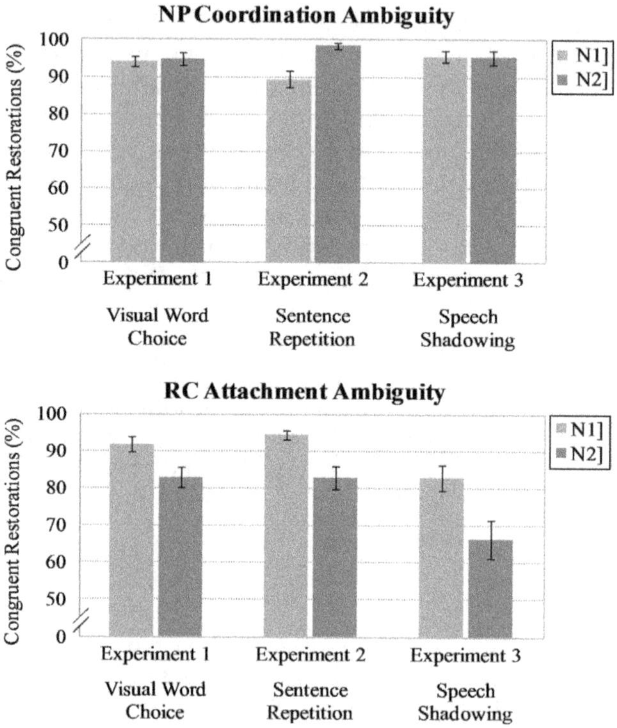

Figure 2. Comparison of data from Experiments 1 (Visual Word Choice), 2 (Sentence Repetition), and 3 (Speech Shadowing), for coordination ambiguity (top panel) and RC attachment ambiguity (bottom panel). (Error bars represent participant-based standard errors.)

$F_2(1, 22) = 6.90$, $p = .015$, as had been anticipated in view of previous experimental findings of such asymmetry in other languages, noted above. In short, the prosody of the stimuli had a powerful effect on sentence comprehension for both constructions, and a contrast emerged between symmetry for the NP coordination ambiguity and asymmetry for the RC attachment ambiguity.

EXPERIMENT 2: SENTENCE REPETITION

Method

Participants

Twenty-four participants (58% female) were drawn from the same population as for Experiment 1. None had participated in Experiment 1.

Materials

Experiment 2 used exactly the same target acoustic stimuli as Experiment 1, also counterbalanced across two lists (12 items in each of the two experimental conditions for each construction). Given the nature of the procedure, the target materials were presented with a reduced number of filler items (the 12 ambiguous fillers only) so that the testing session would not be too lengthy. Each list of targets and fillers was preceded by two practice items and two additional "warm-up" items at the beginning of the testing session.

Procedure

Participants' task was to repeat the sentence aloud immediately after listening to the stimulus. They were told to start speaking as soon as they saw a microphone icon on the screen, which was synchronised with the end of the stimulus. A response time-out was set for 7,000 ms from the point at which the microphone icon appeared on the screen. As in Experiment 1, DMDX controlled the presentation, including the different pseudo-randomisation of the materials for each participant, and collected participant responses.

Data treatment

The dependent measure was which word was produced by the participant in lieu of the noise-replaced word in the stimulus, from which it could be inferred which interpretation had been imposed on the sentence. As for Experiment 1, we report the data as percent congruent phoneme restorations. Missing data in this task are the result of recordings terminated prematurely because of the preset response timeout. Recordings terminated prematurely before the critical word was uttered made up 4.9% of the data.

Results

Data for Experiment 2 are reported in Figure 2 (center panel in each of the bar graphs). They show that for both the NP coordination and the RC attachment constructions, congruent phoneme restorations were again overwhelmingly more frequent (ranging between 83 and 98%).

With regard to detailed effects, in Experiment 2 we again found the expected asymmetry for RC attachment: N1] prosody had a stronger effect on RC attachment than N2] prosody did, in keeping with results from other languages as noted above, $F_1(1, 22) = 11.15$, $p = .003$; $F_2(1, 22) = 14.81$, $p = .001$. We also found an unanticipated asymmetry in the data for the NP coordination materials, in the opposite direction from RC attachment: N2] prosody elicited more congruent restorations than N1] prosody, $F_1(1, 22) = 17.09$, $p < .001$; $F_2(1, 22) = 4.66$, $p = .042$. This effect is absent from our other two experiments, and, as noted above, to our knowledge it has not been reported in the literature. Further experimentation with this construction is required to check whether this effect replicates.

EXPERIMENT 3: SPEECH SHADOWING

Method

Participants

Twenty-four participants (54% female) recruited from the same population as for Experiments 1 and 2, participated successfully in Experiment 3. None had taken part in either Experiment 1 or Experiment 2. Three participants with over 25% missing data (due to recordings terminated prematurely) were rejected and replaced.

Materials

Experiment 3 used the same audio stimuli as Experiment 2, counterbalanced across two lists, and with the same practice and "warm-up" items as in Experiment 2.

Procedure

Participants' task was to shadow the speaker in the stimulus recordings, by speaking the sentence aloud as they were listening to it, with as little delay as possible. As in Experiment 2, the presentation, controlled by DMDX, began with a key press to play a given audio stimulus. Unlike in Experiment 2, the onset of the audio was synchronised with the appearance of a microphone icon on the computer screen and with the beginning of audio recording of the participant's response. The preset response time-out, starting at the appearance of the microphone icon on the screen, was 7,000 ms. Participants were instructed to start repeating the sentence as soon as it began, and to continue as best as they could through to the end.

Data treatment

As in Experiment 2, the dependent measure was which word was produced by the participant in lieu of the noise-replaced item in the stimulus, indicating which interpretation had been imposed on the input sentence. Data were again coded as percent congruent phoneme restorations. The response time-out resulted in some recordings (7% of the complete dataset) being terminated before the participant had produced the critical word.

Results

The participants in Experiment 3 would not be considered "close shadowers" as defined by Marslen-Wilson (1985), since every one of them had a mean latency well over 400 ms. One reason for the longer latencies in our study may be that our participants were shadowing single sentences, rather than connected prose consisting of several sentences. They had to resume shadowing anew for each sentence, which did not allow them to establish a comfortable but rapid pace and maintain it. In future work this could be avoided by embedding target sentences in paragraphs.

As shown in Figure 2 (rightmost panel of each of the bar graphs), Experiment 3 again elicited a clear majority of phoneme restorations congruent with the prosody of the stimuli, for both ambiguities, with means ranging between 66 and 96%. For NP coordination, both prosodies were equally effective in cueing the associated syntactic structure; as in Experiment 1, there was no asymmetry between them ($F_1 < 1$; $F_2 < 1$). Rates of congruent restorations were comparable to those in the other two tasks. With RC attachment materials, congruent phoneme restoration rates were reliably different for the two prosodies, F_1 $(1, 22) = 22.13$, $p < .001$; $F_2(1, 22) = 5.21$, $p = .033$, showing the asymmetry observed in both Experiments 1 and 2, in which N2] prosody has less impact than N1] prosody.

Yet there is a striking difference between this task (Speech Shadowing) and the other two tasks (Visual Word Choice and Sentence Repetition). For the RC construction, both prosodies resulted in rates of congruent restoration that were lower than for the other tasks. This could be ascribed to the difficulty of shadowing, except that a comparable decrement in performance was not observed for NP coordination. Two explanations are possible and can be examined in future research. One is that RC constructions are more difficult to process, even under normal circumstances, than coordinations are, and that a more demanding task impacts difficult constructions disproportionately. Another possibility is that a variety of impinging factors—ranging from the contrast between restrictive and nonrestrictive modification, to prescriptive punctuation rules in the orthography—render the alignment between syntax and prosody more fragile for the RC construction than it is for coordination, making it less resistant to pressures such as the shadowing task imposes.

Also of interest in the Experiment 3 data for the RC attachment ambiguity is that the N2] prosodic phrasing was especially vulnerable, to an extent not fully accounted for by any general processing problem for RCs. Its rate of 66% congruent restorations was by far the lowest in the whole study. However, this has a natural explanation, given that Speech Shadowing with N2] prosody in the RC attachment construction is the only situation across all three experiments in which the participant's reconstruction of the critical word is tapped immediately following the biasing prosodic cue; see Figure 1. We speculate, therefore, that the particular combination of N2] prosody with the instruction to shadow closely affords too little time for prosodic processing to initiate a reliable phoneme restoration.

GENERAL DISCUSSION

The primary motivating question for this project was whether the phoneme restoration protocol can deliver reliable veridical results concerning the prosody–syntax interface. In order to validate a novel methodology, it is necessary to demonstrate that it yields outcomes comparable to those obtained using already existing experimental techniques. For the coordination ambiguity, this turned out to be straightforwardly true. An N1] prosodic break yielded almost exclusively subject coordination responses while an N2] break produced almost only object coordination responses, comporting well with standard observations for coordination, such as for multiple NP coordination in English (though in a somewhat different sentential context than in our materials) by Clifton et al. (2006).

For the RC attachment ambiguity, the results were generally less sharply drawn but still comparable to what is reported in the previous literature. Only the shadowing task was relatively unresponsive to prosody. In all three tasks, an N1] prosodic break yielded a large proportion of low attachment of the RC to N2, while an N2] break produced mostly high attachment of the RC to N1 but to a lesser degree. Both the substantial effect of prosody and this asymmetry match findings reported for RC attachment in languages including Croatian, English, German, Hebrew, and Spanish (see references above).

Why there would be an asymmetry in effectiveness of the two prosodies has been discussed in the literature. A possible explanation is offered by the Rational Speaker Hypothesis (Clifton et al., 2006), which predicts that a prosodic break that could have been motivated by non-configurational considerations has less impact on perceived syntactic structure than a break without such other motivation. In Bulgarian there is a default prosodic break immediately before a RC (comparable to French, as discussed by Fodor, 2002). Speakers almost invariably break at the pre-RC position even for a RC following a single head noun where there is no attachment ambiguity. (Bulgarian RCs are obligatorily preceded by commas in writing, even after a single noun.) Since the N2] breaks in our materials constitute breaks at the left edge of the RC, the N2] breaks would be predictable for hearers and might therefore be discounted as cues to high RC attachment. In contrast, an N1] break is less common in the language, which could make it more likely to be treated as genuinely indicative of the syntactic structure.

For the coordination construction there is no reason to suppose that an N1] break is any more or less likely than an N2] break, so no asymmetry is expected in their impact on perceived syntactic configuration.

A practical question of interest in this project was whether one of the tasks revealing how phonemes were restored by perceivers would prove to be superior to the others for purposes of understanding the interaction of prosody and syntax in normal sentence processing. In fact all three tasks yielded satisfactory and largely parallel results, as documented above. It is clear that in all three tasks, prosodic phrasing strongly influenced ambiguity resolution for both the NP coordination and the RC attachment constructions. The similarity of outcomes across the three tasks is striking, although there are also some mismatches between them as the discussion above has noted.

The indication that shadowing is more taxing than the other tasks was not unexpected. In fact it was more surprising to find that for coordination materials, sensitivity to prosody was not at all diminished in shadowing compared with the other tasks. Thus, by and large, the listeners in our study coped well with the exigencies of the shadowing task. Even so, in future work we would have participants shadow longer passages that provide an opportunity to settle smoothly into shadowing mode before the critical sentence occurs.

The one finding that we have speculated is due specifically to the shadowing methodology is the exceptionally low rate of congruent restorations for RC attachment materials with N2] prosodic breaks. We have suggested that this is because the critical word in the RC sentences is the relative pronoun, which immediately follows the N2] prosodic break, making it likely that the N2] break has not been fully processed in the interval between hearing the acoustic cues to the prosodic boundary and uttering the relative pronoun. This contrasts with the N2] break in the Visual Word Choice and Sentence Repetition tasks, and with the N1] break in the Shadowing task, where there is a more substantial time interval between the break and the listeners' response to it.

HOW ILLUSORY IS THE MISSING PHONEME?

As noted above, the advantages of phoneme restoration for studying ambiguity resolution do not turn on the assumption that participants experience a true perceptual illusion, in which they are convinced that they actually heard the missing phoneme. This is an intriguing question, nonetheless, and is made more so by the vehemence of the phenomenological reports in the literature. In Warren's (1970, p. 392) presentation of his first experiment, he wrote "The illusory perception of the absent phoneme was in keeping with the observation of others (graduate students and staff), who, despite knowledge of the actual stimulus, still perceived the missing phoneme as distinctly as the clearly pronounced sounds actually present". Sherman (1971), in the first experiment on phoneme replacement in a sentential context, having clearly informed the subjects in advance in one condition "that a cough did replace a single speech sound in a sentence", then asked them to judge after each item "whether or not the replaced sound was clearly missing". Subjects gave "no" responses on 57% of trials, even after their fourth hearing of the same item (Sherman, 1971, pp. 12, 16, 37). In later work, Samuel (1981, p. 474) took a more skeptical stance, but he too refers to phoneme restoration as "a powerful auditory illusion".

However, Samuel (1981) raised a doubt as to whether sentential contexts are as effective in creating the illusion as within-word contexts such as *legi█latures* (from Warren) or *fu█erals* (from Samuel), which may be more uniquely constraining.[1] This is an interesting point which deserves to be taken seriously, as we do below. But we wish to be clear that our own experiments were not designed to investigate the phenomenological status of the restoration phenomenon. For Samuel, phoneme restoration as a genuine illusion was a more central concern than it is in our prosody–sensitivity studies, because his aim was to test a basic model of speech perception, specifically "the hypothesis that restoration (and more generally, speech perception) depends on the bottom-up confirmation of expectations generated at higher levels" (p. 474). In pursuit of this, he applied a signal detection theoretic analysis to a discrimination task in which participants were required to judge an item as either "noise-replaced" or "noise-added". If noise-replaced items really sound to listeners as if the phoneme is present beneath the noise, then they should be indiscriminable from noise-added items even to participants clearly alerted to the difference. (Samuel makes it clear that in describing the task to the participants there was no deception: "the nature of the stimuli was clearly explained beforehand" (p. 478).)

At the level of single words, the d' (d-prime, i.e., discrimination) measure was lower for real words than for pseudo-words. That is, noise-replaced and noise-added versions were less well discriminated for real words than they were for nonwords. This indicates that the contextual predictability of a particular phoneme affected perceptual processing, not merely a postperceptual response bias. It thus supports the intuitive claim of a strong perceptual illusion. By contrast, with sentential contexts as in (4) above, d' for the noise-replaced versus noise-added versions did not significantly differ for words that were predictable in the sentence context versus words that were less predictable in that context. There was a significant difference between

[1] We thank an anonymous reviewer for urging us to discuss this point, which to the best of our knowledge has not been addressed since it was raised by Samuel in 1981.

conditions, but it was reflected primarily in the Beta measure, which reflects postperceptual biases. The Beta scores were higher for contextually predictable versus nonpredictable words (e.g., *batter* in the context of *pitcher* versus *batter* in the context of *soldier*), indicating that the sentential contexts did affect restorations, but via postperceptual guessing strategies rather than by an influence on perception.

There could be several reasons for this. Samuel notes that in the sentential materials "the critical words were designed to be multiply restorable" and that possibly "the existence of more than one potential percept inhibited restoration, improving discriminability" (p. 491). This contrasts with the experiments with isolated words, where each target word with a masked or replaced phoneme corresponded to only one possible word in the language. If this is the right explanation for the partial failure of the illusion in the sentential materials, it could apply equally to the materials in our experiments as well. But there are other accounts of Samuel's data which would not apply to ours.

It is possible that the sentential contexts in Samuel's target items (of which the only example given in his paper is the *battle–batter* item in (4) above) were only weakly constraining and did not decisively favour one version of the word over the other (e.g., in the context of (4a), *battle* and *batter* differ in plausibility but neither creates a non-sentence of the language). In that case, Samuel's finding that the phonological illusion is weak would not extrapolate to our experiments if the prosodic contexts in our experiments are more constraining than the pragmatic (world knowledge) contexts in Samuel's. We suspect that they are, but confirmation of that must await further experimentation.

Samuel himself was inclined towards the conclusion that for the sentential contexts "the higher level (syntactic–semantic) information was not being passed down to the lower phonetic–phonological level" (Samuel, 1981, p. 491). However, he also offered an alternative explanation of the greater discriminability in sentential than in lexical contexts by pointing to a flaw in the preparation of his sentential stimuli, which led to "an artifactual cue for discriminating added and replaced versions in sentences" (p. 490). Samuel suggests that the likely culprit "is the influence of prosody (especially pitch contour) in sentences. The replacement version of a sentence will often introduce a break into the prosodic structure, whereas the added version seldom does" (p. 490). In view of this, it remains an open question whether a sentential context—affording either pragmatic/semantic disambiguation or prosodic disambiguation—can effectively limit the construal of an ambiguous word to such an extent that a speech sound is confidently "perceived" in the absence of any acoustic cues from the input. This question could be pursued in a programme of experimentation modelled on Samuel's discrimination paradigm. However, such research cannot be integrated comfortably into studies that employ the phoneme restoration effect as a probe for other phenomena, as in the investigation reported here. This is because the replaced/added discrimination task draws extreme attention to the critical lexical item. Also in Samuel's protocol, the added/replaced discrimination task crucially precedes other tasks, so it would delay the primary response of interest in word choice or repetition, and would be incompatible with shadowing. Thus, in general the d′ methodology would counteract the naturalness of the phoneme restoration phenomenon, which had recommended it for the study of the prosody–syntax interface.

CONCLUSION

The value of phoneme restoration for tapping into ambiguity resolution processes was assessed in this investigation: does it prove itself worthy of use in future research on prosodic (or other) influences on ambiguity resolution? The results were validated by comparison with results from existing methods for "tried and true" ambiguities already known to be open to prosodic influence across a variety of languages. Similar effects of prosodic phrasing were confirmed here for Bulgarian, a language not previously studied from this point of view. This adds strength to the speculation that some basic aspects of the prosody–syntax interface are universal (see Selkirk, 2000).

The phoneme restoration approach has satisfied the demands that we imposed at the outset of our search for a new methodology. Having observed in the past that naïve participants in an experiment can behave oddly in relation to prosody when they become self-conscious and try too hard to be responsive to it, we were especially seeking an experimental procedure that would avoid attracting attention either to the existence of a syntactic/semantic ambiguity, or to the significance of prosody as a means of disambiguating it. To be more specific on this point: there are four kinds of conscious awareness which might arise in such an experiment and which need to be distinguished: (1) awareness of the sentence-level ambiguity; (2) awareness of the relevance of prosody; (3) awareness of a lexical ambiguity in the word with noise replacement; and (4) awareness that the original phoneme(s) were fully replaced, rather than overlaid, by the noise. For our purpose, which is ultimately to assess the role of prosody in the interpretation of spoken language under normal conversational conditions, the paramount concern is to avoid (1) and (2), and preferably also (3), since these could render participants' reactions less spontaneous than in normal language use; by comparison with these, (4) is of negligible importance. Whether or not it is a total illusion, we believe the evidence is strong that the phoneme restoration effect is convincing enough in a natural listening context that participants accept it at face value and respond spontaneously in the experimental task. If future research continues to uphold this conviction, it will provide strong evidence that prosodic influences on ambiguity resolution in perception are independent of awareness on the part of the perceiver that there is an ambiguity to be resolved. This issue parallels the corresponding point for prosody production (viz. whether the production of prosodic cues for ambiguity resolution is independent of awareness on the part of the producer that there is an ambiguity to be resolved), which has emerged as a central issue in recent research on the prosody–syntax interface in language processing (e.g., Kraljic & Brennan, 2005; Snedeker & Trueswell, 2003).

We conclude that the phoneme restoration method is a useful addition to the repertoire of paradigms for investigating ambiguity resolution in sentence processing, with the additional merits that the stimulus sentences are neither anomalous nor incomplete, and the amount of extraneous material (such as comprehension questions) to be processed between the critical word and the response is minimised. Its similarity to the imperfect acoustic conditions typical of everyday life renders the method ecologically authentic. Listening to speech overlaid with sporadic noise is surely even more frequent than listening under ideal acoustic conditions. Hence, what phoneme restoration reveals about prosody in sentence comprehension may be especially representative of normal language processing.

Phoneme restoration methodology has considerable flexibility for the study of prosody perception. Importantly, it shares with the visual world paradigm the merit that it can be used (in its repetition versions) with nonliterate populations, for example to study the developmental course of prosodic sensitivity (since children as young as 5 years old have been reported to be able to restore missing phonemes; Newman, 2004; Walley, 1988). The technique has many other potential applications as well. It could be used to test the influence on ambiguity resolution of nonacoustic factors, such as lexical frequency, discourse context and information structure. And of course, now that its validity has been established, it can be extended to a range of new syntactic ambiguities in Bulgarian and other languages, which have not previously been investigated.

REFERENCES

Augurzky, P. (2006). *Attaching relative clauses in German: The role of implicit and explicit prosody in sentence processing*. Leipzig, Germany: Max Planck Institute for Human Cognitive and Brain Sciences.

Bashford, J. A., & Warren, R. M. (1979). Perceptual synthesis of deleted phonemes. In J. J. Wolf & D. H. Klatt (Eds.), *Speech communication papers presented at the 97th meeting of the Acoustical Society of America* (pp. 423–426). New York, NY: Acoustical Society of America.

Beach, C. M., Katz, W. F., & Skowronski, A. (1996). Children's processing of prosodic cues for phrasal interpretation. *Journal of the Acoustical Society of America*, *99*(2), 1148–1160. doi:10.1121/1.414599

Bley-Vroman, R., & Chaudron, C. (1994). Elicited imitation as a measure of second-language competence. In E. Tarone, S. M. Gass, & A. D. Cohen (Eds.), *Research methodology in second-language acquisition*. Hillsdale, NJ: Lawrence Erlbaum.

Clifton, C. Jr., Carlson, K., & Frazier, L. (2006). Tracking the what and why of speakers' choices: Prosodic boundaries and the length of constituents. *Psychonomic Bulletin and Review*, *13*, 854–861. Available from http://www.ncbi.nlm.nih.gov/pubmed/17328385

Eckstein, K., & Friederici, A. D. (2006). It's early: Event-related potential evidence for initial interaction of syntax and prosody in speech comprehension. *Journal of Cognitive Neuroscience*, *18*(10), 1696–1711. doi:10.1162/jocn.2006.18.10.1696

Fernández, E. M. (2007). How might a rapid serial visual presentation of text affect the prosody projected implicitly during silent reading? *Conferências do V Congresso Internacional da Associação Brasiliera de Lingüística*, *5*, 117–154.

Ferreira, F., Anes, M. D., & Horine, M. D. (1996). Exploring the use of prosody during language comprehension using the auditory moving window technique. *Journal of Psycholinguistic Research*, *25*, 273–290. doi:10.1007/BF01708574

Fodor, J. D. (2002). Prosodic disambiguation in silent reading. In M. Hirotani (Ed.), *Proceedings of the North East Linguistic Society 32* (Vol. 1, pp. 113–132). Amherst, MA: GSLA, University of Massachusetts.

Forster, K. I., & Forster, J. C. (2003). DMDX: A Windows display program with millisecond accuracy. *Behavior Research methods, Instruments, & Computers*, *35*(1), 116–124. Available from http://www.ncbi.nlm.nih.gov/pubmed/12723786

Frazier, L., Clifton, C., & Carlson, K. (2004). Don't break, or do: Prosodic boundary preferences. *Lingua*, *114*(1), 3–27. doi:10.1016/S0024-3841(03)00044-5

Ito, K., & Speer, S. R. (2005). *The effect of intonation on visual search: An eye-tracking study.* Presentation at conference on experimental pragmatics: Exploring the cognitive basis of conversation, April 14–16, 2005 The British Academy, Cambridge, UK.

Kjelgaard, M. M., & Speer, S. R. (1999). Prosodic facilitation and interference in the resolution of temporary syntactic closure ambiguity. *Journal of Memory and Language*, *40*(2), 153–194. doi:10.1006/jmla.1998.2620

Kraljic, T., & Brennan, S. E. (2005). Prosodic disambiguation of syntactic structure: For the speaker or for the addressee? *Cognitive Psychology*, *50*, 194–231. doi:10.1016/j.cogpsych.2004.08.002

Lehiste, I. (1972). The timing of utterances and linguistic boundaries. *Journal of the Acoustic Society of America*, *51*, 2018–2024. doi:10.1121/1.1913062

Lehiste, I., Olive, J. P., & Streeter, L. A. (1976). Role of duration in disambiguating syntactically ambiguous sentences. *Journal of the Acoustical Society of America*, *40*, 1199–1202. doi:10.1121/1.381180

Lovrić, N. (2003). *Implicit prosody in silent reading: Relative clause attachment in Croatian.* Doctoral dissertation, CUNY Graduate Center, New York, NY.

Lust, B., Flynn, S., & Foley, C. (1996). What children know about what they say: Elicited imitation as a research method for assessing children's syntax. In D. McDaniel, C. McKee, & H. S. Cairns (Eds.), *Methods for assessing children's syntax* (pp. 55–76). Cambridge, MA: MIT Press.

Marslen-Wilson, W. D. (1973). Linguistic structure and speech shadowing at very short latencies. *Nature*, *244*, 522–523. doi:10.1038/244522a0

Marslen-Wilson, W. D. (1975). Sentence perception as an interactive parallel process. *Science*, *189*, 226–228. doi:10.1126/science.189.4198.226

Marslen-Wilson, W. D. (1985). Speech shadowing and speech comprehension. *Speech Communication*, *4*, 55–73. doi:10.1016/0167-6393(85)90036-6

Marslen-Wilson, W. D., Tyler, L. K., Warren, P., Grenier, P., & Lee, C. S. (1992). Prosodic effects in minimal attachment. *Quarterly Journal of Experimental Psychology, 45A*, 73–87. doi:10.1080/14640749208401316

Misheva, A., & Nikov, M. (1998). Intonation in Bulgarian. In D. Hirst & A. Di Cristo (Eds.), *Intonation systems: A survey of twenty languages* (pp. 275–287). Cambridge, UK: Cambridge University Press.

Newman, R. S. (2004). Phoneme restoration in infants. *Journal of the Acoustical Society of America, 107*(5), 2857. doi:10.1121/1.429250

Peppé, S., & McCann, J. (2003). Assessing intonation and prosody in children with atypical language development: The PEPS-C test and the revised version. *Clinical Linguistics and Phonetics, 17*(4–5), 345–354. doi:10.1080/0269920031000079994

Peppé, S., McCann, J., Gibbon, F., O'Hare, A., & Rutherford, M. (2007). Receptive and expressive prosodic ability in children with high-functioning autism. *Journal of Speech, Language and Hearing Research, 50*, 1015–1028. doi:10.1044/1092-4388(2007/071)

Samuel, A. G. (1981). Phonemic restoration: Insights from a new methodology. *Journal of Experimental Psychology: General, 110*, 474–494. doi:10.1037/0096-3445.110.4.474

Samuel, A. G. (1996). Phoneme restoration. *Language and Cognitive Processes, 11*, 647–653. doi:10.1080/016909696387051

Schafer, A. J., Speer, S. R., Warren, P., & White, S. D. (2000). Intonational disambiguation in sentence production and comprehension. *Journal of Psycholinguistic Research, 29*(2), 169–182. doi:10.1023/A:1005192911512

Selkirk, E. (2000). The interaction of constraints on prosodic phrasing. In M. Horne (Ed.), *Prosody: Theory and Experiment* (pp. 231–262). Dordrecht: Kluwer.

Shaked, A. (2009). *Sentence processing of complex nominals in Hebrew.* Doctoral dissertation, CUNY Graduate Center, New York, NY.

Sherman, B. L. (1971). *Phonemic restoration: An insight into the mechanisms of speech perception.* Unpublished master's thesis, University of Wisconsin–Milwaukee, Milwaukee, WI, USA.

Snedeker, J., & Trueswell, J. (2003). Using prosody to avoid ambiguity: Effects of speaker awareness and referential context. *Journal of Memory and Language, 48*, 103–130. doi:10.1016/S0749-596X(02)00519-3

Steinhauer, K., Alter, K., & Friederici, A. D. (1999). Brain responses indicate immediate use of prosodic cues in natural speech processing. *Nature Neuroscience, 2*, 191–196. doi:10.1038/5757

Streeter, L. (1978). Acoustic determinants of phrase boundary perception. *Journal of the Acoustical Society of America, 64*, 1582–1592. doi:10.1121/1.382142

Teira, C., & Igoa, J. M. (2007). The prosody-syntax relationship in sentence processing. *Anuario de Psicología, 38*(1), 45–69. Available http://www.raco.cat/index.php/AnuarioPsicologia/article/view/71747/0

Walley, A. C. (1988). Spoken word recognition by young children and adults. *Cognitive Development, 3*, 137–165. doi:10.1016/0885-2014(88)90016-0

Warren, R. M. (1970). Perceptual restoration of missing speech sounds. *Science, 167*, 392–393. doi:10.1126/science.167.3917.392

Warren, R. M. (2008). *Auditory perception: A new analysis and synthesis* (3rd ed.). Cambridge, UK: Cambridge University Press. (Auditory demonstrations available at: http://www4.uwm.edu/APL/demonstrations.html)

Warren, R. M., & Warren, R. P. (1970). Auditory illusions and confusions. *Scientific American, 223*, 30–36. doi:10.1038/scientificamerican1270-30

Watson, D. G., Gunlogson, C. A., & Tanenhaus, M. K. (2006). Online methods for the investigation of prosody. In S. Sudhoff, D. Lenertova, R. Meyer, S. Pappert, P. Augurzky, I. Mleinek, N. Richter, & J. Schlieber (Eds.), *Methods in empirical prosody research* (pp. 259–282). New York, NY: Walter de Gruyter.

LANGUAGE AND COGNITIVE PROCESSES
2010, 25 (7/8/9), 1294

Psychology Press
Taylor & Francis Group

Corrigendum

Please note that in the article entitled "The role of prosody in the English dative alternation" by Arto Anttila, Matthew Adams, and Michael Speriosu, published online ahead of print and in this issue (Volume 25, Issue 7/8/9, Pages 946–981), there was an author error.

In their description of the corpus from which they pulled their data, the authors reported that 100% of their data came from blogspot.com. In fact, only about 81% of the web sites were actually from blogspot.com.

The breakdown of the content of the "Blogspot Corpus" is as follows (The verb "donate" is not included):

All URLs: 1,513 (100%)
Blogspot: 1,231 (81.4%)
Geocities: 51 (3.4%)
Livejournal: 36 (2.4%)
Other: 195 (12.8%) — these are a mix, mainly the verbs "give" and "bring"

http://www.psypress.com/lcp DOI: 10.1080/01690965.2010.525020

Subject Index

For Product Safety Concerns and Information please contact our EU representative GPSR@taylorandfrancis.com
Taylor & Francis Verlag GmbH, Kaufingerstraße 24, 80331 München, Germany

www.ingramcontent.com/pod-product-compliance
Lightning Source LLC
LaVergne TN
LVHW081359011026
849161LV00013BA/2859

* 9 7 8 1 8 4 8 7 2 7 4 0 3 *